Writing
Southern
History

FLETCHER M. GREEN

WRITING SOUTHERN HISTORY

Essays in Historiography
in Honor of
FLETCHER M. GREEN

edited by
Arthur S. Link
&
Rembert W. Patrick

LOUISIANA STATE UNIVERSITY PRESS

FOREWORD

F LETCHER MELVIN GREEN was born at Gainesville, Georgia, in 1895 and was graduated from Emory Academy, Emory University (Ph.B., 1920) and the University of North Carolina (A.M., 1922, and Ph.D., 1927). During World War I he served in the United States Army Expeditionary Force in France. His teaching career began at Lindsey-Wilson Preparatory School at Columbia, Kentucky in 1920. From 1923 to 1924 he taught at Sparks Junior College and during the following year was assistant professor of history at Vanderbilt University. He was assistant professor (1927–1930) and associate professor (1930–1933) at the University of North Carolina. After a three-year tenure as professor at Emory University, he returned to the University of North Carolina in 1936, was appointed Kenan Professor in 1946, and became chairman of the department of history in 1953. On reaching the university's mandatory retirement age for administrators in 1960, he continued his career as a teacher of undergraduate and graduate students. Meanwhile he joined the summer staff of many institutions, was visiting professor at North Carolina College (1941–1944) and Harvard University (1944–1945), and delivered the Fleming Lectures at Louisiana State University and the Young Lectures at Memphis State University.

His interest in the advancement of the historical profession has been demonstrated by his membership and service in national, regional, and state associations. He was president of the Southern Historical Association (1945), the North Carolina Historical Society (1953), the North Carolina Literary and Historical Association (1955), and the Mississippi Valley Historical Association (1960–1961). In addition he was a member of the executive councils of these organizations and the board of editors of the journals published by them. He has held offices in and served on committees of many other historical societies.

Although his writings are a substantial contribution to historical knowledge, Fletcher M. Green is preeminently a teacher. It is characteristic of him that he has never used his graduate students as a means to support a distinctive interpretation of history or contribute chapters for special books. After describing the techniques of a few distinguished teachers, Wendell Holmes Stephenson characterized Professor Green's methods and results in the following paragraph:

Some other seminars with genuine inner life have had a purpose other than producing books from a central seminal idea of the teacher. The director of one at the University of North Carolina since the 1930's cannot identify the spark that sets members on the road to historianship. "I agree," he says, that they "must have the burning desire to learn, to teach, and to write, but under what circumstances and why they come by that zeal I cannot say." Members of the seminar and observers of its fruits may know the answer even if the modest director does not. Numeration does not explain it, though it may serve as an index. One hundred and fifty have completed the master's degree, nearly ninety have attained the doctorate, and twenty-five more are working on their dissertations. A few of the hundred books and two hundred and twenty-five articles in historical journals have been awarded prizes. Thirty former members have won Guggenheim, Ford, Rosenwald, Social Science Research Council, Fulbright, and Institute for Advance Study fellowships. They have taught in half of the states and in England, Germany, Japan, and India. This record equals, if it does not surpass, that attained by Johns Hopkins students under Adams' tutelage.[1]

This book is dedicated to Fletcher Melvin Green, a master teacher.

1 Wendell Holmes Stephenson, *Southern History in the Making: Pioneer Historians of the South* (Baton Rouge, 1964), 24–25. Quoted with permission of the author and publisher.

PREFACE

SOUTHERNERS who lament that they are misunderstood or maligned must admit that in any event their region has not been ignored. Since the colonial era the number of articles and books about the South has multiplied almost in geometric ratio, until southern historiography excels as well as exceeds that of any other region of the United States. No single volume, however, has presented southern historiography systematically, in detail, and in all its immense variety.

This book surveys and analyzes the writing on various segments and aspects of southern history. The essays vary in style, emphasis, and interpretation, for the editors demanded no bridling conformity. Authors and editors had a common purpose—to produce a book of considerable coherence and unity that would do justice to the literature on the history of the South. The articles were written by former students of Fletcher Melvin Green at the University of North Carolina to honor a master teacher. To fulfill this second purpose, every essay was planned and written solely for publication in this volume.

Various proposals for a *festschrift* to honor Professor Green culminated in the election by his former students of a Green Essay Committee composed of Dewey W. Grantham, J. Carlyle Sitterson, and Bennett H. Wall. The committee selected the editors who planned the book and, in consultation with the committee, chose the contributors. Most of the authors began their work in the autumn of 1961, and their articles were completed at various dates from 1962 to 1965. Two contributors, Vernon L. Wharton and Charles E. Cauthen, died before this book went to press. Dean Wharton had completed his essay before his death, and W. Magruder Drake and Amos Simpson took responsibility for seeing it through to publication. Lewis P. Jones completed Professor Cauthen's chapter.

The editors have accumulated a pleasant burden of indebtedness while guiding this work to completion. They are grateful to the members of the Green Essay Committee, particularly its chairman, Professor Wall, for many services and to the contributors for their cooperation and patience. Mary Frances Green, George B. Tindall, and Cornelius O. Cathey, all of Chapel Hill, North Carolina, responded to every request for information about Professor Green. Neva Armstrong, secretary of the Department of History at the University of Kentucky, recorded discussions at conferences, kept files, and typed and mailed more than a thousand letters. Eleanor B. Patrick alphabetized index cards and prepared the detailed index. Beverly Penny gave outstanding editorial assistance. The University of Florida, Princeton University, and the University of Kentucky contributed office supplies and the time of members of their staffs. The editors and authors of course are responsible for whatever errors remain in this book.

ARTHUR S. LINK
REMBERT W. PATRICK

Princeton, New Jersey
Gainesville, Florida
March 25, 1965

CONTENTS

WRITING
SOUTHERN
HISTORY

I

The Colonial South

Hugh F. Rankin

CARL BRIDENBAUGH, in his *Myths and Realities,* maintains that there was no colonial South, but only a heterogeneous people living south of Pennsylvania. There were, he explains, only two creative forces that moved over into the nineteenth century to shape the traditional South: a predominantly rural community and the institution of slavery.[1] But how many forces are necessary to shape a region? Could it not be stated that the harsh climate and hard-scrabble soil of New England were equally instrumental in assigning to that section a future of commerce and industry? So it was that the South's agrarian characteristics and Negro slavery were outgrowths of the inconsistencies of geography.

In rebuttal to those historians who claim that the South did not begin to manifest sectionalist tendencies until the 1820's, John R. Alden argues

1 Bridenbaugh, *Myths and Realities: Societies of the Colonial South* (Baton Rouge, 1952).

3

that the First South arose in opposition to the First North between 1775 and 1789. He supports his conclusions in such basic areas as climate, specialized farming, Negro slavery, and that ever-elusive intangible, a "southern way of life." [2] It seems only a reasonable supposition that if these characteristics were flushed into the open through a revolution, elementary differences and frictions, albeit dormant, existed prior to that time.

The fact that an agrarian community seldom engages in literary pursuits introduces an element of geographical determinism into the historiography of the southern colonies. Concentrating his energies upon "that bewitching vegetable," tobacco, the southern colonial was quite content to cultivate his weed and allow the more literate New Englander to extol the virtues of the Puritan way of life. This negligence has been ironically repaid, for today many a schoolboy (alas, even in the South!) will automatically credit the Pilgrims of Massachusetts with founding the first English settlement on American soil.

Discounting the compilations of the Hakluyts and Hariot's chronicles of Roanoke Island, Virginia fostered the first production of what might be termed historiography in the sometimes garrulous and often self-aggrandizing writings of Captain John Smith. The frequency with which he indulged his flair for the romantic made later historians prone to label the ebullient captain as an imaginative and colossal liar. In recent years, however, Smith has been reconsidered, with implications that he is more reliable than had been intimated, and perhaps even may be forgiven for his, "I know I shall be taxed for writing so much of my selfe: but I care not much." And there must always be the controlling realization that Smith's primary objective was to spotlight the New World as a field for England's future greatness. One recent plea for Smith submits the brief that his fall from grace dates from the period of the American Civil War when northern historians, viewing the gregarious captain as a symbol of southern honor, attacked his veracity.[3]

For nearly a century after the settlement of Jamestown, the primary

2 Alden, *The First South* (Baton Rouge, 1961).
3 Edward Arber and A. G. Bradley (eds.), *Travels and Works of Captain John Smith* (2 vols.; Edinburgh, 1910); J. M. Morse, "John Smith and His Critics," *Journal of Southern History*, I (May, 1935), 123–37; Lewis L. Kropf, "Captain John Smith of Virginia," *Notes and Queries*, IX, 7th series (1890), 1–2, 41–43, 102–104, 161–62, 223–24, 281–82; Bradford Smith, *Captain John Smith: His Life and Legend* (Philadelphia, 1953); Laura Polanyi Striker and Bradford Smith, "The Rehabilitation of Captain John Smith," *Journal of Southern History*, XXVIII (December, 1962), 476–81.

writings of the southern colonists were contained within such sweeping observations as John Oldmixon's *British Empire in America*. Not until 1705, when Robert Beverley published his *History and Present State of Virginia*, was there a significant southern history of local origin. Beverley's approach was the first that could be compared with that of the modern analytical historian in that he dwells at length upon Virginia's dissipation of resources, a fault attributed to the laziness of her people ("climate struck," he calls them). He observes that "where God Almighty is so Merciful as to work for People, they never work for themselves." It is when Beverley deviates from his cause-and-effect matrix and strays into the contemporary political scene that he loses his objectivity. He paints an ugly picture of English control and works himself into a near-hysterical tirade against the wickedness of the governors, especially the incumbent Francis Nicholson.[4]

Although written in 1697, *The Present State of Virginia, and the College*, by Henry Hartwell, James Blair, and Edward Chilton, was not published until 1727. Tinged with personal bias, the observations of these Scotch- and English-born witnesses concentrated upon descriptions of the various agencies of government, but also demonstrated a strong interest in the changes taking place in that civilization transferred from the Old to the New World.[5]

In 1724 the Reverend Hugh Jones published his *Present State of Virginia*, subtitled *From Whence Is Inferred a Short View of Maryland and North Carolina*. There is but scant mention of the adjoining colonies, however, and any impressions must be "inferred" from the discussion of Virginia. At the request of "some gentlemen of distinction" Jones added a rather heavy appendix of suggestions for bettering the colony, among them a recommendation for including an instructor of history in the faculty of the College of William and Mary.[6]

A more sophisticated account, *History of the First Discovery and Settlement of Virginia*, appeared in 1747. The author, William Stith, rector of Henrico Parish and a governor of William and Mary College, proposed to correct some of the "learned Trumpery" of his predecessors. Ending his story with 1624, Stith upheld the writings of Captain John

4 Beverley, *The History and Present State of Virginia*, ed. Louis B. Wright (Chapel Hill, 1947).

5 Hartwell, Blair, and Chilton, *The Present State of Virginia, and the College*, ed. Hunter Dickinson Farish (Williamsburg, 1940).

6 Jones, *The Present State of Virginia: From Whence Is Inferred a Short View of Maryland and North Carolina*, ed. Richard L. Morton (Chapel Hill, 1956).

Smith and stood on the side of the Virginia Company in its dispute with
the Crown.[7]

John Lawson's *History of North Carolina,* published in London in
1709 and 1714 and later plagiarized by Dr. John Brickell, was not unlike a propaganda tract, flavored with descriptions of flora and fauna,
and interspersed with personal experiences. Yet the patient reader may
discover some rather pungent and winsome commentaries on the North
Carolinians of the day.[8]

A unique satirical work by Patrick Tailfer, Hugh Anderson, and
David Douglas appeared in 1741, bearing the title, *A True and Historical
Narrative of the Colony of Georgia in America.* This attack upon Ogle-
thorpe included a parade of panaceas for all ills then plaguing
the colony. The unusual feature does not lie in the polemics of the
authors, but in the running commentaries by one of the trustees of
Georgia, the Earl of Egmont.[9]

There are good reasons for the absence of greater historical activity
among the southern colonists. In the first place, printing presses and book
publication are the marks of an urban civilization. Perhaps a partial explanation can be found in the words of Stephen Vincent Benét:

> And those who came were resolved to be Englishmen,
> Gone to World's End, but English every one.[10]

In their efforts to re-create an England in the wilderness, the early
settlers looked eastward across the Atlantic for their mirror of life. Those
who indulge their vanity in ancestor worship may be tempted to dispute
the basic illiteracy of the southern colonials by calling attention to the
more than 3,600 titles in the personal library of William Byrd, but
Byrd was the exception rather than the rule. Philip Alexander Bruce,
examining more than 18,000 names in the seventeenth-century records

7 Stith, *History of the First Discovery and Settlement of Virginia* (Williamsburg,
1747).

8 Lawson, *Lawson's History of North Carolina, Containing the Exact Description
and Natural History of that Country, Together with the Present State Thereof
and a Journal of a Thousand Miles Travelled through Several Nations of Indians,
Giving a Particular Account of their Customs, Manners, Etc. Etc.,* ed. Frances
Latham Harris (Richmond, 1937); John Brickell, *The Natural History of North
Carolina* (Dublin, 1737); Percy G. Adams, "John Lawson's Alter-Ego—
Dr. John Brickell," *North Carolina Historical Review,* XXXIV (July, 1957),
315–27.

9 Tailfer, Anderson, and Douglas, *A True and Historical Narrative of the Colony
of Georgia in America,* ed. Clarence L. Ver Steeg (Athens, 1960).

10 Benét, *Western Star* (New York, 1943), 116.

of Virginia, determined that nearly one half of the white males (including some judges) and three fourths of the white female population were unable to sign their names. Those fortunate enough to enjoy the printed word directed their interests into the accumulation of works of "useful knowledge," applicable to everyday problems, rather than the interpretations of the past. Thirteen years after Governor William Berkeley thanked God there were no free schools or printing presses to spread "false gospel," the Reverend John Clayton described Jamestown in 1684 with the words: "They have few scholars, so that every one studys to be halfe Physitian, halfe Lawyer, and with a natural accuteness that amuse thee, for want of books they read men the more." [11]

Not until the rise of nationalism and the realization that events of the past were a partial basis for current greatness, was there something of a renaissance in the writing of local history in the South. Accepting this premise as a cue, Virginia took the lead in documenting her heritage. As an example of this and subsequent enthusiasm, a recent bibliography of writings about seventeenth-century Virginia alone totaled seventy-three pages.[12] That class best endowed with the ability and education to analyze the past was often drained off by the lure of a legal or political career. Others literate enough to engage in historical writing were so often steeped in lofty self-respect that there was little attempt to place the colonial South within the framework of the American colonies. George Tucker possibly had the best opportunity to create this perspective in 1856 in his *History of the United States,* but he was so eager to get to the heroic events of the American Revolution and a defense of southern institutions that he did little more than bare the bones of the earlier period. On the other hand, Charles E. A. Gayarré's *Histoire de la Louisiane* was so exceptional that his work is still considered a basic source in that area, and has left him with a reputation as the South's finest historian prior to the Civil War.[13]

There are other early nineteenth-century historians who should not be ignored. Despite the charge of plagiarism leveled against David Ramsay, his *History of South Carolina,* written in 1808, contains much that is useful about social, economic, and scientific developments within that

11 Quoted in Daniel J. Boorstin, *The Americans: The Colonial Experience* (New York, 1958), 304, 305.
12 E. G. Swem, John M. Jennings, and James A. Servies, *A Selected Bibliography of Virginia, 1607–1689,* in E. G. Swem (ed.), *Jamestown 350th Anniversary Historical Booklets* (23 vols.; Williamsburg, 1957).
13 Tucker, *The History of the United States* (4 vols.; Philadelphia, 1856–1857); Gayarré, *Histoire de la Louisiane* (2 vols.; New Orleans, 1846).

colony. And it should be noted in Ramsey's defense that plagiarism in his
day did not carry much onus, and he freely admitted his "great reliance"
upon Alexander Hewat's *Historical Account of the Rise and Progress of
the Colonies of South Carolina and Georgia,* published in London in
1779. Hewat in turn made free use of the earlier writings of Governors
John Glen and John Archdale, along with those of George Milligan. In
a like manner, later South Carolina historians, including J. B. O.
Landrum, and Edward McCrady, were not above paraphrasing Hewat.[14]
Similar in approach to Ramsey's works were John Daly Burk's *History
of Virginia* and Francis L. Hawk's *History of North Carolina,* along
with the histories of that same state by Hugh Williamson and François
X. Martin, all near enough to the colonial period to retain the flavor of
that era. The same might be said for Hugh McCall's *History of Georgia.*[15]

Not until near the end of the nineteenth century, when the South was
beginning to acquire some of those characteristics usually associated with
an urban civilization, were there increased and serious efforts to produce
scholarly studies of the region. By then much had been lost through the
destruction and deterioration of the records. Even then it was not always
possible to escape the affectations of romanticism. For example, John
Esten Cooke's mistitled *Virginia, A History of a People,* which was published in 1883, presented a rhapsodic view of the cavalier planters, and
the work in general was redolent with the scent of magnolias. Fourteen
years later John Fiske wrote brilliantly of *Old Virginia and Her Neighbors.* Although the book still reads well, it mirrors Fiske's tendency to
sacrifice accuracy for the sake of a pretty story or the turn of a neat
phrase. Fiske saw in a band of romantic cavaliers the essence of all that
is good in American history.[16]

Even with the reality of the twentieth century pressing upon them,
many writers, though impressed by the scientific approach, still labored

14 Orin G. Libby, "Ramsey as a Plagiarist," *American Historical Review,* VII
(July, 1902), 697–703; Ramsey, *History of South Carolina, from Its First Settle-
ment in 1670, to the Year 1808* (2 vols.; Charleston, 1809); Elmer D. Johnson.
"Alexander Hewat: South Carolina's First Historian," *Journal of Southern History,*
XX (February, 1954), 50–62.

15 Burk, *The History of Virginia from Its First Settlement to the Commencement
of the Revolution* (3 vols.; Petersburg, 1804–1805); Hawks, *History of North
Carolina* (2 vols.; Fayetteville, 1858–1859); Martin, *The History of North Carolina, From the Earliest Period* (2 vols.; New Orleans, 1892); Williamson, *History
of North Carolina* (2 vols.; Philadelphia, 1812); McCall, *History of Georgia* (2
vols.; Savannah, 1811–1816).

16 Cooke, *Virginia, A History of a People* (Boston, 1883); Fiske, *Old Virginia
and Her Neighbors* (Boston, 1897).

under the nationalistic influences of George Bancroft. Virginia still held the center of the stage, with the president of the College of William and Mary, Lyon G. Tyler, in the vanguard of a group of able writers whose efforts increasingly began to illustrate a modern concept of history. Alexander Brown, whose real forte lay in compiling and editing, brought out his two-volume documentary, *The Genesis of the United States*. It was followed in 1898 by his *The First Republic in America,* a detailed history of Virginia down to 1627 which, as the title implies, suggested that democracy first began to develop in that colony. Prejudices were not always easy to curb, and Lyon Tyler's *The Cradle of the Republic* was a vehicle for expressing his personal animosity toward the dictatorial measures of Captain John Smith and the Virginia Company.[17]

More substantial interpretations appeared in the still-useful works of Philip Alexander Bruce: *Economic History of Virginia in the Seventeenth Century, Institutional History of Virginia in the Seventeenth Century,* and *Social Life of Virginia in the Seventeenth Century*. Each of these titles represents solid research and evaluation; and, although Bruce does not belong to the "Cavalier School" of Virginia history, there was a wistful note in the "many evidences that a large number of the immigrants were sprung from English families of substance." In *Social Life of Virginia,* Bruce comes to the interesting conclusion that there was little to differentiate the rural communities of England from those of Virginia other than the institution of slavery.[18]

In South Carolina during this period Edward McCrady was writing his *History of South Carolina Under the Proprietary Government, 1670–1719,* and *History of South Carolina Under the Royal Government, 1719–1776*. Some critics consider McCrady's series "one of the best state histories written." Especially excellent were his chapters detailing economic and social life in the eighteenth century, though he did ignore relationships between social and political developments. And there were occasions when McCrady found it difficult to control his rampant patriotism; this resulted in a tendency to condemn unjustly when measuring colonial developments by the yardstick of the American

---

17 Brown, *The Genesis of the United States* (2 vols.; Boston, 1890), and *The First Republic in America* (Boston, 1898) ; Tyler, *The Cradle of the Republic* (Richmond, 1907).

18 Bruce, *Economic History of Virginia in the Seventeenth Century* (2 vols.; New York, 1895), *Institutional History of Virginia in the Seventeenth Century* (2 vols.; New York, 1910), and *Social Life of Virginia in the Seventeenth Century* (Richmond, 1907).

Revolution.[19] Equally nationalistic were the writings of Newton D. Mereness on the history of proprietary Maryland.[20]

With the rise of the "Imperial School" of colonial historians and the idea that American history extended beyond local horizons, researchers pushed into European backgrounds with all of the zeal of genealogists. Edward Channing's multivolume *History of the United States* dealt with the imperial theme and devoted as much space to the southern colonies as to his native New England. Channing still offers much to the student of colonial history, even though he does accept the notion of "gentleman volunteers" as being the first settlers of Virginia and thus "the first heroes of American history." [21]

Charles M. Andrews represents the epitome of the Imperial School, and, since his writings concentrated heavily upon the English background, his interest inevitably lags when he focuses on the colonies. This he explains with the statement, "The colonial period of our history is not American, only Anglo-American." [22]

Following Andrews' contention that all thirty British colonies underwent the same colonial experience, Lawrence Henry Gipson, Andrews' most outstanding student and disciple, has followed the imperial path in his multivolume *British Empire Before the American Revolution*. Despite a style and organization sometimes ponderous, there can be no argument about the thoroughness of his research or the meticulous perspective in which Gipson has placed the colonies in their relationship within the Empire. Describing the colonists as a "world of literate people devoted to freedom and opposed to Governmental regulation," he still leaves room for disagreement in his portrayal of a benevolent empire troubled with her petulant children.[23]

19 McCrady, *History of South Carolina Under the Proprietary Government, 1670–1719* (New York, 1897), and *History of South Carolina Under the Royal Government, 1719–1776* (New York, 1899). See also W. R. Smith, *South Carolina as a Royal Province, 1719–1776* (New York, 1903).

20 Mereness, *Maryland as a Proprietary Province* (New York, 1901). For other studies of Maryland in this period see Gaillard T. Lapsley, *The County Palatine of Maryland; A Study in Constitutional History* (New York, 1900); Clayton C. Hall, *The Lords Baltimore and the Maryland Palatinate* (Baltimore, 1902); Bernard C. Steiner, *Beginnings of Maryland, 1631–1639* (Baltimore, 1903), Steiner, *Maryland During the English Civil Wars* (2 vols.; Baltimore, 1906–1907), and Steiner, *Maryland Under the Commonwealth; A Chronicle of the Years 1649–1658* (Baltimore, 1911).

21 Channing, *A History of the United States* (6 vols.; New York, 1905–1925).

22 Andrews, *The Colonial Period of American History* (4 vols.; New Haven, 1934–1938).

23 Gipson, *The British Empire Before the American Revolution* (7 vols.; Caldwell, Idaho and New York, 1936–1949). Four additional volumes are planned.

As graduate schools were established in the South and Southerners began to divorce historical curiosity from ancestor worship, the colonial period was subjected to almost constant reevaluation. The rash of new interpretations and variety of new approaches would indicate that this new breed of historians was accepting literally the advice of Charles M. Andrews: "History shows us the constant waning of the old and waxing of the new. . . . The task of these historians is to discover the character of these processes and the nature of the laws and forces bringing them about . . . and to determine the measure of human freedom involved." [24] Herbert S. Osgood's earlier complaint about too great a concentration of interest on the seventeenth century was obviously premature, for emphasis now seems to have shifted to the eighteenth century, with more attention being given to those forces and laws of which Andrews spoke.

Few since Edward McCrady have been bold enough to attempt to write comprehensive history of a single colony. One exception is Richard L. Morton, whose stately two-volume *Colonial Virginia* appeared in 1960. Although critics have deplored his lack of new interpretations and adherence to traditional viewpoints, it is difficult to imagine how a volume of this nature could be better researched or organized. Certainly it is more comprehensive and balanced than George F. Willison's *Behold Virginia,* which, one reviewer said, "reads as if its author had a bad case of dyspepsia and thoroughly disliked everyone concerned with the settlement of Virginia. About the only person for whom he has a good word is Powhatan, the Indian Chief." [25]

One-volume state histories have partially filled the void of comprehensive colonial coverage by devoting an increasing number of pages to the period.[26] Perhaps some gratitude should be expressed to the so-called "mug books," publications exploiting the vanity of persons willing to pay a handsome price for the privilege of reading their biographies in supplementary volumes to state histories, while the two volumes allotted

---

24 Andrews, "These Forty Years," *American Historical Review,* XXX (January, 1925), 225–50.

25 Morton, *Colonial Virginia* (2 vols.; Chapel Hill, 1960); Willison, *Behold Virginia: The Fifth Crown* (New York, 1952); Louis B. Wright's review of Willison's book in the *American Historical Review,* LVII (July, 1952), 979–80.

26 Some of the better one-volume state histories are Hugh T. Lefler and Albert R. Newsome, *North Carolina: The History of a Southern State* (Chapel Hill, 1954); David D. Wallace, *South Carolina, A Short History* (Chapel Hill, 1951); Kathryn Abbey Hanna, *Florida: Land of Change* (Chapel Hill, 1948); E. Merton Coulter, *Georgia, A Short History* (Chapel Hill, 1947); Matthew Page Andrews, *Virginia, the Old Dominion* (New York, 1937).

to history allow more coverage for the colonial era. Those by R. D. W. Connor and Hugh T. Lefler in North Carolina, Philip Alexander Bruce in Virginia, and David D. Wallace in South Carolina are all well-balanced in their organization.

Writings about the colonial period have all too often focused upon a limited area. There is a tendency for those interested in English settlements to ignore the presence of the Spanish. The fact that they were here first is constantly emphasized in the studies of Herbert Bolton and Woodbury Lowery. Lowery not only covered Spanish activities in the lower South, but advanced the thesis that the Spanish sought not only to forestall foreign encroachments in Spanish Florida, including the present state of Georgia, but also to maintain the Florida peninsula as a Spanish fortress protecting the Bahama Channel. An idea of the extent of earlier Spanish efforts may be gained from the little-known, abortive effort to establish a Jesuit mission in the Chesapeake area between 1570 and 1572.[27]

The efforts of Sir Walter Raleigh to establish a colony are revealed in the documents contained in Conway W. Sam's *The Conquest of Virginia* and David B. Quinn's *The Roanoke Voyages*. Quinn stressed the point that Raleigh's efforts must be examined within the framework of England's long rivalry and wars with Spain. And in his slim volume in the "Teach Yourself History" series, *Raleigh and the British Empire,* Quinn removed much of the glamor surrounding the fate of the so-called "Lost Colony" by suggesting that Raleigh's colonists were lost at sea when they attempted to return to England aboard their small pinnace.[28]

Edward P. Cheney saw the settlement of Virginia as one aspect of the rivalry of English trading companies in expanding their areas of influence. Pointing to the similarities between Jamestown and a settlement in Ireland during the same period, he concluded that the Virginia

27 Lowery, *The Spanish Settlements Within the Present Limits of the United States* (2 vols.; New York, 1959 [Reprint of 1901–1905 edition]) ; Bolton, *The Spanish Borderlands* (New Haven, 1921). See also Frederick W. Lodge and Theodore H. Lewis, *Spanish Explorers in the Southern United States, 1528–1543* (New York, 1907) ; Verne E. Chatelain, *The Defenses of Spanish Florida, 1565 to 1763* (Washington, 1941) ; Edward G. Bourne, *Spain in America, 1450–1580* (New York, 1904) ; Herbert I. Priestley, *The Coming of the White Man, 1492–1548* (New York, 1929) ; Clifford M. Lewis, S.J. and Albert J. Loomie, S.J., *The Spanish Jesuit Mission in Virginia, 1570–1572* (Chapel Hill, 1953) ; John Tate Lanning, *The Spanish Missions of Georgia* (Chapel Hill, 1935).

28 Sams, *The Conquest of Vrginia: The First Attempt* (Norfolk, 1924) ; Quinn, *The Roanoke Voyages, 1584–1590* (2 vols.; London, 1955), and *Raleigh and the British Empire* (London, 1947). See also George B. Parks, *Richard Hakluyt and the English Voyages* (New York, 1928).

effort was not unique in the history of English colonization. The best studies of motives for colonization have been made by Wesley Frank Craven. His *Dissolution of the Virginia Company* showed that the administrators of the company were guilty of such gross mismanagement and negligence that it was only proper that the Crown dissolve the corporation. Economic reasons, said Professor Craven, were responsible for the dissolution rather than the old myth that the breakup of the company represented the termination of a struggle between a "Patriot" party determined to steer American government into popular channels, and a "Court" party bent on oligarchy.[29]

Indeed, Craven's writings are now the necessary point of departure for any study of the southern colonies. His *The Southern Colonies in the Seventeenth Century* is a cogent, fast-moving, and well-documented analysis of the South in its first century of English colonization. Agreeing with Andrews that land hunger was one of the basic individual motivations, Craven notes that the early settlers, who thought of themselves as transplanted Europeans, should not be considered Southerners: any sectional prides and prejudices "bespoke principally the ancient ethnological and political divisions of Britain." There is concentration upon the Chesapeake colonies, but this is logical enough since these were the only well-established southern colonies in the seventeenth century; and, as the author suggests, Virginia was a "mother colony" from which a stream of migrants fanned out into other areas, carrying with them those political and social traditions that were to influence the southern way of life.[30]

As opposed to past emphasis upon the cavalier tradition, modern scholars seem intrigued with a search for the roots of democratic institutions as revealed in colonial political practices. Yet their conclusions usually are based upon the activities of a self-styled aristocracy. Democratic tendencies issued from conflicts between Crown officials and legislatures. Carl Bridenbaugh's examination of Virginia politics, in *Seat of Empire,* sees the upper classes of the colony maintaining a firm local control, with the plantation providing a practical school of people and affairs. Still, and despite their admiration for the English aristocracy,

29 Cheney, "Some English Considerations Surrounding the Settlement of Virginia," *American Historical Review,* XII (April, 1907), 507–508; W. F. Craven, *The Dissolution of the Virginia Company: The Failure of a Colonial Experiment* (New York, 1932), and "The Dissolution of the London Company for Virginia," *American Historical Review,* XXXVII (October, 1931), 14–24.

30 W. F. Craven, *The Southern Colonies in the Seventeenth Century, 1607–1689* (Baton Rouge, 1949).

these people were more American than they knew; it was in order to
protect their own interests that they became advocates of separation
from England. The same author, in *Myths and Realities,* saw the gentry's
ideal of public service as the primary virtue of this society.[31]

Pursuing this idea, Jack P. Greene studied the 630 members who sat
in the House of Burgesses between 1720 and 1776. Of this group, he
discovered that 110 delegates dominated the affairs of the colony. Of
this favored number, 92 engaged in planting or part-time planting, and
at least one half were connected through marriage. Despite the gradual
shifting of the geographical center of political power northward and
westward, the leadership of the tidewater was not breached until the
1740's. In a similar vein, Charles Sydnor, in *Gentlemen Freeholders*
(a study deceptive in its depth because of its readability), suggests that
all was not pure in the politics of Virginia, for candidates were not above
"swilling the planters" to solicit votes. This, in turn, made electioneering such an expensive endeavor that the poor would have been effectively excluded from political participation even had they had the opportunity. On the other hand, had the franchise been expanded, the
landed gentry might well have strengthened their already powerful
position by flooding the polls with their toadies and hangers-on. Sydnor
saw eighteenth-century Virginians as colonial Hamiltonians in their attachment to a government of the wealthy, the well-born and the able,
with the homes of the gentry serving as a nursery of practical politics.
This is carried further in Lucille Griffith's *Virginia House of Burgesses,*
in which she concludes that elections turned on personalities rather than
issues or factions. And the franchise was extended more than is suggested by Sydnor, for 60 percent of all white males above sixteen owned
enough property to vote, and around 45 percent exercised their privilege.[32]

Thomas Jefferson Wertenbaker was among the first to deprecate the
idea that the first settlers of Virginia were preeminent among the aristocracy. He saw seventeenth-century Virginia as a colony of small farmers, comparatively free of Negro slaves, with indentured servants rising
to the level of respectable landholders. It was in the eighteenth century
that Negro slavery developed in response to the real key to Virginia his-

31 Bridenbaugh, *Seat of Empire: The Political Role of Eighteenth-Century Williamsburg* (Williamsburg, 1950), and *Myths and Realities.*

32 Greene, "Foundations of Political Power in the Virginia House of Burgesses,
1720–1776," *William and Mary Quarterly,* XVI, 3rd series (October, 1959), 485–
506; Sydnor, *Gentleman Freeholders: Political Practices in Washington's Virginia*
(Chapel Hill, 1952); Griffith, *Virginia House of Burgesses, 1750–1774* (North-
port, Ala., 1963).

tory, the tobacco madness. The small farmer was forced to compete with slaves, and his political influence faded until there was no longer a "vigorous, intelligent, independent yeomanry." In *Give Me Liberty,* Wertenbaker views Virginia political history as a relentless and purposeful pursuit of self-government from the founding of Jamestown to the American Revolution, with the House of Burgesses arrayed against the governor and council. Willison goes beyond Wertenbaker in saying that early Virginians were little more than the off-scourings of England, but he does concede that out of this group grew an intellectual aristocracy superior to that of any other colony.[33] Yet, Louis B. Wright, in *The First Gentlemen of Virginia,* concluded that something like a cavalier tradition was a source of continuous vitality in the evolution of "the most public-spirited aristocracy this country has ever known." Morton's *Colonial Virginia* viewed the contest between Crown and Burgesses as a proving ground for modern democratic institutions; he makes a point for the cavaliers by noting the number of refugees from Puritan England who were influential in the development of the colony.[34]

Bernard Bailyn, in a succinct essay, implied that there was always a cadre of leaders drawn from the top level of English society during the first fifteen years of Virginia history, but that this group did not survive a single generation. The vacuum created by their disappearance was filled not only by those who were strong enough to survive, but also by men ambitious and shrewd enough to see the advantages of a seat in the legislature. This group, however, did not necessarily spring from the lower class, but included "ambitious younger sons of middle class families who knew well enough what gentility was and sought it as a specific objective." Although speaking of Virginia, he infers that the same generalizations might well apply to all southern colonies. Despite surface harmony there was an area of permanent conflict between political and social leadership at the top level. And, as if to refute those who see colonial Virginia as a seedbed of liberal reform, Professor Bailyn,

33 Wertenbaker, *Patrician and Plebian: Or, The Origin and Development of the Social Classes of the Old Dominion* (Charlottesville, 1910), *Virginia Under the Stuarts, 1607–1688* (Princeton, 1914), *The Planters of Colonial Virginia* (Princeton, 1922), *The Old South: The Founding of American Civilization* (New York, 1942), and *Give Me Liberty: The Struggle for Self-Government in Virginia* (Philadelphia, 1958); Willison, *Behold Virginia.*
34 Wright, *The First Gentlemen of Virginia: Intellectual Qualities of the Early Colonial Ruling Class* (San Marino, 1940); Morton, *Colonial Virginia.* See also Percy S. Flippin, *The Royal Government of Virginia* (New York, 1919); Julian A. C. Chandler, *The History of Suffrage in Virginia* (Baltimore, 1901).

in another essay, views Virginia as more conservative than other colonies.[35]

Donnell MacLane Owings found divergent patterns in the proprietary patronage of Maryland, "for the offices were less important than the men who filled them." Maryland officeholders were, in general, from the conservative element and loyal in their defense of prerogative. Economic considerations were important, for planting alone was insufficient to accumulate fortunes, and it was necessary to increase wealth through land speculation, commercial or industrial activity, the practice of law, and officeholding. Aubrey C. Land's biographical study of the two Dulanys of colonial Maryland not only covers the entire spectrum of eighteenth-century Maryland politics, but also projects political developments into the background of social growth. Using his subjects as examples, Land demonstrated that as a colonial politician leaned toward conservatism, the quality of his political thinking degenerated.[36] This trend toward conservatism may explain the conclusion, reached in Greene's study of the lower houses of legislatures in the eighteenth century, that only Maryland among the southern colonies failed to reach political maturity by 1763.[37]

In North Carolina a strong theme of sectionalism ran throughout colonial politics. Disagreements over representation between 1734 and 1754 created factions and drove the Albemarle and Cape Fear sections apart. Because of this hostility the welfare of the colony suffered, and progress was retarded. Although the older Albemarle area was to remain supreme in politics until the Revolution, back-country discontent manifested itself in the "War of the Regulation." Incompatibility between the tidewater and the West has been attributed to several factors: the disorganized state of the government, a lack of homogeneity among the people, the distance between frontier and the seat of the government, and conflicts arising out of differences in political, religious, and social mores. Because of this multiplicity of ills, the North Carolina

35 Bailyn, "Politics and Social Structure in Virginia," in James Morton Smith (ed.), *Seventeenth-Century America: Essays in Colonial History* (Chapel Hill, 1959), and Bailyn, "Political Experience and Enlightenment Ideas in Eighteenth-Century America," *American Historical Review*, LXVII (January, 1962), 339–51.

36 Owings, *His Lordship's Patronage: Offices of Profit in Colonial Maryland* (Baltimore, 1953); Land, *The Dulanys of Maryland: A Biographical Study of Daniel Dunlany the Younger (1722–1797)* (Baltimore, 1955).

37 Greene, "The Role of the Lower Houses of Assembly in Eighteenth-Century Politics," *Journal of Southern History*, XXVII (November, 1961), 451–74.

Assembly did not gain the upper hand until the 1760's.[38] This coincides
with the complaints of Governor Arthur Dobbs of the "cabals and jun-
tas" arrayed against him during this period, despite the claim of his
biographer that Dobbs was more a man of the people than his adversaries
in the legislature. The lower house gained strength through the usurpa-
tion of some appointive powers of more tractable governors; in later
years it claimed these powers as its right through usage.[39] One factor encouraging chaos in the already turbulent politics of North Carolina was
the land speculations of Henry McCulloh and others in the four decades
prior to the Revolution. This situation, said Charles G. Sellers, Jr., was
by no means unique to North Carolina, and it was through such operations, aided by influential persons in London, that England's "bumbling
colonial policy" emerged. Native politicians resented the intrusions of
McCulloh and other "foreigners," for they wished to control the colony
to their own advantage, and their impatience with the restrictions of
the mother country helped to explain their leadership of the American
Revolution.[40]

Richard Walsh's *Charleston's Sons of Liberty*, primarily concerned
with the Revolutionary activities of the artisans, further illustrates the
familiar structure of political control. Here again the upper classes were
able to maintain their domination through denial of the franchise. Not
until the local market was flooded with imported British goods did the
craftsmen demonstrate their political potential. South Carolina, like
Virginia, had its small, but powerful, political coterie able to exert disproportionate influence. This power was centered in the Royal Council,
where six families exercised dominance through control of the governor.
An equally important pressure group was the mercantile community with
its interlocking partnerships and influence with the board of trade; along
with the six families it was able to control almost 60 percent of the

38 Lawrence F. London, "The Representation Controversy in Colonial North
Carolina," *North Carolina Historical Review*, XI (October, 1934), 255–76;
Alonzo Thomas Dill, *Governor Tryon and His Palace* (Chapel Hill, 1955).

39 Desmond Clarke, *Arthur Dobbs Esquire, 1689–1765: Surveyor-General of Ireland, Prospector and Governor of North Carolina* (Chapel Hill, 1957); Jack P.
Greene, "The North Carolina Lower House and the Power to Appoint Public
Treasurers, 1711–1775," *North Carolina Historical Review*, XL (January, 1963),
37–53.

40 Sellers, "Private Profits and British Colonial Policy: The Speculations of
Henry McCulloh," *William and Mary Quarterly*, VIII, 3rd series (October, 1951),
535–51. See also Charles L. Raper, *North Carolina: A Study in English Colonial
Government* (New York, 1904); Coralie Parker, *The History of Taxation in
North Carolina, 1663–1776* (New York, 1928); John S. Bassett, *The Constitutional
Beginning of North Carolina* (Baltimore, 1894).

council seats. Not until the board of trade decided that men financially dependent upon the Crown were more likely to support prerogative did this coalition's position begin to wane, and then resistance to English authority shifted to the Assembly.[41]

Georgia, it has been said, was slow in developing because of the confusion growing out of the trustees' acceptance of too much responsibility with too little knowledge of American life. A related observation is that the trustees of Georgia, although successful in extracting funds for the colony from Parliament, became involved in political factions and failed to maintain a distinct identity. Too often their decisions were colored by English political considerations, and too often funds were spent injudiciously. Not until Georgia lost its military character did the colony begin to flourish economically under the added stimulus of larger land grants and Negro slavery. In his model study of *The Royal Governors of Georgia,* William W. Abbot suggested that these officials, endowed with greater authority than those in any other colony, championed the causes of the planter class, whose prosperity was dependent upon close ties with Britain, thereby winning the support of the gentry against the lower groups. It was not until 1768 that some of the planters, under pressure, joined the resistance party and thereafter battled Governor James Wright for political control. Abbot likewise implied ragged social and political progress in the statement, "Georgia, a mere lass among matrons, was out of phase." [42]

Even in the less well-developed Floridas, the assemblies were constantly attempting to whittle away the power of the governor. Here, however, the struggle was hampered by the executive's financial independence and a small population that furnished few able delegates. Yet their strength is evident in the legislation disallowed by the Privy

---

41 Walsh, *Charleston's Sons of Liberty: A Study of the Artisans, 1763–1789* (Columbia, 1959); M. Eugene Sirmans, "The South Carolina Royal Council, 1720–1763," *William and Mary Quarterly,* XVIII, 3rd series (July, 1961), 373–92. See also Edson L. Whitney, *The Government of the Colony of South Carolina* (Baltimore, 1895); William A. Schafer, "Sectionalism and Representation in South Carolina," in American Historical Association, *Annual Report, 1900* (Washington, 1901).

42 Boorstin, *The Americans,* 85. See also J. R. McCain, *Georgia as a Proprietary Province* (Boston, 1917); Richard S. Dunn, "The Trustees of Georgia and the House of Commons, 1732–1752," *William and Mary Quarterly,* XI, 3rd series (October, 1954), 551–65; James Etheridge Callaway, *The Early Settlements of Georgia* (Athens, 1948); Trevor Richard Reese, *Colonial Georgia: A Study in British Imperial Policy in the Eighteenth Century* (Athens, 1963); Abbot, *The Royal Governors of Georgia 1754–1775* (Chapel Hill, 1959).

Council.[43] Among those studies on the periphery of colonial politics, yet necessary for full understanding, is Ella Lonn's account of the activities of the agent in London who was not only a lobbyist, but also the overseas voice of the American governments.[44]

Jack Greene, in *The Quest for Power,* a study of the lower houses of the legislatures of Virginia, the Carolinas, and Georgia, comes to the conclusion that it was in the control of finances and the civil list that the representatives won their greatest victories, while at the same time they were usurping many of the functions of the executive. Not only were the Americans of 1776 experienced in representative government, but the Revolution was "in essence a war for political survival." [45]

A flurry of little rebellions broke out along the seaboard between 1660 and 1724. All have been covered in general histories, but the revolt of Nathaniel Bacon in Virginia in 1676 has most titillated the interests of historians. Wertenbaker set off great disagreement in his biography of Bacon, *Torchbearer of the Revolution,* by casting his subject in the role of a seventeenth-century reformer with democratic impulses and representing this internecine struggle as a forerunner of the American Revolution. Craven registers mild disagreement: "Indeed, it might be argued that an interpretation of his rebellion couched in the old-fashioned terms of a sectional contest makes as much sense as the more recent tendency to interpret it in terms of class conflict." Professor Craven saw the rebellion's most significant consequence as a warning to the governing class. A later study, Wilcomb E. Washburn's *The Governor and the Rebel,* with greater reliance on English sources, disputed Wertenbaker's conclusions. Governor William Berkeley appears in a more favorable light, even as something of a defender of liberty, while Bacon is less the champion of democracy than the rabble-rouser who discovered in the unhappy Indian situation and the aggressiveness of the frontiersmen an opportunity for personal political gain. As Bacon's status diminishes, the rebellion shrinks into a dispute over Indian affairs. Washburn gains support from Bernard Bailyn's assertions that the specific grievances leading to the upheaval were later revived, and that no stable political parties or factions arose out of the conflict.

43 Cecil Johnson, *British West Florida, 1763–1783* (New Haven, 1943); C. L. Mowat, *East Florida as a British Province, 1763–1784* (Berkeley, 1943); John Anthony Caruso, *The Southern Frontier* (Indianapolis, 1963).

44 Lonn, *Colonial Agents of the Southern Colonies* (Chapel Hill, 1945).

45 Greene, *The Quest for Power: The Lower Houses of Assembly in the Southern Royal Colonies, 1689–1776* (Chapel Hill, 1963).

Morton suggests that there is more to the Wertenbaker thesis than is usually admitted.[46]

Other outbursts of discontent deserve more detailed examinations as expressions of political or social schisms. The late eighteenth-century "War of the Regulation" in North Carolina, for instance, is no longer considered "the first battle of the American Revolution," but the climax of a revolt of the western people against the oppressive laws and corrupt officials of the tidewater. Conversely, Richard M. Brown in *The South Carolina Regulators*, states that this dispute was not so much a result of frontier-low country relations as a reaction against the lawlessness in the backcountry following the Cherokee war of 1759–1761. These Regulators seem to have been little more than colonial vigilantes attempting to cope with a breakdown in morals.[47]

Inasmuch as the course of politics is so often a reflection of intellectual and social evolution of the community, these activities cannot be isolated from one another. Carl Bridenbaugh, in *Myths and Realities,* reveals the Chesapeake society as a cultural parasite with its greatest weakness being its lack of intellectual growth. He further declares that such men as Madison and Jefferson were but "biological sports in the Chesapeake Society." Admitting that the culture of Charleston was likewise of English origin, Professor Bridenbaugh believes that Charlestonians tried "to cultivate culture." Although life was more vigorous in the back settlements, the frontiersmen emerge as a shiftless, depraved, and reckless breed of what the Reverend Charles Woodmason termed "Vile and Impudent fellows." [48]

Edmund S. Morgan's *Virginians at Home* presents a more attractive picture of Virginians, and, though heavily weighted on the side of the planters, discusses social relationships between the classes when sources permit. Similarly, Maryland is viewed in a more favorable light by

46 Wertenbaker, *Torchbearer of the Revolution: The Story of Bacon's Rebellion and Its Leader* (Princeton, 1940) ; W. F. Craven, *Southern Colonies in the Seventeenth Century,* 389–90; Washburn, *The Governor and the Rebel: A History of Bacon's Rebellion in Virginia* (Chapel Hill, 1957) ; Bailyn, "Politics and Social Structure in Virginia," in J. M. Smith (ed.), *Seventeenth-Century America,* 106; Morton, *Colonial Virginia.*

47 Andrews, *Colonial Period of American History;* W. F. Craven, *Southern Colonies in the Seventeenth Century;* Lefler and Newsome, *North Carolina;* J. S. Bassett, "The Regulators of North Carolina," in American Historical Association, *Annual Report, 1894* (Washington, 1895), 141–212; Richard Maxwell Brown, *The South Carolina Regulators* (Cambridge, 1963).

48 Bridenbaugh, *Myths and Realities;* Richard J. Hooker (ed.), *The Carolina Back Country on the Eve of the Revolution: The Journal and the Writings of Charles Woodmason, Anglican Itinerant* (Chapel Hill, 1953).

Charles A. Barker, who sees social developments in that colony as a growing phase of English culture rooted in foreign soil. Louis B. Wright's *Cultural Life in the American Colonies* emphasizes influences of agrarian life upon southern culture, while in other works he studies and reappraises the impact of non-English immigration upon colonial social growth. Arthur P. Middleton's *Tobacco Coast* likewise attributes the South's cultural dependence to its rural atmosphere. Bailyn's recent evaluation, drawing some of its strength from Wright's findings, concludes that the Virginians "knew themselves to be provincials in the sense that their culture was not self-contained." [49]

Bridenbaugh's major study of the cities of colonial America sees vestiges of urban life in the South only in Charleston. The absence of cities, he contends, was responsible for shaping a culturally sterile South. Delineations of Charleston's culture are likewise presented in Frederick B. Bowes's *The Culture of Early Charleston* and Hennig Cohen's *South Carolina Gazette,* the latter being a graphic example of the value of the colonial newspaper to the historian.[50] Studies of the theater have established the fact that Williamsburg constructed the first theater in the colonies, and that Williamsburg, Annapolis, and Charleston were on the regular itinerary of professional touring companies. Admittedly the colonial theater was of English derivation, but there is some significance in the fact that these communities, especially the two smaller towns, could sustain one of the most attractive ornaments of a civilized society, a repertory theater.[51] James T. Flexner's *American Painting*

49 Morgan, *Virginians at Home: Family Life in the Eighteenth Century* (Williamsburg, 1952) ; Barker, "Maryland Before the Revolution," *American Historical Review,* XLVI (October, 1940), 1–20, and *The Background of the Revolution in Maryland* (New Haven, 1940) ; Wright, *The Cultural Life of the American Colonies, 1607–1763* (New York, 1957), *The Atlantic Frontier: Colonial Civilization (1607–1763)* (New York, 1947), *Culture on the Moving Frontier* (Bloomington, 1955), and *The British Tradition in America* (Birmingham, 1954) ; Middleton, *Tobacco Coast: A Maritime History of the Chesapeake Bay in the Colonial Era* (Newport News, 1953) ; Bailyn, "Politics and Social Structure in Virginia," in J. M. Smith (ed.), *Seventeenth-Century America,* 107.

50 Bridenbaugh, *Cities in the Wilderness: The First Century of Urban Life in America, 1625–1742* (New York, 1938; reissued, 1955), and *Cities in Revolt: Urban Life in America 1743–1776* (New York, 1955) ; Bowes, *The Culture of Early Charleston* (Chapel Hill, 1942) ; Cohen, *The South Carolina Gazette, 1732–1775* (Columbia, 1953). Also see Mrs. St. Julien Ravenal, *Charleston: The Place and the People* (New York, 1927).

51 Robert H. Land, "The First Williamsburg Theater," *William and Mary Quarterly,* V, 3rd series (July, 1948), 359–74; Eola Willis, *The Charleston Stage in the Eighteenth Century* (Columbia, 1924) ; Arthur H. Quinn, *A History of the American Stage* (2 vols.; New York, 1943) ; Hugh F. Rankin, *The Theater in Colonial America* (Chapel Hill, 1965).

includes southern artists, while Margaret Middleton's *Jeremiah Theus,*
with its exposition of central European influences upon New World art
forms, fits a painter into the daily life of Charleston.[52] And Charleston's
St. Cecelia Society—the first American musical organization to support
a paid orchestra—and hospitable reception to concerts by any musical
group is discussed in O. G. Sonneck's *Early Concert-Life in America.*[53]
Although the southern colonies produced little that a modern critic
would deem literature, southern authors are examined in Moses Coit
Tyler's survey, while Jay B. Hubbell places the writings in their proper
perspective. Hubbell also includes a number of valuable bibliographies
for those who would pursue the subject.[54] Wright's *The First Gentlemen of Virginia* examines the significance of social developments by
looking into the literary tastes of the planters. Others have studied personal libraries to determine reading habits, though this technique contains obvious weaknesses, especially when modern book dealers so often
advertise books once owned by well-known colonials with their pages
as yet uncut.[55] And that ever-present female influence in society has
been covered in Julia Cherry Spruill's *Women's Life and Work in the
Southern Colonies.* She testifies that women were responsible for important and lasting contributions to southern culture.[56]

Cultural developments may often be equated with the growth of

52 Flexner, *American Painting: First Flowers of Our Wilderness* (Boston, 1947);
Middleton, *Jeremiah Theus, Colonial Artist of Charles Town* (Columbia, 1953);
Anna Wells Rutledge, *Artists in the Life of Charleston, from Restoration to
Reconstruction* (Philadelphia, 1949).

53 Sonneck, *Early Concert-Life in America, 1731–1800* (New York, 1906).

54 M. C. Tyler, *A History of American Literature During the Colonial Period,
1607–1765* (2 vols.; New York, 1897); Hubbell, *The South in American Literature,
1607–1900* (Durham, 1954). See also Howard M. Jones, *The Literature of Virginia
in the Seventeenth Century* (Boston, 1946).

55 Wright, *The First Gentlemen of Virginia;* William D. Houlette, "Books of
the Virginia Dynasty," *The Library Quarterly,* XXIV (1954), 226–39; Wright,
"The Purposeful Reading of Our Colonial Ancestors," *ELH: A Journal of English
Literary History,* IV (1937), 85–111, and "The 'Gentleman's Library' in
Early Virginia," *Huntington Library Quarterly,* I (October, 1937), 3–61;
Frances L. Spain, "Libraries of South Carolina: Their Origins and Early
History, 1700–1830," *The Library Quarterly,* XVI (1947), 28–42; Stephen B.
Weeks, "Libraries and Literature in North Carolina in the Eighteenth Century,"
in American Historical Association, *Annual Report, 1895* (Washington, 1896);
Julia Cherry Spruill, "The Southern Lady's Library, 1700–1776," *South Atlantic
Quarterly,* XXXIV (1935), 23–41; George K. Smart, "Private Libraries in Colonial
Virginia," *American Literature,* X (1938–1939), 24–52; J. T. Wheeler, "Reading
Interests in Colonial Maryland," *Maryland Historical Magazine,* XXXVI (1941),
281–82; XXXVII (1942), 26–27, 291; XXXVIII (1943), 37–38, 167–68, 273–74.

56 Spruill, *Women's Life and Work in the Southern Colonies* (Chapel Hill, 1938).

communications. Lawrence C. Wroth has molded an example in his examinations of the printing presses of colonial Maryland and of William Parks, colonial journalist. Others have made regional studies, but any inference as to the influence of the press must be found in more general evaluations.[57] The same statement might be applied to the operations of the colonial post office and to transportation and travel accommodations.[58]

Daniel Boorstin's first volume of *The Americans,* though not limited in scope to the South, must be considered for its Turnerian placement of emphasis upon environmental modifications in the intellectual baggage brought by the colonists. And there is a bit of the obvious in one article, which stated that the settlers were too beset by material matters to busy themselves with new and different cultural or intellectual pursuits. Indeed, the authors declared that America and Scotland may be termed "England's Cultural Provinces." One provocative explanation, though open to dispute, is that cultural stagnation in the colonies may be hidden in the thesis that the eighteenth-century learned societies of Europe were becoming more utilitarian in their thought, with their activities leveling off into trivialities.[59]

The rise of a politically and socially dominant class in the southern colonies had many of its origins in slavery, and an institution that permits one human being to enslave another cannot be anything but controversial. In fact, Alexander de Tocqueville once attributed all the differences between North and South to slavery. As a result, the literature of slavery is filled with conflicting views, accusations, and unbalanced interpretations. Earlier historians, almost without question, accepted the fact that the "Twenty Nigars" arriving at Jamestown in 1619 were

57 Wroth, *History of Printing in Colonial Maryland, 1686–1776* (Baltimore, 1922); Parks, *Printer and Journalist of England and Colonial America* (Richmond, 1926); Stephen B. Weeks, *The Press of North Carolina in the Eighteenth Century* (New York, 1891); A. S. Salley, "The First Presses of South Carolina," Bibliographical Society of America *Proceedings and Papers,* II (1907–1908), 26–29; Cohen, *South Carolina Gazette;* Elizabeth C. Cook, *Literary Influences in Colonial Newspapers, 1704–1750* (New York, 1912).

58 William Smith, *The History of the Post Office in British North America, 1639–1870* (Cambridge, 1920); Alice Morse Earle, *Stage-Coach and Tavern Days* (New York, 1935); Elsie Lathrop, *Early American Inns and Taverns* (New York, 1926); F. W. Clonts, "Travel and Transportation in Colonial North Carolina," *North Carolina Historical Review,* III (January, 1926), 16–35.

59 Boorstin, *The Americans: The Colonial Experience;* John Clive and Bernard Bailyn, "England's Cultural Provinces: Scotland and America," *William and Mary Quarterly,* XI, 3rd series (April, 1954), 200–13; Bernard Fay, "Learned Societies in Europe and America in the Eighteenth Century," *American Historical Review,* XXXVII (January, 1932), 255–66.

slaves in fact, if not in law. Bruce, in his *Economic History of Virginia in the Seventeenth Century,* accepted this assumption and distinguished between the treatment of white and black servants with the implication that the Negroes were indentured for life.[60]

The discovery that Virginia's first slavery statute was not adopted until 1660 led James C. Ballagh, in his *A History of Slavery in Virginia,* to conclude that prior to that date, Negroes had the status of servants. Eleven years later, however, John H. Russell in his study, *The Free Negro in Virginia,* noted that slavery, despite the absence of legal sanctions, was fast becoming an accepted fact between 1640 and 1660, a view given credence in the writings of Susie B. Ames. Ulrich B. Phillips, who saw climate as the determining factor in the rise of the plantation system, agreed with Russell. As late as 1949, Craven implied that the white man's natural distaste for the Negro encouraged an early trend toward slavery. Exception was taken by Kenneth Stampp who, in his *The Peculiar Institution,* denied the existence of racial antipathy, declaring that the Negro was only a white man with black skin. Still, there is a case for racial enmity in an examination of the measures taken by the southern colonies to define mulattos (in North Carolina, one-sixteenth Negro blood) and to include such persons in the slave codes.[61]

Seeds of controversy lie in a piquant article by Oscar and Mary Handlin that appeared in the *William and Mary Quarterly* in 1950. They voiced their disagreement with interpretations which implied that racial prejudices were involved. "Negro slavery," they said, "was not spontaneously produced by heat, humidity and tobacco. . . . It emerged rather from an adjustment to American conditions of traditional European institutions." Negroes prior to 1660, the Handlins insist, were indeed indentured servants, but less free than white bondsmen. In a summary of varying interpretations, Winthrop D. Jordan disputes these conclusions and submits the charge "with some candor that the Handlin thesis rests on unsatisfactory documentation." Jordan concludes that a clear distinction between white and black did exist before 1660, and that

60 Bruce, *Economic History of Virginia in the Seventeenth Century.*

61 Ballagh, *A History of Slavery in Virginia* (Baltimore, 1902); Russell, *The Free Negro in Virginia, 1619–1865* (Baltimore, 1913); Ames, *Studies of the Virginia Eastern Shore in the Seventeenth Century* (Richmond, 1940); Phillips, *American Negro Slavery* (New York, 1918). See also T. R. Davis, "Negro Servitude in the United States," *Journal of Negro History,* VIII (July, 1923), 247–83; W. F. Craven, *Southern Colonies in the Seventeenth Century;* Stampp, *The Peculiar Institution: Slavery in the Ante-Bellum South* (New York, 1956); Winthrop P. Jordan, "American Chiaroscuro: The Status and Definition of Mulattoes in the British Colonies," *William and Mary Quarterly,* XIX, 3rd series (April, 1962), 183–200.

economic factors were responsible for an early inclination toward slavery. He also implies that those who assert that prejudice arose after the establishment of slavery have been influenced by problems of contemporary race relations.[62] The Handlins' contradiction of Edward McCrady's generalization that South Carolina's slave code was modeled on that of Barbados was based on a contention that the "labor system of those places [the island colonies] was not fully evolved" when South Carolina drew up its first slave code. This theory, in turn, has been challenged by M. Eugene Sirmans, who declared that seventeenth-century South Carolina gradually accepted the slave pattern of Barbados and developed chattel slavery along Barbadian lines because of early political control by a faction of former Barbadians. Not until after the slave insurrections of 1793 was this approach completely abandoned.[63]

James M. Wright's study of the free Negro in Maryland suggested that slavery existed in that colony almost from its first settlement. John S. Bassett, in *Slavery and Servitude in Colonial North Carolina,* stated that the institution was a phenomenon of the coastal plains, and that the increase in the slave population in that colony was the result of the birth rate rather than importation. It was also his conclusion that the Negro was as much a civilizing influence as the white man.[64] In general, the controversy over the legal status of the Negro seems to have overshadowed the need for a good modern study of the economic and social impact of slavery.

One interesting adjunct to the slavery question is the small number of Negro landowners in seventeenth-century Virginia who not only held black servants, but were sufficiently prosperous to pay the transportation costs of white indentured servants, on each of whom they could claim fifty acres of land.[65] Equally interesting is the attitude of English

62 Oscar and Mary F. Handlin, "Origins of the Southern Labor System," *William and Mary Quarterly,* VII, 3rd series (April, 1950), 199–222; Jordan, "Modern Tensions and the Origins of American Slavery," *Journal of Southern History,* XXVIII (February, 1962), 18–30.

63 McCrady, "Slavery in the Province of South Carolina, 1670–1770," in American Historical Association, *Annual Report, 1895* (Washington, 1896) ; Sirmans, "The Legal Status of the Slave in South Carolina, 1670–1740," *Journal of Southern History,* XXVIII (November, 1962), 462–73.

64 Wright, *The Free Negro in Maryland, 1634–1860* (New York, 1921) ; see also Jeffrey R. Brackett, *The Negro in Maryland* (Baltimore, 1889) ; Bassett, *Slavery and Servitude in the Colony of North Carolina* (Baltimore, 1896).

65 James H. Brewer, "Negro Property Owners in Seventeenth Century Virginia," *William and Mary Quarterly,* XII, 3rd series (October, 1955), 575–80. See also John H. Russell, "Colored Freemen as Slave Owners in Virginia," *Journal of Negro History,* I (July, 1916), 234–37.

mercantilists who, ever desirous of obtaining staple products in exchange for more expensive manufactured goods, were overly apprehensive of high labor costs in America. Although opposing Negro slavery because it opened no new markets, they became reconciled to the system after the first half of the eighteenth century because of the greater utilization of land.[66] One facet of slavery as yet not subjected to close examination in the southern colonies is that of Indian slavery. South Carolina apparently practiced this more than other southern colonies, but most of the savages captured in the war were immediately shipped out to be sold in the West Indies rather than retained as local labor.[67]

Richard B. Morris' study encompassing all the colonies, *Government and Labor in Early America,* discovers the origins of many later labor practices. There was, for instance, the essence of white supremacy in the efforts of the colonial artisans to restrain ruinous competition imposed by slavery, while the roots of the convict-labor system can be seen in the practice of importing convicted criminals. Professor Morris disposes of those who would be prone to view colonial labor practices in modern humanitarian terms in one succinct statement: "In the seventeenth and eighteenth centuries the personal-service contract was specifically enforced as a property right." [68]

A. E. Smith's examination of the status of the indentured servant in America, *Colonists in Bondage,* concluded that this system was not only the most economic method of relieving the labor shortage, but at the same time an effective means of promoting colonization. Those who were strong enough to survive the winnowing processes of the New World, he said, "became the American people." And to critics of the system, Smith replied that the practice of indentures was as fair as could be expected for the times, for those who were indentured were of a group who could expect exploitation wherever they were. There is some disagreement in Mildred Campbell's examination of the middle and late seventeenth-century port records of Bristol and London. Most of the immigrants in that era were not social and economic dregs but were usually farmers or skilled laborers. Warren B. Smith's *White Servitude in South Carolina* comes to the interesting conclusion that white servants

66 C. Robert Haywood, "Mercantilism and Colonial Slave Labor," *Journal of Southern History,* XXIII (November, 1957), 454–64.

67 Almon Wheeler Lauber, *Indian Slavery in Colonial Times Within the Present Limits of the United States* (New York, 1913). See also W. Stitt Robinson, Jr., "Legal Status of the Indian in Colonial Virginia," *Virginia Magazine of History and Biography,* LXI (July, 1953), 247–359.

68 Morris, *Government and Labor in Early America* (New York, 1946).

were desired initially for their labor, later, as a supplemental protective force against Indians and slaves.[69]

Then there were the free laborers, or colonial craftsmen. Carl Bridenbaugh, in his study of these artisans, stated that the southern craftsmen, because of the rural atmosphere and the competition of slave labor, were inevitably drawn into farming by reason of their inability to make a living. Walsh registered some disagreement by arguing that slavery served to advance the white artisans of South Carolina who were able to increase production through the exploitation of cheap Negro labor. In this same vein, Marcus W. Jernigan believed that the diversification of farming in the South led to the employment of slaves in nonagricultural and manufacturing processes, with the slave artisan becoming the most important agency in the development of plantation manufacturing.[70] Other studies of specific craftsmen have been made, but too often they assume the format of spoon-collectors' manuals.

Tobacco is often credited with providing the impetus for the rise of slavery and shaping the economic future of the southern colonies. Sarah Dickson's *Panacea or Bane* is a very readable survey of tobacco in seventeenth-century writings. Joseph C. Robert's *The Story of Tobacco in America* devotes space to the colonial cultivation of the "holy herb." Jerome E. Brooks's *The Mighty Leaf* makes the point that heavy concentration upon the cultivation of the weed brought about the imposition of the factor or consignment system upon the unhappy planters by London mercantile interests, a situation that was to lead Jefferson to describe the Virginians as "a species of property annexed to certain mercantile houses in London." [71] The influence of tobacco culture upon

69 A. E. Smith, *Colonists in Bondage: White Servitude and Convict Labor in America, 1607–1776* (Chapel Hill, 1947); Campbell, "Social Origins of Some Early Americans," in J. M. Smith (ed.), *Seventeenth-Century America*, 63–89; W. B. Smith, *White Servitude in South Carolina* (Columbia, 1961). See also Eugene I. McCormac, *White Servitude in Maryland, (1634–1820)* (Baltimore, 1904); James C. Ballagh, *White Servitude in the Colony of Virginia* (Baltimore, 1895).

70 Bridenbaugh, *The Colonial Craftsman* (New York, 1950); Walsh, *Charleston's Sons of Liberty;* Jernigan, *Laboring and Dependent Classes in Colonial America, 1607–1783* (Chicago, 1931), and "Slavery and the Beginnings of Industrialism in the American Colonies," *American Historical Review*, XXV (January, 1920), 220–40.

71 Dickson, *Panacea or Bane: Tobacco in Sixteenth-Century Literature* (New York, 1954); Robert, *The Story of Tobacco in America* (New York, 1949); Brooks, *The Mighty Leaf: Tobacco Through the Centuries* (Boston, 1952). See also Jacob Price, "The Rise of Glasgow Merchants in the Chesapeake Tobacco Trade, 1707–1775," *William and Mary Quarterly*, XI, 3rd series (April, 1954), 179–99; Lewis C. Gray, "The Market Surplus Problems of Colonial Tobacco,"

the Chesapeake and its tributaries is the theme of Middleton's *Tobacco Coast,* but he also saw the same geographical forces as being instrumental in the development of a flourishing trade and ship-building interests second only to those of New England. Equally interesting is the discussion centered on the seldom-mentioned Chesapeake trade with other colonies and southern Europe "founded on grain." A. J. Doyle's assertions that Carolina tobacco prosperity lagged because of an inferior leaf is challenged by W. Neill Franklin. He argues that lack of suitable waterways and legislative reprisals of Virginia must share the blame.[72]

In the general field of southern agriculture, Lewis C. Gray and Avery Craven look back into the colonial experience to trace fundamental elements in the evolution of southern society and agree that the two primary factors responsible for reduction in tobacco profits were soil exhaustion and mounting burdens of fixed charges and debts.[73] Louis Morton, in *Robert Carter of Nomini Hall,* examines the various social and economic components of the plantation system as reflected in the career of one planter; his revelation of Carter's rather large-scale manufacturing along with other economic enterprises divorced from the raising of tobacco should be noted.[74]

One of the most delightful ventures into a related field is E. G. Swem's model of editorial excellence, "Brothers of the Spade: Correspondence of Peter Collinson of London and John Custis of Williamsburg, Virginia, 1734–1746." Ostensibly a collection of letters, the correspondence furnishes the structural framework for an extensive discussion of colonial botany which is often more valuable than the letters. The biographical study of *Mark Catesby: The Colonial Audubon,* however, illustrates the weaknesses of the eighteenth-century naturalist in his comprehensive range of interests which included botany, ornithology, geology, anthropology, and zoology. John Clayton was influenced by Catesby and became the equal of any botanist of his day; as late as

Agricultural History, II (January, 1928), 1–34; Richard H. Shryock, "British versus German Traditions in Colonial Agriculture," *Mississippi Valley Historical Review,* XXVI (June, 1939), 39–54.

72 Middleton, *Tobacco Coast.* See also Margaret S. Morriss, *Colonial Trade of Maryland, 1689–1715* (Baltimore, 1914); Doyle, *The Colonies Under the House of Hanover* (London, 1907); Franklin, "Agriculture in Colonial North Carolina," *North Carolina Historical Review,* III (October, 1926), 539–74.

73 Gray, *History of Agriculture in the Southern United States to 1860* (2 vols.; Washington, 1933); A. O. Craven, *Soil Exhaustion as a Factor in the Agricultural History of Virginia and Maryland, 1606–1860* (Urbana, 1926). See also Lyman Carrier, *The Beginnings of Agriculture in America* (New York, 1903).

74 Morton, *Robert Carter of Nomini Hall: A Virginia Tobacco Planter of the Eighteenth Century* (Williamsburg, 1945).

1940, his work was still considered fundamental.[75] Other studies have investigated rice culture and the raising of indigo in South Carolina, with the former becoming profitable through the employment of slaves.[76] Those who have examined the silk industry and similar exotic plantings have attributed failure to climate, inattention to colonial conditions, and lack of communication and cooperation. Bacon's rebellion, it has been said, was partially responsible for the abandonment of sericulture in Virginia.[77] And there were two legal practices that have been made much of in the study of colonial agriculture—primogeniture and entail. Bailyn, drawing upon an unpublished dissertation at the University of Chicago, declares that neither primogeniture nor entail was practiced extensively in Virginia by the end of the seventeenth century, that they were never deeply rooted in any colony.[78]

Leila Sellers has studied the business activities of pre-Revolutionary Charleston and explained that physical geography accounts for the commercial dominance of that port. Because navigable streams leading into the Chesapeake gave direct access to the plantations, mercantile activity was appropriated by Scottish or English factors. Conversely, Charleston had a fine harbor, with shallow rivers reaching into the hinterlands that prohibited deep-draft vessels from penetrating the interior. As a consequence, small vessels plied these streams, and Charleston flourished as an entrepôt. C. C. Crittenden, writing on *The Commerce of North Carolina, 1763–1789,* noted that the much-maligned British trade regulations not only stimulated the production of naval stores, but aided rather than hindered the general business activities of

75 E. G. Swem (ed.), "Brothers of the Spade: Correspondence of Peter Collinson of London and of John Custis of Williamsburg, Virginia, 1734–1746," American Antiquarian Society *Proceedings,* LXVIII (April, 1948), 17–190 (reprinted privately, 1957); George Frederick Frick and Raymond Phineas Stearns, *Mark Catesby: The Colonial Audubon* (Urbana, 1961); Edmund Berkeley and Dorothy Smith Berkeley, *John Clayton, Pioneer of American Botany* (Chapel Hill, 1963).

76 Duncan C. Heyward, *Seed from Madagascar* (Chapel Hill, 1937); Harriott H. Ravenel, *Eliza Pinckney* (New York, 1909); Alexander S. Salley, Jr., *The Introduction of Rice Culture into South Carolina* (Columbia, 1919).

77 Marguerite B. Hamer, "The Foundation and Failure of the Silk Industry in Provincial Georgia," *North Carolina Historical Review,* XII (April, 1935), 125–48; Charles E. Hatch, Jr., "Mulberry Trees and Silkworms: Sericulture in Early Virginia," *Virginia Magazine of History and Biography,* LXV (May, 1957), 3–61.

78 Bernard Bailyn citing Clarence R. Keim, "Influence of Primogeniture and Entail in the Development of Virginia" (Ph.D. dissertation, University of Chicago, 1926) in "Politics and Social Structure in Virginia," in J. M. Smith (ed.), *Seventeenth-Century America.*

the colony. There is need for a new evaluation of the effect of piracy upon the commerce of the southern colonies.[79]

The Anglican Church seems to hold the same fascination for historians as does Puritanism in New England, while the dissenting sects are usually left to shift for themselves in denominational histories or surveys of colonial religion.[80] Perhaps the reason for the greater concern about the Anglican Church was the importance of the question of a colonial establishment. There is often the suggestion of a search for democratic impulses in religious affairs. George Maclaren Brydon indicates that the political growth of the colonies is mirrored in the incorporation of local church control within the vestries. Despite an emphasis upon the Anglican organization, he explained that the growth of dissenting sects paralleled the physical expansion of Virginia. Brydon, as an Episcopalian, regretfully reports the impact of George Whitefield's preachings in attracting good Anglicans into other denominational ranks. In the western part of the colony, where Anglicans were a minority, the weaknesses of other sects lay in their variety and number. There has been some agreement that the self-centered and conservative outlook of the Church of England operated to the advantage of those of evangelical fervor. Although the Great Awakening is covered in general works on religion, Wesley M. Gewehr's well-documented *The Great Awakening in Virginia* is a good local study.[81]

Evarts B. Greene maintains that the lack of a bishop in the colonies not only limited the influence of the Church of England, but also deprived the Americans of a powerful conservative voice. A similar, though more recent study, Carl Bridenbaugh's *Mitre and Sceptre,* advances the thesis that the efforts of the Anglican Church to establish itself as a state-supported institution throughout the colonies was one of the fundamental causes of the American Revolution. Dissenters, he believes,

79 Sellers, *Charleston Business on the Eve of the American Revolution* (Chapel Hill, 1934); Crittenden, *The Commerce of North Carolina, 1763–1789* (New Haven, 1936). See also Shirley C. Hughson, *The Carolina Pirates and Colonial Commerce, 1670–1740* (Baltimore, 1894).

80 William W. Sweet, *Religion in Colonial America* (New York, 1942); John M. Mecklin, *The Story of American Dissent* (New York, 1934); Stephen B. Weeks, *The Religious Development in the Province of North Carolina* (Baltimore, 1892).

81 Brydon, *Virginia's Mother Church and the Conditions Under Which It Grew: An Interpretation of the Records of the Colony of Virginia and of the Anglican Church of That Colony, 1607–1727,* I (Richmond, 1947), II (Philadelphia, 1952); Louis B. Wright, *Religion and Empire: The Alliance Between Piety and Commerce in English Expansion, 1558–1625* (Chapel Hill, 1943); Gewehr, *The Great Awakening in Virginia, 1740–1790* (Durham, 1930). See also Stuart C. Henry, *George Whitefield: Wayfaring Saint* (New York, 1957).

organized themselves into pressure groups, not only to weaken the Church but actively to oppose the establishment of any bishop in the colonies.[82]

The importance of a self-perpetuating vestry and the absence of firm policy are listed as prime reasons for the Anglicans never establishing themselves in any colony north of Maryland. This lack of episcopal organization, along with environmental influences and geographical separation, not only allowed the vestry to become influential in church affairs and the watchdogs of morality, but also gained for them some civil jurisdiction. William H. Seiler thinks that the vestries were defending their independence rather than opposing the prerogative when they resisted the governor's attempts to meddle in church affairs.[83] In North Carolina, where religious freedom had been offered as an inducement for settlement, toleration gained strength as a result of indifference, the economic ambitions of the Proprietors, and the prevailing spirit of the times. Toleration waned when religion became involved in politics and there was an attempt to establish the Anglican Church. Still, the Anglican Church was not legally established until a satisfactory vestry act was passed in 1765. Opposition to the establishment by both Anglicans and dissenters was but another facet of the North Carolinians' insistence on local autonomy.[84]

Many early church histories are naive. Too often the works of others have been accepted without additional research or interpretation to substantiate such arguments as "the Separate Baptist Movement in the South was undoubtedly one of the most formative influences ever brought to bear on American religious life." Recent scholars have concentrated on church-state relations rather than denominational studies.[85]

82 E. B. Greene, "The Anglican Outlook on the American Colonies in the Early Eighteenth Century," *American Historical Review*, XX (October, 1914), 64–85; Bridenbaugh, *Mitre and Sceptre* (New York, 1962).

83 H. Shelton Smith, Robert T. Handy, and Lefferts A. Loetscher, *American Christianity: An Historical Interpretation with Representative Documents, 1607–1920* (New York, 1960); Seiler, "The Anglican Parish Vestry in Virginia," in J. M. Smith (ed.), *Seventeenth-Century America*, and "The Anglican Parish Vestry in Colonial Virginia," *Journal of Southern History*, XXII (August, 1956), 310-37.

84 Haskell Monroe, "Religion and Politics in Early North Carolina," *North Carolina Historical Review*, XXXIX (July, 1962), 267–83; Paul Conkin, "The Church Establishment in North Carolina, 1765–1776," *North Carolina Historical Review*, XXXII (January, 1955), 1–30.

85 William L. Lumpkin, *Baptist Foundations in the South: Tracing Through the Separates the Influence of the Great Awakening, 1754–1787* (Nashville, 1961); Robert B. Semple, *A History of the Rise and Progress of the Baptists in Virginia* (Philadelphia, 1894); Leonard J. Trinterud, *The Forming of an American Tradi-*

Some have looked into religious activity among the slaves. Apparently there was little. Economic considerations, meager attention by the church, resistance of political forces, indifference of owners, low mental capacity of the Negro, and social superiority of whites have all been advanced as reasons for the token slave participation in religious affairs. Between 1704 and 1776 the number of conversions increased in proportion to the growth of slave population, but few of the converts led what might be termed a Christian life, for it was the form rather than the substance of Christianity that they accepted. Frank J. Klingberg's account of the work of the Society for the Propagation of the Gospel among Negroes discovers that the SPG's program was based "on the fundamental assumption that the Negro's future would be identified with the white man's fortune." [86]

The tendency to analyze colonial religious activities in the light of their social significance has carried over into the studies of church architecture. For instance, Stephen P. Dorsey, in his text accompanying the photographs in *Early English Churches in America,* though predominantly concerned with church auditories (and Virginia churches at that), implied a close relationship between the various denominations. And George W. Williams, in his study of St. Michael's of Charleston, related the influence of a religious body on the community.[87]

Research has established that southern architecture was derivative in its reliance upon European styles. Harold R. Shurtleff, in his *The Log Cabin Myth,* has shown that this style of architecture was a contribution of the Swedes and Finns nearly fifty years after Jamestown, and that it was not until the eighteenth century that the log cabin became typical of frontier housing. Henry Chandlee Forman, in his studies partially based upon archaeological findings, saw early American homes crude enough to support Jefferson's contention that the "genius of architecture seems to have shed its maledictions over this land." Southern architecture

---

tion: A Re-Examination of Colonial Presbyterianism (Philadelphia, 1949) ; George Howe, *History of the Presbyterian Church in South Carolina* (2 vols.; Columbia, 1870–1883) ; Rufus M. Jones, *The Quakers in the American Colonies* (London, 1911) ; John G. Shea, *The Catholic Church in Colonial Days* (New York, 1886) ; Lee M. Friedman, *Early American Jews* (Cambridge, 1934) ; Albert W. Werline, *Church and State in Maryland* (South Lancaster, Mass., 1948) ; Reba C. Strickland, *Religion and the State in Georgia in the Eighteenth Century* (New York, 1939) ; E. L. Goodwin, *The Colonial Church in Virginia* (London, 1927).

86 Marcus W. Jernigan, "Slavery and Conversion in the American Colonies," *American Historical Review,* XXI (April, 1916), 504–27; Klingberg, *An Appraisal of the Negro in Colonial South Carolina* (Washington, 1941).

87 Dorsey, *Early English Churches in America, 1607–1807* (New York, 1952) ; Williams, *St. Michael's Charleston, 1751–1951* (Columbia, 1951).

during its first two centuries, says Forman, was essentially English medieval in origin.[88] Marcus Whiffen's volumes on the public and private buildings of colonial Williamsburg conclude that the basic concept was English, with modifications being dictated by climate and materials.[89] Morris L. Radoff did not adhere strictly to architectural details in his study of the public buildings of Annapolis, for he considered circumstances leading to their construction, the builders, and the business methods employed in the construction. In general, the frontier influences on colonial architecture have been minimized, and it has been said that only after the Revolution did America contribute to world architecture through its use of classic forms.[90]

The very crudity of colonial medical practices would seem to make this a more attractive subject for research, yet few historians have ventured into the field. No other southern colonies have studies to equal those of Wyndham D. Blanton's on medicine in colonial Virginia.[91] John Duffy's *Epidemics in Colonial America* ranges over all of the colonies and exposes those endemic fevers that periodically ravaged the southern colonies, with an interesting correlation between the epidemics of Canada and the southern colonies. Duffy also maintained that despite the presence of virulent fevers, conditions were healthier in the southern colonies than in Europe; the wealth of good land and the acute labor shortage on the frontier led to better health and a longer life expectancy among the lower economic classes than among their counterparts in the

88 Shurtleff, *The Log Cabin Myth* (Cambridge, 1939); Forman, *Jamestown and St. Mary's: Buried Cities of Romance* (Baltimore, 1938), and *The Architecture of the Old South: The Medieval Style, 1585–1850* (Cambridge, 1948).

89 Whiffen, *The Public Buildings of Williamsburg* (Williamsburg, 1958), and *The Eighteenth-Century Houses of Williamsburg* (Williamsburg, 1960). See also Thomas J. Waterman and J. A. Barrows, *Domestic Colonial Architecture of Tidewater Virginia* (Chapel Hill, 1947).

90 Radoff, *Buildings of the State of Maryland at Annapolis* (Annapolis, 1954); Fiske Kimball, "Architecture in the History of the Colonies and of the Republic," *American Historical Review*, XXVII (October, 1931), 47–57, and Kimball, *Domestic Architecture of the American Colonies and of the Early Republic* (New York, 1927).

91 Blanton, *Medicine in Virginia in the Eighteenth Century* (Richmond, 1931), *Medicine in Virginia in the Seventeenth Century* (Richmond, 1931); Edward Ingle, "Regulating Physicians in Colonial Virginia," *Annals of Medical History*, IV, N.S. (1922), 248–50; J. I. Waring, "Medicine in Charleston, 1750–1775," *Annals of Medical History*, XII, N.S. (January, 1935), 19–26; Joseph Krafka, Jr., "Medicine in Colonial Georgia," *Georgia Historical Quarterly*, XX (1936), 326–44; Francis R. Packard, *History of Medicine in the United States* (2 vols.; New York, 1931); St. Julien Ravenel Childs, *Malaria and Colonization in the Carolina Low Country, 1526–1696* (Baltimore, 1940).

old countries. In the first volume of this same author's edition of *The Rudolph Matas History of Medicine in Louisiana,* there is a contrast between medicine in colonial Louisiana and the British colonies, with the implication that Louisiana lagged behind the eastern seaboard in medical practices.[92]

Historians seem equally reluctant to probe deeply into legal history, certainly to the extent of searching the court records as did Morris in his *Government and Labor in Early America.* Raphael Semmes did a prodigious amount of research for his *Crime and Punishment in Early Maryland,* and, though there is a good review of human frailties, the reader is left to his own interpretation. Cyrus H. Karraker's study of the seventeenth-century sheriff is useful. But older works by Chitwood and Scott on judicial processes of colonial Virginia will be outdated when historians have examined the flood of new materials being made available under Virginia's present vigorous program of microfilming source materials in foreign repositories.[93] The General Court of Colonial Virginia, composed of members of the governor's council, was an agency dispensing justice through judges who were often unskilled in legal knowledge, but who won praise from foreign observers for their development of precedent law. Paul M. McCain found in the county courts of North Carolina the same patterns of social benevolence prevalent in the higher echelons of government, with the wealthy and prominent exercising judicial and administrative control over the community.[94]

Mays's *Pendleton* is an excellent study of a colonial lawyer. Clement Eaton's study reveals that although some lawyers were trained in Edinburgh and London, by far the greater number received their education under an apprentice system. The real rewards of the legal system were

92 Duffy, *Epidemics in Colonial America* (Baton Rouge, 1953), "Eighteenth Century Carolina Health Conditions," *Journal of Southern History,* XVIII (August, 1952), 289–302, and *The Rudolph Matas History of Medicine in Louisiana,* I (2 vols.; Baton Rouge, 1958).

93 Semmes, *Crime and Punishment in Early Maryland* (Baltimore, 1938); Karraker, *The Seventeenth-Century Sheriff: A Comparative Study of the Sheriff in England and the Chesapeake Colonies, 1607–1689* (Chapel Hill, 1930); Oliver P. Chitwood, *Justice in Colonial Virginia* (Baltimore, 1905); Arthur P. Scott, *Criminal Law in Colonial Virginia* (Chicago, 1930).

94 McCain, *The County Court in North Carolina Before 1750* (Durham, 1954); Hugh F. Rankin, "The General Court of Colonial Virginia: Its Jurisdiction and Personnel," *Virginia Magazine of History and Biography,* LXX (April, 1962), 142–53. See also W. C. Guess, *County Government in Colonial North Carolina* (Chapel Hill, 1911); Albert O. Porter, *County Government in Virginia* (Columbia, 1947).

special opportunities which the profession afforded for land speculation and political advancement.[95]

The first volume of the documentary series, Edgar W. Knight's *A Documentary History of Education in the South before 1860,* presents perhaps the best picture of colonial education and again emphasizes the theme of European heritages. Rural education and the tutorial system are best revealed in the diaries of Fithian and Harrower, the latter an indentured servant serving out his time in plantation pedagogy.[96]

The West has received its most careful study from Verner W. Crane, whose *The Southern Frontier* suggested that conflicts in the area arose out of Indian trade rather than Spanish influences. A more detailed application of Indian policy is found in John Alden's *John Stuart and the Southern Colonial Frontier.* South Carolina has been presented as a frontier barrier against the Spanish and the French before the founding of Georgia; and during Queen Anne's War it became evident that the control of the Mississippi Valley was to become the focus of inter-colonial rivalry in America.[97]

It would seem improper to mention the West and ignore Indian-white relations. One modern scholar has said that the distinction in this area is based upon the "natural right" of the Indian as opposed to the "legal

95 David J. Mays, *Edmund Pendleton, 1721–1803* (2 vols.; Cambridge, 1952); Eaton, "A Mirror of the Southern Colonial Lawyer: The Fee Books of Patrick Henry, Thomas Jefferson, and Waightstill Avery," *William and Mary Quarterly,* VIII, 3d series (October, 1951), 520–34; E. H. Alderman, *The North Carolina Colonial Bar* (Chapel Hill, 1913); Aubrey C. Land, "Genius of a Colonial Fortune: Daniel Dulany of Maryland," *William and Mary Quarterly,* VII, 3d series (April, 1950), 255–69.

96 Edgar W. Knight, *European Inheritances* (Chapel Hill, 1949), Volume I of Knight (ed.), *A Documentary History of Education in the South Before 1860* (4 vols.; Chapel Hill, 1949–1953); Hunter Dickinson Farish (ed.), *Journal and Letters of Philip Vickers Fithian, 1773–1774: A Plantation Tutor of the Old Dominion* (Williamsburg, 1943, 1957); Edward Miles Riley (ed.), *The Journal of John Harrower: An Indentured Servant in the Colony of Virginia, 1773–1776* (Williamsburg, 1963). See also Edgar W. Knight, *Public Education in the South* (Boston, 1922); J. P. Corry, "Education in Colonial Georgia," *Georgia Historical Quarterly,* XVI (1932), 136–45; Bernard G. Steiner, *History of Education in Maryland* (Washington, 1894); Edward McCrady, "Education in South Carolina Prior to and During the Revolution," *South Carolina Historical Society Collections,* IV (Columbia, 1887), 7–15.

97 Crane, *The Southern Frontier, 1670–1732* (Philadelphia, 1929), and "The Southern Frontier in Queen Anne's War," *American Historical Review,* XXIX (April, 1919), 379–95; Alden, *John Stuart and the Southern Colonial Frontier* (Ann Arbor, 1944). See also Thomas P. Abernethy, *Three Virginia Frontiers* (Baton Rouge, 1940); R. L. Meriwether, *The Expansion of South Carolina, 1729–1765* (Kingsport, Tenn., 1940); L. K. Koontz, *The Virginia Frontier* (Baltimore, 1925).

right" of the white man, an interpretation related to the basic sovereignty of the Crown. Much of the conflict between the two races, said Wilcomb E. Washburn, may be attributed to "the legal culture of the American Indian [which] tends to regard the fine distinction between law and morality so often made in the Western world as the product of a hypocritical mind." The arguments of Nancy O. Lurie, based on anthropological and sociological conclusions, suggest that the Indian was responsible for his own extinction in his failure to adjust to changing times, despite the many similarities in the basic cultures of the two races. R. S. Cotterill, in *Southern Indians,* implied that the Indians were victims of close contact with the white man and the westward push for land. Corkran in *The Cherokee Frontier* is somewhat more precise in explaining that Cherokee power was broken in the campaigns against them in 1760–1761 by British regulars and Carolina provincials.[98]

In summary, there is one central theme in virtually all the literature of southern colonial history—that it was derivative while undergoing environmental mutations. There can be little disagreement here for, indeed, all colonial cultures are derivative by their very natures. And there is little new in such conclusions, for David Ramsay was noting the affinity of the South Carolinians for British manners as early as 1808. At the beginning of the twentieth century, Herbert L. Osgood said of seventeenth-century Americans, "In their languages and traditions of their culture they were Europeans: but they were transplanted upon a new and distant continent, and felt chiefly the pressure of its environment." [99] Studies of colonial culture in the South have always been limited, by the nature of the sources, to the upper classes; and only an extensive use of the extant legal records and reliance upon contemporary observations can restore any kind of balance.

There is promise in the future of colonial historiography. Not only are more historians directing their interests to this period, but the Institute of Early American History and Culture, sponsored jointly by the College of William and Mary and Colonial Williamsburg, Inc., has become an important agency of such studies. Not only does it provide

98 Washburn, "The Moral and Legal Justification for Dispossessing the Indian," in J. M. Smith (ed.), *Seventeenth-Century America,* 15–32; Lurie, "Indian Cultural Adjustment to European Civilization," in J. M. Smith (ed.), *Seventeenth-Century America,* 33–60; Cotterill, *The Southern Indian: The Story of the Civilized Tribes Before Removal* (Norman, 1954). See also Chapman J. Milling, *Red Carolinians* (Chapel Hill, 1940) ; David M. Corkran, *The Cherokee Frontier, Conflict and Survival, 1740-62* (Norman, 1962).

99 Ramsay, *South Carolina;* Osgood, *The American Colonies in the Seventeenth Century* (3 vols.; New York, 1904–1907).

vigorous leadership, but the institute's journal, the *William and Mary Quarterly*, has been expanded into a distinguished vehicle of changing interpretations of early American history.

In any examination of the historiography of the colonial South, there can be no apology for the heavy emphasis upon Virginia. Not only did the Virginians exhibit an early interest in their past, but they have provided such excellent tools of research as E. G. Swem's *Virginia Historical Index* and the *Virginia Gazette Index,* by Lester J. Cappon and Stella F. Duff.[100] The present-day program of microfilming Virginia materials in foreign archives furnishes a growing stockpile of original sources for the historian. Although many southern states are beginning to demonstrate a more active interest in making available their colonial records, Virginia still remains in the lead and is not likely to be overtaken soon.

---

100 Swem (ed.), *Virginia Historical Index* (2 vols.; Roanoke, 1934–1936) ; Cappon and Duff (eds.), *Virginia Gazette Index* (2 vols.; Williamsburg, 1950).

II

The American Revolution:
Southern Founders of a
National Tradition

Charles G. Sellers, Jr.

THE common experiences of the War for Independence created in
the American people from Georgia to New Hampshire a sense of one
nationality, a tradition of loyalty to a union deriving its essential character from the liberal ideals of the Declaration of Independence. Translated into a written historiography, this Revolutionary tradition has
continued throughout our history to reinforce, against all sectional and
illiberal tendencies, the liberal nationalism of all Americans. This Revolutionary historiography had its brilliant beginning in the work of a
Southerner, Dr. David Ramsay, who resided in that sometime epicenter
of radical Southernism, Charleston, South Carolina.

On July 4, 1778, in the first of all anniversary orations on American
independence, Dr. Ramsay eloquently expressed the emotional and ideological content of the Revolutionary tradition. "When I anticipate in
imagination the future glory of my country, and the illustrious figure it
will soon make on the theatre of the world," he told his fellow Charles-

tonians, "my heart distends with generous pride for being an American."
Ramsay's words make one doubt at the outset whether there could be a
peculiarly "southern" historiography of the Revolution. Nowhere does he
hint at sectional consciousness or sectional jealousy. Instead he concedes
that Pennsylvania and New England have had a larger share of that
political freedom for which the Revolution is being fought; and he concludes in a strain of enthusiastic nationalism:

We have laid the foundations of a new empire, which promises to enlarge
itself to vast dimensions, and to give happiness to a great continent. It is
now our turn to figure on the face of the earth, and in the annals of the
world. . . . Ever since the flood, true Religion, Literature, Art, Empire and
Riches, have taken a slow and gradual course from east to west, and are now
about fixing their long and favourite abode in this new western world. . . .
Our Independence will redeem one quarter of the globe from tyranny and oppression, and consecrate it the chosen seat of Truth, Justice, Freedom, Learning and Religion. We are laying the foundation of happiness for countless
millions. Generations yet unborn will bless us for the blood-bought inheritance, we are about to bequeath them. Oh happy times! Oh glorious days! Oh
kind, indulgent, bountiful Providence, that we live in this highly favoured
period, and have the honour of helping forward these great events, and of
suffering in a cause of such infinite importance.[1]

Ramsay could not have foreseen that the South's "generations unborn"
would one day be trying to use history in order to deny their Americanism. If he had, he would have rejoiced that the Revolutionary tradition
was the one part of the South's history that refused to be so used. Three
quarters of a century after Ramsay's oration, Abraham Lincoln would
invoke "the mystic chords of memory, stretching from every battlefield
and patriot grave to every living heart and hearthstone all over this
broad land" in his efforts to check the disunionism that stemmed from
latter-day Charleston.

While Ramsay's blood-bought inheritance and Lincoln's mystic chords
of memory were not enough by themselves to check the forces of sectional chauvinism in the distraught South of 1861, neither could the
South, even then in its own thinking, sectionalize the staunchly American
tradition of the Revolution. Thus there was never a peculiarly southern
historiography of the Revolution, but only an American historiography,
which included much writing by Southerners and much specialized writ-

1 Ramsay, *An Oration on the Advantages of American Independence: Spoken
before a Publick Assembly of the Inhabitants of Charlestown in South-Carolina,
on the Second Anniversary of That Glorious Aera* (Charlestown, 1778), 14, 20–21.

ing about Revolutionary events and personages within the South.

The American historiography of the Revolution began when the British captured Charleston in 1780 and imprisoned Dr. Ramsay. During his eleven months in a British prison at St. Augustine, Ramsay conceived the idea of writing a history of the Revolution in South Carolina. Upon his release he went busily to work, gaining access to the papers of General Greene and combing through the papers of the Confederation Congress while serving as one of South Carolina's delegates to that body. In 1785 he proudly published his two-volume work,[2] the first substantial account of any phase of the Revolution and a foundation stone for all subsequent study of the Revolution in the South.

But Ramsay was not satisfied. His volumes sold so poorly that the venture cost him several hundred dollars, and he seems to have perceived the importance of establishing a firm historiographical base for the Revolutionary tradition out of which a new nation was growing. Back he went to his documents and writing desk, and in 1789 he published a general history of the Revolution [3] that would stand unrivaled in Amer-

---

2 Ramsay, *The History of the Revolution of South-Carolina, from a British Province to an Independent State* (2 vols.; Trenton, 1785).

3 Ramsay, *The History of the American Revolution* (2 vols.; Philadelphia, 1789); Robert L. Brunhouse, "David Ramsay's Publication Problems, 1784–1808," Bibliographical Society of America, *Papers,* XXXIX (1945), 51–67. Ramsay had completed his history by 1787 but delayed publication in order to include an account of the new Constitution.

The only contemporary work remotely comparable to Ramsay's was William Gordon's *History of the Rise, Progress, and Establishment of the Independence of the United States of America* (4 vols.; London, 1788). Gordon's history was of doubtful American origin, its author being an English clergyman who lived in America only between 1770 and 1786. His account of the southern campaigns was drawn mainly, and often copied bodily, from Ramsay's work on South Carolina, which Ramsay had loaned him in manuscript; and the rest of Gordon's volumes depended as slavishly on the accounts in the British *Annual Register.* Americans criticized Gordon for publishing his history in London and charged that he had softened the anti-British tone of his original manuscript to make it more acceptable in England. The *Annual Register* had similarly been the basis for several even less substantial and more derivative histories of the Revolution by British and French authors. But these were not sufficiently impressive or sympathetic to the American cause to win much attention on this side of the Atlantic. O. G. Libby, "A Critical Examination of William Gordon's History of the American Revolution," American Historical Association, *Annual Report,* 1899, I, 367–88; David D. Van Tassel, *Recording America's Past: An Interpretation of the Development of Historical Studies in America, 1607–1884* (Chicago, 1960), 35–40.

A distinguished competitor to Ramsay appeared when Carlo Botta's history, originally published in Italy in 1809, was translated into English under the title *History of the War of Independence of the United States of America* (3 vols.; Philadelphia, 1820–21).

ican historiography until George Bancroft's great multivolume history reached the Revolutionary period in the 1850's.

Ramsay's commitment to history came straight out of his liberal nationalism. His most important work was written while he was simultaneously engaged in the campaign for a stronger federal government; and his historical writing was a deliberate effort to enshrine the Revolution as the great unifying experience by which the American people sought to establish a utopian republic on the basis of their common liberal ideals. "The Americans knew but little of one another, previous to the Revolution," he wrote. "A continental army, and a Congress composed of men from all the States, by freely mixing together, were assimilated into one mass." At the same time that he was completing his history, in 1788, he published a pamphlet to refute the sectional objections being urged in South Carolina to the new federal constitution. "Indulge no narrow prejudices to the disadvantage of your brethren of the other states," he exhorted his fellow Carolinians. "Consider the people of all the thirteen states, as a band of brethren, speaking the same language, professing the same religion, inhabiting one undivided country, and designed by heaven to be one people." [4]

The simultaneous and happy culmination of Ramsay's labors on his history and his efforts for a stronger national government only confirmed him in his role as expounder-cum-historian of the Revolutionary tradition of liberal nationalism. "We should, above all things, study to promote the union and harmony of the states," he told another Fourth of July gathering in Charleston in 1794. "Perish the man who wishes to divide us into back country, or low country, into a northern and southern, or into an eastern or western interest. . . . We should consider the people of this country, from the Mississippi to the Atlantic, from New-Hampshire to Georgia, as forming one whole, the interest of which should be preferred to that of every part." [5]

In pursuit of this goal he devoted every minute he could spare from his medical practice and extensive public services to historical writing, and in the process he blazed a pioneering trail for every one of the major historical genres that were to compose the Revolutionary historiography of the nineteenth century. As a biographer and maker of a national

4 Ramsay, *History of the American Revolution*, II, 316; *An Address to the Freemen of South-Carolina, on the Subject of the Federal Constitution*. . . . (Charleston [1788]), 11–12.

5 Ramsay, *An Oration, Delivered in St. Michael's Church, before the Inhabitants of Charleston, South-Carolina, on the Fourth of July, 1794*. . . . (Charleston [1794]), 20.

hagiology, he wrote the best of the early one-volume lives of George Washington. Then he turned to state history and, following the example of Jeremy Belknap's history of New Hampshire, produced a superior history of South Carolina. "Had we Belknaps in every state," he wrote to a friend, "we might become acquainted with each other in that intimate and familiar manner which would wear away prejudices, rub off asperities & mold us into an homogeneous people loving esteeming and rightly appreciating each other." He expanded his history of the Revolution into a general history of the United States and devoted his last years to creating a vast account of the whole of human experience as culminating in the American republic.[6]

Ramsay's writings, and especially his *History of the American Revolution,* fed the historical imagination and the growing liberal nationalism of several generations of Americans. His fellow Americans resented with him the refusal of the English public to give a hearing to the truths he expounded; and Congress, by special act in 1789, granted him the first copyright extended to an author by the general government. "America has produced a Ramsay," exulted young James K. Polk, who eagerly devoured Ramsay's works while a student at the University of North Carolina in 1817, "the Tacitus of this western hemisphere to transmit to posterity in the unpolished language of truth, the spirit of liberty which actuated the first founders of our republic." [7]

Ramsay's nationalism arose in part from his personal intersectional experience as a native of Pennsylvania, student at the College of New Jersey and in Philadelphia, and member of the Confederation Congress. Yet his nationalism seems to have been highly congenial to the South Carolina community where he was a leading political and intellectual figure throughout his mature years. The final irony was that his funeral eulogy was delivered by none other than the brilliant young

6 Ramsay, *The Life of George Washington* . . . (Philadelphia, 1807); *The History of South-Carolina, from Its First Settlement in 1670, to the Year 1808* (2 vols.; Charleston, 1809); *History of the United States, from Their First Settlement as English Colonies, in 1607, to the Year 1808 . . . Continued to the Treaty of Ghent, by S. S. Smith . . . and Other Literary Gentlemen* . . . (3 vols.; Philadelphia, 1816–17); *Universal History Americanized* . . . (12 vols.; Philadelphia, 1819). The last two works were completed and brought out posthumously by friends for the benefit of Ramsay's destitute family. The quotation is from Page Smith, "David Ramsay and the Causes of the American Revolution," *William and Mary Quarterly,* XVII (Jan., 1960), 74.

7 Charles Evans (comp.), *American Bibliography* . . . (14 vols.; Chicago and Worcester, 1903–59), VII, 354; James K. Polk, "The Admission of Foreigners into Office in the United States," MS in "Addresses of the Dialectic Society," IV, First Series, University of North Carolina Library.

Charleston lawyer Robert Y. Hayne, later a firebrand of nullification.[8]

Ramsay's reputation was later clouded for professional historians by exaggerated charges of plagiarism from the *Annual Register;* but the most recent professional evaluation places him "in the front rank of American historians."[9] The first quality in Ramsay's history that strikes the modern reader is his temperate and insightful treatment of the behavior and policies of the British. Even more impressive is his sensitive assessment of the many factors that contributed to the Revolutionary movement—the relationship between the American environment and the psychology and political behavior of the Americans, the place of economic considerations in the mixture of motives that influenced the patriots, the influence of age and temperament and chance in the flow of events. Finally and most striking of all, Ramsay's interpretation of the Revolution as essentially a struggle over constitutional principles is the view to which historians have been returning after decades of dalliance with less durable interpretations. "Ramsay offered us," concludes Professor Page Smith, "a wiser and better balanced interpretation than the most expert and 'scientific' of his successors."[10]

These professional successors, the university-trained professors who aspired to write scientific history, were not to appear until the end of the nineteenth century. In the meantime there was to be a vast amount of

8 Hayne, "Biographical Memoir of David Ramsay, M.D.," *Analectic Magazine,* VI (Sept., 1815), 204–24. This, the fullest biographical sketch of Ramsay, was drawn from Hayne's memorial address. Hayne had married a niece of Mrs. Ramsay; and another later nullifier leader, Henry L. Pinckney, founder and editor of the famous fire-eating newspaper, the Charleston *Mercury,* was the brother of Mrs. Hayne and a nephew of Mrs. Ramsay. David D. Wallace, *The Life of Henry Laurens . . .* (New York, 1915), 430–31.

Ramsay was born the son of a Scotch-Irish farmer in Pennsylvania in 1749, attended the College of New Jersey, studied medicine in Philadelphia, settled in Charleston in 1773, and died in 1815, having been shot down in the street by a tailor who had earlier been confined on a judgment by Ramsay and another physician that he was insane.

9 O. G. Libby, "Ramsay as a Plagiarist," *American Historical Review,* VII (July, 1902), 697–703; Smith, "David Ramsay and the Causes of the American Revolution," 77. Early historians of the Revolution almost universally relied heavily on the *Annual Register,* whose excellent contemporary accounts of Revolutionary events were often the best available source until fuller documentation became available. Most of these writers, including the illustrious John Marshall, simply pasted together verbatim passages, paraphrases, and condensations from the *Annual Register* and other sources. Ramsay did more of this than his preface suggests, but less than his contemporaries. The important distinction is that Ramsay fitted derivative passages into a superior interpretive framework that was distinctly his own.

10 Smith, "David Ramsay and the Causes of the American Revolution," 73.

writing about the Revolution by doctors, lawyers, clerics, and occasional self-trained college professors, following down one or another of the trails of national history, state history, or biography that David Ramsay had blazed. But before turning to the work of Ramsay's nonprofessional successors, it is necessary to note the substantial contributions made to Revolutionary historiography by those members of his own generation who recorded their memoirs of the war for independence.

Military aspects of the Revolution were particularly illuminated by the efforts of leading officers on both sides to buttress their reputations and justify their conduct. The British generals, Sir Henry Clinton and Lord Charles Cornwallis, had barely returned to England when they and their friends became engaged in a violent pamphlet controversy over responsibility for the Yorktown debacle. Several of the pamphlets produced by the controversy were promptly reprinted in America and provided an inside view of the operations of the British high command.[11]

The Clinton-Cornwallis feud also stimulated the writing of valuable military histories by lesser British officers. In 1787 Cornwallis' former commander of dragoons, Colonel Banastre Tarleton, published in London *A History of the Campaigns of 1780 and 1781, in the Southern Provinces of North America;* also in London, in 1794, a former commissary officer in Cornwallis' army, Charles Stedman, published his two-volume *The History of the Origin, Progress and Termination of the American War.* Tarleton's work was regarded as anti-Cornwallis and Stedman's as anti-Clinton. Of the two, Tarleton's is much the more valuable. Written with the aid of his mistress, the celebrated actress Mary Robinson, it provides an absorbing first-hand account of the southern campaign. Stedman, on the other hand, copied extensively from both Tarleton and the *Annual Register,* though some of his material is derived from personal experience and independent sources.[12]

---

11 The major pamphlets in the Clinton-Cornwallis controversy are conveniently collected in Benjamin F. Stevens (ed.), *The Campaign in Virginia, 1781 . . .* (2 vols.; London, 1788). Clinton also completed but did not publish an extensive memoir, which has been edited and published by William B. Willcox under the title, *The American Rebellion: Sir Henry Clinton's Narrative of His Campaigns, 1775–1782, with an Appendix of Original Documents* (New Haven, 1954). The editor's introduction to this volume contains a fine analysis of the points in dispute between Clinton and Cornwallis.

12 Tarleton's history seems to have been prompted in considerable measure by a running attack on his conduct of the battle of Cowpens, launched in the London press in 1782 by a fellow-officer, Lieutenant Roderick Mackenzie, and carried on as a minor counterpart to the Clinton-Cornwallis controversy. When Tarleton's history appeared, Mackenzie published a pamphlet of *Strictures on Lt.-Col. Tarleton's History . . .* (London, 1787) which was answered by another officer, George

Thus in the decade following the war, the rivalries of British officers for reputation made available a detailed knowledge of the southern campaigns from the British point of view. American officers, being free from the necessity of shifting the onus of defeat to each other, were much more backward about supplying memoirs. Not until 1802 did Colonel William Moultrie publish his memoirs, telling clumsily about events in which he participated. And it was 1812 before an American officer, General Henry ("Light Horse Harry") Lee, produced an account comparable in value to Tarleton's.[13]

The battle of military reputations on the American side was left to be fought not by the officers themselves, but by their descendants and admirers, as a part of the flood of biography which, during most of the nineteenth century, was the most important form of writing about the Revolution.

No one dared, of course, to question Washington's heroic qualities. Ramsay's biography of Washington remained for many years after its publication in 1807 the soundest brief account, but it was overshadowed by more spectacular productions. "Parson" Mason Locke Weems had brought out the first edition of his flimsy, fanciful, and fantastically successful and influential *Life and Memorable Actions of George Washington* in 1800;[14] and between 1804 and 1807 Chief Justice John Marshall published five ponderous volumes on the subject. For all his verbiage, Marshall added little new knowledge about the Revolution, either in the North or South,[15] but he did inspire a fellow Supreme Court jus-

Hanger, in *An Address to the Army in Reply to Strictures by Roderick M'Kenzie.* For the circumstances under which Tarleton wrote his history, see Robert D. Bass, *The Green Dragon: The Lives of Banastre Tarleton and Mary Robinson* (New York, 1957). Clinton himself attacked Stedman's history in a pamphlet, *Observations on Mr. Stedman's History of the America War* (London, 1794). For a recent evaluation of Stedman's work, see R. Kent Newmyer, "Charles Stedman's *History of the American War,*" *American Historical Review,* LXIII (July, 1958), 924–34.

13 Moultrie, *Memoirs of the American Revolution, So Far as It Related to the States of North and South Carolina, and Georgia* . . . (2 vols.; New York, 1802). Lee, *Memoirs of the War in the Southern Department of the United States* (2 vols.; Philadelphia, 1812). "Despite occasional prejudice and error," Lee's work "is a classic," writes John R. Alden in *The South in the Revolution, 1763–1789* (Baton Rouge, 1957), 412.

14 For a modern edition with an excellent critical introduction, see Mason L. Weems, *The Life of Washington,* ed. Marcus Cunliffe (Cambridge, 1962).

15 Marshall, *Life of George Washington* (5 vols.; Philadelphia, 1804–07). The sections on the Revolution consisted largely of copying and paraphrasing, mainly from William Gordon and the *Annual Register,* according to William A. Foran, "John Marshall as a Historian," *American Historical Review,* XLIII (Oct., 1937), 51–64.

tice to an emulation that furnished new information on the Revolution in the South.

Justice William Johnson of Charleston, South Carolina, seems to have been moved by a desire for literary fame, coupled with a desire to furnish an antidote to the anti-Republican poison contained in Marshall's final volume. Since Washington had been "done," Judge Johnson turned to the next most important Revolutionary general, Nathanael Greene. Traveling to New England in 1818 in search of data, he gained access to the general's papers in the hands of the family; and in 1822 he published a two-volume biography.[16] Drawing fresh information from the Greene papers, Johnson's biography ranks with the works of David Ramsay and Henry Lee among the most substantial southern contributions to the early historiography of the Revolution.

It is a striking fact that Charleston produced two of the South's three important early historians of the Revolution, and that both Ramsay and Johnson coupled ardent nationalism with a strong commitment to liberal republican views. Indeed their careers showed many similarities. Both the doctor and the judge were, of course, professional men. Both had sprung from humble origins, Ramsay's father being a Pennsylvania farmer and Johnson's a New York blacksmith who moved to Charleston before the Revolution (in 1780 the elder Johnson was carried off with Dr. Ramsay to the British prison at St. Augustine). Both future historians were educated at the College of New Jersey, and both rose to political eminence in Charleston, Johnson being appointed to the Supreme Court by President Jefferson.

While Judge Johnson was an uncompromising Jeffersonian Republican in his commitment to civil and religious liberties and democratic government, he explicitly denied that the Virginia Republican doctrine of state rights was a central tenet of Republicanism. "State rights, or United States' rights are nothing," he declared in his biography of Greene, "except as they contribute to the safety and happiness of the people." He went out of his way to praise Greene's efforts for a stronger union; and when his biography was challenged, he stated his purposes in writing it as follows: "1, to trace out and to adhere to the historical truth. 2, to im-

16 William Johnson, *Sketches of the Life and Correspondence of Nathanael Greene . . . in the War of the Revolution* (2 vols.; Charleston, 1822). Johnson paid out of his own pocket for the printing of 1,000 sets; but after four years he still had 400 unsold sets on his hands. Donald G. Morgan has written an excellent biography, *Justice William Johnson, the First Dissenter . . .* (Columbia, S. C., 1954); for Johnson's work as a biographer, see pp. 105–106, 143–52. Johnson's biography of Greene followed by several years a much slighter work, Charles Caldwell, *Memoirs of the Life and Campaigns of the Hon. Nathanael Greene . . .* (Philadelphia, 1819).

press on my countrymen the necessity of hugging to their bosoms the bond which unites us to each other, by exhibiting the toil and hazard to which we were exposed from a want of combined operation and continental feeling in the revolutionary war." [17]

Judge Johnson's life of Greene appeared in the very year that Denmark Vesey's slave insurrection plot accelerated South Carolina's ideological somersault from nationalism to state rights, and Johnson made himself unpopular with many of his fellow Charlestonians by trying to calm the hysteria. But he had been denouncing "the wily serpent of disunion" at least since 1812, when he had followed in Ramsay's footsteps as Charleston's Fourth of July orator. "Long may the love of country be the animating principle of the sons of Carolina," he had said on that occasion. So he was ready when the wily serpent came boldly into the open in 1827 in the *Crisis* essays of Robert Turnbull, the bellwether of nullification. Judge Johnson replied with a pamphlet of over a hundred pages, calling on Americans "to strengthen and consolidate the Union of the States . . . and thus build, on a firm basis, a lofty *national* character and a permanent national prosperity." Only thus, he predicted, would the United States be prepared to play its destined role in the coming climax of the great world struggle between tyranny and freedom.[18]

Although Johnson's book on Greene furnishes further impressive evidence of the importance of the Revolutionary tradition in resisting the South's drift into sectionalism, and though its research findings were an important contribution to knowledge about the Revolution, it was not a popular success. Johnson's prose was too ponderous, and his bluntly expressed prejudices—against High-Church Episcopalianism and Count Pulaski among others—invited counterattacks. Historiographically the most productive of Johnson's attacks were on the Virginia Lees. In 1824 Henry Lee, Jr., responded to the judge's animadversions on the accuracy of his father's memoirs by publishing in Philadelphia a weighty account of *The Campaign of 1781 in the Carolinas; with Remarks, Historical and Critical on Johnson's Life of Greene.* . . . A year later another Lee, Richard Henry, answered Johnson's insinuations that his grandfather and namesake had been involved in the Revolutionary machinations against Washington by publishing in Philadelphia a two-volume *Memoir of the Life of Richard Henry Lee.* . . . Despite their tendentiousness, the embattled Lees further illuminated both the military and the civil side of the Revolutionary struggle in the South.

17 Morgan, *Justice William Johnson,* 150–51, 152n.
18 *Ibid.,* 96–97, 297.

Meanwhile two Southerners had been clothed with the mythic qualities of secondary heroes. The new military hero was the semiliterate, sometimes ruthless, and always daring partisan commander, Francis Marion, whose midnight forays from the swamps had kept American resistance alive after the British overran lowcountry South Carolina. Around 1806 that master myth-maker Parson Weems encountered one of Marion's former lieutenants, Peter Horry, who had been collecting materials and painfully trying to construct a biography. Weems seems to have recognized instantly the romantic appeal of Marion's exploits; and Horry incautiously turned his manuscript over to the famous biographer of Washington with a request that he "make it read grammatically" and also "embellish" it. When Weems published the "embellished" work in 1809, Horry was horrified. "A history of realities turned into a romance. . . . a fictitious invention of the brain," he complained to Weems. "You have carved and mutilated it with so many erroneous statements, your embellishments, observations and remarks, must necessarily be erroneous as proceeding from false grounds. Most certainly 'tis not MY history, but YOUR romance." The plain old soldier was additionally disturbed because he was made to appear the sole author in some of the early editions.[19]

Efforts to correct Weems's romanticizing of Marion failed to overtake the parson's imagined dialogue, invented adventures, and flashing prose.[20] The dashing Swamp Fox, along with Washington, moved into

19 The first edition of *The Life of Gen. Francis Marion* . . . (Philadelphia, 1809) listed no author. For bibliographical data on this and subsequent editions, see A. S. Salley's introduction to the reprint edition of William D. James, *A Sketch of the Life of Brig. Gen. Francis Marion* . . . (Marietta, Ga., 1948) and Paul Leicester Ford, *Mason Locke Weems: His Works and Ways,* ed. Emily E. F. Skeel (3 vols.; New York, 1909), I, 97–127. Horry's complaint is quoted in William Gilmore Simms, "Weems, the Biographer and Historian," *Views and Reviews in American Literature, History and Fiction, Second Series* (New York, 1845 [1847]), 136.

20 Another South Carolinian who had served under Marion, William D. James, published at Charleston in 1821 *A Sketch of the Life of Brig. Gen. Francis Marion* . . . , which was unadorned and unexciting. Over two decades later the South Carolina novelist, William Gilmore Simms, sought to paint a truer picture of Marion, drawing on both Weems and James and checking them against other histories and unpublished documents. Simms admitted that Weems "had rather loose notions of the privileges of the biographer," but concluded that "in reality, he has transgressed much less in his Life of Marion than is generally supposed." Simms, *The Life of Francis Marion* (New York, 1844), 8. A modern biographer, Robert D. Bass, after comparing Weems and James with an even wider range of previously unused sources, has similarly concluded that "the two biographies have about equal validity." Bass, *Swamp Fox: The Life and Campaigns of General Francis Marion* (New York, 1959). 247.

the foreground of the American consciousness of the Revolution. Weems's books, said William Gilmore Simms, "were among my earliest treasures"; they "have had a vast circulation, have exercised a wondrous influence over the young minds of the country, have moulded many of our noblest characters." [21]

While the military exploits of Weems's Marion were captivating the young, their elders were being treated to the legendary civil exploits of another hero of the Revolutionary South. About the time that Parson Weems encountered Peter Horry, an ambitious young lawyer of humble origins, William Wirt, was trying to climb into the leadership of class-conscious Virginia. As part of his campaign for social acceptability, Wirt sought to add a literary reputation to his flashy oratorical attainments. Originally he planned to write a series of sketches of famous Virginians. But one of his projected subjects, like himself a man of modest birth and spectacular rhetorical abilities, so absorbed Wirt that he devoted years to preparing a biography of Patrick Henry. Though Wirt did not, like Weems, put imagined conversations into the mouths of his characters, he did presume to reconstruct verbatim texts of Henry's celebrated orations from the recollections of aged witnesses. Moreover the theme of Henry's rise from obscurity to leadership was so important to Wirt that he exaggerated both the lowliness of Henry's origins and the aristocratic splendor of the Virginia ruling class. Most important, he seized upon the developing strain of Romantic assumptions in American thought to interpret Henry as a force of Nature, a natural genius whose greatness was greatness of soul. This view enabled the biographer to gloss over his subject's intellectual and moral shortcomings, or even to turn them into Romantic virtues. John Taylor of Caroline called Wirt's biography of Henry "a wretched piece of fustian," and even Henry's admirer, John Randolph, thought it "a splendid novel." But these men were anachronistic in an increasingly Romantic society, which quickly adopted Wirt's Henry as its leading civil hero of the Revolutionary movement. And once again the Revolutionary tradition had exercised its nationalizing spell over a southern writer. Patrick Henry, in life the exemplar of Virginia provincialism, emerged from Wirt's pages as a man of national vision.[22]

21 Simms, "Weems, The Biographer and Historian," 125, 127.
22 Wirt, *Sketches of the Life and Character of Patrick Henry* (Philadelphia, 1817). For a suggestive interpretation of Wirt as biographer see William R. Taylor, *Cavalier and Yankee: The Old South and American National Character* (New York, 1961), 67–94; the quotations are from p. 69. Though I derive my view of Wirt from Taylor's insights, I cannot see the basis for his central contention that Wirt's interpretation of Henry was significantly "southern."

By the 1840's the development of a popular market for biography had evoked readable but unoriginal accounts of several southern Revolutionary figures; [23] and the 1850's saw publication of a series of more substantial biographical works based on previously unused sources and comparable to Johnson's study of Greene in their contribution to historical knowledge.[24] Following the Civil War this tendency toward fuller documentation culminated in a series of voluminous biographical works that unfolded their subjects' lives through masses of letters and other documents strung together by minimal narrative connections.[25]

These nonprofessional biographers greatly expanded historical knowledge of the Revolutionary South, but they also exhibited some less happy characteristics of nineteenth-century historical writing. Their works were motivated in part by intense state pride, by a desire to claim for their respective states a larger share of the glory of the Revolution. Kate Mason Rowland dedicated her biography of George Mason "To VIRGINIA the Illustrious, the Dearly Loved Old Dominion"; and the biographer of James Iredell asserted in his preface his purpose to "vindicate the claim of North Carolina to a place in the front rank of the foremost states in the War of the Revolution." This effort to glorify the heroes of one's state was often reinforced by a more directly filiopietistic impulse. Biographies of Richard Henry Lee, Nathanael Greene, and Patrick Henry were written by their grandsons, that of William Pinkney by a nephew, that of James Iredell by the husband of a granddaughter, those of Edmund Randolph and George Mason by more distant kinsmen, and that of Charles Carroll of Carrollton was commissioned by his descendants. "I resolved that nothing should prevent me from

23 In addition to his biography of Marion, William Gilmore Simms wrote *The Life of Nathanael Greene* . . . (New York, 1848) ; and Jared Sparks included in his *Library of American Biography* (25 vols.; Boston, 1834–48) accounts of William R. Davie by F. M. Hubbard, Nathanael Greene by George W. Greene, Patrick Henry by Alexander H. Everett, Benjamin Lincoln by Francis Bowen, and William Pinkney by Henry Wheaton.

24 William Pinkney, *The Life of William Pinkney* (New York, 1853) ; Griffith J. McRee, *Life and Correspondence of James Iredell* . . . (2 vols.; New York, 1857–58) ; Henry S. Randall, *Life of Thomas Jefferson* (3 vols.; New York, 1858) ; and James Graham, *The Life of General Daniel Morgan* . . . (New York, 1859).

25 George Washington Greene, *The Life of Nathanael Greene* . . . (3 vols.; New York, 1867–1871) ; Moncure D. Conway, *Omitted Chapters of History Disclosed in the Life and Papers of Edmund Randolph* (New York, 1888) ; William Wirt Henry, *Patrick Henry: Life, Correspondence and Speeches* (3 vols.; New York, 1891) ; Kate Mason Rowland, *The Life of George Mason, 1725–1792* (2 vols.; New York, 1892) ; Kate Mason Rowland, *The Life of Charles Carroll of Carrollton, 1732–1832, with His Correspondence and Public Papers* (2 vols.; New York, 1898) ; Charles C. Pinckney, *Life of General Thomas Pinckney* (Boston, 1895).

telling the full story of my grandfather's life, and claiming for him the gratitude which is his due from all generations of his countrymen," declared George Washington Greene in the preface to his work. Even Moncure Conway, a notorious dissenter and virtual exile from his Virginia background, felt called upon to defend his remote forbear, Edmund Randolph, at every turn, partly perhaps because he felt that Virginians had unjustly maligned both Randolph's reputation and his own.

Yet in another respect the familial connections of so many of the nineteenth-century biographers with their subjects were an advantage. Often a biography was undertaken partly because the family had the subject's papers; and the biographer made available a mass of precious documentation which might otherwise have been lost and on which historians have depended ever since. In addition to the documents that were lavishly reprinted in the biographies, there were separate editions of the papers of several southern Revolutionary leaders.[26]

The biographers' interest in documents was only one phase of a large-scale movement for documentary collection and publication, which was one of the most important forms of American historical activity in the nineteenth century. The Revolution was a primary focus for this documentary activity. "The more I look into it," declared Jared Sparks, New England minister-turned-historian, in 1827, "the more I am convinced that no complete history of the American Revolution has been written. The materials have never been collected; they are still in the archives of the states, and in the hands of individuals." Sparks made this observation in the course of a three-year documentary survey that took him to all the states and to London and Paris. He never produced the great comprehensive history of the Revolution that was his original aim, but he did help inaugurate a notable era of documentary collection and publication. Sparks himself published the diplomatic correspondence of the Revolution and the papers of Washington, Franklin, and Gouverneur Morris. Simultaneously the federal government embarked on a series of ambitious documentary publication projects, the most important of which for Revolutionary historiography was Peter Force's vast uncompleted

26 Thomas Jefferson Randolph, *Memoir, Correspondence, and Miscellanies, from the Papers of Thomas Jefferson* (4 vols.; Charlottesville, 1829). Congress later purchased the Jefferson papers and underwrote a more complete edition, H. A. Washington (ed.), *The Writings of Thomas Jefferson* . . . (9 vols.; Washington 1853–54). The first of two projected volumes of the *Correspondence of Mr. Ralph Izard* . . . (New York, 1844) was brought out by the subject's daughter, Anne Izard Deas; and William Gilmore Simms edited *The Army Correspondence of John Laurens in the Years 1777–1779* (New York, 1867). Besides these American publications there was Charles Ross (ed.), *Correspondence of Charles, First Marquis Cornwallis* (3 vols.; London, 1859).

American Archives project, of which nine great folio volumes were eventually published.[27]

The great national projects of Sparks and the federal government were paralleled by countless state and private documentary enterprises; and of these the southern states had a large share. In 1841 a Georgia historian, Dr. William B. Stevens, echoed Sparks by complaining that the Revolutionary history of his state "has hitherto, for the want of authenticated documents, been a blank page in our written and traditionary annals." But by this time Georgia and other southern states were well along toward remedying the deficiency. Georgia, in fact, had led the way for the American states by designating Joseph V. Bevan as its official historiographer in 1824 and subsidizing his project to collect and publish documents relating to the state's history. Bevan gained access to the British archives in London for the purpose of copying documents relating to early Georgia history, but he died before any substantial progress was made. The legislature authorized appointment of another agent in the 1830's, and by 1839 he had brought back from London twenty-two folio volumes of transcripts. It was from these materials that Dr. Stevens was able to present in his address to the Georgia Historical Society in 1841 the first accurate and amply documented account of Georgia's role in the coming of the Revolution.[28]

Georgia's discovery of the documentary riches of the British archives prompted other southern states to similar activity. In 1825 the North Carolina legislature authorized a lottery to aid Judge Archibald D. Murphey in his project of gathering documents for an exhaustive history

27 On Sparks, Force, and the documentary movement in general, see John Spencer Bassett, *The Middle Group of American Historians* (New York, 1917); the quotation is from p. 92. Sparks's principal documentary compilations were: *Diplomatic Correspondence of the American Revolution* (12 vols.; Boston, 1829–30); *The Life and Writings of George Washington* (12 vols.; Boston, 1834–37); and *Correspondence of the American Revolution: Being Letters of Eminent Men to George Washington* . . . (4 vols.; Boston, 1853). Peter Force's volumes appeared under the title *American Archives* . . . (4th series, 6 vols.; 5th series, 3 vols.; Washington, 1837–53). There were several earlier and less ambitious efforts to publish the more important Revolutionary documents: Hezekiah Niles, *Principles and Acts of the Revolution in America* . . . (Baltimore, 1822); and Jedidiah Morse, *Annals of the American Revolution* . . . (Hartford, 1824). A later general compilation of enduring value was Frank Moore, *Diary of the American Revolution: From Newspapers and Original Documents* (2 vols.; New York, 1860).

28 Stevens, "Discourse Delivered before the Georgia Historical Society, at the Celebration of Their Second Anniversary [Feb. 12, 1841]," Georgia Historical Society, *Collections*, II (Savannah, 1842), 1–36; quotation from p. 2; Stevens, *A History of Georgia* . . . *to* . . . *1798* (2 vols.; New York, 1847; Philadelphia, 1859), I, viii–ix; Van Tassel, *Recording America's Past*, 105–106.

of the state. Like Georgia's Bevan, Murphey died before materials could be secured from London, but not before he had collected at home a valuable body of documents relating especially to the Revolutionary history of the state. Meanwhile the governor had secured from British officials an index to North Carolina documents in the London archives, which the state finally published in 1843. South Carolina sponsored an agent who spent three years in London locating and copying materials relating to that state. William W. Hening's superbly edited *Statutes at Large* gave Virginia a magnificent corpus of source material for the colonial and Revolutionary periods, and the state's Revolutionary legislative journals were also published.[29]

The movement for state-sponsored historical activities, beginning in the 1820's, was followed closely by the organization of state historical societies. Virginia's historical society was organized in 1831, North Carolina's in 1833, Georgia's in 1839, Maryland's in 1844, and South Carolina's in 1855; and by 1860 there were historical societies in nearly every southern state. While some of these societies were only sporadically active, those in the seaboard southern states made substantial contributions to Revolutionary historiography through the collection and publication of source materials. The North Carolina society maintained and expanded Judge Murphey's collection of documents; the Georgia society built up a library and commissioned a history of the state by Dr. Stevens; and the societies of Georgia, South Carolina, Virginia, and Maryland issued extensive documentary publications.[30] In addition to the documentary activities of the states and the societies, an individual

29 Van Tassel, *Recording America's Past,* 103–107; Bassett, *The Middle Group of American Historians,* 240–42; Guion G. Johnson, *Ante-Bellum North Carolina: A Social History* (Chapel Hill, 1937), 819; William W. Hening (ed.), *The Statutes at Large: Being a Collection of All the Laws of Virginia, from . . . 1619* (13 vols.; Richmond, Philadelphia, 1819–23). Virginia published the journals of its Senate for the years 1778–79 and 1785–90 (2 vols.; Richmond, 1827–28) and the journals of its House of Delegates for the years 1776–1790 (4 vols.; Richmond, 1828).

30 Van Tassel, *Recording America's Past,* 97–98. The Georgia society issued three volumes of *Collections,* 1840–48; the South Carolina society sponsored publication of Plowden C. J. Weston (ed.), *Documents Connected with the History of South Carolina* (London, 1856), and then issued three volumes of *Collections,* 1857–59; the Virginia society issued a single volume of *Collections,* 1834, published historical contributions regularly in the *Southern Literary Messenger,* 1835–37, revived publication 1848–53 through a quarterly *Virginia Historical Register, and Literary Advertiser* issued by its secretary, and then published an annual *Virginia Historical Reporter,* 1854–60; and the Maryland society published in pamphlet form many historical addresses delivered at its meetings as well as some documentary contributions. See Walter Muir Whitehill, *Independent Historical Societies . . .* (Boston, 1962), 134, 163, 177, 184.

compiler published a notable collection of documents on the Revolutionary history of South Carolina.[31]

Though cut short by the Civil War, this flourishing documentary activity showed remarkable hardihood, and by the 1870's and 1880's was
being pushed even more vigorously under the same kind of political and
nonprofessional auspices as it had begun. The Georgia Historical Society resumed publication of its *Collections* in 1873 and the South Carolina society in 1884; and during the same period both the Virginia and
Maryland societies began extensive publication programs. The most
notable development of this period was the inauguration of two great
documentary publication projects: the *Archives of Maryland,* published in Baltimore since 1883, edited by William H. Browne and successors, which would run to over sixty volumes by the 1960's; and the
twenty-six volume *Colonial and State Records of North Carolina* published in Raleigh and Goldsboro from 1886 to 1906, edited by Secretary
of State William L. Saunders and Chief Justice Walter Clark. Virginia
began copying from the London archives, publishing in Richmond from
1875 to 1893 an eleven-volume *Calendar of Virginia State Papers and
Other Manuscripts,* edited by W. P. Palmer *et al.,* and obtaining twenty-
two additional volumes of unpublished transcripts. Spurred by the example of Virginia and North Carolina, South Carolina in the 1890's employed its neighbors' archival agent, W. Noel Sainsbury, to collect
thirty-six volumes of transcripts. Georgia, which had pioneered in the
collection of documents, lost its London transcripts by fire in the 1850's;
and not until the twentieth century did it revive its documentary publication.[32]

The vast store of source materials so industriously accumulated was
not very fully utilized by the nonprofessional historians of the nineteenth
century for studies of the Revolutionary South. Aside from their important contributions in biography, what writing they did was mainly
in the area of state and local history. Much of this writing was motivated

31 Robert W. Gibbes (ed.), *Documentary History of the American Revolution*
(3 vols.; New York, 1853–57).

32 Allen D. Candler (ed.), *The Colonial Records of the State of Georgia* (26
vols.; Atlanta, 1904–16), and *The Revolutionary Records of the State of Georgia*
(3 vols.; Atlanta, 1908). For surveys of the documentary situation at the end of
the nineteenth century, see Stephen B. Weeks, "On the Promotion of Historical
Studies in the South," Southern History Association, *Publications,* I (Jan., 1897),
13–34; Appleton P. C. Griffin, *Bibliography of Historical Societies (The United
States and the Dominion of Canada)* in American Historical Association, *Annual
Report, 1905,* II (Washington, 1907); and Whitehill, *Independent Historical Societies,* 136, 163, 177, 185.

by state and local pride, but the best of the state histories proceeded from an intelligent recognition of the legitimacy and importance of the state as a unit for historical analysis and came close to the standard that a historian of Maryland set for himself. "As a loyal son of Maryland," wrote J. Thomas Scharf, "the writer feels a natural pride in her honorable history; but he has never (to the best of his belief, at least,) allowed himself to be moved from the straight path of truth by any bias in her favor." [33]

Again it was David Ramsay who had shown the way, having followed his pioneering work on the Revolution in South Carolina (1785) with a general history of the state (1809) that remains today unexcelled among state histories for detachment and critical insight. Less critical but also notable among the early state histories was the history of Virginia by the expatriated Irish Republican and playwright, John Daly Burk. Burk wrote partly to combat the custom of contrasting Virginia's "yielding policy with the sturdy patriotism of New-England"; but his Virginia patriotism was far overshadowed by his enthusiasm for American republicanism. He viewed the period of the French and Indian War as a "new and more splendid aera," when the American provinces, "driven into an union by the sense of common danger, . . . sink their local prejudices and lay the foundation of an American character." Burk's closing paragraph was a paean to "the glory of the Revolutionary morning," when "souls of ethereal stamp flocked from the remotest regions, and rallied round the first pure altar, raised to the worship of liberty." [34]

Georgia and North Carolina early had unimpressive histories that were useful in the absence of anything better; [35] but in the 1830's and 1840's better state histories began to be written. Maryland's celebrated and choleric Whig orator, John V. L. McMahon, published in 1831 a his-

---

33 Scharf, *History of Maryland from the Earliest Period to the Present Day* (3 vols.; Baltimore, 1879), I, vii.

34 Burk, *The History of Virginia, from Its First Settlement to the Present Day* (3 vols.; Petersburg, 1804–05), II, 233; III, 167, 468. Burk died before he completed his project, and his three volumes extend only to 1775. In 1816 there was published at Petersburg a fourth volume extending to 1781, entitled *The History of Virginia Commenced by John Burk and Continued by Skelton Jones and Louis Hue Giradin*.

35 Hugh McCall, *The History of Georgia . . . to the Present Day (1784)* (2 vols.; Savannah, 1811–1816), was a derivative work with many errors, written by an army captain who retired to the Savannah jailorship. Hugh Williamson, *The History of North Carolina* (2 vols.; Philadelphia, 1812), was a clumsy stringing together of documents which barely reached the Revolution. A better researched but still poorly written work by a French immigrant to North Carolina who later became a distinguished jurist in Louisiana was Francois Xavier Martin, *The History of North Carolina from the Earliest Period* (New Orleans, 1829).

torical analysis of government in Maryland that to this day commands the respect of professional scholars. Maryland got a more conventional history, a fervent and thinly researched narrative, by James McSherry in 1849; and in 1846–48 Robert R. Howison published a solid history of Virginia extending into the nineteenth century.[36]

By all odds the most distinguished state history written before the Civil War was the history of Georgia published in 1847–59 by Dr. William Bacon Stevens. This versatile New Englander practiced medicine in Savannah after completing his studies at Dartmouth in 1837; entered the Episcopal priesthood and taught for a time at the University of Georgia; moved to a large church in Philadelphia in 1848; and later became Bishop of Pennsylvania and a principal founder of Lehigh University. Dr. Stevens was the major force behind the organization of the Georgia Historical Society at Savannah in 1839 and edited the first two volumes of its *Collections*. It was in response to his notable address on Georgia's role in the Revolution that the society in 1841 requested him to write a history of the state. Dr. Stevens sought to write "not by the secondary helps of former histories, but by the careful study of original, contemporary, and official documents." The result was two detailed, dispassionate volumes, published in 1847 and 1859, which stood until the mid-twentieth century as the most authoritative account of Georgia's history to 1798.[37]

The genre of state history, following the direction set by Dr. Stevens, reached its ultimate development in the late nineteenth and early twentieth centuries in a series of enormously detailed, reliable, and usually unimaginative narratives. These works represented a merging of nonprofessional into professional scholarship. Four of them were written by Confederate veterans: Maryland's J. Thomas Scharf, sometime lawyer, newspaperman, and public official; Georgia's Charles C. Jones, Jr.,

---

36 McMahon, *An Historical View of the Government of Maryland from Its Colonization to the Present Day* (Baltimore, 1831); McSherry, *A History of Maryland from Its First Settlement in 1634 to the Year 1848* (Baltimore, 1849); Howison, *A History of Virginia . . . to the Present Time* (2 vols.; Philadelphia, 1846, and Richmond, 1848).

37 Stevens, *A History of Georgia*, I, x. By the 1840's a popular market for state histories was developing, especially for use in the schools. William Gilmore Simms, *The History of South Carolina . . .* (Charleston, 1840), was a well written summary, based on the best secondary authorities. The versatile literary hack, Timothy Shay Arthur, best known for his temperance tract *Ten Nights in a Barroom and What I Saw There*, collaborated with W. H. Carpenter on a series of state histories including *The History of Virginia from Its Earliest Settlement to the Present Time* (Philadelphia, 1852) and *The History of Georgia from Its Earliest Settlement to the Present Time* (Philadelphia, 1852).

lawyer and one-time mayor of Savannah; South Carolina's Edward Mc-Crady, lawyer-legislator from Charleston and nephew of Justice William Johnson; and North Carolina's Samuel A. Ashe, lawyer, editor and politician. The transition toward academic historians is exemplified by North Carolina's Robert D. W. Connor, school teacher and administrator who had a year of graduate study at Columbia long after he had embarked on historical scholarship and who eventually became a university professor and the first Archivist of the United States. The last and best of the lengthy narrative state histories was written by South Carolina's David D. Wallace, who earned a Ph.D. degree at Vanderbilt in 1899 and taught at Wofford College. Whatever the shortcomings of the earlier of these works, they brought the coverage of the Revolutionary South by nonprofessional historians to a high point of comprehensiveness and authority; and Connor's and Wallace's volumes remain today the fullest and best accounts of the Revolution in the Carolinas. In addition, Wallace attained a degree of critical objectivity about his state that had not been reached since David Ramsay's history of South Carolina more than a century earlier.[38]

A final category of nineteenth-century writings about the Revolutionary South consisted of a variety of works dealing with particular areas or episodes and usually resting heavily upon oral tradition. Justice William Johnson's brother Joseph, a physician, wrote one of the most valuable and interesting books of this type, emphasizing upcountry South Carolina during the Revolution. A similar useful contribution was made by a Virginia Presbyterian minister, William H. Foote, who published several volumes relating to the Presbyterian settlements in Virginia and North Carolina, with emphasis on the Revolutionary

38 Scharf, *History of Maryland from the Earliest Period to the Present Day;* Charles C. Jones, Jr., *The History of Georgia* (2 vols.; Boston, 1883); Edward McCrady, *The History of South Carolina under the Proprietary Government, 1670–1719* (New York, 1897), *The History of South Carolina under the Royal Government, 1719–1776* (New York, 1899), *The History of South Carolina in the Revolution, 1775–1783* (2 vols.; New York, 1901–02); Samuel A. Ashe, *History of North Carolina* (2 vols.; Greensboro, 1908, Raleigh, 1925); Connor, *The Colonial and Revolutionary Periods, 1584–1783,* Volume I of Connor *et al., History of North Carolina* . . . (6 vols.; Chicago and New York, 1919), *North Carolina: Rebuilding an Ancient Commonwealth, 1584–1925* (4 vols.; Chicago and New York, 1929); Wallace, *The History of South Carolina* (4 vols.; New York, 1934). The works by Connor and Wallace included, in addition to the historical narrative, volumes of biographical sketches for which the principal authors were not responsible. Besides the state histories, Connor published a biography of the Revolutionary leader *Cornelius Harnett* . . . (Raleigh, 1909), and Wallace made a major contribution to Revolutionary historiography in *The Life of Henry Laurens* . . . (New York, 1915).

period. A prominent North Carolina politician, John H. Wheeler, published a brief history of the state, to which he attached a lengthy series of county sketches containing much local history and biography. The Virginia historian Hugh Blair Grigsby published an able discourse on the Virginia convention of 1776; and the pioneer collector of frontier Americana, Lyman Draper, finally published in 1881 an account of the battle of Kings Mountain, based on manuscripts and recollections he had been gathering for half a century. After the Civil War, county histories began to appear, some of them like A. S. Salley, Jr.'s history of Orangeburg County, South Carolina, making a substantial contribution to Revolutionary historiography. The works mentioned here had many less distinguished imitators which, in spite of their patent biases and credulity, preserved useful information about local events and personages.[39]

The local pride that was so evident in all nineteenth-century historiography was at its most blatant in some of these local historians. One writer took up his pen because "my heart burned with indignation at the many misrepresentations, of the people of North Carolina, which had so long gone unchallenged." Therefore as "a dutiful son of North Carolina," he "determined to write this book in defence of his native state, and in vindication of the honor and patriotism of her people." Yet the pride and touchiness of the South's Revolutionary historians about their states had in it nothing that was sectionally divisive. On the contrary, southern writers sought to claim for their respective states a larger share in the glorious Revolutionary tradition of liberal nationalism.

39 Joseph Johnson, *Traditions and Reminiscences Chiefly of the American Revolution in the South* . . . (Charleston, 1851); Foote, *Sketches of North Carolina* . . . (New York, 1846) and *Sketches of Virginia* . . . (2 vols.; Philadelphia, 1850–55); Wheeler, *Historical Sketches of North Carolina* . . . (2 vols.; Philadelphia, 1851); Grigsby, *The Virginia Convention of 1776* . . . (Richmond, 1855); Draper, *King's Mountain and Its Heroes* . . . (Cincinnati, 1881); and A. S. Salley, Jr., *The History of Orangeburg County, South Carolina* (Orangeburg, 1898). Other works of varying usefulness and reliability are, in chronological order: John Drayton, *Memoirs of the American Revolution . . . As Relating to the State of South Carolina. . . .* (2 vols.; Charleston, 1821); Alexander Garden, *Anecdotes of the American Revolutionary War* . . . (2 vols.; Charleston, 1822–28; reprinted, 3 vols,; Brooklyn, 1865); Joseph Seawell Jones, *A Defense of the Revolutionary History of the State of North Carolina from the Aspersions of Mr. Jefferson* (Boston, 1834); George White, *Statistics of the State of Georgia* . . . (Savannah, 1849) and *Historical Collections of Georgia* . . . (New York, 1854); Eli W. Caruthers, *Revolutionary Incidents . . . in the "Old North State"* (2 vols.; Philadelphia, 1854–56); Cyrus L. Hunter, *Sketches of Western North Carolina* . . . (Raleigh, 1877); David Schenck, *North Carolina, 1780–'81* . . . (Raleigh, 1889); and Major William A. Graham, *General Joseph Graham and His Papers on North Carolina Revolutionary History* . . . (Raleigh, 1904).

David Ramsay had made the developing tradition of liberty central to his interpretation of South Carolina history. "The love of liberty had taken deep root in the minds of carolinians long before the revolution," he wrote; the "similarity of state and condition" produced by the early settlers' struggle to subdue the wilderness had "inculcated the equality of rights" and "taught them the rights of man." Ramsay's successors simply echoed this theme with greater competitive stridency on behalf of their respective states. "There is no state in our Union whose early history is marked by purer patriotism, more unsullied devotion to liberty, or more indomitable opposition to every form of tyranny than North Carolina," wrote John H. Wheeler in 1851. Indeed William Gilmore Simms had gone so far in his younger days as to admit that "The Yankee is the man, who first hung out the banner of liberty . . . and determined to be free." [40]

As a matter of fact, a modern reader could almost go through the whole corpus of southern writings about the Revolution without finding any evidence that a southern sectional consciousness ever existed or that a sectional war ever took place. There are, of course, exceptions to this generalization. As early as 1835 the *Southern Literary Messenger* attacked Bancroft's first volume on the ground that it was "intended to dispose us to acquiesce in the new notion 'that the people of the colonies, all together, formed one body politic before the Revolution.' " [41] Richard Hildreth also drew attacks from southern reviewers; [42] but over against these sectional reactions to national histories written by sometimes unsympathetic Northerners must be set the fact that a southern historian could dedicate his work to Bancroft as "the only historian who has done justice to North Carolina"; while another Southerner could himself write an impressive national history showing little sectional consciousness and acknowledging special indebtedness to Bancroft. [43]

40 Schenck, *North Carolina, 1780–'81*, 12, 471; Ramsay, *History of South Carolina*, II, 384; Wheeler, *Historical Sketches of North Carolina*, xvii; Simms, quoted in John Higham, "The Changing Loyalties of William Gilmore Simms," *Journal of Southern History*, IX (May, 1943), 211.

41 Quoted in Van Tassel, *Recording America's Past*, 117. For another southern attack on Bancroft, see James P. Holcombe, *Sketches of the Political Issues and Controversies of the Revolution* (Richmond, 1856).

42 For a condescending reference to the South, see Richard Hildreth, *The History of the United States of America* (Rev. ed.; New York, 1856), III, 97. *DeBow's Review* commented of Hildreth that "Never before was history so prostituted to gratify personal or party malevolence." Van Tassel, *Recording America's Past*, 140n.

43 Wheeler, *Historical Sketches of North Carolina*, v; George Tucker, *The History of the United States . . . to . . . 1841* (4 vols.; Philadelphia, 1856–57).

Only once did the debate over the Revolutionary contributions of the respective states degenerate into a rancorous squabble over the relative merits of North and South. In 1853 William Gilmore Simms published a 177-page reply to certain animadversions on South Carolina's Revolutionary record by Lorenzo Sabine, and the quarrel reverberated through the rest of the decade. This was the same Simms who in a series of lectures to the Georgia Historical Society in 1841 had asked, "where in *our* history, are the epochs, and what the materials, which, in the hands of the future poet and romancer, shall become the monuments of our nation—shall prove the virtues of our people,—declare and assert, to the unborn ages, the fame of our achievements?" Simm's novels, as well as his biographies of Greene and Marion and his history of South Carolina, were part of his effort to create through poetry and romance a historical tradition more national than sectional. Only under the extreme pressure of sectional crisis, and then only in polemical settings, could southern writers escape the powerful influence of the tradition of liberal nationalism in dealing with the Revolution. In their historical writings they continued to assume, with Dr. William B. Stevens, that the Revolutionary age was "The heroic age of American history," and that "To trace the progress of free principles in America would be to epitomize her whole history," including the history of the southern states.[44]

At least three antebellum southern historians, Eli Caruthers, Robert R. Howison, and George Tucker, followed out the logic of the Revolutionary tradition by publicly denouncing slavery. Of those who lived through the Civil War, all whose positions have been discovered opposed secession, except Charles C. Jones, Jr., and Edward McCrady. After the Civil War, the Revolution lost its place as the primary object of historical interest. But in the writing about the Revolution that did appear, the note of sectional bitterness was sounded only through General Fitzhugh Lee's preface to Kate M. Rowland's biography of George Mason. "The withdrawal of some of the States from the Union in 1861 was in accordance with the theories of the Fathers of the Government, endorsed in the earlier history of the republic by the great masses of the people . . . ," wrote this unreconstructed Confederate. "We have before us the life of a patriot who labored by tongue and pen to erect a

44 A Southron [W. G. Simms], *South-Carolina in the Revolutionary War* . . . (Charleston, 1853) ; quotations from W. G. Simms, *Views and Reviews in American Literature, History and Fiction, First Series,* ed. C. Hugh Holman (Cambridge, 1962), 47; and W. B. Stevens, "Discourse before the Georgia Historical Society," 1–2.

bulwark between Federal power and State rights, so strong, that the hand of an oppressor could never take away the liberties of the people." [45]

Lee's comment with regard to one of the great codifiers of Revolutionary liberalism reminds us that the South's Revolutionary experience was always susceptible to a particularistic, sectionally chauvinistic interpretation. The failure of the general's sentiment to find an echo anywhere in the vast body of southern Revolutionary historiography is conclusive evidence of the pervasiveness and power of the Revolutionary tradition of liberal nationalism for Southerners as for other Americans.

By the time General Lee composed his anachronistic preface in 1892, there was even less room for a southern historiography of the Revolution than before. The writing of southern history was being taken over by men who had gone north to seminars at Columbia and Johns Hopkins to receive Ph.D.'s before returning to teach in southern colleges and universities. These professional scholars and their multiplying successors belonged emphatically to a national community of inquiry; and what they wrote about the Revolutionary South was guided by the seminal ideas current among all American historians.

At Johns Hopkins by the end of the century the seminal idea was Professor Herbert Baxter Adams' preoccupation with the evolution of political institutions. Adams was not particularly concerned with the Revolution or the South, but his colleague Professor J. C. Ballagh encouraged investigations into southern history. These twin influences stimulated a series of monographs that constituted the earliest substantial body of professional scholarship on the Revolutionary South. John A. Silver led the way in 1895 with a study tracing the evolution of Maryland's Revolutionary government "from its germ in the non-importation agreements of 1773 and 1774 through its gradual exercise and assertion of sovereign authority until it found itself the only power in the Colony." Over the next several decades, other Hopkins-trained scholars extended Silver's study of Maryland's Revolutionary government; made similar studies for other southern states; explored church-state relations, an aspect of institutional history that especially interested Adams, in Revolutionary Virginia; and wrote broader accounts (one of them in the form of a biography of a royal governor) of the Revolution in several southern areas.[46] Several similar institutional studies of government in

45 Rowland, *The Life of George Mason*, I, x-xi.
46 Most of these studies were published in the "Johns Hopkins University Studies in Historical and Political Science" (Baltimore), as follows: Silver, *The Provisional Government of Maryland (1774–1777)*, XIII, No. 10 (1895), quotation from p. 60; Bernard C. Steiner, *Life and Administration of Sir Robert Eden*, XVI, Nos.

the pre-Revolutionary and Revolutionary South came from the seminars at Columbia.[47]

By the end of the First World War the burst of scholarly energy in the area of institutional history had about run its course, and other approaches were competing for the attention of historians. Frederick Jackson Turner was emphasizing the frontier experience and the development in colonial times of a democratic "Old West" whose conflicts with the more conservative coastal settlements had had an important bearing on the course of Revolutionary events. A new emphasis on economic causation reached Revolutionary historiography with the publication of Arthur M. Schlesinger's *Colonial Merchants and the American Revolution* in 1918. Schlesinger pictured the Revolutionary ferment as arising from the economic objections of colonial businessmen to British policies, reinforced by agitation from democratic-minded lower orders in the colonial towns. And a 1924 book by Allan Nevins, *The American States during and after the Revolution,* explored internal conflicts and political and social changes of the period.

Southern historians were surprisingly slow to utilize any of these approaches, and in fact the 1920's and 1930's were lean years for publications about the Revolutionary South. Schlesinger's economic emphasis found an echo in 1926, when Isaac S. Harrell published a doctoral dissertation on Virginia Loyalism, urging the importance of planter debts as a cause for Revolution. Schlesinger's theme was even more directly explored by two studies of the mid-thirties on commerce in North Carolina and in Charleston. Southern students of the Revolution did not do

---

7–9 (1898) ; Enoch W. Sikes, *The Transition of North Carolina from Colony to Commonwealth,* XVI, Nos. 10–11 (1898); William Taylor Thom, *The Struggle for Religious Freedom in Virginia: The Baptists,* XVIII, Nos. 10–12 (1900); Steiner, *Western Maryland in the Revolution,* XX, No. 1 (1902); Beverly W. Bond, *State Government in Maryland, 1777–1781,* XXIII, Nos. 3–4 (1905); James M. Leake, *The Virginia Committee System and the American Revolution,* XXXV, No. 1 (1917). Published outside the series were: Hamilton J. Eckenrode, *Separation of Church and State in Virginia* (Richmond, 1910), and *The Revolution in Virginia* (Boston, 1916) ; Percy S. Flippin, "The Royal Government in Georgia, 1752–1776," *Georgia Historical Quarterly,* VIII (1924), 1–37, 81–120, 243–91; IX (1925), 187–245; X (1926), 1–25, 251–76; XII (1928), 326–52; XIII (1929), 128–53. Steiner's *Sir Robert Eden* and Eckenrode's *Revolution in Virginia* were particularly comprehensive accounts for Maryland and Virginia respectively. Beverly W. Bond, in addition to his monograph on Maryland, wrote a careful study of *The Quit-Rent System in the American Colonies* (New Haven, 1919), which included much material on the colonial and Revolutionary South.

47 W. Roy Smith, *South Carolina As a Royal Province, 1719–1776* (New York, 1903) ; Charles R. Lingley, *The Transition in Virginia from Colony to Commonwealth* (Columbia University, "Studies in History, Economics, and Public Law," XXXVI, No. 2 [New York, 1910]).

much with Turner's interest in the West until Turner's disciple Charles H. Ambler issued a study of Washington and the West in 1936. This was followed in the next year by Thomas P. Abernethy's exhaustive (and exhausting) study of land speculation in relation to the Revolution, which seriously qualified some of Turner's assumptions. Meanwhile, Nevins' pioneering work on internal political developments during the Revolutionary era had been followed by Fletcher M. Green's study of constitutional development in the southern states.[48]

The golden age of scholarly writing about the Revolutionary South dates from 1940. Since then almost every year has seen the publication of several good books. Some of this outpouring has been devoted to the themes of economic causation and sectional and class conflict introduced to Revolutionary historiography by Turner, Schlesinger, and Nevins. Following Merrill Jensen's overenthusiastic statement of the internal-conflict thesis in 1948, Elisha P. Douglass impressively documented, with heavy emphasis on the southern states, the vigorous contest over the degree of democracy in the new state governments created during the Revolution. Carl Bridenbaugh briefly adduced new evidence of a split between conservative and liberal wings of the Virginia gentry, and Robert D. Meade pushed this view even further in his biography of Patrick Henry. The question of Virginia planter debts has been further debated, the latest conclusion being that Virginians did not rebel for the purpose of fleecing their creditors. Finally Richard Walsh's study of the Charleston artisans reinforced Schlesinger's claims about radical pressure from the lower echelons of colonial society, though Walsh did not seem to credit fully these implications of his data.[49]

48 Harrell, *Loyalism in Virginia: Chapters in the Economic History of the Revolution* (Durham, 1926) ; Leila Sellers, *Charleston Business on the Eve of the American Revolution* (Chapel Hill, 1934) ; C. C. Crittenden, *The Commerce of North Carolina, 1763–1789* (New Haven, 1936) ; Ambler, *George Washington and the West* (Chapel Hill, 1936) ; Abernethy, *Western Lands and the American Revolution* (New York, 1937) ; Green, *Constitutional Development in the South Atlantic States, 1776–1860* (Chapel Hill, 1930).

49 Merrill Jensen, *The Articles of Confederation: An Interpretation of the Social-Constitutional History of the American Revolution* (Madison, 1948) ; Douglass, *Rebels and Democrats: The Struggle for Equal Political Rights and Majority Rule during the Revolution* (Chapel Hill, 1955) ; Bridenbaugh, *Seat of Empire: The Political Role of Eighteenth-Century Williamsburg* (Williamsburg, 1950) ; Meade, *Patrick Henry: Patriot in the Making* (Philadelphia, 1957) ; Lawrence H. Gipson, "Virginia Planter Debts before the American Revolution," *Virginia Magazine of History and Biography*, LXIX (1961), 259–77; Emory G. Evans, "Planter Indebtedness and the Coming of the Revolution in Virginia," *William and Mary Quarterly*, XIX (Oct., 1962), 511–33; Walsh, *Charleston's Sons of Liberty: A Study of the Artisans, 1763–1789* (Columbia, 1959).

Yet the bulk of recent scholarship about the Revolutionary South has been little concerned with any particular thesis. Through a variety of specialized approaches to the Revolutionary era, scholars have delineated a pattern of such diversity and complexity that overarching generalizations seem, by implication at least, to be ruled out.

One group of modern historians has carried forward the work of the older state historians by analyzing with greater detail and sophistication the varying patterns of Revolutionary events in the individual states.[50] Another group of historians has illuminated Revolutionary events through the highly perfected modern form of historical biography. The distinguished biographical works by Brant, Malone, Freeman, and Mays have been followed in many less ambitious but scholarly and revealing studies of secondary Revolutionary figures.[51] Still other his-

50 For Maryland: Charles A. Barker, *The Background of the Revolution in Maryland* (New Haven, 1940) ; Philip A. Crowl, *Maryland during and after the Revolution* (Baltimore, 1943). For Georgia: Albert B. Saye, *New Viewpoints in Georgia History* (Athens, 1943), and *A Constitutional History of Georgia, 1732–1945* (Athens, 1958) ; W. W. Abbot, *The Royal Governors of Georgia, 1754–1775* (Chapel Hill, 1959). For North Carolina: Alonzo Thomas Dill, *Governor Tryon and His Palace* (Chapel Hill, 1955), and the series of more detailed and fully documented articles from which the book is drawn, in the *North Carolina Historical Review*, XIX–XXIII (Apr., 1942; Oct., 1943; Jan. 1945–Oct., 1946) ; Charles G. Sellers, Jr., "Making a Revolution: The North Carolina Whigs, 1765–1775," in J. Carlisle Sitterson (ed.), *Studies in Southern History in Memory of Albert Ray Newsome* . . . (Chapel Hill, 1957), 23–46. For Virginia: Freeman H. Hart, *The Valley of Virginia in the American Revolution, 1763–1789* (Chapel Hill, 1942) ; Thad W. Tate, "The Coming of the Revolution in Virginia: Britain's Challenge to Virginia's Ruling Class, 1763–1776," *William and Mary Quarterly*, XIX (July, 1962), 323–43.

51 Irving Brant, *James Madison* (6 vols.; Indianapolis, 1941–61) ; Dumas Malone, *Jefferson and His Time* (3 vols.; Boston, 1948–) ; Douglas S. Freeman, *George Washington: A Biography* (6 vols.; New York, 1948–54) ; David J. Mays, *Edmund Pendleton, 1721–1803: A Biography* (2 vols.; Cambridge, 1952) ; Richard H. Barry, *Mr. Rutledge of South Carolina* (New York, 1942) ; Bass, *The Green Dragon: The Lives of Banastre Tarleton and Mary Robinson,* and *Swamp Fox: The Life and Campaigns of General Francis Marion;* Thomas Boyd, *Light-Horse Harry Lee* (New York, 1931) ; North Callahan, *Daniel Morgan, Ranger of the Revolution* (New York, 1960) ; William M. Dabney and Marion Dargan, *William Henry Drayton and the American Revolution* (Albuquerque, 1962) ; Chalmers Davidson, *Piedmont Partisan: The Life and Times of Brigadier-General William Lee Davidson* (Davidson, N.C., 1951) ; Hamilton J. Eckenrode, *The Randolphs: The Story of a Virginia Family* (Indianapolis, 1946) ; Anne King Gregorie, *Thomas Sumter* (Columbia, 1931) ; Don Higginbotham, *Daniel Morgan, Revolutionary Rifleman* (Chapel Hill, 1961) ; Aubrey C. Land, *The Dulanys of Maryland* (Baltimore, 1955) ; Meade, *Patrick Henry;* Samuel W. Patterson, *Horatio Gates, Defender of American Liberties* (New York, 1941) ; Blackwell P. Robinson, *William R. Davie* (Chapel Hill, 1957) ; Theodore Thayer, *Nathanael Greene, Strategist of the American Revolution* (New York, 1960) ; Alice Noble Waring, *The Fighting Elder: Andrew Pickens (1739–1817)* (Columbia, 1962).

torians have approached the Revolution through some of the significant social groups involved: the Loyalists, Virginia's officeholding gentry, and North Carolina's Highland Scots.[52] And one historian has explored Indian policy on the colonial frontier as it related to the coming of the Revolution.[53] Finally the military history of the Revolution in the South has been receiving renewed attention from able scholars.[54]

By 1957, when John R. Alden undertook to integrate this wealth of modern scholarship into a single comprehensive volume, the picture he painted was one of baffling diversity and complexity. It was not even clear that an identifiable "South" existed at the time of the Revolution. Alden himself could marshall only scant evidence for his contention that "By the end of the Revolutionary era . . . the South had emerged as a section and the Southerners as a people different from Northerners"; while another able historian asserted flatly that "In 1776 there was no South; there never had been a South," and that the people of the area were "without question the least homogeneous human group in all America." [55]

Whether historians thought of a "South" or of a "South-that-was-to-be," they were equally confused about the nature and meaning of the Revolutionary transformation that had now been so fully delineated for the region. Insofar as a trend in interpretation was observable, they seemed to be following the lead of Edmund and Helen Morgan in viewing the Revolution as a struggle over constitutional principles and home rule. Indeed the most substantial recent contribution to southern Revo-

52 Robert O. DeMond, *The Loyalists of North Carolina during the Revolution* (Durham, 1940); Joseph W. Barnwell, Jr., "Loyalism in South Carolina, 1765–1785" (Ph.D. dissertation, Duke University, 1941); Charles S. Sydnor, *Gentleman Freeholders: Political Practices in Washington's Virginia* (Chapel Hill, 1952); Duane Meyer, *The Highland Scots of North Carolina, 1732–1776* (Chapel Hill, 1961). This category also includes two works cited earlier: Harrell, *Loyalism in Virginia*, and Walsh, *Charleston's Sons of Liberty*.

53 John R. Alden, *John Stuart and the Southern Colonial Frontier . . . 1754–1775* (Ann Arbor, 1944).

54 In addition to the biographies of military figures cited above, see: William B. Willcox, "The British Road to Yorktown: A Study in Divided Command," *American Historical Review*, LII (1946), 1–35; John R. Alden, *General Gage in America* (Baton Rouge, 1948); Alexander A. Lawrence, *Storm over Savannah: The Story of Count d'Estaing and the Siege of the Town in 1777* (Athens, Ga., 1951); Eric Robson, "The Expedition to the Southern Colonies, 1775–1776," *English Historical Review*, LXVI (1951), 535–60.

55 Alden, *The South in the Revolution, 1763–1789*, 2; Bridenbaugh, *Myths and Realities: Societies of the Colonial South* (Baton Rouge, 1952), vii. Alden argues for the early emergence of a distinctive South more explicitly if not more convincingly in *The First South* (Baton Rouge, 1961).

lutionary historiography, announced for publication while this essay was being written, is Jack P. Greene's study of the long struggle for autonomy by the southern colonial assemblies.[56]

Thus by the 1960's, the sophisticated professional American historiography of the Revolution seemed to be finding its way back to the interpretation that had been so impressively thought out in a British prison by that southern father of American Revolutionary historiography David Ramsay. Having survived a century of southern sectionalism and three generations of critical professional scholarship, Ramsay's Revolutionary tradition of liberal nationalism may long impart to Americans, from Charleston to Honolulu, a livelier and truer sense of who they are and what they are about.

---

56 Edmund S. and Helen M. Morgan, *The Stamp Act Crisis: Prologue to Revolution* (Chapel Hill, 1953); Jack P. Greene, *The Quest for Power: The Lower Houses of Assembly in the Southern Royal Colonies, 1689-1776* (Chapel Hill, 1963).

III

"The Critical Period,"
the Constitution,
and the New Nation

Ernest M. Lander, Jr.

A MERICAN historians have been intrigued for more than a century by the critical period, when their forefathers thus laid constitutional foundations and built viable political institutions. But only in the past three decades have chroniclers given adequate attention to the South during this period.

For example, southern sectionalism during the Confederation period was not thoroughly explored until John R. Alden published *The First South*.[1] Earlier general histories, like Andrew C. McLaughlin's *The*

1 Alden, *The First South* (Baton Rouge, 1961). Edmund C. Burnett published an important but little noticed article entitled "Southern Statesmen and the Confederation," *North Carolina Historical Review*, XIV (October, 1937), 343–60. He recalled Edward Rutledge's alarm over Dickinson's draft of the Articles of Confederation, which would, Rutledge feared, subject some states to a government by "Eastern Provinces." This was the keynote of the South's political philosophy, said Burnett. Unfortunately, the author rambled widely, and only at his conclusion did he briefly, though somewhat vaguely, anticipate Alden. Burnett listed seven

Confederation and the Constitution, 1783–1789, either ignored or denied the existence of a North-South cleavage. The subject fared no better
in R. S. Cotterill's *The Old South,* published in 1936, which denied that
there was a southern consciousness before the Missouri controversy in
1820. Such appears to have been the view of William B. Hesseltine,
writing in the same year, and of Francis B. Simkins as recently as 1953.[2]
Clement Eaton's *A History of the Old South* took brief note of the
"strong consciousness of sectional interests" at the Philadelphia Convention,[3] and Hesseltine, in collaboration with David L. Smiley, also
gave some account of sectional discord at Philadelphia.[4] Otherwise,
these authors generally overlooked sectionalism during the 1780's.

Merrill Jensen's *The New Nation: A History of the United States
During the Confederation, 1781–1789,* included, somewhat incidentally,
accounts of: sectional strife over methods of apportioning requisitions
(land or slaves) ; Robert Morris' monopoly of tobacco sales to France;
Jay's proposal to close the Mississippi; the South's new indebtedness to
creditors in Philadelphia and Baltimore; Kentucky's statehood petition
of 1787; methods of paying the national debt (by the states or by the
central government) ; alleged exploitation of Southerners by northern
shippers; and disunion sentiment in the Northeast. In fact, Jensen said,
"Many roots of antagonism that ultimately led to war between the North
and the South are to be found in the era of the American Revolution." [5]

But Jensen made no effort to unify his discussion of sectionalism, and
it remained for Alden to give the first comprehensive picture of southern
sectionalism during the Confederation. His *The First South* showed
numerous disagreements, beginning with the Revolution, over use of
Negro troops, nonexportation, the Articles of Confederation, and the
personnel of the peace delegation to Paris. Alden also covered those con-

---

examples wherein southern statesmen "gave a rather better account of themselves"
than the Northerners in the conduct of the government. These cases, such as the
Southerners' defense of free navigation of the Mississippi, often revealed sectional
animosity.

2 McLaughlin, *The Confederation and the Constitution, 1783–1789* (New York
and London, 1905) ; Cotterill, *The Old South: The Geographic, Economic, Social,
Political, and Cultural Expansion, Institutions, and Nationalism of the Antebellum South* (Glendale, Calif., 1936), 142–43; Hesseltine, *A History of the South*
(New York, 1936) ; Simkins, *A History of the South* (New York, 1953).

3 Eaton, *A History of the Old South* (New York, 1949), 146.

4 Hesseltine and Smiley, *The South in American History* (2nd ed.; Englewood
Cliffs, N. J., 1960), 91–99.

5 Jensen, *The New Nation: A History of the United States During the Confederation, 1781–1789* (New York, 1950), 74, 170–74, 191–92, 202–203, 238, 335, 397–404,
417–18.

troversies discussed by Jensen, and he then carried the story through the Philadelphia Convention and the state ratifying conventions.[6]

Allan Nevins made the first serious attempt to cover the history of individual southern states during the Confederation period in *The American States During and After the Revolution, 1775–1789*.[7] Nevins said little new about Maryland, but his treatment of Virginia politics was detailed and interpretive. He found the Old Dominion conservatively oriented and in favor of a vigorous central government until the mid-1780's, at which time a strong antinationalist party under Patrick Henry arose and remained a powerful force in Virginia politics until 1789. Nevins further indicated that constitutional reform and pressing economic problems accentuated an East-West sectionalism within the state during 1785–1788. Nevins also reviewed North Carolina's problems of debts, paper money, treatment of Loyalists, and relations with the Confederation government. South Carolina faced virtually the same problems. Noteworthy was Nevins' account of the activities of the Charleston "radicals" led by Commodore Gillon—a class struggle, Nevins decided. As for Georgia, Nevins discovered that the main outlines of its history during the Confederation period closely resembled those of South Carolina. Though now outdated, *The American States During and After the Revolution* is still a useful point of departure.

A monograph of vital importance is Fletcher M. Green's *Constitutional Development in the South Atlantic States, 1776–1860; A Study in the Evolution of Democracy*. Green pointed to three distinct phases of constitutional change from 1776 to 1800: first, South Carolina's revision in 1778; second, the struggle for constitutional reform as a political and sectional issue in all states; and third, the revisions and changes resulting from the adoption of the Federal Constitution of 1787. In judging the results, Green discovered sweeping changes in South Carolina and Georgia, few in North Carolina and Maryland, and none in Virginia. In the latter state, however, the democratic element forced through the legislature measures which would have been secured in other states via constitutional reform. On the whole it was "a period of reaction, experiment, and readjustment." [8]

---

6 For criticism of Alden's failure to weigh the unifying factors in the nation, see review by Jackson T. Main in *Mississippi Valley Historical Review*, XLVIII (March, 1962), 696–97.

7 Nevins, *The American States During and After the Revolution, 1775–1789* (New York, 1924).

8 Green, *Constitutional Development in the South Atlantic States, 1776–1860; A Study in the Evolution of Democracy* (Chapel Hill, 1930) 100–41.

Jensen's *The New Nation* supplemented Nevins' state-by-state survey of the problems of the Revolutionary and Confederation periods, such as taxes, paper money, debts, agriculture, tariff laws, and treatment of Loyalists. Jensen contended that the southern states came closer to solving their problems than earlier historians had admitted. He further indicated that southern state tariff laws were fairly uniform and not discriminatory against other states, only against some foreign countries, especially Great Britain.[9] His view of the tariff was amply supported by William F. Zornow in a more recent evaluation of the tariff laws of Virginia, the Carolinas, and Georgia.[10] A valuable supplement to Jensen's work is E. James Ferguson, "State Assumption of the Federal Debt During the Confederation." [11]

The last one hundred pages of John R. Alden's *The South in the Revolution, 1763–1789* [12] have provided by far the best balanced and most up-to-date analysis of the southern post-Revolutionary scene. Alden found the southern states remarkably lenient toward the Tories, laggard in public education, and slow to change their criminal codes, Virginia excepted. Alden also gave attention to the unsuccessful attempts in the upper South to abolish slavery. On economic matters he adhered to Jensen's thesis that the South recovered rapidly from the war. By 1789, he concluded, Virginia, Maryland, and South Carolina had achieved stability, and the outlook in North Carolina and Georgia had vastly improved. On state constitutional developments, Alden supported Green's interpretations. Alden's treatment of the Philadelphia Convention and the state ratifying conventions, though adequate, was more fully developed in his later volume *The First South.*

Significant accounts and interpretations of the South's part in making the Constitution are to be found in the recent works, Forrest McDonald, *We the People,* and Jackson T. Main, *The Antifederalists.* McDonald launched a mighty attack on Beard's economic interpretation and in so

9 Jensen, *The New Nation,* 216–17, 235–36, 274–81, 298–335, 350–54.

10 Zornow, "Georgia Tariff Policies, 1775–1789," *Georgia Historical Quarterly,* XXXVIII (March, 1954), 1–10, and "The Tariff Policies of Virginia, 1775–1789," *Virginia Magazine of History and Biography,* LX (July, 1954), 306–19, and "Tariff Policies in South Carolina, 1775–1789," *South Carolina Historical Magazine,* LVI (January, 1955), 31–44, and "North Carolina Tariff Policies, 1775–1789," *North Carolina Historical Review,* XXXII (April, 1955), 151–64.

11 Ferguson, "State Assumption of the Federal Debt During the Confederation," *Mississippi Valley Historical Review,* XXXVIII (December, 1951), 403–24.

12 Alden, *The South in the Revolution, 1763–1789* (Baton Rouge, 1957). Of all the general histories on the South, only Hesseltine and Smiley, *A History of the South,* 86–99, makes any serious effort to cover the Confederation period. Even so, their account is brief.

doing gave the most incisive critique yet to appear on the political and economic forces behind ratification in each of the five southern states. Main clarified the position of the opponents of the Constitution and how the Federalists converted enough waverers to ensure success. He too gave a state-by-state survey, adhering to a modified Beardian interpretation. He agreed with Beard that there were economic divisions over the Constitution but said that they conformed more nearly to geographic than to class lines. This led Main to dissent from some of McDonald's conclusions.[13]

Consideration must also be given to important works on individual states during the Confederation. Worthy of special mention are the multivolume histories of Virginia, South Carolina, Georgia, and Tennessee, written respectively by Lyon G. Tyler, David D. Wallace, Walter G. Cooper, and Philip M. Hamer, and published under the auspices of the American Historical Society.[14] Of the four, Hamer included the fullest and probably the most satisfactory account of his state during the Confederation (and the Federalist era, too), Wallace, the scantiest. Hugh T. Lefler's recent two-volume *History of North Carolina* is of high quality.[15]

Beverly W. Bond, Jr.'s monograph on Maryland government from 1777 to 1791 is still useful. To this may be added Bernard C. Steiner's article, "Maryland's Adoption of the Federal Constitution," a detailed narrative devoid of interpretation.[16] But the most important work on Maryland during the 1780's is Philip A. Crowl's *Maryland During*

13 McDonald, *We the People: The Economic Origins of the Constitution* (Chicago, 1958); Main, *The Antifederalists: Critics of the Constitution, 1781–1788* (Chapel Hill, 1961). For their disagreements see Main, "Charles A. Beard and the Constitution: A Critical Review of Forrest McDonald's *We the People;* with a Rebuttal by Forrest McDonald," *William and Mary Quarterly,* XVII, 3rd series (January, 1960), 86–110.

14 Tyler, *The Federal Period, 1763–1861,* Volume II of *History of Virginia* (3 vols.; Chicago and New York, 1924); Hamer (ed.), *Tennessee, A History, 1673–1932* (2 vols.; New York, 1933); Wallace, *The History of South Carolina* (3 vols.; New York, 1934); Cooper, *The Story of Georgia* (3 vols.; New York, 1938).

15 Lefler, *History of North Carolina* (2 vols.; New York, 1956). See also William K. Boyd, *History of North Carolina: The Federal Period, 1783–1860* (Chicago, 1919).

16 Bond, *State Government in Maryland, 1777–1791* (Baltimore, 1905); Steiner, "Maryland's Adoption of the Federal Constitution," *American Historical Review,* V (December, 1899), 207–24. Of minor importance is Max P. Allen, "William Pinkney's First Public Service," *Maryland Historical Magazine,* XXXIX (December, 1944), 277–92; and Everett D. Obrecht, "The Influence of Luther Martin in the Making of the Constitution of the United States," *Maryland Historical Magazine,* XXVII (September, 1932), 173–90, (December, 1932), 280–96.

and After the Revolution: A Political and Economic Study. There was
no "critical period" of threatening anarchy in Maryland after the war,
Crowl concluded. The state was dominated by a relatively small group
of planters, lawyers, and merchants. The last two chapters, dealing with
Maryland and the Constitution, Crowl later revised and enlarged in an
article entitled "Anti-Federalism in Maryland, 1787–1788." He found
no class struggle in Maryland and no debtor class consisting exclusively
of small farmers. Many once-wealthy merchants and lawyers were also
in debt. The people of Maryland paid little attention to the Philadelphia
Convention; nevertheless, a majority of the ruling clique favored ratification. A small faction within this ruling oligarchy, headed by Samuel
Chase, William Paca, and Luther Martin, led the fight against ratification. Most of them had speculated heavily in confiscated Tory property
or had attempted to pay prewar British debts in depreciated state currency.[17] Incidentally, both Main and McDonald relied heavily on Crowl's
research.

Virginia during the Confederation period has been the subject of
several studies published since 1900, beginning with Charles H. Ambler's
Sectionalism in Virginia from 1776 to 1861. Its thesis was that sectionalism, accentuated by geographic, racial, religious, and economic differences, was the dominant issue at almost every legislative session.[18]
A thorough and well-documented work on one of Virginia's sections is
Freeman H. Hart's *The Valley of Virginia in the American Revolution,
1763–1789.* The Valley was not a typical frontier region and rapidly developed a cattle-hog-corn-wheat economy. Its delegates voted unanimously in 1788 to approve the Constitution because by 1785 the Valley
had deserted its Southside allies on two major issues: a grant to Congress of power over commerce, and collection of British debts. The first,
Valley residents apparently believed, would benefit Potomac River commerce, and the second would influence British withdrawal from the
Northwest posts.[19] Articles in 1953 by Robert E. Thomas and W. A.
Low furnished further information on economic aspects of Virginia
politics in the 1780's. Low, on the basis of limited research, surmised
that by 1784 Britain's monopoly of Virginia's carrying trade and credit
had been largely revived, thus creating new friction. Thomas presented

17 Crowl, *Maryland During and After the Revolution: A Political and Economic
Study* (Baltimore, 1943), and "Anti-Federalism in Maryland, 1787–1788," *William
and Mary Quarterly,* IV, 3rd series (October, 1947), 446–69.
18 Ambler, *Sectionalism in Virginia from 1776 to 1861* (Chicago, 1910).
19 Hart, *The Valley of Virginia in the American Revolution, 1763–1789* (Chapel
Hill, 1942). See especially pp. 183-87.

economic data to offer "substantial proof that the leaders of both the Federalist and Anti-Federalist parties [Virginia Convention, 1788] came from the *same* class . . . and that the conflict, for whatever reasons, was only sectional." [20]

Jackson T. Main has now modified previous findings and interpretations for the years 1781–1787 in Virginia, with the publication of two articles of unusually high merit. In the first, "The Distribution of Property in Post-Revolutionary Virginia," Main revealed that from one half to three fourths of the adult males, exclusive of town dwellers, were poor, landless tenants or hired laborers. They were most numerous in the Northern Neck and Tidewater, the more densely populated and earlier-settled areas. This and other pertinent information Main gleaned from little used records of Virginia's annual census in the 1780's.[21] A second and more significant article, "Sections and Politics in Virginia, 1781–1787," sought to discover if Virginia counties voted according to some consistent pattern. The two major political opponents were the nationalistic, big farmer-poor tenant Northern Neck and the particularistic, small-farmer Southside. Neither section commanded a majority of the state. Main carefully studied the voting habits of the other sections and their relations to the two chief political regions. His paramount interpretation, cogently but not conclusively presented, was that the most meaningful division in Virginia was between counties of the major river valleys and those lacking access to navigable streams.[22]

The chief work on North Carolina politics in the 1780's is Louise I. Trenholme's *The Ratification of the Federal Constitution in North Carolina.* The real opposition to the Constitution, she concluded, came from western agrarian and religious groups. Decentralization of this agricultural state, plus ignorance of national affairs, helped to defeat the Constitution at the Hillsboro convention. Federalist victory at the second (Fayetteville) convention resulted from economic pressure by the First Congress, Federalist propaganda, need for protection against Indians, and proposals for amendments.[23]

20 Thomas, "The Virginia Convention of 1788: A Criticism of Beard's *An Economic Interpretation of the Constitution," Journal of Southern History,* XIX (February, 1953), 63–72; Low, "Merchant and Planter Relations in Post-Revolutionary Virginia, 1783–1789," *Virginia Magazine of History and Biography,* LXI (July, 1953), 308–18.

21 Main, "The Distribution of Property in Post-Revolutionary Virginia," *Mississippi Valley Historical Review,* XLI (September, 1954), 241–58.

22 Main, "Sections and Politics in Virginia, 1781–1787," *William and Mary Quarterly,* XII, 3rd series (January, 1955), 96–112.

23 Trenholme, *The Ratification of the Federal Constitution in North Carolina* (New York, 1932).

Albert R. Newsome, writing in 1940, gave a brief review of North Carolina's ratification. He generally agreed with Mrs. Trenholme, but on the change of sentiment between the two conventions, he placed more emphasis on economic factors. At the same time, he ignored religious motivation, probably correctly so, and pointed out that, contrary to tradition, the second convention ratified the Constitution without knowing whether or not another state had approved any of the twelve amendments that Congress had submitted.[24] Trenholme's and Newsome's studies are well supplemented by William C. Pool's detailed article "An Economic Interpretation of the Ratification of the Federal Constitution in North Carolina." It proved that men owning substantially the same amounts of the same kinds of property were equally divided on the matter of adoption or rejection.[25]

C. Christopher Crittenden recounted much of the economic history of North Carolina in *The Commerce of North Carolina, 1763–1789*. This monograph revised the "critical period" thesis insofar as the Tar Heel state was concerned. North Carolina rapidly recovered its prosperity and commerce after the war, its tonnage clearance in 1788 being two thirds as much as South Carolina's.[26]

An early but still standard study of South Carolina politics during the Confederation period is Ulrich B. Phillips' "The South Carolina Federalists," appearing in two installments in the *American Historical Review* in 1909. The first installment dealt entirely with the 1780's, during which time South Carolina experienced the usual postwar turmoil and economic problems. But from 1785 onward planters and merchants began to realize that political independence had not brought economic independence, hence their increasing desire for a stronger central government—which might, incidentally, help to keep radicals in check.

24 Newsome, "North Carolina's Ratification of the Federal Constitution," *North Carolina Historical Review*, XVII (October, 1940), 287–301.

25 Pool, "An Economic Interpretation of the Ratification of the Federal Constitution in North Carolina," *North Carolina Historical Review*, XXVII (April, 1950), 119–41, (July, 1950), 289–313, (October, 1950), 437–61. McDonald relied heavily on Pool, as evidenced by pp. 310–21 of *We the People*. See also Main, *The Antifederalists*, 242–48. For further information on North Carolina politics during the Confederation see Blackwell P. Robinson, "Willie Jones of Halifax," *North Carolina Historical Review*, XVIII (January, 1941), 1–26, (April, 1941), 133–70; and Alice B. Keith, "William Blount in North Carolina Politics, 1781–1789," in J. Carlyle Sitterson (ed.), *Studies in Southern History in Memory of Albert Ray Newsome* (Chapel Hill, 1957), 47–61.

26 Crittenden, *The Commerce of North Carolina, 1763–1789* (New Haven, 1936). In addition, see Alice B. Keith, "John Gray and Thomas Blount, Merchants, 1783–1800," *North Carolina Historical Review*, XXV (April, 1948), 194–205.

Yet, unaccountably, as Phillips pointed out, even the Charleston radicals were supporting a stronger government by 1787.[27] Allan Nevins incorporated the chief points of Phillips' first installment in his *American States During and After the Revolution.*

Not until 1941 did another author make a serious study of South Carolina politics in the 1780's. Then Charles G. Singer undertook to examine South Carolina history "from the point of view of federalism and those factors which determined [its] relations . . . with Congress." Singer believed that South Carolina was probably more loyal in meeting congressional requests than any other state, and he attributed the state's growing tendency toward a stronger federal government to Revolutionary experiences, war debts held by South Carolinians, and, as Phillips also said, the desire of Charleston merchants for national control of commerce.[28] Forrest McDonald's later research clearly revealed that some merchants stood to profit, others to lose, through federal control of commerce.[29] Unfortunately, Singer's monograph, valuable in several respects, was poorly edited and contains numerous factual errors. George C. Rogers, Jr., in 1961 published "South Carolina Ratifies the Federal Constitution," valuable for its revelation of the close rapport between the northern élite and the prominent South Carolinians and discussion of British mercantile influence in securing Charleston's support for ratification of the Constitution.[30]

Until the past decade Georgia's history in the 1780's has been neglected, excepting some general studies and a brief article of some worth by Amanda Johnson. Robert S. Lambert's "The Repossession of Georgia, 1782–1784" and William W. Abbot's "The Structure of Politics in Georgia, 1782–1789" began to remedy this deficiency in 1957. Lambert briefly discussed the serious problems that the patriots faced after the British evacuated Savannah, while Abbot splendidly surveyed the whole gamut of Georgia politics during the Confederation period. He noted that Georgia's whole structure of government was Assembly dominated, that nineteen men rose to the top and remained there during the decade—

27 Phillips, "The South Carolina Federalists," *American Historical Review,* XIV (April, 1909), 529–43, and (July, 1909), 731–43.

28 Singer, *South Carolina in the Confederation* (Philadelphia, 1941), 162.

29 McDonald, *We the People,* 205–16.

30 Rogers, "South Carolina Ratifies the Federal Constitution," in South Carolina Historical Association, *Proceedings, 1961* (Columbia, 1962), 41–62. The positions of the state's four delegates are analyzed in Ernest M. Lander, Jr., "The South Carolinians at the Philadelphia Convention, 1787," *South Carolina Historical Magazine,* LVII (July, 1956), 134–55.

though suffrage requirements were nominal—that land was the crux of men's interest in government, that a low country-upcountry cleavage developed early, and that capable upcountry leaders moved to the forefront in 1785–1786. Abbot concluded his article with examples of greed, dishonesty, and stupidity in land, Loyalist, and Indian policies.[31]

Two years later Kenneth Coleman published *The American Revolution in Georgia, 1763–1789,* based on extensive research at home and abroad. The final one hundred pages gave the best account yet available on Georgia's Confederation history, especially on social and economic changes. In politics, Coleman explained that the upcountry played a dominant role earlier than in most states due to its temporary political control during the Revolution and to the Indian menace afterward.[32]

Concerning southern history during the Federalist period, the older studies by Bassett and Channing hardly touched North-South disputes and almost completely overlooked state and regional political developments. On the other hand, Charles A. Beard, as early as 1914, took note of strong southern opposition to Hamilton's funding and assumption. Writing in 1930, Jesse T. Carpenter conceded that the South was a "conscious minority" from the Philadelphia Convention onward. The early 1790's, according to Carpenter, revealed the North and South to be "hanging by a thread upon the shoulders of their common president, George Washington." [33] Cotterill, Hesseltine and Smiley, and Eaton followed in due course, as we have seen, with general histories of the South, but only Hesseltine and Smiley did justice to the Federalist period. In a chapter entitled "The Beginnings of Sectional Conflict," the authors reviewed southern opposition to Hamilton's program, southern leadership in the Republican party, and the development of southern constitutional ideas. They also noted that the "first evidence of conflicting sectional interests" in the First Congress arose with the introduction of antislavery petitions from Pennsylvania.

John C. Miller's *The Federalist Era, 1789–1801,* despite some ques-

31 Johnson, "A State in the Making: Georgia (1783–1798)," *Georgia Historical Quarterly,* XV (March, 1931), 1–27; Lambert, "The Repossession of Georgia, 1782–1784," in South Carolina Historical Association, *Proceedings, 1957* (Columbia, 1958), 14–25; Abbot, "The Structure of Politics in Georgia, 1782–1789," *William and Mary Quarterly,* XIV, 3rd series (January, 1957), 47–65.

32 Coleman, *The American Revolution in Georgia, 1763–1789* (Athens, 1959).

33 John S. Bassett, *The Federalist System, 1789–1801* (New York, 1906); Edward Channing, *Federalists and Republicans, 1789–1815* (New York, 1917), Volume IV of his *A History of the United States* (6 vols.; New York, 1905–1925); Beard, "Some Economic Origins of Jeffersonian Democracy," *American Historical Review,* XIX (January, 1914), 282–98; Carpenter, *The South as a Conscious Minority, 1789–1861* . . . (New York, 1930), 18–19.

tionable interpretations, is probably the best general history of the period. Miller emphasized the growing sectionalism of the 1790's, repeatedly pointing to North-South alignments in congressional voting on issues ranging from assumption through the Sedition Act. Accepting recent revisionist views, Miller confirmed Madison in his role as chief opponent of Hamilton, chief organizer of the Republican party, and formulator of Republican constitutional theories. Other southern leaders, Jefferson included, did not fare so well in Miller's hands, Washington perhaps excepted.[34]

Two articles appeared in 1962 and shed significant additional light on early sectionalism: Whitney K. Bates, "Northern Speculators and Southern State Debts: 1790," and E. James Ferguson, "Public Finance and the Origins of Southern Sectionalism." Bates made a detailed statistical analysis from official records of the state debts of Virginia and the Carolinas and confirmed the traditional view that much of the indebtedness of these states was to outsiders, principally New Yorkers. This fact intensified a developing economic sectionalism and encouraged Southerners to take the lead in forming an anti-Hamilton party.[35] Ferguson, relying primarily on research included in his book *The Power of the Purse,* gave penetrating insight into the South's opposition to Hamilton's financial program. On assumption, for instance, Northerners questioned the validity of many southern claims on the grounds of poor records. Hence, when Madison and Jefferson made their deal with Hamilton about the location of the federal capital, the bargain included a not-too-well-noticed concession to the South: a liberal accounting of state debts to be assumed by the federal government.[36]

Thomas P. Abernethy brought out his long-awaited *The South in the New Nation, 1789–1819* in 1961. It was a disappointment, for, after two chapters on the South Atlantic states, Abernethy turned to the West and returned to the East only occasionally during the balance of the book.[37] For more detailed information readers must rely on biographies, monographs, and other special works.

34 Miller, *The Federalist Era, 1789–1801* (New York, 1960). For adverse criticism see review by Merrill Jensen in *Journal of Southern History*, XXVII (November, 1961), 533–36.

35 Bates, "Northern Speculators and Southern State Debts: 1790," *William and Mary Quarterly*, XIX, 3rd series (January, 1962), 30–48; Ferguson, "Public Finance and the Origins of Southern Sectionalism," *Journal of Southern History*, XXVIII (November, 1962), 450–61.

36 Ferguson, *The Power of the Purse: A History of American Public Finance, 1776–1790* (Chapel Hill, 1961).

37 Abernethy, *The South in the New Nation, 1789–1819* (Baton Rouge, 1961).

Of particular value are the recent multivolume biographies of the South's three outstanding national figures of the period: Madison, Jefferson, and Washington. Irving Brant led the way with his fresh treatment of Madison, a six-volume study entitled *James Madison*. The second volume, covering the years 1780–1787, portrayed Madison as a tireless worker for a stronger central government, a resourceful, determined, and ingenious leader, and a politician with a "passion for anonymity." Most of Brant's reviewers heaped high praise on this volume, Merrill Jensen dissenting in one respect. He accused Brant of accepting the Federalist party's "chaos and patriots to the rescue" version of the period.[38]

Brant ran on treacherous shoals in his third volume, covering the years 1787–1800. While aptly showing that Jefferson built upon foundations laid by Madison, Brant painted Madison and his friends too white, their opponents too black. But Brant's most serious flaw, according to most critics, was his unsatisfactory explanation of Madison's shift in political philosophy during the formative years of the new Republic.[39] Brant supplemented his third volume with a provocative article on Madison's leadership in the Republican party. He attributed the traditional view of Madison's "secondary" role largely to Federalist and Republican propaganda in Madison's day. With persuasive, though not conclusive, evidence, Brant maintained, for instance, that both features of the compromise over assumption and location of the capital came from Madison and "so did the idea of linking them." [40]

It is not without significance that Brant's estimate of "Little Jimmy" has been supported to a considerable degree by numerous other writers. The judicious Dumas Malone, in *Jefferson and the Rights of Man*, revealed that Madison led the early Virginia movement against Hamilton's measures. Malone, in *Jefferson and the Ordeal of Liberty*, further pointed out that Madison, not Jefferson, was the real leader of the Republican

38 Brant, *James Madison, the Nationalist, 1780–1787* (Indianapolis, 1948). See review by Jensen in *Journal of Southern History*, XIV (August, 1948), 412–13. The scope of this essay does not permit examination of the numerous one-volume biographies or special monographs dealing with limited aspects of the careers of Madison, Jefferson, and Washington.

39 Brant, *James Madison: Father of the Constitution, 1787–1800* (Indianapolis, 1950). Its harshest critic, J. H. Powell, wrote: "Brant never seems to come close to the mind or humanity of Madison." *Mississippi Valley Historical Review*, XXXVII (March, 1951), 710–12.

40 Brant, "James Madison and His Times," *American Historical Review*, LVII (July, 1952), 853–70. See especially p. 856.

party until the latter became Vice-President in 1797.[41] Adrienne Koch had previously given additional evidence about the two Virginians' relationship in 1950. As she pointed out, the two great statesmen, who had deep regard for each other, were not always in agreement. Jefferson "concentrated on individual rights, and on that fateful phase of opposition when the underdog minority becomes the legal ruling majority." Madison "spent his political strength in effecting order and a reasonable atmosphere for civilized compromise." [42]

Brant's deficiencies, such as they may have been, in analyzing Madison's political philosophy were corrected, at least in part, by Neal Riemer in "The Republicanism of James Madison." Riemer, believing Madison to be "one of the least understood of major American political thinkers," convincingly argued that the great driving force behind Madison's political philosophy was his republican faith, not economic interests, social class, or sectional outlook. In appraising Madison's influence as a party leader, Riemer, with insufficient evidence, called him "the most original, most understanding, and most effective champion of republicanism against its enemies." Such adulation weakened an otherwise objective article.[43]

Revisionism continued with the appearance in 1955 of three essays on the origins of the American party system by the late Joseph Charles. He portrayed Madison and John Beckley as early leaders of the Republicans, who did not take the offensive until 1794 and then on the issue of Jay's Treaty. Charles saw Jefferson as a latecomer, largely in retirement from 1794 to 1797, who was forced to the front by a popular movement.[44] Noble E. Cunningham hastened to furnish evidence to show that Charles had gone too far in denigrating Jefferson's influence, especially during his years as Vice-President. He also believed there was more party organization prior to 1794 than Charles's essays suggested.

41 Malone, *Jefferson and the Rights of Man* (Boston, 1951), Volume II of *Jefferson and His Time* (2 vols.; Boston, 1948–1951) ; Malone, *Jefferson and the Ordeal of Liberty* (Boston, 1962), Volume III of *ibid.*

42 Koch, *Jefferson and Madison: The Great Collaboration* (New York, 1950). See especially pp. 293–94.

43 Riemer, "The Republicanism of James Madison," *Political Science Quarterly,* LXIX (March, 1954), 45–64.

44 Charles, "Hamilton and Washington: The Origins of the American Party System," *William and Mary Quarterly,* XII, 3rd series (April, 1955), 217–67, and "Adams and Jefferson: The Origins of the American Party System," *William and Mary Quarterly,* XII, 3rd series (July, 1955), 410–46, and "The Jay Treaty: The Origins of the American Party System," *William and Mary Quarterly,* XII, 3rd series (October, 1955), 581–630. These articles were published in book form as *The Origins of the American Party System: Three Essays* (Williamsburg, 1956).

These points Cunningham expanded in *The Jeffersonian Republicans: The Formation of Party Organization, 1789–1801,* a meritorious monograph on the workaday world of politics. Additionally, Cunningham showed that party growth was slow, that the Republicans were becoming "a party of system and concerted action" by 1796, and that Southerners, led by Madison and Jefferson (after 1796), played the dominant part in shaping national party policies.[45]

George Washington's post-Revolutionary career to 1793 has been fully and objectively treated by Douglas S. Freeman in the sixth volume of his life of the great Virginian. After Freeman's untimely death, John A. Carroll and Mary W. Ashworth, two of Freeman's researchers, completed the seventh volume, covering the period 1793–1799. Both volumes are excellent for detailed information about Washington's personal and political life but are lacking in interpretation. Both credit him with sound judgment and great statesmanship. Only occasionally do they depict the great man unfavorably. Sadly absent is an evaluation of Washington, which Freeman had planned to include in the final volume.[46]

The South's reaction to the Alien and Sedition Acts, as evidenced by the Virginia and Kentucky resolutions, has long interested historians. Frank M. Anderson in 1899, Edward Channing in 1915, and several later scholars did the first work on the motives and conduct of the major participants.[47] In 1948, Adrienne Koch and Harry Ammon offered some startling new interpretations. They concluded, "for the present," that the resolutions were primarily intended as a defense of civil liberties against the Alien and Sedition Acts, that Jefferson and Madison collaborated closely and were the only major authors, and that the initiative was Jefferson's. For his part, Madison reined in his spirited friend and produced the well-guarded Virginia Resolutions and more carefully defined Report of 1800. Jefferson, these authors went on, assessed the

---

45 Cunningham, *The Jeffersonian Republicans: The Formation of Party Organization, 1789–1801* (Chapel Hill, 1957). See also Cunningham, "John Beckley: An Early American Party Manager," *William and Mary Quarterly,* XIII, 3rd series (January, 1956), 40–52, and his review of Charles's work in *William and Mary Quarterly,* XIV, 3rd series (April, 1957), 294–96.

46 Freeman, *Patriot and President* (New York, 1954), Volume VI of *George Washington: A Biography* (7 vols.; New York, 1948–1957); Carroll and Ashworth, *First in Peace, March 1793–December 1799* (New York, 1957), Volume VII of *ibid.*

47 Anderson, "Contemporary Opinion of the Virginia and Kentucky Resolutions," *American Historical Review,* V (December, 1899), 225–52; Channing, "Kentucky Resolutions of 1798," *American Historical Review,* XX (January, 1915), 333–36; Philip G. Davidson, "Virginia and the Alien and Sedition Laws," *American Historical Review,* XXXVI (January, 1931), 336–42.

true design of the Alien and Sedition Acts to be political terrorism against Republican opponents. This, in his opinion, was tantamount to an illegal muzzling of his forthcoming presidential campaign.[48] The only prosecution in a southern state was the Richmond trial of James T. Callender. James M. Smith has told this story in *Freedom's Fetters: The Alien and Sedition Laws and American Civil Liberties.*[49]

State studies for the Federalist era abound, except for Maryland and Georgia.[50] Virginia has proved to be a fertile field for historians, especially biographers. Dice R. Anderson's study of William B. Giles led the way for modern scholars.[51] Albert J. Beveridge in 1916 produced the first two volumes of *The Life of John Marshall.* The second volume, covering the years 1788–1801, was a real contribution to knowledge of Marshall and contemporary politics.[52] Henry H. Simms published a standard biography of John Taylor of Caroline in 1932, and Bernard Drell's article, "John Taylor of Caroline and the Preservation of an Old Social Order," further clarified Taylor's political philosophy. The chief threat to his beloved agrarian order, Taylor feared, was not democracy but the new endeavors: manufacturing, commerce, and banking.[53] Edmund Pendleton has been the subject of two biographies in recent years. The first, written in 1939 by Robert L. Hilldrup, was too biased in favor of Jefferson's conservative occasional opponent. The second, in two volumes by David J. Mays in 1952, was the product

---

48 Koch and Ammon, "The Virginia and Kentucky Resolutions: An Episode in Jefferson's and Madison's Defense of Civil Liberties," *William and Mary Quarterly,* V, 3rd series (April, 1948), 145–76. In citing the above article, Brant, *Madison, 1787–1800,* 506, stated: "All earlier accounts have serious factual errors or omissions."

49 Smith, *Freedom's Fetters: The Alien and Sedition Laws and American Civil Liberties* (Ithaca, 1956).

50 But see the useful Bernard C. Steiner, *The Life and Correspondence of James McHenry* (Cleveland, 1907); Ellen H. Smith, *Charles Carroll of Carrolton* (Cambridge, 1942). Of limited use on Maryland politics is Max P. Allen, "William Pinkney's Public Career, 1788–1796," *Maryland Historical Magazine,* XL (September, 1945), 211–29. Of minor value on Georgia history in the 1790's is Ulrich B. Phillips, "Georgia and States Rights . . . ," in American Historical Association, *Annual Report, 1901,* Volume II (2 vols.; Washington, 1902); and Louise F. Hays, *Hero of Hornet's Nest, A Biography of Elijah Clarke, 1733–1799* (New York, 1946). The best work on Georgia history for the period is William O. Foster, Sr., *James Jackson: Duelist and Militant Statesman, 1757–1806* (Athens, 1960).

51 Anderson, *William Branch Giles . . .* (Menasha, Wisc., 1914).

52 Beveridge, *The Life of John Marshall* (4 vols.; Boston and New York, 1916–1919).

53 Simms, *Life of John Taylor . . .* (Richmond, 1932); Drell, "John Taylor of Caroline and the Preservation of an Old Social Order," *Virginia Magazine of History and Biography,* XLVI (October, 1938), 286–98.

of difficult and careful research in primary sources.[54] Two biographies have given full treatment to George Mason. The first, by Helen Hill, emphasized Mason's valuable work as consultant and adviser, particularly to Jefferson. The second, by Robert A. Rutland, more clearly revealed Mason's character.[55] It was a followup of his monograph *The Birth of the Bill of Rights, 1776–1791*, deserving mention here because it detailed the role of Mason and other Southerners in formulating and obtaining adoption of the Bill of Rights.[56] Patrick Henry's post-Revolutionary years have not received adequate study. Jacob Axelrad's biography in 1947 was too laudatory and exhibited little serious research, while Robert D. Meade's proposed second volume is still in preparation. Significant, though brief and undocumented, was Bernard Mayo's reinterpretation of Henry's "enigma." He attempted to steer between the "dark" and "bright" images of the Revolutionary hero but leaned toward the latter.[57]

One of the most significant syntheses of Virginia politics during the 1790's is Harry Ammon's "The Formation of the Republican Party in Virginia, 1789–1796." It contradicted Beard, confirmed Charles's work, and furnished much material for Cunningham's more general study. Ammon depicted the struggle over ratification of the Constitution in Virginia as being one between two agrarian groups. He noted that most Federalists of 1788 were Antifederalists in the 1790's and that some of the opponents in the First Congress to Hamilton's program were merely temporary protestors. Virginia opposition coalesced during the Second Congress on principles of strict construction, agrarianism, and republicanism. Nevertheless, Virginia Republicans avoided Hamilton's fiscal program as the rallying point for a popular movement. Instead, they chose Washington's policy of neutrality toward France in 1793 as their point of departure, and this as a matter of political expediency. The next year Jay's Treaty solidified party lines in Virginia.[58]

Scholarly work on North Carolina during the Federalist period began

---

54 Hilldrup, *The Life and Times of Edmund Pendleton* (Chapel Hill, 1939); Mays, *Edmund Pendleton, 1781–1803: A Biography* (2 vols.; Cambridge, 1952).

55 Hill, *George Mason, Constitutionalist* (Cambridge, 1938); Rutland, *George Mason, Reluctant Statesman* (Williamsburg, 1961).

56 Rutland, *The Birth of the Bill of Rights, 1776–1791* (Chapel Hill, 1955).

57 Axelrad, *Patrick Henry: The Voice of Freedom* (New York, 1947); Mayo, "The Enigma of Patrick Henry," *Virginia Quarterly Review*, XXXV (Spring, 1959), 177–95; Meade, *Patrick Henry: Patriot in the Making* (Philadelphia, 1957).

58 Ammon, "The Formation of the Republican Party in Virginia, 1789–1796," *Journal of Southern History*, XIX (August, 1953), 283–310.

in 1903 with the publication of William E. Dodd's *The Life of Nathaniel Macon*. Then came Henry M. Wagstaff's "Federalism in North Carolina" in 1910.[59] A considerable superstructure has been built on these foundations. Delbert H. Gilpatrick, *Jeffersonian Democracy in North Carolina, 1789–1816*, devoted much attention to the pre-1789 background and the forces that made for sharp political division in 1789. Nascent Republicans controlled the state until 1796, when European broils led to temporary Federalist control. In 1800 the Republicans overwhelmingly returned to power. Gilpatrick concluded that North Carolina geography, discouraging to commerce, was a prominent factor in causing this "small farmer" state to vote Republican.[60] Gilbert L. Lycan, "Alexander Hamilton and the North Carolina Federalists," supplied valuable information on patronage and the reasons for the Federalist party's failure in North Carolina.[61] Blackwell P. Robinson's *William R. Davie* recounted the story of this Federalist governor's political career and his part in founding the University of North Carolina.[62]

For Federalist activities in South Carolina, U. B. Phillips' lengthy article, cited above, is still the standard work. Senator Ralph Izard, Izard's son-in-law, William Loughton Smith, and Robert Goodloe Harper were the chief agents in holding South Carolina conservatives firmly to nationalistic policies and Federalist alignment. Phillips, noting early opposition to Hamilton's program, found the fruition of party development in South Carolina clearly evidenced in the bitter presidential contest of 1796. The Federalists largely defaulted the election to the Republicans in 1800. J. Harold Wolfe's *Jeffersonian Democracy in South Carolina* somewhat revised Phillips' picture. Wolfe went to great effort to prove that the Federalists did not control South Carolina in the 1790's. He found the control about evenly divided: Republican victory in 1796, a slight swing to Federalism in 1798, and Republican victory in 1800.[63]

59 Dodd, *The Life of Nathaniel Macon* (Raleigh, 1903); Wagstaff, "Federalism in North Carolina," in *The James Sprunt Historical Publications,* IX (Chapel Hill, 1910), 3–44.

60 Gilpatrick, *Jeffersonian Democracy in North Carolina, 1789–1816* (New York, 1931). See also Eugene P. Link, "The Democratic Societies of the Carolinas," *North Carolina Historical Review,* XVIII (July, 1941), 259–77.

61 Lycan, "Alexander Hamilton and the North Carolina Federalists," *North Carolina Historical Review,* XXV (October, 1948), 442–65.

62 Robinson, *William R. Davie* (Chapel Hill, 1957).

63 Wolfe, *Jeffersonian Democracy in South Carolina* (Chapel Hill, 1940). One of the causes of South Carolina's disaffection for Federalism was the Senate's re-

Historians have written a more comprehensive story of the trans-montane region than of the Seaboard states, and there are now available full accounts of western land policies, land speculation, early settlement and political developments in Tennessee and Kentucky, foreign intrigue, and Indian relations. Payson J. Treat in *The National Land System, 1785–1820,* one of the earliest studies, showed that the Ordinance of 1785 was a compromise between New Englanders, who wanted land to be sold only in contiguous township plots, and Southerners, who wished to sell tracts on an individual basis anywhere within the surveyed area.[64]

The history of the first western "state"—Franklin—was the subject of Samuel C. Williams' monograph published in 1924. Williams' work, still regarded as the standard study, contained good chapters on social and economic conditions and attempted to show that the main driving force behind John Sevier and his supporters was separatism.[65] Thomas P. Abernethy sharply challenged this view in *From Frontier to Plantation in Tennessee: A Study in Frontier Democracy,* averring that land, not freedom, was the key to settlement and politics in Tennessee. He clearly demonstrated that most outstanding Tennessee patriots were deeply involved in the "Great Land Grab." Franklin was the scene of a tug of war between two rival groups of land speculators.[66] Williams' thesis, on the other hand, was confirmed in articles by Walter F. Cannon and Paul M. Fink, and by Carl S. Driver's carefully-researched biography of the colorful Sevier.[67]

On Tennessee statehood, Samuel C. Williams' "Admission of Tennes-

---

fusal to approve the appointment of John Rutledge to the Supreme Court. See George S. McCowan, Jr., "Chief Justice John Rutledge and the Jay Treaty," *South Carolina Historical Magazine,* LXII (January, 1961), 10–23. Rutledge is also the subject of a readable but unscholarly and superficial biography by Richard Barry, entitled *Mr. Rutledge of South Carolina* (New York, 1942).

64 Treat, *The National Land System, 1785–1820* (New York, 1910). See especially pp. 34–36.

65 Williams, *History of the Lost State of Franklin* (Johnson City, Tenn., 1924). Also note Stanley J. Folmsbee, "Samuel Cole Williams: An Evaluation," *Tennessee Historical Quarterly,* VII (June, 1948), 101–104; Archibald Henderson, *The Conquest of the Old Southwest . . . 1740–1790* (New York, 1920).

66 Abernethy, *From Frontier to Plantation in Tennessee: A Study in Frontier Democracy* (Chapel Hill, 1932).

67 Cannon, "Four Interpretations of the History of the State of Franklin," in East Tennessee Historical Society *Publications,* No. 22 (1950), 3–18; Driver, *John Sevier, Pioneer of the Old Southwest* (Chapel Hill, 1932) ; Fink, "Some Phases of the History of the State of Franklin," *Tennessee Historical Quarterly,* XVI (September, 1957), 195–213. Cannon listed the four theories as the democratic, the ingrate, the speculative, and the separatist, and he added that Sevier's personal vanity influenced the fortunes of Franklin.

see into the Union" is a valuable study. Williams explained that statehood was difficult to achieve because of the delays of the territorial governor, William Blount, the middle Tennesseans' fear of domination by East Tennessee, and Federalist dilatory tactics in Congress.[68] John D. Barnhart's article on the Tennessee constitutional convention of 1796 is a noteworthy supplement. He found that upper class, conservative frontiersmen controlled the convention.[69] William H. Masterson's more recent *William Blount* carefully followed this ambitious, resourceful, and unscrupulous politician and land speculator through North Carolina Confederation politics into Tennessee, until his expulsion from the Senate for involvement in a British plot against Spain.[70] The "Blount Conspiracy" itself has been investigated by several writers, whose research Abernethy combined with his own in *The South in the New Nation*.[71]

Historians have disagreed as much about the background of Kentucky statehood as about the origins of the State of Franklin. E. Merton Coulter's "Early Frontier Democracy in the First Kentucky Constitution" briefly catalogued the first nine Kentucky conventions seeking self-government and then centered on the political agitation preliminary to the convention of 1792. Coulter gave no detailed discussion of the convention itself, nor did he give much attention to motivation.[72] Huntley Dupree's "The Political Ideas of George Nicholas," a brief biography of the most influential member of the Kentucky convention of 1792, emphasized the liberal origins of Nicholas' political philosophy. In "State Building in Kentucky," Clifton S. Lowry, while stressing the Lockeian influence on Kentuckians, insisted that their concern over slavery rights and valid land titles largely motivated their desire for autonomy.[73] Lowry's views were strengthened by the thorough research

68 Williams, "Admission of Tennessee into the Union," *Tennessee Historical Quarterly,* IV (December, 1945), 291–319.

69 Barnhart, "The Tennessee Constitution of 1796: A Product of the Old West," *Journal of Southern History,* IX (November, 1943), 532–48.

70 Masterson, *William Blount* (Baton Rouge, 1954).

71 See Walter B. Posey, "The Blount Conspiracy," *Birmingham Southern College Bulletin,* XXI (December, 1929), 11–21; Isabel Thompson, "The Blount Conspiracy," East Tennessee Historical Society *Publications,* No. 2 (1930), 3–21; Frederick J. Turner (ed.), "Documents on the Blount Conspiracy, 1795–1797," *American Historical Review,* X (April, 1905), 574–606.

72 Coulter, "Early Frontier Democracy in the First Kentucky Constitution," *Political Science Quarterly,* XXXIX (December, 1924), 665–77.

73 Dupree, "The Political Ideas of George Nicholas," *Register of the Kentucky Historical Society,* XXXIX (July, 1941), 201–23; Lowry, "State Building in Kentucky," *Filson Club History Quarterly,* XVI (October, 1942), 199–207.

of Pratt Byrd, who noted that the Kentucky frontier had disappeared by 1792 under the impact of land speculation and litigation. The rising aristocrats, in control of the convention, nevertheless compromised to some extent with the democratic forces, who, albeit, presented no novel ideas.[74]

Perhaps the most important study of early southwestern politics, and certainly the most controversial, was John D. Barnhart's reexamination of the constitutional beginnings of Kentucky, Tennessee, and other Ohio Valley states from 1775 to 1818. Kentucky and Tennessee, he concluded, symbolized the failure of the democratizing frontier due to eastern planter influence, in contrast to the emerging states of the Old Northwest.[75] Questioning the validity of this thesis, Fletcher M. Green recalled that some southern states were the first to provide for popular election of judges and others permitted free Negroes to vote long after states north of the Ohio limited suffrage to adult white males.[76] Another reviewer, Thomas D. Clark, presented his own view that Kentuckians had been variously motivated. The finished constitution—a curious document, said Clark—revealed an aristocratic fear of democracy and a frontier fear of taxation, confirmed Bluegrass political control, contained an airtight slavery clause, and omitted an educational clause.[77]

Two recent monographs on social and economic developments in Tennessee and Kentucky are Everett Dick's *The Dixie Frontier* and Harriette S. Arnow's *Seedtime on the Cumberland*. Dick's book, lacking quantitative evaluations, pictured the folkways and mores of frontier society down to 1860. Mrs. Arnow's study, the product of more careful and complete research, was confined in time to the period 1763–1803 and in area to the Cumberland River Valley.[78] More limited in scope is Albert C. Holt's "Economic and Social Beginnings of Tennessee." It included a wealth of poorly digested material.[79]

74 Byrd, "The Kentucky Frontier in 1792," *Filson Club History Quarterly*, XXV (July, 1951), 181–203, and (October, 1951), 286–94.

75 Barnhart, *Valley of Democracy: The Frontier Versus the Plantation in the Ohio Valley, 1775–1818* (Bloomington, 1953).

76 Green, review in *Mississippi Valley Historical Review*, XLI (December, 1954), 506–507.

77 Clark, review in *American Historical Review*, LX (January, 1955), 383–85.

78 Dick, *The Dixie Frontier: A Social History of the Southern Frontier . . .* (New York, 1948); Arnow, *Seedtime on the Cumberland* (New York, 1960). Covering much the same ground is John A. Caruso, *The Appalachian Frontier, America's First Surge Westward* (Indianapolis, 1959).

79 Holt, "Economic and Social Beginnings of Tennessee," *Tennessee Historical Magazine*, VII (October, 1921), 194–230, and (January, 1922), 252–313, and VIII (April, 1924), 24–86. Significant aids in rounding out the economic and

Probably the most confusing and complicated aspect of southwestern history for the period 1783–1800 is that which deals with foreign intrigues and Indian relations. Fortunately, in recent years historians have delved into foreign archives and discovered much hitherto unknown information about international intrigue. Their work, long in process, is now virtually complete.

Archibald Henderson was one of the first American historians to take the "Spanish Conspiracy" in the Southwest seriously. Covering much the same ground, Arthur P. Whitaker published two articles in 1925–1926 giving a more detailed and somewhat different picture of Spanish intrigue.[80] Studying the same period was Samuel F. Bemis, whose *Pinckney's Treaty* was a significant addition to southwestern history, though the author's main concern was the negotiations leading to the Treaty of San Lorenzo. But Bemis devoted two chapters to Spanish intrigues with western leaders. His researches confirmed the old suspicions of James Wilkinson and supported Whitaker's view that the Tennesseans probably trafficked with Spain in order to wring concessions from North Carolina.[81]

Only a year after the publication of *Pinckney's Treaty*, Whitaker published the first of two superb volumes on the Southwest, *The Spanish-American Frontier, 1783–1795*. He placed much more emphasis on events and conditions in the West than Bemis had done, and he concluded that the costliness of frontier intrigue plus the fear of an Anglo-American alliance pushed Spain into momentous concessions at San Lorenzo.[82] The second volume, *The Mississippi Question, 1795–1803*, discussed the dénouement of Pinckney's Treaty: Spain's gradual retreat and abandonment of her southern Indian allies, increased American

---

social picture of the region are Margaret Deschamps [Moore], "Early Days in the Cumberland Country," *Tennessee Historical Quarterly*, VI (September, 1947), 195–229; Lowell H. Harrison, "John Breckinridge of Kentucky: Planter, Speculator, and Businessman," *Filson Club History Quarterly*, XXXIV (July, 1960), 205–27; and Harriette S. Arnow, "The Pioneer Farmer and His Crops in the Cumberland Region," *Tennessee Historical Quarterly*, XIX (December, 1960), 291–327.

80 Henderson, "The Spanish Conspiracy in Tennessee," *Tennessee Historical Magazine*, III (December, 1917), 229–43; Whitaker, "Spanish Intrigue in the Old Southwest: An Episode, 1788–89," *Mississippi Valley Historical Review*, XII (September, 1925), 155–76, and Whitaker, "The Muscle Shoals Speculation, 1783–89," *Mississippi Valley Historical Review*, XIII (December, 1926), 365–86.

81 Bemis, *Pinckney's Treaty: A Study of America's Advantage from Europe's Distress, 1783–1800* (Baltimore, 1926).

82 Whitaker, *The Spanish-American Frontier, 1783–1795: The Westward Movement and the Spanish Retreat in the Mississippi Valley* (Boston, 1927).

commerce on the Mississippi, American filibustering efforts in the Southwest, the end of the Kentucky intrigue of Wilkinson and others, Spain's willing surrender of Louisiana to France, and American schemes to seize Louisiana rather than let it fall into the hands of France.[83] These two volumes are probably the finest works on the Southwest for the period 1783–1803.

The story of western intrigue is further revealed in biographies and articles about some of the participants. Temple Bodley attempted to rehabilitate the damaged reputation of George Rogers Clark, the unfortunate Revolutionary hero.[84] Her story was refuted in turn by James Alton James, whose definitive biography of Clark was based on patient research in the monumental Draper Collection at the University of Wisconsin.[85] The other major figure in western intrigue, James Wilkinson, has been the subject of two biographies of limited value.[86]

These previously cited biographies and monographs, particularly those by Whitaker, Bemis, Abernethy, Driver, and Masterson, shed much light on the all-important subject of the federal government's relations with the southwestern Indians. Several significant works dealt solely with this topic. In "Federal Indian Management in the South, 1789–1825," R. S. Cotterill concentrated on two Indian agents, William Blount and Benjamin Hawkins, and their efforts to extend United States influence over the tribes.[87] Randolph C. Downes clarified Blount's role further in "Indian Affairs in the Southwest Territory, 1790–1796." [88]

83 Whitaker, *The Mississippi Question, 1795–1803: A Study in Trade, Politics, and Diplomacy* (New York, 1934).

84 Bodley, *George Rogers Clark, His Life and Public Services* (Boston and New York, 1926).

85 James, *The Life of George Rogers Clark* (Chicago, 1928).

86 James R. Jacobs, *Tarnished Warrior: Major-General James Wilkinson* (New York, 1938); Thomas R. Hay and M. R. Werner, *The Admirable Trumpeter: A Biography of General James Wilkinson* (New York, 1941). For activities of others involved in the conspiracies, see Archibald Henderson, "Isaac Shelby and the Genet Mission," *Mississippi Valley Historical Review,* VI (March, 1920), 451–69; Arthur P. Whitaker (ed.), "Harry Innes and the Spanish Intrigue, 1794–1795," *Mississippi Valley Historical Review,* XV (September, 1928), 236–48; John C. Parish, "The Intrigues of Doctor James O'Fallon," *Mississippi Valley Historical Review,* XVII (September, 1930), 230–63; Elizabeth Warren, "Benjamin Sebastian and the Spanish Conspiracy in Kentucky," *Filson Club History Quarterly,* XX (April, 1946), 107–30; Samuel C. Williams, "French and Other Intrigues in the Southwest Territory, 1790–96," East Tennessee Historical Society *Publications,* No. 13 (1941), 21–35.

87 Cotterill, "Federal Indian Management in the South, 1789–1825," *Mississippi Valley Historical Review,* XX (December, 1933), 333–52.

88 Downes, "Indian Affairs in the Southwest Territory, 1790–1796," *Tennessee Historical Magazine,* III (January, 1937), 240–68.

In two other well-documented articles, Downes discussed Creek-American relations from 1782 to San Lorenzo.[89] John K. Mahon, "Military Relations between Georgia and the United States, 1789–1794," recounted the almost continuous friction between Georgia and the federal government over policies of frontier defense.[90] Merritt Pound's scholarly biography of Benjamin Hawkins adequately appraised the career of the man who was primarily responsible for the Georgia-Creek rapprochement of 1796.[91] Alexander McGillivray, the remarkable one-fourth Creek who was probably the most important border leader of his time, has been the subject of biographies by A. P. Whitaker and John W. Caughey.[92] R. S. Cotterill's *The Southern Indians: The Story of the Civilized Tribes before Removal* covered the period between McGillivray's death and the removal of the tribes.[93]

In sum, modern researchers, led by Henderson, Williams, Bemis, Whitaker, Abernethy, James, Driver, and Barnhart, have covered well the political and diplomatic history of the Old Southwest. Their major findings have been incorporated either in Alden's *The South in the Revolution, 1763–1789* or, more especially, in Abernethy's *The South in the New Nation, 1789–1819*. Moreover, Williams, Arnow, Dick, and Caruso have written ably on cultural and economic developments on the Tennessee-Kentucky frontier. There is now no substantial unexplored gap in the history of the Southwest for the period 1783–1800.

The history of the South Atlantic region has not been as exhaustively written. For political developments during the Confederation years, Crowl's work on Maryland, Ambler's, Hart's, and Main's on Virginia, Trenholme's on North Carolina, Coleman's and Abbot's on Georgia are

89 Downes, "Creek-American Relations, 1782–1790," *Georgia Historical Quarterly*, XXI (June, 1937), 142–84, and "Creek-American Relations, 1790–1795," *Journal of Southern History*, VIII (August, 1942), 350–73. Richard K. Murdoch, *The Georgia-Florida Frontier, 1793–1796* . . . (Berkeley and Los Angeles, 1951), competently treats a brief period of frontier relations, though it adds little to the story.

90 Mahon, "Military Relations between Georgia and the United States, 1789–1794," *Georgia Historical Quarterly*, XLIII (June, 1959), 138–55.

91 Pound, *Benjamin Hawkins, Indian Agent* (Athens, 1951).

92 Whitaker, "Alexander McGillivray, 1783–1789," *North Carolina Historical Review*, V (April, 1928), 181–203, and "Alexander McGillivray, 1789–1793," *North Carolina Historical Review*, V (July, 1928), 289–309; Caughey, *McGillivray of the Creeks* (Norman, 1938).

93 Cotterill, *The Southern Indians: The Story of the Civilized Tribes before Removal* (Norman, 1954).

significant studies, but South Carolina has yet to be adequately treated.[94] Additionally, state constitutional changes and ratification of the Federal Constitution have been thoroughly investigated. Then Alden's excellent study admirably tied the regional story together for the Confederation years.

For the Federalist period Wolfe, Gilpatrick, and Ammon have skill-fully interpreted political movements in South Carolina, North Carolina, and Virginia, respectively, and Cunningham and Charles have dealt with the entire South. But these writers, having mainly centered their studies on the Jeffersonians, neglected southern Federalists. Additionally, Jeffersonian beginnings in Georgia and Maryland need further study, as do many of the individual political leaders in all the South Atlantic states except Virginia. In the latter, biographers have done excellent work.

The economic history of the South Atlantic region has fared badly for the years 1783–1800. There are some outstanding works such as Crittenden's on North Carolina commerce, Zornow's on tariff, and Ferguson's on finance, but the gaps are large. The greatest deficiency, however, was Abernethy's failure to make an adequate survey of the South Atlantic states from 1789 to 1819, thus failing to give continuity to the preceding and succeeding volumes in *A History of the South* series published by the Louisiana State University Press. And, as noted earlier, until the present decade there has been a tendency for the general histories of the South to brush lightly over the years 1783–1800, giving the impression that time largely stood still from the end of the Revolution until the accession of the Jeffersonians to power.

---

94 This deficiency may have been remedied by George C. Rogers, Jr., *Evolution of a Federalist: William Loughton Smith of Charleston, (1758–1812)* (Columbia, 1962). This biography appeared too late for examination and inclusion in this study.

IV

Jeffersonian Democracy
and the Origins
of Sectionalism

Malcolm C. McMillan

EACH generation forms its own conceptions of the past, and the history of an era is never fixed or final. Even historians writing in the same generation may see the past differently because of their different backgrounds, convictions, or philosophies of life. This process of continually rewriting the past is well illustrated in the case of the Jeffersonian period in southern history.[1]

Indeed, historians have tended to portray all of American history in terms of Jefferson *versus* Hamilton, so basic to the country's later de-

1 Material on the historiography of Jeffersonian democracy can be found in Michael Kraus, *The Writing of American History* (Norman, Okla., 1953) ; William T. Hutchinson (ed.), *The Marcus W. Jernegan Essays in American Historiography* (New York, 1958) ; Harvey Wish, *The American Historian* (New York, 1960) ; William H. Cartwright and Richard L. Watson, Jr. (eds.), *Interpreting and Teaching American History* (National Council for the Social Studies, Washington, D. C., 1961) ; John Higham (ed.), *The Reconstruction of American History* (New York, 1962). The best study of Jeffersonian historiography is Merrill D. Peterson, *The Jefferson Image in the American Mind* (New York, 1960).

velopment were the issues between these two political giants in their day.[2] This process began early in our history in regular Hegelian fashion (with Hamilton as the thesis and Jefferson the antithesis) and remains in effect, though recent revisionists have done some violence to the idea. This interpretation probably reached its climax in the pro-Jeffersonian works of Claude G. Bowers, especially his *Jefferson and Hamilton: The Struggle for Democracy in America* and *Jefferson in Power: The Death Struggle of the Federalists.*[3] They relate a kind of battle of Armageddon between Jefferson and Hamilton and the imprint they left on the character of the new republic. Jefferson's faith in democracy prevailed over Hamilton's distrust of it, and the hard-fought battle, closing with the collapse of the Federalist party, determined that this should be not only a republic, but "a democratic republic."

However, this dialectical interpretation in reverse was more common in the nineteenth century. Federalist-Whig historians represented Hamilton and Marshall as symbolic of the rising tide of nationalism in the new nation, which was saved by the Civil War; they depicted a Jefferson devoted to state rights and a weak central government. The pinnacle of this interpretation came in the twentieth century when Albert J. Beveridge wrote his great life of John Marshall, called by Douglass Adair "the most sustained and thorough attack ever made on Jefferson and all his works." [4] In his last two volumes, entitled *Conflict and Construction, 1800–1815* and *The Building of the New Nation, 1815–1835,* Beveridge depicts Marshall, the wise statesman *versus* his able adversary, Thomas Jefferson, leader of a mad tide of Jacobins.

Charles M. Wiltse in 1935 focused attention on what Jefferson's ideas had meant in the evolution of the American system of government and life in his *The Jeffersonian Tradition in American Democracy.*[5] Merrill Peterson traced the cycles in Jefferson historiography from Jefferson's death in 1826 to his bi-centennial in 1943.[6] Peterson, Wiltse, Douglass

2 James Truslow Adams, "Jefferson and Hamilton Today; the dichotomy in American Thought," *Atlantic Monthly,* CXLI (April, 1928), 443–50; Kraus, *The Writing of American History,* 4, 374.

3 Bowers, *Jefferson and Hamilton: The Struggle for Democracy in America* (Boston and New York, 1925), and *Jefferson in Power: The Death Struggle of the Federalists* (Boston, 1936).

4 Douglass Adair, "The New Thomas Jefferson," *William and Mary Quarterly,* 3rd series, III (January, 1946), 125; Albert J. Beveridge, *The Life of John Marshall* (4 vols.; Boston, 1916–1919).

5 Wiltse, *The Jeffersonian Tradition in American Democracy* (Chapel Hill, 1935). See also Clement Eaton, "The Jefferson Tradition of Liberalism in America," *South Atlantic Quarterly,* XLIII (January, 1944), 1–10.

6 Peterson, *The Jefferson Image.*

Adair, and the authors of general works on American historiography
have all found a definite correlation between the Jeffersonian image
produced by a particular writer's party politics, sectional background,
economic propensity, class predilections, and other influences, as well as
the image produced by the nation's predominant "climate of opinion" at
the time a work on Jeffersonian democracy was prepared.[7] That the New
Deal profoundly affected interpretations of Jefferson's democracy was
shown by Charles M. Wiltse's book, written in the middle of that
upheaval.[8]

Since most of the main actors in the "Age of Jefferson"—Jefferson,
Madison, Monroe, Marshall, Clay, Calhoun, John Randolph, and others
—were southern, there is a definite relationship between what historians
have said at different times about the period and the existing historical
image of the South in the nation. In the political sphere, southern history
is so much the history of southern leadership in the nation during these
years (three of the four Presidents were members of the "Virginia
Dynasty") that one finds it hard to separate southern and national
history. In fact, it is much easier to write the history of New England
as a section, in the days of the Essex Junto and Hartford Convention,
than that of the South. Only when the writer reaches the struggle over
slavery in Missouri is sectionalism so pronounced in the South.

Since the ascendancy of Jeffersonian democracy was first made possible by a combination of southern and western support (a winning
combination on many later occasions for the party that Jefferson
founded), any interpretation of Jeffersonian democracy is also tied to
emphasis or de-emphasis on Frederick Jackson Turner's frontier hypothesis. And in this day of the accentuation of the class struggle, an
explanation of these years is equally bound to what a particular writer
may think of Marxian economic determinism. The application of this
principle to the Jefferson period began in earnest with Charles A.
Beard's *Economic Origins of Jeffersonian Democracy*.[9]

Few Presidents were more bitterly hated during their lifetimes than
Jefferson, and all of the pre-Civil War writings on Jefferson were
partisan. One Jefferson scholar has found that "no work in literature

7 *Ibid.;* Adair, "The New Thomas Jefferson," 123–33, and "Bibliographical
195–224.
Essay," in Charles M. Wiltse, *The New Nation, 1800–1845* (New York, 1961),
8 Wiltse, *The Jeffersonian Tradition in American Democracy*, 238–67. In line with
the New Deal's emphasis on the welfare state, Wiltse's last chapter on "Social
Democracy" discusses the socialistic potentials of Jefferson's philosophy.
9 Beard, *Economic Origins of Jeffersonian Democracy* (New York, 1915).

takes higher rank for sheer malice than Henry Lee's *Observations on the Writings of Thomas Jefferson.*[10] George Tucker's *The Life of Thomas Jefferson* answered Lee's slanders but was too calm and judicious for many Jeffersonians and too partisan for most conservatives. The Democratic historian George Bancroft was favorable to Jefferson, but the pages on Jefferson in the history by Richard Hildreth, the Massachusetts Whig historian, read like a Federalist polemic.[11]

Jefferson historiography took a great stride forward with the publication, on the eve of the Civil War, of Henry S. Randall, *The Life of Thomas Jefferson.*[12] Then, as death removed the first generation of Jefferson's enemies, his reputation rose somewhat in the North and declined in the South. Although William H. McGuffey taught at the University of Virginia from 1845 to 1873, his *Readers* extolled Hamilton but ignored Jefferson.[13] William E. Dodd, a disciple of Jefferson, made one of the first scholarly studies of the decline of Jeffersonian liberalism in the South. It revealed a section moving from support of Jefferson to support of Calhoun, and finally to conservative revolt under Davis. W. G. Bean's, "Anti-Jeffersonianism in the Ante-bellum South," concluded that in "the period from 1820 to 1860 the political idealism of Jeffersonianism had been discarded by the governing class in the South; the axioms of Jeffersonian democracy had been supplanted by those of an 'Africanized' democracy; and only the Jeffersonian doctrine of states rights remained to justify secession." Clement Eaton found that "from Jefferson to Calhoun. . . . a great change took place in the Southern States. . . . [as] the liberal ideas of the eighteenth century were in large part discarded. . . . In place of the appeal to reason the suppression of radical criticism was substituted." A similar theme can be found in Vernon L. Parrington's *The Romantic Revolution in America,* Virginius Dabney's *Liberalism in the South,* and Wilbur J. Cash's *The Mind of the South.* Joseph C. Robert traced the strong trend in Virginia away from Jeffersonian liberalism in his *Road from Monticello.* And Henry T. Shanks, in "Conservative Constitutional Tendencies in the Virginia Secession Convention," depicted that body

10 Peterson, *The Jefferson Image,* 115. Lee's book was published in Richmond in 1932.

11 Tucker, *The Life of Thomas Jefferson* (Philadelphia, 1837) ; Bancroft, *History of the United States* (10 vols.; Boston, 1883–85) ; Hildreth, *The History of the United States* (6 vols.; New York, 1849–56).

12 Randall, *The Life of Thomas Jefferson* (3 vols.; New York, 1858).

13 Peterson, *The Jefferson Image,* 114; Clement Eaton, *The Old South* (New York, 1949), 477.

as turning the clock back on democratic reforms made in Virginia by the constitutional conventions of 1829–30 and 1850.[14]

Peterson has shown that Jefferson, despite his detractors, became after his death both the Father of Democracy and the Father of State Rights.[15] This claiming of Jefferson by opposite political and social groups has continued to this day. It makes Jefferson extraordinarily important in the interpretation of American history, but at the same time a very complex figure for the historical interpreter. Unlike Washington, Hamilton, Lincoln and others, he has represented many different things to many men, factions, and generations. By one group, Jefferson has been considered the father of the symbolic creed that shielded the South (so interpreted even by twentieth-century southern States' Righters and agrarians[16]) ; by another, the creator of the symbolic creed that threatened to destroy it.

Beginning in the 1830's, antislavery men in the North had been quick to claim Jefferson. Harking back to Jeffersonian liberalism and opposition to slavery, the new sectional party which elected Abraham Lincoln in 1860 made Jefferson its patron saint and deliberately christened the party Republican after Jefferson's old party.[17] Preeminence in the Republican Pantheon was soon given to the martyred Lincoln, however, and the Republican party, captured by "big business," turned to Hamilton for its ideas.

During the last quarter of the nineteenth century, the Federalist or Nationalistic historians generally held Jefferson in low esteem. They considered his faith in the people, his advocacy of an extended franchise,

---

14 Dodd, *Statesmen of the Old South; or, From Radicalism to Conservative Revolt* (New York, 1911). Bean, "Anti-Jeffersonianism in the Ante-bellum South," *North Carolina Historical Review*, XII (April, 1935), 124; Eaton, *Freedom of Thought in the Old South* (Durham, 1940), vii; Parrington, *The Romantic Revolution in America*, Vol. II of *Main Currents in American Thought* (3 vols.; New York, 1927–30) ; Cash, *The Mind of the South* (New York, 1941), 72–110; Dabney, *Liberalism in the South* (Chapel Hill, 1932), 1–153; Robert, *The Road from Monticello: A Study in the Virginia Slavery Debate of 1832* in ("Historical Papers of the Trinity College Historical Society," XXIV [Durham, 1941]) ; Shanks, "Conservative Constitutional Tendencies" in Fletcher M. Green (ed.), *Essays in Southern History* (Chapel Hill, 1941), 28–48. The decline of Southern liberalism is also the theme of Charles S. Sydnor, "The Southerner and the Laws," *Journal of Southern History*, VI (February, 1940), 3–23.

15 Peterson, *The Jefferson Image*, 162–226.

16 See Twelve Southerners, *I'll Take My Stand: The South and the Agrarian Tradition* (New York, 1930).

17 Wilfred E. Binkley, *American Political Parties: Their Natural History* (New York, 1958), 215–16; Charles A. Beard and Mary Beard, *The Rise of American Civilization* (2 vols.; New York, 1944) II, 22–23.

and his emphasis upon democracy generally as but a prelude to the corruption of government by the "mob democracy" of the Jackson period. Their obvious Federalist-Whig predilections caused them to deplore his "leveling" tendencies which gave democracy a wider base and decreased the power of the "rich, the wise and the well born." They were also writing in the aftermath of the Civil War and the defeat of the agrarian South, which now had little influence in the Union. The bankruptcy of Jeffersonian statesmanship, particularly with the embargo, was the standard theme of Federalist historians.[18]

Perhaps the extreme nationalist, Hermann E. von Holst, was this school's most zealous critic of Jefferson. "Ambition," von Holst wrote of the Virginian, "was the sovereign trait in his character. He was always ready to sacrifice much of his favorite theories to his feverish thirst for power and distinction." [19] Von Holst also painted a doleful picture of a South where the "peculiar institution" permeated and blighted everything. He "clearly never understood . . . Jefferson, whom he suspected of wishing to disrupt the Union." [20] John Bach McMaster was almost as hostile to Jefferson. His treatment may have been determined in part by Hildreth's interpretation, which he had read.[21]

Henry Adams, still the most important historian of the Jeffersonian era, was also the first of the scientific school of American historians. He once wrote that he had "published a dozen volumes of American history . . . to satisfy himself whether, by the severest process of stating, with the least possible comment, such facts as seemed sure, in such order as seemed rigorously consequent, he could fix for a familiar moment a necessary sequence of human movement." [22] This he accomplished for the Jefferson and Madison administrations in his masterpiece, *History of the United States During the Administrations of Jefferson and Madison.*[23]

18 Peterson, *The Jefferson Image,* 130–31, 137. Also, see essays on each of the Federalist historians studied in Hutchinson (ed.), *The Marcus W. Jernegan Essays in American Historiography.*

19 von Holst, *The Constitutional and Political History of the United States* (8 vols.; Chicago, 1876–92), I, 159.

20 Charles R. Wilson, "Hermann Eduard von Holst," in Hutchinson (ed.), *The Marcus W. Jernegan Essays in American Historiography,* 79.

21 McMaster, *A History of the People of the United States from the Revolution to the Civil War* (8 vols.; New York, 1883–1913), II, 439–635 and III, 1–358; William T. Hutchinson, "John Bach McMaster," in Hutchinson (ed.), *The Marcus W. Jernegan Essays in American Historiography,* 140.

22 Adams, *The Education of Henry Adams* (New York, 1931), 382.

23 Adams, *History of the United States During the Administrations of Jefferson and Madison* (9 vols.; New York, 1889–91).

The first fruit of Adams' research into the age of Jefferson was *The Life of Albert Gallatin*.[24] This classic biography gains coherence from the theme of the rise and fall of democratic idealism in the Jefferson period. (Raymond Walters' recent biography of Gallatin manifests a deeper interest in Gallatin's personality and shows the greater interest brought about by the growth of historical knowledge, but supplements rather than replaces Adams' great work.) [25]

Adams, who was the great grandson and grandson of conservative Presidents, wrote his *History* to show also that the Jeffersonian Republicans had actually adopted and implemented the very Federalist policies they had once opposed. This thesis, like so many other of Adams' ideas, has long since become an accepted interpretation in history texts. Adams seemed to think that Jefferson's actions in office disproved the genuineness of his idealism. He found the career of Jefferson as President to be tragi-comedy: "History's solution of the nation's problems was to go counter to every dogma of the Virginian, and he was to be history's instrument. The advocate of negative government was in the end to increase government's scope." [26] Madison, to Adams, was a far less attractive personality than Jefferson and by no means as great a historical figure. So much time and space is given to Jefferson that there is little left for Madison.[27]

Adams was ever conscious of the southern heritage of the administrations about which he wrote. The federal government under the Virginia leaders, he said, "was in the main controlled by ideas and interests peculiar to the region south of the Potomac, and only to be understood from a Southern standpoint. Especially its foreign relations were guided by motives in which the northern people felt little sympathy." [28] A sectional bias, which is seldom pronounced in his history, is more evident in his *John Randolph*.[29] On the whole, Adams wrote without personal animus about the political enemies of his presidential ancestors. "Adams naturally found it impossible to divest himself of his great grandfather's distrust of Jefferson," wrote Edward Channing, "but in general the work is impersonal." [30]

24 Adams, *The Life of Albert Gallatin* (Philadelphia, 1879).
25 Walters, *Albert Gallatin: Jeffersonian Financeer and Diplomat* (New York, 1957).
26 Elizabeth Stevenson, *Henry Adams: A Biography* (New York, 1955), 249.
27 Adams, *History*, VI, 176–219, 412–44.
28 Quoted in Michael Kraus, *The Writing of American History*, 181–82.
29 Adams, *John Randolph* (Boston and New York, 1882).
30 Channing, *Federalists and Republicans, 1789–1815* (New York, 1917), 272, Volume IV of his *A History of the United States* (6 vols.; New York, 1905–25).

The *History* is founded on patient research, with extended use of American and foreign archives, and heavy emphasis on diplomatic history. Its focus is on the central diplomatic and military themes—the coming of the War of 1812 and the war itself. But for a broad view of American life at the beginning of the new century, there is no better source than the first six chapters of Adams' history, three of the chapters being on the "intellect" of the southern, middle and New England states respectively.[31] Adams failed to integrate social and political developments and neglected economic forces, but he occasionally anticipated the Turner thesis of the influence of the West.[32] In addition, Adams was conscious of environmental factors in American history. "Already in 1817 the difference between Europe and America was decided," he wrote. "American character was formed, if not fixed," [33] but fortuitous circumstances and not Jeffersonian policy had brought about the results.

Nearly all the numerous critiques of the *History* agree that it is a supreme intellectual and artistic achievement which has influenced the interpretation of the Jeffersonian period more than any single work.[34] "It is not an exaggeration . . . ," writes Henry Steele Commager, "to insist that the *Gallatin* is the best political biography, the *Administrations of Jefferson and Madison* the finest piece of historical writing, in our literature." [35]

Adams paved the way, and professional historians took over the business of writing the history of the period. Edward Channing, a twentieth-century "scientific historian" and one-time student of Adams at Harvard, abandoned his plans for early research on the Jefferson period when he saw advanced sheets of Adams' history. But he later relied heavily on Adams' research to supplement his own contributions, which were mainly factual rather than interpretive, in *The Jeffersonian System, 1801–1811* and in *Federalists and Republicans, 1789–1815*.[36] Although

31 The first six chapters have been printed separately. See Henry Adams, *The United States in 1800* (Ithaca, New York, 1957).

32 Kraus, *The Writing of American History*, 184.

33 Adams, *History*, IX, 220–21.

34 For studies of Henry Adams see Ernest Samuels, *Henry Adams: The Middle Years* (Cambridge, 1958) ; William H. Jordy, *Henry Adams: Scientific Historian* (New Haven, 1952) ; Elizabeth Stevenson, *Henry Adams: A Biography* (New York, 1955) ; J. C. Levenson, *The Mind and Art of Henry Adams* (Cambridge, 1957) ; George Hochfield, *Henry Adams: An Introduction and Interpretation* (New York, 1962).

35 Henry Steele Commager, "Henry Adams" in Hutchinson (ed.), *The Marcus W. Jernegan Essays in American Historiography*, 195.

36 Channing, *The Jeffersonian System, 1801–1811* (New York, 1906), Volume XII of *The American Nation Series* (28 vols.; New York, 1904–08) ; Channing, *Federalists and Republicans, 1789–1815*.

Channing was inclined toward the Federalist view of history and wrote from the vantage point of New England, he was not always unfriendly to Jefferson. Woodrow Wilson, who also wrote history from the Federalist point of view, thought Hamilton an abler statesman than Jefferson.[37] William E. Dodd, who did much both as a teacher and writer to arouse an interest in southern history, is also significant in early professional Jeffersonian historiography. Dodd saw Thomas Jefferson "as peasant planter, aristocratic leveler, religious liberal, educated politician, advocate of democracy, symbol of the first American West, [and] 'political saint to Abraham Lincoln.' " [38]

According to one scholar, "Frederick Jackson Turner and Charles Beard together . . . succeeded in making 'Jeffersonianism' intellectually respectable for the first time since the Civil War." [39] Beard saw American history as a struggle between an agrarian society and a rising industrial order. His studies and those inspired by him reveal the continuing vitality of the Jefferson economic tradition in American politics. And Turner's studies on the significance of the frontier and sections in American history gave a native blessing and a certain aura to Jeffersonianism, which earlier historians who had found the roots of Jefferson's thinking in Europe had never been able to project.[40] Turner also broadened and enriched the older interpretation of American history as being primarily a struggle between the North and South by establishing the importance of a third factor, the West, in the development of the American civilization. Jefferson in his eyes was the first prophet of American democracy, the first voice of the West against the East.[41]

Beard, in his *Economic Origins of Jeffersonian Democracy*, took issue

37 See also Woodrow Wilson, *A History of the American People* (5 vols.; New York, 1902) ; Marjorie L. Daniel, "Woodrow Wilson: Historian," *Mississippi Valley Historical Review*, XXI (December, 1934), 361–74; Arthur S. Link, *Wilson: The Road to the White House* (Princeton, 1947), 29, 381.

38 See "William E. Dodd: Historian of Democracy," in Wendell H. Stephenson, *The South Lives in History* (Baton Rouge, 1955), 45–46. See also Lowry Price Ware, Abstract of "The Academic Career of William E. Dodd" (Ph.D. dissertation, University of South Carolina, 1956), in *Dissertation Abstracts*, XVII (Ann Arbor, 1957), 843.

39 Douglass Adair, "The New Thomas Jefferson," *William and Mary Quarterly*, 3rd series, III (January, 1946), 125.

40 Turner's two books on sectionalism—*The Significance of Sections in American History* (New York, 1932), and the posthumously published, *The United States, 1830–1850, the Nation and Its Sections* (New York, 1935)—are very significant in southern history. They provided historians with controversial democratic and sectional themes about the South for decades to come.

41 Frederick Jackson Turner, *The Frontier in American History* (New York, 1962), 250.

with any such western or democratic thesis. "Jeffersonian Democracy simply meant," Beard said, "the possession of the federal government by the agrarian masses led by an aristocracy of slave-owning planters, and the theoretical repudiation of the right to use the Government for the benefit of any capitalistic groups, fiscal, banking, or manufacturing." [42] With this view Arthur M. Schlesinger was essentially in agreement. Arguing that "Jeffersonian democracy did not . . . cause the doom of the caste principle in American society and government. . . . [but] perpetuated it in a more enlightened and less offensive form," he said, "it is clear that political power had shifted from a mercantile aristocracy built on English models to a landed aristocracy fully acclimated to the American environment." [43] Leonard D. White's administrative history of the Jeffersonian era further confirms this viewpoint. He found that Jeffersonian administration was in fact a projection of the Federalist tradition of a strong executive, with widely varying degrees of success, and of the gentleman in political life.[44]

Fletcher M. Green in *Constitutional Development in the South Atlantic States, 1776–1860: A Study in the Evolution of Democracy,* found society, as measured in terms of constitutional reform, growing progressively more democratic in Jefferson's day. But he concluded that reforms grew out of local conditions and would have come about "had there been no New West beyond the Allegheny Mountains." [45] Thus Green accepted Turner's estimate as to the genuineness of Jeffersonian democracy but rejected his frontier hypothesis. Green also disagreed with the historians cited earlier in this essay who emphasized the decline of Jeffersonian liberalism and democracy in the South before 1860. In his *Constitutional Development* and in "Democracy in the Old South," his presidential address for the Southern Historical Association, Green relates a progressive development of constitutional and governmental

42 Beard, *Economic Origins of Jeffersonian Democracy* (New York, 1915), 467. See also Charles A. Beard, "Some Economic Origins of Jeffersonian Democracy," *American Historical Review,* XIX (January, 1914), 282–98.

43 Schlesinger, *New Viewpoints in American History* (New York, 1925), 84. A fascinating essay by Dixon Wecter, "Thomas Jefferson: The Gentle Radical," in Wecter, *The Hero in America* (Ann Arbor, 1963), emphasizes the mildness of Jefferson's reforms.

44 White, *The Jeffersonians: A Study in Administrative History, 1801–1829* (New York, 1951).

45 Green, *Constitutional Development in the South Atlantic States, 1776–1860: A Study in the Evolution of Democracy* (Chapel Hill, 1930), 199. See Green's chapter entitled "The Democratic Awakening, (1800–1830)," in *ibid.,* 171–200.

democracy from Jefferson, through Jackson, to the Civil War.[46]

Thomas Perkins Abernethy, a student of Turner's, has been one of the most persistent critics of the frontier-democratic thesis. "Thomas Jefferson," he wrote, "belonged to the second generation of Piedmont society, and was a fairly typical representative of eastern Virginia culture. His ideas of democracy came from European philosophy rather than from frontier equalitarianism, whatever our historians, steeped in Jacksonian and Lincolnian traditions, may have said to the contrary." [47] In his Fleming lectures at Louisiana State University in 1940, Abernethy explained Jeffersonian democracy in terms of liberal leadership (upper class down) rather than democratic leadership (lower class up).[48] Thus Jeffersonian democracy owed much more to the European Enlightenment than to the democratizing frontier. In another study, in which he took Tennessee for analysis, Abernethy detailed the triumph of privilege and opportunism over democracy in frontier Tennessee of the late eighteenth and early nineteenth centuries. Emphasizing events in terms of a single motivating influence—land speculation—he found that "from the Revolution to the War of Secession the government remained in the hands of the few." [49] In his recent *The South in the New Nation, 1789–1819*, Abernethy pictured the movement of the planter west to the best lands and "the poorer people . . . to the Piney woods, the 'pennyroyal' and wiregrass country. . . . Thus a democracy and a landed gentry grew up side by side." [50]

Scholarly biographies of Jefferson did not begin to appear until the 1920's. Bowers' first book on Jefferson, already mentioned, appeared in 1925. The following year, A. J. Nock's biography depicting Jeffer-

---

46 Green, "Democracy in the Old South," *Journal of Southern History*, XII (February, 1946), 3–23. See also Green's review of John Allen Krout and Dixon Ryan Fox, *The Completion of Independence, 1790–1830* (New York, 1944), in *William and Mary Quarterly*, 3rd series, II (November, 1945), 415, in which Green states that "in general the various sections were developing together and that similarities rather than differences of the sections were most marked."

47 Abernethy, "Democracy and the Southern Frontier," *Journal of Southern History*, IV (February, 1938), 5.

48 Abernethy, *Three Virginia Frontiers* (Baton Rouge, 1940).

49 Abernethy, *From Frontier to Plantation in Tennessee* (Chapel Hill, 1932), 363–64. A recent study at the University of Texas follows the Turnerian thesis, saying that "Tennessee's formative period was frontier America maturing in miniature." Abstract of William A. Walker, Jr., "Tennessee, 1796–1821" (Ph.D. dissertation, University of Texas, 1959), *Dissertation Abstracts*, XX (Ann Arbor, 1959), 2265–66.

50 Abernethy, *The South in the New Nation, 1789–1819* (Baton Rouge, 1961), x–xi.

son as "the father of American democracy" appeared. Three years later Gilbert Chinard's influential *Thomas Jefferson: The Apostle of Americanism* was published. It concluded that Jefferson developed his own ideas without dependence on French or English philosophers.[51]

As a result of the Depression of 1929, the Democratic party of Jefferson, after many lean years, became the Democratic party of Franklin Roosevelt. But the Liberty Leaguers, stressing states' rights, claimed Jefferson; and early New Dealers were embarrassed by Jefferson the states' righter and advocate of local government. However, Jefferson furnished good precedent for Roosevelt's assault on the Supreme Court, and Jefferson the advocate of liberty took on new meaning in the context of the totalitarian threat from Europe. New Dealers, having had time for thought, now argued that Roosevelt was using Hamiltonian means to attain Jeffersonian ends, the welfare of all the people. And as America fought for liberty in the Second World War, the final canonization of Thomas Jefferson was consummated. Scholars now went to work as never before to study the complexities of his life and personality. In the postwar years, Jefferson the architect, scientist, economic thinker, and educator, was added to the image of Jefferson the philosopher-statesman. In the meantime the people were constantly being reminded of the apotheosis by a Jefferson stamp, a Jefferson coin, and the Jefferson Memorial in Washington.[52]

A mere listing of some of the studies on Jefferson published since 1942 will indicate what Jefferson has come to mean in our civilization: Elbert D. Thomas, *Thomas Jefferson: World Citizen;* Adrienne Koch, *The Philosophy of Thomas Jefferson;* Frank L. Mott, *Jefferson and the Press;* Edward Dumbauld, *Thomas Jefferson, American Tourist;* Karl Lehman, *Thomas Jefferson: American Humanist;* D. J. Boorstin, *The Lost World of Thomas Jefferson;* Edwin T. Martin, *Thomas Jefferson:*

51 Bowers, *Jefferson and Hamilton, The Struggle for Democracy in America* (Boston, 1925); Nock, *Jefferson* (New York, 1926); Chinard, *Thomas Jefferson* (Boston, 1929).

52 Peterson, *The Jefferson Image*, 355–78, 432–39; Douglass Adair, "The New Thomas Jefferson," *William and Mary Quarterly*, 3rd series, III (January, 1946), 127–28; Clement Eaton, *The Old South* (New York, 1949), 175. Previous to the New Deal, there had been a revival of interest in Jefferson during the Populist revolt. Thomas E. Watson, a leading Georgia Populist, published his *The Life and Times of Thomas Jefferson* (New York, 1903). William Jennings Bryan cited Jefferson in defense of the farmer, and liberal Democrats in almost every southern state called themselves "Jeffersonian Democrats" in opposition to "Organized Democracy." See C. Vann Woodward, *Origins of the New South, 1877–1913* (Baton Rouge, 1951), 244–45, 249–50; and Richard Hofstadter, *The American Political Tradition and the Men Who Made It* (New York, 1948), 38–39.

Scientist; Caleb Perry Patterson, *Constitutional Principles of Thomas Jefferson;* Phillips Russell, *Jefferson, Champion of a Free Mind;* James B. Conant, *Thomas Jefferson and the Development of American Public Education;* Robert M. Healey, *Jefferson on Religion in Public Education;* Dumas Malone, *Thomas Jefferson as a Political Leader.*[53]

Most recent biographies of Jefferson, particularly Saul K. Padover's *Jefferson,* are adulatory; but in Nathan Schachner's *Thomas Jefferson,*[54] the hero is clearly Hamilton. Although Jefferson has recently attracted many biographers we do not yet have a full-length scholarly study of his long and eventful life. What will perhaps be the definitive work, Dumas Malone's *Jefferson and His Time,* goes only to 1800.[55] Three volumes by Marie Kimball, which carry the story down to 1789, will never be added to because of the author's death.[56] A great work of scholarship still in progress is *The Papers of Thomas Jefferson* (17 vols.; 1950——), edited by Julian P. Boyd of Princeton University.[57]

One of the most significant recent trends in Jeffersonian historiography has been the upgrading of James Madison. Studies of the formation of the Republican party show that Madison was the important leader before 1796.[58] And Adrienne Koch, in *Jefferson and Madison, the Great*

---

53 Thomas, *Thomas Jefferson: World Citizen* (New York, 1942); Koch, *The Philosophy of Thomas Jefferson* (New York, 1943); Mott, *Jefferson and the Press* (Baton Rouge, 1943); Dumbauld, *Thomas Jefferson, American Tourist* (Norman, Okla., 1946); Lehman, *Thomas Jefferson: American Humanist* (New York, 1947); Boorstin, *The Lost World of Thomas Jefferson* (New York, 1948); Martin, *Thomas Jefferson: Scientist* (New York, 1952); Patterson, *Constitutional Principles of Thomas Jefferson* (Austin, Texas, 1953); Russell, *Jefferson, Champion of a Free Mind* (New York, 1956); Conant, *Thomas Jefferson and the Development of American Public Education* (Berkeley, 1962); Healey, *Jefferson on Religion in Public Education* (New Haven, 1962); Malone, *Thomas Jefferson as a Political Leader* (Berkeley, 1963). In *Jefferson and Civil Liberties: The Darker Side* (Cambridge, 1963), Leonard W. Levy strikes a critical note quite different from the trend established by the above works.

54 Padover, *Jefferson* (New York, 1942); Schachner, *Thomas Jefferson* (2 vols.; New York, 1951).

55 Malone, *Jefferson and His Time* (3 vols.; Boston, 1948——). The three volumes are *Jefferson the Virginian* (1948), *Jefferson and the Rights of Man* (1951), and *Jefferson and the Ordeal of Liberty* (1962).

56 Kimball, *Jefferson* (3 vols.; New York, 1943–1950). The three volumes are *Jefferson; The Road to Glory, 1743–1776* (1943), *Jefferson; War and Peace 1776–1784* (1947), and *Jefferson; The Scene of Europe, 1784–1789* (1950).

57 See also Bernard Mayo (ed.), *Jefferson Himself: The Personal Narrative of a Many-Sided American* (Boston, 1942); Saul K. Padover (ed.), *The Complete Jefferson* (New York, 1943); Adrienne Koch and William Peden (eds.), *The Life and Selected Writings of Thomas Jefferson* (New York, 1944).

58 Noble E. Cunningham, Jr., *The Jeffersonian Republicans: The Formation of Party Organization, 1789–1801* (Chapel Hill, 1957); William Nisbet Chambers,

Collaboration, concludes that the political philosophy known simply as "Jeffersonian" is actually an amalgam of ideas which owes much to James Madison.[59] Madison, the philosopher-statesman and forceful leader, is fully resurrected in Irving Brant, *James Madison,*[60] the fifth and sixth volumes of which deal with his presidency. Although very partial to its subject, the biography is a great work of scholarship.

No one has published a study of Jeffersonian democracy in the South equivalent to William A. Robinson's *Jeffersonian Democracy in New England.*[61] But Delbert H. Gilpatrick's monograph on North Carolina and John Harold Wolfe's on South Carolina indicate what has to be done on the state level before a regional study is possible.[62] As Virginia in Jefferson's era was exercising extraordinary influence in the South and the nation, histories of Virginia and its institutions should furnish an unusual insight into Jeffersonian democracy. Unfortunately, no one has written a study of the Old Dominion in the late eighteenth and early nineteenth centuries comparable to Philip A. Bruce's earlier works on the seventeenth century. But Bruce himself has partially compensated for this lack in his *History of the University of Virginia, 1819–1919,*[63] an excellent study of the great university that Jefferson founded. Bruce analyzes Jefferson's educational ideas and shows how they developed, in this history of the university that continues to be a center of Jefferson scholarship.[64] In *The Educational Work of Thomas*

Political Parties in a New Nation: The American Experience, 1776–1809 (New York, 1963) ; Joseph Charles, *The Origins of the American Party System* (Williamsburg, 1956).

59 Koch, *Jefferson and Madison, the Great Collaboration* (New York, 1950).

60 Brant, *James Madison* (6 vols.; Indianapolis, 1941-1961).

61 Robinson, *Jeffersonian Democracy in New England* (New Haven, 1916).

62 Gilpatrick, *Jeffersonian Democracy in North Carolina, 1789–1816* (New York, 1931) ; Wolfe, *Jeffersonian Democracy in South Carolina* (Chapel Hill, 1940). The latter disagrees with Ulrich B. Phillips, "The South Carolina Federalists," *American Historical Review,* XIV (April and July, 1909), 529–43, 731–43, who found the Federalists strong in South Carolina after 1800. See also Harry Ammon, "The Jeffersonian Republicans in Virginia, An Interpretation," *Virginia Magazine of History and Biography,* LXXI (April, 1963), 153–67; and David K. McCarrell, "The Formation of Jefferson's Party in Virginia" (Ph.D. dissertation, Duke University, 1937).

63 Bruce, *History of the University of Virginia, 1819–1919: The Lengthened Shadow of One Man* (5 vols.; New York, 1920–22). See also Thomas Perkins Abernethy, *Historical Sketch of the University of Virginia* (Richmond, 1948).

64 Thomas Perkins Abernethy and Bernard Mayo of the University of Virginia's faculty are both Jefferson scholars, and the following doctoral dissertations on the period have been written there since 1947: Raymond C. Dingledine, Jr., "The Political Career of William Cabell Rives" (1947) ; Harry Ammon, "The Republican Party in Virginia, 1789 to 1824" (1948) ; John S. Pancake, "The General

Jefferson, Roy J. Honeywell deals not only with the university but also with Jefferson's life-long fight for education in Virginia.[65] Others have been interested in Jefferson's libraries, both private and public.[66] It is in connection with the University of Virginia, where Jefferson designed the first buildings, that Jefferson the architect comes into focus. The second chapter in Lewis Mumford, *The South in Architecture,* emphasizes Jefferson, the gifted amateur architect. Fiske Kimball, *Thomas Jefferson and the First Monument of the Classical Revival in America,* highlights the importance of the Virginia state capitol. *Thomas Jefferson*

---

from Baltimore: A Biography of Samuel Smith" (1949); William Harris Gaines, Jr., "Thomas Mann Randolph of Edgehill" (1950); Newton Bond Jones, "Charlottesville and Albemarle County, Virginia, 1819–1860" (1950); William Minor Dabney, "Jefferson's Albemarle: History of Albemarle County, Virginia, 1727–1819" (1951); Joseph Hobson Harrison, Jr., "The Internal Improvement Issue in the Politics of the Union, 1783–1825" (1954); Malcolm Lester, "Anglo-American Diplomatic Problems Arising from British Naval Operations in American Waters, 1793–1802" (1954); Norris Watson Preyer, "The South's Experiment with Protective Tariffs, 1816–1820" (1954); George Green Shackelford, "William Short, Jefferson's Adopted Son, 1778–1849" (2 vols.; 1955); Joseph Carroll Vance, "Thomas Jefferson Randolph" (1957); Mary P. Adams, "Jefferson's Military Policy with Special Reference to the Frontier, 1805–1809" (1958); Edwin Metcalf Gaines, "Outrageous Encounter! The Chesapeake-Leopard Affair of 1807" (1960); Norman K. Risjord, "The Old Republicans: Southern Conservatives in Congress, 1806–1824" (1960); James Marvin Helms, Jr., "The Early Career of Nathaniel Macon, A Study in 'Pure Republicanism'" (1962); Jerry Wayne Knudson, "The Jefferson Years: Response by the Press, 1801–1809" (1962). An even greater number of master's theses might be listed. Among the more significant are: Esmond Wright, "An Eighteenth Century Pragmatist: A Study of the Sources of Thomas Jefferson's Political Ideas" (1940); Hamilton M. Hutton, "Southern Nationalism, 1790 to 1817" (1940); Rex Beach, "Judge Spencer Roane, a Champion of State Rights" (1941); Elizabeth Weston, "The Early Career of James Monroe" (1942); Winifred Julia Loss, "Thomas Jefferson and the West" (1943); William Upson Cawthon, "The Federal Government and the Yazoo Speculation" (1945); Nicia Luz, "Spanish and French Views on the Burr Conspiracy" (1946); Norris W. Preyer, "The Congressional Fight over the Admission of Kentucky, Tennessee, Louisiana, and Alabama to the Union" (1950); James M. Helms, Jr., "Land Tenure in Territorial Mississippi, 1798–1809" (1955); Norman K. Risjord, "The Republican Quids: Political Puritans" (1957).

65 Honeywell, *The Educational Work of Thomas Jefferson* (Cambridge, Mass., 1931).

66 Elizabeth Cometti (ed.), *Jefferson's Ideas on a University Library; Letters from the Founder of the University of Virginia to a Boston Bookseller* (Charlottesville, Va., 1950); William Peden, "Some Notes Concerning Thomas Jefferson's Libraries," *William and Mary Quarterly,* 3rd series, I (July, 1944), 265–72; E. Millicent Sowerby (ed.), *The Catalogue of the Library of Thomas Jefferson* (5 vols.; Washington, D. C., 1952–1959).

and the National Capital deals with Jefferson's role in planning and landscaping the national capital.[67]

It is in the lives of Jefferson's southern lieutenants that the story of Jefferson as Virginian and Southerner is best told. Here the reader finds emphasis on localism, states' rights, strict construction, and agrarianism without the complex image of the many-sided Jefferson. Here, also, one discovers local conditions and political cross currents that scarcely appear in secondary writings of other kinds or in biographies of Jefferson, Madison, or Monroe.

John Taylor of Caroline County, Virginia, the scholar and publicist of Jeffersonian democracy and penetrating critic of Hamilton and Marshall, has been the subject of studies by William E. Dodd, Henry H. Simms, E. T. Mudge and Benjamin F. Wright.[68] Jefferson never wrote down in succinct form what Jeffersonian democracy meant; his *Notes on Virginia* (Philadelphia, 1801) is his most concise statement. Taylor, in contrast, wrote many pamphlets and books in which he attempted to do what Jefferson failed to do—give organized articulation to Jeffersonian democracy.[69] Spencer Roane, a justice of the Virginia

67 Mumford, *The South in Architecture* (New York, 1941); Kimball, *Thomas Jefferson and the First Monument of the Classical Revival in America* (Harrisburg, Pa., and Washington, 1915); Padover (ed.), *Thomas Jefferson and the National Capital* (Washington, D. C., 1946). See also Fiske Kimball, *Thomas Jefferson, Architect* (Boston, 1916); William B. O'Neal, *Jefferson's Buildings at the University of Virginia: The Rotunda* (Charlottesville, 1960).

68 Dodd, "John Taylor of Caroline: Prophet of Secession," *John P. Branch Papers of Randolph-Macon College,* II (June, 1908), 214–52; Simms, *Life of John Taylor: The Story of a Brilliant Leader in the Virginia State Rights School* (Richmond, 1932); Wright, "John Taylor, The Philosopher of Jeffersonian Democracy," *American Political Science Review,* XXII (November, 1928), 870–92; Mudge, *The Social Philosophy of John Taylor of Caroline: A Study in Jeffersonian Democracy* (New York, 1939). The latter is probably the best study.

69 Taylor's works, which would be better known were they not so labored and prolix that they almost need translation, include *A Definition of Parties* (Philadelphia, 1794) and *An Inquiry into the Principles and Tendency of Certain Public Measures* (Philadelphia, 1794), in which he attacked Hamilton's financial policies. Although a states' righter and a strict constructionist, he defended Jefferson's purchase of Louisiana in *A Defense of the Measures of the Administration of Thomas Jefferson* (Washington, D. C., 1804). His greatest work, *An Inquiry into the Principles and Policy of the Government of the United States* (Fredericksburg, Va., 1814), which is a sympathetic study of Jeffersonian democracy, has been called one of the few notable contributions to political science written in America. In *Construction Construed and Constitutions Vindicated* (Richmond, 1820), *Tyranny Unmasked* (Washingon, D. C., 1822), and *New Views of the Constitution* (Washington, D. C., 1823), he attacked Marshall's court and the growing power of the Federal government. Although he died in 1824, Dodd thought his writings prophetic,

supreme court, whom Jefferson wanted to make Chief Justice of the United States in place of Marshall, is the subject of a study by Clyde Christian Gelbach.[70] John Randolph of Roanoke, another Virginia contemporary and an eccentric and powerful figure in Congress during Jefferson's presidency, is the subject of biographies by Henry Adams, already cited, William Cabell Bruce, and Gerald W. Johnson.[71] Russell Kirk, *Randolph of Roanoke, A Study in Conservative Thought*, supplements Bruce's work in emphasizing Randolph's ideas and influence. The book argues convincingly that Randolph was the father of southern nationalism, the creator of the bitterly irreconcilable minority of 1860.[72] William E. Dodd has written the only biography of another of the statesrights Jeffersonians, Nathaniel Macon of North Carolina.[73] William Branch Giles, a Jefferson spokesman in Congress, is treated sympathetically in Dice Robinson Anderson's biography.[74] Thomas Ritchie, a newspaper editor and Democratic politician who outlived both Jefferson and Jackson, is the subject of a penetrating study by Charles Henry Ambler.[75] A recent biography of James Jackson, governor of Georgia and ardent Jeffersonian until his death in 1806, though by no means definitive, has increased our knowledge of Jeffersonian democracy in

---

making him the connecting link between Jefferson, John C. Calhoun, and Jefferson Davis. One historian thinks there was a "vital cleavage" between Jefferson's ideas and those of Taylor, which "Jefferson seems never to have recognized." Leland D. Baldwin, *The Stream of American History* (2 vols.; New York, 1952) I, 346.

70 Gelbach, "Spencer Roane of Virginia, 1762–1822: A Judicial Advocate of State Rights" (Ph.D. dissertation, University of Pittsburg, 1955), in *Dissertation Abstracts*, XV (Ann Arbor, 1955), 2179. For a good discussion of the struggle between John Marshall on one side and Spencer Roane, John Taylor and other Virginia leaders on the other, see William E. Dodd, "Chief Justice Marshall and Virginia, 1813–1821," *American Historical Review*, XII (July, 1907), 776–87.

71 Adams, *John Randolph* (Boston and New York, 1882); Bruce, *John Randolph of Roanoke* (2 vols.; New York, 1922). Johnson, *Randolph of Roanoke: A Political Fantastic* (New York, 1929), is based largely on Bruce's work.

72 Kirk, *Randolph of Roanoke, A Study in Conservative Thought* (Chicago, 1951). H. J. Eckenrode, *The Randolphs: The Story of a Virginia Family* (Indianapolis, 1946), suggests that the Randolph philosophy of life, essentially patrician and aristocratic, was overturned in the end by one who was himself a Randolph, Thomas Jefferson.

73 Dodd, *Life of Nathaniel Macon* (Raleigh, 1903), 400–401. Also see Abstract of James Marvin Helms, Jr., "The Early Career of Nathaniel Macon: A Study in 'Pure Republicanism'" (Ph.D. dissertation, University of Virginia, 1962) in *Dissertation Abstracts*, XXIII (Ann Arbor, 1963), 2883–84.

74 Anderson, *William Branch Giles: A Study in the Politics of Virginia and the Nation from 1790 to 1830* (Menasha, Wisconsin, 1914).

75 Ambler, *Thomas Ritchie: A Study in Virginia Politics* (Richmond, 1913).

his state.[76] In short, most of the leaders of the Southeast during the Jeffersonian era have been given appropriate biographical treatment. A notable exception is William H. Crawford, studied only in a laudatory, inadequate, and out-dated little volume by John E. D. Shipp.[77]

State-making, land speculation, local politics, and other such concerns of the West and Southwest dominate the biographies of their leaders during the Jeffersonian era.[78] The "Southern Biography Series" of Louisiana State University Press includes the biographies of three Southwesterners of the Jefferson era: Felix Grundy, Edward Livingston, and Edmund Pendleton Gaines.[79]

Western state-making went on apace during the Jefferson period, and five new southern states had joined the original five when Alabama entered the Union in 1819. John D. Barnhart, E. Merton Coulter, W. Magruder Drake, and Malcolm C. McMillan have studied the first Tennessee, Kentucky, Mississippi and Alabama constitutions. Barnhart found the constitution of Tennessee modeled largely after that of North Carolina with some added democratic features; Drake showed the part that George Poindexter played in turning the Mississippi Constitution of 1817 into a conservative document. Coulter saw "early frontier Democracy in the First Kentucky Constitution," and McMillan attributed the democratic nature of the Alabama Constitution of 1819 to the joint efforts of frontier democracy and an enlightened planter leadership affected by Jeffersonian liberalism.[80] Clarence E. Carter's *The Territorial*

76 William Omer Foster, Sr., *James Jackson, Duelist and Militant Statesman, 1757–1806* (Athens, 1960).

77 Shipp, *Giant Days: Or, The Life and Times of William H. Crawford* (Americus, Ga., 1909).

78 Mack Swearingen, *The Early Life of George Poindexter: A Story of the First Southwest* (New Orleans, 1934); William B. Hamilton, *Thomas Rodney: Revolutionary and Builder of the West* (Durham, 1953); Weymouth T. Jordan, *George Washington Campbell of Tennessee: Western Statesman* (Tallahassee, 1955); Joseph T. Hatfield, "The Public Career of William C. C. Claiborne" (Ph.D. dissertation, Emory University, 1962).

79 Joseph H. Parks, *Felix Grundy: Champion of Democracy* (Baton Rouge, 1940); William B. Hatcher, *Edward Livingston: Jeffersonian Republican and Jacksonian Democrat* (Baton Rouge, 1940); James Silver, *Edmund Pendleton Gaines: Frontier General* (Baton Rouge, 1949).

80 Coulter, "Early Frontier Democracy in the First Kentucky Constitution," *Political Science Quarterly*, XXXIX (1924), 665–77; Barnhart, "The Tennessee Constitution of 1796: A Product of the Old West," *Journal of Southern History*, IX (November, 1943), 532–48; Drake, "Constitutional Development in Mississippi, 1817–1865" (Ph.D. dissertation, University of North Carolina, 1954); McMillan, *Constitutional Development in Alabama, 1798–1901: A Study in Politics, the Negro, and Sectionalism* (Chapel Hill, 1955); McMillan, "The Alabama Constitution of 1819: A Study in Constitution Making on the Frontier," *The Alabama Review*, III (October, 1950), 263–85.

Papers of the United States contains a vast mine of information on political, social, economic, and other conditions in the Southwest of Jefferson's day.[81]

Avery O. Craven has commented on the striking failure of the general frontier historians to include the old Southwest within their ken.[82] But monographs go a long way toward providing a reliable record. Walter B. Posey has studied three denominations in the old Southwest during the frontier period.[83] Randle B. Truett's *Trade and Travel Around the Southern Appalachians Before 1830* depicts the growth of roads, inns, taverns, and trade, but it fails to bring the development of the region as a whole into focus. Perhaps the best treatment of the expansion of the population westward into the Gulf region is contained in Thomas Perkins Abernethy's *The Formative Period in Alabama, 1815–1828*. Expansion into western Tennessee is considered in Samuel C. Williams, *Beginnings of West Tennessee in the Land of the Chickasaws, 1541–1841*. The southward movement into Florida is discussed in Sidney W. Martin, *Florida During the Territorial Days*.[84] A case study in migration from Iredell County, North Carolina, to Alabama has been done by Hugh H. Wooten. The great part that Virginia played in the building of the nation as its sons moved westward is told by Richard Beale Davis in "The Jeffersonian Virginia Expatriate in the Building of the Nation." [85]

81 See volumes on the territories of Mississippi, Alabama, Orleans, Louisiana, and Louisiana-Missouri in Carter (ed.), *The Territorial Papers of the United States* (18 vols.; Washington, D.C., 1934–1952).

82 Craven, "The 'Turner Theories' and the South," *Journal of Southern History*, V (August, 1939), 291–314. Frederic L. Paxson, *History of the American Frontier, 1763–1893* (Boston, 1924), all but leaves the South out; Thomas D. Clark, *The Rampaging Frontier* (Indianapolis, 1939), emphasizes only the upper South; and Everett N. Dick, *The Dixie Frontier* (New York, 1948), has relatively little material on the Gulf states. John Anthony Caruso's *The Appalachian Frontier: America's First Surge Westward* (Indianapolis, 1959), recapitulates the often recorded history of the extension of civilization from the coastal regions of Virginia and the Carolinas to Tennessee and Kentucky.

83 Posey, *The Development of Methodism in the Old Southwest, 1783–1824* (Tuscaloosa, 1933), and *The Presbyterian Church in the Old Southwest, 1778–1838* (Richmond, 1952), and *The Baptist Church in the Lower Mississippi Valley, 1776–1845* (Lexington, 1957).

84 Truett, *Trade and Travel Around the Southern Appalachians Before 1830* (Chapel Hill, 1935); Abernethy, *The Formative Period in Alabama, 1815–1828* (Montgomery, Ala., 1922); Williams, *Beginnings of West Tennessee in the Land of the Chickasaws, 1541–1841* (Johnson City, Tenn., 1930); Martin, *Florida During the Territorial Days* (Athens, Ga., 1944).

85 Wooten, "Westward Migration from Iredell County, 1800–1850," *North Carolina Historical Review*, XXX (January, 1953), 61–71; Davis, "The Jeffersonian

One of the great controversies of Jefferson's day, the Yazoo land speculations, has not yet found a historian. The story must be pieced together from general histories and special studies.[86] Much, however, has been written on land policy and land speculation as motivating factors in the settlement of the Gulf plains. Both Payson J. Treat, *The National Land System, 1785–1820,* and Roy M. Robbins, *Our Landed Heritage: The Public Domain, 1776–1936,*[87] are general treatments which contain material on the South. Robert S. Cotterill, "The National Land System in the South, 1803–1812," [88] is more specialized. Paul W. Gates' "Private Land Claims in the South" [89] deals with clouded land titles caused by duplicating by France, Britain, Spain, the older southern states, and finally the federal government. Hugh C. Bailey's "John W. Walker and the Land Laws of the 1820's" and his recent *John Williams Walker: A Study in the Political, Social, and Cultural Life of the Old Southwest* [90] discuss the origins of the land laws of the 1820's in the difficulties which the federal government encountered under the law of 1800. Gordon T. Chappel, in "Some Patterns of Land Speculation in the Old Southwest," [91] recounts the fabulous speculation in Tennessee Valley lands about the time that Alabama came into the Union. Ulrich B. Phillips' "The Origin and Growth of Southern Black Belts" [92] argues that the planter took over the best lands and pushed the farmer into the Piedmont and the hills. Frank L. Owsley's "The

Virginia Expatriate in the Building of the Nation," *Virginia Magazine of History and Biography,* LXX (January, 1962), 49–61.

86 See Charles H. Harkins, "The Yazoo Land Companies," in American Historical Association *Papers,* V (1891), No. 4, pp. 61–103; A. M. Sakolski, *The Great American Land Bubble* (New York, 1932); George White, *An Accurate Account of the Yazoo Fraud, Compiled from Official Documents* (Marietta, Ga., 1852).

87 Treat, *The National Land System, 1785–1820* (New York, 1910); Robbins, *Our Landed Heritage: The Public Domain, 1776–1936* (Princeton, 1942).

88 Cotterill, "The National Land System in the South, 1803–1812," *Mississippi Valley Historical Review,* XVI (March, 1930), 495–506.

89 Gates, "Private Land Claims in the South," *Journal of Southern History,* XXII (May, 1956), 183–204.

90 Bailey, "John W. Walker and the Land Laws of the 1820's," *Agricultural History,* XXXII (April, 1958), 120–26, *John Williams Walker: A Study in the Political, Social, and Cultural Life of the Old Southwest* (University, Ala., 1964).

91 Chappel, "Some Patterns of Land Speculation in the Old Southwest," *Journal of Southern History,* XV (November, 1949), 463–77.

92 Phillips, "The Origin and Growth of Southern Black Belts," *American Historical Review,* XI (July, 1906), 798–816.

Pattern of Migration and Settlement on the Southern Frontier" [93] contends that the pattern was much more democratic, with planter and small farmer living side by side.

The Burr conspiracy, which highlights the sectionalism and nationalism of the Southwest in Jefferson's day, has been the subject of much historical and biographical writing. Walter Flavius McCaleb's study, first published in 1903, was republished in 1936 with a laudatory introduction by Charles A. Beard.[94] It argued that Burr did not commit or even conspire to commit treason and that his whole enterprise was directed against Spain. Samuel H. Wandell and Meade Minnigerode, in a work published in 1925, were pro-Burr and add a bitter anti-Jefferson and anti-Hamilton touch in order to enhance Burr's reputation.[95] In *Aaron Burr: The Proud Pretender,* Holmes Alexander followed Henry Adams closely in attributing to Burr motives of disloyalty and overweening ambition. He uses few primary sources and makes extensive use of the old studies by Matthew L. Davis and James Parton.[96] On the other hand Nathan Schachner follows McCaleb in clearing Burr by representing him as a protagonist of independence for Mexico.[97] A recent study by Thomas Perkins Abernethy has found Burr guilty and perhaps finally turned the tide against him. Using sources not available to earlier scholars, Abernethy asserts that Burr's major objective was the separation of the western states from the Union.[98]

Burr's compatriot in intrigue in the Southwest (and key figure in the Spanish conspiracy of the 1780's) was General James Wilkinson. No less colorful or controversial than Burr, he has been the subject of many biographies and articles. He is perhaps the perfect example of a subject being fascinating because of his faults rather than his virtues.

---

93 Owsley, "The Pattern of Migration and Settlement on the Southern Frontier," *Journal of Southern History,* XI (May, 1945), 147–76. See also William O. Lynch, "The Westward Flow of Southern Colonists before 1861," *Journal of Southern History,* IX (August, 1943), 303–27.

94 McCaleb, *The Aaron Burr Conspiracy: A History Largely from Original and hitherto Unused Sources* (New York, 1903) ; Beard's Introduction to *ibid.* (New York, 1936), ix–xi.

95 Wandell and Minnigerode, *Aaron Burr* (2 vols.; New York, 1925).

96 Alexander, *Aaron Burr: The Proud Pretender* (New York, 1937) ; Davis, *Memoirs of Aaron Burr* (2 vols.; New York, 1836–37) ; Parton, *The Life and Times of Aaron Burr* (New York, 1858).

97 Schachner, *Aaron Burr: A Biography* (New York, 1937).

98 Abernethy, *The Burr Conspiracy* (New York, 1954). See also Abernethy, "Aaron Burr in Mississippi," *Journal of Southern History,* XV (February, 1949), 9–21; I. J. Cox, "The Louisiana-Texas Frontier During the Burr Conspiracy," *Mississippi Valley Historical Review,* X (December, 1923), 274–84.

Two modern biographers, Royal O. Shreve in 1933 and James Ripley Jacobs in 1938, have dealt with him in high disapproval.[99] A more balanced biography was published by Thomas R. Hay and M. R. Werner in 1941. They followed a credit and debit course in assessing Wilkinson's character and accomplishments.[100] In a short biography, written like a lawyer's brief, Wilkinson's great-grandson has attempted to clear his name.[101]

One of the prime objectives of the Jefferson administration was the acquisition of West Florida. To this subject Isaac J. Cox devoted years of study, and his *West Florida Controversy, 1798–1813* [102] remains the best book on the subject. In two articles, Cox credited Jefferson with a "Pan American" vision and traced Jefferson's determination to the very end of his second administration to acquire West Florida by fair means or foul, using even the unsavory Wilkinson, whom Jefferson knew to be untrustworthy.[103] In a third article, "The American Intervention in West Florida," [104] Cox discussed the filibustering activities of certain Southerners against West Florida and concluded that the seizure of West Florida was forced by the demands of settlers in Alabama and Mississippi for an outlet to the Gulf, even as the opening of the Mississippi had been motivated earlier by similar pressures. A similar situation on the Georgia-Florida border has been treated by I. J. Cox in "The Border Missions of General George Mathews," [105] and even more fully in Rembert Patrick, *Florida Fiasco: Rampant Rebels on the Georgia-Florida Border, 1810–1815.* [106]

99 Shreve, *Finished Scoundrel* (Indianapolis, 1933); Jacobs, *Tarnished Warrior: Major-General James Wilkinson* (New York, 1938).

100 Hay and Werner, *The Admirable Trumpeter: A Biography of General James Wilkinson* (Garden City, New York, 1941). Hay, "Some Reflections on the Career of General James Wilkinson," *Mississippi Valley Historical Review,* XXI (March, 1935), 471–94, is sympathetic to Wilkinson and portrays him as a self-centered adventurer, no "less ready to deceive his Spanish paymasters than to betray the interests of his own government."

101 James Wilkinson, *Wilkinson, Soldier and Patriot* (New York, 1935).

102 Cox, *West Florida Controversy, 1798–1813* (Baltimore, 1918).

103 Cox, "General Wilkinson and His Later Intrigues with the Spaniards," *American Historical Review,* XIX (July, 1914), 794–812, and "The Pan American Policy of Jefferson and Wilkinson," *Mississippi Valley Historical Review,* I (September, 1914), 212–39.

104 Cox, "The American Intervention in West Florida," *American Historical Review,* XVII (January, 1912), 290–311.

105 Cox, "The Border Missions of General George Mathews," *Mississippi Valley Historical Review,* XII (December, 1925), 309–33.

106 Patrick, *Florida Fiasco: Rampant Rebels on the Georgia-Florida Border, 1810–1815* (Athens, Ga., 1954).

The diplomacy that subsequently brought about the transfer of Florida to the United States is treated in an old but still useful study by Herbert Bruce Fuller in 1906.[107] The best study, however, is P. C. Brooks, *Diplomacy and the Borderlands: The Adams-Onís Treaty of 1819,* supplemented by A. P. Whitaker, *The United States and the Independence of Latin America, 1800–1830.* Samuel Flagg Bemis has an excellent discussion of the whole matter in his *John Quincy Adams and the Foundations of American Foreign Policy.*[108]

Jeffersonian nationalism is reflected not only in the expansion into the Floridas, but also in the war with the Barbary pirates, the embargo, the War of 1812, the nationalist program after the war, and most particularly in the Louisiana Purchase. The latter was significant in southern history for numerous reasons, not the least of which was the possibility presented for the extension of the plantation-slavery system westward and the fight over slavery in the territories which brought on the Civil War. But historians have also seen the purchase as epitomizing the ideal of American democracy. "It is significant," writes Adrienne Koch, "that Jefferson first began to use the term 'empire for liberty' after the acquisition of Louisiana—when he had already decided that real national power was essential for survival in a world where aggressive and unscrupulous great powers were carving out their empires in bloody battle." [109]

All the aforementioned general works and biographies of Jefferson that go through his first administration discuss the Louisiana Purchase in varying detail, and several monographs provide additional detail. Arthur P. Whitaker's *The Mississippi Question, 1795–1803* is good on the background.[110] E. Wilson Lyon studied the cession from the standpoint of Paris in his *Louisiana in French Diplomacy, 1759–1804.*[111]

107 Fuller, *The Purchase of Florida: Its History and Diplomacy* (Cleveland, 1906). See also Charles C. Griffin, *The United States and Disruption of the Spanish Empire, 1810–1822* (New York, 1937).
108 Brooks, *Diplomacy and the Borderlands: The Adams-Onís Treaty of 1819* (Berkeley, 1939); Whitaker, *The United States and the Independence of Latin America, 1800–1830* (Baltimore, 1941); Bemis, *John Quincy Adams and the Foundations of American Foreign Policy* (New York, 1949).
109 See chapter on "Jefferson and the Pursuit of Happiness," in Adrienne Koch, *Power, Morals, and the Founding Fathers* (Ithaca, New York, 1961), 48.
110 Whitaker, *The Mississippi Question, 1795–1803* (New York, 1934). See also A. B. Darling, *Our Rising Empire, 1763–1803* (New Haven, 1940); Louis Pelzer, "Economic Factors in the Acquisition of Louisiana," Mississippi Valley Historical Association *Proceedings (1912–13),* VI, 109-28; and W. Edwin Hemphill, "The Jeffersonian Background of the Louisiana Purchase," *Mississippi Valley Historical Review,* XXII (September, 1935), 177–90.
111 Lyon, *Louisiana in French Diplomacy, 1759–1804* (Norman, Okla., 1934).

Everett S. Brown's book concentrates on the many constitutional aspects of the purchase, including Jefferson's *volte face* on strict construction.[112] George Dangerfield's *Chancellor Robert R. Livingston of New York, 1746–1815* [113] is a significant study of one of the participants in the purchase. P. C. Brooks, in "Spain's Farewell to Louisiana, 1803–1821," [114] shows Spain's bitterness at Napoleon's sale of Louisiana and traces Spain's persistent efforts to win the area back through diplomacy, including intrigue in New Orleans as late as 1817.

The perils of neutrality during the great Napoleonic Wars were of course Jefferson's main cause of concern during his second administration. The two best studies of Jefferson's effort to prevent war through the use of the embargo are those of Walter Wilson Jennings and Louis Martin Sears.[115] The former is an economic study, with particular reference to the effect that the embargo had in encouraging industry at the same time that it blighted agriculture and commerce. Sears' broader study, less influenced by the Beardian thesis, analyzes the attitude toward the embargo of New England, the middle states, and the South. Sears has an interesting theory that the South suffered more than any other section as a result of the embargo.[116] While New England exporters turned to manufacturing, the South had no such recourse. Yet, according to Sears the Southerners obeyed the law while New Englanders defied it almost to the point of treason. Unlike Jennings, Sears believed "the actual pressure was severe, and [the embargo] came far nearer to producing the desired result than the enemies of Jefferson, or even his friends, perceived." [117]

The two best introductions to historical writing on the causes of the War of 1812, one of the most studied topics in American history, are Warren H. Goodman, "The Origins of the War of 1812: A Survey of Changing Interpretations," [118] and Reginald Horsman, *The Causes of*

112 Brown, *Constitutional History of the Louisiana Purchase* (Berkeley, 1920).

113 Dangerfield, *Chancellor Robert R. Livingston of New York, 1746–1815* (New York, 1960).

114 Brooks, "Spain's Farewell to Louisiana, 1803–1821," *Mississippi Valley Historical Review*, XXVII (June, 1940), 29–42.

115 Jennings, *American Embargo: 1807–1809* (Iowa City, 1921); Sears, *Jefferson and the Embargo* (Durham, 1927).

116 See also Louis Martin Sears, "The South and the Embargo," *South Atlantic Quarterly*, XX (July, 1921), 254–75.

117 Sears, *Jefferson and the Embargo*, viii.

118 Goodman, "The Origins of the War of 1812: A Survey of Changing Interpretations," *Mississippi Valley Historical Review*, XXVIII (September, 1941), 171–86.

the War of 1812,[119] orginally written as a doctoral dissertation at Indiana University. Goodman's study, cited for many years for its commentary on the clash of interpretations, is ably done but is somewhat evasive in its conclusions. The more recent Horsman study has the advantage of later research and makes a more forthright appraisal of the historical arguments.

It is interesting to note that the appraisals of the causes of the war have gone full cycle—beginning with Henry Adams' emphasis on maritime causes and finally coming back to a similar emphasis by other historians in recent years. The main weakness of this theory stems from the fact that all of the maritime complaints were acute long before 1812. Adams' *History* gave some attention to western causation.[120] The maritime rights interpretation remained the conventional one, however, modified by emphasis on the sectional character of the war and intimations that the War Hawks had entertained aggressive designs upon Canada, until the end of the century.

In the twentieth century, an increasing number of scholars, seeking to explain western and southern bellicosity, turned their backs on the seaboard and looked to the West and South for causation. Howard T. Lewis argued in 1911 that Westerners wanted the rich lands of Canada and were willing to go to war to secure them.[121] A similar "land hunger" thesis presented by Louis M. Hacker in 1924 [122] met an immediate and strong rebuttal from Julius W. Pratt who placed his emphasis on the desire of the West to take Canada because of the Indian menace and the determination of southern expansionists for Florida.[123]

The most recent "western" interpretation has in a sense completed the cycle by bringing us back over a circuitous route to the maritime thesis. George R. Taylor opened fresh, fertile ground in 1931 by arguing

119 Horsman, *The Causes of the War of 1812* (Philadelphia, 1961). See also Reginald Horsman, "Western War Aims, 1811–1812," *Indian Magazine of History,* LIII (March, 1957), 1–18.

120 The young Republicans from the South and West, said Adams, were "bent on war with England, they were willing to face debt and probable bankruptcy on the chance of creating a nation, of conquering Canada, and carrying the American flag to Mobile and Key West." Adams, *History,* VI, 123.

121 Lewis, "A Re-analysis of the Causes of the War of 1812," *Americana,* VI (New York, 1911), 506–16, 577–85.

122 Hacker, "Western Land Hunger and the War of 1812: A Conjecture," *Mississippi Valley Historical Review,* X (March, 1924), 365–95.

123 Pratt, "Western War Aims in the War of 1812," *Mississippi Valley Historical Review,* XII (June, 1925), 36–50, and *Expansionists of 1812* (New York, 1925). Parks, *Felix Grundy: Champion of Democracy,* gives strong support to the Pratt thesis.

that the disruption of commerce on the high seas by the British brought falling prices and economic depression to the agrarian West, which demanded war in retaliation.[124] Margaret K. Latimer applied the same thesis to South Carolina and found that depressed prices in cotton and other commodities there forced the issue of war or peace.[125] Although he did not ignore the Canadian problem, Canadian-born A. L. Burt [126] stressed the complexity of the impressment and ship-seizure controversies—a treatment very reminiscent of Henry Adams' *History*. A more recent student, Norman K. Risjord,[127] rejects the economic interpretations of the coming of the war as unproved or too narrowly sectional. With the exception of New England, he finds national honor the unifying force behind the war—a new twist to the maritime causes stressed by nineteenth-century historians.

Bernard Mayo's biography of the chief of the War Hawks, *Henry Clay: Spokesman of the New West*,[128] is excellent on the growth of the war spirit but brings Clay's life only to 1812. The author does not subscribe to the thesis that Clay blackmailed Madison into war, but he does argue that the aggressive Kentuckian used his powers as speaker of the House in 1811–12 to push a reluctant Madison toward war. Charles M. Wiltse's *John C. Calhoun: Nationalist, 1782–1828* [129] is also excellent on the coming of the war.

For many years most historians followed Henry Adams in writing that Madison, unlike John Adams who opposed war with France in 1798, was a weakling, pushed into war by a Congress which he could not control.[130] As has already been indicated, recent revisionists have done much to upgrade Madison's reputation as President. Brant sees Madison as a forceful leader encouraging the war movement, as does

124 Taylor, "Prices in the Mississippi Valley Preceding the War of 1812," *Journal of Economic and Business History*, III (November, 1930), 148–63, and "Agrarian Discontent in the Mississippi Valley Preceding the War of 1812," *Journal of Political Economy* XXXIX (August, 1931), 471–505.

125 Latimer, "South Carolina: A Protagonist of the War of 1812," *American Historical Review*, LXI (July, 1956), 914–29.

126 Burt, *The United States, Great Britain, and British North America from the Revolution to the Establishment of Peace after the War of 1812* (New Haven, 1940).

127 Risjord, "1812: Conservatives, War Hawks, and the Nation's Honor," *William and Mary Quarterly*, XVIII, 3rd series (April, 1961), 196–210.

128 Mayo, *Henry Clay: Spokesman of the New West* (Boston, 1937).

129 Wiltse, *John C. Calhoun: Nationalist, 1782–1828* (Indianapolis, 1944).

130 See Adams, *History*, VI, 176–219. Adams heads one of his chapters "Madison as Minerva," and another, "Hesitations."

Abbot Smith in his cogent article, "Mr. Madison's War." [131] On the other hand, Bradford Perkins, using the same materials as Brant, declared Madison a complete failure in 1812: "The war came, not because of the President, but despite him." [132]

A really good study of the Indian wars in the South, a very important part of the War of 1812, is yet to appear. *Benjamin Hawkins, Indian Agent,* by Merritt B. Pound, sheds some light on the subject.[133] George D. Harmon, *Sixty Years of Indian Affairs,*[134] contains material on the Creek War. The best accounts of the role of Andrew Jackson, the key figure in the war in the Southwest, is to be found in Marquis James, *The Border Captain,* and John Spencer Bassett, *Life of Andrew Jackson.*[135] Two recent accounts of the battle of New Orleans have appeared: Jane Lucas De Grummond's *The Baratarians and the Battle of New Orleans,* which probably claims too much for Jean Laffite and his privateers; and Charles B. Brooks' *The Siege of New Orleans,* which is more dramatic and more likely to appeal to the general reader.[136]

The diplomacy of the War of 1812 has been treated as unit by Frank A. Updyke, *The Diplomacy of the War of 1812,*[137] but the best studies

131 Irving Brant, *James Madison: The President, 1809–1812,* 427–30, 478–83; Abbot Smith, "Mr. Madison's War," *Political Science Quarterly,* LVII (1942), 229–46.

132 Perkins, *Prologue to War, England and the United States, 1805–1812* (Berkeley and Los Angeles, 1961), 426. William Ray Barlow has written an interesting account of the problems of Congress during the War of 1812: "Congress During the War of 1812" (Ph.D. dissertation, Ohio State University, 1961).

133 Pound, *Benjamin Hawkins, Indian Agent* (Athens, Ga., 1951). See also Merritt B. Pound, "Colonel Benjamin Hawkins—North Carolinian—Benefactor of the Southern Indians," *North Carolina Historical Review,* XIX (January and April, 1942), 1–21, 168–86; Henry T. Malone, *Cherokees of the Old South: A People in Transition* (Athens, Ga., 1956); Annie H. Abel, "The History of Events Resulting in Indian Consolidation West of the Mississippi," American Historical Association, *Annual Report, 1906* (Washington, 1908); Robert S. Cotterill, *The Southern Indians: The Story of Civilized Tribes before Removal* (Norman, Okla., 1954), and "Federal Indian Management in the South, 1789–1825," *Mississippi Valley Historical Review,* XX (December, 1933), 333–52.

134 Harmon, *Sixty Years of Indian Affairs* (Chapel Hill, 1941).

135 Marquis James, *The Border Captain,* Volume I of his *The Life of Andrew Jackson* (2 vols.; Indianapolis, 1933–1937); Bassett, *Life of Andrew Jackson* (2 vols.; New York, 1925).

136 De Grummond, *The Baratarians and the Battle of New Orleans* (Baton Rouge, 1961); Brooks, *The Siege of New Orleans* (Seattle, 1961).

137 Updyke, *The Diplomacy of the War of 1812* (Baltimore, 1915). See also Charles M. Gates, "The West in American Diplomacy, 1812–1815," *Mississippi Valley Historical Review,* XXVI (March, 1940), 499–510. A study of what Virginians thought of Napoleon is Joseph I. Shulim, *The Old Dominion and Napoleon Bonaparte* (Columbia, 1952).

of the three southern secretaries of state and their diplomacy during the Jefferson and Madison administrations (other than Henry Adams' monumental *History* which makes diplomatic history an art and a science) are C. E. Hill's "James Madison," C. C. Tansill's, "Robert Smith," and Julius W. Pratt's "James Monroe." [138]

Charles M. Wiltse, *John C. Calhoun: Nationalist, 1782–1828*,[139] is perhaps the best starting point for southern nationalism after the war. In this second volume of his trilogy, Wiltse features Calhoun the War Hawk, advocate of tariff protection, federal aid to roads and waterways, a national bank, and a strong army and navy. Essentially, as Henry Adams had pointed out long before, this was the Hamiltonian program, which Jefferson's party, including Calhoun and many other Southerners, was now supporting.[140] Henry Clay's nationalism after the War of 1812, his American System, and his work as the "Great Compromiser" in 1820 and later are well related by Carl Schurz, Glyndon G. Van Deusen, and Clement Eaton.[141] Clay emerges as the master politician who more than any other statesman of his era helped to preserve the Union.

Both volumes in the recent "A History of the South" series dealing with the period under discussion have been published, the line of division

138 Bemis (ed.), *The American Secretaries of State and Their Diplomacy* (10 vols.; New York, 1927–29) III, 80–276.

139 Wiltse, *John C. Calhoun: Nationalist, 1782–1828.* Other volumes in Wiltse's trilogy are: *John C. Calhoun, Nullifier, 1829–1839* and *John C. Calhoun: Secessionist, 1840–1850* (3 vols.; Indianapolis, 1944–1951). The best one-volume life of Calhoun is Margaret Coit, *John C. Calhoun: American Portrait* (Boston, 1950), which is descriptive, dramatic, and imaginative, but not as good on interpretation. Seldom has history so reversed itself as upon the interpretation of Calhoun. The *bete noir* of the Federalist historians, today the erstwhile champion of slavery and the "lost cause" has been resurrected as one of America's most original thinkers, the exponent and defender of all minority rights everywhere. See August O. Spain, *The Political Theory of John C. Calhoun* (New York, 1951). A penetrating and interpretive study of Calhoun is "John C. Calhoun: The Marx of the Master Class," in Richard Hofstadter, *The American Political Tradition and the Men Who Made It* (New York, 1948), 67–91. Robert L. Meriwether (ed.), *The Papers of John C. Calhoun, 1801–1817,* I (Columbia, S. C., 1959), is excellent for the period under consideration.

140 Henry Adams, *History,* IX, 104–25. A good monograph on the bank is Ralph C. H. Catterall, *The Second Bank of the United States* (Chicago, 1903). See also Joseph Dorfman, *The Economic Mind in American Civilization* (3 vols.; 1946–1949).

141 Carl Schurz, *Life of Henry Clay* (2 vols.; Boston, 1887), was marred by Schurz's strong antislavery and nationalist bias; Van Deusen, *The Life of Henry Clay* (Boston, 1937); Clement Eaton, *Henry Clay and the Art of American Politics* (Boston, 1957). See also John F. Hopkins and Mary W. M. Hargreaves (eds.), *The Papers of Henry Clay: The Rising Statesman, 1797–1814* (Lexington, Ky., 1959).

being the Panic of 1819, when southern nationalism began to recede. Thomas Perkins Abernethy, *The South in the New Nation, 1789–1819*,[142] virtually ignores the South Atlantic states and concentrates on the Southwest, Louisiana and the Floridas, Spanish intrigues, Indian wars, the westward movement, and land speculation. Charles S. Sydnor, *The Development of Southern Sectionalism, 1819–1848*,[143] treats the internal history of the South along with the region in its relation to the nation. Emphasizing and integrating economic, social, and cultural history, the author ploughs new ground. As the title indicates, the book traces and emphasizes the course of the South from nationalism to sectionalism.

Neither James Monroe nor John Quincy Adams has had a "Henry Adams," and Monroe has not attracted biographers; William P. Cresson's posthumously published *James Monroe*[144] is the best available. Monographs and interpretative studies, other than those on southern sectionalism, are lacking for the domestic history of both administrations, and one must piece together special studies about southern politics.[145] It was definitely a period of transition from Jeffersonian to Jacksonian democracy with the South moving gradually from nationalism to sectionalism.[146] The best study of the period as a whole is George Dangerfield's brilliant *Era of Good Feeling*.[147] Perhaps the chief criti-

142 Abernethy, *The South in the New Nation, 1789–1819*.

143 Sydnor, *The Development of Southern Sectionalism, 1819–1848* (Baton Rouge, 1948), Volume V of Stephenson and Coulter (eds.), *A History of the South*.

144 Cresson, *James Monroe* (Chapel Hill, 1946).

145 See Charles S. Sydnor, "The One Party Period of American History," *American Historical Review*, LI (1946), 439–51, which is a good survey of the decade before the election of 1824; A. R. Newsome, *The Presidential Election of 1824 in North Carolina*, in ("James Sprunt Studies in History and Political Science" XXIII [Chapel Hill, 1939]) ; Paul C. Nagle, "The Election of 1824, A Reconsideration based on Newspaper Opinion," *Journal of Southern History*, XXVI (August, 1960), 315–29, agrees with A. R. Newsome that bitter sectional issues were more important in the campaign than personalities—the latter being the generally accepted interpretation. See also Harry Ammon, "James Monroe and the Era of Good Feeling," *Virginia Magazine of History and Biography*, LXVI (October, 1958), 387–98. Both Ruth K. Nuermberger, " 'The Royal Party' in Early Alabama Politics," *Alabama Review*, VI (April, and July, 1953), 81–98, 198–212, and Hugh C. Bailey, "John W. Walker and the Georgia Machine in Early Alabama Politics," *Alabama Review*, VIII (July, 1955), 179–195, show how William H. Crawford, secretary of treasury under Monroe, used the patronage to build up a machine in Alabama.

146 Edward Channing subtitles his fifth volume: *The Period of Transition, 1815–1848*. See Channing, *A History of the United States* (6 vols.; New York, 1905–25).

147 Dangerfield, *Era of Good Feeling* (New York, 1952).

cism of the book is its title, a dubious one when used for Monroe's administrations and absurd for John Quincy Adams'.

Only on the origins and promulgation of the Monroe Doctrine do we have anything like definitive work for the Monroe administrations. Dexter Perkins, who has done the most careful work on the origins of the doctrine, thinks that though John Quincy Adams had great influence, the initiative came from Monroe himself.[148] Samuel Flagg Bemis, in his more recent *John Quincy Adams and the Foundations of American Foreign Policy*,[149] argued with great force that Adams was the main author of the document, though he does not deny that it was also shaped by others.

Sectionalism in New England previous to and during the War of 1812 is linked with that in the South thereafter. Writing in 1948, Charles S. Sydnor complained that most historians explain southern sectionalism "in terms of subsequent southern political frustration instead of beginning, as chronology requires, with previous New England political frustration." [150] And economic historians have interpreted the phenomena in each section in terms of economic determinism— federal policy *versus* local self-interest.

Slavery, perhaps the most important cause of southern sectionalism, is dealt with in a later chapter. Among those who cite self-interest and not abstractions, the tariff, next to slavery, is the most often emphasized cause of southern sectionalism. Nearly all writing on the subject has until recently been colored by the pro- or antitariff convictions of the writer. Stanwood's protariff history treated the subject in great detail, emphasizing the political aspects of the tariff, but was largely nonanalytical. The work by F. W. Taussig, a group of essays which the long-time economist at Harvard University had previously printed, first appeared together in book form in 1888. This work, critical of protection, went through many editions. Neither of the above studies has the advantage of recent historical scholarship or is especially oriented to-

148 Perkins, *The Monroe Doctrine, 1823–1826* (Cambridge, 1927), 74.

149 Bemis, *John Quincy Adams and the Foundations of American Foreign Policy* (New York, 1949). Other historians have emphasized Jefferson's part in the Monroe Doctrine. See T. R. Schellenberg, "Jeffersonian Origins of the Monroe Doctrine," *Hispanic American Historical Review*, XIV (February, 1934), 1–31. Gilbert Chinard, *Thomas Jefferson, the Apostle of Americanism* (Boston, 1929), 467–88, has a discussion of Jefferson and the "doctrine of two spheres."

150 Sydnor, *The Development of Southern Sectionalism, 1819–1848*, 370. See also Ames (ed.), *State Documents on Federal Relations: The States and the United States* (Philadelphia, 1907); Henry Adams (ed.), *Documents Relating to New England Federalism, 1800–1815* (Boston, 1877). Both are excellent documentary collections, illustrative of sectionalism.

ward an understanding of the South's position.[151] The South was overwhelmingly antitariff after 1816. However, as Taylor found, in his introduction to *The Great Tariff Debate, 1820–1830,* most of the issues in regard to the tariff were not clearly focused until 1824.[152]

An informative study of the opposition of South Carolina to the tariff acts of 1820, 1824, and 1827 is that of John L. Conger, which shows the interrelations of the early tariffs with other issues.[153] The thesis that Southerners hoped and expected that textile manufacturing would develop in their section, generally given by historians as a cause for strong Southern support of the 1816 tariff, has been attacked by Norris W. Preyer. He found that "it was not a desire for manufacturing, but a combination of prosperity, patriotism, and promises that had swayed Southerners" to vote against their economic self-interest in 1816. With waning prosperity and the lessening of the danger of war with England, economic self-interest became paramount and "the South turned almost unanimously against the tariff bill of 1820." [154] On the other hand, Joseph H. Harrison, Jr., found the South turning against federal aid to internal improvements in the early 1820's for psychological and political reasons. They feared anything which enhanced the power of a potentially less southern federal government.[155]

Frederick Jackson Turner stressed sectionalism based on geographic and economic factors more than slavery as a cause of growing southern sectionalism. Correlating the falling prices of cotton and the growing opposition of the South to each tariff after the Panic of 1819, Turner

---

151 Edward Stanwood, *American Tariff Controversies in the Nineteenth Century* (2 vols.; Boston and New York, 1903), I, 39–159; Taussig, *The Tariff History of the United States* (New York, 1914). In explaining the South's reversal of support on the tariff between 1816 and 1820, Taussig wrote: "It is possible that the Missouri Compromise struggle had opened their eyes to the connection between slavery and free trade," 73.

152 George Rogers Taylor (ed.), *The Great Tariff Debate, 1820–1830* (Boston, 1953), v, in George Rogers Taylor (ed.), *Problems in American Civilization* (Boston, 1949——). See also Taylor, *The Transportation Revolution, 1815–1860* (New York, 1951), 360–65. Both John C. Calhoun and William Lowndes of South Carolina took a prominent part in support of the tariff of 1816, but a majority of Southerners under the leadership of John Randolph voted against the bill. For a record of the vote, see Wiltse, *John C. Calhoun: Nationalist, 1782–1828,* Appendix B, 403.

153 Conger, "South Carolina and the Early Tariffs," *Mississippi Valley Historical Review,* V (March, 1919), 415–33.

154 Preyer, "Southern Support of the Tariff of 1816—A Reappraisal," *Journal of Southern History,* XXV (August, 1959), 306–22.

155 See Abstract of Joseph H. Harrison, Jr., "The Internal Improvement Issue in the Politics of the Union, 1783–1825" (Ph.D. dissertation, University of Virginia, 1954), *Dissertation Abstracts,* XIV (Ann Arbor, 1954) 1694–95.

attributes the region's growing sectionalism between 1820 and 1830 to economic self-interest. About Calhoun's vote against the tariff of 1827, Turner said: "Sectional economic interests had dominated the political philosophy of the greatest Southern statesman since Jefferson and the South had entered on the long struggle that culminated in the Civil War." [156] Beard turned to class analysis for an explanation—the irrepressible struggle between industrial-commercial interests and the planters, which began very early but became more accentuated with the passage of time. "Many an orator," he said, "who might have forgiven the South for maintaining a servile labor system could not forgive it for its low tariff doctrines and its opposition to centralized finance." [157]

Although historians disagree as to when southern sectionalism became pronounced, most of them agree that the Missouri controversy marked the turning point in the attitude of the South toward the Union. An old but still useful study of the compromise, by James A. Woodburn, concludes that the South on this occasion stood "at the threshold of the struggle that produced the Civil War." [158] An important contribution to the understanding of the origins of the bitter Missouri controversy is Albert F. Simpson, "The Political Significance of Slave Representation, 1787–1821." [159] Glover Moore's excellent study, The Missouri Controversy, 1819–1821,[160] begins with a chapter on the background of sectionalism in which he finds threads of sectionalism going back to the constitutional convention. The overall significance of the compromise, as he shows, is that it set for several decades the pattern used to preserve a balance in the North-South conflict. An earlier work which describes and analyzes conditions in Missouri itself is Floyd C. Shoemaker, Missouri Struggle for Statehood, 1804–1821.[161]

Jesse Thomas Carpenter, in The South as a Conscious Minority, 1789–1861,[162] argues that the South was a self-conscious minority struggling with the problem of political control by northern majorities

156 Turner, "The South, 1820–1830," American Historical Review, XI (April, 1906), 573.

157 Quoted in Harvey Wish, The American Historian: A Social-Intellectual History of the Writing of the American Past (New York, 1960), 279.

158 Woodburn, "The Historical Significance of the Missouri Compromise," in American Historical Association, Annual Report, 1893 (Washington, 1894), 296.

159 Simpson, "The Political Significance of Slave Representation, 1787–1821," Journal of Southern History, VII (August, 1941), 315–42.

160 Moore, The Missouri Controversy, 1819–1821 (Lexington, Ky., 1953).

161 Shoemaker, Missouri Struggle for Statehood, 1804–1821 (Jefferson City, Mo., 1916).

162 Carpenter, The South as a Conscious Minority, 1789–1861 (New York, 1930).

from the formation of the Constitution in 1787 to the decision of 1860–61. The main weakness of this book is its failure to consider the North-South struggle for the support of the West, one of the strongest motivations in the politics of the period. Ulrich B. Phillips, *Georgia and State Rights*,[163] is a case study of the application of the states' rights principle in one southern state, organized around such issues as federal aid to internal improvements, Indian removal, the Second United States Bank, the tariff, and slavery. John G. Van Deusen's *The Economic Bases of Disunion in South Carolina*[164] details growing sectionalism based on land exhaustion, depressed agriculture, and inadequate finance in South Carolina after the Panic of 1819.

Intrastate sectionalism based on geography, soil, isolation, and other conditions was a powerful force in most southern states and had to subside before Southern sectionalism could mature. On the Atlantic the pattern was generally East *versus* West (true also of Tennessee) ; on the Gulf it was North *versus* South. Fletcher M. Green featured intrastate sectionalism in his study of constitutional reform in the South Atlantic states, and studies of intrastate sectionalism presenting similar themes exist for Virginia, South Carolina, Tennessee, and Alabama.[165]

Although much has been done, the role of the South in the age of Jefferson remains a fertile and challenging field of study. It is apparent that with the exception of Henry Adams' *History,* most of the scholarly work on the period is of recent date. Much interest is manifest in the causes of the War of 1812, in diplomacy and foreign affairs, expansion and intrigue along the southern and southwestern border, and in biographical studies of Jefferson and his colleagues. Much less has been done on the Indians and Indian wars in the South, the westward movement

---

163 Phillips, *Georgia and State Rights,* in American Historical Association, *Annual Report, 1901* (Washington, D.C., 1902), II, 3–224.

164 Van Deusen, *The Economic Bases of Disunion in South Carolina* (New York, 1928). In *The Coming of the Civil War* (New York, 1942), Avery O. Craven finds the seeds of Southern sectionalism in the rural depression of 1800–1832, pp. 39–66. Soil exhaustion as a cause of southern sectionalism is treated in a later chapter.

165 Green, *Constitutional Development in the South Atlantic States, 1776–1860: A Study in the Evolution of Democracy* (Chapel Hill, 1930) ; Charles Henry Ambler, *Sectionalism in Virginia from 1776 to 1861* (Chicago, 1910) ; William A. Schaper, *Sectionalism and Representation in South Carolina* (Washington, 1901) ; Stanley J. Folmsbee, *Sectionalism and Internal Improvements in Tennessee, 1796–1845* (Knoxville, 1939) ; Theodore H. Jack, *Sectionalism and Party Politics in Alabama, 1819–1842* (Menasha, Wisc., 1919) ; Malcolm C. McMillan, *Constitutional Development in Alabama, 1798–1901: A Study in Politics, the Negro, and Sectionalism,* in ("The James Sprunt Studies in History and Political Science" [Chapel Hill, 1955]).

into the Gulf plains, and the social and economic history of banking, internal improvements, agriculture, and like matters.

Additional research is needed on the state and local level, where fresh and unique information is often revealed. Practically all the territories of Jefferson's day await a historian. As already indicated, monographic studies on Jeffersonian democracy exist only for North Carolina and South Carolina. And very little has been done in southern domestic history for the Monroe and Adams administrations. The nationalism of the South before 1820 has been inadequately presented. Historians, in their eagerness to explain the Civil War and to keep the South in character, have read southern sectionalism back into a period in which the South was perhaps the most nationalistic part of the Union.

Recent historical trends include a growing emphasis on the importance of James Madison, a de-emphasis on the differences between Jefferson and Hamilton, and an unusual interest in the rich intellectual and cultural history of the Jeffersonian years.[166] In spite of the growing interest in Madison, however, it is the versatile and complex Jefferson who has most fascinated recent biographers and historians. Although future followers of Clio will build on recent scholarship, they will without doubt overturn some of the recent interpretations, introduce others, and present new hypotheses as they attempt to make the age of Jefferson meaningful for their own generations.

---

166 The most recent study of intellectual history is Richard Beale Davis, *Intellectual Life in Jefferson's Virginia, 1790–1830* (Chapel Hill, 1964).

V

The Jacksonian Era

Edwin A. Miles

THE manner in which scholars have viewed American and southern history in general and the antebellum period in particular has naturally influenced the way in which they have interpreted the role of the South in the eventful era that Arthur M. Schlesinger, Jr., has called the "Age of Jackson." During the late nineteenth century, for example, patrician historians of the Gilded Age generally held the Jacksonian era in low esteem. Above all, their ardent Federalist-Whig predisposition caused them to deplore the triumph of mediocrity, vulgarity, corruption, and mob democracy, which they regarded as the most deleterious political innovations of that period. On the other hand, such Social Darwinists as William Graham Sumner and Carl Schurz, while deprecating the motives behind the Jacksonian policies, grudgingly approved their anti-mercantilistic tendencies. But they were writing in an age when the South possessed an ineffectual voice in the nation's political life and was not sharing fully in the triumph of industrialism which Jacksonian laissez-faire principles had apparently facilitated. Thus the South did not loom large in the appraisal by these historians of the significance of the Jacksonian period.[1]

Furthermore during the late nineteenth century many historians, retaining trenchant memories of the Civil War, looked upon the so-called Middle Period primarily as a prelude to that epochal conflict. For decades after the war the abolitionist interpretation of antebellum southern society prevailed. According to this view, the southern white population prior to 1861 had consisted almost entirely of two elements: the wealthy planters, who comprised a small, haughty ruling class, and the poor whites, a depraved, ignorant, downtrodden people, under the sway of their political and social superiors. Richard Hildreth's earlier description of the prewar commonwealths below Mason and Dixon's line as "aristocracies of the sternest and most odious kind" remained the standard interpretation.[2] James Schouler, who cast animadversions upon both the South and Andrew Jackson, traced the origins of the Civil War in part to Old Hickory's "unconscious bias to the side of the South." His "treacherous policy of Mexican dismemberment and annexation for the sake of slavery," according to Schouler, made him partly responsible "for the worst that followed after he set the ball in motion." [3]

In the early twentieth century, the Civil War continued to overshadow the Jacksonian era for many historians who argued that commitment to states' rights principles was the South's most significant development during that period. Between 1896 and 1928 there were three full-length studies of the nullification movement in South Carolina.[4] Ulrich B. Phillips' monograph, "Georgia and State Rights," set the fashion for similar studies that laid stress upon the relationship between the state

1 For general surveys of the historiography of the Jacksonian period consult Alfred A. Cave, *Jacksonian Democracy and the Historians* (Gainesville, 1964) ; Charles G. Sellers, Jr., "Andrew Jackson versus the Historians," *Mississippi Valley Historical Review*, XLIV (March, 1958), 615–34; Harry Stevens, "Jacksonian Democracy, 1825–1849," in William H. Cartwright and Richard L. Watson, Jr. (eds.), *Interpreting and Teaching American History* (*Thirty-First Yearbook of the National Council for the Social Studies;* Washington, 1961), 75–86; John W. Ward, "The Age of the Common Man," in John Higham (ed.), *The Reconstruction of American History* (New York, 1962), 82–97.

2 Hildreth, *Despotism in America; An Inquiry into the Nature, Results, and Legal Basis of the Slave-Holding System of the United States* (Boston, 1854), 8.

3 Schouler, *History of the United States of America under the Constitution* (7 vols.; New York, 1880–1913), IV, 272.

4 David Franklin Houston, *A Critical Study of Nullification in South Carolina* (Cambridge, 1896) ; Chauncey Samuel Boucher, *The Nullification Controversy in South Carolina* (Chicago, 1916) ; Frederic Bancroft, *Calhoun and the South Carolina Nullification Movement* (Baltimore, 1928).

and the federal union as the paramount political question facing antebellum southern statesmen.[5] In a later essay Phillips declared that "the
great central body of southern Whigs were the cotton producers, who
were first state-rights men pure and simple and joined the Whigs from
a sense of outrage at Jackson's threat of coercing South Carolina"—an interpretation accepted by Arthur C. Cole, E. Malcolm Carroll, and a
whole generation of historians.[6] These scholars, Charles G. Sellers later
declared, portrayed the South as a "section unified as early as the 1820's
in its devotion to state rights doctrines and its hostility to the nationalistic, antislavery, capitalistic North." [7]

Such an interpretation comported well with the sectional approach to
American history advocated by Frederick Jackson Turner. Turner was
highly influential in shaping both the manner in which historians considered the role of the South in the Jacksonian period and also the
way in which they treated southern state politics of that era. While
recognizing the diverse components of the Jacksonian coalition, Turner
attached preeminent importance to its western or frontier elements.
Aware of the strong sentiment for Old Hickory in the seaboard southern
states, as well as in the newer states west of the Appalachian mountains,
he asserted that "the South Atlantic section had deceived itself" in supporting Jackson's candidacy. "It," Turner went on, "had aided in placing
in the White House a man of the frontier, and as a result the West took
the reins of authority." [8] Jackson was the "very personification" of a
frontier democracy which "came, stark and strong and full of life, from
the American forest." [9] Only as long as the Southwest remained pri-

5 Phillips, "Georgia and State Rights," in American Historical Association, *Annual
Report, 1901*, II, 1–224; Henry McGilbert Wagstaff, *State Rights and Political
Parties in North Carolina, 1776–1861* (Baltimore, 1906); Cleo Hearon, "Nullification in Mississippi," Mississippi Historical Society, *Publications (1912)*, XII,
37–71; E. Merton Coulter, "The Nullification Movement in Georgia," *Georgia Historical Quarterly*, V (March, 1921), 1–39.

6 Phillips, "The Southern Whigs, 1834–1854," *Essays in American History Dedicated to Frederick Jackson Turner* (New York, 1910), 209; Arthur Charles Cole,
The Whig Party in the South (Washington, 1913); E. Malcolm Carroll, *Origins
of the Whig Party* (Durham, 1925); Henry H. Simms, *The Rise of the Whigs
in Virginia, 1824-1840* (Richmond, 1929); Jesse T. Carpenter, *The South as a
Conscious Minority, 1789–1861; A Study in Political Thought* (New York, 1930).

7 Sellers, "Who Were the Southern Whigs?" *American Historical Review*, LIX
(January, 1954), 135.

8 Turner, *The United States, 1830-1850; The Nation and Its Sections* (New York,
1935), 37.

9 Turner, "Contributions of the West to American Democracy," *Atlantic Monthly*,
XCI (January, 1903), 87, and "The Problem of the West," *Atlantic Monthly*,
LXXVIII (September, 1896), 294–95.

marily "western" rather than "southern," according to Turner, was it a potent influence in the development of American democracy.[10]

Turner's contention that "the spread of cotton culture, and the development of great plantations" had destroyed the southwest's "natural democratic tendencies" met widespread concurrence.[11] William E. Dodd, who similarly believed that "democracy could not exist in the presence of great fortunes in slaves and land," maintained that the South, forsaking its liberal Revolutionary heritage, had adopted a political philosophy based upon the inequality of man by the time of the Civil War. According to him, Southerners "turned their backs upon democracy . . . and accepted a new social faith, which, as they said, was more consistent with the facts of life." [12] William Gleason Bean later traced through the writings of the region's spokesmen the ideological movement from Jefferson to Calhoun, during which the South's dominant group repudiated majoritarian democratic principles.[13] Thus for many historians the stirrings of the Age of Jackson made little impact upon the South, which continued under the dominance of the aristocratic planters. As Arthur M. Schlesinger, Sr., put it, "Jacksonian democracy . . . never disturbed their seats of power within the borders of their own states." [14]

Turner's emphasis upon sectionalism as a force in national politics during the Jacksonian era inspired many studies dealing with intrastate sectionalism during the same period.[15] Theodore H. Jack's statement

10 Turner, "Contributions of the West to American Democracy," 89. While regarding the frontier influence with varying degrees of favor and disfavor, John W. Burgess, Carl Russell Fish, William M. Meigs, William E. Dodd, John Spencer Bassett, and Frederick A. Ogg all shared the view that it was the most significant force upon Jacksonian politics. See Cave, Jacksonian Democracy and the Historians, Chap. 2. Consult also Avery O. Craven, "The 'Turner Theories' and the South," Journal of Southern History, V (August, 1939), 291–314.

11 The quotation is from Turner, "Contributions of the West to American Democracy," 89.

12 Dodd, "The Social Philosophy of the Old South," American Journal of Sociology, XXIII (March, 1918), 736, 737. See also Dodd, Statesmen of the Old South; or, From Radicalism to Conservative Revolt (New York, 1911). For a similar interpretation consult D. Huger Bacot, "Constitutional Progress and the Struggle for Democracy in South Carolina following the Revolution," South Atlantic Quarterly, XXIV (January, 1925), 61–72.

13 Bean, "Anti-Jeffersonianism in the Ante-Bellum South," North Carolina Historical Review, XII (April, 1935), 103–24.

14 Schlesinger, New Viewpoints in American History (New York, 1922), 91.

15 W. A. Schaper, "Sectionalism and Representation in South Carolina," in American Historical Association, Annual Report, 1900, I, 237–463; Charles Henry Ambler, Sectionalism in Virginia from 1776 to 1851 (Chicago, 1910); Theodore Henley Jack, Sectionalism and Party Politics in Alabama, 1819–1842 (Menasha, Wisconsin, 1919).

that "the growth of a spirit of sectionalism" in Alabama was the "most striking and significant feature in the history of the State" during the 1820's and 1830's was typical of the conclusions drawn by such scholars.[16] Stanley J. Folmsbee, in his later study of internal improvements in Tennessee, concluded that the fomenting of sectional antagonisms was "one of the most unfortunate results" of the debates over the building of transportation facilities in that state.[17]

Turner's conception of the forces operating upon Jacksonian America did not go unchallenged even in his own day. Edward Channing, a Harvard colleague, was one of the few historians of the early twentieth century to attribute far-reaching importance to the southern influence upon Jacksonian policies. Declining to accept Turner's seemingly inflexible differentiation between the South Atlantic and the South Central states, Channing asserted that "Jackson was really chosen to the presidency by the solid South, as was quite proper as he was a Southern man, a slaveholder, and a cotton grower." In his opinion, Jackson was "not only the representative of the rising democracy of Pennsylvania and New York and of frontier radicalism, he was more particularly the representative of the cotton planters." [18]

Thomas Perkins Abernethy, a student of Turner at Harvard, became one of his mentor's most persistent critics among southern historians.[19] His study of Tennessee politics during the era of transition from frontier to plantation reached several conclusions which were at variance with Turner. Abernethy, like Channing, concluded that Jacksonian policies were generally more beneficial to seaboard planters than to western frontiersmen. He also called into question the strength of the "much vaunted democracy of the west" and impugned Jackson's reputation as a democratic leader.[20] Emphasizing the contributions of the land speculator in the development of the Southwest, he declared that a small minority friendly to such interests controlled the political institutions during the early days of settlement. "What we recognize as Western democracy," he wrote, "really developed after the actual frontier stage had been

16 Jack, *Sectionalism and Party Politics in Alabama*, vii.

17 Folmsbee, *Sectionalism and Internal Improvements in Tennessee, 1796–1845* (Knoxville, 1939), 266–67.

18 Channing, *A History of the United States* (6 vols.; New York, 1904–1925), V, 375–76, 380, 422, 423.

19 Abernethy's Ph.D. dissertation, *The Formative Period in Alabama, 1815–1828* (Montgomery, 1922), gave little indication that he would later assume that role.

20 Abernethy, *From Frontier to Plantation in Tennessee; A Study in Frontier Democracy* (Chapel Hill, 1932), 351, 353–54.

passed." [21] Calling attention to Jackson's own speculative ventures in land, his conservative associates, and his highly personal view of politics, Abernethy declared that to the Old Hero "Democracy was good talk with which to win the favor of the people and thereby accomplish ulterior objectives. Jackson never really championed the cause of the people; he only invited them to champion his." [22]

Abernethy was one of the few American historians of his generation who did not write with a decidedly democratic bias. His attitude toward popular government, if not consistently hostile, was at least ambiguous. He asserted in 1932 that Jacksonian democracy had not fundamentally altered the American political system; in fact, he implied that democracy had been an illusion throughout the course of the nation's history.[23] Yet in his presidential address before the Southern Historical Association some years later he maintained that there were genuine political changes "in the direction of mass government" during the Jacksonian period, though he observed the consequences with regret.[24] Abernethy also proposed criteria for judging democratic leaders that few men who have generally been regarded as such could meet. Writing in the year that Franklin D. Roosevelt was first elected President, he denied Jackson's pretensions to that distinction partly on the grounds that he was a member of the privileged class and "never possessed . . . class consciousness." [25]

Most historians of the antebellum South who wrote during the era of the New Deal and the Second World War did not share Abernethy's point of view. The prevailing opinion that the Civil War had been a needless conflict led naturally to the idea that the sections had not been so different after all, while the bewildered mood of the Depression years was particularly responsive to the Marxian concept of the class

21 Abernethy, "Democracy and the Southern Frontier," *Journal of Southern History*, IV (February, 1938), 11.

22 Abernethy, *From Frontier to Plantation in Tennessee*, 248.

23 *Ibid.*, 364.

24 Abernethy, "Democracy and the Southern Frontier," 11.

25 Abernethy, *From Frontier to Plantation in Tennessee*, 357. See also the following articles by Abernethy: "Andrew Jackson and the Rise of the Southwestern Democracy," *American Historical Review*, XXXIII (October, 1927), 64–77; "The Origin of the Whig Party in Tennessee," *Mississippi Valley Historical Review*, XII (March, 1926), 504–22; "The Early Development of Banking in Tennessee," *Mississippi Valley Historical Review*, XIV (December, 1927), 311–25; "Social Relations and Political Control in the Old Southwest," *Mississippi Valley Historical Review*, XVI (March, 1930), 529–37; "The Political Geography of Southern Jacksonism," East Tennessee Historical Society *Publications*, III (January, 1931), 35–41.

struggle, as evidenced in Roger Shugg's study of nineteenth-century Louisiana politics.[26] But insofar as southern Jacksonian history was concerned, the most significant development during the "Age of Franklin Roosevelt" was the higher socio-economic standing awarded the Old South's "forgotten man"—the yeoman farmer.

Elsewhere in this volume James C. Bonner discusses the revolution in southern historiography during the 1930's and 1940's which led to the acceptance of the view that the prewar South had been a dynamic economic democracy rather than a society ruled by an aristocratic planter oligarchy.[27] Although earlier historians had recognized that the middle-class yeomanry constituted a majority of the antebellum South's population, Frank L. Owsley, aided by his wife and his students at Vanderbilt University, led the successful movement to accord that class a more elevated status. Owsley's affectionate concern for the South's agrarian past, as expressed in his essay in *I'll Take My Stand,* undoubtedly prompted these studies, but it was the New Deal's stress upon the common man that assured them a sympathetic reception.[28] So ardently did the members of the "Owsley School" assail the planter poor-white stereotype of southern society that Fabian Linden, who disputed both their methodology and their conclusions, wrote in 1946 that "it is the debunking of the 'two class' fallacy that has now become the tedious cliché." [29] A decade later Clement Eaton cautioned that the tendency to exalt the Old South's yeomanry might lead to the "danger of historians and novelists sentimentalizing and romanticizing the common man in the same way that they had previously glamorized the Southern planter." [30]

The general acceptance of the idea that there was a measure of economic democracy in the Old South probably facilitated the favorable reception of the concept that the region was also more politically demo-

---

26 Shugg, *Origins of Class Struggle in Louisiana; A Social History of White Farmers and Laborers during Slavery and after, 1840-1875* (Baton Rouge, 1939). See also William G. Carleton, "The Conservative South—A Political Myth," *Virginia Quarterly Review,* XXII (Spring, 1946), 179–93.

27 See pp. 147–74.

28 Owsley, "The Irrepressible Conflict," in Twelve Southerners, *I'll Take My Stand: The South and the Agrarian Tradition* (New York, 1930), 61–91.

29 Linden, "Economic Democracy in the Slave South," *Journal of Negro History,* XXXI (April, 1946), 187.

30 Eaton, "Recent Trends in the Writing of Southern History," *Louisiana Historical Quarterly,* XXXVIII (April, 1955), 35.

cratic than was formerly believed.[31] Whereas William E. Dodd and
William Gleason Bean had earlier portrayed a once-democratic South
renouncing majoritarian principles, Fletcher M. Green perceived a once-
conservative South becoming democratic. In "Democracy in the Old
South," his presidential address prepared for the Southern Historical
Association in 1945, Green declared that the South kept pace with the
nation as a whole in embracing political democracy during the age of
Jackson. "The establishment of white manhood suffrage, the abolition of
property qualifications for office holders, the election of all officers by
popular vote, and the apportionment of representation on population
rather than wealth, with periodic reapportionment," he wrote, "dealt a
death blow to the political power of the landed, slaveholding aristocracy
of the Old South." Disagreeing with Turner, Green concluded that the
frontier influence upon democratic progress had been negligible. Reiterat-
ing an observation made in his earlier *Constitutional Development in
the South Atlantic States,* he asserted that in the seaboard South "the demands for reform grew out of local conditions and would have arisen
had there been no 'New West' beyond the Appalachians." [32] In *Valley
of Democracy,* John D. Barnhart, a disciple of Turner, argued that
Green exaggerated the efficacy of the democratic reform movement in
the South and underestimated the democratic pressures emanating from
the West. Barnhart maintained that "the frontier on both sides of the
mountains created fluid social and economic conditions which set the
stage for reform." [33]

Two of Green's students, Malcolm Cook McMillan and Winbourne
Magruder Drake, later wrote studies of nineteenth-century constitutional
development in Alabama and Mississippi, respectively. McMillan attributed the democratic nature of the Alabama constitution of 1819 to
the joint efforts of frontier and aristocratic elements. Planters, McMillan

31 Years earlier Gustavus W. Dyer, instructor in Sociology and Economics at
Vanderbilt University, had presented a case for the democratic nature of antebellum
southern society, but his *Democracy in the South before the Civil War* (Nashville,
1906) attracted little attention. "All [Southerners]," he wrote, "believed they were
living under a democracy; all believed they were enjoying the inalienable rights of
life, liberty, and the pursuit of happiness; all believed that they were free, and were
living under governments that gave equal rights to all and special privileges to
none," 38–39.

32 Green, "Democracy in the Old South," *Journal of Southern History,* XII (February, 1946), 15, 17–18, and *Constitutional Development in the South Atlantic
States, 1776-1860; A Study in the Evolution of Democracy* (Chapel Hill, 1930),
300.

33 Barnhart, *Valley of Democracy: The Frontier versus the Plantation in the
Ohio Valley, 1775–1818* (Bloomington, 1953), 274.

wrote, "furnished the leadership of the convention and dominated the Committee of Fifteen which wrote the liberal original draft of the constitution. However, to the 'plain men,' those who came mostly from the 'white counties,' must go the credit for amending the document into an even more democratic constitution." [34] On the other hand, Drake, in his analysis of the Mississippi constitution of 1832, noted that "the representatives of the aristocratic Natchez area supported democratic measures when they thought it was to their advantage to do so. Conversely, the representatives of the usually more democratic frontier and small farmer region did not hesitate to support undemocratic features of the constitution if they stood to gain thereby." Joining issue with Barnhart, Drake argued that "the democratization of Mississippi's basic law" refuted the interpretation that "political democracy did not flourish in the antebellum South because of the domination of the aristocratic planters." [35]

Charles S. Sydnor, in his *Development of Southern Sectionalism*, averred, with Green, that the "obvious roots" of the democratic reform movement "ran back into the local situation in the South." He wrote: "Seldom if ever have the governments of the Southern states been subjected to more vigorous domestic criticism than during the 1820's or to more thoroughgoing constitutional reformation than during the 1830's." Sydnor accepted with some reservations Green's interpretation of the overall success of the crusade for democracy in the South: "In a few states the conservatives held their power unimpaired; more often they were compelled to compromise; and in some states the radicals won a complete victory." But he implicitly rejected Green's conclusion that "in spirit and administration as well as in form" the southern states "had progressively become more and more concerned with the rights and interests of the people." Pointing out that the most notable progress in public education was made in the more conservative southern states, he declared that "political democracy was vigorous, active, and noisy; but the people gained little in return for their votes. To use a phrase attributed to David Crockett: the social program of the democrats was like shearing a pig: big squeal and little wool." [36]

34 McMillan, *Constitutional Development in Alabama, 1798–1901: A Study in Politics, the Negro, and Sectionalism* (Chapel Hill, 1955), 46.
35 Drake, "The Mississippi Constitutional Convention of 1832," *Journal of Southern History*, XXIII (August, 1957), 370. See also Drake, "Constitutional Development in Mississippi, 1817–1865" (Ph.D. dissertation, University of North Carolina, 1954).
36 Sydnor, *The Development of Southern Sectionalism, 1819–1848* (Baton Rouge, 1948), Chap. 12.

Arthur M. Schlesinger, Jr.'s *Age of Jackson,* one of the most widely publicized volumes in American history to appear since the Second World War, was also an impressive challenge to the Turnerian interpretation of the Jacksonian era. But the South mattered little in Schlesinger's analysis of the significance of Jacksonian democracy, in which he often saw the New Deal in embryonic form. Rejecting Channing's concept of a Solid South, and adopting Turner's distinction between the seaboard South and the Southwest, Schlesinger viewed the seaboard Republican planters primarily as "keepers of the Jeffersonian conscience" and held that southwestern (and all western) influence upon Jacksonian democracy was inconsequential. Though he declared that the period could be better understood in terms of classes rather than sections, his interpretation nevertheless had the effect of directing the attention of historians from one section to another, for he maintained that the laboring class, concentrated largely in the cities of the eastern states, was the most fermenting element in the Jacksonian coalition.[37]

Most of Schlesinger's numerous critics shared his disavowal of Turner's sectional interpretation of Jacksonian democracy but declined to accept *The Age of Jackson* as an accurate analysis of the class influences upon the movement. In fact, some of them repudiated either implicitly or explicitly Schlesinger's thesis that Jacksonian democracy could be understood as "a problem . . . of classes." Bray Hammond and Richard Hofstadter agreed with Schlesinger that eastern urban influences were paramount, but they criticized his evaluation of the role of labor, stressing instead the entrepreneurial elements of the Jacksonian party.[38] Joseph Dorfman, Edward Pessen, and Walter Hugins challenged Schlesinger's understanding of the nature of the workingmen's movement itself.[39] Discussing the psychological aspects of Jackson's appeal and the "Jacksonian persuasion," John W. Ward and Marvin Meyers minimized both sectional and class differences, while Louis Hartz argued

37 Schlesinger, *The Age of Jackson* (Boston, 1945).

38 Hammond, *Banks and Politics in America, from the Revolution to the Civil War* (Princeton, 1957); Hofstadter, *The American Political Tradition and the Men Who Made It* (New York, 1948), 44–66.

39 Dorfman, "The Jackson Wage-Earner Thesis," *American Historical Review,* LIV (October, 1948), 296–306; Pessen, "The Workingmen's Movement of the Jacksonian Era," *Mississippi Valley Historical Review,* XLIII (December, 1956), 428–43; Hugins, *Jacksonian Democracy and the Working Class; A Study of the New York Workingmen's Movement, 1829–1837* (Stanford, 1960).

that virtually all Americans, Whig and Democrat, Northerner and Southerner, were attracted to a common liberal creed.[40]

Because most historians who have written in recent years about Jacksonian democracy as a national movement have either concentrated upon eastern urban influences or have de-emphasized sectional and class differences, few of them have considered the role of the South in that era as a worthwhile topic for their deliberation. Even so, the past three decades have seen publication of a host of biographical studies of Southerners prominent in the political battles of the period.[41] Many, but for-

40 Ward, *Andrew Jackson, Symbol for an Age* (New York, 1955) ; Meyers, *The Jacksonian Persuasion: Politics and Belief* (Stanford, 1957) ; Hartz, *The Liberal Tradition in America; An Interpretation of American Political Thought since the Revolution* (New York, 1955).

41 These include: Wendell Holmes Stephenson, *Alexander Porter, Whig Planter of Old Louisiana* (Baton Rouge, 1934) ; Herbert Everett Putnam, *Joel Roberts Poinsett; A Political Biography* (Washington, 1935) ; J. Fred Rippy, *Joel R. Poinsett, Versatile American* (Durham, 1935) ; Carl Brent Swisher, *Roger B. Taney* (New York, 1935) ; Charles W. Smith, *Roger B. Taney: Jacksonian Jurist* (Chapel Hill, 1937) ; Henry H. Simms, *Life of Robert M. T. Hunter; A Study in Sectionalism and Secession* (Richmond, 1935) ; Arthur Styron, *The Cast-Iron Man; John C. Calhoun and American Democracy* (New York, 1935) ; Charles M. Wiltse, *John C. Calhoun* (3 vols.; Indianapolis, 1944–1951) ; Margaret L. Coit, *John C. Calhoun, American Portrait* (Boston, 1950) ; Gerald M. Capers, *John C. Calhoun, Opportunist; A Reappraisal* (Gainesville, 1960) ; Edwin L. Green, *George McDuffie* (Columbia, S. C., 1936) ; James Byrne Ranck, *Albert Gallatin Brown, Radical Southern Nationalist* (New York, 1937) ; Oliver Perry Chitwood, *John Tyler, Champion of the Old South* (New York, 1939) ; William B. Hatcher, *Edward Livingston: Jeffersonian Republican and Jacksonian Democrat* (Baton Rouge, 1940) ; Joseph Howard Parks, *Felix Grundy: Champion of Democracy* (Baton Rouge, 1940) ; Dallas C. Dickey, *Seargent S. Prentiss: Whig Orator of the Old South* (Baton Rouge, 1946) ; Lillian Adele Kibler, *Benjamin F. Perry, South Carolina Unionist* (Durham, 1946) ; J. Herman Schauinger, *William Gaston, Carolinian* (Milwaukee, 1949) ; Francis Fry Wayland, *Andrew Stevenson, Democrat and Diplomat, 1785–1857* (Philadelphia, 1949) ; Joseph Howard Parks, *John Bell of Tennessee* (Baton Rouge, 1950) ; Thomas B. Alexander, *Thomas A. R. Nelson of East Tennessee* (Nashville, 1956) ; Charles Grier Sellers, *James K. Polk, Jacksonian, 1795–1843* (Princeton, 1957) ; Ruth Ketring Nuermberger, *The Clays of Alabama, A Plantation-Lawyer-Politician Family* (Lexington, 1958) ; James P. Shenton, *Robert John Walker, A Politician from Jackson to Lincoln* (New York, 1961) ; Herbert J. Doherty, *Richard Keith Call, Southern Unionist* (Gainesville, 1961) ; Alvin Laroy Duckett, *John Forsyth, Political Tactician* (Athens, 1962) ; Albert D. Kirwan, *John J. Crittenden: The Struggle for the Union* (Lexington, 1962) ; Claude H. Hall, *Abel Parker Upshur, Conservative Virginian, 1790–1844* (Madison, 1963) ; Edward M. Steel, Jr., *T. Butler King of Georgia* (Athens, 1964). The only full-length biography of Andrew Jackson published during the past three decades is Marquis James, *The Life of Andrew Jackson* (2 vols. in 1; Indianapolis, 1938). Recent biographical studies of Henry Clay relating to his career during the Jacksonian era are George R. Poage, *Henry Clay and the Whig Party* (Chapel Hill, 1936) ; Glyndon G. Van Deusen, *The Life of Henry Clay* (Boston, 1937) ; and Clement Eaton, *Henry Clay and the Art of American Politics* (Boston, 1957).

tunately not all, of these biographies have devoted relatively little attention to the broader developments of the period in which the central figure played his role or to the relationship between national and state political developments. Charles G. Sellers, whose *James K. Polk, Jacksonian* warrants no such criticism, has regretfully noted the indifference of most historians "to the local and particular ends that are often the springs of political behavior" and has warned that the American political system can never be fully comprehended "so long as able scholars confine themselves to congressional and cabinet level materials, while regarding investigations at the base of political life as work for inferior talents." [42]

Since World War II there have been numerous detailed examinations of southern politics during the Jacksonian period, many of them undertaken by students of Fletcher M. Green at the University of North Carolina.[43] These and other postwar studies offered no simple interpretation of the era, but most of them reflected the changing currents in American historiography. As the Civil War gradually retreated into the more distant past, American historians became impressed less by the rupture between the North and the South in 1861 than by the temporary nature of that breach and the permanence of the reunion since Appomattox.[44] As writers began to describe a "vanishing South" in the twentieth century, some of them were led to wonder whether that region had ever been characterized by qualities clearly distinguishing it from the rest of the nation.[45] In addition, scholars nurtured in the liberal environment of the New Deal-Fair Deal era were less inclined to regard seriously the states' rights debates of an earlier age, because such arguments had become the stock-in-trade of conservatives who embraced a contrary economic and social philosophy. "The issue of Federal relations never

42 Sellers, "Jackson Men with Feet of Clay," *American Historical Review*, LXII (April, 1957), 551. Glyndon G. Van Deusen's volume, *The Jacksonian Era, 1828–1848,* in ("The New American Nation Series" [New York, 1959]), has been criticized for its "neglect of political machinery and of politics at the grass roots." See Review by John A. Munroe, *Mississippi Valley Historical Review*, XLVI (September, 1959), 309.

43 Students of Green cited in this chapter are Jack N. Averitt, Herbert J. Doherty, Winbourne Magruder Drake, Alvin Laroy Duckett, Thomas P. Govan, William S. Hoffmann, Ernest M. Lander, Jr., Malcolm C. McMillan, Edwin A. Miles, Paul Murray, Jack B. Scroggs, Charles G. Sellers, Edward M. Steel, Jr., D. Allen Stokes, and Carolyn Andrews Wallace.

44 See, for example, David M. Potter, "The Historian's Use of Nationalism and Vice Versa," *American Historical Review*, LXVII (July, 1962), 924–50.

45 See Thomas P. Govan, "Was the Old South Different?" *Journal of Southern History*, XXI (November, 1955), 447–55; Charles G. Sellers (ed.), *The Southerner as American* (Chapel Hill, 1960).

loomed as large in Southern politics," Paul Murray wrote in the year of the Dixiecrat revolt, "as it has in the writings which have followed Ulrich B. Phillips' work on that subject in 1901."[46] And Charles G. Sellers warned in 1954 that "recent events should make the student wary of state rights banners, especially when raised by conservative men against national administrations not conspicuously devoted to the interests of the propertied."[47]

The changing interpretation of American history during the 1950's also affected the manner in which historians of the South studied the region's politics during the Jacksonian era. Economic determinism went into an eclipse during the relatively prosperous Eisenhower years. Undoubtedly the world-wide struggle between communistic and democratic ideologies contributed further to the diminishing popularity of a view of the past associated with Marxist philosophy. The Cold War with Russia as well as the attenuation of class animosities in the United States doubtless prompted many scholars to emphasize points of consensus rather than cleavage in the American past. These so-called "consensus" historians stressed that throughout the nation's history Americans had been fundamentally a middle-class people with no serious doctrinal arguments. The political conflicts of the past, according to this opinion, had been primarily between the "ins" and "outs" and had not reflected serious class or ideological disputes.[48] Since some historians maintained that the roots of American democracy went back to a much earlier period than the Jacksonian era, there was a lessening tendency to represent that period as one of social and political upheaval.[49]

In recent years historians have displayed a curious ambivalence toward Andrew Jackson and the movement linked with his name. Although some scholars have treated him sympathetically because of his identification with the rise of democracy, others have been repelled by the concept of a negative government which he and his party appeared to endorse. The equivocal attitude of mid-twentieth-century historians toward Jacksonian democracy is well illustrated by William S. Hoffmann's conclu-

[46] Murray, The Whig Party in Georgia, 1825–1853 (Chapel Hill, 1948), 205.

[47] Sellers, "Who Were the Southern Whigs?" American Historical Review, LIX (January, 1954), 346.

[48] See John Higham, "The Cult of the 'American Consensus': Homogenizing Our History," Commentary, XXVII (February, 1959), 93–100.

[49] See Richard P. McCormick, "New Perspectives on Jacksonian Politics," American Historical Review, LXV (January, 1960), 288–301. For a recent example of a work supporting the case for the eighteenth-century origins of democracy in a southern colony, see Robert E. Brown and B. Katherine Brown, Virginia, 1705–1786: Democracy or Aristocracy? (East Lansing, 1964).

sions regarding North Carolina politics during that era. "The Democrats," he wrote, "were honest men who did little good; the Whigs were ambitious schemers whose policies would have been best for the country." [50] Carolyn Andrews Wallace, in her study of David L. Swain, concluded that the North Carolina Democrats constituted the party of the status quo, whose leaders were "satisfied with the economic, social, and cultural conditions of the state," while the Whigs were the party of change who favored an "active, paternalistic government." [51]

On the other hand, several postwar writers have disputed Thomas P. Abernethy's assertion that Jackson's pre-presidential career disqualified him as a *bona fide* democratic leader. Arda S. Walker declared that "Jackson was one of the democracy's great exponents in Tennessee before he became the exponent of democracy for working people throughout the nation." [52] Albert Somit took issue with Abernethy's statement that Jackson possessed no political philosophy. And Charles G. Sellers, stressing Jackson's "Old Republican hostility to the social effects of a paper system of any kind," challenged the contention that Old Hickory had no deep-seated anti-bank animus prior to 1828.[53] Sellers also argued that Jackson had displayed an "increasingly manifest social philosophy" during the 1820's which distinguished him from his conservative associates in Tennessee.[54] Herbert J. Doherty published a letter written by Jackson endorsing universal white manhood suffrage in the territory of Florida in order to refute a statement by Harold C. Syrett, who, following Abernethy, contended that before he became President, the Old Hero "did not once espouse a policy that was designed to aid the majority or to weaken the control of the minority over the government." [55]

---

50 Hoffmann, *Andrew Jackson and North Carolina Politics* (Chapel Hill, 1958), 122.

51 Wallace, "David Lowry Swain, the First Whig Governor of North Carolina," in J. Carlyle Sitterson (ed.), *Studies in Southern History* (Chapel Hill, 1957), 77–78.

52 Walker, "Andrew Jackson: Frontier Democrat," East Tennessee Historical Society *Publications (1946)*, XVIII, 59–86.

53 Somit, "Andrew Jackson: Legend and Reality," *Tennessee Historical Quarterly*, VII (December, 1948), 291–313, and "Andrew Jackson as a Political Theorist," *Tennessee Historical Quarterly*, VIII (June, 1949), 99–126; Sellers, "Banking and Politics in Jackson's Tennessee," *Mississippi Valley Historical Review*, XLI (June, 1954), 61–84.

54 Sellers, "Jackson Men with Feet of Clay," 537–51.

55 Doherty, "Andrew Jackson on Manhood Suffrage: 1822," *Tennessee Historical Quarterly*, XV (March, 1956), 57–60. See Harold C. Syrett, *Andrew Jackson: His Contribution to the American Tradition* (Indianapolis, 1953), 22.

Sellers has made the point that Jackson "had been quicker than most of his contemporaries to sense that the changes in American society revealed by the Panic of 1819 dictated a shift from politics based on personal friendship to politics based on convictions about public policy." Nevertheless, several studies have suggested that personal friendship with the Old Hero often accounted for his following in the South, particularly in newer states and territories.[56] Joseph G. Tregle emphasized the role of Martin Gordon, the collector of customs at New Orleans, who apparently convinced the President as well as himself that "he *was* the Jackson *party* in Louisiana." [57] Edwin A. Miles stressed the part played by the so-called "Mississippi Regency," headed by Samuel and William M. Gwin, old Tennessee friends of Jackson, who became "the virtual dictators of federal patronage in Mississippi." [58] In Arkansas, as Ted R. Worley, Lonnie J. White, D. Allen Stokes, Jr., and Jack B. Scroggs have pointed out, there was the clique, variously called the "Family Combine," the "Bourbon Dynasty," and "Sevier's Hungry Kinfolks," led by Ambrose H. Sevier, another old friend of Jackson.[59] And in Florida, so Herbert J. Doherty and Arthur W. Thompson have written, there was the "Nucleus," composed of Jackson's cronies from his brief tenure as territorial governor.[60]

Tregle, Worley, and Miles have advanced the proposition that the personal popularity of Jackson was of more consequence than the policies he supported in sustaining his party's popularity in Louisiana, Arkansas, and Mississippi.[61] Perhaps the youthful nature of society in such states,

56 The quotation by Sellers is from "Banking and Politics in Jackson's Tennessee," 84.

57 Tregle, "The Political Apprenticeship of John Slidell," *Journal of Southern History*, XXVI (February, 1960), 57–60. See also Tregle, "Louisiana in the Age of Jackson: A Study in Ego-Politics" (Ph.D. dissertation, University of Pennsylvania, 1954).

58 Miles, *Jacksonian Democracy in Mississippi* (Chapel Hill, 1960), 170.

59 Worley, "The Control of the Real Estate Bank of the State of Arkansas, 1836–1855," *Mississippi Valley Historical Review*, XXXVII (December, 1950), 403–26; White, *Politics on the Southwestern Frontier: Arkansas Territory, 1819–1836* (Memphis, 1964); Stokes, "The First State Elections in 1836," *Arkansas Historical Quarterly*, XX (Summer, 1961), 126–48; Scroggs, "Arkansas Statehood: A Study in State and National Political Schism," *Arkansas Historical Quarterly*, XX (Autumn, 1961), 227–44.

60 Doherty, "Andrew Jackson's Cronies in Florida Territorial Politics," *Florida Historical Quarterly*, XXXIV (July, 1955), 3–29, and "Political Factions in Territorial Florida," *Florida Historical Quarterly*, XXVIII (October, 1949), 131–42; Thompson, *Jacksonian Democracy on the Florida Frontier* (Gainesville, 1961).

61 Tregle, "Louisiana in the Age of Jackson," 464–67; Worley, "Arkansas and the Money Crisis of 1836–1837," *Journal of Southern History*, XV (May, 1949), 178–91; Miles, *Jacksonian Democracy in Mississippi*, 168–69.

as Tregle speculated, led to this result. But as William S. Hoffmann and Jack Nelson Averitt revealed, Jackson's popularity in the older states of North Carolina and Georgia was so remarkable that well-established rival factions in those states both endorsed his candidacy in 1828.[62] Whatever the influence of the South upon the political developments of the Jacksonian era, it is quite evident that Jackson exerted considerable impact upon southern state politics, though the impact varied from state to state. Howard Braverman, in his study of the Virginia Conservatives, showed how the "Democratic party in Virginia fell apart when it no longer had the cohesive force of Andrew Jackson's leadership around which to rally"; [63] yet Ernest M. Lander's analysis of South Carolina politics during the same period indicated that Jackson's retirement made possible the reunion of the Calhounites and the Unionists in the Palmetto State.[64] In territorial Florida, so Arthur W. Thompson argued, Jackson failed to serve as a rallying symbol for the Democratic party primarily because so many of his original supporters had defected to the Whigs.[65]

The increasing inclination of mid-twentieth-century historians to stress the personal motives of politicians rather than impersonal forces like sectionalism, economic considerations, or constitutional arguments, may be due in part to the wider availability of manuscript sources, which more often than newspapers or published speeches come closer to exposing the wellsprings of human behavior. Despairing of explaining antebellum Tennessee politics "on the basis of geography, soil, slaveholding, urbanization, and concentration of capital or business and professional men," Thomas B. Alexander stressed "the considerable effect of prestigious leadership in establishing traditional party alignments." [66] The peculiar personal alliances and animosities within each state render it hazardous to venture generalizations about southern politics in the Jack-

62 Hoffmann, *Andrew Jackson and North Carolina Politics,* Chap. 3; Averitt, "The Democratic Party in Georgia, 1824–1837" (Ph.D. dissertation, University of North Carolina, 1956), Chap. 5.

63 Braverman, "The Economic and Political Background of the Conservative Revolt in Virginia," *Virginia Magazine of History and Biography,* LX (April, 1952), 266–87.

64 Lander, "The Calhoun-Preston Feud, 1836–1842," *South Carolina Historical Magazine,* LIX (January, 1958), 24–37.

65 Thompson, *Jacksonian Democracy on the Florida Frontier,* 57.

66 Alexander, "Thomas A. R. Nelson as an Example of Whig Conservatism," *Tennessee Historical Quarterly,* XV (March, 1956), 17, and *Thomas A. R. Nelson of East Tennessee,* 21.

sonian era. Consider, for example, the movement for Philip P. Barbour's vice-presidential candidacy in 1832 as it affected North Carolina and Georgia. According to William S. Hoffmann, "almost all" of the Nullifiers in North Carolina supported the Jackson-Barbour ticket, while the Unionists favored the Jackson-Van Buren slate of electors. Yet in Georgia, as Jack N. Averitt has pointed out, those most sympathetic to nullification supported Van Buren, while the Unionists favored Barbour! The Georgia Unionists disliked Van Buren because of his earlier association with William H. Crawford, one-time leader of the rival Crawford-Troup faction.[67] Certainly the studies of Jacksonian politics in the southern states indicate that Roy Franklin Nichols' observation regarding the party structure of the 1850's was equally appropriate to the 1830's: "The national parties . . . were but loose federations of state machines. . . . Each represented a separate state with its individual social organization, personal antagonisms, economic interests, and political issues. Each was subject to local attitudes and prejudices, to internal rivalries and struggles for leadership." [68]

Recent studies concerning the early Jackson movement in the South have also accentuated the personal ambitions and aspirations of individual men. "Whatever the roots of the Jackson party elsewhere," Mark H. Haller wrote in 1962, "in Maryland it grew primarily out of practical political needs, out of the search for alliances and for office by displaced politicians, and out of the external pressures created by the formation of national parties dedicated to Andrew Jackson and John Quincy Adams." [69] Haller's article, "The Rise of the Jackson Party in Maryland," and Shaw Livermore's *Twilight of Federalism*, which described the support for Jackson among northern Federalists, indicate that a study of the role of the southern Federalists in the Jackson movement might be a fruitful one.[70] Norman K. Risjord has analyzed the part played in Jackson's campaign for the presidency by another disaffected group, the Old Republicans, who supported Old Hickory "with an almost blind faith" in 1828. But Risjord concluded: "It was not the conservative Southern agrarian, but the Northern or Western businessman—

---

67 Hoffmann, *Andrew Jackson and North Carolina Politics,* Chap. 6; Averitt, "The Democratic Party in Georgia, 1824–1837," Chap. 8.

68 Nichols, *The Disruption of American Democracy* (New York, 1948), 6.

69 Haller, "The Rise of the Jackson Party in Maryland," *Journal of Southern History,* XXVIII (August, 1962), 307–26.

70 Livermore, *The Twilight of Federalism; The Disintegration of the Federalist Party* (Princeton, 1962).

nationalist or economic liberal as it suited his interests—who triumphed in the election of Andrew Jackson." [71]

Elsewhere Charles G. Sellers has emphasized the business-minded orientation of southern Whiggery. In an article entitled "Who Were the Southern Whigs?" he took sharp issue with those historians who asserted that "the Whig party in the South mainly reflected the state rights proclivities of the great planters" and who maintained that "political strife within the Old South was confined largely to struggles over intrastate sectional issues between upcountry and low country, hill country and 'black belt.' " According to Sellers, the Whig party in the South "was controlled by urban commercial and banking interests, supported by a majority of the planters, who were economically dependent on banking and commercial facilities." The Whig party in the South, he wrote, "rapidly shook off its state rights adherents and by 1841 was almost solidly in support of the nationalistic policies of Henry Clay." Regarding banking as the key issue of the Jacksonian era, Sellers maintained that Southerners divided on this and other issues in much the same way as other Americans did.[72]

Some historians, in contrast, have questioned whether the Whigs were a class party at all. Owsley's assertion that most antebellum Southerners were independent yeomen and Green's argument that political democracy flourished in the South as well as in the North made it difficult to entertain Arthur C. Cole's view that the Whigs, who often commanded majorities in the southern states, were exclusively "a broadcloth and silk stocking party embracing a large part of the wealth, intelligence, and blue blood of the South." [73] Based upon his searching inquiry into voting patterns in North Carolina under its dual electoral system adopted in 1835, Richard P. McCormick concluded that the upper economic electoral class in that state divided between the Whigs and Democrats

71 Risjord, "The Old Republicans: Southern Conservatives in Congress, 1806–1824" (Ph.D. dissertation, University of Virginia, 1960), 494–96. Joseph Hobson Harrison, Jr., in an article entitled "Martin Van Buren and His Southern Supporters," stressed Van Buren's hostility to Clay's American System as the primary bond between the New Yorker and his southern allies. "But such a policy," Harrison wrote, "however agreeable to the constitutional susceptibilities of the Southern Atlantic States, did little for their badly deficient systems of communication." *Journal of Southern History,* XXII (November, 1956), 458.

72 Sellers, "Who Were the Southern Whigs?" 335–46. Three decades earlier Chauncey S. Boucher had similarly argued that during the 1830's and 1840's party loyalty generally transcended sectional loyalty in the South. Boucher, "In Re That Aggressive Slavocracy," *Mississippi Valley Historical Review,* VIII (June–September, 1921), 15–19.

73 The quotation is from Cole, *The Whig Party in the South,* 69.

in almost the same proportions as the lower economic electoral class.[74] Grady McWhiney, in an analysis of Whig and Democrat leaders in Alabama, discovered them to be remarkably alike in economic and social status. He acknowledged that "in the state as a whole it may have indeed been true that more large planters were Whigs than Democrats," but he maintained that the "Whigs were no more exclusively the 'silk stocking' party in Alabama than the Democracy was exclusively the party of the 'common man.' " [75] William H. Adams, noting that in Louisiana "leaders in both parties were seemingly equal in wealth and education," also found it difficult to believe that the Whig party in that state was a class party.[76]

Other scholars have come to very different conclusions. Paul Murray, in his critical study of the Georgia Whigs, concluded that the basic weakness of the earlier economic interpretation of antebellum southern politics was its failure to account for the "farmers, preachers, overseers, 'patty-rollers,' and other hangers-on to the slave system" who were often allied with the large planters in politics.[77] Herbert J. Doherty, though conceding that "Whigs and Democrats in Florida both appealed to and drew their strength from the all-pervading middle class," designated the Whigs as "primarily the party of the rich, earlier settled, plantation areas of Middle Florida, while the Democrats were primarily the party of the new, frontier, small-farmer regions of East and South Florida." Doherty protested against the consensus historians whose writings gave the impression "that there was or is no difference between political parties except that one is in and one is out." He wrote that "though the differences may often be differences of degree and may often appear to be slight, generally the active and influential interest groups in opposing parties have clear-cut and often sharply conflicting desires." Doherty's conclusions derived from his examination of Florida politics suggested that Sellers' generalizations regarding southern Whig-

74 McCormick, "Suffrage Classes and Party Alignments: A Study in Voter Behavior," *Mississippi Valley Historical Review*, XLVI (December, 1959), 397–410.

75 McWhiney, "Were the Whigs a Class Party in Alabama?" *Journal of Southern History*, XXIII (November, 1957), 510–22. A more recent study has concluded that "the traditional view of Whiggery may have considerable validity in the hill section but not in the Black Belt of Alabama." Thomas B. Alexander, Kit C. Carter, Jack R. Lister, Jerry C. Oldshue, and Winfred G. Sandlin, "Who Were the Alabama Whigs?" *Alabama Review*, XVI (January, 1963), 5–19. See also Carlton Luther Jackson, "A History of the Whig Party in Alabama, 1828–1860" (Ph.D. dissertation, University of Georgia, 1962).

76 Adams, "The Louisiana Whig Party" (Ph.D. dissertation, Louisiana State University, 1960).

77 Murray, *The Whig Party in Georgia, 1825–1853*, p. 177.

gery might require further examination. Whereas Sellers contended that the southern business class exerted extraordinary influence upon the planters, Doherty attributed the Democratic leanings of certain commercial counties partly to the influence of the strongly Democratic region in Georgia which they served.[78] Furthermore recent studies concerning the divided mind of business interests in other periods of American history indicate that Sellers may have attributed to southern commercial leaders of the Jacksonian era a greater degree of unanimity on political issues than they actually possessed.[79]

Many aspects of southern politics during the Jacksonian era remain to be explored. For example, we need a more thorough critical examination of politics in South Carolina and Kentucky, where the towering figures of Calhoun and Clay have monopolized the attention of scholars, and in Virginia, whose historians have been primarily interested in epochs during which the Old Dominion played a more dramatic part in the nation's history. As Charles G. Sellers has pointed out, there is also a lack of studies relating to banking and the urban business class in the South.[80] Milton S. Heath's investigation of "constructive liberalism" in Georgia indicates that further inquiries should be made into the role of the state government in the economic development of other southern states, particularly studies that relate the political and economic trends of the time.[81]

If, as Edward H. Carr has stated, history is a "continuous process of interaction between the historians and the facts," the behavioral scientists can offer the students of history valuable insights, illuminating concepts, and new methodological techniques to assist them in the "unending dialogue between the present and the past." [82] Richard Hofstadter maintained in 1956 that "some of the discoveries made by modern social research about current mass political behavior and political influence will revise some of the historian's assumptions about political

78 Doherty, *The Whigs of Florida* (Gainesville, 1959), Chap. 5.

79 See, for example, Robert H. Wiebe, "Business Disunity and the Progressive Movement, 1901–1914," *Mississippi Valley Historical Review*, XLIV (March, 1958), 664–85; Stanley Coben, "Northeastern Business and Radical Reconstruction: A Re-examination," *Mississippi Valley Historical Review*, XLVI (June, 1959), 67–90; Forrest McDonald, *We The People; The Economic Origins of the Constitution* (Chicago, 1958) ; Robert P. Sharkey, *Money, Class and Party; An Economic Study of Civil War and Reconstruction* (Baltimore, 1959).

80 Sellers, "Who Were the Southern Whigs?" 341–43.

81 Heath, *Constructive Liberalism; The Role of the State in Economic Development in Georgia to 1860* (Cambridge, 1954).

82 Carr, *What Is History?* (New York, 1962), 35.

behavior in the past." [83] Lee Benson later demonstrated the potentialities of utilizing such discoveries in his painstaking inquiry into New York politics during the Jacksonian era, or—as he prefers to call it—"the Age of Egalitarianism." [84]

Students of Jacksonian politics in the South should certainly consider the investigations by social psychologists of such influences upon political behavior as, to mention only a few, reference groups, cross pressures, and the failure of most voters to make political decisions on ideological grounds. Although the behaviorists have been less successful in revealing the connection between voting decisions and the actual implementation of political programs, they can aid the historian materially by acquainting him with the complexity of the influences that bear upon the political process. If the realization of these widely diverse considerations makes more laborious the historian's compilation of data and more hazardous his task of generalization, he is at least spared the temptation to offer overly simple interpretations. Paradoxically, some of the hypotheses advanced by the social scientists indicate that perhaps some of the older historians not now in favor might have been closer to the truth than was once believed. Robert E. Lane's conclusion that Americans have usually preferred political divisions along regional rather than class lines because "sectional conflict does not raise such questions of neighbor against neighbor" is suggestive that some recent historians may have disparaged too much Frederick Jackson Turner's approach to state and national politics.[85]

There are hazards as well as benefits to be derived by historians from a study of the concepts and techniques of the social scientists. Because the laboratory of the behaviorists has necessarily been the political setting of contemporary America, there is the danger that in applying their tentative findings to previous eras the historian's representation of an earlier age might be less a faithful record than an illusory projection of the present into the past. Perhaps there is a connection between the tendency of recent historians to de-emphasize class conflict in the nation's past and the surveys of American voting by the University of Michigan Survey Research Center which reveal that class polarization in the United States has diminished appreciably in the past twenty

83 Hofstadter, "History and the Social Sciences," in Fritz Stern (ed.), *The Varieties of History, from Voltaire to the Present* (New York, 1956), 364.
84 Benson, *The Concept of Jacksonian Democracy: New York as a Test Case* (Princeton, 1961).
85 Lane, *Political Life; Why People Get Involved in Politics* (Glencoe, 1959), 24.

years.[86] Furthermore, social psychologists have devoted so much study to the considerations that modify the political effect of socio-economic class that they have sometimes given the impression that income and occupational status are not very consequential political determinants. In 1960, however, Seymour M. Lipset, the political sociologist, re-affirmed the view that there is now and has generally been an important relationship between class and political affiliation in American society.[87]

Intellectual humility is the most valuable quality in the historian who seeks to understand southern political behavior during the Jacksonian period. He owes a debt of gratitude to those scholars who have blazed the trail before him. He is usually more aware of the effect of the social and political environment of earlier historians upon their interpretation than he is of similar influences upon his own. He should realize that no historical interpretation is final and that some of them, like yesterday's fashions, are discarded only to return in an altered form at a later date. He may be impressed by the degree of sophistication displayed by his own generation of historians, but it is doubtful that the followers of Clio have advanced as remarkably as scholars in some other disciplines. The social scientists can suggest new questions for him to ponder in his study of the past, but the historian will have to discover the answers for himself. The role of the South in the Age of Jackson remains for him a challenging and fruitful field of inquiry.

86 See Angus Campbell, Philip E. Converse, Warren E. Miller, and Donald E. Stokes, *The American Voter* (New York, 1960), Chap. 13.
87 Lipset, *Political Man; The Social Bases of Politics* (New York, 1960), Chap. 9.

VI

Plantation and Farm:
The Agricultural South

James C. Bonner

JOHN BACH McMASTER in the last quarter of the nineteenth century departed from the custom of his predecessors when he refused to confine historical writing to the great currents of political change. A disciple of Thomas B. Macaulay, he attempted a broader and more faithful interpretation of America's past by a consideration of its social and economic aspects.[1] This nonpolitical historical writing was the precursor of agricultural history, one of the earlier areas of specialization.

Interest in this subject began in the United States Department of Agriculture as early as 1862, when bits of agricultural history were included in its annual reports.[2] But for more than half a century after-

1 Theodore Clark Smith, "The Writing of American History from 1884 to 1934," *American Historical Review*, XI (April, 1933), 439-50.
2 Everett E. Edwards, "Agricultural History and the Department of Agriculture," *Agricultural History*, XVI (July, 1942), 129-36.

wards, the subject received only incidental attention in the publications of that department. Sound scholarly interest in the history of agriculture in the United States began at the University of Wisconsin where, in 1893, Frederick Jackson Turner developed his essay on the significance of the frontier. At Wisconsin and later at Harvard, Turner introduced research in agricultural history to many of his students, a number of whom were Southerners. These in turn introduced the subject to their own students.[3]

Lewis Cecil Gray began his monumental *History of Agriculture in the Southern United States to 1860* soon after commencing graduate study at Wisconsin in 1908.[4] Eleven years later, after he had become chief of the Division of Land Economics in the United States Department of Agriculture, he completed this work. In the meantime, however, printed works on the plantation had appeared, and these caused him to rework his original materials.[5] When this task was completed in 1933, the entire work had consumed twenty-five years. It became and has remained one of the outstanding contributions to the study of agricultural economics and techniques in the Old South, as well as to the social history of the era.

General historical scholarship dealing specifically with the southern region received its initial impetus at Johns Hopkins University in the 1890's, under the leadership of Herbert Baxter Adams and James G. Ballagh. The latter organized a course in southern history there in 1896. George Petrie, an Adams student, began teaching at Alabama Polytechnic Institute in the 1880's. Among the undergraduate students who later

3 *Ibid.*, 128.

4 Gray, *History of Agriculture in the Southern United States* (2 vols.; Washington, 1933). It was reprinted in 1941 in New York.

5 Henry C. Taylor, "L. C. Gray, Agricultural Historian and Land Economist," *Agricultural History,* XXVI (October, 1952), 165. Some of the more significant works on southern agriculture which appeared before 1919 are Matthew B. Hammond, "The Cotton Industry; An Essay in American Economic History," American Economic Association *Publications,* new series, I (New York, 1897); J. R. Commons, Ulrich B. Phillips, *et al.* (eds.), *A Documentary History of American Industrial Society* (10 vols.; Cleveland, 1910–1911); Clarence P. Gould, *The Land System in Maryland, 1720–1765* (Baltimore, 1915); Ulrich B. Phillips, *American Negro Slavery: A Survey of the Supply, Employment and Control of Negro Labor as Determined by the Plantation Regime* (New York, 1918); U. B. Phillips, *A History of Transportation in the Eastern Cotton Belt to 1860* (New York, 1908); Alfred H. Stone, "The Cotton Factorage System of the Southern States," *American Historical Review,* XX (April, 1915), 557–65; James L. Watkins, *King Cotton; A Historical and Statistical Review, 1790–1908* (New York, 1908); Thomas J. Wertenbaker, *Patrician and Plebeian in Virginia* (Charlottesville, 1910); Henry G. Ellis, "Edmund Ruffin: His Life and Times," *John P. Branch Historical Papers of Randolph-Macon College,* III (Ashland, 1910).

came under his tutelage were Walter Lynwood Fleming, Frank Lawrence Owsley, and Herman Clarence Nixon. Near the turn of the century another Hopkins man, John Spencer Bassett, was writing some of the earliest monographs on slavery. These alluded only in general terms to cotton plantations and to rice and tobacco production.

Professor William Archibald Dunning of Columbia University attracted as graduate students such early scholars as William Kenneth Boyd, Walter L. Fleming, Ulrich Bonnell Phillips, Benjamin Burks Kendrick, Charles Ramsdell, Thomas Staples, Mildred Thompson, and J. G. de Roulhac Hamilton.[6] To this older generation of southern scholars also belongs William E. Dodd, who was something of a maverick in any generic classification of historians. Born in North Carolina, educated at a technical school and abroad, he began to attract attention as a historian of the South after he became a professor of history at the University of Chicago in 1908. His writings, notably *The Cotton Kingdom,*[7] exercised great influence in the 1920's, but this influence waned considerably with the subsequent appearance of more definitive scholarship.

Of these writers, it was Phillips who became the first historian of the southern plantation and its related institutions. Brought up in the Georgia cotton belt, at LaGrange and at Milledgeville, he was educated at the University of Georgia before entering Columbia to study under Dunning. Later he came into close contact with Turner at Wisconsin. Later still, at Tulane, Michigan, and Yale, he offered graduate courses on the antebellum South while pursuing research in this field. He was the first to use effectively such essential documents as plantation records, letters, journals, diaries, and account books, all of which gave to his studies a realistic social and economic content. Phillips, having demonstrated in *Life and Labor in the Old South* [8] both a captivating style and an effective use of hitherto untapped sources, influenced dozens of younger scholars in the next three decades. They followed his pattern and filled in many details.

Phillips was a scholar who hated to draw conclusions, claiming that the more research he did the less willing he was to generalize. The central theme of southern history, which he stated in 1928, is his most notable generalization. This unifying theme, he said, was the determination of the white folk that the region should remain "a white man's coun-

6 Wendell H. Stephenson, "A Half Century of Southern Historical Scholarship," *Journal of Southern History,* XI (February, 1945), 3–4.
7 Dodd, *The Cotton Kingdom: A Chronicle of the Old South* (New Haven, 1921).
8 Phillips, *Life and Labor in the Old South* (Boston, 1931).

try." A conscious determination to maintain white supremacy, he continued, whether professed by political demagogues or by dignified gentlemen, is the cardinal test of a Southerner and the central theme of the section's history.[9]

This theme appears to have been stated in its essential form as early as 1903 by Senator John Sharp Williams of Mississippi and also by William Garrott Brown of Alabama. William E. Dodd recognized one of its essential characteristics when he noted the intense fear which poor whites had of free Negroes and he explained that the ownership of slaves did not divide Southerners until after the outbreak of the Civil War, when Confederate conscription laws exempted certain slaveowners.[10]

The failure of slaveownership to divide Southerners before the Civil War has been demonstrated by practically all subsequent writers in southern history. Roger W. Shugg, for example, working backward from Populism in the 1890's, found this movement to be a class struggle without any roots other than the economic depression of that period.[11] The rich planters did not excite resentment in the less fortunate majority around them; consequently the latter did not use their franchise to strike down or disrupt the economy of their more affluent neighbors.[12] Wilbur J. Cash, in *The Mind of the South,* has aptly described slavery and the plantation as introducing a "vastly ego-warming and ego-expanding distinction between the white man and the black." [13] Nearly all contemporary observers of poor whites recognized the strength and the depth of their attachment to slavery—a kind of group consciousness based upon instinctive self-interest.

If the presence of the Negro and the desire of the white man to keep him subjugated formed the central theme of southern history, this theme came into existence because of the plantation. This institution in turn

9 Phillips, "The Central Theme of Southern History," *American Historical Review,* XXXIV (October, 1928), 30–43.

10 Charles S. Sydnor, "The Southern Experiment in Writing Social History," *Journal of Southern History,* XI (November, 1945), 455–68; Wendell H. Stephenson, "William Garrott Brown: Literary Historian and Essayist," *Journal of Southern History,* XII (August, 1946), 313–44; Dodd, "The Plantation and Farm Systems in Southern Agriculture," in Julian A. C. Chandler *et al.* (eds.), *The South in the Building of the Nation* (13 vols.; Richmond 1909), V, 77–79.

11 Roger W. Shugg, *Origins of Class Struggle in Louisiana: A Social History of White Farmers and Laborers During Slavery and After, 1840–1875* (Baton Rouge, 1939), i–ix.

12 *Ibid.,* 28.

13 Wilbur J. Cash, *The Mind of the South* (New York, 1941), 38.

rested on staple crops, the principal factor in the success of which was climate.[14] Thus, according to Phillips, the delineation of the South's history should begin with a consideration of the region's climate.

Other historians have minimized climate as a factor in making the South a distinctive community. The most recent of these is William A. Foran, who has suggested that it was a "climate of opinion" rather than climate of weather which was a deterministic absolute.[15] Avery O. Craven, in *Edmund Ruffin, Southerner* (New York, 1932), saw two non-climatic factors which had contributed to the making of a unique South. These were the Old World ideal of a country gentleman and the presence of Negroes in large numbers. The former, transplanted from England, flourished naturally in the South simply because that region was overwhelmingly agricultural.[16] Craven in 1942 emphasized that by far the greater proportion of the South's white population was middle-class yeomen, and that despite the section's diversity there were *three* forces which worked for southern nationalism. The added factor was "a climate in part more mellow than other sections enjoyed." [17]

The most vocal dissenter from the climatic theory of the plantation is Edgar T. Thompson, a sociologist at Duke University. His most serious objection to this theory was its failure to account for the transition from plantation to farm, or vice versa, in an area where the climatic factor remains constant. Plantations are largely concentrated in the tropics, says Thompson, not because of climate but because tropical regions constitute a highly important and accessible trade and agricultural frontier. He emphasized the fact that the plantation is always an institution of the frontier. The contrast between farm and plantation is an aspect of the difference between peasant agriculture and estate agriculture throughout the world generally. In many countries these represent distinct and competing systems of agricultural production within the same climatic area. Indeed, the plantation and farm had existed side by side in the South since the days of colonial settlement. Instead of explaining the plantation through climate, Thompson claims that it is

14 Phillips, *Life and Labor in the Old South*, 1.

15 Foran, "Southern Legend: Climate or Climate of Opinion," South Carolina Historical Association, *Proceedings, 1956* (1956), 6–22.

16 Craven, *The Repressible Conflict, 1830–1861* (Baton Rouge, 1939), 14–23. See also Francis B. Simkins, "The Everlasting South," *Journal of Southern History*, XIII (August, 1947), 309.

17 Craven, *The Coming of the Civil War* (New York, 1942), 33.

a political institution to be accounted for like other political institutions based upon the principle of authority.[18] In describing plantation agriculture as "military agriculture," Thompson has suggested one explanation of the martial spirit which has been associated not only with the South's history but also with that of such agrarian civilizations as those of Assyria, Sparta, and Rome. While Thompson himself has not extended the idea of military agriculture to connect it emphatically with the military tradition, this relationship has been considered briefly but unsatisfactorily by one or two recent writers.[19]

The plantation epoch of the ancient Mediterranean world was based upon oil and wine. The next epoch appeared with the colonization of the New World in the development of an export trade in tobacco, rice, and cotton. Finally, the modern system based on rubber, tea, and coffee is found largely around the borders of the Indian Ocean and on certain islands of the Pacific. These three plantation epochs, involving three distinct areas, should provide a basis for a highly rewarding comparative study by students of southern history. A complete understanding of the plantation as an institution and of the societies based upon it must therefore await expansion of research into other areas than the American South and other periods than the eighteenth and nineteenth centuries.

While recognizing the overwhelming superiority in numbers of farms and farmers over plantations and planters, none of the writers before the 1930's accorded the former the attention which either their numbers or their importance deserved. Receiving proportionately much more attention, but perhaps as little understood, was the poor-white element which occupied the lowest rung of the white man's society. Gray presented a somewhat clearer picture of the middle class and poor whites than did either Dodd or Phillips, but he touched only a specialized phase of the problem. The common people had few apologists, and they left fewer records than the more articulate plantation masters. The poor whites often were illiterate and could be seen only through the eyes of some disdainful contemporary. Rupert Vance explains the paucity of historical material about these two groups by suggesting that few of

18 Thompson, "The Climatic Theory of the Plantation," *Agricultural History,* XV (January, 1941), 49, and "Purpose and Tradition in Southern Rural Society," *Social Forces,* XXV (March, 1947), 272.

19 Robert D. Meade, "The Military Spirit of the South," *Current History,* XXX (April, 1929), 55; James C. Bonner, "The Historical Basis of Southern Military Tradition," *Georgia Review,* IX (Spring, 1955), 3–14; John Hope Franklin, *The Militant South, 1800–1861* (Cambridge, 1956).

their survivors have wanted to preserve proof of descent either from poor white or yeoman farmer.[20]

All leading historians who wrote before 1930 recognized that the planter minority exercised an influence in southern society incompatible with its number, but none made a serious effort to assemble and study materials which would reveal the life of the majority group. Hence the role of the common folk was left unresolved in Dodd's works and was inadequately treated by Phillips and Gray. The latter held that there was a high degree of segregation of planter and yeoman farmer in the South, and that planters held the better lands. As the plantation system expanded, slaveholders tended to buy up the land of their less affluent neighbors with particular regard for their more productive fields. These two writers attributed the origin of the plantation system largely to the territorial expansion of slaveholders at the expense of small farmers.[21] Dodd emphasized this tendency also, but he limited the phenomenon to the 1850's, explaining it by reference to the booming cost of Negro slaves which soared out of proportion to the price received for cotton during that decade. This situation, claimed Dodd, made it impossible for many to enter the planting class.[22]

The first serious challenge to the Phillips-Gray-Dodd thesis came from Frank L. Owsley and his students at Vanderbilt University. As early as 1905 Gustavus W. Dyer, instructor in economics and sociology at Vanderbilt, published a little volume entitled *Democracy in the South before the Civil War* which foreshadowed the later studies of Owsley and his students at the same institution. Dyer referred briefly to the printed census reports to show that no more than a third of the farmers in the South owned any slaves at all, and that the great mass of non-slaveholders did not deserve the appellation "poor white." Owsley's students used local tax records, wills, and trial records in addition to exploring intensively for the first time the voluminous manuscript census data of the last three decades before the Civil War. Phillips had made abbreviated use of the census records as early as 1906, but the Vanderbilt historians were the first to use them exhaustively.[23] Departing some-

20 See Vance's Review of Frank L. Owsley, *Plain Folk of the Old South* (Baton Rouge, 1950) in *Journal of Southern History*, XVI (November, 1950), 545–47.

21 Ulrich B. Phillips, "The Origin and Growth of the Southern Black Belts," *American Historical Review*, XI (July, 1906), 799–800; L. C. Gray, *History of Agriculture in the Southern United States*, II, 474.

22 Dodd, "The Plantation and Farm System in Southern Agriculture," 77–79.

23 For a description of these records and Owsley's technique for their use, see Frank L. and Harriet C. Owsley, "The Economic Basis of Society in the Late Ante-Bellum South," *Journal of Southern History*, VI (January, 1940), 24–26;

what from the orthodox position, Owsley questioned seriously the competency of travelers and other critics who wrote during the antislavery crusade. On the other hand, while some might question the accuracy of individual entries in the drab and prosaic census returns, and discover numerous omissions, none could successfully challenge the disinterestedness of census enumerators.

These researchers applied the *coup de grâce* to the idea of a completely aristocratic society, the oldest and most firmly intrenched legend in the literature of the Old South. Beginning in the 1830's with novels about plantation society by Beverly Tucker, William Alexander Carruthers and John P. Kennedy, this type of writing was continued by John Esten Cooke and others.[24] In these novels the great planter played the leading role, leaving the yeoman farmer and the poor whites in a shadowy background. The role of the Negro was limited to that of a faithful retainer. At the time that these novels were romanticising the colonial plantation life of the Upper South, the novels of Sir Walter Scott were also becoming popular. Reflecting this influence is the fact that rising cotton planters of the Lower South were naming their plantations after famous Virginian and Scottish country seats. Simultaneously, the abolitionists were contributing to this literary image by portraying a three-class structure of southern society, consisting only of plantation masters, poor whites, and Negroes.

This aristocratic tradition not only set a pattern for the *nouveaux riches* of the cotton belt but also helped to establish an ideal for yeoman farmers. Many of the latter were able to achieve their ambition to become masters of slaves before 1860. This tradition was not lost on the Negro freedman who often was known to take great pride in the escutcheon of the white family to which he had been attached. The literary tenacity of this tradition was manifested more than a century later in Margaret Mitchell's *Gone With the Wind*,[25] yet Augustus Baldwin Longstreet's *Georgia Scenes* exposed the invalidity of this tradition a full century before the appearance of Miss Mitchell's novel.[26] Later, such writers

---

Owsley and Owsley, "The Economic Structure of Rural Tennessee, 1850–1860," *Journal of Southern History*, VIII (May, 1942), 16. For another criticism of U. B. Phillips' thesis see Richard Hofstadter, "U. B. Phillips and the Plantation Legend," *Journal of Negro History*, XXIX (April, 1944), 109–24.

24 Francis Pendleton Gaines, *The Southern Plantation: A Study in the Development and the Accuracy of a Tradition* (New York, 1925), 18.

25 Clement Eaton, *The Growth of Southern Civilization, 1790–1860* (New York, 1961), 150.

26 Longstreet, *Georgia Scenes, Characters, Incidents, etc.* (New York, 1840). These stories appeared first in small Georgia papers between 1832 and 1835.

as Sherwood Bonner,[27] a Mississippian whom Longfellow admired, and Richard Malcolm Johnston wrote stories which gave faithful portrayals of the slaveless farmer.[28]

Among the first of the trained historians to draw attention to the inaccuracy of the aristocratic tradition of literature, stage, and song was John Spencer Bassett who, in 1899,[29] exploded the idea of a three-class feudal society in the Old South. A little later William Garrott Brown criticized the rhetorical tendency of the older historians to contrast Virginia Cavaliers with New England Puritans.[30] Thomas J. Wertenbaker made a frontal attack on the aristocratic legend with his realistic *Patrician and Plebian in Virginia,* published in Charlottesville in 1910. Fourteen years later, Francis Pendleton Gaines also compared the traditional concept with historical realities. He admitted, however, that the plantation ideal was dominant and widespread in southern life—the *ne plus ultra* of the section's society.[31]

The Owsley group, which came into prominence during the "Age of Franklin Roosevelt," held that the yeomanry represented a true middle class and enjoyed a high degree of prosperity in the last decade before the Civil War.[32] Owsley stated that in comparison with the situation in most advanced countries at that time, the southern white folk were one of the most literate major groups in the entire world.[33] In a provocative paper entitled "The Fundamental Causes of the Civil War: Egocentric Sectionalism," [34] the Vanderbilt professor used his thesis to argue that the Civil War was not a struggle on the part of the South to destroy

27 Bonner, *Like Unto Like* (New York, 1878), 150.

28 Johnston, *Dukesboro Tales* (New York, 1892).

29 Bassett, *Slavery in the State of North Carolina* (Baltimore, 1899).

30 Brown, *The Lower South in American History* (New York, 1903), 6–7.

31 Gaines, *The Southern Plantation,* 27.

32 The New Deal provided an ideal climate in which the Owsley thesis could thrive. In 1909, for example, Julia Flisch had sought to refute the idea that the influence of the common people of the Old South had been a negligible factor in the development of that region's civilization. Her work attracted little attention at that time. Julia Flisch, "The Common People of the Old South," American Historical Association, *Annual Report, 1908* (Washington, 1909), I, 133–42.

33 Owsley, *Plain Folk of the Old South,* 146. For later discussions of the class structure, see for Alabama, Owsley and Owsley, "The Economic Basis of Society in the Late Ante-Bellum South," 24–26; for Tennessee see Blanche Henry Clark, *The Tennessee Yeoman, 1840–1860* (Nashville, 1942); for Louisiana see Harry L. Coles, Jr., "Some Notes on Slave ownership and Land ownership in Louisiana, 1850–1860," *Journal of Southern History,* IX (August, 1943), 381; for Mississippi see Herbert Weaver, *Mississippi Farmers* (Nashville, 1945).

34 Owsley, "The Fundamental Causes of the Civil War: Egocentric Sectionalism," *Journal of Southern History,* VII (February, 1941), 3–18.

free government and personal liberty, nor one on the part of the North to preserve them. He maintained that the exact opposite was closer to historical truth. While the East owned or controlled the nation's means of production in industry and commerce, the slaveholders of the South owned scarcely any of the land outside of a limited area known as the black belt. Actually the basic means of production even in the black belt, as well as in the South as a whole, was well distributed among all classes of the white population. Even 70 percent of the nonslaveholders, he claimed, owned the land which they farmed.

Owsley's position has been both praised and condemned. The sociologist Rupert Vance struck a common note of discord in a brilliant review of Owsley's *Plain Folk of the Old South*. The author, Vance averred, was "much too innocent of the use and resources of modern statistical method" and there was much more to his material than met the eye.[35] The most penetrating criticism of the Owsley school had been made earlier by Fabian Linden, an erstwhile graduate student at the University of North Carolina. None of the Vanderbilt monographs, he said, had provided well-focused definitions of the class to which their generalizations applied, nor had they used adequate samplings. Moreover, the studies did not show what proportion of the general population was represented in each class, nor did they indicate the distribution of property other than land. Since slaveholding figures were not recorded, the proposition that property holdings were well distributed or widely diffused had not been convincingly demonstrated. In challenging the use of land distribution alone as an especially sensitive indicator of economic stratification, Linden cited numerous variables such as location, quality, condition, and crops to which land might be particularly adapted.[36]

Whether one accepts fully the validity of these criticisms or not, it must be admitted that the Vanderbilt group accomplished a minor revolution in historical interpretation. They not only directed attention to the importance of the yeoman farmer, but also made historians aware of the value of the manuscript census records as source material for studying the social and economic history of the Old South. Before the Owsley

35 Review of Owsley's *Plain Folk of the Old South*, by Rupert Vance, in *Journal of Southern History*, XVI (November, 1950), 546.

36 Linden, "Economic Democracy in the Slave South: An Appraisal of Some Recent Views," *Journal of Negro History*, XXXI (April, 1946), 140–89. In his reply to Linden's review of Weaver's *Mississippi Farmers*, Owsley claimed that Linden failed to recognize that the primary object of the author was to analyze land tenure and not to make a study of slavery, and also that the reviewer "damns by the simple process of assertion." *American Historical Review*, LII (July, 1947), 845–49.

group began its researches, historians had relied for statistics on such works as Timothy Pitkins' *Statistical View* (1817–1835), Adam Seybert's *Statistical Annals* (1818), *Niles' Weekly Register* (1811–1849), *Hunt's Merchants' Magazine* (1839–1870), and James D. B. DeBow's *The Industrial Resources of the Southern and Western States* (1852–1853).

The value of the census records for research purposes was brought to the attention of scholars early in the present century by Joseph A. Hill of the census bureau. It was soon after this that Dyer and Phillips made the earliest, though very abbreviated, use of them. Perhaps the best description of these records, together with a discussion of a technique for their use, has been presented by Barnes F. Lathrop of the University of Texas.[37] His *Migrations into East Texas, 1835–1860* focuses attention on the nature of information found in these sources, and his discussion of methodology takes precedence over his actual findings. No student contemplating a scholarly scrutiny of the census records could well ignore Lathrop's discussion.[38]

Detailed census enumerations have so far not been used extensively in a definitive study of the poor whites of the antebellum South. Researchers have found it difficult to categorize that amorphous group of white men which occupied the periphery of agricultural society. Among them were a large number of unskilled laborers, wood-cutters, squatters, hunters, fishermen, and the rising entrepreneurs about whom too little has been learned except through observations of their more literate contemporaries. The poor white tradition has been greatly exaggerated in historical literature as a result of travel accounts by authors seeking journalistic sensationalism. Abolitionist writers tended to classify all nonslaveholding whites as poor, illiterate, and degenerate. Many northern soldiers who wrote of their war experiences south of the Potomac understandably perpetuated this image long after the sixties.

Typical of the comments which created a false picture of the poor whites are those of George Weston who, in 1856, declared that approximately three-fourths of all southern whites were of this group. "Confined to the low wages of agriculture and forced to a companionship

37 See the following works by Barnes F. Lathrop: "History from the Census Returns," *The Southwestern Historical Quarterly,* LI (April, 1948), 293–312; *Migrations into East Texas 1835–1860: A Study From the United States Census* (Austin, 1949).

38 See also Joseph Schafer, "The Wisconsin Domesday Book: A Method of Research for Agricultural Historians," *Agricultural History,* XIV (January, 1940), 23–32.

with slaves," he wrote, "they lived a semi-savage life on the outskirts of civilization sinking deeper and more hopelessly into barbarism with each succeeding generation." [39] Daniel R. Hundley, a native of Alabama, became the first critic of this stereotype. "God help me to present the truth in a form acceptable to the public," he wrote in his diary on October 28, 1856. His *Social Relations in Our Southern States,* published in New York in 1860, presented one of the earliest and most accurate pictures of agricultural classes in the antebellum South. His delineations of gentry, middle class, yeoman, and poor white have been largely sustained by recent historians.[40] Paul H. Buck, who used the categories of slaveholder, yeoman, farmer, artisan, and poor white, described the last group as comprising the slum element of the agricultural South and explained their existence by the absence of industry which would have produced its own type of slum. "Southern society before the Civil War provided no position that the poor white could fill that was not already being satisfactorily filled by others," he wrote. He also described the poor white man as a stranded frontiersman, being separated from the real frontier by a belt of plantations beyond the pine barrens, wherein he most frequently was found.[41] Thus it was that the old frontier of the eighteenth century, moving westward with the advance of the cotton plantation, had simply passed him by.

The poor whites of the Piedmont and lowlands have been adequately distinguished from the slaveless subsistence farmers of the mountains. The latter, as poor and ignorant as any people, have been described generally as brave, enterprising and self-respecting. Horace Kephart's *Our Southern Highlanders,* first published in 1913, is more in the pattern of the old and somewhat unreliable travel account than a collection of scientific observations. He described the lowland poor as descending from English convicts and indentured servants. This was in contrast to the mountain people who he claimed were of Swiss, Palatine German, and Scotch-Irish stock.[42] A. N. J. Den Hollander, writing in 1934, related the characteristics of the lowland poor to their ill health which was caused chiefly by hookworm and malaria. He suggested that the relative disappearance of the poor whites in the twentieth century may be more the result of modern medical discovery than of the dilution of the ethnic

39 Weston, *The Poor Whites of the South* (Washington, 1856), 5.

40 Blanche Henry Clark Weaver, "D. R. Hundley: Subjective Sociologist," *Georgia Review,* X (Summer, 1956), 222–34.

41 Buck, "The Poor Whites of the Ante-Bellum South," *American Historical Review,* XXXI (October, 1925), 41–54.

42 Kephart, *Our Southern Highlanders* (Rev. ed.; New York, 1936), 428–51.

stock from which they might have sprung.[43] Shields McIlwaine has given the most recent appraisal of this group. Combining literary with social history, he made a critical study of the literature dealing with this group, but his study is not definitive.[44] Clement Eaton's brief discussion of the subject in *The Growth of Southern Civilization* probably is as accurate a general account as can be found.[45]

Often as little understood as the poor white was the overseer. Students of the Old South have recognized him as a vital cog in plantation structure, but they have too often based their interpretation of him upon prejudiced accounts by his dissatisfied employer. The overseer was too busy with the details of managing Negroes and operating the plantation or too badly educated to do much writing of a leisurely character. Members of his class seldom answered criticisms, if indeed they often were aware of the real extent of vilifications against them. It was their duty to enforce discipline among the slaves and to see that they performed. Their social position in the community was similar to that of underpaid prison wardens of a later era, or perhaps to traffic policemen in rural southern towns. As a class they were not lovable men but hard and ruthless by necessity. To the leisurely and more articulate groups who observed them, they seemed to be anything but gracious and congenial companions.

As a result of such observations by their contemporaries, overseers have been described by Carl Bridenbaugh as brutal and unscrupulous.[46] Lewis Cecil Gray depicted them as "men with little education, with narrow vision and sympathies; at worst cruel, licentious tyrants . . . and in numerous instances . . . unreliable and dishonest." [47] Ulrich B. Phillips was no more generous when he described them as "crude in manner, barely literate, commonplace in capacity, capable only of ruling slaves by severity in a rule of thumb routine and needing fairly constant oversight by their employers." [48] John Spencer Bassett in 1925 edited approximately two hundred letters of overseers on James K. Polk's

---

43 Den Hollander, "The Tradition of Poor Whites," in W. T. Couch (ed.), *Culture in the South* (Chapel Hill, 1935), 403–31.

44 McIlwaine, *The Southern Poor White: From Lubberland to Tobacco Road* (Norman, 1939).

45 Eaton, *The Growth of Southern Civilization*, 150–76.

46 Bridenbaugh, *Myths and Realities: Societies of the Colonial South* (Baton Rouge, 1952), 63.

47 Gray, *History of Agriculture in the Southern United States*, I, 502, 557.

48 Phillips, *Life and Labor in the Old South*, 310.

plantation in Mississippi.[49] Although severely limited in scope, these
letters showed the overseer's life and character from many angles, and
this work remained the only reliable treatment of the subject for almost
four decades. Until 1961 only two or three short papers had dealt further with the subject. At this late date William K. Scarborough completed an extensive study of the plantation overseer.[50]

Scarborough's work, which shows painstaking research, covers the
period from colonial times to the Civil War. It goes far toward revising
the traditional concept of the man who often carried both a gun and a
whip. Using census records extensively, he found a total of 26,000 overseers in seven southern states in 1860, and less than 38,000 in the entire
country. Among those in the Lower South were a large number of
transients generally inexperienced and incompetent, who apparently
provided the stereotyped image for the entire group. Scarborough agrees
with Owsley that only an insignificant number of overseers were illiterate.[51] The most talented and capable overseers were found in the rice
and sugar regions, where often they belonged to the category of stewards
and received relatively high compensation for their services. Elsewhere
the pay was small, but fringe benefits were high.[52]

No discussion of the historiography of the plantation and farm would
be complete without a consideration of the Turner frontier thesis. Turner
in 1893 presented a method of interpreting American history which
thereafter could not be ignored in a study of the southern plantation.[53]
While Fulmer Mood has traced the frontier concept somewhat from
census analyzers and statisticians, recent investigation indicates that the
Turner idea was also suggested before 1890 by European writers, nota-

49 Bassett (ed.), *The Plantation Overseer as Revealed in His Letters* (Northamp-
ton, 1925).

50 Scarborough, "The Southern Plantation Overseer" (Ph.D. dissertation, University of North Carolina, 1961). A revision of this dissertation is scheduled for
publication by the Louisiana State University Press in 1966.

51 Owsley, *Plain Folk of the Old South*, 146.

52 U. B. Phillips observed that the crop-share system of compensation for the
overseer's work was replaced in the nineteenth century by the payment of fixed
wages in order "to diminish the inducement for over-driving." *American Negro
Slavery*, 281. However, scaling salaries according to the crop called forth the same
evil. Also the crop-share system was never completely abandoned.

53 Mood, "The Historiographic Setting of Turner's Frontier Essay," *Agricultural
History*, XVII (July, 1943), 153; James C. Malin, "Space and History: Reflections
on the Closed Space Doctrines of Turner and MacKinder . . . ," *Agricultural
History*, XVIII (April, 1944), 65.

bly the Italian economist, Achille Loria.[54] He urged the study of American colonial life as an aid to understanding the stages of European development, affirming that colonial settlement is to the economic scientist what the mountain is to the geologist. Each brings to the surface primitive stratifications. Loria believed that America, which he thought of as itself having no history, would "reveal luminously the course of universal history." A general application of the Turner thesis has been made by Paul L. MacKendrick, a classical scholar, who believed it to be of great value in understanding the expansion of Roman agriculture. Donald W. Treadgold, a student of Russian history and a number of Russian historians, notably V. O. Kliuchevskii and Lobanov-Rostovsky, have perceived the thesis to be suitable both to the Siberian and Chinese frontiers. On the other hand, the Mexican historian, Silvio Zavala, does not agree with this thesis when applied to Hispanic frontiers, particularly to the common frontiers of Mexico and the United States.[55]

At the time that the Turner thesis was stated, in 1893, the general narrative historian was being supplanted by the specialist who already was beginning to produce monographs. Herbert B. Adams of Johns Hopkins, importing the German seminar methods, stimulated a large number of these, while others soon were produced at Columbia, Harvard, and Chicago. Turner, who had received his degree at Hopkins, was not satisfied with Adams' generic approach to historical research, so far as social institutions were concerned. Instead of stressing continuity and the transit of European culture across the Atlantic, Turner, like so many young students of all periods, was looking for meaning and significance. He sought a historical summit from which to view American history. An environmentalist, he stressed differences rather than continuing similarities. His frontier hypothesis was something of an agricultural interpretation of American history at a time when the country was fast entering an urban-industrial age.[56] His writing was not in the form of a monograph but rather a short essay representing the results of historical thinking and synthesis springing from a fertile and resourceful mind.

Turner made a profound contribution to scholarly interest in agricul-

54 Lee Benson, "Achille Loria's Influence on American Economic Thought," *Agricultural History*, XXIV (October, 1950), 182. See also Benson, *Turner and Beard: American Historical Writing Reconsidered* (Glenco, Illinois, 1960).

55 Donald W. Treadgold, "Russian Expansion in the Light of Turner's Study of the American Frontier," *Agricultural History*, XXVI (October, 1952), 147; Walker D. Wyman and Clifton B. Krocher (eds.), *The Frontier in Perspective* (Madison, 1957).

56 Malin, "Space and History," 65.

tural history and incidentally to the history of the southern plantation and farm. This interest can be traced from or to Turner through at least three Southerners who were or who later became professional historians. For over thirty years the Wisconsin professor was a friend and colleague of Ulrich B. Phillips, and it was Turner who invited the Georgian to teach southern history at Madison. Phillips later described Turner's ability to stimulate young scholars in exactly the same manner in which Phillips' students later described their own master. Phillips spoke of Turner's inspiration as "a ripple which, though it must lessen in the lapse of time and the spread of space, never quite reaches an end," [57] and he did not fail to cite the frontier thesis in his earliest writings.[58] On his part, Turner claimed that through conversation with Woodrow Wilson, also a Hopkins graduate, his own ideas and ambitions had broadened, and that Wilson's lectures expounding politics in a larger sense had made a profound impression upon him. Through Wilson he had come to see the larger meaning of sectionalism and to acquire new ideas of the South and an awareness that its history possessed some dynamic factors.[59]

One of the most influential of Turner's students is Avery O. Craven. Although he registered a minor disagreement with his master in 1941,[60] he has shown in numerous writings that Turner's approach has a considerably wider application to the antebellum South than has usually been supposed. Craven has suggested that the South's early frontier, with its free range cattle industry possessing such accoutrements as rustling, fighting, and drinking, possessed a distinctly western flavor.[61] Those who have published works on the trans-Mississippi West have neglected to explore the roots of their story in the expanding and westward-moving plantation. Craven has noted this in his review of Dan Elbert Clark's *The West in American History*, in which he voiced sharp disappointment with that author's handling of the Southwest during the Middle period. "Some day it will be understood," he wrote, "that the expansion of the plantation system, slavery and all things Southern into a wilderness is just as much a Western story with its own unique

57 Phillips, "The Traits and Contributions of Frederick Jackson Turner," *Agricultural History*, XIX (January, 1945), 21.

58 Phillips, *A History of Transportation*, 48.

59 Wendell Stephenson, "The Influence of Woodrow Wilson on Frederick Jackson Turner," *Agricultural History*, XIX (October, 1945), 249.

60 Craven, *Democracy in American Life* (Chicago, 1941), 38–67.

61 A. O. Craven, "The Turner Thesis and the South," *Journal of Southern History*, V (August, 1939), 303. See also James C. Bonner, "The Open Range Livestock Industry in Colonial Georgia," *Georgia Review*, XVII (Spring, 1963), 85–92.

results on men and institutions as that of farmers and free laborers to
the Northwest." [62] Edward Everett Dale, in *The Range Cattle Industry*,[63] gave recognition to the Turner thesis when he wrote that the range
cattle industry of the Great Plains was a phase of the development of
the whole American wilderness, characterized by the appearance of successive stages of development in which the herder and pioneer farmer
followed one another in the same region in more or less rapid succession,
depending upon topography and climate. Like Clark, however, he failed
to give adequate attention to the early cattle range developments of the
Southeast. Paul C. Henlein, in *The Cattle Kingdom of the Ohio Valley,
1782–1860,* was equally negligent when he suggested that the cattle industry of Texas was an extension of the Ohio Valley kingdom.[64] Others
have contended that the Texans took over the open-range industry from
the Spaniards to the south and transmitted it with modifications to the
Great Plains and the Rocky Mountain region. On the other hand, Joseph
Schafer, in *The Social History of American Agriculture,* shows clearly
that the trans-Mississippi cattle business had its forerunner in the
southern Piedmont in the period of the Revolution.[65] Thus the Virginia
cowboy might well have been the one described by Owen Wister in the
first western novel which, significantly, is entitled *The Virginian.*

The westward-moving plantation system, according to Walter Prescott
Webb, came to a halt at approximately the hundredth meridian where
Webb pictured an "institutional fault." Every institution which was
carried west of this point was either broken, remade, or else greatly
altered. East of this meridian, civilization had stood on the tripod of
water, land, and timber. Westward there was but one leg to stand on,
land. Webb's key word was contrast, and he insisted that the West could
not be understood as a mere extension of the East.[66] Research in the
history of the South has yet to produce a definitive study of this region's
early range-cattle industry which might help to sustain or to modify
Webb's theory. A few short articles have suggested that there is much
more to this subject than is generally known.

62 For Craven's review of Dan Elbert Clark, *The West in American History*
(New York, 1937), see *American Historical Review,* XLIII (January, 1938), 401.
63 Dale, *The Range Cattle Industry* (Norman, 1930).
64 Henlein, *The Cattle Kingdom of the Ohio Valley, 1782–1860* (Lexington, 1959).
65 Schafer, *The Social History of American Agriculture* (New York, 1936).
66 Webb, *The Great Plains* (Boston, 1931), 507–10. Henry C. Allen's *Bush and
Backwoods* (East Lansing, 1959) is a comparison of the frontier in Australia to
that in the United States. It illustrates a type of comparative study which adds a
new dimension to knowledge of the frontier.

A famous sentence in Turner's thesis described westward migration. "Stand at the Cumberland Gap," he wrote, "and watch the procession of civilization, marching single file—the buffalo following the trail to the salt springs, the Indians, the fur trader and hunter, the cattle raiser, the pioneer farmer—and the frontier has passed by." Clarence W. Alvord and Ray Allen Billington have rejected this aspect of Turner's thesis. The former described the migration as more resembling a flood, and he criticized Turner for ignoring the existence of the land speculator who played a major role in the march of civilization.[67] Only since 1930 have historians been fully aware of the omission of the speculator. A few scholars have recognized the potential of this topic,[68] but it has not yet commanded a definitive study.

The most noted studies of this phase of agricultural history have been made by Thomas P. Abernethy. His *Western Lands and the American Revolution* does not present a flattering picture of the fathers of the Republic,[69] some of whom appeared quite willing to sacrifice national interests for protection of their land claims. The works of this author and those of Paul W. Gates,[70] both of whom are antagonists of the frontier thesis, parade the twin roles of the land speculator and the plantation aristocrat as evidence that the frontier was not as democratic as Turner had described it. Abernethy's story does not go beyond the

67 Gene M. Gressley, "The Turner Thesis—A Problem in Historiography," *Agricultural History*, XXXII (October, 1958), 227; Fulmer Mood, "The Concept of the Frontier," *Agricultural History*, XIX (January, 1945), 24–30.

68 These works include Ray Allen Billington, "The Origin of the Land Speculator as a Frontier Type," *Agricultural History*, XIX (October, 1945), 204; Robert S. Cotterill, "A Chapter of Panton, Leslie and Company," *Journal of Southern History*, X (August, 1944), 275; Frank L. Owsley, "The Pattern of Migration and Settlement on the Southern Frontier," *Journal of Southern History*, X (May, 1945), 47; Thomas P. Abernethy, *Western Lands and the American Revolution* (New York, 1937); Arthur P. Whitaker, "The Muscle Shoals Speculation, 1783–1789," *Mississippi Valley Historical Review*, XXIII (January, 1936), 27–48; J. C. Ballagh, *Southern Economic History: Tariff and Public Land*, in American Historical Association *Reports, 1898*, 221–63; J. O. Callahan, "The War Veteran and the Public Lands," *Agricultural History*, XXVIII (October, 1954), 163–68; Elgin Williams, *The Animating Pursuits of Speculation: Land Traffic in the Annexation of Texas* (New York, 1949).

69 Abernethy, *Western Lands and the American Revolution* (New York, 1937). See also Thomas P. Abernethy, *From Frontier to Plantation in Tennessee; A Study in Frontier Democracy* (Chapel Hill, 1932), *Three Virginia Frontiers* (Baton Rouge, 1940), and "Democracy on the Southern Frontier," *Journal of Southern History*, IV (February, 1938), 3–13; Paul W. Gates, "Research in the History of American Land Tenure," *Agricultural History*, XXVIII (July, 1954), 121–26.

70 See for example Paul W. Gates, "The Homestead Law in an Incongruous Land System," *American Historical Review*, XLI (July, 1936), 652–81.

Confederation period. It should be carried much beyond this limit to make the full significance clear. We do not yet know the full effect of the speculator upon the settlement process, whether it hastened or retarded the advance of the frontier.

There are few problems more vital to the life of the people than those relating to the distribution, tenure, and use of land. As early as 1910 Payson J. Treat made a study of public land policies for the period 1785 to 1820,[71] and Benjamin H. Hibbard and others later wrote additional segments of this story.[72] These works deal only incidentally with the situation in the South.[73] There were at least ten different survey systems employed on the original Georgia grant alone, a fact which makes the region between the Savannah and the Mississippi rivers a surveyor's museum. The plats and records of the original distribution of both federal and state lands in the entire southern region are almost complete. These are being increasingly used by lawyers in making abstracts of land titles, an activity which has assumed great importance since World War II with the rising value of southern timber and pulpwood. These abstracts, which might be available for historical research, are a valuable untapped source of ready information for historians seeking answers to the problems of land distribution, settlement, migration, and tenure.

The basic difference between the Turner approach and that of Herbert B. Adams has already been noted. The latter stressed the roots of American institutions in their European background at a time when no serious attempt had been made to study the history of agriculture. Somewhat as a result of the twin emergence of agricultural history and the Turner school, all of the early investigations of southern economic institutions, particularly the plantation, have been largely under the Turner aegis. It is not surprising that there is a paucity of general knowledge of the Old World background of southern agriculture. Richard H. Shryock has protested against the tendency to overemphasize the Ameri-

71 Payson J. Treat, *National Land System, 1785–1820* (New York, 1910); Beverly W. Bond, Jr., *The Quit Rent System in the American Colonies* (New Haven, 1919).
72 Hibbard, *A History of the Public Land Policies* (New York, 1924); Roy M. Robbins, *Our Landed Heritage: The Public Domain, 1776–1936* (Princeton, 1942); William D. Pattison, *The Beginnings of the American Rectangular Land Survey System, 1784–1800* (Chicago, 1957); R. S. Cotterill, "The National Land System in the South," *Mississippi Valley Historical Review*, XVI (March, 1930), 459–506; Marshall D. Harris, *The Genesis of the Land Tenure System of the United States* (Urbana, 1945). For the better articles on the history of the public lands which have appeared in historical and other journals, see Vernon Carstensen (ed.), *The Public Lands: Studies in the History of the Public Domain* (Madison, 1963).
73 On a significant phase of the land problem in the South see Samuel G. McLendon, *History of the Public Domain of Georgia* (Atlanta, 1924).

can environment and the failure of the southern historian to start with
the original stock of humanity which settled the American wilderness.
In comparing the agricultural practices of the German settlers with
those of the English, for example, he concluded that the Anglo-Ameri-
cans exploited the resources of the soil for immediate advantage while
the German Americans improved the land for posterity. Hence it was
that the dominance of the English group in the Old South led to soil
exhaustion and colonial dependence upon England.[74]

Shryock's discussion suggests that a look at the European background
of southern agriculture might prove as rewarding to students in this
field as is the Magna Carta or the Petition of Rights to those who study
political institutions. Indeed, this return to the Adams approach seems
to be a natural consequence of a declining isolationist accent in historical
writing. Such a retrospective view might also encompass the classical
world wherein such writers as Cato, Varro, Vergil, and Pliny wrote
of plantation management, overseers, and slaves. An excellent example
of the simple "linguistic approach" to history is given in a paper by
Allen W. Read entitled "The Comment of British Travelers on Early
American Terms Relating to Agriculture." [75] Certain modifications of
British agriculture are seen in the use of such American terms as
"worn out" land, "worm" fences, and "patch," which were unknown
to English visitors who came to the South. On the other hand, the early
Virginia overseer often was called the bailiff, an English designation for
those who managed large estates. A book-length study of antebellum
southern agriculture as viewed by foreign observers would be extremely
valuable in tracing modifications which the American environment
wrought upon European practices.

Thomas J. Wertenbaker has done for architecture, the arts, crafts,
and land tenure what needs to be done for the entire range of economic
life.[76] Beginning with the knowledge, customs, and arts brought by
settlers from the Old World, he discussed changes wrought not only by
the physical environment but also by intercultural conflicts along the seaboard. He considered cultural history as a changing, developing process.
Another illustration of the synthesis and amalgamation of conflicting
elements in agricultural traditions is found in Richard Lyle Power's

74 Shryock, "Cultural Factors in the History of the South," *Journal of Southern
History*, V (August, 1939), 333–46.

75 Read, "The Comment of British Travelers on Early American Terms Relating
to Agriculture," *Agricultural History*, VII (July, 1933), 99.

76 Wertenbaker, *The Old South: The Founding of American Civilization* (New
York, 1942).

Planting Corn Belt Culture.[77] This writer depicts a dramatic conflict in the Old Northwest between southern and New England emigrants. The Yankees did not like the way that southern emigrants farmed, and they made fun of their cattle. "The cow-milking Yankee Puritans" could never understand why their southern-bred neighbors never made cheese, and they rated them as inefficient husbandmen. This cultural conflict extended to the manner of keeping house and growing fruits and vegetables, and it found expression at the race track and the market place. According to Power, neither won out in the end, for both were moulded by the region into Midwesterners.

Of the various special aspects of agricultural history which have been studied, the most intensive research has been devoted to the cotton industry, soil exhaustion, and agricultural reform, and the staple crops of tobacco, rice, sugar cane, and hemp, somewhat in the order named. None of the staple crops, however, with the possible exception of sugar cane, has been treated exhaustively. It is surprising that a general history of cotton is yet to be written.[78] Of the many works on the subject, only state and period histories are available. Typical of the better treatments of the cotton industry by states are those by Charles S. Davis on Alabama and Charles E. Allred and Benjamin D. Raskopf on Tennessee. Tobacco has received fairly comprehensive treatment by Joseph C. Robert.[79] The rice grower was somewhat neglected by Ulrich B. Phillips, but he has since been treated by Duncan C. Heyward [80] and James H. Easterby.[81] The scholar who has most recently devoted attention to this topic is Albert V. House, Jr., who has produced several articles and a book dealing with planter management of rice plantations.[82] His work

77 Power, *Planting Corn Belt Culture: The Impress of the Upland Southerner and Yankee in the Old Northwest* (Indianapolis, 1953).

78 David L. Cohn's *The Life and Times of King Cotton* (New York, 1956) is a popular general account which begins with the 1790's. Compiled from a limited number of well-known sources, it added little to what was already general knowledge.

79 Robert, *The Tobacco Kingdom: Plantation, Market, and Factory in Virginia and North Carolina, 1800–1860* (Durham, 1938). Robert's *The Story of Tobacco in America* (New York, 1949) includes technical aspects of the industry.

80 Heyward, *Seed From Madagascar* (Chapel Hill, 1937).

81 Easterby (ed.), *The South Carolina Rice Plantation* . . . (Chicago, 1945). See also Easterby, "The South Carolina Rice Factor as Revealed in the Papers of F. W. Allston," *Journal of Southern History*, VII (May, 1941), 160–72.

82 House, "The Management of a Rice Plantation in Georgia, 1834–1861 . . . ," *Agricultural History*, XIII (October, 1939), 208–17. See also the following works by House: *Planter Management and Capitalism in Ante-Bellum Georgia: The Journal of Hugh Frazer Grant, Rice Grower* (New York, 1954), "Charles

involves an interpretative analysis of financing, milling, and marketing of Georgia rice which is of particular significance. Specialized economic studies of sugar production appeared under the auspices of the United States Bureau of Foreign and Domestic Commerce in 1913, and again in 1917, and in numerous short papers published in professional journals thereafter. The first scholarly attempt to tell the overall story of this industry appeared in 1953, when J. Carlyle Sitterson produced a study of the industry in the South extending from 1753 to 1950.[83] He has brought together and analyzed many plantation records and diaries dealing with day-to-day operations. His studies include methods of cultivation and manufacture as well as financing and marketing arrangements.

The 1950's saw a study by James F. Hopkins on the hemp industry in Kentucky. This crop provided farmers in that state with their chief source of cash from 1792 to 1861 and was the economic basis of slavery in Kentucky.[84] The author points out that hemp also accounts in some measure for Clay's "American System" and the Whig party's fight for high tariffs. In a doctoral dissertation on hemp in colonial Virginia, George Melvin Herndon found that hemp-growing regions coincided roughly with large concentrations of Scotch-Irish settlers who had acquired skills in growing the crop in the Old World.[85] Both of these studies indicate that this minor staple may have been of greater consequence in the South's history than has been supposed. Professor Hopkins' study has a peculiar significance because of its consideration of the interrelations between certain political movements and underlying agricultural factors. Such relationships in the South Carolina cotton belt had been earlier demonstrated by Robert R. Russel [86] and John G. Van Deusen.[87] This pattern of historical study might profitably be extended

Manigault's Essay on the Open Planting of Rice," *Agricultural History,* XVI (October, 1942), 184–92; "Labor Management Problems on a Georgia Rice Plantation, 1840–1860," *Agricultural History,* XXVIII (October, 1954), 149–54.

83 Sitterson, *Sugar Country: The Cane Sugar Industry in the South, 1753–1950* (Lexington, 1953).

84 Hopkins, *A History of the Hemp Industry in Kentucky* (Lexington, 1957).

85 Herndon, "The Story of Hemp in Colonial Virginia" (Ph.D. dissertation, University of Virginia, 1959). For a discussion of the beginnings of the flax and hemp industries in the Cumberland region, see Harriette S. Arnow, "The Pioneer Farmer and His Crops in the Cumberland Region," *Tennessee Historical Quarterly,* XXIX (December, 1960), 291–327.

86 Russel, *Economic Aspects of Southern Sectionalism, 1840–1861* (Urbana, 1923). See also Alfred G. Smith, Jr., *Economic Readjustment of an Old Cotton State* (Columbia, 1958).

87 Van Deusen, *Economic Basis of Disunion in South Carolina* (New York, 1928).

to cover a broader topical scope and a more comprehensive geographic area.

Nothing of importance has been written on the non-staple crops grown in the antebellum South such as grains, vegetables, and fruits. There are no works dealing with southern farm livestock except for rather sketchy and inadequate treatment of livestock production in the Tennessee-Kentucky region. Lewis C. Gray and most scholars who have followed his path have stressed the large number of farm animals in the slave states, but they have devoted too little attention to their quality and distribution. Professor Owsley described what he believed to be a thriving livestock industry in the region, and he used this to support his thesis of a prosperous and expanding yeomanry. Eugene D. Genovese recently has challenged this view in a short paper which needs to be expanded for convincing proof of his assertion that the Old South had a very poor record in livestock enterprises.[88] The younger scholar ignores the successful experimentation with Angora goats, European breeds of hogs and cattle, and Spanish sheep, as well as the introduction into Georgia of Brahma cattle from India in the 1850's. Also, the fact that the South possessed fine and diversified breeds of poultry in this period has been universally ignored.[89]

Four or five special studies of general agriculture in particular southern states or localities have been written. Two of them—Cornelius O. Cathey's study of antebellum North Carolina agriculture and John H. Moore's study of Mississippi—are among the better local agricultural histories for the entire country. Moore's work provides an excellent discussion of cotton as a capitalistic enterprise and contains perhaps the best treatment of cotton breeding which is available. James C. Bonner has completed a study on Georgia agriculture to 1860.[90] Other such state

88 Genovese, "Livestock in the Slave Economy of the Old South—A Revised View," *Agricultural History*, XXXVI (July, 1962), 143–49.

89 See for example James C. Bonner, "The Angora Goat: A Footnote in Southern Agricultural History," *Agricultural History*, XXI (January, 1947), 42–46; Bonner, "Advancing Trends in Southern Agriculture, 1840–1860," *Agricultural History*, XXII (October, 1948), 248–59. Samuel W. Geiser in 1945 published a study on horticulture in early Texas. Its narrow geographical and chronological scope fails to provide a suitable sampling for the southern region. Geiser, *Horticulture and Horticulturists in Early Texas* (Dallas, 1945).

90 These agricultural histories of southern states or regions are: James C. Bonner, *A History of Georgia Agriculture, 1732–1860* (Athens, 1964); Edwin A. Davis, *Plantation Life in the Florida Parishes of Louisiana, 1836–1846* . . . (New York, 1943); Cornelius O. Cathey, *Agricultural Developments in North Carolina* (Chapel Hill, 1956); John H. Moore, *Agriculture in Ante-Bellum Mississippi* (New York, 1958); Alfred G. Smith, Jr., *Economic Readjustment of an Old Cotton State, South*

histories are needed, as well as a study of agriculture among the five civilized tribes in the Lower South.

Most of the local and state histories on agriculture have given considerable attention to soil exhaustion, which phenomenon indeed ran like a red thread throughout the history of the South. Thus, it was among the first topics to attract the attention of historians. Edward Channing and Frederick Jackson Turner each gave a gloomy picture of agriculture in Virginia during the first forty years of the republic. Planting economy was described as struggling with an impoverished soil and declining social organization to which, according to Channing, commercial warfare and the conflict with England in 1812 gave the death stroke. The early national historians, however, did not comprehend the agricultural rebirth which followed close on the heels of the first decline.[91]

Avery O. Craven's *Soil Exhaustion as a Factor in the Agricultural History of Virginia and Maryland, 1606–1860* demonstrated that economic and political forces over which the planter had no control were responsible for agricultural decline in the Chesapeake region.[92] Craven followed this pioneer monograph with two papers on John Taylor's early attempts at agricultural reform in the Upper South,[93] but his most significant contribution to the history of agricultural revival and reform in this area was *Edmund Ruffin, Southerner*.[94]

Agricultural reform subsequently became the subject of numerous articles and a few monographs.[95] Appearing in the first number of *Agricultural History* in 1927 was a discussion by Ellis Merton Coulter of the movement for agricultural reorganization of the cotton South during

Carolina, 1820–1860 (Columbia, South Carolina, 1958). See also Gilbert Fite, "Development of the Cotton Industry by the Five Civilized Tribes," *Journal of Southern History*, XV (August, 1949), 342–53.

91 Kathleen Bruce, "Virginia Agricultural Decline to 1860: A Fallacy," *Agricultural History*, VI (January, 1932), 3–13. See also Theodore Saloutos, "Efforts at Crop Control in Seventeenth Century America," *Journal of Southern History*, XII (February, 1946), 45–64.

92 Craven, *Soil Exhaustion as a Factor in the Agricultural History of Virginia and Maryland, 1606–1860* (Urbana, Ill., 1932).

93 Craven, "Agricultural Reformers of the Ante-Bellum South," *American Historical Review*, XXXIII (January, 1928), 302–14, and "John Taylor and Southern Agriculture," *Journal of Southern History*, IV (May, 1938), 37–42.

94 Craven, *Edmund Ruffin, Southerner* (New York, 1932).

95 The depression of the early 1930's stimulated great interest in this subject and it has shown few signs of abatement. A recent treatment is Alfred Glaze Smith, Jr., *Economic Readjustment of an Old Cotton State, South Carolina, 1820–1860*.

the Civil War.[96] Coulter later followed with a paper on the relationship
between southern nationalism and agriculture.[97] "The leaders of the
agricultural reform movement," he wrote, "knew that the soul of the
South was embedded in the Southern soil and that no program which
did violence to this fact could be made to succeed." [98]

Earlier writers repeatedly alleged that the plantation system devoured
the soil while the farming system did not. Phillips, in an article published posthumously in 1938, frankly challenged this assertion.[99] There
was, he wrote, sharpest competition between farmer and planter in the
Piedmont, where the soil was thin. All growers were tempted to sell
their soil in the form of lint and then move westward. According to
Phillips, planters were more successful in resisting this temptation than
were farmers. While the former most commonly improved his land, the
latter "cleared, cropped, and cleared out."

Most of Phillips' conclusions have been challenged by Eugene D.
Genovese's recent doctoral dissertation,[100] which emphasizes the low
productivity of southern labor and maintains that slavery led to agricultural methods which depleted the soil and forced the region to adopt
the exploitive methods of the frontier. The agricultural reform movement
waned with each upswing in cotton prices, Genovese points out, and
general agricultural reform was impossible in conjunction with slave
labor. Genovese therefore differs with most specialists in contending
that it was not the Civil War and Reconstruction which brought to a
temporary end the agricultural reform movement.

It is doubtless true that the war and Reconstruction were not as
cataclysmic to antebellum nonpolitical institutions as they have often
been depicted as being. While they speeded up some processes already
well on their way and retarded others, they left untouched far more
agricultural traditions and habits than they changed. Even the labor
situation was not a complete revolution from that which existed before
the Thirteenth Amendment, for the freedman remained for many decades,
economically at least, a quasi-slave. Despite these facts, the Genovese

96 Coulter, "The Movement for Agricultural Reorganization in the Cotton South
During the Civil War," *Agricultural History*, I (January, 1927), 3–17.

97 Coulter, "Southern Agriculture and Southern Nationalism Before the Civil
War," *Agricultural History*, IV (July, 1930), 77–91.

98 *Ibid.*, 86.

99 Phillips, "Plantations with Slave Labor and Free," *Agricultural History*, XII
(January, 1938), 77–91.

100 Genovese, "The Limits of Agrarian Reform in the Slave South" (Ph.D. dissertation, Columbia University, 1960).

theory seems to reveal a few disconcerting evasions. For example, agricultural reform was much more than a program for diversification on which Genovese largely rests his case for its unsuitability to slave labor. Actually, the movement involved factors ranging from architecture of the plantation house, better marketing techniques for cotton, and the use of guano in its production, to improved care, housing, and management of Negro slaves.[101] One of its more notable achievements was in mitigating the effects of soil erosion on the large plantations of the rolling Piedmont region.

In a study devoted to soil erosion, Arthur R. Hall has stated that the methods of terracing employed in the southern Piedmont "are indigenous to the region, having been developed by trial, error, and experimentation there with practically no borrowings from foreign practice." [102] These techniques evolved from horizontal plowing and hillside ditching, and they are distinctive contributions made principally by large planters of the region to the art of agriculture. Dr. Hall's study contains probably the best discussion available on the history of terracing in the South. Unfortunately it is less satisfactory in its discussion of soil culture techniques and of plows, of which a small but significant number were developed locally after 1840.

The paucity of published works on certain other cognate aspects of the plantation and farm is keenly felt by students of agricultural history. More biographies of agricultural leaders are needed, despite outstanding works by Avery O. Craven, E. Merton Coulter, Wendell H. Stephenson, and Weymouth T. Jordan. There is a great need for full-length biographies of Thomas Affleck, Richard Peters, H. W. Vick, Daniel Lee, David Dickson, John Skinner, James H. Hammond, Thomas Mann Randolph, and many others.[103] The routine day-to-day and season-to-

101 See Chester M. Destler, "David Dickson's System of Farming and the Agricultural Revolution in the Deep South, 1850–1885," *Agricultural History,* XXXI (July, 1957), 30–39; James C. Bonner, "Plantation Architecture of the Lower South on the Eve of the Civil War," *Journal of Southern History,* XI (August, 1945), 370–88.

102 Hall, "Soil Erosion and Agriculture in the Southern Piedmont: A History" (Ph.D. dissertation, Duke University, 1948).

103 Edward J. Davis, *Titans of the Soil: Great Builders of Agriculture* (Chapel Hill, 1949), gives biographical sketches of seventeen American agricultural leaders of whom none were identified with the Lower South. Short biographies of several southern agricultural leaders have appeared in *Agricultural History* from time to time. See for example, Chester M. Destler, "David Dickson's System of Farming," 30–39; Robert W. Williams, "Thomas Affleck: Missionary to the Planter, the Farmer, and the Gardener," in Vol. XXXI (July, 1957), 40–48; and Weymouth T. Jordan, "Noah B. Cloud and the *American Cotton Planter,*" Vol. XXXI (October, 1957), 44–49.

season plantation management could be seen best in the detailed biography of some yeoman farmer.

Too little is known about the commercial life of the Old South, particularly the financing and marketing of the staple crops. It has been noted that Professor Sitterson has dealt somewhat extensively with cane sugar, and Charles S. Davis has effectively described the cotton factorage system in Alabama.[104] However, the latter gave little attention to the small farmer, and that part of his study which deals with the factorage system is of limited geographic scope. Charles C. Crittenden has produced a work on the commerce of North Carolina in which naval stores, lumber, and tobacco were described in the period from 1783 to 1789.[105] Ralph H. Haskins has completed a dissertation on the cotton factor in the first sixty years of the nineteenth century,[106] while Milton S. Heath, Clement Eaton, and Lewis E. Atherton have included the problem briefly in general works.[107] These writers agree in substance that credit was a major problem in the antebellum South, which made it a profound influence upon the agricultural economy of the region. Bennett H. Wall, who has in progress a study of the plantation factor from 1783 to 1861, disagrees with most authorities concerning the alleged control which this factor and other town merchants exercised over the operations of planters.[108]

Just as the planters' factors were most often town merchants, professional groups also had country patrons, and many prospering townsmen were absentee planters and looked toward the plantation for retirement. Town life in the Old South was in many localities a reflection of the plantation and the farm, in both sentiment and interest. The towns of the plantation belt differed to a great extent from those in the areas

104 Davis, *The Cotton Kingdom in Alabama* (Montgomery, 1939).

105 Crittenden, *The Commerce of North Carolina 1763–1789* (New Haven, 1936).

106 Haskins, "The Cotton Factor, 1800–1860, a Study in Southern Economic and Social History" (Ph.D dissertation, University of California, 1956).

107 Heath, *Constructive Liberalism, The Role of the State in Economic Development in Georgia to 1860* (Cambridge, 1954), 159–220, 293–335; Eaton, *The Growth of Southern Civilization, 221–70;* Atherton, *The Southern Country Store, 1800–1860* (Baton Rouge, 1949). See also Atherton, "The Problem of Credit Rating in the Ante-Bellum South," *Journal of Southern History* (November, 1949), 534–56.

108 On the eve of the Revolution Thomas Jefferson said that he and his neighbors were merely a species of property, annexed to certain mercantile houses of London, and later Oliver Wolcott attributed the Whigism of Virginia to planter indebtedness. More than a century later Arthur M. Schlesinger and others largely corroborated these statements. B. B. Kendrick, "The Colonial Status of the South," *Journal of Southern History,* VIII (February, 1942), 3–23.

of small farms, and these in turn were quite different in character from the river ports and coastal cities. The subject of plantation and farm architecture for the entire southern region in itself offers a fascinating opportunity for research.

While it is recognized that a comprehensive view of southern town life is needed to complete the overall story of the region's agriculture, this view will have to await the appearance of additional research on specific communities. Unfortunately, of the numerous local histories which have been published, few have dealt with the entire range of social and economic life which would elevate them to regional and national significance. Scholarly work on local history is therefore a fertile and unworked field to which scholars at institutions with limited archival collections could devote their skills with satisfaction to themselves and for the advancement of professional knowledge.[109]

109 An example of the type of work needed is that of Gerald M. Capers, who, in 1939, produced a study of Memphis as a river port. Outside of the treatment of the Old New Orleans no other work of such a scholarly and comprehensive nature has been produced. See Capers, *The Biography of a River Town, Memphis: Its Heroic Age* (Chapel Hill, 1939). Two examples of a study made of small agricultural areas are James C. Bonner, "Profile of a Late Ante Bellum Community," *American Historical Review*, XLIX (July, 1944), 663–80; and Edward W. Phifer, "Slavery in Microcosm: Burke County, North Carolina," *Journal of Southern History*, XXVIII (May, 1962), 137–65.

VII

African Slavery

Bennett H. Wall

HISTORIANS of the United States, especially those writing about the South, have been unable to write on the subject of slavery without rather obvious bias. Indeed, few subjects have so readily lent themselves to periodic and cyclical reinterpretation, perhaps because the easily available documentation for any thesis has led to polemical writing more appropriate to the courtroom than to scholarship. A distinguished historian has succinctly explained the problem:

Slavery was always two things: (1) an abstract idea,—which, involving the idea of a human being as property, is repulsive to all American ethical & democratic values. As such it can only be denounced as something which had no place in the Modern world—(2) But slavery was also an historical fact,—the labor system employed, first in all the colonies, then gradually reduced to a Southern institution—Thus the problem became one of what, as a human institution, *it could be*—(and it *could be* brutal and inhuman in practice)—or it *could be* considerate and paternal in practice—

So slavery must always be dealt with as both an abstraction and as an historical fact. You can never forget *what it could be* like in practice,—nor can you forget its bitter abstract, inherent character.

Few historians writing on slavery have been able to divorce themselves from the ugly fact that slaves were property or from what this historian so aptly called "the tangle of abstraction and reality." [1]

Among the most cogent explanations for this lack of objectivity on the part of historians is that advanced by Stanley M. Elkins in his volume, *Slavery; A Problem in American Institutional and Intellectual Life.* Elkins wrote: "How a person thinks about Negro slavery historically . . . tends to locate him morally in relation to a whole range of very immediate political, social, and philosophical issues which in some way refer back to slavery." [2]

Many aspects of the antebellum South have long been neglected. From the earliest writings on slavery, the tendency has been to ignore or gloss over such basic problems as the economic, social, and psychological effects created by the institution. Far too much writing on slavery has been an almost conditioned reflex to outside attacks.

Slavery in the South did not exist accidentally. It grew. Its effects are still felt by every American in the twentieth century, especially southern Americans. No American historian writing on the period before the Civil War has been able to avoid entirely the grim reality of slavery; no American historian writing on the period since the Civil War has been able to escape its shadow.

Although slavery by 1800 was essentially a southern institution, it rapidly became a national problem. An anachronism in the western world after 1830, slavery became each year a larger moral issue with increasing political overtones. The emergence and growth in numbers of extremists—both abolitionists and proslavery men—as the anachronism was politically agitated made it a dominant political question. The Civil War would not have occurred had not slavery existed in the South.

Historians who have written about the South and slavery have usually been grounded in political history, with some training in the loosely defined field of social history. My analysis of writing on slavery in the South indicates that interpretation has been influenced by the social atti-

1 Avery O. Craven to Bennett H. Wall, August 27, 1962, in possession of author.
2 Elkins, *Slavery; A Problem in American Institutional and Intellectual Life* (Chicago, 1959, and New York, 1963), 1. Citations here are to the latter edition.

tudes of the particular generation of the writer. This analysis covered the publications of many modern historians who, despite an obvious effort toward impartiality, treat slavery subjectively.

The subject of slavery as a part of a known economic system, though carefully discussed, has not been analyzed in the light of new materials or methodologies.[3] The literature of slavery reveals much heat on the question of morality but little illumination of other aspects of the institution. It represents to a large degree patternized cataloguing and is all too often more descriptive than analytical. Other than Elkins' volume, the only instance of a recent interdisciplinary approach to the subject is that of two economists, Alfred H. Conrad and John R. Meyer, on the question of the profitability of slavery.[4]

Rembert W. Patrick has divided the population of the antebellum South into five classes: planters with twenty or more slaves, yeomen, poor whites, free Negroes, and slaves. He then added, "Any valid history of the Old South must encompass all of these classes."[5] The principal difficulty in writing southern history is that few valid records exist for the slave, the free Negro, and the poor white. Yet these groups must be studied because historical analysis of one class is valid only in its larger context. A study of slavery is therefore relative to the entire research problem of the antebellum South.

There are certain imponderables about southern slavery which render treatment difficult. Only the slave could describe what it meant to be enslaved, but slaves left few records. As one scholar has said, "History can never record with exactness the innermost feelings of slaves when they contemplated their inferior position, their hopelessness in a system that closed the door to personal independence and responsibility."[6] Most accounts of slavery written contemporaneously, either by fugitive or freed slaves, or memoirs of slavery are more valuable as records of propaganda than as accounts of bondage.

3 The anti-slavery, abolitionist, and pro-slavery literature has been copiously treated. See Louis Filler, *The Crusade Against Slavery, 1830–1860* (New York, 1960); William S. Jenkins, *Pro-Slavery Thought in the Old South* (Chapel Hill, 1935); Dwight L. Dumond, *Anti-Slavery: The Crusade for Freedom in America* (Ann Arbor, 1961), and Dumond, *A Bibliography of Anti-Slavery in America* (Ann Arbor, 1961).

4 Conrad and Meyer, "The Economics of Slavery In the Ante Bellum South," *The Journal of Political Economy,* LXVI (April, 1958), 95–130. These scholars have developed a very useful actuarial table on slavery.

5 Patrick, *Race Relations In The South* (Tallahassee, 1958), 1–2.

6 Wendell H. Stephenson, *A Basic History of the Old South* (Princeton, 1959), 90.

Sources available for scholars interested in writing on slavery are extremely particularized. Plantation records, vast and important, are valuable as reflections of extensive agricultural operations in the South and for case studies of individual plantation operations. Letters of planters expressing views of slavery are valid evidence of managerial or administrative opinion. Overseers left few records. The literature of slavery on the yeoman farm is limited in scope, in fact virtually nonexistent. Rare indeed are the records of such extraordinary individuals as the free Negro, William Johnson, whose comments, however excellent, are still illustrative of the exceptional.[7] From the interstate slave traders there are only scattered records; from their chattels, none. Abolitionists saw what they wanted to see; pro-slavery writers found what they sought in the institution.

In the last three decades several scholars have sought to synthesize southern history. Robert S. Cotterill produced the first one-volume history of the Old South,[8] but he did not devote much space to slavery. The second one-volume history of the South, that of William B. Hesseltine, also gave little space to slavery and the slave. However, Hesseltine emphasized the debate over slavery and the rise of the sectional controversy more fully than did Cotterill.[9] Francis B. Simkins began his history of the South with the injection of the issue of slavery into national politics in the Missouri Compromise debates of 1819–1820. His sketch of slavery before 1820 is brief; indeed, he largely ignores the economic and social effects of the slave system on the antebellum South. In keeping with his announced purpose, he stresses those political and social traits that make the region "a cultural province conscious of its identity." His preoccupation with politics and culture left little space for a discussion of the effects of slavery on the Negro or the white man.[10] Clement Eaton de-

7 Recently, Edward W. Phifer in an excellent article dealing with backcountry slavery has thrown considerable new light on the institution of yeomen farms as well as the operation of the institution in noncommercialized crop areas. Phifer, "Slavery in Microcosm: Burke County, North Carolina," *Journal of Southern History,* XXVIII (May, 1962), 137–65. See also William R. Hogan and Edwin A. Davis (eds.), *William Johnson's Natchez* (Baton Rouge, 1951); Edwin A. Davis and William R. Hogan, *The Barber of Natchez* (Baton Rouge, 1954).

8 Cotterill, *The Old South* (Glendale, Calif., 1936 and 1939). William E. Dodd, *The Old South. Struggles For Democracy* (New York, 1937), is not a history of the South, nor does his *The Cotton Kingdom* (New Haven, 1919) purport to be a history of the South.

9 Hesseltine, *A History of the South* (New York, 1936). See also William B. Hesseltine and David L. Smiley, *The South in American History* (New York, 1960).

10 Simkins, *The South Old and New: A History, 1820–1947* (New York, 1947). Revised edition, *A History of The South* (New York, 1956).

voted a chapter of his *A History of the Old South* to "Black Labor," thereby providing the most complete coverage to be found in a textbook. Eaton utilized most of the printed research and writings on slavery and many manuscript sources. He considered carefully such topics as the efficiency of slave labor and its profitability. Eaton also discussed slavery on the smaller plantations and farms. Wendell H. Stephenson, in *A Basic History of the Old South,* placed slavery in perspective. Each paragraph on the subject of slavery, though brief, is packed with opinion based on sound research and skillful judgment. The documents that Stephenson appended to his text support his interpretations. *A Basic History of the Old South* provides the best brief synthesis of the Old South as well as of slavery.[11]

To the reader comparing general textbooks on the history of the United States, sections on the South and slavery appear to have been written according to a formula. Textbook presentation supports the conclusion that the subject of slavery is touched as lightly as possible. The trend has recently been to emphasize the political and propagandistic aspects and to minimize the institution as a social and economic system. The authors uniformly agree that there were a few ameliorating factors, but that the institution was an injustice both to black and white. Abolitionist propaganda is equated with desegregation literature. Attention to the development of the system is minimal in edited documents, problems, and readings. Slavery was evil, its effects were bad; with textbook space at a premium, any qualifying features are treated superficially if at all.

Of the textbooks examined for this essay,[12] that by Hofstadter, Mil-

11 Eaton, *A History of the Old South* (New York, 1949); Stephenson, *A Basic History of the Old South.*

12 John R. Alden, *Rise of the American Republic* (New York, 1963), 169–71, 323–26; John M. Blum, Bruce Catton, Edmund S. Morgan, Arthur M. Schlesinger, Jr., Kenneth M. Stampp, and C. Vann Woodward, *The National Experience* (New York, 1963), 200–205; Harry J. Carman and Harold C. Syrett, *A History of the American People* (2 vols.; New York, 1952), I, 414–38; Oliver P. Chitwood, Rembert W. Patrick, and Frank L. Owsley, *The American People* (2 vols.; Princeton, N. J., 1962), I, 103–104; Avery O. Craven and Walter Johnson, *The United States* (Boston, 1962), 226–29; Richard N. Current, T. Harry Williams, and Frank Freidel, *American History* (New York, 1961), 327–29; T. Harry Williams, Richard N. Current, and Frank Freidel, *A History of the United States* (2 vols.; New York, 1959), I, 486–87; Harold U. Faulkner, *American Political and Social History* (New York, 1948), 306–12; John D. Hicks, *A History of the United States* (2 vols.; Boston, 1957), I, 451–56; John D. Hicks and George E. Mowry, *A Short History of American Democracy* (Boston, 1946), 289–94; Richard Hofstadter, William Miller, and Daniel Aaron, *The American Republic* (2 vols.; Englewood Cliffs, N. J., 1959), I, 505–28; Richard W. Leopold and Arthur S. Link (eds.), *Problems in American History* (New York, 1952), 319–426; Samuel E. Morison and Henry S. Commager, *The Growth of the American Republic* (2

ler, and Aaron gives the most complete and informed treatment of slavery in the Old South. It contains a thoughtful chapter on "The Southern Nation" with a balanced discussion of slavery. Carman and Syrett devote a full chapter to the southern farmer with an illuminating section on slavery. They present the physical aspects of slavery and then discuss the question of the profitability of slavery. Harold Faulkner has an excellent summary chapter on "The Old South," including some discussion of slavery. The texts of Craven and Johnson; Chitwood, Patrick, and Owsley; and Williams, Current, and Freidel generally integrate treatment of slavery with other material. All of these present slavery both as an historical fact and a moral wrong. Morison and Commager have dropped the "Sambo" designation and other characterizations of the Negro that caused the student uproar at Queens College, New York City, in 1951. Though they have not eliminated all clichés, their chapter on the South remains a brilliant summary conforming to the modern concern over the issue of race. Alden's text contains a good general statement on slavery. Stampp, writing in a multi-authored text, has an excellent brief and balanced discussion of slavery. Charles G. Sellers, in a brief synopsis to accompany the *Berkeley Series in American History*, virtually ignores the subject of slavery. Of the texts examined, Hicks' *The Federal Union* is the most favorable to the South.

Perhaps spatial limitations imposed by publishers have affected the treatment of slavery and other topics. Only comparison of authors' manuscripts with suggested editorial changes and published textbooks can establish whether the publisher, impelled by profits, or the historian, impelled by the desire to publish, is responsible for the polite skirting of controversial topics such as slavery, the Negro, or currently the United Nations. Certainly historians cannot live or write in a vacuum. Thus it is patently impossible to determine whether the renewed interest in states rights exhibited by political moderates and economic conservatives, or the heated agitation of the race question in the United States and the world, has influenced textbook or other writing. Still it is not without significance that in current American history textbooks there is measur-

---

vols.; New York 1962), I, 524–29; Charles G. Sellers, Jr., and Henry May, *A Synopsis of American History* (Chicago, 1963), 157–59. For recent special anthologies, see Katharine M. Jones, *The Plantation South* (Indianapolis, 1957); Willard Thorp, *A Southern Reader* (New York, 1955); and Ina W. Van Noppen, *The South, A Documentary History* (Princeton, N. J., 1958). Use of Morison and Commager's text was discontinued at Queens College in 1951 because it contained clichés about the institution of slavery and the slave. See *Time* (February 26, 1951), 48–49.

ably less space devoted to slavery, the Old South, and the Negro than in textbooks of a generation past.

There is in progress a multivolume *History of the South,* of which five volumes have been completed on the Old South. W. Frank Craven, in his study, *The Southern Colonies in the Seventeenth Century, 1607–1689,* carefully analyzed the development of commercialized agriculture based on slavery. Slavery in the South, as Craven treats it, was the unplanned result of the aspirations of several generations of settlers. The pattern of large plantations resulted from individual interests rather than common objectives. The evolution of the plantation system and the emergence of African slavery are thereby interlocked.[13] John R. Alden's *The South in the Revolution, 1763–1789,* perhaps properly devoted little attention to slavery.[14] Thomas P. Abernethy, in *The South in the New Nation, 1789–1819,* has only passing references to the institution, largely ignoring the questions of the unprofitableness of slavery in the post-Revolutionary era and the bases of emancipation sentiment before 1819.[15] Charles S. Sydnor, in the next volume, *The Development of Southern Sectionalism, 1819–1848,* devoted surprisingly little attention to the institution of slavery. However, he discussed the relation of slavery and abolition to southern politics.[16] Avery O. Craven, in his *The Growth of Southern Nationalism, 1848–1861,* briefly discussed slavery with relation to problems confronting the South after 1848.[17] This multivolume history of the South does not tell the reader what slavery was, how it operated, how slaves lived and worked, whether or not slavery was profitable, the effect of slavery on the South, or a host of other answers necessary for understanding the southern past. Political and social history (narrowly defined) dominates these volumes. The reader can rightly question whether this portrait of the South is balanced.

The New American Nation Series thus far includes two volumes dealing with the question of slavery in the South. Louis Filler's *The Crusade Against Slavery, 1830–1860,* described the abolitionist and anti-slavery crusade with sympathetic insight largely in keeping with present-day

13 W. F. Craven, *The Southern Colonies in the Seventeenth Century, 1607–1689* (Baton Rouge, 1949).

14 Alden, *The South in the Revolution, 1763–1789* (Baton Rouge, 1957).

15 Abernethy, *The South in the New Nation, 1789–1819* (Baton Rouge, 1961).

16 Sydnor, *The Development of Southern Sectionalism, 1819–1848* (Baton Rouge, 1948).

17 A. O. Craven, *The Growth of Southern Nationalism, 1848–1861* (Baton Rouge, 1953).

concern over the race issue. Despite his obvious effort to be fair, few abolitionists would quarrel with his summary.[18] Clement Eaton in *The Growth of Southern Civilization, 1790–1860* presented a well-written and carefully organized history of the South. Eaton exhibited mastery of specific detail. His book is a series of well-selected essays on southern development. Only the careful reader is able to glean Eaton's opinion, for he is more given to meticulous presentation of evidence than to illuminating interpretations.[19] The bibliographies in these two books are valuable to the student of slavery.

Three important monographs have been concerned solely with the subject of slavery: Ulrich B. Phillips, *American Negro Slavery;* Kenneth M. Stampp, *The Peculiar Institution;* and Stanley M. Elkins, *Slavery.*[20] Stampp's volume was largely an effort to refute Phillips. Stampp did not cover the subject, especially the evolutionary aspects of slavery, as completely as did Phillips. While Stampp benefited a great deal from researches completed and materials collected in the years after Phillips' volume was printed, his research in many areas indicates haste and is inadequate. Phillips drew largely from records of the large plantations, for few other sources were available when he wrote his study in 1918. He also labored under the handicap of emotional ties to the South. Stampp's organization was virtually patterned after that used in Phillips' volume. Fully one fourth of the Phillips volume is still the best available source of information on the institution. Phillips ignored anthropological evidence and erred in expressing his conviction of the inherent racial inferiority of the slave, while Stampp's distillation reflects to a degree the latter-day abolitionist view of slavery.

Both Stampp and Richard Hofstadter have correctly accused U. B. Phillips of writing from the basic premise of Negro inferiority and of disregarding contrary evidence.[21] Wendell H. Stephenson, after study of Phillips' letters, papers, and notes, concluded that the errors of Phillips were the result of a closed mind. Stephenson believed that "within a decade after he [Phillips] attained his doctorate his concepts

---

18 Filler, *The Crusade Against Slavery, 1830–1860* (New York, 1960).

19 Eaton, *The Growth of Southern Civilization, 1790–1860* (New York 1961).

20 Phillips, *American Negro Slavery* (New York, 1918) ; Stampp, *The Peculiar Institution* (New York, 1956) ; Elkins, *Slavery. A Problem in American Institutional and Intellectual Life* (New York, 1963).

21 Stampp, "The Historian and Southern Negro Slavery," *American Historical Review,* LVII (April, 1952), 613–24; Richard Hofstadter, "U. B. Phillips and the Plantation Legend," *Journal of Negro History,* XXIX (April, 1944), 109–24.

were formulated," and that "all of his basic views were the product of his early research and thought." [22]

Phillips argued that the institution of slavery was declining while Stampp found it vigorous. Their arguments are anticipated both by the two authors' premises and their selection of materials. On the one hand, slavery, if it was a relatively humane institution, necessarily had to decline; on the other hand, if it was a brutal and profitable institution, it had to be maintained and defended aggressively. One is inclined to question the criticism directed at Phillips by Hofstadter: "Phillips handled a truly extraordinary mass of original source material which he used to great advantage . . . in accordance with principles of selection governed by his personal bias." [23] Despite such blatant criticisms, Ulrich B. Phillips still overshadows, and dictates response to, the subject of slavery in the Old South.[24]

Phillips' argument that slavery was a declining institution received strong support in 1929 from Charles W. Ramsdell's article, "The Natural Limits of Slavery Expansion." Ramsdell stated that "by 1860 the institution of slavery had virtually reached its natural frontiers in the West." Instead of seeking to answer the question of the profitability of slavery, Ramsdell assumed that the institution was profitable in the 1850's despite the high price of slaves caused by the supply of fresh lands opening for the cultivation of cotton. He then proceeded to point out that improved transportation was the key factor in this expansion and prosperity. However with transportation assumed, the quantity of lands made available would inevitably serve to depress both cotton and slave prices. Ramsdell concluded: "In an era of over-stocked plantations and low cotton prices, the planter would have found that he was rearing slaves, as well as growing cotton at a loss. . . . It [slavery] had reached its limits in both profits and lands. . . . Even those who wished it de-

22 Stephenson, *The South Lives In History* (Baton Rouge, 1955), 94. Compare Wood Gray, "Ulrich Bonnell Phillips," in William T. Hutchinson (ed.), *The Marcus W. Jernegan Essays in American Historiography* (Chicago, 1937), 334–73. Gray essentially agrees with Stephenson.

23 Hofstadter, "U. B. Phillips and the Plantation Legend," 122.

24 See David M. Potter, Jr. (comp.), "A Bibliography of the Printed Writings of Ulrich Bonnell Phillips," *Georgia Historical Quarterly,* XVIII (September, 1934), 270–82; and Everett E. Edwards (comp.), "A Bibliography of the Writings of Professor Ulrich Bonnell Phillips," *Agricultural History,* VIII (October, 1944), 199–218. In this study on slavery I have cited Phillips, *American Negro Slavery* exclusively since the chapter in Phillips' *Life and Labor in The Old South* (Boston, 1929) is largely drawn from the earlier volume.

stroyed had only to wait a little while—perhaps a generation, probably less." [25]

Elkins wrote the most controversial volume yet to appear on the subject of slavery. He immersed himself in the available secondary material as well as many printed sources. There is, however, no evidence that he has used available manuscript source records of slavery to any extent. His conclusions are based on a dubious analogy—the utilization of psychological researches based on the concentration-camp experiences of Nazi captives for purposes of comparison with and insight into the infantilism of American slaves. This lack of direct citation and the false analogy serve to destroy much of the impact of Elkins' book. Nevertheless it is an important contribution.

Part of the value of Elkins' volume lies in the polarization of ideas concerning the effect of bondage on the slave and the comparison of slavery in the United States with slavery in other countries in the hemisphere. Fresh as is Elkins' approach, functionally his volume may best serve to point out vast areas of the subject still in need of scholarly exploration. Thus Elkins used "standard" sources in his description of and conclusions about the intra-African slave trade. Yet at the 1958 Newberry Library conference devoted to exploration of the slave stereotype, "Sambo," anthropologist K. Onwuka Dike pointed out that these sources were "highly dubious." Similarly Arthur F. Corwin believes that Elkins' comparison of slavery in the South with slavery in other American nations is based on equally questionable sources. Corwin failed to find slavery as practiced in Cuba actually "open" as categorized by Elkins. The list of areas covered by Elkins and still open to scholarly investigation could be extended. But Elkins *did* face these problems. Regardless of the disagreement over his answers, Elkins asked many of the right questions. *Slavery; A Problem in American Institutional and Intellectual Life* is an interesting contribution to the literature of slavery in the southern United States, despite its magisterial tone, which is hardly justified in a pioneering interdisciplinary study.[26]

25 Ramsdell, "The Natural Limits of Slavery Expansion," *Mississippi Valley Historical Review*, XVI (September, 1929), 151–71.

26 Elkins, *Slavery; A Problem in American Institutional and Intellectual Life*, 81–139, 223–30. See "The Question of 'Sambo,'" A Report of the Ninth Newberry Library Conference on American Studies, *The Newberry Library Bulletin*, V (December, 1958), 14–41. See the review of Elkins' book by Harvey Wish in *Mississippi Valley Historical Review*, XLVII (September, 1960), 319–20. There are no psychological researches in the experiences of slaves nor is there any record indicating the number of slaves who were never free, either those brought to America or those born in slavery in America. See also Arthur F. Corwin, "Spain

The abolitionist-influenced strictures of Hermann E. von Holst and James Ford Rhodes[27] had no detectable influence on students at Johns Hopkins University's famous graduate school, where the first scholarly studies of slavery in the various states began to appear in 1890. These studies, in keeping with the theory that historians could be objective, were largely institutional, legalistic, and diplomatic. Since few plantation records were available, the various scholars depended largely on laws, court cases, collected letters of public figures, newspapers, and treaties for their sources. Because of their detached tone and lack of conclusion or interpretation, they created no great comment and had little lasting influence.[28]

It was Phillips who was the real pioneer and formative scholar,[29] and his influence is readily apparent in later state studies by Charles S. Davis, Ralph B. Flanders, James B. Sellers, Charles S. Sydnor, Rosser H. Taylor, Joe Gray Taylor, and Orville W. Taylor.[30] Sydnor's volume *Slavery in Mississippi* is the most significant.

Before Stampp's volume appeared, the only noticeable variation from

---

and the Problem of Abolishing Slavery in Cuba, 1817–1873" (Ph.D. dissertation, University of Chicago, 1958).

27 von Holst, *The Constitutional and Political History of the United States* (8 vols.; Chicago, 1876–1892), II, 80–406; Rhodes, *History of the United States from the Compromise of 1850* (7 vols.; New York, 1893–1906), I, 303–83.

28 In order of their appearance, the Johns Hopkins University Studies (Baltimore) on slavery were Jeffrey R. Brackett, *The Negro in Maryland* (1889); John H. T. McPherson, *History of Liberia* (1891); Edward Ingle, *The Negro in the District of Columbia* (1893); Bernard C. Steiner, *History of Slavery in Connecticut* (1893); James C. Ballagh, *White Servitude in the Colony of Virginia* (1895); Edson L. Whitney, *Government in the Colony of South Carolina* (1895); Henry S. Cooley, *Slavery in New Jersey* (1896); John S. Bassett, *History of Slavery in North Carolina* (1899); Eugene I. McCormac, *White Servitude in Maryland* (1904); James C. Ballagh, *A History of Slavery in Virginia* (1902); Harrison A. Trexler, *Slavery in Missouri, 1804–1865* (1914). Two additional studies are Ivan E. McDougle, *Slavery in Kentucky, 1792–1865* (Lancaster, 1918); and Caleb P. Patterson, *The Negro in Tennessee, 1790–1865* (Austin, 1922). Their approach is similar to that of the Hopkins school.

29 See Stephenson, *The South Lives In History*, 59; Gray, "Ulrich Bonnell Phillips," 367–73; and Elkins, *Slavery. A Problem in American Institutional and Intellectual Life*, 10–26.

30 Davis, *The Cotton Kingdom in Alabama* (Montgomery, 1939); Flanders, *Plantation Slavery in Georgia* (Chapel Hill, 1933); Sellers, *Slavery in Alabama* (University, 1950); Sydnor, *Slavery in Mississippi* (New York, 1933); R. H. Taylor, *Slaveholding in North Carolina: An Economic View* (Chapel Hill, 1926); J. G. Taylor, *Negro Slavery in Louisiana* (Baton Rouge, 1963); O. W. Taylor, *Negro Slavery in Arkansas* (Durham, N. C., 1958). J. Winston Coleman, Jr., *Slavery Times in Kentucky* (Chapel Hill, 1940) is a study that does not precisely follow this pattern.

Phillips' pattern was Guion Griffis Johnson's volume on antebellum North Carolina. Mrs. Johnson's volume stands out because she, in keeping with her subtitle, placed the institution more nearly in the proper social and economic perspective.

In 1957 Chase C. Mooney published an analysis of slavery in selected Tennessee counties using the manuscript census and other records to statistically relate slavery to land tenure and agricultural production. This intensive study offers a challenge that has not been met by other scholars. As in all such cases where selected sample data are projected, scholars may question Mooney's projection of selected counties to describe the institution of slavery in the state. But *Slavery in Tennessee* offers a new and different approach and provides a guidepost against which stereotypes regarding slavery may be tested elsewhere.[31]

The findings of nearly all these scholars added to the burden of evidence that slavery was not profitable. All of them followed Phillips in organization and coverage. Each recounts the beginning of slavery in the particular state. Then follow chapters on the types of plantations, plantation management, plantation labor, plantation life, the domestic trade, runaways, the slave and the law, the economics of slavery, slave health, and free and town Negroes. Some of the scholars included chapters on religion and hired slaves. But essentially the presentation and the picture are the same.[32] Even Stampp could not escape reacting to Phillips. Controls and checks, where hypothecated by Phillips, appear to have become the substance rather than guideposts. Nor have the various authors ever pointed up sharply the variations in the operation of slavery. Rather they have sought the average or composite.

The subject of slavery needs fresh examination by the case method, using census returns, tax records, county records, and other available material for continuity and statistical indices. If Frank L. Owsley and Herbert and Blanche Henry Weaver could arrive at challenging interpretations on the yeoman of the South by using such evidence[33] then other scholars should certainly use these materials for the study of the slave, the free Negro, and the poor white.

It is also time to cast a sharp eye on travelers' comments on slavery

31 Guion G. Johnson, *Ante-Bellum North Carolina: A Social History* (Chapel Hill, 1937) ; Mooney, *Slavery in Tennessee* (Bloomington, 1957) ; Phifer, "Slavery in Microcosm."

32 Compare chapter headings in the volumes above cited, footnote 30, with those in Phillips, *American Negro Slavery*.

33 See above, pp. 155 ff.

and the South.[34] Highly critical accounts preponderate. This, perhaps, is not surprising. But much of the travel literature falls into the class of "hearsay" evidence and has been used with little discrimination. These accounts have much value as descriptions of operations of slavery in a particular time and place, but historians have yet to be as critical in using travel accounts as they have been in evaluating secondary works. Richard Hofstadter's statement, "I believe that a fuller and more accurate knowledge of the late antebellum South can be obtained from the volumes of [Frederick Law] Olmsted than from Professor Phillips' own writings," [35] is, perhaps as he intended, startling. But few scholars who have worked in the sources would agree. Essentially there is more to evidence than the fact that it is contemporary. Valid generalizations for the antebellum period cannot be made from what any traveler in the South saw on a given day. Even Olmsted erred.

Abolitionists' accounts of slavery, the stories inspired by abolitionists but told by slaves, and the accounts by proslavery apologists should be carefully checked by scholars who are concerned with the quality of current historical writing. Analyses should be made of both factual and propagandist data. There are a number of ways by which such sources could be tested for accuracy. These involve use of census records, county and state archives, plantation records, and the checking of pertinent papers, letters and other materials.

Beyond question, the greatest single contribution to antebellum southern history was that of Lewis C. Gray in his *History of Agriculture in the Southern United States to 1860*. Gray carefully analyzed the evolution of and developments in agriculture. Covering in detail plantations and small farms, he concluded that slavery was profitable: "The belief, however, that in 1860 slavery in the South was on the point of being 'strangled for lack of room to expand' is a wholly mistaken interpretation of actual conditions." Gray was the first prominent scholar to take issue with Phillips.[36]

In the same year that Gray published his volumes, Charles S. Sydnor concluded in his volume, *Slavery in Mississippi,* that there was less re-

34 See Thomas D. Clark (ed.), *Travels in the Old South, A Bibliography* (3 vols.; Norman, Okla., 1956–1959) ; Volume III, *The Ante-Bellum South, 1825–1860.*

35 Hofstadter, "U. B. Phillips and the Plantation Legend," 121. For a gentle but thorough analysis on this point, see Stephenson, *The South Lives In History,* 78–79. Interestingly enough, Phillips classified Olmsted as expert and cited him quite often.

36 Gray, *History of Agriculture in the Southern United States to 1860* (2 vols.; Washington, 1933).

turn on investment in slaves in 1860 than could be obtained from other properties. "From an economic standpoint," he wrote, "it is very questionable whether slaves were a good investment year in and year out even in Mississippi." [37] The issue of the profitability of slavery was again joined.

Allan Nevins devoted much of the first volume of his *Ordeal of the Union* to a judicious analysis of the system of slavery. His approach to slavery appears in the preface: Slavery, an utterly different labor system, was but one of the barriers to be overcome by strong movement toward national unification. To Nevins, the slavery question was overemphasized into a heated moral issue when the "one really difficult problem was that of permanent race-adjustment." Thus while "slavery was the great peculiar institution of the South," the overriding fact was the social problem: "The South was an area where two races had somehow to live side by side." [38] Therefore, to the planter-lawyer-merchant group the economic issue was subordinate to the larger social issue of white supremacy. Nevins' discussion of the problem of slavery, along with general economic and social development, is both balanced and enlightened. Slavery was "the greatest curse to white and black alike that America has ever known. . . ." But "the South needed compassion and help, not condemnation." [39]

Invaluable to the scholar interested in slavery are two multivolume collections of sources: *Judicial Cases Concerning American Slavery and the Negro,* edited by Helen T. Catterall, and *Documents Illustrative of the History of the Slave Trade to America,* edited by Elizabeth Donnan.[40] Miss Catterall's work is more valuable when used in conjunction with the compilations of the antislavery jurist, John C. Hurd, *The Law*

---

37 Sydnor, *Slavery in Mississippi,* 200. Sydnor indicated no awareness of the paper read by Gray in Durham, N. C. on January 1, 1930, at the joint meeting of the Agricultural History Society and the American Historical Association entitled "Economic Efficiency and Competitive Advantages of Slavery under the Plantation System." In revised form this paper was also published in *Agricultural History,* IV (April, 1930), 31–47. If Sydnor was aware of either the paper or the *History* he does not so indicate. Nor did he indicate awareness of the fact that Gray announced in the paper and in the article the virtual completion and forthcoming publication of his *History of Agriculture in the Southern United States to 1860.* Both Sydnor's *Slavery in Mississippi* and the Gray volumes appeared in 1933.

38 Nevins, *Ordeal of The Union* (4 vols.; New York, 1947–1950), I, 413.

39 *Ibid.,* I, 461.

40 Catterall (ed.), *Judicial Cases Concerning American Slavery and the Negro* (5 vols.; Washington, 1926–1937); Donnan (ed.), *Documents Illustrative of the History of the Slave Trade to America* (4 vols.; Washington, 1930–1935).

of Freedom and Bondage in the United States,[41] and that of the pro-slavery jurist, Thomas R. R. Cobb, *An Inquiry into the Law of Negro Slavery in the United States of America.*[42] Significantly, the work of Catterall is not only invaluable for the study of the slave, slave law, the plantation, and the slave system, but also because it contains valuable material on slavery on small farms, in towns, and elsewhere. Miss Donnan's introductory comments to each volume of her documents are of especial value; her insight into and analysis of the problem of slave trade serve as base points for using the documents she selected.

The most important work supplementing and interpreting Miss Donnan's work is Warren S. Howard, *American Slavers and the Federal Law.*[43] Howard pointed out the hypocrisy in the alleged British effort to end the African slave trade and the inadequate American efforts to prevent smuggling of slaves after 1808. He established the existence of slave trade to the South in the 1840's and 1850's, though he expressed doubt that there was a considerable amount of such traffic. The appendices to this work are useful and informative. The author challenged and discounted several much-used sources on the slave trade.[44] In addition to Donnan, Howard used little known documents and court records. W. E. B. DuBois, *The Suppression of the African Slave Trade,*[45] long the standard volume on the subject, has been partially superseded by that of Howard. However, many areas of the DuBois volume are largely untouched by Howard, and DuBois remains an important source of information.

Of less value than Howard is *Black Cargoes,* by Daniel P. Mannix in collaboration with Malcolm Cowley.[46] However, it does include some fresh material along with many standard sources. It gives a long-range picture of the slave trade, has excellent illustrations, and is well written. The picturesqueness of this volume was obtained in some degree by

41 Hurd, *The Law of Freedom and Bondage in the United States* (2 vols.; Boston, 1858).

42 Cobb, *An Inquiry into the Law of Negro Slavery in the United States of America* (Philadelphia, 1858).

43 Howard, *American Slavers and the Federal Law* (Berkeley and Los Angeles, 1963).

44 For example, George Francis Dow, *Slave Ships and Slavery* (Salem, 1927); Captain Theodore Canot, *Adventures of an African Slaver,* ed. Malcolm Cowley (New York, 1928); and Charles A. L. Lamar "A Slavetrader's Letter Book," *North American Review,* CCCLX (November, 1886), 421–46.

45 DuBois, *The Suppression of the African Slave Trade To The United States of America, 1638–1870* (New York, 1896).

46 Daniel P. Mannix, in collaboration with Malcolm Cowley, *Black Cargoes* (New York, 1962).

uncritical use of sources; even so, *Black Cargoes* is an interesting and very useful book.

The most informative volumes yet written on the background of the slave are Melville J. Herskovits, *The Myth of the Negro Past*,[47] and Basil Davidson, *The Lost Cities of Africa*.[48] Research and writing on the cultural survivals of the African experience should complement these two volumes. There are several useful studies on this subject,[49] the most significant pioneer work being that of two University of North Carolina scholars, Guion Griffis Johnson and her husband, Guy B. Johnson.[50] Though limited in scope, their researches show how other disciplines could be used in analyzing slavery and suggest significant new areas of inquiry.

There have been a number of efforts to generalize on slavery topically and on problems arising from slavery. On the subject of the domestic slave trade, Frederic Bancroft's *Slave Trading in the Old South* is still the only monograph.[51] Bancroft grounded his study on the propagandist work, John E. Cairnes's *The Slave Power*, and thereby destroyed its value to a large degree. An indispensable offset to the abolitionist bias of Bancroft is Wendell H. Stephenson's judicious biography, *Isaac Franklin, Slave Trader and Planter of the Old South*.[52]

Herbert Aptheker published his pioneering work, *American Negro Slave Revolts*, in 1943,[53] but it has been aptly described as "so subjective and lacking in discrimination that the book—in any of its forms—scarcely deserves to be classed as history." [54] Joseph C. Carroll, *Slave Insurrections in the United States, 1800–1865*, sifted rumors with greater care, concentrating on major insurrections.[55] Significantly neither of these

47 Herskovits, *The Myth of the Negro Past* (New York, 1941).

48 Davidson, *The Lost Cities of Africa* (Boston, 1959).

49 As an example of a volume opening this subject to investigation, see Newton M. Puckett, *Folk Beliefs of The Southern Negro* (Chapel Hill, 1926).

50 G. G. Johnson, *A Social History of the Sea Islands* (Chapel Hill, 1930); and G. B. Johnson, *Folk Culture on St. Helena Island, South Carolina* (Chapel Hill, 1930).

51 Bancroft, *Slave Trading in the Old South* (Baltimore, 1931). See also Jacob E. Cooke, *Frederic Bancroft* (Norman, 1957); and John E. Cairnes, *The Slave Power* (2nd ed.; London, 1863).

52 Stephenson, *Isaac Franklin, Slave Trader and Planter of the Old South* (Baton Rouge, 1938).

53 Aptheker, *American Negro Slave Revolts* (New York, 1943).

54 Chase C. Mooney, "The Literature of Slavery: A Re-evaluation," *Indiana Magazine of History*, XLVII (September, 1951), 255. See also Stephenson, *The South Lives in History*, 85.

55 Carroll, *Slave Insurrections in the United States, 1800–1865* (Boston, 1938).

volumes is concerned with explaining why there were so few revolts and insurrections. The nature of the plantation operated to isolate slaves,[56] but this does not explain why there were so few group efforts for freedom. Nor does the explanation lie in the law, the patrol, or the dictatorial position of the planter and overseer, for these all varied in time and place. Slavery existed in the towns, and few actual revolts occurred and almost as few conspiracies were discovered in them.[57] Richard C. Wade, who has carefully examined slavery in the cities, concluded that some accounts of insurrections in towns were based on error and overdrawn. For example, concerning the Denmark Vesey insurrection of 1822, he wrote, "It grew out of worsening relations between Negroes and whites in Charleston where a rumor of a plot set off a swift retaliation. I am convinced there was no significant conspiracy." [58]

Even the grim warning of impaled heads of rebels, as cited by Joe Gray Taylor, could not have affected many slaves.[59] There were no tom-toms to communicate from plantation to plantation. Fear as described by Stampp[60] operated to keep some of the slaves docile.[61] The slave system could not have operated without a special system of control. Negro slavery endured a long time in the United States—too long. Still the question of the vitality of slavery needs examination. The damning indictment of Elkins may be the answer: ". . . there were elements in the very structure of the plantation system . . . that could sustain infantilism as a normal feature of behavior. These elements, having less to do with 'cruelty' per se than simply with the sanctions of authority, were effective and pervasive enough to require that such infantilism be characterized as something much more basic than mere 'accommodation.' " [62] Why most enslaved Africans accepted slavery as they did and why their children continued to accept it requires careful exploration and

56 Edgar T. Thompson, "The Natural History of Agricultural Labor in the South," David K. Jackson (ed.), *American Studies in Honor of William Kenneth Boyd* (Durham, N. C., 1940), 113–17, hereinafter cited as Thompson, "Natural History of Agricultural Labor."

57 See the review of Carroll, *Slave Insurrections,* by Harvey Wish in *The Journal of Southern History,* V (May, 1939), 265.

58 Richard C. Wade to Bennett H. Wall, January 2, 1964, in possession of author. See also Richard C. Wade, "The Vesey Plot: A Reconsideration," *The Journal of Southern History,* XXX (May, 1964), 143–61 and his *Slavery and the Cities* (New York, 1964).

59 J. G. Taylor, *Negro Slavery in Louisiana,* 213.

60 Stampp, *The Peculiar Institution,* 141–91.

61 On this point, see Stephenson, *The South Lives in History,* 84–86.

62 Elkins, *Slavery. A Problem in American Institutional and Intellectual Life,* 86.

research. Certainly this subject, like that of the slave trade, needs fresh investigation.

The only volume on the actual physical conditions of slavery is William D. Postell, *The Health of Slaves on Southern Plantations.*[63] Postell accepted too much material uncritically, cited endless notes without interpretation, and made few generalizations. Still his is the only volume in an area obviously in need of new research.

Although virtually every travel account, article, and volume on the antebellum South treats the physical conditions of slavery, perhaps it is appropriate to point out to historians that the first valid table illustrating the life expectancy of slaves was that of the economists Conrad and Meyer, which has been referred to previously. Further enlightenment regarding the physical well-being of slaves could be obtained if scholars, using this or similar tables, would analyze slavery on plantations and farms by the case method, using the table prepared by Conrad and Meyer as a control.

John Hope Franklin, in his volume *From Slavery to Freedom,* made a significant contribution to understanding the role of the Negro both as slave and citizen.[64] He succeeded in his objective of placing the Negro in perspective across his more than three hundred years in America. Interestingly, Franklin, in a far more controversial volume, *The Militant South,* found that the presence of the Negro tended to strengthen both the cavalier and military traditions of the South.[65] But the tradition of violence that has coursed through the South from colonial times to the present was not completely based on race, for slaves and free Negroes fought almost as readily as white planters and yeomen.[66]

Another significant general work is that of the sociologist, E. Franklin Frazier, *The Negro in The United States.*[67] Frazier, using the basic techniques that Gunnar Myrdal employed in *An American Dilemma,*[68] sought to explain the process by which African culture was replaced by

63 Postell, *The Health of Slaves on Southern Plantations* (Baton Rouge, 1951). See the interesting chapter entitled "Negro Peculiarities," in Weymouth T. Jordan, *Ante-Bellum Alabama, Town and Country* (Tallahassee, 1957), 84–105. See also the articles and books of John Duffy and Jo Ann Carrigan on antebellum medicine.

64 Franklin, *From Slavery to Freedom* (New York, 1947).

65 Franklin, *The Militant South* (Cambridge, Mass., 1956), 12–79. Fundamentally this volume lacks perspective, though the monistic approach does serve a useful purpose.

66 *Ibid.,* 12.

67 Frazier, *The Negro in The United States* (New York, 1949).

68 Myrdal, *An American Dilemma* (2 vols.; New York, 1944).

American. Though Frazier's treatment of slavery is brief, it is neverthe-less rewarding.

Contemporary students of slavery in the antebellum South have just begun to reappraise the institution, but their volumes are in no wise definitive. State studies of slavery are but guideposts to the wealth of material so belatedly collected. We need a new appraisal of the cultural aspects of slavery and of the socio-psychological effects of slavery on black and white. Moreover—to speak more broadly—the entire field of southern history must be reexamined. Areas peripheral to slavery need detailed exploration on the state level and synthesis on the regional level. Among the major pioneer studies of this nature that have been neither emulated nor paralleled are Avery Craven, *Soil Exhaustion as a Factor in the Agricultural History of Virginia and Maryland;* Robert R. Russel, *Economic Aspects of Southern Sectionalism;* Lorenzo J. Greene, *The Negro in Colonial New England;* Roger W. Shugg, *Origins of Class Struggle in Louisiana;* Francis P. Gaines, *The Southern Plantation;* Joseph C. Sitterson, *Sugar Country: The Cane Sugar Industry in The South, 1753–1950;* Joseph C. Robert, *The Tobacco Kingdom, Plantation, Market, and Factory in Virginia and North Carolina, 1800–1860;* and James F. Hopkins, *A History of The Hemp Industry in Kentucky.* Then there is the parallel study, Richard Morris, *Government and Labor in Early America.* Studies of antebellum agriculture like John H. Moore's on Mississippi are vital to understanding slavery. Whatever merits historians may attribute to these monographs,[69] all have in common a coverage of a vital area or topic bearing directly on both the South and slavery. Comparable studies for all the southern states or the South would open the antebellum South to reexamination.[70]

The most intellectually stimulating and challenging essays on slavery

69 A. O. Craven, *Soil Exhaustion as a Factor in the Agricultural History of Virginia and Maryland* (Urbana, Ill., 1926) ; Russel, *Economic Aspects of Southern Sectionalism, 1840–1861* (Urbana, 1924) ; Greene, *The Negro in Colonial New England 1620–1776* (New York, 1942) ; Shugg, *Origins of Class Struggle in Louisiana* (Baton Rouge, 1939) ; Gaines, *The Southern Plantation* (New York, 1925) ; Sitterson, *Sugar Country: The Cane Sugar Industry in The South, 1753–1950* (Lexington, 1953) ; Robert, *The Tobacco Kingdom, Plantation, Market, and Factory in Virginia and North Carolina, 1800–1860* (Durham, N. C., 1938) ; Hopkins, *A History of The Hemp Industry in Kentucky* (Lexington, 1951) ; Morris, *Government and Labor in Early America* (New York, 1946) ; Moore, *Agriculture in Ante-Bellum Mississippi* (New York, 1958).

70 Perhaps preoccupation with the end product of slavery—the Civil War—has led historians of the South to abandon their craft. A careful checking of the major historical periodicals leads to the conclusion that for some reason there is relatively little basic research now conducted in many phases of the history of the South.

in recent years have been written by historians interested in sociology and economics, and by economists. One of them, apparently little known and rarely cited, is Edgar T. Thompson, "The Natural History of Agricultural Labor in the South." Thompson was concerned primarily with the economic development of slavery and the sharecrop system. To him, impersonal forces operated to develop such institutions as slavery. He dismissed the charge that slaves were generally oppressed, except as viewed through present-day concepts of oppression: "On ante-bellum plantations slavery was not an abstract problem of right and justice to be debated. . . . Slavery was a set of concrete and very commonplace relationships with individual Negroes . . . for the very practical purpose of making a crop of cotton or tobacco." [71] Thompson described plantation agriculture as military agriculture. Slave labor, or forced labor in America, was, therefore, "mainly a defensive measure against the effects of the frontier on the labor market."

A second interesting article was Alfred H. Conrad and John R. Meyer, "The Economics of Slavery in the Ante Bellum South." [72] These scholars sought to resolve the question of the profitability of slavery. This they have done better than any other writers on the subject. Using the term "modern capital theory" rather than the accounting concept of profitability, they considered the slave both as a producer and an investment. Conrad and Meyer prepared very accurate tables based on the best available data. They found that slavery was profitable for the entire South and that investments in slaves yielded returns which compared favorably to investments in property in the free states. As they put it, "It was profitable—at least as profitable as most other enterprises of the time in the United States." These authors contended: "The failure of southern development [in the antebellum period] can no longer be explained by assertions of the unprofitability of slavery or the inefficiency of the slave labor market." [73]

Douglas F. Dowd pointed out in a provocative reply that it was most difficult to make a meaningful distinction between the social and economic factors of slavery, especially since the two were in a state of continuous interaction. Dowd, charging that slavery inhibited the development of entrepreneurial capitalism, contended that if slavery was profitable, the "profit" came high:

71 Thompson, "Natural History of Agricultural Labor," 110–74.
72 Conrad and Meyer, "The Economics of Slavery in the Ante Bellum South," 95–131.
73 Conrad and Meyer, "Reply," *Journal of Political Economy,* LXVI (October, 1958), 443.

. . . it was at a price: the domination of southern society by the slave issue. This in turn meant the suppression of that kind of social rationality which has been, for better or for worse, associated with the development of industrial capitalism. . . . For the Southerner to convert himself to beliefs and behavior which would support and comport with slavery required a concentration so intense that all else became secondary—including the process of capital accumulation.[74]

Coincidentally, Conrad and Meyer, in their reply to Dowd, pointed out other areas of study regarding slavery not yet explored by historians: entrepreneurship and the socio-psychological problem of explaining the failure of planters to invest profits rather than consume them.[75] Perhaps these subjects will soon attract historians of the South and slavery.

Dowd tackled another difficult problem of great concern to scholars of slavery and the South. In an article comparing the economic development of the South and West, he concluded that the South deliberately chose to be a separate country, first because of slavery and afterward because of race. The Negro, whether slave or free, was to Dowd, as Phillips had already said,[76] the central theme of southern history. To Dowd this was the basic difference in the development of the South and the West, and the price paid was second-class citizenship for the former section.[77]

Another stimulating article on the question of profitability was Thomas P. Govan, "Was Plantation Slavery Profitable?" Govan, refuting the conclusion that slavery was not profitable, found that Sydnor's own figures in *Slavery in Mississippi* when used accurately, showed the hypothetical planter making a handsome profit. Govan also emphasized that slavery was less an economic system than "a social order to permit two unlike peoples to live together." [78] This point, while neither unique nor new, needs further study and elaboration.

Little used but nevertheless still one of the half-dozen best essays yet to appear on the controversy over the effects of slavery is Robert R. Russel, "The General Effects of Slavery upon Southern Economic

74 Dowd, "The Economics of Slavery in the Ante Bellum South: A Comment," *Journal of Political Economy,* LXVI (October, 1958), 440–42.

75 Conrad and Meyer, "Reply," 443.

76 Phillips, "The Central Theme of Southern History," *American Historical Review,* XXIV (October, 1928), 30–43.

77 Dowd, "A Comparative Analysis of Economic Development in the American West and South," *Journal of Economic History,* XVI (December, 1956), 558–74.

78 Govan, "Was Plantation Slavery Profitable?" *Journal of Southern History,* VIII (November, 1942), 513–35.

Progress." Perhaps this article has been ignored largely because Russel realistically refuted the argument that slavery—through "skinning" the land, degrading manual labor, retarding population growth, foreclosing economic opportunities, and preventing accumulation of capital—was responsible for the relative economic lag of the South. Russel charged that "the importance of Negro slavery as a factor determining the character and extent of the economic development of the South has been greatly overestimated." [79] Essentially, Conrad and Meyer substantiated the thesis of Russel: "Slavery did not make the Cavalier any more than slavery invented speculation in cotton." [80]

Harold D. Woodman, in a provocative article, "The Profitability of Slavery: A Historical Perennial," has sifted the work of both antebellum and modern writers. Woodman pointed out that there has been no general agreement on the question of profits or the effects of slavery. He made an excellent contribution through his clarification of the varying bases used by writers in arriving at conflicting conclusions on the subject of the profitability of slavery and its economic and social effects.[81]

Robert W. Smith added the point that it was erroneous to use current slave prices in assessing the capital investment of planters. Smith stated that it was "perhaps simpler and more accurate to consider the total slave force of a planter in determining his labor investment." He suggested that the cost of maintaining a slave born on the plantation, along with the time lost from work by the mother, represented the sole capital investment until the slave became productive. He further pointed out that the maintenance cost-production value ratio of slaves was so overbalanced by the production figure that southwestern planters on fresh lands bid the price of slaves up, and the same imbalance led to the migration of eastern planters or to the sale of their surplus slaves.[82]

In challenging essays Fabien Linden and Eugene D. Genovese have explored the effects of slavery on the development of manufacturing and the home market.[83] While controversy may be expected over their con-

79 Russel, "The General Effects of Slavery Upon Southern Economic Progress," *Journal of Southern History,* IV (February, 1938), 35–54.
80 Conrad and Meyer, "The Economics of Slavery in the Ante Bellum South," 120.
81 Woodman, "The Profitability of Slavery: A Historical Perennial," *Journal of Southern History,* XXIX (August, 1963), 303–25.
82 Smith, "Was Slavery Unprofitable in the Ante-Bellum South?" *Agricultural History,* XX (January, 1946), 62–64.
83 Linden, "Repercussions of Manufacturing in the Ante-Bellum South," *North Carolina Historical Review,* XVII (October, 1940), 313–31; Genovese, "The Significance of the Slave Plantation for Southern Economic Development," *Journal of Southern History,* XXVIII (November, 1962), 422–37.

clusions, these two articles should serve to stimulate further research in the social and political as well as economic effects of slavery on southern development.

In an essay in the *William and Mary Quarterly* on the "Origins of the Southern Labor System," Oscar and Mary Handlin used considerable new material to reappraise the thesis that the first Negroes in Virginia had the rather uncertain status of being neither slave nor free. Essentially, this essay amplified James C. Ballagh's contention that slavery did not begin in 1619.[84]

Slavery and its effects have prompted other scholars to write significant articles.[85] However, those cited bear out the statement that, insofar as analyses and a fresh point of view are concerned, the most stimulating work on slavery is being done by scholars interested in the economics of slavery and the effects of the capital investment in slavery on other aspects of southern life and development. To a large degree, articles on other aspects of slavery tend to supplement or amplify the details in Phillips and Stampp.[86]

Analysis of the historical literature on slavery defies completion. Of more interest than work completed is that still unwritten.

All aspects of southern history invite research, but none more than slavery. In recent years the image of the American abroad has too often been the image of a southern racist. The background of slavery helped to produce a person not understood even by Americans. Reconstruction of the actuality of slavery by imaginative historians exploring all facets of the material available will help us to understand this person.

---

84 Oscar and Mary F. Handlin, "Origins of the Southern Labor System," *William and Mary Quarterly,* 3rd Series, VII (April, 1950), 199–222; Ballagh, *A History of Slavery in Virginia* (Baltimore, 1902).

85 For example, see Fletcher M. Green, "Democracy in The Old South," *Journal of Southern History,* XII (February, 1946), 1–23; James C. Bonner, "Profile of a Late Ante-Bellum Community," *American Historical Review,* XLIX (July, 1944), 663–80; Harry L. Coles, "Some Notes on Slaveownership and Landownership In Louisiana, 1850–1860," *Journal of Southern History,* IX (August, 1943), 381–94.

86 For example, Bennett H. Wall, "Medical Care of Ebenezer Pettigrew's Slaves," *Mississippi Valley Historical Review,* XXXVII (December, 1950), 451–70.

VIII

The Mind of
The Antebellum South

Herbert J. Doherty, Jr.

A SURVEY of historical literature on the mind of the antebellum South immediately forces one to decide upon definitions. In this essay the "mind" of the South is defined to include the history of literature, publishing, religion, education, science, and architecture and the arts. The "antebellum South" refers to the states in which slavery flourished between 1815 and 1861. This period is chosen because during these years a distinctive southern culture was most apparent, southern sectionalism was most virulent, and southern attempts to be distinct from the remainder of the nation were most determined. Indeed, many historians believe that there was no marked southern consciousness until the rise of the slavery controversy following the War of 1812. Southern intellectuals who were preeminently national figures have been omitted; hence Jefferson and John Marshall do not figure in these pages.

One standard approach to the writing of general histories of the South has been to describe the varieties of geographical regions which comprise it. Similarly, one who attempts to study the "mind" of the Old South soon perceives that there were many "southern minds." Much of the more rarified cultural activity—such as art, *belles lettres*, literary criticism, music and the theater, and liberal theological speculation—was carried on almost exclusively in the urban centers. Foremost were Baltimore, Richmond, Charleston, and New Orleans, while towns such as Savannah, Natchez, and Nashville assumed secondary importance. The character of each of these differed. New Orleans' languid, superficially metropolitan Creole culture probably reached its highest development in the theatrical arts. Baltimore's bustling, commercial, Yankee-oriented society encouraged national-minded economic writers and journalists. In between were Richmond, symbol of a decaying upper-South plantation regime, and Charleston, seat of absentee landlords orienting themselves to the tastes of English aristocrats, ignoring their imminent economic decline, and producing a community which has been called the literary capital of the Old South. Beyond the city-bound cultural patterns of the Old South were those of the plantation, the Negro, and the poor white and the middle class folk of the hills, the Mississippi Valley, and the Southwest. Their "minds" are more difficult to understand because of the lack of extant sources, but glimpses into them can be gained in Negro spirituals, frontier humor, newspapers, farm periodicals, and the activities of frontier preachers and churches.

Some aspects of the antebellum southern mind have been written about continuously, voluminously, and usually uncritically since the Civil War. This is most true of literature and religion, areas in which nineteenth-century writing is usually defensive, contentious, provincial, and of little lasting value except as it indirectly testifies to the state of intellectual activity in the post-Civil War South. Near the end of the century, however, the rise of the trained scholar began to have an impact on the writing of southern history. Foremost among this group was William Peterfield Trent of Richmond, who was attracted to Johns Hopkins University in 1887 by the fame of Herbert Baxter Adams.[1] As interest in antebellum southern thought grew, moreover, scholars of other sections contributed to its study, while more and more *southern* writers and historians made respectable contributions to various aspects of antebellum intellectual history. But not until a generation ago did modern concepts of intellectual history gain acceptance and bring new vitality into southern historiography. Not until about 1930 did serious students

1 Wendell H. Stephenson, "William P. Trent as a Historian of the South," *Journal of Southern History*, XV (May, 1949), 151–77.

begin to appear who were interested in showing the interrelationships of the major institutions and values of southern culture, placing ideas and cultural patterns in the total context of their times, and showing how these patterns were shaped and altered by the currents of history.

One of the earliest systematic attempts to bring the best scholarship to bear upon the history of the South was the publication, early in the twentieth century, of the thirteen-volume series, *The South in the Building of the Nation.*[2] This impressive series sought to cover virtually every aspect of the South, and four volumes touch upon social, cultural, and intellectual history. Two of these are of little lasting value. *History of Southern Fiction,* edited by Edwin Mims, is mostly a selection of writings by southern authors, and *History of Southern Oratory* is a compilation of speeches almost exclusively by political orators with an introductory history by Thomas E. Watson. The volume, *Social Life,* edited by Samuel Chiles Mitchell, is of more value and includes essays on art, sculpture, architecture, religious denominations, education, and reform movements. Many of the essays, however, tend to be narrowly conceived, briefly executed, and statistical or descriptive in nature rather than analytical or reflective. The treatment of antebellum education is defensive. Beyond all measure, the best of these volumes is the one edited by John Bell Henneman, *History of the Literary and Intellectual Life of the South.* This work contains first rate commentary on southern literature and essays on contributions by Southerners to natural history, science, mathematics, law, medicine, and music. The literary historian, William P. Trent, maintained that the antebellum South had not rivaled New England or the Middle Atlantic states in intellectual contributions, but he remarked that this volume showed that the range of southern intellectual activity was "far wider than the outside world or most Southerners seem to have thought."[3]

Almost twenty years passed before antebellum southern thought again received significant attention. Then, in 1927, Vernon L. Parrington devoted a substantial part of *The Romantic Revolution in America* to "The Mind of the South."[4] Parrington's work was limited to southern

2 Julian A. C. Chandler *et al.* (eds.), *The South in the Building of the Nation* (13 vols.; Richmond, 1909–1913).

3 Trent, "Introduction," in Henneman (ed.), *History of the Literary and Intellectual Life of the South,* xvi, Volume VII of Chandler *et al.* (eds.), *The South in the Building of the Nation.* Professor Henneman, editor of this volume, died before its completion, and the volume was finished and its introduction written by Professor Trent.

4 Parrington, *The Romantic Revolution in America* (New York, 1927), 3–179, Volume II of *Main Currents in American Thought* (3 vols.; New York, 1927–30).

literature, however, and will be discussed at greater length later in this essay. Virginius Dabney followed in 1932 with *Liberalism in the South*.[5] Though his theme encompassed economics, literature, religion, art, and education, he did not exercise much critical judgment.

The greater interest shown in cultural and intellectual history since the Great Depression has resulted in several major contributions to the history of the southern mind. Most of them were foreshadowed by Clement Eaton's pioneering *Freedom of Thought in the Old South*.[6] He sees the southern mind in this era as being in transition from aristocratic liberalism to militant authoritarianism. Central themes in the development of this story are southern defensiveness on slavery and orthodoxy in religion. Eaton's view of this transformation is one that raised the ire of several historians.[7] Nonetheless, this book is an historiographical landmark. On its heels came the provocative, imaginative volume of Wilbur J. Cash, *The Mind of the South*.[8] His treatment, literary and intuitive rather than scholarly, is not a balanced intellectual history, for it hardly touches on important contributions to political theory, philosophy, or science. Rather, it attempts to portray the mind of the average Southerner. Like Eaton, Cash saw that mind strait-jacketed by slavery but tormented by a conscience made uneasy because of that institution.

Volumes in the long-planned *History of the South* series began to appear after the Second World War. Charles S. Sydnor's *The Development of Southern Sectionalism, 1819–1848* appeared in 1948, but the succeeding volume, Avery O. Craven's *The Growth of Southern Nationalism, 1848–1861*, did not come from the press until 1953.[9] Both are integrated narratives of southern history, valuable for showing the interrelationships between political, economic, cultural, and intellectual development in the era when efforts to encourage a southern mind were most intense. Rollin G. Osterweis, in his monograph *Romanticism and Nationalism in the Old South*, saw the cult of chivalry, the plantation system, and Negro slavery as the three factors most important in shap-

5 V. Dabney, *Liberalism in the South* (Chapel Hill, 1932).

6 Eaton, *Freedom of Thought in the Old South* (Durham, N. C., 1940).

7 See especially reviews by R. S. Cotterill in *Mississippi Valley Historical Review*, XXVII (September, 1940), 299–300; and Frank L. Owsley in *Journal of Southern History*, VI (November, 1940), 558–59.

8 Cash, *The Mind of the South* (New York, 1941). A recent volume, similar in concept and execution, is Henry Savage, Jr., *Seeds of Time, the Background of Southern Thinking* (New York, 1959).

9 Sydnor, *The Development of Southern Sectionalism, 1819–1848* (Baton Rouge, 1948); Craven, *The Growth of Southern Nationalism, 1848–1861* (Baton Rouge, 1953).

ing a distinctively southern mind.[10] It was the first of this trio that interested Osterweis most, but he emphasized the cult of chivalry as but one phase of the whole romantic movement that swept the South between 1815 and 1860. He saw southern nationalism as the most important element in that romanticism.

A most suggestive article, pointing to the fact that Southerners found more to occupy their minds than slavery and politics, appeared in the *Journal of Southern History* in 1957.[11] James W. Patton, who presides over the impressive Southern Historical Collection at the University of North Carolina, in his article, "Facets of the South in the 1850's," did an exceedingly good job of showing the provincialisms and prejudices of the antebellum Southerner and the difficulty he had in evaluating alien cultures objectively.

The seventh decade of the twentieth century has seen two more important contributions by Clement Eaton to cultural and intellectual history. His *The Growth of Southern Civilization, 1790–1860* was a summing up of the scholarly work of a lifetime. This volume depicts the distinctive social patterns of southern life, but does not concentrate upon cultural and intellectual developments. Such materials Eaton saved for a later book, *The Mind of the Old South*.[12] Both works show us a southern mind which ran deeper than that seen by Osterweis and which was more diverse and impressively detailed than that seen by Cash. Professor Eaton brings a surer grasp and a firmer ordering to the comprehensive mass of information he commands than does any other author writing on southern cultural and intellectual history today.

Several notable social histories of individual southern states have been published within the last generation. Each makes a greater or lesser contribution and illustrates regional differences better than the general studies do. Minnie Clare Boyd's *Alabama in the Fifties: A Social Study* amassed from newspaper sources a quantity of new information on religion, education, law, and journalism, but the book fell short on appraisal and interpretation.[13] Probably the best of the state studies was that of Guion Griffis Johnson, *Ante-Bellum North Carolina: A Social*

10 Osterweis, *Romanticism and Nationalism in the Old South* (New Haven, 1949).

11 Patton, "Facets of the South in the 1850's," *Journal of Southern History,* XXIII (February, 1957), 3–24.

12 Eaton, *The Growth of Southern Civilization, 1790–1860* (New York, 1961), in Henry Steele Commager and Richard B. Morris (eds.), *The New American Nation;* and Eaton, *The Mind of the Old South* (Baton Rouge, 1964).

13 Boyd, *Alabama in the Fifties: A Social Study* (New York, 1931).

History.[14] More comprehensive than the others, it included treatment of education, religion, newspapers and periodicals, and the intellectual awakening of the 1850's. Indeed, the Johnson study was a model for social history and reflected the brilliant work being done in sociology and history at Chapel Hill in the 1930's. Less impressive was Rosser H. Taylor's *Ante-Bellum South Carolina: A Social and Cultural History*.[15] It brought together widely scattered information on medicine, education, religion, the theater and the arts, literature, and publishing. Generally, however, Taylor reviewed South Carolina culture through rose-colored glasses.

Kentucky has been the subject of two recent monographs. F. Garvin Davenport's *Ante-Bellum Kentucky: A Social History, 1800–1860* assembled information on many subjects but presented little that was new.[16] More stimulating was Arthur K. Moore's *The Frontier Mind: A Cultural Analysis of the Kentucky Frontiersman*, which emphasized the anti-intellectual impact of the frontier.[17] Moore was mainly concerned with the growth of a native literature, and his study centers upon hindrances to literary production. His analysis is original and provocative.

We still have few broadly conceived treatments of cultural life in the cities of the Old South, except for three cities in the Mississippi River Valley. Some of the most interesting work pertains to life in Natchez. Charles S. Sydnor's study of Benjamin L. C. Wailes, *A Gentleman of the Old Natchez Region*, is actually a history of the civilization of the area from 1800 to 1860.[18] Wailes was an educator, historian, naturalist, planter, and traveler, and Sydnor takes his life as a point of departure for the story of the social, scientific, and cultural interests of the area. The result is a fascinating and enlightening view of life in a near-legendary southern river town. Supplementary to Professor Sydnor's

14 G. G. Johnson, *Ante-Bellum North Carolina: A Social History* (Chapel Hill, 1937).

15 R. H. Taylor, *Ante-Bellum South Carolina: A Social and Cultural History* (Chapel Hill, 1942).

16 Davenport, *Ante-Bellum Kentucky: A Social History, 1800–1860* (Oxford, Ohio, 1943).

17 Moore, *The Frontier Mind: A Cultural Analysis of the Kentucky Frontiersman* (Lexington, Kentucky, 1957). Niels Henry Sonne, *Liberal Kentucky, 1780–1828* (New York, 1939), is a rather narrow view of the struggle between religious liberalism and Protestant orthodoxy and is examined in another connection later in this essay.

18 Sydnor, *A Gentleman of the Old Natchez Region: Benjamin L. C. Wailes* (Durham, N. C., 1938).

volume, and showing a different side of life in Natchez, are two books by Edwin A. Davis and William Ransom Hogan. One was their edition of the diary of William Johnson, a free Negro of Natchez.[19] This gave a wonderfully detailed and intimate picture of the city between 1835 and 1851 as seen by an intelligent man who moved in both white and Negro circles and really belonged to neither. It is a rare primary source on free Negro life with valuable insights into the cultural life open to this uneasy class of people. The second was *The Barber of Natchez,* a popularized history based largely on the Johnson diary but illuminated by additional research to produce an interesting volume of social history containing a fair amount of material on intellectual and cultural interests.[20]

F. Garvin Davenport had less fertile soil to till than Sydnor, Davis, and Hogan, but his *Cultural Life in Nashville on the Eve of the Civil War* [21] shows that culture was making headway against the harsh frontier by mid-nineteenth century. He treats of schools, the theater, religion, writers, newspapers, and bookstores; and he points up the obstacles to and the superficiality of cultural achievement.

An interesting footnote to the history of old New Orleans was contributed in 1952 by Joseph D. Tregle, Jr., in the *Journal of Southern History.*[22] Challenging the traditional romantic views of Creole society, he said that it was shallow, provincial, unlettered, and unskilled. It was a society without cultural attainments, to which literature, art, and science did not appeal, and which gave only sparing support even to the theater.

Insofar as topical examinations of southern intellectual interests are concerned, the field of literature, particularly *belles lettres,* is the most thoroughly worked area. It was not always so. Few studies of lasting value appeared between 1865 and the 1890's. The literature produced by the slavery regime seemed discredited by the South's defeat in war, and even Southerners were content to let the memories of their writers die. A new era in southern literary historiography began with the work by William Peterfield Trent in the early 1900's. His first great work,

19 Hogan and Davis (eds.), *William Johnson's Natchez: The Ante-Bellum Diary of a Free Negro* ("Source Studies in Southern History," No. 1 [Baton Rouge, 1951]).

20 Davis and Hogan, *The Barber of Natchez* (Baton Rouge, 1954).

21 Davenport, *Cultural Life in Nashville on the Eve of the Civil War* (Chapel Hill, 1941).

22 Tregle, "Early New Orleans Society: A Reappraisal," *Journal of Southern History,* XVIII (February, 1952), 20–36.

Southern Writers, is an anthology, with biographical sketches, of eighty-six writers.[23] Trent's treatment was not provincial, did not respect southern sensitivities, and coincided in some respects—notably his disparagement of antebellum literary productivity and his attribution of its poor quality to the deadening influence of slavery—with the earlier views of Hinton Rowan Helper.[24] Trent was most famous for his *William Gilmore Simms,* about which more will be said later. A notable northern literary historian who made a valiant attempt to encompass southern writing was Montrose J. Moses.[25] He, however, knew too little about the South, and his work is marred by frequent elementary errors.

The third decade of the twentieth century witnessed a literary study that surpassed all others at the time—the second volume of Vernon L. Parrington's *Main Currents in American Thought,* which contained a masterful survey of the writers of the Old South.[26] Not restricted to *belles lettres,* this volume touched also upon political and economic theory, proslavery literature, and humor. Parrington's famous Jeffersonian bias did not prevent his serious and extended analysis of anti-Jeffersonian writers. Critical scholarship of such high quality was increasingly being brought to bear on the traditions of southern literature by the end of the 1920's. The strain of romanticism—so marked in the 1850's—was reexamined. It had come to be visualized as embracing an all-pervasive admiration of the medieval romances of Sir Walter Scott. Important exceptions to this impression were taken by Grace Warren Landrum in two articles in *American Literature.*[27] Her writings were important for showing that the emphasis on Scott ignored the broad range of southern reading—Shakespeare, Byron, Bulwer, Cooper, Dickens, Thackeray, and Thomas More—and that the very faults which modern critics condemn in Scott were also seen by antebellum southern critics.

In 1940 a landmark article by Jay B. Hubbell, foreshadowing his greater work to come, was published in *American Studies in Honor of William Kenneth Boyd.*[28] It was "Literary Nationalism in the Old

23 Trent, *Southern Writers* (New York, 1905).

24 Helper, *The Impending Crisis of the South: How to Meet It* (New York, 1857).

25 Moses, *Literature of the South* (New York, 1910).

26 Parrington, *The Romantic Revolution in America,* 3–179.

27 Landrum, "Sir Walter Scott and his Literary Rivals in the Old South," *American Literature,* II (November, 1930), 256–76, and "Notes on the Reading of the Old South," *American Literature,* III (March, 1931), 60–71.

28 Hubbell, "Literary Nationalism in the Old South," in David Kelley Jackson (ed.), *American Studies in Honor of William Kenneth Boyd* (Durham, N. C., 1940), 175–220.

South," which focused upon the political motivation behind sectional literature and the barriers to literary accomplishment. Hubbell concluded that there was little demand for a distinctively southern literature before 1830, and that demand was in direct correlation to the intensity of the slavery controversy after that date. The attempt, however, was doomed to failure from the outset, for the economic vassalage of the South to the North left the publishing business a near-monopoly of the North. Hubbell further observed, "Great literature has not ordinarily resulted from a demand based upon patriotic motives." [29]

Hubbell's *magnum opus, The South in American Literature, 1607–1900,* appeared in 1954.[30] A dispassionate, accurate study, it deals with almost every southern writer worth remembering and is so broad in scope as to have some claim to being called a general intellectual history rather than a literary history. This is a monumentally definitive book even though it concentrates on history, not criticism. Unlike nineteenth-century critics, Hubbell is unwilling to judge antebellum southern literature as being either insignificant or distinctive. It was American, "an essential part of the nation's literature," but relatively less meritorious than that produced in other sections.[31]

Romanticism in the Old South gave rise to what has been called the plantation tradition. John Pendleton Kennedy's *Swallow Barn,* published in 1832, is generally accepted as the beginning of that tradition. Kennedy received his most complete biographical treatment at the hands of Henry T. Tuckerman in 1871.[32] It was a well-balanced book and appears to be one of the best literary biographies of the late nineteenth century. Edward M. Gwathmey's study, published in 1931, is briefer and contains some material overlooked by Tuckerman.[33]

The first general scholarly work was Francis Pendleton Gaines, *The Southern Plantation.*[34] The most recent contribution is William R. Taylor, *Cavalier and Yankee: The Old South and American National Character.*[35] Focusing more on the Southerner than the Yankee, this book

---

29 *Ibid.,* 217.

30 Hubbell, *The South in American Literature, 1607–1900* (Durham, N. C., 1954).

31 *Ibid.,* 327–28.

32 Tuckerman, *The Life of John Pendleton Kennedy* (New York, 1871).

33 Gwathmey, *John Pendleton Kennedy* (New York, 1931).

34 Gaines, *The Southern Plantation: A Study in the Development and Accuracy of a Tradition* (New York, 1925).

35 W. R. Taylor, *Cavalier and Yankee: The Old South and American National Character* (New York, 1961).

describes the "Cavalier image" of the Southerner which developed in the fictional literature of the first sixty years of the nineteenth century. Convincing, brilliantly written, abounding in valuable insights, Taylor's book has been hailed as "superior to almost everything else that has been done about the state of mind of the antebellum South." [36]

The single most important southern man of letters before the Civil War, William Gilmore Simms, has not received full-scale biographical treatment since William P. Trent's pioneering biography in 1892.[37] In this, his most important historical writing, Trent delineated his characteristic view of Southern intellectual life as being stunted, stagnant, and stifling. He, like Helper, blamed slavery for the poor quality of southern literary accomplishments. By the standards of Trent's day, this was a superior work. Today scholars view it as being excessively harsh. For example, John R. Welsh, writing in the *Journal of Southern History*, argues that Simms saw the South with more critical perception than has been admitted—a critical understanding extending from intellectual and economic matters to politics.[38]

Whether or not Boston-born Edgar Allan Poe should be ranked among southern writers is open to question. Educated at the University of Virginia, intermittently a resident of Richmond, and briefly though brilliantly the editor of the *Southern Literary Messenger,* Poe really belonged to the world. His major kinship with the South lay perhaps in his romanticism, yet, unlike other southern writers, his was a romanticism tied neither to time nor place. Poe's southern background is best treated by David K. Jackson and Agnes Bondurant. Jackson's volume, *Poe and the Southern Literary Messenger,* traces the writer's journalistic career in the South.[39] He concludes that Poe was "the magazinist" with few if any equals in nineteenth-century America, who pioneered in American literary criticism in the pages of the *Messenger.* Miss Bondurant, in *Poe's Richmond,* is concerned with the churches,

36 Review by Louis D. Rubin, Jr., in *Mississippi Valley Historical Review,* XLVIII (March, 1962), 704–706.

37 Trent, *William Gilmore Simms* (Boston, 1892). But see Edd Winfield Parks, *William Gilmore Simms as a Literary Critic* ("University of Georgia Monographs," No. 7 [Athens, Georgia, 1961]).

38 Welsh, "William Gilmore Simms, Critic of the South," *Journal of Southern History,* XXVI (May, 1960), 201–14. For a parallel earlier view, see John W. Higham, "The Changing Loyalties of William Gilmore Simms," *Journal of Southern History,* IX (May, 1943), 210–23.

39 Jackson, *Poe and the Southern Literary Messenger* (Richmond, 1934).

books, libraries, theaters, and amusements of the city as they might have influenced Poe.[40]

Poetry was a scarce commodity in the Old South and, aside from Poe, individual poets have received relatively scant historical notice. Perhaps the most notable were the Charlestonians, Henry Timrod and Paul Hamilton Hayne. Henry T. Thompson's *Henry Timrod: Laureate of the Confederacy* is useful but not really satisfactory.[41] The only biography of Hayne, Kate Harbes Becker, *Paul Hamilton Hayne: His Life and Letters,* overlooks much available material.[42] Jay B. Hubbell's edition of *The Last Years of Henry Timrod* contains much interesting material on both poets.[43] In the lower South, the foremost poets were Georgia's Thomas Holley Chivers and Richard Henry Wilde. The best works on Chivers are those by S. Foster Damon and Landon C. Bell, which debate whether Chivers copied Poe or Poe copied Chivers.[44] There is no good biography of Wilde. West of the mountains, Kentucky's Theodore O'Hara was undoubtedly the most talented poet. His story has been well told in Edgar Erskine Hume, *Colonel Theodore O'Hara: Author of The Bivouac of the Dead.*[45]

If, as many have claimed, romanticism in southern literature was an imitation of European literary fashions, the literary productions of the lower South and the Southwest have been more indigenous. These regions produced a realistic and earthy humorous literature which was often published in newspapers and therefore was thought to be common and of little account. John D. Wade's *Augustus Baldwin Longstreet: A Study of the Development of Culture in the South* was an almost definitive biography of the founder of this school. It marked the beginnings of scholarly work on southwestern frontier humorists.[46] W. Stanley Hoole's fine biography of Johnson Jones Hooper, another

40 Bondurant, *Poe's Richmond* (Richmond, 1942). See also Philip A. Bruce, "The Background of Poe's University Life," *South Atlantic Quarterly,* X (July, 1911), 212–26; E. A. Alderman, "Edgar Allan Poe and the University of Virginia," *Virginia Quarterly Review,* I (April, 1925), 78–84; W. S. Hoole, "Poe in Charleston, S. C.," *American Literature,* VI (March, 1934), 78–80.

41 Thompson, *Henry Timrod: Laureate of the Confederacy* (Columbia, S. C., 1928).

42 Becker, *Paul Hamilton Hayne: His Life and Letters* (Belmont, N. C., 1951).

43 Hubbell (ed.), *The Last Years of Henry Timrod* (Durham, N. C., 1941).

44 Damon, *Thomas Holley Chivers: Friend of Poe* (New York, 1930); Bell, *Poe and Chivers* (Columbus, Ohio, 1931).

45 Hume, *Colonel Theodore O'Hara: Author of The Bivouac of the Dead* (Charlottesville, Virginia, 1936).

46 Wade, *Augustus Baldwin Longstreet: A Study of the Development of Culture in the South* (New York, 1924).

frontier humorist, was published in 1952.[47] Though no definitive biography of Joseph G. Baldwin has appeared, an outstanding biographical and critical treatment published in 1901 by G. F. Mellen was interestingly supplemented in 1952 by Eugene Current-Garcia.[48] Cecil D. Eby, Jr., in 1960 published a life of David Hunter Strother, an independent-minded artist and author who wrote about all sections and in all modes but who was judged to be at his best when employing the style and mood of the humorists.[49] Henry Clay Lewis, the "Louisiana Swamp Doctor," remained something of a mystery until the researches of John Q. Anderson showed him to be a young physician who died at twenty-five. Writing in the guise of an elderly rural doctor, Lewis published some twenty humorous "Big Bear" tales in the New York *Spirit of the Times* in the 1840's.[50] The most distinguished representative of this school was Thomas Bangs Thorpe, a Louisiana newspaper editor. Thorpe turned out hundreds of humorous stories for the *Spirit of the Times* and other national periodicals and was something of a painter as well. Milton Rickels has portrayed him as a prime shaper of America's first important realistic tradition, that of the frontiersman.[51] The man who did most to give a national audience to these regional humorists was William T. Porter of the New York *Spirit of the Times*. He published more than a thousand pieces of their work over a thirty-year period. The importance of his magazine to southern frontier writers is made clear in Norris W. Yates, *William T. Porter and the* Spirit of the Times: *A Study of the Big Bear School of Humor*.[52]

Discussions of southern political literature inevitably center upon the writings of John C. Calhoun who is often viewed as one of the few Americans to have made original contributions to political theory. Writings about Calhoun range from extended biographical works to brief specialized articles and vary in viewpoint from the unconcealed animosity

---

47 Hoole, *Alias Simon Suggs: The Life and Times of Johnson Jones Hooper* (University, Alabama, 1952).

48 Mellen, "Joseph G. Baldwin and the 'Flush Times,'" *Sewanee Review*, IX (April, 1901), 171–84; Current-Garcia, "Joseph Glover Baldwin: Humorist or Moralist?" *Alabama Review*, V (April, 1952), 122–41.

49 Eby, *"Porte Crayon": The Life of David Hunter Strother* (Chapel Hill, 1960).

50 Anderson, *Louisiana Swamp Doctor: The Life and Writings of Henry Clay Lewis* (Baton Rouge, 1962).

51 Rickels, *Thomas Bangs Thorpe: Humorist of the Old Southwest* (Baton Rouge, 1962).

52 Yates, *William T. Porter and the* Spirit of the Times: *A Study of the Big Bear School of Humor* (Baton Rouge, 1957).

of Hermann E. von Holst to the adoration of Gustavus M. Pinckney.[53]
Twentieth-century Calhoun biographers generally may be termed
scholarly but sympathetic. Without doubt the definitive multivolume
Calhoun biography is that of Charles M. Wiltse, while the best one-
volume treatment now available is that of Margaret Coit.[54] Both writers
are so devoted to Calhoun that their enthusiasm weakens their critical
judgment when dealing with their hero's intellectual contributions.
Wiltse's discussion of Calhoun's political philosophy has been judged
"superficial as well as brief." [55] Both Wiltse and Miss Coit seem to
believe that the South Carolinian's doctrines are applicable to the present.
Perhaps the closest approximation to a rigorous analysis of Calhoun's
political theory was Charles E. Merriam's essay in *Studies in Southern
History and Politics Inscribed to William Archibald Dunning*.[56] The
much later study by August O. Spain illuminates many facets of Calhoun's mind and shows the derivations of his thought, but is short on
analysis and evaluation and long on defense.[57] Valuable insights can be
found in the sketches of Calhoun by William E. Dodd, Vernon L. Parrington, Richard Hofstadter, and Richard N. Current.[58]

John Randolph of Roanoke and John Taylor of Caroline were pre-
cursors of Calhoun's political thought and are often seen as links between the thought of Jefferson's day and that of Calhoun's. Henry
Adams' famous biography of Randolph is brilliant, entertaining, and
mercilessly partisan.[59] William Cabell Bruce's later study of Randolph
is the most complete biography, but it is enlivened only by Bruce's
denunciation of the Adams biography.[60] In recent years Randolph's
political ideas have been subject to investigation by latter-day conservatives in search of an intellectual foundation. One result of this search was

53 von Holst, *John C. Calhoun* (Boston, 1882) ; Pinckney, *Life of John C. Calhoun*
(Charleston, S. C., 1903).

54 Wiltse, *John C. Calhoun* (3 vols.; Indianapolis, 1944, 1949, 1951) ; Coit, *John
C. Calhoun: American Portrait* (Boston, 1950).

55 Review by Richard N. Current in *Mississippi Valley Historical Review*,
XXXVIII (March, 1952), 707–709.

56 Merriam, "The Political Philosophy of John C. Calhoun," in *Studies in Southern
History and Politics Inscribed to William Archibald Dunning* (New York, 1914),
319–40.

57 Spain, *The Political Theory of John C. Calhoun* (New York, 1951).

58 Dodd, *Statesmen of the Old South* (New York, 1911), 91–167; Parrington,
The Romantic Revolution in America, 69–82; Hofstadter, *The American Political
Tradition and the Men Who Made It* (New York, 1949), 67–91; Current, *John C.
Calhoun* (New York, 1963).

59 Adams, *John Randolph* (Boston, 1882).

60 W. C. Bruce, *John Randolph of Roanoke* (2 vols.; New York, 1922).

Russell Kirk's *Randolph of Roanoke: A Study in Conservative Thought*.[61] John Taylor of Caroline has a full scale biography by Henry H. Simms.[62] Half of the book is devoted to a review of Taylor's political writings, but the analysis of his ideas is weak. The work does not satisfactorily relate Taylor's political ideas to their economic basis. Parrington's earlier essay is helpful in this respect.[63]

The single outstanding general survey of antebellum southern political theory is Jesse T. Carpenter's *The South as a Conscious Minority*.[64] Carpenter organizes much information on political thought from Jefferson to Davis, but writes legalistically, shows little recognition of the social and economic milieu in which political theory took shape, seems unduly sympathetic to the southern position, and gives little attention to men who opposed sectionalism. Indeed, few students have been interested in antebellum Southerners whose views ran counter to Calhoun's.[65]

Work in economic theory was rarely if ever produced apart from political theory in the antebellum South. One of the earliest studies of this literature was the essay that Ulrich B. Phillips contributed to the volume on intellectual history in *The South in the Building of the Nation*.[66] Parrington also gave some attention to the economic ideas of southern publicists, particularly John Taylor of Caroline. But the most interesting and comprehensive survey appeared in the second volume of Joseph Dorfman's *Economic Mind in American Civilization*.[67] One of Dorfman's most important contributions is his delineation of the variety of economic viewpoints that prevailed in the antebellum South and his description of their relation to political and social attitudes. His work

61 Kirk, *Randolph of Roanoke: A Study in Conservative Thought* (Chicago, 1951).

62 Simms, *Life of John Taylor: The Story of a Brilliant Leader in the Early Virginia State Rights School* (Richmond, 1932).

63 Parrington, *The Romantic Revolution in America*, 14–19.

64 Carpenter, *The South as a Conscious Minority, 1789–1861: A Study in Political Thought* (New York, 1930).

65 A handful of good biographies exist of opponents of the nullifiers and secessionists. See especially Lillian A. Kibler, *Benjamin F. Perry, South Carolina Unionist* (Durham, N. C., 1946); Joseph H. Parks, *John Bell of Tennessee* (Baton Rouge, 1950); Percy S. Flippin, *Hershel V. Johnson of Georgia, State Rights Unionist* (Richmond, 1931); J. Fred Rippy, *Joel R. Poinsett, Versatile American* (Durham, N. C., 1935); and Herbert J. Doherty, Jr., *Richard Keith Call: Southern Unionist* (Gainesville, Fla., 1961).

66 Phillips, "Economic and Political Essays in the Ante-Bellum South," in Henneman (ed.), *History of the Literary and Intellectual Life of the South*, 173–99.

67 Dorfman, *The Economic Mind in American Civilization* (3 vols.; New York, 1946–1949).

is unusual, too, in setting southern doctrines in their national context.

The literature of economic theory frequently touched upon slavery and was bound up in the proslavery argument after 1820. Almost all the writings descriptive of this literature are the products of modern scholarship. The monumental treatise is William Sumner Jenkins, *Pro-Slavery Thought in the Old South*.[68] It traces the origins of both pro- and antislavery thought, but only briefly relates it to its social and economic backgrounds. An interesting article that relates the proslavery argument to Malthus' theories on population was published a year after Jenkins' book by Joseph J. Spengler in the *Journal of Southern History*.[69] The story of the rapid swing of southern public opinion to the "positive good" viewpoint has been told by Joseph Clarke Robert in *The Road from Monticello*.[70] Robert's focus is upon the Virginia slavery debates of 1832, which he views as a major turning point in southern attitudes on the peculiar institution. One of the leading proslavery spokesmen, George Fitzhugh, found a skillful biographer in Harvey Wish.[71]

Recent studies of attitudes toward Negro slavery have been influenced by the civil rights controversies of the 1950's and 1960's. The most significant, William Stanton's *The Leopard's Spots,* analyzes "scientific attitudes" toward race in America from 1815 to 1859. It concentrates on three individuals, of whom Josiah Clark Nott of Mobile was the most important Southerner. The major figures were all "racists," but Stanton gives due attention to their main opponent and critic, the Reverend John Bachman of Charleston.[72]

Vernon Loggins' *The Negro Author: His Development in America* was a pioneering attempt to discover the Negro contribution to American cultural life. Loggins contended that religion was the main channel of expression for the slave and that the spiritual was his chief literary contribution during the antebellum period. Mason Crum's work on the sea island Negroes, published in 1940, broadened our knowledge of Negro culture.[73] Dealing with dialect and way of life as well as songs

68 Jenkins, *Pro-Slavery Thought in the Old South* (Chapel Hill, 1935).
69 Spengler, "Population Theory in the Ante-Bellum South," *Journal of Southern History,* II (August, 1936), 360–89.
70 Robert, *The Road from Monticello, A Study of the Virginia Slavery Debate of 1832* ("Historical Papers of the Trinity College Historical Society," Series XXIV [Durham, N. C., 1941]).
71 Wish, *George Fitzhugh: Propagandist of the Old South* (Baton Rouge, 1943).
72 Stanton, *The Leopard's Spots: Scientific Attitudes toward Race in America, 1815–1859* (Chicago, 1960).
73 Loggins, *The Negro Author: His Development in America* (New York, 1931); Crum, *Gullah: Negro Life in the Carolina Sea Islands* (Durham, N. C., 1940).

and religion, this volume's merit lay largely in its discussion of spirituals. By 1953 Miles Mark Fisher could argue that sacred and secular songs formed a body of literature which tells the history of the Negro in this country during slavery.[74]

As contemporaries often noted, book publishing did not flourish in the Old South. Some of the problems of selling books in the South and of publishing southern authors were related in Warren S. Tryon, "The Publications of Ticknor and Fields in the South, 1840–1865." [75] This revealing article is a survey of the connections of southern readers and northern publishers, based on the records of the predecessors of the Houghton-Mifflin Company. Periodical literature did flourish in four southern cities—Charleston, Richmond, Baltimore, and New Orleans— and provided the surest outlet for southern writers. For the most part Charleston was the home of the most important magazines and was the closest thing to a literary center which the antebellum South possessed. Edwin Mims's essay, "Southern Magazines," in volume seven of *The South in the Building of the Nation,* was the earliest general history of antebellum southern periodical journalism. Other general and more recent studies are in the first two volumes of Frank Luther Mott's *History of American Magazines* and Jay B. Hubbell's essay, "Southern Magazines." [76] The single most important southern magazine was *The Southern Literary Messenger,* published at Richmond. A commemorative volume by its editor and publisher from 1843 to 1847, Benjamin Blake Minor, was published in 1905.[77]

Modern scholarship again must be credited with most of the more specialized work on southern periodical literature. David K. Jackson's *The Contributors and Contributions to The Southern Literary Messenger* is important for identifying the often anonymous material appearing in that review.[78] Linda Rhea's biography of Hugh Swinton Legaré tells us much about one of the chief Charleston magazines, the *Southern Re-*

---

74 Fisher, *Negro Slave Songs in the United States* (Ithaca, N. Y., 1953). See review by Margaret Walker in *Journal of Southern History,* XX (May, 1954), 265–66.

75 Tryon, "The Publications of Ticknor and Fields in the South, 1840–1865," *Journal of Southern History,* XIV (August, 1948), 305–30.

76 Mims, "Southern Magazines," in Henneman (ed.), *History of the Literary and Intellectual Life of the South,* 437–69; Mott, *A History of American Magazines* (3 vols.; Cambridge, Mass., 1930–1938); Hubbell, "Southern Magazines," in W. T. Couch (ed.), *Culture in the South* (Chapel Hill, 1935), 159–82.

77 Minor, *The Southern Literary Messenger* (New York, 1905).

78 Jackson (comp.), *The Contributors and Contributions to the Southern Literary Messenger* (Charlottesville, Virginia, 1936).

view.[79] The most notable periodical in the Lower South, *DeBow's Review,* edited by James Dunwoody Brownson DeBow in New Orleans, has been thoroughly covered by Otis C. Skipper.[80] *Niles Register,* the preeminent periodical in the Upper South, found a faithful chronicler in Norval Neil Luxon.[81]

Three surveys of periodical publications centering on two southern states and one city have been produced within the last generation. William Stanley Hoole, in 1936, prepared a checklist of Charleston periodicals published between 1732 and 1864 and introduced it with a historical resumé suggesting fields for fresh research and shedding light upon the lack of popular support for literary pursuits. Bertram Holland Flanders' work on Georgia literary magazines before 1865 analyzed twenty-four journals and their editors and contributors. Rhoda C. Ellison's history of the Alabama literary scene focused on authors and topics that appealed to Alabama readers between 1807 and 1870.[82] Notable listings of newspapers for a few states have been completed. Lester J. Cappon compiled a bibliography of Virginia newspapers, 1821–1935, with a long introduction. Miss Ellison performed a similar task for Alabama newspapers in 1954. Less a bibliography than a series of historical and biographical essays was the volume published by James Owen Knauss in 1926, *Territorial Florida Journalism.* It is an invaluable contribution to the early history of Florida.[83] Robert N. Elliott, Jr.'s recent *The Raleigh Register* is the only good history of an antebellum southern newspaper.[84]

Though editors of southern literary magazines might have wrung their hands over lack of support, the editors of agricultural journals had no such problems, for they served better the utilitarian interests of the reading public. Albert L. Demaree's *The American Agricultural Press,*

79 Rhea, *Hugh Swinton Legaré, A Charleston Intellectual* (Chapel Hill, 1934).

80 Skipper, "J. D. B. DeBow, the Man," *Journal of Southern History,* X (November, 1944), 404–23, and *J. D. B. DeBow: Magazinist of the Old South* (Athens, Georgia, 1958).

81 Luxon, *Niles' Weekly Register: News Magazine of the Nineteenth Century* (Baton Rouge, 1947).

82 Hoole, *A Check-List and Finding-List of Charleston Periodicals, 1732–1864* (Durham, N.C., 1936); Flanders, *Early Georgia Magazines: Literary Periodicals to 1865* (Athens, Georgia, 1944); Ellison, *Early Alabama Publications: A Study in Literary Interest* (University, Alabama, 1947).

83 Cappon, *Virginia Newspapers, 1821–1935, A Bibliography with Historical Introduction and Notes* (New York, 1936); Ellison, *History and Bibliography of Alabama Newspapers in the Nineteenth Century* (University, Alabama, 1954); Knauss, *Territorial Florida Journalism* (DeLand, Fla., 1926).

84 Elliott, *The Raleigh Register, 1799–1863* ("James Sprunt Studies in History and Political Science," Vol. 36 [Chapel Hill, 1955]).

1819–1860, shows that more than 400 such periodicals were published in all parts of the country in the antebellum period.[85] This solid study has a general survey of the farm press and detailed sketches of sixteen important journals, five of which were published in the South. Religious periodicals were possibly more widely read than farm journals in the South, and Henry Smith Stroupe found that at least 159 church journals were published in the South Atlantic states between 1802 and 1865.[86] His worthwhile study has an all too brief introduction, but it is a useful reference work.

Denominational and religious history, so long the province of defensive partisans, has now happily become a burgeoning field for scholars whose works are genuine contributions to intellectual history. The most notable is William Warren Sweet whose books have general currency today as the best studies of American religious history.[87] Fully as important for the South is Walter B. Posey, who further refined Sweet's frontier thesis as applied to church history. *The Development of Methodism in the Old Southwest, 1783–1824* was Posey's earliest volume. Though based almost entirely on printed sources, it was one of the most careful pieces of scholarship in its field when it appeared. It analyzed the factors in the expansion of the Methodist Church and was hailed as containing the best description of the camp meeting ever written. Almost twenty years later came Posey's *The Presbyterian Church in the Old Southwest, 1778–1838.* Though concentrating on Kentucky and Tennessee, Posey sought to portray the general impact of the democratic church on frontier life. On the heels of that study came *The Baptist Church in the Lower Mississippi Valley, 1776–1845.*[88] This volume draws important parallels between Methodist and Presbyterian development. In all these works Posey discussed church leadership, educational

85 Demaree, *The American Agricultural Press, 1819–1860* ("Columbia University Studies in the History of American Agriculture," No. 8 [New York, 1941]).

86 Stroupe, *The Religious Press in the South Atlantic States, 1802–1865: An Annotated Bibliography with Historical Introduction and Notes* ("Historical Papers of the Trinity College Historical Society," Series XXXII [Durham, N. C., 1956]).

87 See especially Sweet, *Revivalism in America: Its Origin, Growth, and Decline* (New York, 1944), *Religion in the Development of American Culture, 1765–1840* (New York, 1952), and the volumes edited by Sweet, *Religion on the American Frontier: The Baptists, 1783–1830* (New York, 1931), *Religion on the American Frontier: The Presbyterians, 1783–1840* (New York, 1936), and *Religion on the American Frontier: The Methodists* (Chicago, 1946).

88 Posey, *The Development of Methodism in the Old Southwest, 1783–1824* (Nashville, 1933), *The Presbyterian Church in the Old Southwest, 1778–1838* (Richmond, 1952), *The Baptist Church in the Lower Mississippi Valley, 1776–1845* (Lexington, Kentucky, 1957).

efforts, work among Indians and slaves, organization, and expansion. In all of them he relied heavily on published works and largely avoided theological and doctrinal analyses. It is surprising that nothing comparable to Posey's work has been done for the old seaboard states or the trans-Mississippi Southwest.

One of the most impressive contributions to intellectual history, however, is the essay done in 1940 by Clarence Ghodes on the Unitarian Church in the antebellum South.[89] Ghodes saw orthodoxy as the greatest foe of Unitarianism and associated the decline of that persuasion with the mounting conformism and intolerance produced in the South by the slavery controversy. He shows that Unitarianism had its greatest appeal in cities like Baltimore, Charleston, Louisville, Richmond, New Orleans, and Nashville. In contrast, historians have not done well by either Catholics or Jews. John Gilmary Shea's monumental Catholic study is helpful as a reference work. Michael Kenny's *Catholic Culture in Alabama* recounts the founding and fostering of Spring Hill College on Mobile Bay.[90] One of the oldest Jewish communities in America is that in Charleston, and its history has been told by Charles Reznikoff and Uriah Z. Engelman.[91]

The history of the Negro and his churches remains to be told in comprehensive objective fashion. One of the earlier twentieth-century studies, Carter G. Woodson's *History of the Negro Church,* is of no great value. More to the point are the article by Haven P. Perkins, "Religion for Slaves: Difficulties and Methods," and the book, *The Negro's God,* by Benjamin H. Mays.[92]

One pronounced characteristic of southern education in the antebellum period was its tendency away from foreign and northern influences. John S. Ezell's article, "A Southern Education for Southrons," deals mostly with higher education and gives some attention to the problem

---

89 Ghodes, "Some Notes on the Unitarian Church in the Ante-Bellum South: A Contribution to the History of Southern Liberalism," in Jackson (ed.), *American Studies in Honor of William Kenneth Boyd,* 327–66.

90 Shea, *History of the Catholic Church in the United States* (4 vols.; New York, 1886–1892) ; Kenny, *Catholic Culture in Alabama: Centenary Story of Spring Hill College, 1830–1930* (New York, 1931). An interesting biography of a Catholic is Peter Guilday, *The Life and Times of John England, First Bishop of Charleston, 1786–1842* (2 vols.; New York, 1927).

91 Reznikoff and Engelman, *The Jews of Charleston: A History of an American Jewish Community* (Philadelphia, 1950).

92 Woodson, *History of the Negro Church* (Washington, 1945) ; Perkins, "Religion for Slaves: Difficulties and Methods," *Church History,* X (September, 1941) ; Mays, *The Negro's God* (Boston, 1939).

of securing "proper" textbooks for a "southern education." [93] Education in the antebellum South was most highly developed at its upper level—colleges and universities. Histories of individual colleges abound, but the earlier ones have little value except to students or alumni of specific institutions. They are generally chronicles organized around presidential administrations, lacking in analysis, and failing to relate the history of the institution to the educational, political, and cultural trends of the times. However, several classics stand out. Kemp P. Battle's two-volume *History of the University of North Carolina* is a significant study by a man whose life was closely linked to the university. Somewhat more campus-centered is Philip A. Bruce, *History of the University of Virginia, 1819–1919*. This work contributes to the history of architecture as well as education. [94]

By the end of the third decade of the twentieth century, professionally trained historians with an eye to the many facets and complexities of educational history were beginning to move into this field. E. Merton Coulter in 1928 produced *College Life in the Old South,* a historical gem as yet undimmed. [95] With a view to depicting the role of the college and the college community in shaping the antebellum South, Professor Coulter minutely examined the University of Georgia as typical. James H. Easterby's volume on the College of Charleston sheds light on the intellectual life of Charleston and points up its important support of a fine museum of natural history. [96] Yet it does not satisfactorily relate the College to the history of education in South Carolina or the nation. Its focus is local, and its flavor, eulogistic.

West of the Appalachian Mountains, the oldest institution of higher education was Transylvania University at Lexington, Kentucky. Under the presidency of Connecticut-born Horace Holley beginning in 1818, this school became the foremost institution of learning in the West, noted for its law and medical schools. Holley's liberalism was his undoing, and the University declined in influence after his departure in 1826. Holley's story has been told briefly and rather superficially in Romie Dustin Judd, *The Educational Contributions of Horace Holley.* More stimulating and provocative is Niels Henry Sonne, *Liberal Kentucky,*

---

93 Ezell, "A Southern Education for Southrons," *Journal of Southern History,* XVII (August, 1951), 303–27.

94 Battle, *History of the University of North Carolina* (2 vols.; Raleigh, N.C., 1907–1912) ; P. A. Bruce, *History of the University of Virginia, 1819–1919* (5 vols.; New York, 1920–1922).

95 Coulter, *College Life in the Old South* (New York, 1928).

96 Easterby, *A History of the College of Charleston* (Charleston, S. C., 1935).

1780–1828, which views the struggle in Kentucky between religious liberalism and Protestant orthodoxy as focusing in the fight for control of Transylvania. This work, however, bears the impress of the doctrinaire liberalism frequently found in scholarly circles in the 1930's; too-sharp lines are drawn separating antagonists into "Calvinists" and "liberals." [97]

Not until after the Second World War were two university histories produced which could stand as models for students of intellectual history. Nora Campbell Chafin's landmark study of Duke University was hailed as mirroring "an epoch in the development of civilization in the United States." [98] It is a work of careful scholarship and balanced judgment. Shortly thereafter, Daniel Walker Hollis' *South Carolina College,* the first volume of his *University of South Carolina,* appeared.[99] Obviously a superior contribution, it reveals the cosmopolitan influences of the early days of South Carolina College and tells how growing orthodoxy and conformity marked the passage of the years toward Civil War. For individual church colleges, the best is George W. Paschal, *History of Wake Forest College,* the first volume of which covers the antebellum period. The best general study is Albea Godbold, *The Church College of the Old South.*[100] Though restricted to Episcopal, Baptist, Presbyterian, and Methodist colleges in Virginia, North and South Carolina, and Georgia, it marshals a considerable quantity of general information. The motives behind the founding of church colleges and their strengths and weaknesses are analyzed, and interesting discussions of curriculum, college life, and literary and debating societies are included.

As in other fields of intellectual activity, the education of the Negro has been neglected. Perhaps the most complete survey is the old work by Carter Woodson, *The Education of the Negro Prior to 1861.*[101]

The United States Bureau of Education, between 1888 and 1903, published a number of circulars tracing the history of education. One exists for almost every southern state; they are among the earliest objective

97 Judd, *The Educational Contributions of Horace Holley* (Nashville, 1936); Sonne, *Liberal Kentucky, 1780–1828* (New York, 1939).

98 Chafin, *Trinity College, 1839–1892: Beginnings of Duke University* (Durham, N. C., 1950). Reviewed by Richard D. Mosier in *American Historical Review,* LVI (October, 1950), 227–28.

99 Hollis, *South Carolina College* (Columbia, S. C., 1951), Volume I of *University of South Carolina.*

100 Paschal, *History of Wake Forest College* (3 vols.; Wake Forest, N. C., 1935–1943); Godbold, *The Church College of the Old South* (Durham, N. C., 1944).

101 Woodson, *The Education of the Negro Prior to 1861* (New York, 1915).

surveys of education in the South.[102] The first general study was Edgar W. Knight, *Public Education in the South*. Its thesis is the growth of democratic principles of education in the South. The connections between economic, social, political, and religious factors and education are emphasized, and more than half the volume is devoted to the antebellum period. Considerable attention is also given to the apprenticeship system and the academy movement. Articles by E. Merton Coulter, James W. Mobley, Ralph M. Lyon, and Margaret L. Coit may also be profitably consulted on the academy movement.[103] Useful, but not inspired, is the two-volume *Universal Education in the South* by Charles William Dabney.[104] The state-by-state treatment bears out the author's generalization that only North Carolina and Kentucky had any semblance of a system of public schools before the Civil War. Today almost every southern state has a history of education, if only the texts used in its teachers' colleges, but few of them are outstanding, and most give greatest emphasis to the period after 1865.

There are chapters on antebellum southern scientific interests and work in *The South in the Building of the Nation,* but the best work on this subject is Thomas Cary Johnson, *Scientific Interests in the Old South.*[105] He argues that scientific interests were so widespread as to have been all but universal. He also emphasizes scientific education in colleges and academies, the popularity of scientific hobbies, articles, and lectures, and the significance of New Orleans and Charleston as cities where original research of some importance was carried on. Yet the book is marred by a defensive, argumentative tone and a tendency to make the evidence prove too much. He does not clearly define "scientific interests," relate such interests to those in other regions, or clarify the relations between science and other activities within the South.

Biographers have made notable contributions to the history of science in the South. One of the most gifted scientists of the region was Matthew Fontaine Maury, a pioneer in oceanography who has been called

102 These are listed in United States Bureau of Education, *List of Publications of the United States Bureau of Education, 1867–1910* (Washington, 1910).

103 Knight, *Public Education in the South* (Boston and New York, 1922); Coulter, "The Ante-Bellum Academy Movement in Georgia," *Georgia Historical Quarterly,* V (December, 1921), 11–42; Lyon, "Moses Waddell and the Willington Academy," *North Carolina Historical Review,* VII (July, 1931), 284–99; Mobley, "The Academy Movement in Louisiana," *Louisiana Historical Quarterly,* XXX (July, 1947), 738–78; Coit, "Moses Waddell: A Light in the Wilderness," *Georgia Review,* V (Spring, 1951), 34–47.

104 C. W. Dabney, *Universal Education in the South* (Chapel Hill, 1936).

105 T. C. Johnson, Jr., *Scientific Interests in the Old South* (New York, 1936).

the "father of the United States Weather Bureau." [106] The first adequate biography of this aristocratic Virginian was by Charles Lee Lewis;
it concentrates chiefly on his accomplishments in oceanography. However, a full-scale and thoroughly-documented study by Frances Leigh
Williams was published in 1963.[107] Like Poe, John James Audubon is
difficult to classify. Francis Hobart Herrick argues that he was born
in Haiti, not near New Orleans as many claim.[108] At any rate, though
much of his work sheds light on the South and its scientific interests,
Audubon was primarily a national, not a sectional figure. Crawford W.
Long's experimentation in the 1840's with ether as an anesthetic has
been well-delineated by Frances Taylor and Frank Kells Boland. The
"father of modern gynecology," Dr. J. Marion Sims, is the subject of a
careful, detailed biography by Seale Harris. It sheds much light on the
state of medical practice in South Carolina and Alabama during the
1830's and 1840's. Though Dr. Daniel Drake operated through the
Ohio River Valley region, he played an important role in raising standards of medical education in Kentucky. Emmett Field Horine objectively
but somewhat woodenly tells Drake's story and relates his connection
with the first medical schools in Lexington and Louisville.[109]

   "Schools of the Old South" is one of the eight major divisions of
William F. Norwood's *Medical Education in the United States Before
the Civil War*.[110] Easily the outstanding state medical history is *The
Rudolph Matas History of Medicine in Louisiana*.[111] John Duffy,
though listed as its editor, actually wrote this study from materials collected by the late Rudolph Matas. The first volume covers the period
1825–1860. These monumental volumes deal with public health, hos-
pitals, medical education, medical writings, medical societies, and regulations governing medical practice. Two articles from the *Journal of*

106 Eaton, *A History of the Old South* (New York, 1949), 520.

107 Lewis, *Matthew Fontaine Maury* (Annapolis, Maryland, 1927); Williams,
Matthew Fontaine Maury, Scientist of the Sea (New Brunswick, New Jersey,
1963).

108 Herrick, *Audubon the Naturalist. A History of His Life and Time* (New
York, 1917).

109 F. L. Taylor, *Crawford W. Long and the Discovery of Ether Anesthesia* (New
York, 1928); Boland, *The First Anesthetic: The Story of Crawford Long* (Athens,
Georgia, 1950); Harris, *Woman's Surgeon; The Life Story of J. Marion Sims*
(New York, 1950); Horine, *Daniel Drake: Pioneer Physician of the Midwest*
(Philadelphia, 1961).

110 Norwood, *Medical Education in the United States Before the Civil War*
(Philadelphia, 1944).

111 John Duffy (ed.), *The Rudolph Matas History of Medicine in Louisiana* (2
vols.; Baton Rouge, 1958, 1962).

Southern History are notable impressionistic surveys of southern medical problems and practices: Martha Carolyn Mitchell, "Health and the Medical Profession in the Lower South, 1845–1860"; and John Duffy, "Medical Practice in the Ante-Bellum South." [112]

Little of significance to the intellectual historian has been produced about southern architecture, though quantities of books—usually picture books—have been turned out on the homes of many regions of the South. Lewis Mumford's *The South in Architecture* is disappointing for its neglect of the antebellum era.[113] One essay on Jefferson as an architect is its contribution, and he is viewed as one of the last to express the rational forms and classic ideals of the eighteenth century. Talbot F. Hamlin's *Greek Revival Architecture in America* is an important study of what the author sees as our first national architectural style.[114] He shows how the architectural styles of each region were influenced by the Greek revival, but his study is descriptive at the expense of analysis. One of the more important studies is Joseph Frazer Smith, *White Pillars, Early Life and Architecture of the Lower Mississippi Valley*.[115] A fine combination of architecture and history, this is a remarkably thorough survey of the dwellings of southern planters from Kentucky to Louisiana. James C. Bonner has analyzed the reaction against the Greek revival in an article in the *Journal of Southern History*. On the same subject, there is *The Architecture of the Old South: The Medieval Style, 1585–1850*, by Henry Chandlee Forman.[116]

As a remarkable cultural center, Charleston has received considerable attention from students interested in the fine arts. Many little studies exist of Charleston architecture, but one of the most interesting is a work on the homes of the city by Alice R. Huger Smith and D. E. Huger Smith.[117] They view Charleston homes as reflective of English

112 Mitchell, "Health and the Medical Profession in the Lower South, 1845–1860," *Journal of Southern History*, X (November, 1944), 424–46; John Duffy, "Medical Practice in the Ante-Bellum South," *Journal of Southern History*, XXV (February, 1959), 53–72.

113 Mumford, *The South in Architecture* (New York, 1941).

114 Hamlin, *Greek Revival Architecture in America* (New York, 1944).

115 J. F. Smith, *White Pillars, Early Life and Architecture of the Lower Mississippi Valley* (New York, 1941).

116 Bonner, "Plantation Architecture of the Lower South on the Eve of the Civil War," *Journal of Southern History*, XI (August, 1945), 370–88; Forman, *The Architecture of the Old South: The Medieval Style, 1585–1850* (Cambridge, Mass., 1948).

117 A. R. Huger Smith and D. E. Huger Smith, *Dwelling Houses of Charleston, South Carolina* (Philadelphia, 1917).

middle-class dwellings, modified by local conditions and the Greek revival of the nineteenth century.

Since most areas of the South were rural and had a near-subsistence
economy, art and artists usually found their patronage in urban centers
such as Baltimore, Charleston, Richmond, and New Orleans. Of these
four cities, Charleston gave the greatest support to art. Anna Wells
Rutledge, *Artists in the Life of Charleston,* traces the art history of that
city from colonial days to 1865.[118] Comparable specialized studies on
the other urban centers of the Old South remain to be done. Biographical
sketches of frontier artists may be found in Samuel W. Price, *The
Old Masters of the Bluegrass,* and in Fern Helen Rusk, *George Caleb
Bingham, the Missouri Artist.* The latter was the most talented native
painter of the Southwest, and his story has been told most recently by
A. Christ-Janer.[119]

The history of the antebellum theater in Charleston has been more
thoroughly recorded than that of any other southern city in W. Stanley
Hoole, *The Ante-Bellum Charleston Theater.* Antebellum New Orleans was also one of the more important theatrical centers of the country,
and its story has recently been told by a journalist, John S. Kendall. Including all the better-known theaters from the 1790's to the early
twentieth century, Kendall's book is enormously detailed, covering plays
and players.[120] Negro contributions to drama in the form of the minstrel
have been interestingly surveyed in Carl Wittke, *Tambo and Bones: A
History of the American Minstrel Stage,* which examines minstrelsy
from the early 1800's to its decline at the end of the century and emphasizes the double caricature involved.[121] Wittke says that Negroes
originally adapted white plantation melodies and that the minstrels in
turn adapted the Negro plantation adaptations.

"The new frontier in Southern historiography . . . is destined to ad-

118 Rutledge, *Artists in the Life of Charleston, Through Colony and State, From
Restoration to Reconstruction* ("American Philosophical Society Transactions,"
N.S., XXXIX, pt. 2 [Philadelphia, 1949]).

119 Price, *The Old Masters of the Bluegrass* (Louisville, Kentucky, 1902); Rusk,
George Caleb Bingham, the Missouri Artist (Jefferson City, Mo., 1917); Christ-
Janer, *George Caleb Bingham of Missouri* (New York, 1940).

120 Hoole, *The Ante-Bellum Charleston Theater* (Tuscaloosa, Alabama, 1946);
Kendall, *The Golden Age of the New Orleans Theater* (Baton Rouge, 1952).
Articles of some interest are Martin S. Shockley, "American Plays in the Richmond Theater, 1819–1838," *Studies in Philology,* XXXVII (January, 1940), 100–
19; William G. Dodd, "Theatrical Entertainment in Early Florida," *Florida Historical Quarterly,* XXV (October, 1946), 121–74.

121 Wittke, *Tambo and Bones: A History of the American Minstrel Stage* (Durham, N. C., 1930).

vance into the area of intellectual history," Clement Eaton wrote a decade ago.[122] There are now numerous signs that historians are discovering their opportunities in this field and are recognizing that intellectual and cultural history offers an exceedingly promising field for new and fresh contributions to southern history. The past generation has contributed much, particularly in the fields of literature, political theory, and religion. But we stand today only on the threshold of this historiographical frontier.

122 Eaton, "Recent Trends in the Writing of Southern History," *Louisiana Historical Quarterly*, XXXVIII (April, 1955), No. 2, p. 41.

IX

The Coming of
The Civil War

C. E. Cauthen,
with the collaboration of Lewis P. Jones

N O segment of southern political history has received more attention from historians than the period of sectional controversy culminating in the outbreak of war in 1861. Writers have been seeking ever since the guns were stilled at Appomattox, and even before, answers to the question of why it all happened. Satisfactory explanations have been sought by a host of both southern-born and northern-born historians. In addition, since southern history of the late antebellum period is so largely concerned with interstate and federal relations, the role of the South in the sectional quarrel has necessarily been interpreted by national historians and by historians of other sections. Interest in the subject seems to have increased with each generation since 1865. It was greatly stimulated by the widespread establishment of graduate schools toward the end of the nineteenth century and mounted to a climax in the 1930's and 1940's, when such a flood of books and articles flowed from the presses of the country that even the specialist found it difficult to keep abreast. By mid-twentieth century the accumulation of historical literature on the South in the pre-Civil War era was massive.

Historical writing on the late antebellum period is not only voluminous; in variety of interpretation, it probably surpasses that of any other period of American history. From generation to generation, and within each generation, historians have viewed the successive developments of the 1846–61 era through different lenses. Thus they have sharply disagreed in assessing the relative importance of geographical, economic, social, political, psychological, and other forces operating in North and South which produced the great American tragedy.

The writers of this short essay can hardly hope in limited space to analyze fully or to characterize with complete fairness the works of a great number of general, regional, and local historians who have described the South and its people as they moved toward secession and war. Brief comment on one point of view of a single historian involves the inevitable risk of giving the impression that the historian failed to recognize the importance of additional forces operating in the period. Limitation of space also prevents mention of numerous historians whose contributions have been more or less substantial.

Although there has never been total agreement among historians of southern secession, broad chronological patterns of changing interpretations are more or less evident. These have been described by numerous writers, notably by Howard K. Beale and Thomas J. Pressly, both of whom point out that the basic idea of nearly every later and more elaborate interpretation can be found expressed by writers in the early postwar period.[1] One broad development since about 1900 had been the obvious movement toward a more balanced treatment by professional historians of the South's own part in the sectional quarrel. It seemed to one protesting northern writer in 1962 that "the work of vindication has been conducted with such skill that the southern viewpoint has come to permeate the writings of historians from every section of the coun-

1 Beale, "What Historians Have Said About the Causes of the Civil War," Social Science Research Council Bulletin 54, Theory and Practice in Historical Study: A Report of the Committee on Historiography (New York, 1946); Thomas J. Pressly, Americans Interpret Their Civil War (Princeton, 1954). The writers are deeply indebted to these and a host of others who have appraised, in books, journal articles, book reviews, and historiographical essays, the works of historians dealing with the secession era. In some cases we have relied entirely upon them, and in all possible instances we have compared their judgments with our own.

try." [2] This is an overstatement of the case, because it implies a degree of unanimity and of sectional bias that does not exist. As will be pointed out later in this essay, there remain substantial differences among historians born and educated in the South as well as between those of different backgrounds. Southerners, however, have made large contributions to a trend that did occur.

In the late nineteenth century, before pioneering southern historians exerted great influence, a pro-northern explanation of the coming of the war had gained rather general acceptance, thus seemingly confirming Jefferson Davis's fears that this might become the South's greatest war loss. Most professional historians had dismissed as mere lawyers' briefs the arguments of Davis, Stephens, and other southern apologists that the South was driven from the Union by a long series of northern aggressions against southern constitutional rights; that the war had its origins in opposing views of the nature and powers of the general government, not in southern defense of its labor system; that the question of slavery in the territories only illustrated northern disregard of the Constitution and the North's "systematic and persistent struggle to deprive the Southern States of equality in the Union"; that slavery, at most, was an incident in the constitutional struggle, perhaps furnished an occasion for the war, but was "far from being the cause of the conflict." [3]

Historians at the same time had also moved away from the emotion-packed interpretations of the coming of the war earlier set forth by northern writers such as Henry Wilson, John A. Logan, and Hermann von Holst. According to them, there had been wickedness only south of Mason and Dixon's line. Southern leaders had been guilty of a diabolical plot to destroy a sacred union which they could no longer selfishly control, for the purpose of perpetuating and extending the hideous institution of slavery. Against an aggressive southern "slavocracy," a nobly motivated northern people had defended national morality, democracy, and liberty. To the South was assigned the villain's role in the successive events of the 1846–61 era. The annexation of Texas was a dark southern conspiracy. The Mexican War was a war of aggression to seize from a weak neighbor some or all of its territory for expansion of slavery and

2 Fawn W. Brodie, "Who Won the Civil War, Anyway?" *New York Times Book Review* (August 5, 1962), 1.

3 Jefferson Davis, *The Rise and Fall of the Confederate Government* (2 vols.; New York, 1881), I, 78, 83, *passim*. Other classic southern defenses are Edward A. Pollard, *The Lost Cause. A New Southern History of the War of the Confederates* (New York, 1866); Alexander H. Stephens, *A Constitutional View of the Late War Between the States* (2 vols.; Philadelphia, 1868–1870).

continued southern control of the federal government. When prevented from carrying slavery into all of the newly acquired territory, southern leaders were unsuccessful in their disunion plot but did succeed in forcing into the Compromise of 1850 an unspeakable fugitive-slave law which outraged northern people. Pro-slavery elements were inspired by Stephen A. Douglas in 1854 to pass the Kansas-Nebraska Act and repeal the Missouri Compromise, and in the subsequent violent struggle to control Kansas they were the only real offenders. In such unholy activities the South prostituted the Democratic party in its purposes and received support from such sycophantic Presidents as Franklin Pierce and James Buchanan. Southern leaders and Buchanan conspired with the Supreme Court to give judicial sanction to the southern cause in the Dred Scott decision. Finally, southern conspirators deliberately disrupted the Democratic party in 1860 in the belief that a Republican victory would enable them to consummate secession and establish a southern confederacy. It was the South that defeated compromise after the election of Abraham Lincoln and the South that precipitated war at Fort Sumter. Southern slaveowners were evil men lacking even the rudiments of Christian morality, while northern abolitionists and the Republican party were as pure as driven snow.[4]

This was what Howard K. Beale and others have called the "devil theory" of history—that *"the* cause" of the war was a conspiracy of selfish and wicked men. But the conspiracy hypothesis has two sides, since there were northern "devils" as well as southern "devils." Southerners tried hard during the period 1861–1900 to exhume the Yankee demons but enjoyed less success. Their rivals had the advantage of speaking for "freedom," "progress," and—most important—the winning side.[5]

The first steps toward a more impartial treatment had been taken by the turn of the century. This is faintly evident in the work of the Union veterans, James Schouler and John W. Burgess. They still pinned all war guilt on a South greedy for extension of slavery but de-emphasized the conspiracy theory and had a few kind words for some southern individuals.[6] James Ford Rhodes went much further. Without much

4 Henry Wilson, *History of the Rise and Fall of the Slave Power in America* (3 vols.; Boston, 1872–1877); John A. Logan, *The Great Conspiracy: Its Origin and History* (New York, 1886).

5 Beale, "What Historians Have Said about the Causes of the Civil War," 58–60.

6 Schouler, *History of the United States of America Under the Constitution* (7 vols.; New York, 1880–1913); Burgess, *The Middle Period, 1817–1858* (New York, 1897), and *The Civil War and the Constitution, 1859–1865* (2 vols.; New

lingering sectional animosity, he found some sections of southern society worthy of praise and conceded that the southern oligarchy included gentlemen of honor, good breeding, and culture. The South in his view was to be pitied as the victim of slavery, not saddled with the sole responsibility for its existence. Even so, Rhodes wrote history from a sectional bias. He painted slavery in its darkest colors; and although he judiciously reviewed developments of the late antebellum period, in most cases he rendered verdicts favoring the North. He found that a southern-controlled Democratic party was responsible for all that was shameful in the 1846–61 era and that the Republican party, of all those in American and perhaps world history, was the purest and most intelligent in dedication to a noble cause. To him, the war's single cause was northern and southern disagreement on the morality of slavery.[7]

The emphasis on the moral issue of slavery as a single explanation of the Civil War has not been abandoned by later historians. But even as the professionally untrained Rhodes was preparing his great work, a new era of historical scholarship was dawning in which academically trained historians were to challenge or modify the Rhodesian interpretation. Some were young Southerners who were inspired and trained in the writing of "objective" and "scientific" history at various graduate schools, notably at the Johns Hopkins University under Herbert Baxter Adams and at Columbia University under William Archibald Dunning.[8]

The years between the 1890's and about 1930 were what may be

York, 1901); Pressly, *Americans Interpret Their Civil War,* 129–32; Lewis E. Ellis, "James Schouler," *Mississippi Valley Historical Review,* XVI (September, 1929), 212–22.

7 Rhodes, *History of the United States from the Compromise of 1850* (7 vols.; New York, 1893–1906); Robert Cruden, *James Ford Rhodes: The Man, the Historian, and his Work* (Cleveland, 1961); Pressly, *Americans Interpret Their Civil War,* 135–49.

8 Wendell H. Stephenson has judiciously discussed the work of pioneering southern historians in *The South Lives in History: Southern Historians and their Legacy* (Baton Rouge, 1955) and in a number of journal articles, among which are: "A Half Century of Southern Historical Scholarship," *Journal of Southern History,* XI (February, 1945), 3–32; "William Garrott Brown: Literary Historian and Essayist," *Journal of Southern History,* XII (August, 1946), 313–44; "William P. Trent as Historian," *Journal of Southern History,* XV (May, 1949), 151–77; "Charles W. Ramsdell: Historian of the Confederacy," *Journal of Southern History,* XXVI (November, 1960), 501–25; "John Spencer Bassett as a Historian of the South," *North Carolina Historical Review,* XXV (July, 1948), 289–317; "Some Pioneer Alabama Historians," *Alabama Review,* I (July, October, 1948), 164–79, 261–78, and II (January, 1949), 45–62; "Herbert B. Adams and Southern Historical Scholarship at The Johns Hopkins University," *Maryland Historical Magazine,* XLII (March, 1947), 1–20. The rejection of rampant sectional prejudice can be seen in *Studies in Southern History and Politics. Inscribed to William Archibald Dunning* (New York, 1914) by his former pupils.

called the transition period in the historiography of the background of the Civil War. Writers from both North and South sought to understand and interpret, not to indict. No longer were sectionalists concerned with pinning war guilt on leaders of the other section. If they varied with one another in the discussion of slavery, it was concerning its importance as a cause of the split in the Union, not over its morality or desirability. These pioneers among a second generation of historians of the 1846–61 era were laying foundations for later scholars and demonstrating the kind of maturity that had been absent among the "devil theory" prosecutors who had perpetuated heat and provided little light. Using the growing volume of southern records and source materials,[9] the transitional historians abandoned the old concentration on a single cause and opened the way for later pluralistic interpretations and syntheses.

French E. Chadwick in 1906 saw the South as having opposed "the broad liberal movement of the age," [10] but he challenged those who had castigated Southerners as depraved. He anticipated many later scholars by saying that secession came because there was no feeling of kinship left, and the Civil War was fought "by one form of society against another form of society." [11] Many other non-southern writers contributed to the trend away from the simplistic, pro-northern view. Frederick Jackson Turner, for example, emphasized the importance of the West in the North-South confrontation and concluded that sectional schism came from many issues other than states' rights and slavery. In his view, the slavery issue never would have come to a head had there been no westward expansion, and the South's insecurity stemmed from the new alignment of West with East. As Pressly has written, Turner broadened "the time-honored concepts of a North-South struggle over slavery and state sovereignty" and thereby "broadened long established explanations of the coming of war." Justin H. Smith's multi-archival studies of the annexation of Texas and the Mexican War destroyed the theory that these events were mere episodes in slavocracy's conspiratorial ac-

9 J. G. de Roulhac Hamilton, "History in the South: A Retrospect of Half a Century," *North Carolina Historical Review*, XXXI (April, 1954), 173–81, "Three Centuries of Southern Records, 1607–1907," *Journal of Southern History*, X (February, 1944), 3–36. See also E. Merton Coulter, "What the South Has Done About Its History," *Journal of Southern History*, II (February, 1936), 3–28.

10 Chadwick, *Causes of the Civil War, 1859–1861* (New York, 1906), 14, Volume XIX of A. B. Hart (ed.), *The American Nation* (28 vols.; New York, 1904–1918).

11 *Ibid.*, 149.

tivities.[12] Frank H. Hodder de-emphasized the slavery, and magnified the railroad, background of the Kansas-Nebraska Act and its repeal of the Missouri Compromise.[13] Chauncey S. Boucher challenged the whole aggressive slavocracy thesis, holding that the South was so badly divided that conspiratorial action was impossible. Southerners in his view wanted to maintain political power for defense, not aggression.[14]

Perhaps most significant of the non-Southerners was Charles A. Beard. He stressed clashing economic interests as the most important of the complex forces which produced the "irrepressible conflict." In his view, both slavery and states' rights were minor issues in comparison with the desire of the North to gain control of the government for enactment of measures deemed essential to the progress of northern industry and commerce and with the determination of the South to remain in a position to defeat such measures disadvantageous to it. The South therefore seceded in response to the victory of a tariff and homestead party, and the war was a "social cataclysm in which the capitalists, laborers, and farmers of the North and West drove from power . . . the planting aristocracy of the South." [15]

Beard had already given economic determinism a great boost in his classic, *An Economic Interpretation of the Constitution* (New York, 1913), and from that time on the economic aspects of the sectional controversy did not escape scrutiny. Beard's analysis of the background of the Civil War, published in 1927, had been foreshadowed by Vernon Louis Parrington's similar views in *Main Currents in American Thought* (New York, 1920) and Robert R. Russel's *Economic Aspects of Southern Sectionalism, 1840–1861* (New York, 1924). A parallel emphasis came in 1928 with publication in New York of J. G. Van Deusen's

12 Turner, *The United States, 1830–1850* (New York, 1935), and *The Frontier in American History* (New York, 1920); Pressly, *Americans Interpret Their Civil War*, 176; Justin H. Smith, *The Annexation of Texas* (New York, 1911), and *The War with Mexico* (2 vols.; New York, 1919).

13 Hodder, "The Railroad Background of the Kansas-Nebraska Act," *Mississippi Valley Historical Review*, XII (June, 1925), 3–22.

14 Boucher, "*In Re* that Aggressive Slavocracy," *Mississippi Valley Historical Review*, VIII (June–September, 1921), 13–79.

15 Charles A. and Mary R. Beard, *The Rise of American Civilization* (2 vols.; New York, 1927), II, 3–51, 54; Howard K. Beale (ed.), *Charles A. Beard: An Appraisal* (Lexington, 1954), 115–59. Beard's ideas continued to be dominant in the economics-conscious 1930's, but later historians again turned their attention to slavery and other factors. The Beard thesis is criticized by Carl N. Degler, *Out of Our Past* (New York, 1959), 193–94, who charged that the impetus for war came from southern agrarians. As will be seen later, southern writers prior to 1927 also reflected some economic determinism.

Economic Bases of Disunion in South Carolina. It also discounted slavery as the chief cause of the conflict.

The clashing-societies interpretation was reaffirmed in 1925 by Edward Channing's influential general history, which saw a conflict between "two distinct social organisms." [16] Channing concluded that slavery would eventually have disappeared. A New Englander, he showed better understanding of the South than earlier general historians had. Although more a narrator than an interpreter, Channing ventured into the role of an economic determinist when he suggested that men who voted for Lincoln were not abolitionists but persons primarily interested in effecting a change in the economic policies of the federal government.[17] He also criticized the abolitionists' propaganda, which aroused the fears of Southerners. But he put much responsibility for the final tragedy on southern extremists.[18]

Pioneering Southerners also contributed much to changing interpretations from the 1890's to 1930. Some of them, while shifting the discussion away from a debate over the morality of slavery, were at least removing their section from "the bench of the accused" in the historians' court and liberating the South from further incriminations as a convicted sinner. But the leaders of this group, William E. Dodd, Ulrich B. Phillips, William Garrott Brown, members of the Dunning school, and other professionals could write favorably about the South and not be castigated for it. Such new scholars made their point: the era of 1846–61 deserved study, not sermons. Not only did this new generation of "scientific" historians cut loose from traditions, but they were able quickly to achieve respect and an audience. Both northern and southern historians were harmonious in the early 1900's, with reviews not being marked by acrimony even when some of their interpretations were favorable to one section or the other. As one student of historiography saw it, the future of southern history seemed bright in 1913, with William A. Dunning as president of the American Historical Association and Woodrow Wilson as President of the United States.[19]

No southern historian produced a more balanced treatment of the sectional conflict than did Woodrow Wilson, whose brief *Division and*

16 Channing, *A History of the United States* (6 vols.; New York, 1905–1925), VI, 3. The title of this sixth volume was "The War for Southern Independence," a far cry from earlier northern titles about something labeled "The Rebellion."

17 Channing, *History of the United States,* VI, 253.

18 *Ibid.,* VI, 114, 254.

19 David D. Van Tassel, "The American Historical Association and the South, 1884–1913," *Journal of Southern History,* XXIII (November, 1957), 482.

Reunion reflected as early as 1893 both a continental outlook and a sympathetic understanding of the Old South. On the states' rights issue he believed that the South correctly interpreted the Constitution as of 1787 but failed to understand that national developments had given it a new meaning by 1860. The South stood still because of slavery, while the North and West progressed toward nationalism.

In general, the Southerners among these careful historians of the transitional period exhibited a gentle feeling toward the Old South, but some of the earlier ones were nationalistic in viewpoint and found much to criticize in southern society. William P. Trent, for example, thought that the Old South was primitive, unprogressive, intolerant, and arrogant because of the influence of slavery.[20] William Garrott Brown, a literary historian more important as an interpreter than a researcher, held that the Union was split not by the tariff, nor economic problems, nor an aggressive slavocracy, nor the institution of slavery—but by the race problem.[21] But he did not weep for the Lost Cause, noting that the South had broken faith with old traditions.[22] Other early southern writers also saw the conflict of the 1860's as an irresistible one between an old-fashioned, rural South blocking the path of "progress" and a materialistic North determined to crush all opposition.[23]

A pioneer professional historian who developed as many disciples and as much respect among the devotees of Clio as did any scholar also made his appearance in the transitional era—Ulrich B. Phillips. He was one of the first to say that the conflict of 1861 was repressible, and he was also definitely sympathetic to the South without claiming all virtue for the region. His "Central Theme"—that southern self-consciousness was a product of racial consciousness—was actually evident in his "Georgia and State Rights." [24] The idea was later restated

20 See Stephenson, "William P. Trent as a Historian of the South," 151–77, for a thoughtful appraisal of Trent's *William Gilmore Simms* (Boston, 1892), *Southern Statesmen of the Old Regime* (New York, 1897), and *Robert E. Lee* (Boston, 1899). Trent was at Sewanee from 1887 to 1900 and founded the *Sewanee Review,* which published articles by John Spencer Bassett, U. B. Phillips, W. L. Fleming, J. G. de Roulhac Hamilton, D. D. Wallace, Colyer Meriwether, *et al.*

21 Brown, *Lower South in American History* (New York, 1902), 74. See also W. H. Stephenson, "William Garrott Brown: Literary Historian and Essayist," 313–44.

22 Brown, *Lower South in American History,* 111–12.

23 For example, Allen Tate, *Rise and Fall of Jefferson Davis* (New York, 1929). Such southern interpretation of "progress" was the opposite of Tate's "Southern agrarian" point of view of 1930.

24 Phillips, "Georgia and State Rights," in American Historical Association *Annual Reports,* 1901, II, 15–224.

in his widely accepted thesis that it was southern determination to maintain white supremacy in the interest of orderly government and Caucasian civilization that made the South a separate entity. Slavery, he held, was but an instrument in this overriding "common resolve . . . that it . . . be and remain a white man's country." [25] In Phillips' view, other causes for southernism and secession were secondary.

Nor did Southerners leave economic interpretations entirely to Yankees. William K. Boyd as early as 1910 underscored the variety of economic interests in antebellum North Carolina.[26] The impassioned William E. Dodd in 1915 anticipated Beard's economic interpretation.[27] Richard H. Shryock, by examining events in Georgia, concluded that unionism accompanied prosperity, so long as the social system seemed in no danger. A contrast of Georgia and South Carolina in the 1847–52 period seemed to bear out this thesis—and to show how far from "devil theories" historical writing had moved.[28]

The regional ramparts were manned once more in 1930 in a mild flurry of sectional pride reminiscent of the war-guilt debate of earlier years, when twelve southern "agrarians" took their stand "to support a Southern way of life against what might be called the American or prevailing way." One of the "agrarians," Frank L. Owsley, a student of William E. Dodd, praised the Dunning school for not having been conquered by the northern intellectual offensive during the "devil theory" days. Certainly Owsley had not been subdued by anyone seeking to pin guilt on the South; now he deplored the fact that northern smugness and pharisaical judgments still remained.[29] Like most interpreters during the next decade, he acknowledged that the Civil War had complex causes. But, he said, it stemmed primarily from a conflict between a commercial, industrial society and an agrarian society. In saying so, he followed others in exploding the myth of a southern aristocratic society. He saw the states' rights emphasis [30] as no mere defense mechanism

25 Phillips, "The Central Theme of Southern History," *American Historical Review,* XXXIV (October, 1928), 31. It was summarized again in his famous *Life and Labor in the Old South* (1929).

26 Boyd, "North Carolina on the Eve of Secession," in American Historical Association *Annual Report, 1910,* pp. 165–77.

27 Dodd, *Expansion and Conflict* (Boston, 1915); Stephenson, *The South Lives in History,* 42–43.

28 Shryock, *Georgia and the Union in 1850* (Durham, 1926).

29 Owsley, "The Irrepressive Conflict," in Twelve Southerners, *I'll Take My Stand* (New York, 1930), 67.

30 See also A. M. Schlesinger, *New Viewpoints in American History* (New York, 1922), 220–43, wherein he de-fused what he called the "State Rights

to protect slavery only—but to protect social and economic interests as well.[31]

A rather obvious watershed in the writings about the coming of the Civil War was reached about 1930, and interest in the topic intensified rather than receded afterward. Between 1930 and 1963 there were no fewer than ninety-eight respectable works published which might have included the phrase "The Coming of the Civil War" in their titles or sub-titles.[32] With this flood also came intensified historical debate. Between 1900 and 1930, historians had generally been credited with objectivity. Of course, reviewers did not always agree, but criticisms were usually in good spirit. In the 1930's and particularly in the late 1940's, historians sometimes became so acrimonious as to engage in name-calling, much of the argument centering around the repressibility of the Civil War.

It is certainly true, as David M. Potter said, that "though every de-cade has brought general agreements, . . . the historiography of the Civil War has seen the facts construed in every possible way and the causes of the war interpreted from every possible position." In so doing, historians have reflected by their positions the changes of intellectual climate, and their literature has thus reflected "the impact of Marxist thought, the post-Versailles disillusionment with war in general, the declining influence of moral and legal absolutes, and the changing em-phasis upon economic determinism." [33] Yet almost every interpretation in the 1930–63 period had been set forth earlier by some pioneer writer. Some of the controversy over historical writing stemmed from the fact that interpretations reflected a new period of sectional strains, new tensions over the proper role of the Negro in American life, and con-cern about the South's continuing colonial status.[34] In the 1930's and 1940's historians were also busy arguing over the responsibility of in-dividuals for the war—the roles of Pierce, Buchanan, Yancey, or Lin-

Fetish" by pointing out that the "in's" have always tended to be strong nationalists and loose constructionists in order to get their program enacted and implemented, while the "out's" have been states' rights supporters and strict constructionists, in order to hamper and hamstring their rivals.

31 Later Owsley said that the war was not a moral crusade but a by-product of egocentric sectionalism which led the North to drive the South out of the Union. See his "Fundamental Cause of the Civil War: Egocentric Sectionalism," *Journal of Southern History*, VII (February, 1941), 3–19.

32 Such a flood overwhelms these writers who are primarily trying to summarize rather than to pass judgment. Making the task more difficult is the fact that there are at least thirty-nine articles that can be classed as historiographical studies.

33 Potter's Review of Pressly, *Americans Interpret Their Civil War*, in *Journal of Southern History*, XX (August, 1954), 400.

34 Pressly, *Americans Interpret Their Civil War*, 239–43.

coln—and the responsibility of one group of extremists or the other.

Although not defending slavery, much of the post-1930 writing did try to explain more accurately, though not always necessarily to justify. Roy F. Nichols saw this "southern interpretation" as "no mean part of a southern renaissance," all the "more convincing because it seemed 'scientific' " and also as providing a " 'scientific' blessing of a folk-legend long current in the land where the 'Lost Cause' has never been forgotten." [35] Most outspoken and obvious of these "southern vindicators" was F. L. Owsley, who rejected the morality or immorality of slavery as the only cause of the war and saw more complex causes stemming from "a state of mind in both sections which explains their conduct," with war resulting when one section (the North) failed to respect the self-respect of the other.[36] The writers sympathetic with the South "believed the war had fundamental causes, but not of a moral, political, or economic nature." [37] Some observers have felt that U. B. Phillips might be considered the founder of this modern school of scientific writers who have been gentle with the South.

The flood of books in the 1930's gave much attention to the major causes of the war. Kenneth M. Stampp listed seven categories for such studies—or seven schools of thought about what was *the* major causative factor: (1) "Slave power" versus "Black Republicans," (2) state rights versus nationalism, (3) economic sectionalism, (4) blundering politicians and irresponsible agitators, (5) the right versus wrong of slavery, (6) majority rule versus minority rights, (7) conflict of cultures.[38] Robert

35 Nichols, "American Democracy and the Civil War," in American Philosophical Society, *Proceedings,* XCI (April 5, 1947), 143–49.

36 Owsley, "The Fundamental Cause of the Civil War: Egocentric Sectionalism," 7, 18. To a lesser extent, Charles W. Ramsdell can be put in the group "whose Southernism showed through."

37 T. Harry Williams, "Disruption of the Union: The Secession Crisis, 1860–1861," in Leonard W. Levy and Merrill D. Peterson (eds.), *Major Crises in American History* (2 vols.; New York, 1962), I, 466. If "southern vindicators" should mean those who were quite critical of abolitionists, the list might include Avery O. Craven, Benjamin B. Kendrick, F. L. Owsley, and James G. Randall. Recent writers who have been comparatively "soft" on abolitionists include A. C. Cole, Bernard DeVoto, Dwight D. Dumond, Allan Nevins, Russell B. Nye, and A. M. Schlesinger, Jr. The term "southern vindicator" may be an overstatement; it does not imply blindness to southern faults nor an aim of blindly "whitewashing" the South.

38 Stampp (ed.), *Causes of the Civil War* (Englewood Cliffs, N. J., 1959). This collection, with extracts from both opinions of contemporaries and historians, is typical of many such works prepared for undergraduate students so that they can read for themselves the opposing views and interpretations. Other useful ones are Edwin C. Rozwenc (ed.), *The Causes of the American Civil War* (Boston, 1961),

C. Black pointed out that no modern historians appeared conspicuously any longer under any one banner, but that some of the most popular causes supported included the following: defense of slavery, defense of state rights, economic determinism, development of southern nationalism, emotionalism and fear, and deficient statesmanship.[39] Other lists and other categories could be noted.

Appearing concurrently with the southern vindicators and sharing many of their opinions were the revisionists who held that the Civil War could have been avoided. They were part of a whole generation disillusioned about war. Some questioned the wisdom of intervention in 1917, while the revisionist school that developed in the 1930's especially questioned the irrepressibility of war in 1861.

Actually, William P. Trent had held some revisionist ideas in the 1890's,[40] criticizing "the logic of passion" and blaming southern political leaders for lack of statesmanship. Mary Scrugham might also be labeled an early-day revisionist since she had stressed the view in 1921 that the vast majority of peoples in 1861 were either indifferent or opposed to war.[41] Before trained historians had embraced revisionism, Gerald W. Johnson, that astute and thought-provoking journalist, alleged that the real truth was, "Everybody, in short, was right; no one was wrong."[42]

and Rozwenc (ed.), *Slavery as a Cause of the Civil War* (Boston, 1963); and Norton Garfinkle (ed.), *Lincoln and the Coming of the Civil War* (Boston, 1959).

39 Black, "Thoughts on the Confederacy," in Donald Sheehan and Harold C. Syrett (eds.), *Essays in American Historiography: Papers Presented in Honor of Allan Nevins* (New York, 1960), 30. In preparation of this essay, the authors had a number of charts with such labels as the above—and many more ("South Combative"; "To save slavery"; "White supremacy"; etc.). It is soon evident that few historians can be "fixed" in one chart, for each name soon appears in several of the lists. For the sake of simplicity, this essay will not consider each never-definitive category along with its ardent disciples. To a degree, Howard K. Beale's excellent study, "What Historians Have Said About the Causes of the Civil War," does approach this problem by noting different categories and some of the varying spokesmen attracted to each.

40 See Stephenson, "William P. Trent as a Historian of the South," 151–77.

41 Scrugham, *Peaceable Americans of 1860–1861: A Study in Public Opinion* (New York, 1921). She did not consider the morality of slavery to have been a key issue in the election of 1860.

42 Johnson, *Secession of the Southern States* (New York, 1933), 13. David Potter has labeled this "forceful little volume" as "in some ways the most vigorous statement of the revisionist view." See Potter's Review of Pressly, *Americans Interpret Their Civil War*, 405–406. Avery Craven, to be as famous as any revisionist, called Johnson's book "a masterpiece of historical interpretation, which, in spite of some startling inaccuracies of fact, comes nearer to a correct interpretation of this major crisis in American life than any previous study." Cited in *Book Review Digest*, 1933, p. 488.

The revisionists denied that the war had one fundamental cause. They rejected the idea that sectional differences had been irreconcilable. To them it was a "needless war" brought on by a "blundering generation" of irresponsible leaders, or as Avery Craven termed them, "politicians and pious cranks." [43] To the revisionists, the differences between sections were not acute enough by themselves to bring on war. Furthermore, as Pressly has summarized their thesis, the moderates *should* have been more successful, and the extremists *should not* have become so powerful. The latter simply emotionalized issues that were not in themselves fundamental.

Charles W. Ramsdell argued in 1929 that the natural limits of slavery had already been reached before 1860; hence there was no longer justification for sectional controversy over its extension. If the artificial issue of slavery in the territories had not been made a political football, then—ergo—war could have been avoided. Then why was it not? Because ambitious politicians wanted to exploit the issue, average citizens were not adequately informed (for example, about the impracticality of the further extension of slavery), and emotionalism made settlement or compromise difficult.[44] Ramsdell a few years later repeated that slavery had reached a peak by 1860 and was bound to decline or to be abolished by Southerners themselves.[45]

Avery O. Craven, author of several articles and four books between 1936 and 1959,[46] was the dean of the "repressible war" school. Somewhat pro-southern, he held that war became inevitable when passions took over. The conflict seemed to him to result from the drive against a labor system which broadened into a moral attack on the character and whole way of life of Southerners, with the differences between North and South being exaggerated into rights and wrongs under the play of emotionalism. Craven claimed not to be trying to explain the causes of the war but said he was trying to explain how the democratic process

43 Avery O. Craven, "Coming of the War Between the States," *Journal of Southern History,* II (August, 1936), 305.

44 Ramsdell, "The Natural Limits of Slavery Expansion," *Mississippi Valley Historical Review,* XVI (September, 1929), 151–71.

45 Ramsdell, "The Changing Interpretations of the Civil War," *Journal of Southern History,* III (February, 1937), 23. He liked Phillips' "Central Theme" but thought that it could be pushed too far. He saw the clash as a result of "emotional appeals carefully matured, joined with sublimated economic motives, and cleverly developed into intersectional hatred."

46 Craven, *The Repressible Conflict: 1830–1861* (Baton Rouge, 1939), *The Coming of the Civil War* (New York, 1942), *The Growth of Southern Nationalism, 1848–1861* (Baton Rouge, 1953) ; and *Civil War in the Making, 1815–1860* (Baton Rouge, 1959).

had broken down under stress. In his later works, Craven modified his views somewhat as he saw deep social and economic forces sublimated into moral issues which placed "the conflict of high emotional charge" beyond the possibility of solution.[47]

Another important revisionist was James G. Randall. He saw a "blundering generation" victimized by demagoguery, prejudice, and intolerance. The Civil War was not "in any real sense a conflict of cultures or economic systems." It showed the imperfections of the American democratic system. An examination of its causes would expose irrational conduct and stupidity. This useless war was a "stupendous fraud" fought over sectional differences that were not irreconcilable. Randall's mood is seen in his use of such words as "fanaticism," "bogus leadership," "misrepresentation," and "a blundering generation." [48]

Roy F. Nichols, recognizing the causes of the conflict as complicated and emphasizing "hyperemotionalism," found the catalyst "in the nature of our political behavior," [49] the problem being not how to maintain a balance among the states but how to balance emotional units or attitudes. To him, the parties failed the nation by splitting into sectional blocs.[50] As he phrased it, "In the last analysis the war was the product of the chaotic lack of system in ascertaining the public will, a chaos exploited by irresponsible and blind operators of local political machinery without adequate central organization." This point is the main thesis of his distinguished *Disruption of American Democracy*.[51]

47 See Kenneth Stampp's Review of Craven, *The Growth of Southern Nationalism,* in *Saturday Review,* XXXVI (August 29, 1953), 17. Another scholar summarized it thus: "In his later writings . . . Craven has recognized that, when concrete issues are simplified into abstract principles and symbols, the historian is confronting patterns of social behavior that are very real indeed. Hence the problem is to understand how abstract issues of right and wrong can cause a breakdown of the democratic process." Rozwenc, *Causes of the American Civil War,* 171.

48 Randall, *Civil War and Reconstruction* (Boston, 1937), "The Blundering Generation," *Mississippi Valley Historical Review,* XXVII (June, 1940), 3–28, "The Civil War Restudied," *Journal of Southern History,* VI (November, 1940), 439–57, *Lincoln and the South* (Baton Rouge, 1946). On the whole Revisionist group, see T. N. Bonner, "Civil War Historians and the Needless War Doctrine," *Journal of the History of Ideas,* XVII (April, 1956), 193–216.

49 Nichols, "American Democracy and the Civil War," in American Philosophical Society *Proceedings,* XCI, No. 2 (April 5, 1947), 144. In this article he listed five dangerous breeders of conflict: "southernism," "metropolitanism," territorialism, antislaveryism, and "New Englandism" plus Protestantism and romanticism.

50 This idea is also noted in Herbert Agar, *The Price of Union* (Boston, 1950).

51 Nichols, *Disruption of American Democracy* (New York, 1948), 7. Nichols has at least four books and five articles on this stormy era. See Pressly's comments on him in *Americans Interpret Their Civil War,* 286–88.

One political interpretation was David Donald's suggestion that an excess of democracy helped to cause the war.[52] He argued that emphasis needs to be put on too much democracy, too much liberty, and the desire to throw off authority.[53]

George Fort Milton, one of the most important revisionists, also has been concerned with the role of politics in the break, agreeing with Alexander H. Stephens that if the extremists of the South had not triumphed, Stephen A. Douglas would have prevailed and war would have been averted. He also pinned much blame on President James Buchanan as the villain largely responsible for the failure of popular sovereignty in Kansas. Like most recent writers, he also recognized many complex underlying causes.[54] Another one who stressed political and psychological forces as more important than economic and social was Henry H. Simms. His synthesis of the 1850's also exposed the decade's emotionalism, need of sounder statesmanship, and party rivalry.[55]

Rebuttal was bound to come, even though it had to await a new national mood and new concerns. New nationalists, appearing mostly after the Second World War, suggested that the issues of 1860 definitely *were* important enough to fight about and implied that deemphasizing slavery as an uncompromisable moral issue amounted to condoning it. Like the nationalists of the late nineteenth century, they saw determination to preserve the Union as a basic cause of war—a determination clearly worth fighting for. These critics, who were usually liberals and progressives, were much involved in the fight for Negro rights in mid-century. Inevitably, their thinking about the Civil War was shaped by this involvement.

Most outspoken in this group was Arthur M. Schlesinger, Jr. He apparently thought that war was necessary to abolish slavery since the

52 Donald, *An Excess of Democracy: The American Civil War and the Social Process* (Oxford, 1960). In connection with it, see "an alternative": A. E. Campbell, "An Excess of Isolation: Isolation and the American Civil War, *Journal of Southern History,* XXIX (May, 1963), 161–74.

53 Other works by Donald reflect his thinking on this era: *Charles Sumner and the Coming of the Civil War* (New York, 1961), *Lincoln Reconsidered: Essays on the Civil War Era* (New York, 1956), and "American Historians and the Causes of the Civil War," *South Atlantic Quarterly,* LIX (Summer, 1960), 351–55.

54 Milton, *Eve of Conflict: Stephen A. Douglas and the Needless War* (Boston, 1934).

55 Simms, *A Decade of Sectional Controversy, 1851–1861* (Chapel Hill, 1942), and *Emotion at High Tide: Abolition as a Controversial Factor, 1830–1845* (Baltimore, 1960).

South had organized itself against "human dignity and freedom." [56]
Pieter Geyl also refused to condone what he said was blindness to the
moral question by a South which cut itself off from Western civilization.[57] Other noted historians have also recently emphasized slavery
and the moral issue. Bernard DeVoto, writing in *Harper's* in 1946,
criticized Revisionists for suggesting that appeasement was the answer
to the problems of 1846-61 [58] Samuel Eliot Morison said that modern
historians "should have pointed out that war does accomplish something"
and condemned the mood of historians of the 1930's (though not the
revisionists specifically) as he held them to a degree to blame for
"American spiritual unpreparedness for World War II" [59] More biting
has been John Hope Franklin, who charged many latter-day southern
historians with a lack of objectivity. Franklin's view of the Old South
was hardly one of an attractive or cultured society.[60] Even more vitriolic
was Charles H. Wesley's judgment on the "misinterpretation and mis-
representation" of southern historians who, he says, engaged in "actual
falsification under the guise of rewriting history . . . to justify the
physical repression and the present exclusion of millions of people of
color." [61] Another reviewer inveighed against the "deep guilt of the
South, transformed by the apparatus of scholarship" and "filtered into
American consciousness by way of textbooks." [62]

56 A. M. Schlesinger, Jr., "The Causes of the American Civil War: A Note on
Historical Sentimentalism," *Partisan Review,* XVI (October, 1949), 968–81.

57 Geyl, "The American Civil War and the Problem of Inevitability," *New England Quarterly,* XXIX (1951), 147–68.

58 DeVoto, "The Easy Chair," *Harper's,* CXCII (February and March, 1946),
123–26, 234–37. He alleged that few southern historians are free from the myth
of the Old South.

59 Morison, "Faith of a Historian," *American Historical Review,* LVI (January,
1951), 261–75.

60 Franklin, *Militant South, 1860–61* (Cambridge, Mass., 1956). The work was
praised by C. Vann Woodward as a "fresh and significant contribution to the
understanding of the mind of the South," but Fletcher M. Green called it a "one-
sided, exaggerated, and distorted picture of Southern life." Woodward's Review,
New York Times Book Review (September 23, 1956), 3; Green's Review, *Mississippi Valley Historical Review,* XLIV (June, 1957), 140–41.

61 Wesley, "The Civil War and the Negro American," *Journal of Negro History,*
XLVII (April, 1962), 96. In the same vein and no less inhibited is Fawn M. Brodie,
"Who Won the Civil War, Anyway?" 1, 22, 23. She commends Allan Nevins,
Bruce Catton, Kenneth Stampp, and Carl Sandburg for not being "ashamed to be
indignant over slavery." Presumably, to satisfy the new nationalists, one not
only cannot consider the Civil War repressible but also must write with righteous
indignation against the South.

62 L. Jesse Lewisch, "Who Won the Civil War Anyway?" *The Nation,* CXCII
(April 8, 1961), 300–302.

Most historians since 1930, however, have not been concerned with proving whether the war was inevitable or not. Even some of the revisionists underwent a metamorphosis and placed less emphasis on the question.[63] Allan Nevins, one of the most prolific of American historians, has often been referred to as a "synthesist," bridging the gulf between revisionists and new nationalists. Recognizing many contributing causes of the break of the Union, Nevins nevertheless stressed—like Phillips—the basic race factor as crucial to a complete cultural schism. Although he saw the issue as being much more complex than Rhodes did, Nevins has been compared to the northern nationalists, obsessed sometimes not with the importance of slavery but with its morality. As Fletcher Green has put it, "Like the abolitionists of the period of which he writes, Nevins seems to be blinded by his sense of moral values." [64] To Nevins, the Civil War was part of a movement to unify the nation.[65] But in his grippingly-told narrative, he touched many factors—emotion, incompetent Presidents, moral issues, economic factors, and most of the others.[66]

Many writers in recent decades have increasingly stressed the war as a contest of two nationalisms, while not agreeing on the major common denominator that made for southern separateness. Phillips had exercised considerable influence with his "Central Theme" earlier. Robert S. Cotterill in his *The Old South* also stressed southern "consciousness of kind" that created a nationalism rather than a sectionalism since it was based on sentiment rather than interest.[67] Benjamin B. Kendrick stressed the evolution and importance of a southern nationality, secession being depicted as a strategy to protect vital southern interests by winning *de jure* recognition of southern nationalism. Particularly galling, he insisted, was the South's colonial status which could be ended only

63 By no means have all Revisionists been discussed individually here—but only some of the leaders, and particularly those who have been subjected to considerable criticism.

64 Green, Review of Nevins, *Ordeal of the Union,* in *Mississippi Valley Historical Review,* XXXV (June, 1948), 128.

65 Allan Nevins, *Ordeal of the Union* (2 vols.; New York, 1947), I, viii–ix.

66 The economic he minimizes: "The war was caused primarily by social, moral, and political, not economic forces." *Ibid.,* II, 244. For further comments on Nevins, see Pressly, *Americans Interpret Their Civil War,* 310 ff.; and Harvey Wish, "Allan Nevins and Recent Historiography," *The American Historian* (New York, 1960), 321–50.

67 Cotterill, *The Old South* (Glendale, Calif., 1936), 143. This volume has been labeled the first attempt at a synthesis.

by secession. Without blaming either side, Kendrick said that the Old South needed a decent burial—not Reconstruction.[68]

Several scholars have chosen to discuss more nebulous aspects of the southern mind and character. Wilbur J. Cash, a North Carolina journalist with keen insight, a frank but friendly critic of his region, noted the Southerner's chip-on-shoulder attitude, his combativeness and violence, his tendency toward romanticism and unreality. All of this he interpreted as a defense mechanism in a region acutely aware of its shrinking power in a growing nation. Militancy—not unique to a frontier agricultural society—was brutalized by the presence of slavery and accompanied by a loss of tolerance among a southern aristocracy that was simply "the natural flower of the backcountry grown prosperous." [69] It was the conflict with the Yankee, driven by emotion and fantasy, that really made the South.[70] Clement Eaton, a trained scholar (unlike Cash), also saw the southern mind as constructed of a curious combination of romanticism and reality. De-emphasizing economic factors as motivating and marking the South, he emphasized "limited vision in politics" and noted "ruinous provincialism and overweening pride." [71] What the South "desperately needed" in 1860 was "the free exercise of the critical spirit." [72] What it actually had was restraint of all dissent, as freedom of thought was circumscribed in a South that "would not accept the nineteenth century." [73] Rollin G. Osterweis is more generally associated with the interpretation that southern nationalism derived from romanticism. In his *Romanticism and Nationalism in the Old South* (New Haven, 1949), he represented southern nationalism as resting on a stool of three legs: the Negro, the plantation, and romanticism. He has emphasized the latter, with a cult of chivalry "focused on manners, women, military affairs, the ideal of Greek democracy, and romantic oratory"—a cult which made the Southerner *feel* himself to be different. A more recent study by T. Harry Williams has also emphasized the ability of the region to deceive itself rather than to accept realistically the logic of events. Southerners, Williams says, took refuge

68 Kendrick and Alex Matthews Arnett, *The South Looks at Its Past* (Chapel Hill, 1935), 103.

69 Cash, *Mind of the South* (New York, 1941), 20.

70 *Ibid.*, 65. He saw a North, however, determined to destroy the southern way of life and make the region over in the national image.

71 Eaton, *Growth of Southern Civilization, 1790–1860* (New York, 1961), 323.

72 *Ibid.*, 313.

73 On this topic, see Eaton, *Freedom of Thought in the Old South* (Durham, 1940).

in a dream world and insisted that others accept their "castle in the sky" —even as they proceeded to commit nearly "every political error in the book" while identifying all issues with slavery and thereby alienating the West.[74]

Jesse T. Carpenter's *The South as a Conscious Minority* has been useful in showing the successive positions in political or constitutional thought adopted by the minority South as it fell back from one defense line to another between 1789 and 1860: local self-government in 1820; concurrent voice in 1830–1850; constitutional guarantees in the 1850's; and secession in 1860–61.[75] But the peak of emphasis upon southern separateness may have been reached with the publication of Professor Avery Craven's *Growth of Southern Nationalism, 1848–61,* in 1953.[76] He told the story of "sectional quarrel, as seen through the evolution of Southern attitudes toward national events" and explained the drift to war "through the breakdown of the democratic process in government." [77] In it all, he saw a growing emotionalism over the social and economic forces which Southerners sought to repudiate as threats to their peculiar civilization.

Despite the new syntheses and emphasis on many factors, slavery and abolition have continued to attract writers. One of them, Dwight L. Dumond, has pursued a somewhat irregular course. He was a Revisionist in his *The Secession Movement,* published in 1931, holding the war to have been repressible, and being considered then by J. G. de Roulhac Hamilton as strongly sympathetic to the southern viewpoint.[78] With publication of *Anti-Slavery Origins of the Civil War* in 1939, Dumond gave evidence of being a neo-abolitionist.[79] By 1961 Dumond was writing about "America's present responsibility in human relationships," and, on a Christian basis, emotionally condemning inequalities. In so

74 Williams, *Romance and Realism in Southern Politics* (Athens, Georgia, 1961).

75 Carpenter, *The South as a Conscious Minority, 1789–1861: A Study in Political Thought* (New York, 1930).

76 Craven, *The Growth of Southern Nationalism, 1848–1861.* In a favorable review, Kenneth M. Stampp saw the book as partially modifying, clarifying, and qualifying Craven's *Coming of the Civil War.* See *Saturday Review,* XXXVI (August 29, 1953), 16–17.

77 Fletcher M. Green, Review, *Mississippi Valley Historical Review,* XL (December, 1953), 535.

78 Dumond, *The Secession Movement, 1860–61* (New York, 1931); Hamilton's Review, in *Mississippi Valley Historical Review,* XIX (December, 1932), 430–32. Also, see Charles W. Ramsdell's Review, in *North Carolina Historical Review,* X (October, 1933), 331–33.

79 Dumond, *Anti-Slavery Origins of the Civil War in the United States* (Ann Arbor, 1939).

doing, he included polemics against slaveholders and almost beatified abolitionists.[80]

Gilbert H. Barnes also revived interest in the antislavery crusade in 1934 with publication of his influential *Anti-Slavery Impulse,* portraying Theodore Dwight Weld and other ministers as more important than such better known radicals as William Lloyd Garrison because over the years the ministers—in a relatively quiet or mild way—convinced the average Northerner of the moral wrong of slavery.[81] A quarter century later, Louis Filler's *Crusade Against Slavery* returned the emphasis to New England. Filler also suggested that the slavery struggle remained basically moral.[82] Russell B. Nye revived the idea of a conspiracy by the "slavocracy" in 1946 and gave it a new twist. He suggested that the slave power aimed at suppressing civil liberty in both North and South, thereby making its "defense of slavery" really a counterattack against free institutions.[83]

Most recent writers have duly noted emotionalism which produced fear, but perhaps none has been more effective than Arnold Whitridge in showing how fanatics fostered phobias and hatreds to drive people to a war they did not want. But for these fanatics, that war could have been avoided despite the real economic differences. After examining colorful partisans and sincere fanatics, Whitridge concluded that "by the end of 1860, extremists had so manipulated the minds of the voters that few men were in a position to think, speak and act for themselves." [84]

Of somewhat narrower scope have been the writings on the dramatic period between the presidential election in November, 1860, and the attack on Fort Sumter in April, 1861; and tempers have flared over

80 Dumond, "Democracy and Christian Ethics," *Journal of Negro History,* XLVI (January, 1961), 1–11, and *Anti-Slavery: The Crusade for Freedom in America* (Ann Arbor, 1961). D. M. Potter observed that Dumond "adopts the dogmatic and polemical tone of the anti-slavery literature itself and also the anti-slavery view that everything that the abolitionists did was almost holy, while any opposition to them was utterly iniquitous." Review, *American Historical Review,* LXVII (July, 1962), 1063–65.

81 Barnes, *The Anti-Slavery Impulse, 1830–1844* (New York, 1933).

82 Filler, *The Crusade Against Slavery, 1830–1860* (New York, 1960).

83 Nye, "The Slave Power Conspiracy: 1830–1860," in *Science and Society,* X (Summer, 1946), 262–74, and *Fettered Freedom: Civil Liberties and the Slavery Controversy, 1830–1860* (East Lansing, Mich., 1949). Frank Freidel, reviewing the latter, warns lest readers might "wrest these themes from their political and economic context in order to revert to the old over-simplification that the Civil War is explainable almost entirely in terms of the moral implications of the slavery issue." *Mississippi Valley Historical Review,* XXXVI (March, 1950), 708.

84 Whitridge, *No Compromise!* (New York, 1960), and "Fanaticism North and South," *Virginia Quarterly Review,* XXXVIII (Summer, 1962), 494–509.

questions about Lincoln's role. Charles W. Ramsdell fired the first shot in this skirmish in 1937 by suggesting that Lincoln hoped that the provisioning of Fort Sumter would provoke the South to fire the first shot, thereby unifying the North, solidifying the Republican party, and giving an excuse for war.[85] James G. Randall accepted Lincoln's word that in effect he would have abandoned Fort Sumter if Fort Pickens could have been reinforced.[86] David M. Potter, in his significant *Lincoln and His Party in the Secession Crisis,* also denied Ramsdell's thesis, arguing that Lincoln was in complete control of his party and was trying sincerely to save the Union short of war. In Potter's view, Lincoln would have drawn the support of southern moderates by offering compromise. But he overestimated and misunderstood the nature of southern unionism, and he rejected conciliation in an effort to preserve the Union. Thus Fort Sumter may have been a blunder, but it was not a deliberate provocation.[87] As Potter later said, Lincoln did not want war but merely accepted what seemed inevitable, hoping that the Confederates would shoot first if there had to be a war.[88] Kenneth M. Stampp entered the fray in 1950 with his *And the War Came.* He stood between the Ramsdell and the Randall-Potter interpretations. He saw politicians, both North and South, thinking too much of personal and party advantage. The slavery issue symbolized and crystallized many other topics of dispute. Political and economic motives were rationalized into freedom, democracy, etc., against wickedness, slavery, etc. Perhaps the South had blundered in failing to abide by the verdict of the election, and perhaps the North blundered by failing to accept southern separation. But Lincoln did not deliberately seek to provoke a war; he took a "calculated risk" to preserve the Union. In the final analysis, however, both Lincoln and southern leaders preferred war to submission.[89] The latest study on

85 Ramsdell, "Lincoln and Fort Sumter," *Journal of Southern History,* III (August, 1937), 259–88. This thesis was elaborated in a partisan book by John S. Tilley, *Lincoln Takes Command* (Chapel Hill, 1941).

86 Randall, "Sumter," Chap. XII of *Lincoln the President* (2 vols.; New York, 1945), I. See also Randall, "When War Came," *Abraham Lincoln Quarterly,* I (March, 1940), 3–42.

87 Potter, *Lincoln and His Party in the Secession Crisis* (New Haven, 1942).

88 From notes taken on a panel discussion at a meeting of the Southern Historical Association, in *Journal of Southern History,* XXV (February, 1959), 100–101.

89 Stampp, *And the War Came: The North and the Secession Crisis, 1860–1861* (Baton Rouge, 1950). See also, Stampp, "Lincoln and the Strategy of Defense in the Crisis of 1861," *Journal of Southern History,* XI (August, 1945), 297–323, in which he shows Lincoln as concerned more with the Union than the issue of peace or war, preferring peace but accepting war if necessary to preserve the Union. His plan was "a strategy of defense which avoided even the appearance of initiating hostilities."

Lincoln's role is Richard N. Current's *Lincoln and the First Shot* (1963), which also disagrees with both the Ramsdell thesis and the Randall-Potter view. Its last chapter is a delightful summary of the historiographical controversy. Current believed that Lincoln was not very hopeful of peace but did not deliberately provoke war. Lincoln thought that his actions would probably lead to hostilities, but he was determined that if such should be the unhappy result, the shooting would have to be initiated by the Confederates.[90]

Space forbids more than a brief comment on the numerous monographs on individual states during the approach of war and secession. Generally, these state studies, usually written by native Southerners, have been noncontroversial in tone, have emphasized politics, and have shown considerable scholarship and judgment. They have tended to recognize the overriding importance of the slavery (or racial) issue in the Lower South, and they have pointed out that in the Upper South it was a matter of choosing between northern or southern nationalism. This is evident in two of the better studies—that of Virginia by Henry T. Shanks and that of North Carolina by J. Carlyle Sitterson.[91] The contention that large planters tended to moderate views and Whiggism is upheld in several state studies,[92] though Ralph Wooster's statistical study of votes in the state secession conventions somewhat challenges this view.[93] Many of these studies of southern states on the road to war are useful in making an examination of the degree of unionism, moderation, and radicalism that existed in the 1850's.

Perhaps appropriately enough, it was the popular historians who wrote the most widely-read syntheses in the 1950's and 1960's. Clifford Dowdey, a Virginian and a novelist, touched on many causes of divergence between sections in *The Land They Fought For*.[94] In general, he was pro-southern and embraced many revisionist interpretations. Bruce Catton, popular Civil War historian, has also not neglected the coming of the war. Seeing many causes, he recognized that slavery was not the only factor but the catalyst for most of the subsidiary causes

90 Current, *Lincoln and the First Shot* (Philadelphia, 1963).
91 Shanks, *The Secession Movement in Virginia, 1847–1861* (Richmond, 1934); Sitterson, *The Secession Movement in North Carolina* (Chapel Hill, 1939).
92 For example: Richard H. Shryock, *Georgia and the Union in 1850* (Durham, 1926); Perry L. Rainwater, *Mississippi, Storm-Center of Secession, 1856–1861* (Baton Rouge: Otto Claitor, 1938); and Clarence P. Denman, *The Secession Movement in Alabama* (Montgomery, 1933).
93 Wooster, *The Secession Conventions of the South* (Princeton, 1962).
94 Dowdy, *The Land They Fought For* (Garden City, 1955). He notes various changing interpretations on pp. 3–5, "The Cold War."

that produced bloodshed. In his view, two definite societies had emerged by 1861, and Lincoln made too many mistakes in 1861. Like the revisionists, Catton saw the war as needless and said that it "settled nothing that reasonable men of good will could not have settled" if they had been willing to try.[95]

Several problems have plagued these ambitious scholars who have sought to understand the background and causes of the great American tragedy. One is the ever-present temptation of "presentitis." Consciously or not, historians are conditioned in their thinking by their own times and circumstances. As Herbert Butterfield has remarked, "the study of the past with one eye on the present" is indeed "the source of all sins and sophistries in history." [96] This problem has been especially acute for historians of the antebellum era, since federal-state relations and race relations, two problems still very much alive, were much at issue. The judgment of modern historians too often reflects their attitudes on these thorny issues. In some instances, one can predict rather accurately certain historians' reactions to certain books—if one knows the thesis of the book and the point of view of a contemporary-minded historian. As early as 1934, Theodore C. Smith was already worried lest the goal of writing objective history might not already have begun to be eroded by the assumption that contemporary political and social values should affect historical writing. Smith warned that history was being used this way by European dictatorships.[97] However, when one considers all the strong feelings that developed during the Civil War and which seared the nation too long after it, one must note that historians have come far toward objectivity as they have worked with biased source materials and sought to tell accurately a story involving their own sections, mores, and traditions. It is perhaps worth noting that twentieth-century scholars who are native Southerners have on the whole been remarkably moderate in tone, free of bias, and more objective than journalists, politicians, and professional Southerners. Indeed, the most important things to be said about historians on this subject is that sectional origins have long since

95 Catton, *The Coming Fury* (New York, 1961). See also, Bruce Catton and William B. Catton, *Two Roads to Sumter* (New York, 1963). Bruce Catton, editor of *American Heritage,* has been called the last survivor of both armies.

96 Quoted in Boyd C. Shafer, "The Study of History in the United States," Association of American University Professors *Bulletin,* L (September, 1964), 237.

97 Smith, "The Writing of American History in America, from 1884 to 1934," *American Historical Review,* XL (April, 1935), 439–49. For a brief summary of the "changes in the intellectual climate since 1865 [that] have conditioned the reactions of each generation," see David M. Potter's Review of Pressly, *Americans Interpret Their Civil War,* 400.

ceased to matter, that they have arrived at a more or less general consensus, and that they recognize that the Civil War was the product of many causes.

Scholars have noted areas where further research might yet uncover evidence which could strengthen or clarify what is already known. But this is about all that remains to be done. As David Donald has observed, this once-controversial subject is now so dead that historians have turned to historiography.[98] He gives four reasons for this decline in interest: the topic has already been exhaustively examined many times; a significant new synthesis would require complex, difficult, technical, and expensive research; there is the knowledge that the subject, long so controversial, is "mined with semantic booby traps"; and young historians are more interested in "tracing elements of continuity and consensus rather than conflict." [99]

Although historiographers may be overwhelmed by the topic, some historians still see point in a pursuit which can never reveal, "objectively and with mathematical precision, what caused the Civil War." [100] Edwin Rozwenc has shown why the search for war causes has no end, for it is a puzzle which historians have helped to create. To Rozwenc, however, the game is worth the candle, for "in the search for causes in human affairs, to come to understand more clearly the springs of human thought and action, we learn to know ourselves, and we discover the destinies which our historical evidence will allow us to choose." [101] Nowhere has this search been more intensive than in the study of the coming of the Civil War. Perhaps it is often disillusioning to see some of the "springs of human thought and action," but there is always the hope that we may yet profit from such lessons and thereby pursue a destiny less fraught with tragedy and conflict than was the era of 1846 to 1861.

98 Donald, "American Historians and the Causes of the Civil War," 351.
99 Ibid., 353–54.
100 Stampp (ed.), Causes of the Civil War, vi.
101 Rozwenc (ed.), Causes of the American Civil War, vii-viii.

X

The Confederate States of America: The Homefront

Mary Elizabeth Massey

CHARLES WILLIAM RAMSDELL, in the middle 1930's, pointed to the need for a "full and comprehensive history of the Confederacy" which would not place "undue emphasis upon any particular phase of the story" but would include everything "that materially affected the people." He believed that it was too soon for one historian to undertake the task of untangling "all the complexities of the subject," for he noted that there were many unexplored areas, among them more than a dozen relating to the homefront. Although some have since been the subject of monographs, others remain in the realm of the unexplored.[1] What Professor Ramsdell did not say, but may have thought, is that any history which includes both military and homefront developments cannot be confined to one volume if it is to be "full and comprehensive."

1 Ramsdell, "Some Problems Involved in Writing the History of the Confederacy," *Journal of Southern History,* II (1936), 133–47.

A cursory survey of books and articles relating to the Confederate homefront reveals a profusion of published materials. But when these are subjected to critical analysis the historian will find that many aspects of the problem have been completely ignored or inadequately studied. More has been written about the battles and campaigns than about life within Confederate lines, and what has been said of the homefront too often spotlights the leaders and upper classes. Much of the detailed information available on domestic conditions is found in scholarly articles published in the professional journals, but these include only a part of the story. It is the lack of space that prevents their being cited as often as they merit, and, with few exceptions, attention must be accorded them in this summary manner. The same is true of the primary and secondary accounts found in the files of *The Southern Historical Society Papers*, *Publications of the Southern History Association*, *Confederate Veteran*, and the late nineteenth century issues of many periodicals, notably *Century Illustrated Magazine*, *Atlantic Monthly* and *Harper's*. All who have ever searched for materials relating to the Confederate homefront recognize that these are a storehouse of information.

Failure to cite is not to be implied as failure to realize the value of biographies and well-edited personal records of those who lived during the war, but rarely can they be mentioned individually. In most instances biographies written in the generation following the war are of little value, for research materials were either unavailable or were not used, and their authors lacked the perspective, detachment, and objectivity which scholarly historians would like to think they possess. These early biographers usually wrote to defend or defame but, ironically, theirs are the only accounts we have of many leaders. Reminiscences and memoirs of the wartime generation are generally less valuable than diaries, journals, or letters. But the value of any diary, journal, or collection of letters will depend in part on the person whose record it is and the editor's knowledge of history and his ability to explain or interpret events and conditions described by the writer. There are dozens of personal accounts written by Southerners and travelers which reflect homefront conditions as no historian has been able to do, but these will receive scant recognition. It should be noted, however, that many illuminating letters and diaries still await an editor.

Whether or not an anthology is of great value depends entirely on the editor. He must know intimately the period with which he is dealing, and he must select carefully, organize sensibly, and comment accurately. Unfortunately, most anthologies consist entirely or primarily of selections from published works with which historians are already familiar. The general Civil War anthologies which cover northern and southern military, naval, diplomatic, and homefront conditions do not devote proportionate space to the Confederate homefront. The two most comprehensive anthologies of this type are *The Blue and the Gray* and *The Tragic Years*,[2] but the two combined do not present as complete a picture of southern economic and social conditions as does *The Confederacy*, edited by Albert D. Kirwan. He carefully chose and brilliantly edited a cross-section of contemporary writings which touch on political, economic, social, cultural, and religious developments in the wartime South. Moreover, he arranged them to reflect the mounting criticism, bitterness, and despondency of the people.[3] Because it portrays only civilian life, Professor Kirwan's anthology surpasses *The Confederate Reader*, edited earlier by Richard Barksdale Harwell.[4] *Mississippi in the Confederacy*, edited by John K. Bettersworth and James W. Silver, and *The Alabama Confederate Reader*, by Malcolm C. McMillan, are excellent portrayals of the experiences of civilians caught in a war. Told by contemporaries and interpreted by able scholars, these anthologies give insight to the problems and reactions of all groups.[5] Even more localized are *Richmond in Time of War* and *Ladies of Richmond*, both arranged chronologically. The former presents a more complete picture of all classes of society, but Katharine Jones, editor of the latter, concentrated on the upper class women and girls who lived in the capital.[6] Miss Jones' *Heroines of Dixie* also represents primarily the writings of the upper classes from broad areas of the Confederacy and includes selections from manuscripts as well as from published works.[7]

Most general histories of the Civil War have tended to emphasize the North rather than the South and the military rather than the civilian side of the story. When the southern homefront is mentioned it is to examine political and economic factors, while either ignoring or casually mentioning social, religious, and cultural developments. Of the his-

2 Henry Steele Commager (ed.), *The Blue and the Gray: The Story of the Civil War As Told By Participants* (2 vols.; Indianapolis, 1950); Paul M. Angle and Arthur Schenck Miers (eds.), *Tragic Years, 1860–1865: A Documentary History of the American Civil War* (2 vols.; New York, 1960).

3 Kirwan (ed.), *The Confederacy* (New York, 1959).

4 Harwell (ed.), *The Confederate Reader* (New York, 1957).

5 Bettersworth and Silver (eds.), *Mississippi in the Confederacy* (2 vols.; Baton Rouge, 1961); Malcolm C. McMillan (ed.), *The Alabama Confederate Reader* (Tuscaloosa, 1963).

6 William J. Kimball (ed.), *Richmond in Time of War* (New York, 1959); Jones (ed.), *Ladies of Richmond* (Indianapolis, 1962).

7 Jones (ed.), *Heroines of Dixie* (Indianapolis, 1955).

torians publishing general studies before 1920, James Ford Rhodes wrote a more satisfactory account than any other, even though it was far from comprehensive. His emphasis was on the North and on military affairs, but he made interesting observations about causes of the Confederacy's failure: financial instability, scarcities, impressment, the breakdown of transportation, and the blockade. Out of deference to social and religious factors he included a few brief remarks about women, Negroes, and revivals.[8] Edward Channing, writing in the twenties, was more attentive to the Confederate homefront than his predecessors or general historians writing since, excepting David Donald. Professor Channing carefully examined economic conditions within the Confederacy but concluded that they were not responsible for its failure. "Governments" he said "have often operated most effectually when bankrupt." The South's greatest weakness lay in its people, who could "have held out for a long time" had they chosen to do so. As "utter demoralization" swept over the land in the last year of the war, the Confederacy "collapsed with speed and thoroughness." Interesting also was Channing's interpretation of President Davis, whose task he described as "stupendous," and whose enemies as vigorous and venomous "little men and selfish politicians." [9]

The only general work confined to the nonmilitary, nonpolitical aspects of Civil War history is *The Irrepressible Conflict* which covers the years 1850–65, but so little space is devoted to Confederate affairs that it does not contribute appreciably to the subject.[10] Carl Russell Fish died before completing his Civil War study, and the one volume which was published is inadequate.[11] In *Conflict: The American Civil War,* George Fort Milton emphasized that the South did not utilize its resources properly or efficiently.[12] It is probably unfair to comment on an unfinished study, but the first two volumes of Allan Nevins' monumental undertaking, *The War for the Union,* are disappointing to one who hopes to find a thorough appraisal of conditions within the Confederacy. Professor Nevins has set the stage for future troubles when he says that the Southerners erred in predicting a short war, relying on cotton to gain them recognition abroad, and endorsing an extremely shortsighted

8 Rhodes, *History of the Civil War, 1861–1865* (reprint, New York, 1961), 366–97. See also Rhodes, *History of the United States from the Compromise of 1850* (8 vols.; reprint, New York, 1902–1920).

9 Channing, *A History of the United States* (6 vols.; New York, 1905–1925), VI, 404–405, 412, 612–28.

10 Arthur Charles Cole, *The Irrepressible Conflict, 1850–1865* (New York, 1934).

11 Fish, *The American Civil War: An Interpretation* (New York, 1937).

12 Milton, *Conflict: The American Civil War* (New York, 1941).

financial program which was insufficient to their needs.[13] The best balanced general history of the war is *The Divided Union,* the complete text of which is also found in David Donald's revision of James Garfield Randall's *The Civil War and Reconstruction.* Professor Donald has greatly expanded Randall's treatment of internal conditions of the war-time South and, after a scholarly and comprehensive appraisal of both the North and South, he offers no single cause for the South's collapse.[14]

The first histories of the Confederacy were written by those who lived during the conflict, and none in this group are balanced accounts. Most are inaccurate and subjective, many are caustic or evasive, and some are nothing more than rationalizations. Edward A. Pollard began publishing his history while the war was being fought, one volume for each year of the conflict. After the war these were combined and published, then reedited and republished. Pollard's hatred of President Davis and other officials permeated everything he wrote, and each edition was more vituperative and malicious than the one preceding it. For much of his information on homefront conditions he relied on the Richmond *Examiner* which he edited, but he could never forget his hatred long enough to present an accurate, unbiased picture of anything. His works have the great value of showing the malevolence of Davis' critics.[15] It was Pollard's interpretation of affairs in Richmond that was first circulated, and there is little indication that Frank H. Alfriend's refutation of Pollard and defense of Davis had any appreciable effect.[16]

When Jefferson Davis wrote his accounts of the war years he added very little to the story since he confined his discussion primarily to military and financial affairs and, in the guise of history, defended his policies. He omitted far more than he included of the inner workings of the government and, except for dedicating the first volume to the women of the Confederacy, he evidenced slight concern over civilian struggles.[17]

13 Nevins, *The Improvised War, 1861–1862* (New York, 1959), Volume I of his *The War for the Union* (New York, 1959——), and *The War Becomes Revolution, 1862–1863* (New York, 1960), Volume II of *ibid.*

14 Randall and Donald, *The Divided Union* (Boston, 1961); Randall and Donald, *The Civil War and Reconstruction* (Boston, 1961).

15 Pollard, *Southern History of the War* (2 vols.; New York, 1866), *The Lost Cause: A New Southern History of the War* (New York, 1866), and *Life of Jefferson Davis, With a Secret History of the Southern Confederacy, Gathered "Behind the Scenes in Richmond"* (Philadelphia, 1869).

16 Alfriend, *Life of Jefferson Davis* (Cincinnati, 1868).

17 Jefferson Davis, *The Rise and Fall of the Confederate Government* (2 vols.; New York, 1881), and *A Short History of the Confederate States of America* (New York, 1890).

When Mrs. Davis wrote about him she attempted to explain his deficiencies while emphasizing the pressures of the office and his wretched
health. Her greatest contribution was her portrait of the President as a
devoted father and husband.[18] Because Davis became an issue during
the war and has remained one since, historians as well as biographers
have presented many interpretations of the man. These have run the
gamut from Pollard's brutal appraisal in the 1860's to Hudson Strode's
extremely defensive one in the 1960's, but there is no completely satisfactory biography of the Confederate President. Among the more favorable of the recent works are those of Elizabeth Cutting and Allen
Tate.[19] Robert W. Winston stated that Davis was the best man for the
position because he represented the planter class, and Rembert W.
Patrick agreed that he should have been President because of his military
training, political experience, character, and courage, though Patrick
says that he lacked finesse.[20] Hamilton J. Eckenrode, Robert McElroy,
and Burton J. Hendrick have not only been critical of Davis but have
singled him out as primarily responsible for the South's defeat.[21] Allan
Nevins found him lacking in warmth, ability to lead the people in "action
and . . . sacrifice," passion, patience, and understanding of the "cataclysmic nature of the era." He was not, says Nevins, "a nation-builder." [22]
Hudson Strode has described Davis as "the warmest of men." His extreme sensitivity was offset by his "deep humanity," and his pride was
that of "the heroes in Greek tragedy." [23] In his analysis of the President,
Bell Irvin Wiley judiciously discussed his virtues and shortcomings and
concluded that there was "more to condemn than to praise." [24]

Alexander Hamilton Stephens made no significant contribution to
Confederate history with his rambling, involved account, two-thirds of

18 Varina Howell Davis, *Jefferson Davis, Ex-President of the Confederate States
of America* (New York, 1890).

19 Cutting, *Jefferson Davis, Political Soldier* (New York, 1930) ; Tate, *Jefferson
Davis: His Rise and Fall: A Biographical Narrative* (New York, 1929).

20 Winston, *High Stakes and Hair Trigger: The Life of Jefferson Davis* (New
York, 1930) ; Patrick, *Jefferson Davis and His Cabinet* (Baton Rouge, 1944).

21 Eckenrode, *Jefferson Davis: President of the South* (New York, 1923) ;
McElroy, *Jefferson Davis the Unreal and the Real* (New York, 1937) ; Hendrick,
Statesmen of the Lost Cause: Jefferson Davis and His Cabinet (New York, 1939).

22 Nevins, *The Statesmanship of the Civil War* (New York, 1953), 5–6, 17–23,
26–47.

23 Strode, *Jefferson Davis: Confederate President* (New York, 1959), xii–xiv.

24 Wiley, *The Road to Appomattox* (Memphis, 1956). See also Wiley's introduction to Jefferson Davis, *The Rise and Fall of the Confederate Government* (2
vols.; New York, 1958).

which related to the period before the war. His emphasis was on the constitutional aspects of the struggle, and he frequently mentioned his love of liberty. But Stephens' rationalization made him seem to be a bigger man than has recent scholarship which implies that his "history" was an evasive fabrication. Commenting on the Vice-President's love of liberty, James Z. Rabun has said that he loved it "as a bigot." While Stephens reiterated that his relations with Davis were cordial despite certain differences, Rabun has published a letter written in 1864 by Stephens to his half-brother Linton, which refutes this assertion. The Vice-President referred to the President as "an unprincipled, untruthful, unreliable, bad man, . . . a weak, sly, hypocritical, aspiring knave." Both Rudolph von Abele, his most recent biographer, and Rabun have interpreted Stephens as a neurotic trouble-maker who determined to have things his way and, when he could not, devoted himself to undermining and hindering the President and his program. Von Abele says that Stephens' behavior during 1864–65 "forms the least creditable chapter of his career," but had he been "more stable, he would have been a great man." In comparing Davis and Stephens, both scholars imply that the President was the greater man.[25]

Thomas Cooper DeLeon wrote a better-balanced history of the Confederacy than did Pollard, Davis, or Stephens. Despite its errors, *Four Years in Rebel Capitals* is valuable today as a homefront study, and although the author stated that he did not "aspire to the heights of history," he did accomplish his purpose—to write about conditions "within the Confederacy." As the title suggests, Richmond and Montgomery were the principal locales, but DeLeon covered all facets of life as he saw them—leaders and their policies, people's problems and reactions, and growing uncertainty and despair. Discussed also were the effects of the blockade, impressment, inflation, and factionalism, and contributions in literature, art, music, and the theatre. Seventeen years after writing this account, DeLeon published *Belles, Beaux and Brains of the 60's*. It told of social leaders, their wartime activities and postwar careers. The author reflected a more romantic view of the past than he had in his first work, and his second volume is not as well balanced as the first

25 Stephens, *A Constitutional View of the Late War Between the States: Its Causes, Character, Conduct and Results* (2 vols.; Philadelphia, 1870); Rabun, "Alexander H. Stephens and Jefferson Davis," *The American Historical Review*, LVIII (1953), 290–321; Rabun (ed.), *A Letter for Posterity: Alexander H. Stephens to His Brother Linton, June 3, 1864* (Atlanta, 1954); von Abele, *Alexander H. Stephens, A Biography* (New York, 1946), 191, 200, 320, 326.

because he never got beyond the upper classes and social affairs.[26]

Jabez L. M. Curry was another of the war generation to write history, and he primarily treated political, diplomatic, and financial affairs while mentioning the privations and ingenuity of southern people. This work is superficial and filled with understatements. He dismissed the grave financial conditions with the sentence, "They became a question of greatest concern." Of Joseph E. Brown he said, "He and his State were in fullest sympathy with the Southern Cause, but not always in harmony with the administration." The work's greatest weakness as history stems from the author's apparent desire to forget the unpleasantness which existed within the Confederacy.[27]

Since the First World War seven general histories of the Confederacy have been written. The first of these was Nathaniel W. Stephenson's small volume, *The Day of the Confederacy,* a brilliant if not an exhaustive interpretation of the Confederate homefront. Touching on all developments behind the lines, he stressed the economic problems which he attributed to the blockade, inadequate transportation, and speculation.[28] Next to appear was Robert Selph Henry's study of the Confederacy, which is accurate and readable but emphasizes military affairs.[29] Clifford Dowdey had contributed two studies, *Experiment in Rebellion* and *The Land They Fought For,* both of which leave the impression of having been written from a window in Richmond. Dowdey has evidenced greater interest in military than homefront developments, but his descriptions of the wartime leaders and events in Richmond are especially vivid and colorful. He has an aversion to footnotes and an inclination to generalize, but he does catch the spirit of the times. Dowdey is decidedly anti-Davis as he depicts the President living with his fantasies and believing in his own infallibility while the Confederacy collapsed around him.[30]

E. Merton Coulter has written the most comprehensive account of the Confederate homefront, *The Confederate States of America, 1861–1865.* It covers military developments but emphasizes political, economic,

26 DeLeon, *Four Years in Rebel Capitals: An Inside View of Life in the Southern Confederacy From Birth to Death* (Mobile, 1890), and *Belles, Beaux and Brains of the 60's* (New York, 1907).

27 Curry, *Civil History of the Government of the Confederate States With Some Personal Reminiscences* (Richmond, 1901), 109, 166, 170.

28 Stephenson, *The Day of the Confederacy: A Chronicle of the Embattled South* (New Haven, 1919).

29 Henry, *The Story of the Confederacy* (Garden City, 1931).

30 Dowdey, *Experiment in Rebellion* (New York, 1946), and *The Land They Fought For: The Story of the South as the Confederacy* (New York, 1955).

social, and cultural currents within the South. His presentation has breadth and, in most instances, depth. That some subjects are handled superficially may be explained by limited space, complexities of the problem, and lack of monographs on many important topics. However, this is the best general account of the Confederate homefront. Professor Coulter recognized that there were many factors which contributed to the collapse of the Confederacy, but he said that they could "be summed up in this one fact: The people did not will hard enough and long enough to win." [31] Clement Eaton, in *A History of the Southern Confederacy*, attained a better balance between military and civilian affairs, proving his ability to select, appraise, and synthesize materials in a limited space. Among many provocative interpretations is Professor Eaton's conclusion that the South did not fail because of economic weaknesses but because of insufficient and ineffective propaganda combined with the highly effective work of the obstructionists.[32] *The Confederacy*, by Charles P. Roland, touches on homefront conditions; especially noteworthy is his account of city life. His volume does not supplement or replace those by Coulter and Eaton.[33]

Scholarly state studies contribute appreciably to our knowledge of the Confederate homefront. The passing years have made Walter Lynwood Fleming's history of Alabama inadequate, but he was a pioneer when he wrote of schools, churches, shortages, styles, and other aspects of wartime life.[34] Among the more recent scholarly, comprehensive state histories are those of Louisiana, Mississippi, and Georgia written by Jefferson Davis Bragg, John K. Bettersworth, and T. Conn Bryan, respectively. All three relegate military affairs to a secondary place and emphasize political, economic, and social developments. The histories of Mississippi and Georgia are more complete and achieve greater depth than does that of Louisiana.[35] Charles Edward Cauthen's study of South Carolina stresses secession but devotes very little space to the war years.[36]

Few monographs can be more interesting and informative than well-

31 Coulter, *The Confederate States of America, 1861–1865* (Baton Rouge, 1950), 566.

32 Eaton, *A History of the Southern Confederacy* (New York, 1954).

33 Roland, *The Confederacy* (Chicago, 1960).

34 Fleming, *Civil War and Reconstruction in Alabama* (New York, 1903).

35 Bragg, *Louisiana in the Confederacy* (Baton Rouge, 1941); Bettersworth, *Confederate Mississippi: The People and Policies of a Cotton State in Wartime* (Baton Rouge, 1943); Bryan, *Confederate Georgia* (Athens, 1953).

36 Cauthen, *South Carolina Goes to War, 1861–1865* (Chapel Hill, 1950).

written urban histories based on careful research. Tens of thousands of people in search of employment, protection, and companionship flocked into southern towns and cities during the Civil War. Unfortunately, few satisfactory accounts of the urban areas have been written, and most of those are not noteworthy contributions. It is natural that Richmond should have been the subject of more volumes than any other city, but all of these have decided limitations. Alfred Hoyt Bill stressed primarily the activities of the upper classes and a few leaders; Stanley Kimmel was preoccupied with the seamier side of life in the capital.[37] Rembert Patrick concentrated on the three days when the government fled and the Federals occupied the capital. Alfred Jackson Hanna covered a part of the same period, but he follows high-ranking officials in their flight from Richmond.[38]

Several Georgia communities recently have inspired histories, but the only one which satisfactorily covers the entire four years and gives adequate attention to civilian life is Florence Fleming Corley's study of Augusta. A. A. Hoehling's *Last Train from Atlanta* is an exciting presentation of both military and civilian affairs but is confined to the period between July and November, 1864. Diffee William Standard's fifty-one page account of Columbus touches economic and social developments only very superficially, while Alexander A. Lawrence's story of Savannah gives too little attention to civilian problems and activities.[39] None of these accounts is as satisfactory as Peter F. Walker's scholarly, balanced history of Vicksburg during the period of secession and war. This is truly the account of "a people at war." Walker discusses the politics, social life, and economic conditions through the early attacks, siege, and fall to the end of the war.[40] Historians will find no better model for urban history. There is a need for similar studies of other southern communities, notably the permanent and provisional state capitals and port cities. It is difficult to understand, for example, why no historian has written a scholarly account of New Orleans during the war, for there is an abundance of primary materials on the subject. Charles L. Dufour's recent account of New Orleans' fall brought citizens

37 Bill, *The Beleagured City: Richmond, 1861–1865* (New York, 1946); Kimmel, *Mr. Davis' Richmond* (New York, 1958).

38 Patrick, *The Fall of Richmond* (Baton Rouge, 1960); Hanna, *Flight into Oblivion* (Richmond, 1938).

39 Corley, *Confederate City: Augusta, Georgia, 1860–1865* (Columbia, 1960); Hoehling, *Last Train from Atlanta* (New York, 1958); Standard, *Columbus, Georgia in the Confederacy* (New York, 1954); Lawrence, *A Present for Mr. Lincoln: The Story of Savannah from Secession to Sherman* (Macon, 1961).

40 Walker, *Vicksburg: A People at War, 1860–1865* (Chapel Hill, 1960).

into the story, and Elizabeth Joan Doyle has written several scholarly articles on conditions in the occupied city, but a full-scale account for the four years is yet to be published.[41]

There are a great many monographs which concentrate on political developments within the Confederacy. Some of these are primarily factual accounts and others are interpretative, but most analyze political conditions in an effort to determine whether or not they caused or contributed to the collapse of the Confederacy. Roy F. Nichols has studied the problem and discovered, as have others, that factionalism and personal animosities played a significant role. He asked if they were not "as significant as the military campaigns" in bringing about the South's defeat, and he urged historians to "give careful study to . . . the functioning of democracy in time of trouble." [42] The tendency has been to study southern leaders who shaped policies and to generalize about the ordinary citizens' reactions to the individuals and their programs.

The executive branch of the Confederate government has been the subject of more than a dozen monographs devoted to Cabinet officials, departments, and related problems. The most scholarly, satisfactory treatment of the Cabinet and its relations with President Davis is Rembert W. Patrick's well-organized, concise account, *Jefferson Davis and His Cabinet*. Every official who served in a Cabinet post is sketched and his work carefully evaluated. Patrick concludes that they were the "ablest men in Southern political life" and would compare favorably with those holding similar positions in any period of American history. For this reason, Patrick concludes that the civil authorities were not responsible for the failure of the Confederacy, nor was President Davis the despot some writers have depicted.[43] Burton Hendrick's *Statesmen of the Lost Cause: Jefferson Davis and His Cabinet* has a misleading title. It is as much a diplomatic history as an analysis of Cabinet officials, and it emphasizes other political figures who had little or no place in the Richmond government. Hendrick was critical of President

41 Dufour, *The Night the War Was Lost* (Garden City, 1960); Doyle, "Greenbacks, Car Tickets and the Pot of Gold: The Effects of Wartime Occupation on the Business Life of New Orleans," *Civil War History*, V (1959), 347–62, and "Nurseries of Treason: Schools in Occupied New Orleans," *The Journal of Southern History*, XXVI (1960), 161–79.

42 Nichols, "The Operation of American Democracy, 1861–1865; Some Questions," *The Journal of Southern History*, XXV (1959), 31–32, 52. See also Nichols, *The Stakes of Power, 1845–1877* (New York, 1961).

43 Patrick, *Jefferson Davis and His Cabinet*, 366–68.

Davis whom he condemned for being shortsighted, stubborn, and opinion-
ated. While Patrick believed that Judah P. Benjamin's appointment as
Secretary of State was a mistake, Hendrick thought him the best choice
for the post. His admiration of Benjamin is evident throughout the
study. Hendrick concluded that it was not lack of military strength
which brought the Confederacy to its knees, but "internal dissension
and factionalism" and Europe's "distrust of the Confederacy," both
of which resulted from having weak men in control of the government.[44]

There are two monographs devoted exclusively to Confederate diplomatic history, both of which emphasize internal political affairs. James
Morton Callahan wrote the first in 1901; he stressed the homefront
conditions which impeded the government's efforts to win recognition
abroad. Among these were political factionalism and dissension, especially that caused by states' rights obstructionists, and an unstable financial
structure.[45] Frank Owsley, writing thirty years later, emphasized the
South's cotton policy as the cause for the diplomatic fiasco and demonstrated that Confederate officials erred in believing that withholding
cotton from England and France would produce a famine which would
inevitably compel them to recognize the Confederacy. Although Professor
Owsley criticized President Davis for his part in this policy, he also
placed blame on Congress, other officials, and the newspapers. *King
Cotton Diplomacy* is the most satisfactory treatment of Confederate
diplomacy, but it fails to stress the people's views, hopes, and disappointments.[46]

Milledge L. Bonham's study of British consuls in the Confederacy reveals an interesting facet of the diplomatic homefront story.[47] There is
no similar study of French consuls, but Gordon Wright made a contribution to homefront history in a scholarly paper reflecting their views
on economic conditions within the Confederacy. They recorded their
complaints about scarcities, high prices, and the numerous inconveniences
and occasional hardships which they were compelled to endure. These
they most often attributed to the blockade. More revealing, however,
were their comments about state and Confederate economic policies,

44 Hendrick, *Statesman of the Lost Cause,* 389.

45 Callahan, *The Diplomatic History of the Southern Confederacy* (Baltimore,
1901).

46 Owsley, *King Cotton Diplomacy: Foreign Relations of the Confederate States
of America* (Rev. ed.; Chicago, 1958).

47 Bonham, *The British Consuls in the Confederacy* (New York, 1911).

the increasing demoralization of the people, and specific outbreaks such as the Bread Riot in Richmond.[48]

The Department of Justice has been so thoroughly and comprehensively investigated by William M. Robinson, Jr., that his study, *Justice in Grey: A History of the Judicial System,* merits being designated "definitive." It is a scholarly and judicious appraisal of the organization, administration, and operation of Confederate, state, territorial, and military courts. It also includes a discussion of the Patent Office and the Bureau of Printing, both a part of the Department of Justice, and gives valuable attention to individuals who held positions in the organization.[49] There are many articles relating to southern courts but that of Joseph Grégoire deRoulhac Hamilton, "The State Courts and the Confederate Constitution," offers an especially significant interpretation. Noting that it was the state courts which interpreted the legality of such issues as conscription, impressment, and the suspension of habeas corpus, Professor Hamilton found that decisions were often slow in coming but the wondrous thing was that "so much uniformity was finally attained and the Confederate government so generally upheld." [50]

It is difficult to single out works dealing with the Treasury Department, for many studies have been made which emphasize the government's financial program. However, there are two which interpret the department's role as the originator and administrator of the policies. Ernest Ashton Smith's *A History of the Confederate Treasury* is now somewhat outdated, but it was long the best account of the inner workings of the Treasury and the relations of Secretaries Memminger and Trenholm with President Davis, Congress, and the people. The author criticized Memminger for shortsighted policies which helped to wreck the Confederacy, but he also cited popular unwillingness to pay the high taxes necessary to sustain a government at war.[51] A later study by Richard Cecil Todd handles the problem more thoroughly, comprehensively, and concisely. Todd agrees with Smith that taxes and loans were neither heavy nor broad enough to meet the needs of the time, but he places the blame primarily on Congress and not on the Secretaries. Todd discusses several developments which were either ignored or merely

48 Wright, "Economic Conditions in the Confederacy as Seen by French Consuls," *The Journal of Southern History,* VII (1941), 195–214.

49 William M. Robinson, Jr., *Justice in Grey: A History of the Judicial System of the Confederate States of America* (Cambridge, 1941).

50 Hamilton, "The State Courts and the Confederate Constitution," *The Journal of Southern History,* IV (1938), 425–48.

51 E. A. Smith, *The History of the Confederate Treasury* (Richmond, 1901).

mentioned by Smith, among these being the relocation of the note-signers in Columbia, the shortages of necessary equipment, and the problem of counterfeiting.[52]

Discussion of the War and the Navy departments is omitted here— even though their policies often touched civilians in numerous ways— because they are emphasized in many of the monographs cited elsewhere in this essay. The Post Office has not yet inspired a scholarly monograph, though August Dietz made an excellent study of Confederate stamps and cancellations and, in the same volume, included all postal legislation. But his is not a thorough treatment of the mail service.[53] There is mention of the subject in various studies, and there are several articles relating to it, but no one has undertaken a full-scale evaluation of its problems, successes, failures, and relation to southern morale.

Wilfred Buck Yearns has written the only study of the Confederate Congress. It is a scholarly, unprejudiced, factual presentation of the major legislation enacted by the body. His monograph lacks luster be- cause he devoted little space to individual legislators, and he rarely at- tempted interpretation except to maintain that President Davis was always in control of Congress despite his losing some support late in the war.[54] Because little has been written about the men who served in the Confederate Congress, Bell I. Wiley's edition of Warren Akin's letters is especially significant. Here the Georgia congressman comes to life as he reveals personal experiences during his months in Richmond and as his wife tells of her problems as a refugee.[55] There is a need for a study of congressmen to supplement the volume by Yearns.

Several wartime political issues referred to in other works have been treated separately in monographs. Frank Owsley was not the first his- torian to suggest that application of the states' rights theory weakened the Confederacy, but he was the first to say that it alone was responsible for the South's collapse. Owsley cited specific Confederate legislation, policies, and officials who so aroused state authorities, notably Governors

---

52 Todd, *Confederate Finance* (Athens, 1954).

53 Dietz, *The Postal Service of the Confederate States of America* (Richmond, 1929).

54 Yearns, *The Confederate Congress* (Athens, 1960).

55 Wiley (ed.), *The Letters of Warren Akin, Confederate Congressman* (Athens, 1959). For contemporary accounts of political affairs in Richmond see John Beauchamp Jones, *A Rebel War Clerk's Diary* (New York, 1935); Edward Younger (ed.), *Inside the Confederate Government: The Diary of Robert Garlick Hill Kean* (New York, 1957); Mary Boykin Chesnut, *A Diary from Dixie* (New York, 1950); Judith Brockenbrough McGuire, *Diary of a Southern Refugee* (New York, 1867).

Joseph E. Brown of Georgia and Zebulon Vance of North Carolina, that they adopted obstructionist tactics which eventually resulted in the demise of the Confederacy.[56] Louise Biles Hill confirmed Owsley's interpretation of Brown as she traced his "assaults" on the Richmond officials and showed the governor of Georgia to be a power-hungry, adamant, uncooperative man who was determined "to rule or ruin." All controversial issues were unresolved until "settled his way," and the damage that he did was not confined to Georgia but spread into other areas of the South.[57] Richard E. Yates is more defensive of Zebulon Vance whom he says was loyal to the cause but who had pressures within his "sturdily individualistic state" with which he could not always cope.[58]

Albert Burton Moore's monograph on conscription revealed another major source of conflict within the Confederacy. He concluded that the obstructionist leaders were more to blame for opposition to conscription than the people who, when hearing the officials voice objections, felt justified in their complaints. He suggested that state conscription "might have been more agreeable" but that there then "would have been the problem of central control of the forces" which would have been necessary and which would have provoked dissension.[59]

Disloyal elements within the Confederacy posed a problem for both military and civil authorities, but no satisfactory study has been made of all aspects of this subject. Georgia Lee Tatum studied the disloyal and the reasons for their refusal to support the Confederate cause, but her major contribution was her discussion of their organizations in all Confederate states except Louisiana.[60] James Welch Patton studied Unionism in Tennessee for the period 1860–68, with emphasis on the political developments; and E. Merton Coulter's biography of William G. Brownlow is a scholarly treatment of East Tennessee's most prominent Unionist.[61] Others have recently published studies of Unionist leaders elsewhere in the South, but the most original and informative account of the number of Unionists in the Confederacy is Frank W.

56 Owsley, *State Rights in the Confederacy* (Chicago, 1925).

57 Hill, *Joseph E. Brown and the Confederacy* (Chapel Hill, 1939), 52, 79, 138, 194, 249–53.   ,

58 Yates, *The Confederacy and Zeb Vance* (Tuscaloosa, 1958), 50.

59 Moore, *Conscription and Conflict in the Confederacy* (New York, 1924), 354–60.

60 Tatum, *Disloyalty in the Confederacy* (Chapel Hill, 1934).

61 Patton, *Unionism and Reconstruction in Tennessee, 1860–1868* (Chapel Hill, 1934); Coulter, *William G. Brownlow: The Fighting Parson of the Southern Highlands* (Chapel Hill, 1937).

Klingberg's *The Southern Claims Commission*. His painstaking research has revealed that thousands of Southerners, many of them
planters, provided Federal forces with commodities and services worth
millions of dollars.[62] That historians are interested in the disloyal
elements is evidenced in the many articles which have appeared in
professional journals, but an exhaustive study is yet to be written.[63]

The peace movement during the last year of the war became a political issue, but the only monograph on this development is Edward
Chase Kirkland's study which includes more information on the North
than on the South. He cites Georgia, under Alexander H. Stephens'
leadership, as the southern "center of rising dissatisfaction," and he
stresses the war weariness of the people as the "decisive" factor in the
Confederacy's collapse. He also thinks that Jefferson Davis erred in
not accepting the terms offered at the Hampton Roads Conference.[64]

Economic studies of the Confederacy have gained favor in the twentieth century, but practically all of these attribute the South's failure to
the government's economic program. John Christopher Schwab, writing
in 1901, discussed the Confederacy's innumerable economic problems,
most of which he blamed on an inadequate financial program, the blockade, and the citizens' "lack of restraint and want of discipline" which
presented a "revolting picture . . . not appreciably modified by . . .
religious revivals." [65] Writing a few years later, William Garrott Brown
found that the South's resources were sufficient for its needs, but that
lack of industrial equipment, inadequate transportation, and the financial
structure prevented proper utilization and development of these resources. He believed that heavier, more equitably distributed taxes
might have saved the Confederacy despite impractical political leaders
and a "weak and undistinguished" Congress.[66]

During the last quarter-century of his life Charles Ramsdell evidenced
a profound interest in the economic problems of the Confederacy, and

62 Klingberg, *The Southern Claims Commission: A Study in Unionism* (Berkeley,
1955). See also Klingberg, "The Case of the Minors: A Unionist Family Within
the Confederacy," *Journal of Southern History*, XIII (1947), 27–45.

63 Hugh C. Bailey, "Disaffection in the Alabama Hill Country, 1861," *Civil War
History*, IV (1958), 183–93, and "Disloyalty in Early Confederate Alabama,"
Journal of Southern History, XXIII (1957), 523–28; Barnes Lathrop, "Disaffec-
tion in Confederate Louisiana: The Case of William Hyman," *Journal of Southern
History*, XXIV (1958), 308–18; Claude Elliott, "Union Sentiment in Texas, 1861–
1865," *Southwest Historical Quarterly*, L (1947), 449–77.

64 Kirkland, *The Peacemakers of 1864* (New York, 1927), 1–2, 212, 257.

65 Schwab, *The Confederate States of America, 1861–1865: A Financial and
Industrial History of the South During the Civil War* (New York, 1901), 227–83.

66 Brown, *The Lower South in American History* (New York, 1903).

when he inaugurated the Fleming Lectures in 1937 he chose as his subject the economic struggles of the southern people. His lectures, published posthumously as *Behind the Lines in the Southern Confederacy,* provide a provocative and brilliant analysis of the financial situation's effect on both citizens and the war effort. Ramsdell traced the emergence of economic problems which military and political officials failed to solve and of state socialistic legislation which the people supported despite their political principles. He emphasized the growing despondency and demoralization on the homefront, attributing this primarily to financial conditions. Throughout the study the author reiterated the insurmountable problems confronting Southerners as they sought to stabilize a new government while fighting invading armies.[67]

Inadequate and inefficient transportation is often cited by historians as one of the major weaknesses of the Confederacy. Francis R. C. Bradlee published a superficial summary of the blockade, railroads, postal service, telegraph, and Southern Express Company, but, with the possible exception of the blockade, his discussion is of little value other than pointing to the need for a history of transportation and communication.[68] The railroads have been more thoroughly studied than any other type of transportation in the Confederacy, and Robert C. Black, III, has written the most comprehensive account of the southern railroads. He discusses the organization, operation, and maintenance of the roads, as well as the men whose job it was to keep them running. Black criticizes the government's lack of a sound railroad policy and Jefferson Davis' failure to enforce the laws at his command, but he cites also the states-rights obstructionists and the owners, managers, and employees of the railroads for failing "to make serious sacrifice of their own personal interests" in order to aid the Confederacy. In emphasizing the war's effect on the railroads, the author failed to stress the civilians' effect on the facilities which they insisted on using whenever the spirit or the enemy moved them.[69] George Edgar Turner included both northern and southern railroads in his monograph emphasizing their effect on the war,[70] and Angus James Johnston, II, confined his study to Virginia railroads and stressed military rather than civilian matters.[71] An inter-

---

67 Ramsdell, *Behind the Lines in the Southern Confederacy* (Baton Rouge, 1944).

68 Bradlee, *Blockade Running During the Civil War and the Effect of Land and Water Transportation on the Confederacy* (Salem, Mass., 1925).

69 Black, *The Railroads of the Confederacy* (Chapel Hill, 1952), 294.

70 Turner, *Victory Rode the Rails: The Strategic Place of Railroads in the Civil War* (Indianapolis, 1953).

71 Johnston, *Virginia Railroads in the Civil War* (Chapel Hill, 1961).

esting little monograph could be written about the travel experiences of southern civilians whose contemporary accounts contain comic and pathetic episodes as they and their baggage moved about the Confederacy. Needed also are studies of other forms of transportation.

Many volumes have been written about the blockade, but most of these stress the daring exploits of the runners rather than the blockade's effect on the homefront. However, the recent study by Hamilton Cochran includes vivid detail on several southern cities which were markets for blockade goods. Cochran stated that the Confederate government erred in not efficiently organizing the blockade so that it would have more adequately supplied both the armed forces and the civilians.[72] Interesting also is Louise Biles Hill's account of the Confederate government's belated "socialistic" commercial and financial policy. It went into effect too late to be decisive, she says, but without it "the Confederacy would have collapsed a year earlier." [73] Domestic trade, business affairs, and banking have been treated primarily in articles rather than monographs.[74]

There are other relatively unexplored areas of Confederate economic history. One of these is southern industry, accounts of which may be found in Schwab's old, outdated work and in general histories of the Confederacy. Most scholarly articles on the subject concentrate primarily on ordnance plants. However Charles Ramsdell wrote of the Confederate government's attempt to regulate production of "clothing, blankets, tents, shoes, wagons, saddles and harness" needed by the army. He concluded that Confederate officials were not interested in developing industry "but only in exploiting it." [75] Even more ironic than the lack of an industrial study is the absence of an agricultural history of the Confederacy. Many volumes mention the numerous wartime problems of the farmers and planters, state laws curtailing cotton and tobacco production, and the effects of impressment, tax-in-kind and foraging parties. But no one has combined these and other agricultural developments into one comprehensive study. Charles P. Roland has written

72 Cochran, *Blockade Runners of the Confederacy* (Indianapolis, 1958).

73 Hill, *State Socialism in the Confederate States* (Charlottesville, 1936), 28–31.

74 E. Merton Coulter, "Commercial Intercourse with the Confederacy in the Mississippi Valley, 1861–1865," *Mississippi Valley Historical Review*, V (1919), 377–95; Joseph H. Parks, "A Confederate Trade Center under Federal Occupation: Memphis, 1862–1865," *Journal of Southern History*, VII (1941), 289–314; Edwin B. Coddington, "The Activities and Attitudes of a Confederate Business Man: Gazaway B. Lamar," *Journal of Southern History*, IX (1943), 3–36.

75 Ramsdell, "The Control of Manufacturing by the Confederate Government," *Mississippi Valley Historical Review*, VIII (1921), 231–49.

about the Louisiana sugar plantations during the war years, and Cornelius O. Cathey has published an excellent essay which tells of the war's effect on North Carolina agriculture. Except for a few published plantation records, compilations of planters' letters, and scholarly articles, very little has been written, and most of these accounts do not tell the story of the small farmer.[76]

Few homefront problems were mentioned more often by contemporaries than that of shortages, and those who later recalled the scarcities paid tribute to the peoples' ingenuity in devising makeshifts; but the historian was slow to piece together the overall situation. Ella Lonn devoted a monograph to the salt shortage, emphasizing the need for the commodity and the Confederate and state governments' attempt to locate new sources of supply.[77] Mary Elizabeth Massey wrote of the general problem as it pertained to the homefront and stressed both the shortages and the substitutes devised to replace scarce or unobtainable items.[78]

The civilian population has been the subject of several studies, beginning with Thomas Cooper DeLeon's *Belles, Beaux and Brains of the 60's*. Bell I. Wiley devoted his Fleming Lectures to *The Plain People of the Confederacy*—the common soldier, the homefolk, and Negroes. In the second essay he told of the privations, frustrations, increasing dissatisfaction, and declining morale of the southern citizenry as he touched on the economy, educational problems, religious activities, and social diversions.[79] What he has done in one brief essay should be expanded into a book which has as its theme the "plain people." This is the group about which very little is known. Professor Wiley has also written the most complete account of southern Negroes for the war period. In this monograph he discusses those who remained behind Confederate lines and those who came under Federal control. He investigates every facet of the problem as he shows both the war's effect on Negroes and their effect on the war, including the relation of master

76 Roland, *Louisiana Sugar Plantations During the American Civil War* (Baton Rouge, 1957); Cathey, "The Impact of the Civil War on Agriculture in North Carolina," in *Studies in Southern History in Memory of Albert Ray Newsome* (Chapel Hill, 1957), 97–110. See also E. Merton Coulter, "The Movement for Agricultural Reorganization in the Cotton South during the Civil War," *Agricultural History*, I (1927), 3–17, and "Planters' Wants in the Days of the Confederacy," *Georgia Historical Quarterly*, XIII (1928), 38–52; Charles William Ramsdell, "Materials for Research in the Agricultural History of the Confederacy," *Agricultural History*, IV (1930), 18–22.

77 Lonn, *Salt as a Factor in the Confederacy* (New York, 1933).

78 Massey, *Ersatz in the Confederacy* (Columbia, 1952).

79 Wiley, *The Plain People of the Confederacy* (Baton Rouge, 1944).

and slave and that of the Negro with Federal and Confederate authorities. Wiley states that although the Negro welcomed his freedom, he was docile and well-behaved in most instances as long as he was within Confederate lines. Wiley suggests that a movement for emancipation would probably have progressed had the South won its independence.[80] Most of the early works relating to the women were romantic and eulogistic in tone,[81] and the only scholarly monograph is *The Women of the Confederacy* by Francis B. Simkins and James W. Patton. Here women's wartime work, hardships, contributions, and experiences are detailed, but also mentioned are women who created problems, "danced" through the war, and were not in sympathy with the Confederacy.[82] Because of the lapse of time since this volume was published, discovery of additional manuscript materials and publication of additional records, a new interpretative account evidencing greater understanding of the women's role should be written. The foreign element in the Confederacy has been so comprehensively treated in Ella Lonn's scholarly monograph that it is doubtful that anyone will ever improve upon it. All groups are brought into her story, as are their contributions in all fields, their problems, and those that they caused. Miss Lonn found that the majority of the foreigners were loyal to the Confederacy and that the Confederate government did its best to protect their interests. In most instances the foreign-born people were assets to the South.[83] The published accounts of foreign travelers are an extremely valuable source of information on homefront conditions.[84]

It seems strange that historians have so generally shied away from writing about the men who did not fight in the war. In this group were all classes who were too infirm, old, or young to enlist, as well as those who were exempt or who avoided conscription. Professional and business groups, planters, dirt farmers, and day laborers were part of the civilian population, and they merit study as much as do others. Nor has anyone

80 Wiley, *Southern Negroes, 1861–1865* (New York, 1953).

81 John L. Underwood, *The Women of the Confederacy* (New York, 1906); Matthew Page Andrews, *The Women of the South in War Times* (Baltimore, 1920); Francis Warrington Dawson, *Our Women in the War* (Charleston, 1885).

82 Simkins and Patton, *The Women of the Confederacy* (Richmond, 1936).

83 Lonn, *Foreigners in the Confederacy* (Chapel Hill, 1940).

84 William Howard Russell, *My Diary North and South* (Boston, 1863); Fitzgerald Ross, *Cities and Camps of the Confederate States,* ed. Richard B. Harwell (Urbana, 1958); James Arthur Lyon Fremantle, *The Fremantle Diary . . . Three Months in Southern States,* ed. Walter Lord (Boston, 1954). See also E. Merton Coulter (ed.), *Travels in the Confederate States: A Bibliography* (Norman, 1948, 1961).

written a social history of the Confederacy which would include not only all groups of people but also their activities. Research materials are fugitive, but an imaginative historian should be able to organize and write an account which would be rich in human interest.

The cultural, intellectual, and religious fields of Confederate history have been more neglected than the political, economic, and social areas. There is no study of fiction other than Robert Lively's volume, *Fiction Fights the Civil War,* and the author never intended that this be confined to the war years, though he does include a few works of fiction written during the war.[85] Lawrence F. London has contributed a discussion of the authors and publishers of the Confederacy, with emphasis on their common problem.[86] There are several compilations of wartime poetry beginning with those of William Gilmore Simms and Thomas Cooper DeLeon in the 1860's, but these are not critical analyses.[87] Even more amazing is the lack of a scholarly study devoted to the Confederate press, especially since northern newspapers and reporters have been the subject for several volumes. There are general histories of some newspapers and articles relating to specific aspects of the subject, but, except for Rabun L. Brantley's monograph, *Georgia Journalism of the Civil War Period,* there is no volume devoted entirely to the newspapers in a state or in the Confederacy.[88] Although much has been written about the hardships and sad experiences of the southern people, very little attention has been paid to humorists. Charles H. Smith, better known as "Bill Arp," has been the subject of a Ph.D. dissertation, and his Civil War writings were compiled and published after the war; but he and other humorists, professional and amateur, have been neglected.[89]

Confederate music has been treated more thoroughly than has the literature. Since 1951, when Richard Harwell published his volume on the subject, three additional books and several articles have appeared.

85 Lively, *Fiction Fights the Civil War: An Unfinished Chapter in the Literary History of the American People* (Chapel Hill, 1957). See also Lawrence S. Thompson, "The Civil War in Fiction," *Civil War History,* II (1956), 83–95.

86 London, "Confederate Literature and Its Publishers," in *Studies in Southern History in Memory of Albert Ray Newsome* (Chapel Hill, 1957).

87 Simms, *War Poetry of the South* (New York, 1866); DeLeon, *South Songs: From the Later Days* (New York, 1866); Lee Steinmetz, *The Poetry of the Civil War* (East Lansing, 1960).

88 Brantley, *Georgia Journalism of the Civil War Period* (Nashville, 1929).

89 Anne Christie, "Bill Arp," *Civil War History,* II (1956), 103–19. See also Christie (Ph.D. dissertation, University of Chicago, 1949). Charles H. Smith, *Bill Arp, So Called. A Side Show of the Southern Side of the War* (New York, 1866), and *Bill Arp's Peace Papers* (New York, 1873).

In some instances these have supplemented Harwell's work but none have replaced it. His account is an excellent evaluation of Confederate composers, compositions, and publishers, and in the latter half of the book Harwell lists 648 pieces of sheet music published in the Confederacy.[90] The theatre has virtually escaped the notice of the historian except for occasional mention and a few articles. A dissertation has been written on the subject, but it has not been published.[91] Amateur and professional productions were a major social diversion of the southern people, and more should be known about the plays, tableaux, and skits and the problems encountered in their presentation.

Two very important institutions in the Confederacy—schools and churches—have not been adequately studied. Unless one consults general histories of education, the war, or specific institutions, or unless he relies on a few articles and essays, he will find nothing about primary, secondary, and higher education in the Confederacy. Nor is there a general account of the role of the churches during the war, though there are histories of individual denominations which include the war years, and there are a few articles on the churches and church leaders. James W. Silver has written an interesting, informative monograph, *Confederate Morale and Church Propaganda,* which emphasizes the church as the most effective propaganda agency in the Confederacy and as the single most successful institution in building and maintaining civilian morale.[92] His study points to the need for both a history of religion in the Confederacy and a scholarly appraisal of all propaganda agencies at work in the wartime South.

It has been noted throughout this essay that historians have searched diligently for explanations as to why the South lost the war. Some have found the answer in one specific condition, others have emphasized several political or economic factors, but very few have taken the eclectic approach. Most studies conclude with a statement as to why the South

90 Harwell, *Confederate Music* (Chapel Hill, 1950), and *Songs of the Confederacy* (New York, 1951); Manly Wade Wellman, *Rebel Songster: Songs of the Confederates* (Charlotte, 1959); Irwin Sibler (ed.), *Songs of the Civil War* (New York, 1960); Willard A. Heaps and Porter W. Heaps (eds.), *The Singing Sixties: The Spirit of Civil War Days Drawn from the Music of the Times* (Norman, 1960).

91 Iline Fife, "The Theatre during the Confederacy" (Ph.D. dissertation, Louisiana State University, 1949); O. G. Brockett and Lenyth Brockett, "Civil War Theatre: Contemporary Treatments," *Civil War History,* I (1955), 229–50; Richard Barksdale Harwell, "The Richmond Stage," *Civil War History,* 295–304.

92 Silver, *Confederate Morale and Church Propaganda* (Tuscaloosa, 1957). See also Silver, "Propaganda in the Confederacy," *Journal of Southern History,* XI (1945), 487–503.

failed, but there are three noteworthy monographs which deal exclusively with this question. The first of these is *The Collapse of the Confederacy* by Charles H. Wesley. The author stressed internal factors rather than military failures as the primary cause of the South's defeat. Several factors which he mentioned had previously been the subject of monographs, among them states' rights, cotton diplomacy, and desertion; but he brought these together, along with economic problems and social issues, to show that troubles within the Confederacy were so numerous and staggering that they broke the spirit and morale of the people. He concluded that there were many reasons for the collapse and that to attribute it to only one "is indefensible." [93]

Bell I. Wiley explains the reasons for the South's failure in *The Road to Appomattox*. After carefully analyzing Jefferson Davis' virtues, shortcomings, and problems, Wiley concludes that the President was in part responsible. He found a second cause in the political and economic policies of the Confederate government, among these impressment, tax-in-kind, and the failure to halt speculation. These and others worked a hardship on the people who, in turn, lost confidence in the government. In the last essay, "Failures That Were Fatal," Professor Wiley emphasizes the disharmony, factionalism, and contentiousness which developed in the Confederacy. This was in part due to the government's failure to keep the people informed of changing conditions and the necessity for adopting certain programs, but it was also the result of the failure of Southerners to understand the northern people or the European situation. The author explains that Southerners did not cooperate during the war because of their provincialism and exaggerated individualism. Important also was the frustration which developed as the people found themselves at war with a powerful adversary.[94]

Why the North Won the Civil War is a compendium of five scholars' re-examination of reasons previously cited as causes for the South's defeat. Only T. Harry Williams concerned himself with military affairs. Richard Current appraised the economic conditions and noted that the North's resources were so superior to those of the South that "it would have taken a miracle, a direct intervention of the Lord" to have made possible a Confederate victory. Norman A. Graebner found the explanation in the South's diplomatic failures which were the result of the Confederacy's not realizing that European conditions and traditions prevented recognition until independence was won. David Donald stated

93 Wesley, *The Collapse of the Confederacy* (Washington, 1937), 167–68.
94 Wiley, *The Road to Appomattox* (Memphis, 1956).

that the Confederacy "Died of Democracy," pointing out that civil
liberties were unimpaired in the South, that public criticism was permitted to weaken the war effort, and that both the soldiers and the
civilians were unable or unwilling to discipline themselves for the good
of the cause. David Potter contended that political conditions were responsible for the defeat. He mentioned President Davis' failures as a
leader and the lack of a two-party system in the South which made it
difficult to organize the opposition in such a way as to provide constructive criticism.[95]

Despite the number of Civil War books published in recent years,
relatively few contribute appreciably to our knowledge of homefront
conditions. Were Professor Ramsdell alive today he would probably
say that there are insufficient monographs now available to permit one
person to write a "full and comprehensive" history of the Confederacy. Many of the unexplored areas that he mentioned in the thirties
have not yet been subjected to thorough investigation. One might ask,
as he did then, what is known about the small farmer, the businessman,
banking and banks, industries, the supply system which "reached into
almost every community," southern families left in occupied areas,
families of the poor and the prewar "animosities held over" into the
war years?[96] If these and other unstudied facets of the Confederate
homefront are to be subjects for monographs, the trained historian must
write them, for amateurs, gifted and otherwise, are primarily synthesists
of published materials, and their purpose is to write for the market, not
to find new information. Historians should remember that the most
unique feature of the Civil War in the history of the United States was
that it was fought over a wide area of this country. It became a war
against civilians as well as between armies, and the effects of the struggle
on the southern people and their way of life have not entirely vanished
from our sight.

---

95 David Donald (ed.), *Why the North Won the War* (Baton Rouge, 1960),
22, 90, 102.
96 Ramsdell, "Some Problems Involved in Writing the History of the Confederacy," 137–38, 139, 144–47.

XI

The Confederate States of America
At War
On Land and Sea

John G. Barrett

FOR countless Americans the Civil War is the great single event of United States history.* Certainly this nation never faced a crisis more strange and bitter than the conflict of 1861–65. The people were never so deeply divided as by this struggle which sought only to unite them. "It would seem," says Robert C. Black, "as if American historiography, American folklore, even the American mind itself, were revolving about a dominant center of gravity called the Civil War." [1]

---

* Because of the great number of books on the Civil War, I have attempted in this chapter to confine myself, as much as possible, to southern accounts. Even then a lack of space limits me to the examination of comparatively few volumes.

1 Black, "Thoughts on the Confederacy," in Donald Sheehan and Harold C. Syrett (eds.), *Essays in American Historiography. Papers Presented in Honor of Allan Nevins* (New York, 1960), 20.

Some people are drawn to the subject by mere curiosity because it provides a bright splash of color.[2] For others the attraction is to a lost cause or to figures like Lee and Grant. Southerners, who seem more emotional and who produced the more interesting soldiers, take the lead here, but the process is general.

More, however, than mere sentiment and curiosity are responsible for the American obsession with the Civil War. That conflict's roots reach deep into the American character and tradition. It was an all-American war—fought by Americans over American issues on American soil. And it was a civil war which, pitting brother against brother, leaves far deeper and more enduring scars than conflicts between sovereign powers. Emotionally and psychologically the struggle did not end with Appomattox.

The continuing importance of the Civil War lies also in the fact that it was this country's great tragic experience. Americans, obsessed with the terrors of the present and future, find themselves increasingly compelled to brood over this first tragic chapter in their past. Bruce Catton thinks it is this "tragic quality which justifies everything that . . . [the] Round Tables are doing, that justifies the work of the Civil War Centennial Commission . . . that justifies even the continuing flood of books."

In addition, the Civil War confirmed much of the nation's political tradition. It proved that a republican form of government could endure. It marked the triumph of nationalism over states' rights and at the same time laid the foundation for the modern industrial United States.

2 In determining why there is so much interest in the Civil War today the following sources were examined: Alan Barker, *The Civil War in America* (New York, 1961), 1–10; John G. Barrett, *Sherman's March Through the Carolinas* (Chapel Hill, 1956), 15–16; Hal Bridges, *Civil War and Reconstruction* (Washington, 1957), 1–19; D. W. Brogan, "A Fresh Appraisal of the Civil War," *Harper's Magazine*, CCXX (1960), 122–23; Alastair Buchan, "The Brother's War," *New Statesman*, LIX (1960), 192–93; Bruce Catton, "Why a Civil War Centennial Observance?" *Civil War Times*, I (1960), 1–3; Bruce Catton, *America Goes to War* (Middletown, 1958), 1–126; Henry S. Commager (ed.), *The Blue and the Gray. The Story of the Civil War as Told by Participants* (2 vols.; New York, 1950), I, xiii–xxiv; Cyril Falls, "A Window on the World. Historians in Shirt-Sleeves," *Illustrated London News* (September 13, 1952); Ulysses S. Grant, III, "Civil War: Fact and Fiction," *Civil War History*, II (1956), 29–40; Otis A. Singletary, "Civil War and Reconstruction," in William H. Cartwright and Richard L. Watson, Jr. (eds.), *Interpreting and Teaching American History* (Washington, 1961), 120–32; Frank E. Vandiver, "The Civil War: Its Theory and Practice," *The Texas Quarterly*, II (1959), 102–108; Robert P. Warren, *The Legacy of the Civil War. Meditations on the Centennial* (New York, 1961), 3–109; Bell I. Wiley, "The Memorable War," *Missouri Historical Review*, LIII (1959), 99–104; T. Harry Williams, *Americans at War. The Development of the American Military System* (New York, 1962), 47–126.

Furthermore, the war was concerned with issues, such as Negro rights, that are still alive today.

Not only are the issues still present but, thanks to the National Park Service, the visible memorials of this conflict are preserved for all to see. The battlefields of Gettysburg, Antietam, Vicksburg, and others serve as constant reminders of this epic period of American history.

The Civil War was also a big war—bigger in most respects than any the world has ever known. It was big with respect to distances involved. Land operations extended across the continent and naval operations around the world. Approximately 3,500,000 men donned uniforms of either blue or gray to participate in one or more of the war's 6,800 separate contests. These engagements involved almost every known form of warfare: large-scale battles, skirmishes, guerrilla fighting, trench warfare, sieges, forays behind enemy lines, amphibious landings, privateering, blockade running, and submarine operations. Above all, the war was big in respect to casualties. Over 618,000 servicemen lost their lives during this four-year period—more than in all other American wars combined.

The conflict of the sixties was both the last of the old-fashioned and the first of the modern wars. It was the last of the wars in which the participants observed on a large scale such amenities as allowing high-ranking military officers to resign their commissions in order to help organize a rebellion. It was not unusual for pickets to fraternize, and more than once soldiers aided a wounded foe lying between the lines or cheered his heroism on the battlefield. When Mrs. George E. Pickett, wife of the Confederate hero of Gettysburg, presented her husband with a "young recruit," Grant's staff even went so far as to celebrate with bonfires. It was, moreover, the last war in which the cavalry was to play an essential role, the last before high explosive shells would drive soldiers underground, the last in which men moved into battle in closed formation, the last in which a bishop (Leonidas Polk) commanded troops, and probably the last in which a general commanded his army personally on the field of battle.

But it was also a modern war. It was the first to necessitate something approaching total mobilization of all human and material resources. Furthermore, it was the first in which the railroad and the telegraph played a major role, and modern weapons such as the breech-loading and repeating rifles, land and naval mines, grenades, rockets, flame throwers, and iron-clad ships were used.

However, the most distinguishing thing about modern war is that it is a matter of absolutes. The South wanted complete independence while the North labored for an absolute Union. Once blood was shed at Fort Sumter there was no chance of compromise, for neither side was then willing to stop short of complete victory. In these circumstances the accepted rules of war had to be transgressed. General Sherman, a foremost exponent of total war, considered all Southerners as enemies of the Union and used his military forces against the civilian population as well as the armies of the Confederacy.

Since photography had passed its infancy by 1861, the destructive effects of total war have been fully recorded in various photographic histories. Whereas the Crimean conflict had yielded only a fair crop of photographs, the Civil War produced them in vast quantities.[3] Certainly one of the chief reasons why this brother's war compels so much interest today is that few crises in human affairs have been more graphically recorded.

This great interest in the struggle of the sixties is nowhere more clearly manifest than in the great number of Civil War books coming off the nation's presses. A paper war of astounding size has developed because of the appeal of the war years. This period of American history has, undoubtedly, captured the fancy of the American reading public in a way that no other incident ever has before. Only the Puritan Revolution of England and the French Revolutionary and Napoleonic wars boast a comparable literature. But, says a leading Civil War historian,

even here the literature is not really comparable. For the American Civil War affected the whole population and . . . it was a highly literate population. Almost everyone could write, and almost everyone, it seems, did. Surely no other chapter of modern history has been so faithfully or so elaborately recorded by ordinary men and women; in the American Civil War Everyman, was, indeed, his own historian. A disproportionate body of the available material is, to be sure, from officers or from statesmen; these were the more articulate members of the population and those who could better arrange for the publication of what they wanted to say. But to a remarkable degree the privates kept records, and so too did the folks back home.[4]

Reminiscences, recollections, diaries, and letters can be found in book, pamphlet, and periodical form, with publishers ranging from local patriotic societies to established firms. Also in print are large military

3 The most complete, but not the best, pictorial history of the war is Francis T. Miller, *The Photographic History of the Civil War* (10 vols.; New York, 1911). David Donald (ed.), *Divided We Fought* (New York, 1952), is a better work.
4 Commager, *The Blue and the Gray,* I, xix.

histories, regimental accounts, naval studies, campaign and battle records, and biographies. In fact, so comprehensive is the coverage of the military phase of the war that virtually every major engagement has its own extensive and controversial literature.

This flood of books has varied in volume but has never ceased since the early stages of the war itself. As early as 1866, John Russell Bartlett published his *Literature of the Rebellion,*[5] enumerating 6,073 books and magazines about slavery and the war. Since then the number has run into tens of thousands. There is hardly an aspect of the subject that has not been covered.

Even before the end of the war, writers produced lives of "Stonewall" Jackson;[6] yet no one could have planned much earlier to write a history of the conflict than James B. McCabe, Jr., who in "May, 1861, commenced to collect such papers and documents, both official and unofficial, relating to the war, as [he] . . . could procure." By the end of the struggle, McCabe had on hand more than fifteen thousand papers, and in 1866 he brought out the *Life and Campaigns of General Robert E. Lee.*[7]

Among the South's most prolific writers during the war years was Edward A. Pollard, the Richmond newspaper editor and bitter critic of Jefferson Davis. Between 1859 and 1872, Pollard wrote at least twenty books, the best known of these being his works on each of the war years, published separately but later combined as *Southern History of the War.*[8] Pollard's works were highly partisan and unreliable except for facts that came under his immediate personal observation. Still they were very popular and had a wide sale.

The influence of Pollard's writings was enhanced in the postwar years when the North, fresh from victory on the battlefield, set out to consolidate victory on the printed page. Scores of books appeared, most of them distasteful to ex-Confederates. Southerners replied with a verbal barrage of their own. Suffering the pain and humiliation of Re-

5 Bartlett, *The Literature of the Rebellion* (Boston, 1866).

6 Markinfield Addey, *The Life and Military Career of Thomas Jonathan Jackson* (New York, 1863) ; John E. Cooke, *Life of Stonewall Jackson* (New York, 1863).

7 McCabe, *Life and Campaigns of General Robert E. Lee* (Atlanta, 1866). No less interesting than the early formal lives of Lee and Jackson were the travel accounts written by British war correspondents and observers. See William H. Russell, *My Diary North and South* (London, 1863) ; Arthur L. Fremantle, *Three Months in the Southern States* (New York, 1864).

8 Pollard, *Southern History of the War* (New York, 1866).

construction, they had but one recourse left—to write history. Benjamin H. Hill put it this way:

Thus, denied by our enemies the opportunity of silencing, by the solemn judgements of their own courts, the fierce accusations of criminality in secession; and denied, by our enemies and the follies of our people, the glorious chance of vindicating our cause in high debate, and face to face with the chosen champions of our accusers we have but one resource left us for our defense or vindication. That resource is history—impartial and unpassioned, unoffice-seeking history.[9]

In this new struggle former soldiers became historians and conservers of history. Less than four months after the close of the war, General Lee was making plans to write a history of his campaigns. His intentions were not so much to set the record straight as to pay a last tribute to his men. On July 3, 1865, he wrote a letter to most of his general officers in which he said: "I am desirous that the bravery and devotion of the Army of Northern Virginia be correctly transmitted to posterity. This is the only tribute that can now be paid to the worth of its noble officers and soldiers." [10]

For a time Lee set about collecting material, but he found it increasingly difficult to secure the necessary papers. It is said that the War Department refused him the use of certain documents in its possession. But there is no positive proof that he ever made an official request.[11] After a while the general abandoned his intentions to write a history, and perhaps it is well that he did. His character was such that he never could have brought himself to place blame where it was due. Any detailed military account from his pen would have raised more questions than it answered.

Although General Lee failed to record for posterity the bravery and devotion of the Army of Northern Virginia, one of his lieutenants, D. H. Hill, made a significant contribution toward preserving for future generations the southern view of the war. In May, 1866, he established at Charlotte, North Carolina, *The Land We Love,* a periodical devoted in part to military history.

While Hill was attempting to make his journal a depository for war

9 Hill, *Senator Benjamin H. Hill of Georgia. His Life, Speeches and Writings* (Atlanta, 1893), 405–406.

10 J. William Jones, *Personal Reminiscences of General Robert E. Lee* (New York, 1874), 180.

11 E. Merton Coulter, "What the South Has Done about its History," *Journal of Southern History,* II (1936), 17.

records and memoirs, a number of former Confederate generals, who had been adjudged failures, were writing their apologiae. Jubal A. Early published his *Memoirs of the Last Year of the War* in 1866.[12] The next high-ranking southern officer to write the history of his campaigns was Joseph E. Johnston. His *Narrative*[13] appeared in 1874, and, although the volume was widely read, it did little to enhance the author's reputation as a soldier. Johnston's aversion to Jefferson Davis was too clearly evident for an effective presentation of his own defense. Johnston's *Narrative* prompted John B. Hood to prepare his memoirs. This apologia, written in 1878–79, was posthumously published for the benefit of the general's orphans under the title, *Advance and Retreat*.[14] General P.G.T. Beauregard, too, made an appeal to posterity. The *Military Operations of General Beauregard* [15] is, nonetheless, a controversial book only in that the general felt compelled to show how wrong everyone was who disagreed with him.

The principal monument of self-justification for officers, both North and South, is the *Battles and Leaders* series published by *Century Magazine*. More by chance than otherwise this periodical contained in its July, 1883, issue two papers on John Brown's Raid, written from opposite points of view. These accounts were so well received that the editor of *Century Magazine,* Clarence C. Buel, decided to run a series of eight or ten articles on the major battles of the war. They were to be written by surviving high-ranking officers of both sides who had participated in the engagements. This rather small project developed into several score articles, long and short, which ran from November, 1884, to the corresponding month in 1887. Circulation of the magazine almost doubled within six months.

Controversies began with the account of the first battle of Bull Run. Johnston took umbrage at some of General Beauregard's assertions about his part in directing the fight and replied. Beauregard rejoined. This helped sales, "but to the South it was humiliating to have two old soldiers disputing over a battle concerning which, two decades before, each had sought to outdo the other's compliments." [16]

12 Early, *A Memoir of the Last Year of the War of Independence* (Toronto, 1866).

13 Johnston, *Narrative of Military Operations* (New York, 1874).

14 Hood, *Advance and Retreat. Personal Experiences in the United States and Confederate Armies* (New Orleans, 1880).

15 Alfred Roman, *The Military Operations of General Beauregard in the War Between the States* (2 vols.; New York, 1883). Although this work bears Roman's name as author, it is generally regarded as autobiographical.

16 D. S. Freeman, *The South to Posterity* (New York, 1939), 82.

The popularity of the different articles caused the editors to reprint the entire series in four volumes under the title *Battles and Leaders of the Civil War*.[17] This set provides the student of the war period with much useful material, but it should be used with caution. "Human nature being what it is," comments Clyde C. Walton in a recent article, "it is exceedingly rare for a man to admit in writing . . . that he or his military unit were found wanting in any real crisis. Most particularly is this true when the author of a memoir or narrative had to exercise the decisions of command." [18]

Relatively little appeared in the *Century* series concerning three of the South's outstanding generals—Albert Sidney Johnston, J.E.B. Stuart and Richard Taylor. Johnston, who was killed at Shiloh, fortunately left his papers almost intact, and his son brought out the *Life of Gen. Albert Sidney Johnston* in 1878.[19] For a biography published so soon after the end of the war, it had some merit. H. B. McClellan, Stuart's adjutant, wrote a careful biography of his commander,[20] and Taylor, before his death in 1879, completed his memoirs, *Destruction and Reconstruction*.[21] It is an important volume covering both the fighting in Virginia and in the West. Since the author possessed considerable literary talent, his narrative is also fascinating and delightful.

As a source of Confederate military history *The Southern Historical Papers* are equally if not more valuable than many personal narratives and early postwar biographies. The first volume of the *Papers* appeared in 1876. It ran for fourteen years as a monthly, then became an annual publication, and finally an occasional publication. It is a storehouse of documentary information.

The federal Congress had meanwhile in 1874 authorized publication of the greatest of all documentary records relating to the conflict—*War of the Rebellion: A Compilation of the Official Records of the Union and Confederate Armies*.[22] The collection of materials for the *Official Records* began in 1864, but the final volume, the index, was not printed until 1901. In the "bulk of materials concerning a single subject and

17 R. U. Johnson and C. C. Buel (eds.), *Battles and Leaders of the Civil War* (4 vols.; New York, 1888).

18 Walton, "Recent Civil War Writing," *Midwest Quarterly* (Autumn, 1959), 81.

19 William P. Johnston, *Life of Gen. Albert Sidney Johnston* (New York, 1878).

20 McClellan, *Life and Campaigns of Major General J.E.B. Stuart* (Boston, 1885).

21 Taylor, *Destruction and Reconstruction: Personal Experiences of the Late War* (New York, 1878).

22 *The War of the Rebellion: A Compilation of the Official Records of the Union and Confederate Armies* (70 vols. 128 pts.; Washington, D. C., 1880–1901).

the length of time needed for completion of the task no other governmental undertaking has surpassed" this project. When completed the set ran to the staggering total of 70 volumes of 138,579 pages, plus a series of 1,006 maps and sketches in a separate atlas. The total cost of publication was approximately $2,858,000, with annual appropriations varying from $20,000 to more than $250,000.

Despite its size and cost, the *Official Records* did not contain all of the important reports. As a result, former officers requested permission to furnish postwar papers. Many of them also wanted to revise their original reports before they were published. In response to this demand, Congressman David Davis of Illinois introduced a bill in Congress (June 19, 1882) which would have allowed the Secretary of War to receive altered reports. This bill did not pass, and the War Department stated that it continued its policy of excluding postbellum matter. Nevertheless, one cannot help but wonder if everything in the 70 volumes is contemporary and unamended.[23]

If it be true that the Civil War is the most thoroughly studied of modern conflicts, and few deny this, the reason is the availability of the *Official Records*. However, in using this valuable source the student should guard against examining material out of context or selecting only documents which fit into the design of a preconceived opinion. Otherwise, this vast amount of material can be employed to prove almost any point.[24]

The appearance of the *Official Records* stimulated demands for publication of naval records, and Congress adopted legislation on July 4, 1884, permitting employment of a small clerical force by the Navy Department to copy and classify such documents as were available in departmental files or could be obtained from other reliable sources. By 1897 five volumes of documents were in print. Altogether thirty-one volumes came out, the final one in 1927. *Official Records of the Union and Confederate Navies in the War of the Rebellion,*[25] although far from complete, is still the basic collection of printed materials for the naval operations during the war.

Almost a decade before the appearance of the initial volume of the naval records in 1894, J. Thomas Scharf brought out his *History of the*

23 Joseph L. Eisendrath, Jr., "The Official Records—Sixty-three Years in the Making," *Civil War History,* I (1955), 89–94.

24 For some comments on the use of the *Official Records,* see Walton, "Recent Civil War Writing," 79–83.

25 *Official Records of the Union and Confederate Navies in the War of the Rebellion* (31 vols.; Washington, D. C., 1884–1927).

Confederate States Navy.[26] This large, unwieldy book (824 pages) is still the best general history of southern naval operations. Since the author had access to very few official papers, except those of Raphael Semmes of *C.S.S. Alabama,* he had to rely mainly on the aid and assistance of Confederate naval officers.[27] These men, in reply to letters sent out by Scharf, provided much valuable information. In addition, the author used his own large collection of naval material, newspapers, private correspondence, and journals.

As noted above, Scharf had used the Semmes papers. During the war this Confederate officer had sent some of his papers to a London publishing house—Saunders, Otley and Company—which brought them out in 1864 as *The Cruise of the Alabama and the Sumter.* (*From the Private Journals and Other Papers of Commander R. Semmes, C. S. N. and other Officers.*) Semmes also wrote his memoirs, published in 1869.[28]

A number of former captains of blockade runners wrote reminiscences between 1865 and 1900. The accounts of John Wilkinson, William Watson, Augustus C. Hobart-Hampden, Tom E. Taylor, and others throw much light on this interesting phase of the war at sea.[29]

The 1890's also saw the beginning of serious historical work on the Civil War. Trained historians, writing on the subject for the first time, gave considerable attention to the decade of the sixties. The one historian who devoted more than usual attention to the war, especially military matters, and attempted to write objectively was James Ford Rhodes, whose seven-volume *History of the United States from the Compromise of 1850* [30] and *History of the Civil War, 1861–1865,*[31] set new standards of balanced judgment and fairness. Unfortunately, southern writers

26 Scharf, *History of the Confederate States Navy from Its Organization to the Surrender of Its Last Vessel* (New York, 1887).

27 W. H. Parker's *Recollections of a Naval Officer 1841–1865* (New York, 1883), was available at this time, and it contained much valuable information on the fighting on inland waters.

28 Semmes, *Memoirs of Service Afloat During the War Between the States* (Baltimore, 1869).

29 Wilkinson, *The Narrative of a Blockade Runner* (New York, 1877); Watson, *The Adventures of a Blockade Runner, or, Trade in Time of War* (London, 1892); Hobart-Hampden, *Never Caught. Personal Adventures Connected with Twelve Successful Trips in Blockade-Running During the American Civil War* (London, 1867); Taylor, *Running the Blockade: A Personal Narrative of Adventure, Risks and Escapes During the American Civil War* (New York, 1896).

30 Rhodes, *History of the United States from the Compromise of 1850* (7 vols.; New York, 1893–1906).

31 Rhodes, *History of the Civil War, 1861–1865* (New York, 1917).

were slow in adopting Rhodes's objectivity. They continued to view the war as a remembered personal experience rather than as history. James Longstreet's *From Manassas to Appomattox*,[32] which appeared in 1896, was a rebuttal to southern charges that he alone was responsible for the disaster at Gettysburg. The two biographies of Lee[33] and the one of Leonidas Polk[34] written in the 1890's were overly sympathetic. The latter volume had value, though, because it dealt with the Army of Tennessee.[35] G. F. R. Henderson, in his life of "Stonewall" Jackson published in 1898,[36] captured the spirit of the Army of Northern Virginia but refused to admit Jackson's errors.[37]

The largest work of this period was the twelve-volume subscription set entitled *Confederate Military History*.[38] As stated in the preface, the first and last volumes "comprise such subjects as the justification of the Southern States in seceding from the Union and the honorable conduct of the war by the Confederate states government. . . ." The remainder of the set is devoted to different state studies. The design was better than the execution. Most of the volumes were poorly done. An exception is the narrative of military operations in Virginia written by Jed Hotchkiss.[39] And D. H. Hill's North Carolina story,[40] in spite of its poor composition, is informative. The most useful parts of each volume are the sketches of virtually all of the Confederate generals credited to individual states. Facts that otherwise might be unavailable today are recorded in these laudatory descriptions.[41]

The most important contribution to Civil War history in the 1890's was the *Histories of the Several Regiments and Battalions from North Carolina in the Great War 1861–65,* of which Judge Walter Clark was

---

32 Longstreet, *From Manassas to Appomattox: Memoirs of the Civil War in America* (Philadelphia, 1896).

33 Fitzhugh Lee, *General Lee* (New York, 1894); Henry A. White, *Robert E. Lee and the Southern Confederacy* (New York, 1897).

34 William M. Polk, *Leonidas Polk: Bishop and General* (New York, 1893).

35 See p. 290.

36 Henderson, *Stonewall Jackson and the American Civil War* (2 vols.; New York, 1898).

37 Freeman, *The South to Posterity,* 165.

38 C. A. Evans (ed.), *Confederate Military History* (12 vols.; Atlanta, 1899).

39 *Ibid.,* III.

40 *Ibid.,* IV.

41 Another valuable depository for obscure facts is *The Confederate Veteran,* a monthly magazine published in Nashville, Tennessee, from January, 1893, to December, 1932.

the general editor.[42] Publication was delayed for various reasons until 1901, but the work when completed comprised five volumes and contained material not only on the individual regiments but also on a variety of other subjects. Since North Carolina contributed more troops to the Confederate army than any other state and had soldiers in all of the major battles of the war (especially those in Virginia), these volumes are invaluable. No other southern state has a publication to compare with these regimental histories.

Interest in the Civil War began to wane after the observance of Lee's centenary in 1907, "when the South presented its appeal to posterity," [43] and creditable books on military subjects and personalities slowed almost to a trickle. Charles A. and Mary R. Beard could remark in the twenties and thirties "how unimportant the actual fighting was and how grass soon covered the . . . battlefields." [44] Among the relatively small number of war books published during this period there were, nevertheless, several first-rate works. General E. P. Alexander's *Memoirs*[45] is an excellent commentary on the operations of the Army of Northern Virginia, still universally relied upon and quoted. William M. Robinson, Jr.'s *Confederate Privateers*[46] is the best monograph on that subject. Frances B. C. Bradlee, *Blockade Running During the Civil War*, and James M. Morgan, *Recollections of a Rebel Reefer,* are valuable additions to the naval story.[47] A sound treatment of the war in the West is Thomas R. Hay, *Hood's Tennessee Campaign.*[48] The artillery of the Army of Northern Virginia is thoroughly analyzed by Jennings C. Wise in *The Long Arm of Lee.*[49] The problems of rounding up deserters from the southern army is admirably covered in works

42 Walter Clark (ed.), *Histories of the Several Regiments and Battalions from North Carolina in the Great War 1861–65*, by Members of the Respective Commands (5 vols.; Goldsboro, 1901).

43 Freeman, *The South to Posterity*, 197.

44 Bridges, *Civil War and Reconstruction*, 9.

45 Alexander, *Military Memoirs of a Confederate* (New York, 1907).

46 Robinson, *The Confederate Privateers* (New Haven, 1928).

47 Bradlee, *Blockade Running During the Civil War* (Salem, 1925); Morgan, *Recollections of a Rebel Reefer* (Boston, 1917). See also James Sprunt, *Chronicles of the Cape Fear River, Being Some Accounts of Historic Events on the Cape Fear River* (Raleigh, 1914).

48 Hay, *Hood's Tennessee Campaign* (New York, 1928). See also Bromfield L. Ridley, *Battles and Sketches of the Army of Tennessee* (Mexico, 1906).

49 Wise, *The Long Arm of Lee; or, The History of the Artillery of the Army of Northern Virginia* (Lynchburg, 1915).

by Ella Lonn and Georgia L. Tatum.[50] And Robert S. Henry's concise
Story of the Confederacy is good for the military phases of the war,[51]
as is John W. Thomason's *Jeb Stuart*.[52]

In 1934, after nineteen years of almost constant labor, Douglas
Southall Freeman brought out two volumes of his long awaited biography of Robert E. Lee. The final two came shortly thereafter.[53] The
completed work was hailed "as the greatest piece of biographical writing
in American literature." [54] Certainly it is the definitive life of the Confederate general and a landmark in the writing of southern history.

The author, who was both a trained historian and a newspaper editor,
uncovered a vast store of material dealing with Lee's strategy. But in
using it he adopted the rather unusual device of allowing the reader no
more knowledge than Lee possessed at the time of any battle or campaign. This policy of viewing the battle scene through the eyes of the
commanding general is subject to criticism on the grounds that it gives
an incomplete picture. It must be remembered, however, that *R. E. Lee*
is a biography first, and military history afterward. By this means, also,
the author established a useful principle of selection of materials and
described the unfolding of strategy more realistically.

It would be an understatement to say that Freeman admired his subject. After completing the biography of Lee, he stated that it had been
his privilege "to live, as it were, for more than a decade in the company
of a great gentleman. . . . What he seemed, he was—a wholly human
gentleman, the essential elements of whose positive character were two
and only two, simplicity and spirituality." [55]

Freeman continued his study of Lee and published in the early 1940's
the three-volume *Lee's Lieutenants: A Study in Command*.[56] In this
work he was concerned with military leadership in terms of the men in
command in the Army of Northern Virginia. It is a thorough study of

50 Lonn, *Desertion During the Civil War* (New York, 1928) ; Tatum, *Disloyalty in the Confederacy* (Chapel Hill, 1934).

51 Henry, *The Story of the Confederacy* (Indianapolis, 1931).

52 Thomason, *Jeb Stuart* (New York, 1930).

53 Freeman, *R. E. Lee, A Biography* (4 vols.; New York, 1934–1935). This work has been condensed into one volume by Richard Harwell, *Lee, An Abridgment in One Volume* (New York, 1961).

54 James I. Robertson, Jr., "The Continuing War," *Civil War History*, VII (1961), 443.

55 Freeman, *R. E. Lee*, IV, 494; Michael Kraus, *A History of American History* (New York, 1937), 569.

56 Freeman, *Lee's Lieutenants: A Study in Command* (3 vols.; New York, 1944).

the relations of the general to his subordinates. The development of the leaders and not the strategy of the campaigns is the theme.

Freeman's writings did much to revive interest in the conflict of the sixties,[57] but, it was the Second World War that provided the greatest stimulus to the study and writing of military history. As Robert Penn Warren observed in his *Legacy of the Civil War:*

> When a people enters upon a period of crisis it is only natural that they look back upon their past and try to find therein some clue to their destiny. . . . World War II merely initiated the period of crisis through which we are passing, and it is only natural that the Civil War looms larger now than ever before. There was a time when the custody of the War was for the most part relegated to Southerners, but now things are different. We can see this simply from the enormous number and sale of books on the War.[58]

Since 1946, biographies of southern military commanders have been turned out in astonishing numbers, even though the war careers of many of these men have been available either in book or periodical form since shortly after the end of hostilities in 1865. Three biographies were published on "Stonewall" Jackson alone in one brief period recently. Burke Davis published a popular biography, *They Called Him Stonewall* in 1954.[59] This was followed by excellent scholarly works authored by Frank E. Vandiver and Lenoir Chambers.[60] The latter, a two-volume study, is the authoritative work on Jackson. Anything further on the Confederate general is unnecessary. T. Harry Williams' *Beauregard* [61] and Charles P. Roland's *Albert Sidney Johnston*[62] are also fine biographical achievements. Williams is judicious and displays a thorough understanding of the strategy and the historic importance of the engagements in which Beauregard took part. Roland is completely objective in the treatment of his subject, pointing out that it can never be positively known whether Johnston had the talents of a great general. He was killed at Shiloh, his one battle as a combat commander. Here he made

---

57 The publication in the 1930's of two novels, Stark Young's *So Red the Rose* and Margaret Mitchell's *Gone with the Wind,* also helped to end public apathy as far as Civil War history was concerned.

58 Warren, *The Legacy of the Civil War,* 79–80.

59 Davis, *They Called Him Stonewall: A Life of Lt. General T. J. Jackson, C. S. A.* (New York, 1954).

60 Vandiver, *Mighty Stonewall* (New York, 1957) ; Chambers, *Stonewall Jackson* (2 vols.; New York, 1959).

61 Williams, *P.G.T. Beauregard: Napoleon in Gray* (Baton Rouge, 1955).

62 Roland, *Albert Sidney Johnston, Soldier of Three Republics* (Austin, 1964).

both wise and unwise decisions. Hal Bridges, on the other hand, in his *Lee's Maverick General* [63] deals too sympathetically with the ill-tempered, hard fighting D. H. Hill. Although Bridges, through prodigious research, turned up some interesting new items, his picture of Hill is almost identical with Lee's (and Freeman's) estimate of the man —a fearless soldier who was at the same time an endless complainer and critic. Another effort to rehabilitate a Confederate commander is *A Different Valor: The Story of General Joseph E. Johnston, C. S. A.,* by Gilbert E. Govan and James W. Livingood.[64] As in Johnston's *Narrative* and Robert M. Hughes' biography of the general (1893)[65] Davis emerges as the second protagonist. He is depicted as a vindictive President more concerned with hindering Johnston than with winning the war. This excessively one-sided picture of the Johnston-Davis feud detracts considerably from the usefulness of the volume. A. P. Hill, long neglected by biographers, is the subject of a recent work by William W. Hassler.[66] The author calls Hill Lee's forgotten general and attempts to rescue him from relative obscurity. Hassler, though, falls far short of his objective, and Hill remains a neglected figure. John Pelham and Sandie Pendleton were both in their twenties when killed in battle, but their services entitle them to full length biographies. W. G. Bean's life of Pendleton[67] fills a gap mentioned by Freeman in his *Lee's Lieutenants*. It is a historian's account drawn from the records. Charles G. Milham uncovered few Pelham papers; yet by utilizing other available sources he was able to write an enjoyable and authentic biography.[68]

Not only military biographies but straight military histories have also flooded the market since the end of the Second World War. Freeman's volumes on the Army of Northern Virginia remain the outstanding work in this field, though the northern writers, Kenneth P. Williams (*Lincoln Finds a General*)[69] and Bruce Catton (*Mr. Lincoln's Army, Glory*

---

63 Bridges, *Lee's Maverick General, Daniel Harvey Hill* (New York, 1961).

64 Govan and Livingood, *A Different Valor: The Story of General Joseph E. Johnston, C.S.A.* (New York, 1956).

65 Hughes, *General Johnston* (New York, 1893).

66 Hassler, *A. P. Hill: Lee's Forgotten General* (Richmond, 1957). See also Martin Schenek, *Up Came Hill: The Story of the Light Division and Its Leaders* (Harrisburg, 1958).

67 Bean, *Stonewall's Man, Sandie Pendleton* (Chapel Hill, 1959).

68 Milham, *Gallant Pelham: American Extraordinary* (Washington, 1959).

69 Williams, *Lincoln Finds a General: A Military Study of the Civil War* (5 vols.; New York, 1949–1959).

Road, and *Stillness at Appomattox*),[70] have made significant contributions to Civil War literature. Frank Vandiver's *Jubal's Raid* [71] also merits attention as a thoroughly documented, vividly written account of General Early's raid on Washington in 1864. While Vandiver does not rate Early a second "Stonewall" Jackson, he does consider him the equal, at least, of Ewell, his predecessor in command of Lee's Second Corps. Dee A. Brown's *Bold Cavaliers,*[72] the story of the Second Kentucky Cavalry raiders, is another well-researched, fast-moving narrative. Brown writes with the full knowledge that his subject is significant in the history of cavalry strategy and tactics. Virgil C. Jones, in his lively history of the Virginia partisans,[73] advances the thesis that these Confederate guerrilla fighters were so effective that they delayed for months the final collapse of Lee's Army. Edward C. Boykin has an interesting account of one of the war's most daring exploits—Wade Hampton's pilfering of 2,468 beeves under the guns of the Federal army.[74] *Daredevils of the Confederate Army*[75] describes the dramatic Confederate raid on the little Vermont town of St. Albans. Unfortunately, the author, Oscar A. Kinchen, misses completely the action, intrigue, and excitement of the operation. Even though more has been written on Gettysburg than any other battle of the Civil War, Glenn Tucker, George R. Stewart, and Clifford Dowdey, to name just a few, undertake to tell the story again. Tucker, relying almost exclusively on secondary sources, fails to uncover any new facts but tells his story well.[76] Stewart's volume, the product of careful study and extensive research, is a microhistory of the preparation, execution, and immediate results of Pickett's charge.[77] Dowdey, in *Death of a Nation,*[78] defends Lee's overall strategy and

70 Catton, *Mr. Lincoln's Army* (New York, 1951), *Glory Road; The Bloody Route from Fredericksburg to Gettysburg* (New York, 1952), and *A Stillness at Appomattox* (New York, 1953).

71 Vandiver, *Jubal's Raid: General Early's Famous Attack on Washington in 1864* (New York, 1960).

72 Brown, *The Bold Cavaliers; Morgan's 2nd Kentucky Cavalry Raiders* (Philadelphia, 1959).

73 Jones, *Gray Ghosts and Rebel Raiders* (New York, 1956).

74 Boykin, *Beefsteak Raid* (New York, 1960).

75 Kinchen, *Daredevils of the Confederate Army: The Story of the St. Albans Raiders* (Boston, 1959).

76 Tucker, *High Tide at Gettysburg* (Indianapolis, 1958).

77 Stewart, *Pickett's Charge: A Microhistory of the Final Attack at Gettysburg* (Boston, 1959).

78 Dowdey, *Death of a Nation; The Story of Lee and His Men at Gettysburg* (New York, 1958).

conduct of the Gettysburg campaign. In a subsequent work, *Lee's Last Campaign*,[79] he records the victories and defeats of the Army of Northern Virginia after Gettysburg. This is the story of the Wilderness, Spotsylvania, Cold Harbor, Petersburg, and Appomattox. Lee again is the hero; Davis, Longstreet, Ewell and others come in for critical scrutiny. Dowdey's latest volume treats the Seven Days battle around Richmond.[80] His hero this time, aside from Lee, is A. P. Hill of whom he draws a very attractive portrait. Fairfax Downey's *Clash of Cavalry: The Battle of Brandy Station*[81] and Edward J. Stackpole's *Chancellorsville: Lee's Greatest Battle*[82] are both superficial. John M. Gibson's *Those 163 Days*[83] covers, from a southern point of view, Sherman's march through Georgia and the Carolinas. The author pictures the Federal army as a mob turned loose to ravage the countryside.

Several general histories of the Confederacy have been published recently. The most comprehensive of these is E. Merton Coulter's *The Confederate States of America*.[84] Since Coulter stresses economic and social conditions, his excellent study is of little value to the military historian. Charles P. Roland's short volume on the Confederacy[85] attains a good balance between military and civil affairs, but he tries unsuccessfully to compress all aspects of Confederate life into 194 pages of text. Nearly half of Clement Eaton's *A History of the Southern Confederacy*[86] is devoted to the military aspects of the war. The chapter on logistics is the best analysis to be found anywhere of Confederate problems of supply. Clifford Dowdey has two books on the Confederacy, both written for the general public. The setting for the first, *Experiment in Rebellion*,[87] is Richmond, and the principal character is Jefferson Davis. The author depicts the Confederate President as a quarrelsome executive constantly interfering with military plans and forgiving his favorites, such as Braxton Bragg, for costly mistakes. Although Dowdey

79 Dowdey, *Lee's Last Campaign; The Story of Lee and His Men at Gettysburg* (New York, 1959).

80 Dowdey, *The Seven Days: The Emergence of Lee* (Boston, 1964).

81 Downey, *Clash of Cavalry: The Battle of Brandy Station* (New York, 1959).

82 Stackpole, *Chancellorsville: Lee's Greatest Battle* (Harrisburg, 1958). Stackpole is a prolific writer of Civil War military history, but his works contribute little that is new in fact or interpretation.

83 Gibson, *Those 163 Days* (New York, 1961).

84 Coulter, *The Confederate States of America, 1861–1865* (Baton Rouge, 1950).

85 Roland, *The Confederacy* (Chicago, 1960).

86 Eaton, *A History of the Southern Confederacy* (New York, 1946).

87 Dowdey, *Experiment in Rebellion* (New York, 1946).

touches on a variety of subjects in *The Land They Fought For*,[88] the volume is essentially military history. Next to Lee, Jackson is accorded the most praise, but lesser military figures are given their share of attention. Dowdey criticizes a number of cavalry leaders for their tactics; at the same time he barely mentions Bedford Forrest's successful exploits in Mississippi, Tennessee, and Alabama.

The most recent significant development in the writing of military history has been the increased interest shown in a hitherto neglected theater of war, the West. Literature on the fighting in the East is still more voluminous than that on the West, but this imbalance is being corrected. Charles Dufour, in *The Night the War Was Lost*,[89] contends —and many of his arguments are difficult to refute—that the capture of New Orleans by Union forces in April, 1862 pointed the way to Appomattox. Both Glenn Tucker and Fairfax Downey see the Chickamauga-Chattanooga campaigns of 1863 as a struggle for control of the western theater.[90] The Confederate defeat opened the gateway to the deep South and made possible Sherman's march through Georgia a few months later. This is hardly a new thesis. Stanley Horn maintains that the battle of Nashville (December, 1864),[91] in which the Confederate Army of Tennessee was virtually destroyed, was the decisive engagement of the war. He thinks that the fate of the Confederacy might have been different had fortune smiled on Hood in Tennessee. The Army of Tennessee is also treated in Joseph H. Park's biography of General Leonidas Polk.[92] The author's conclusion, that Polk was a competent corps commander, is not always apparent from the book.

The best general account of military operations in the trans-Mississippi West is Jay Monaghan, *Civil War on the Western Border*.[93] The most significant additions are Stephen B. Oates, *Confederate Cavalry West of the River*,[94] and Joseph H. Parks, *General Edmund Kirby*

88 Dowdey, *The Land They Fought For; The Story of the South as the Confederacy* (New York, 1955).

89 Dufour, *The Night the War Was Lost* (New York, 1960).

90 Tucker, *Chickamauga: Bloody Battle in the West* (Indianapolis, 1961); Downey, *Storming of the Gateway: Chattanooga, 1863* (New York, 1960).

91 Horn, *The Decisive Battle of Nashville* (Rev. ed.; Baton Rouge, 1957). Horn also has a history of the Army of Tennessee, *The Army of Tennessee: A Military History* (Indianapolis, 1941). It is pedestrian.

92 Parks, *General Leonidas Polk, C.S.A.: The Fighting Bishop* (Baton Rouge, 1962).

93 Monaghan, *Civil War on the Western Border, 1854–1865* (Boston, 1955).

94 Oates, *Confederate Calvary West of the River* (Austin, 1961).

Smith, C.S.A.[95] Oates' field of investigation is original, and his monograph discloses for the first time that southern cavalry west of the Mississippi was an autonomous arm. Parks' scholarly, objective biography shows that Smith failed as commanding general of the trans-Mississippi department due to his lack of training as a civilian administrator, want of transportation, lack of cooperation from the people, and inadequacy of resources. Albert E. Castel's thoroughly documented study of Kansas, 1861–1865,[96] has a political emphasis. *Gray Ghosts of the Confederacy,* by Richard S. Brownlee,[97] despite its subtitle *Guerrilla Warfare in the West,* remains basically an analysis of the war in Missouri. The author's most valuable contribution is a detailed explanation of guerrilla warfare and its development under such partisans as William Quantrill, "Bloody Bill" Anderson, and George Todd. Quantrill is also the central figure in a thinly researched work by Carl W. Breihan,[98] based for the most part on old volumes by John N. Edwards and William E. Connelley.[99] It adds little to the understanding of the struggle on the frontier. Ray C. Colton's *The Civil War in the Western Territories* [100] gives a comprehensive coverage of the fighting in the Southwest. He pays particular attention to General Sibley's invasion of the New Mexico Territory. This Confederate operation, the major campaign in the region, is, moreover, the subject of specialized studies by Martin H. Hall and Robert L. Kerby.[101] All three books are competently researched, well written, and in essential agreement on major points. But they supplement, rather than change appreciably, the commonly held views on the fighting in New Mexico.

Another recent significant trend in Confederate historiography is concern for the common soldier. Here Professor Bell I. Wiley has done the best work. His *Johnny Reb* and *Billy Yank* [102] take the enlisted man

95 Parks, *General Edmund Kirby Smith, C.S.A.* (Baton Rouge, 1954).

96 Castel, *A Frontier State at War; Kansas, 1861–1865* (Cornell, 1958).

97 Brownlee, *Gray Ghosts of the Confederacy: Guerrilla Warfare in the West, 1861–1865* (Baton Rouge, 1958).

98 Breihan, *Quantrill and His Civil War Guerrillas* (Denver, 1959).

99 Edwards, *Noted Guerrillas, or Warfare on the Border* (St. Louis, 1877); Connelley, *Quantrill and the Border Wars* (Cedar Rapids, 1910).

100 Colton, *The Civil War in the Western Territories* (Norman, 1959).

101 Hall, *Sibley's New Mexico Campaign* (Austin, 1960); Kerby, *The Confederate Invasion of New Mexico and Arizona, 1861–1862* (Los Angeles, 1958).

102 Wiley, *The Common Soldier in the Civil War* (New York, 1958). This volume contains the author's *The Life of Billy Yank* and *The Life of Johnny Reb,* previously published separately.

out of battle and show how he lived in camp and what, in general, he thought about the war and the issues of the day.

Current writers have likewise shown an increased interest in matters of strategy and command. However, a great deal of work remains to be done in this field. There is no study of the organization and administration of the Confederate army comparable to Fred A. Shannon's full, scholarly treatment of the Union forces.[103] Frank Vandiver's *Rebel Brass* [104] is a forceful and clear yet extremely brief account of the failings of the Confederate command system. A larger work in defense of the high command is *Confederate Strategy from Shiloh to Vicksburg*,[105] by Archer Jones. He argues that Confederate authorities adopted a realistic defensive strategy in the western theater. "Its implementation through a decentralized departmental command system was wise," he says, "and the measure of central control was adequate." [106] T. Harry Williams, in a provocative essay on why the North won the war,[107] stresses superior northern leadership. He claims more genius for Grant than earlier historians have been willing to concede to him; at the same time he attempts to penetrate the myth that surrounds Lee. It is Williams' contention that southern generalship did not grow. Confederates won the first battles with Jominian strategy, and they saw no reason to change. Lee and his lieutenants were pretty much the same at the end of the war as at the beginning. They were good; still they never freed themselves from the accepted rules of warfare. The North, on the other hand, finally brought forward officers like Grant and Sherman who were able to grow and who could shed themselves of traditional doctrines. Williams, readily admitting that many of the tributes to Lee as a commander are deserved, points out that the general never had a chance to demonstrate his ability on a larger scale than a theater. His preoccupation with the war in Virginia constituted, in Williams' mind, a tragic command limitation in a modern war.

Although the conflict at sea has not appealed to the current student of the war as much as the fighting on land, there is, nevertheless, consider-

---

103 Shannon, *The Organization and Administration of the Union Army 1861–1865* (2 vols.; Cleveland, 1928).

104 Vandiver, *Rebel Brass: The Confederate Command System* (Baton Rouge, 1956).

105 Jones, *Confederate Strategy from Shiloh to Vicksburg* (Baton Rouge, 1961).
106 *Ibid.*, 240.

107 Williams, "The Military Leadership of North and South," in David Donald (ed.), *Why the North Won the Civil War* (Baton Rouge, 1960). See also Bruce Catton, *U. S. Grant and the American Military Tradition* (Boston, 1960); John F. C. Fuller, *Grant and Lee* (Bloomington, 1957).

able literature on naval affairs. Recently two books on the blockade, three on Confederate raiders, and two on ironclads have appeared.[108] Of these only R. W. Daly's *How the Merrimac Won* is scholarly. Daly gives the barest possible attention to the actual *Monitor-Merrimac* clash, which he classifies as a lazy little skirmish. Instead, he argues that the *Merrimac* won a strategic victory by frustrating and delaying McClellan's push up the peninsula—an argument used by Harrison A. Trexler in a much earlier work.[109] Allen Gosnell and Fletcher Pratt have readable books concerning the struggle on western waters.[110] While these volumes are informative, they do not equal in coherence and comprehensiveness A. T. Mahan's *The Gulf and Inland Waters*,[111] published some eighty years ago. Bern Andersen, *By Sea and By River*, and Virgil Jones, *The Civil War at Sea*, are general histories of the navy during the Civil War.[112] Both are written for the general reader and contribute very little to the known facts of the war at sea, especially Confederate operations. A chapter in Anglo-American relations is ably treated by W. D. Jones in *The Confederate Rams at Birkenhead*.[113] Presenting the story of the Laird rams through the eyes of the British government, Jones interprets the activities of its members on the basis of documents found in the British Museum and the Public Records Office. He puts his findings together in a pleasant, unexcited, easy style. The result is a useful little book.

Monographs on special aspects of the war are so numerous as to defy classification. Confederate ordnance, transportation, and medicine,

108 Hamilton Cochran, *Blockade Runners of the Confederacy* (Indianapolis, 1958); Robert Corse, *Blockade. The Civil War at Sea* (New York, 1958); Stanley F. Horn, *Gallant Rebel: The Fabulous Cruise of the C.S.S. Shenandoah* (New Brunswick, 1947); Edward Boykin, *Ghost Ship of the Confederacy; The Story of the Alabama and Her Captain Raphael Semmes* (New York, 1957), and Boykin, *Sea Devil of the Confederacy. The Story of the Florida and Her Captain, John Newland Maffitt* (New York, 1959); Robert MacBride, *Civil War Ironclads: The Dawn of Naval Armor* (Philadelphia, 1962); R. W. Daly, *How the Merrimac Won: The Strategic Story of the C.S.S. Virginia* (New York, 1957).

109 Trexler, *The Confederate Ironclad "Virginia" ("Merrimac")* (Chicago, 1938).

110 Gosnell, *Guns on the Western Waters: The Story of River Gunboats in the Civil War* (Baton Rouge, 1949); Pratt, *Civil War on Western Waters* (New York, 1956).

111 Mahan, *The Gulf and Inland Waters* (New York, 1883).

112 Anderson, *By Sea and By River; The Naval History of the Civil War* (New York, 1962); Virgil C. Jones, *The Civil War at Sea* (3 vols.; New York, 1960–1962).

113 Wilbur D. Jones, *The Confederate Rams at Birkenhead: A Chapter in Anglo-American Relations* (Tuscaloosa, 1961).

along with the roles played by reporters and engineers, are but a few of many topics which have been investigated.[114] State studies [115] and regimental histories [116] are available. Even minority groups have come in for their share of attention.[117]

These recent trends in Civil War writing have given more balance to the military accounts and also greatly expanded the Civil War audience. Yet they have seldom altered the known facts of the war. Enthusiasm and interest, unfortunately, have not stimulated or even encouraged good historical work. Indeed, there has been a decided trend toward mediocrity since the end of the Second World War. There have been, as Frank Vandiver recently wrote, "the potboiler biography (often written by journalists with pretensions to be Nevinses, Cattons, or Freemans), which says nothing new, is based on no real sources, but abounds in blood and gore. . . . the jazzed-up regimental history. . . . the 'Day Book' [and] the new 'Book of Hours'. . . . Some are good, if perspective is kept in mind, but many are disjointed, twist facts out of content and violate historical continuity." [118] It is not surprising, therefore, that there are many who agree with Allan Nevins in saying that "it is unfortunate . . . [that] ninety-nine in a hundred [books] are on military topics and leaders." [119] But these critics remain a minority, for the American public still shows a strong predilection for reading about armies, battles, and heroes.

114 Frank E. Vandiver, *Ploughshares into Swords: Josiah Gorgas and Confederate Ordnance* (Austin, 1952); Robert C. Black, *The Railroads of the Confederacy* (Chapel Hill, 1952); Angus J. Johnston, *Virginia Railroads in the Civil War* (Chapel Hill, 1961); Horace H. Cunningham, *Doctors in Gray: The Confederate Medical Service* (Baton Rouge, 1958); James L. Nichols, *Confederate Engineers* (Tuscaloosa, 1957); W. Stanley Hoole, *Vizetelly Covers the Confederacy* (Tuscaloosa, 1957).

115 John G. Barrett, *The Civil War in North Carolina* (Chapel Hill, 1963); John E. Johns, *Florida During the Civil War* (Gainesville, 1963); John D. Winters, *The Civil War in Louisiana* (Baton Rouge, 1963).

116 William G. Bean, *The Liberty Hall Volunteers; Stonewall's College Boys* (Charlottesville, 1964); James I. Robertson, Jr., *The Stonewall Brigade* (Baton Rouge, 1963).

117 Frank Cunningham, *General Stand Waite's Confederate Indians* (San Antonio, 1959); Benjamin Quarles, *The Negro in the Civil War* (Boston, 1953); Bertram W. Korn, *American Jewry and the Civil War* (Philadelphia, 1951); and especially Bell I. Wiley, *Southern Negroes, 1861–1865* (New Haven, 1938).

118 Vandiver, "The Civil War: Its Theory and Practice," 107–108.

119 Nevins, "The Glorious and the Terrible," *Saturday Review,* XLIV (1961).

XII

Reconstruction

Vernon L. Wharton

E. MERTON COULTER'S *The South During Reconstruction,* published in 1947, is a masterful summation of an interpretation of southern Reconstruction that was three quarters of a century in the making. This interpretation became the standard of general histories, college and high school textbooks, and popular fiction. In the preface to his book, Coulter stated:

As each generation feels constrained to rewrite the past, points of view and methods of approach necessarily change, and so revisionists arise. If they remain within the reasonable bounds of established facts, they may well make lasting contributions in fresher interpretations and in the presentation of new information; but if they depart from the old channels to attract attention novel and unsubstantiated points of view, they themselves may soon be revised. The author of this work feels that there can be no sensible departure from the well-known facts of the Reconstruction program as it was applied to the South.[1]

In another preface, published in 1961, David Donald said:

For the Southern states during the Reconstruction years I have taken full advantage of the important revisionist work that has been completed in recent years and have tried to show the Negroes, carpetbaggers and scalawags in a fuller, and I hope fairer light.[2]

And again, in the section on bibliography:

While drawing heavily upon the factual research of the Dunning-school writers and on the insights of the Marxists, the present work adopts the position of the Revisionists as to the general pattern of Reconstruction.[3]

Donald's announcement in 1961 of a "Revisionist" approach was only one of many indications of a general realignment of forces on "the dark and bloody ground"[4] of Reconstruction historiography. The story of southern Reconstruction which had come to be almost completely accepted by about 1930 told of the defeat of an outnumbered South in the Civil War and of devastation and poverty within the region at the close of hostilities. The poverty and devastation were often contrasted with the wealth, the gracious living, and the social stability of the South in the antebellum period. There usually followed a discussion of the presidential "plan" for Reconstruction, designed by Lincoln and attempted by Johnson. Then came a description of the gradual capture of the Reconstruction process by a radical minority in the Congress, determined to give political security to the industrial and financial interests of the North, and, especially, to the Republican party. Generally, there was detailed discussion of the various theories of the "Constitutional" position of the southern states vis-à-vis the federal union.

Following the Radical triumph in the elections of 1866, the impeachment and near-conviction of Johnson in 1868, and the election of Grant in the same year, there was the period of "radical" or "black" Recon-

---

1 Coulter, *The South During Reconstruction, 1865–1877* (Baton Rouge, 1947), xi.

2 James Garfield Randall and David Herbert Donald, *The Civil War and Reconstruction* (Boston, 1961), vii. The use of the term "revisionist" continues to be confusing. In earlier works, it was often used to refer to such men as John W. Burgess, James Ford Rhodes, William A. Dunning, and members of the Dunning School.

3 *Ibid.*, 777.

4 Bernard A. Weisberger, "The Dark and Bloody Ground of Reconstruction Historiography," *Journal of Southern History*, XXV (November, 1959), 427–47.

struction. This phase was marked by the degradation of the South under the corrupt and incompetent rule of carpetbaggers, Negroes, and a small number of scalawags; and by comparable inefficiency and dishonesty in the Grant administration on the national scene. The debauchery in the South finally goaded the white citizens of that region into determined and united action to overcome Negro and carpetbagger rule. By the mid-1870's, the abuses of southern Reconstruction had become so apparent that the program was generally unpopular throughout the North. In the disputed election of 1876, a Republican President could be elected only through a deal which would give him the electoral vote of some of the southern states. The deal was made; federal troops were withdrawn; home rule was restored to the southern whites; a mistaken and dreadful experiment was unsuccessfully completed; and the entire nation had learned an expensive but valuable lesson.

In extreme form, the story was written into popular fiction by Thomas Dixon, Jr., in books [5] that sometimes were listed as standard readings in the history classes of high schools and colleges. D. W. Griffith, drawing from Dixon's *The Clansman,* released in 1915 America's first "spectacular" motion picture, "The Birth of a Nation." Claude G. Bowers' historical version of the story, *The Tragic Era,*[6] was as violent and extreme as the fiction of Dixon and Griffith. It became a national bestseller and a selection of the Literary Guild of America.

There was and is an abundance of source material to support even the most hostile interpretations of Radical Reconstruction. There was a firm base in the reports of Benjamin C. Truman, Harvey Watterson, and Generals Grant, Steedman, and Fullerton to President Andrew Johnson; in thousands of pages of reports, documents, and sworn testimony in publications of governmental agencies; in hundreds of travel accounts, reminiscences, and autobiographies; and in thousands of issues of newspapers and magazines. In such circumstances, the historian could only attempt to find the truth in terms of his own knowledge, convictions, and values. It is important, therefore, to take some notice

5 Dixon, *The Leopard's Spots: A Romance of the White Man's Burden, 1865–1890* (New York, 1902), *The Clansman: An Historical Romance of the Ku Klux Klan* (New York, 1905), and *The Traitor: A Story of the Fall of the Invisible Empire* (New York, 1907).

6 Bowers, *The Tragic Era: The Revolution after Lincoln* (Boston, 1929). Carl Neumann Degler, in *Out of Our Past: The Forces That Shaped Modern America* (New York and Evanston, 1959), 440, stated that this work has "probably done more than any other book to delineate the view now so commonly accepted regarding the enormities of Reconstruction."

of the atmosphere of the time during which the generally accepted interpretation of southern Reconstruction was being developed.

The period between 1875 and 1910 was a time when "social Darwin-
ism" was accepted in the United States as a basic assumption in the
social sciences. It produced the laissez-faire sociology of William G.
Sumner and the racist political science of John W. Burgess, while it
welcomed the importation of the harsh economic doctrines of David
Ricardo and Alfred Marshall. It was the time when presidents and professors of great universities joined newspaper editors and Supreme
Court justices in scientific condemnation of any effort to relieve the lot
of those whose poverty and wretchedness were adequate proof of innate
inferiority; and when the recorded lynchings of almost 2,000 Negroes
in twenty years could be shrugged off, defended as necessary, or applauded. Finally, it saw Anglo-Saxonism, Teutonism, or Aryanism, in
extreme form, become basic tenets in a variety of fields of learning, and
especially in history. The preservation of "white Anglo-Saxon civilization" against Indians, Negroes, Orientals, and the new immigrants
from southern and eastern Europe became a theme of both popular and
scholarly writing. It was in this atmosphere that the basic structure of
Reconstruction historiography was formed, basic histories were written,
and teachers were trained. In such an atmosphere, Radical Reconstruction could be viewed only as an evil.

This interpretation of Reconstruction is commonly attributed to
Professor William Archibald Dunning of Columbia University and his
"southern" students. Actually, the Dunning School merely gave elaborate and expert documentation to a story already generally accepted.

One of the earliest full treatments of the theme may be found in
Carpetbag Rule in Florida, published in 1888 by John Wallace, a Negro
Republican who was a member of the Florida legislature for twelve
years. Wallace's book defends Florida's harsh Black Code. The Freedmen's Bureau is thoroughly discredited and described as "the worst
curse of the race," having served to mislead, debase, and betray the
Negroes. Bureau officials are said to have established a "reign of terror,"
and, deliberately, to have provoked "deadly hostility" between native
whites and blacks, who otherwise "would have passed through the ordeal of reconstruction without a jar or disturbance." There is detailed
exposure of the greed, corruption and criminality of carpetbaggers of
every stripe, and almost every evil of Reconstruction is attributed to
that group, with which, ostensibly, Wallace was allied for many years.
On the other hand, Wallace has nothing but praise for native southern

whites. Finally, the book declares that the triumph of the Democrats in 1876 was a "blessing in disguise" for Negroes; racial prejudice was passing away, Negroes were achieving education and prosperity, and the future was full of hope.[7]

Thus, nine years before Dunning published the first edition of his *Essays on the Civil War*,[8] and thirteen years before the appearance of the first monograph by a Dunning student, the so-called Dunning-School interpretation had been elaborately presented, in a relatively extreme form, by a "Southern Negro Republican."

The work ascribed to Wallace has been used as a source by scores of writers, without attention to evidence that suggests that the book was a forgery and that Wallace was a tool of the powerful Democratic leader, William D. Bloxham. Wallace was employed by Bloxham immediately after the Civil War and was closely associated with him in later years. One historian, who said he received the information directly from Bloxham, described *Carpetbag Rule in Florida* as "produced under the general supervision of Wm. D. Bloxham, Democratic leader and enlightened politician, who befriended the Negro Wallace and aided him in producing this volume." [9] It seems probable that in the historiography of southern Reconstruction Bloxham has not received proper attention.

In 1890, Hilary Abner Herbert edited and published a series of brief essays which gave for each of the southern states an interpretation of Reconstruction similar to that which the Wallace book had presented for Florida.[10] The fact that Walter Lynwood Fleming would later describe the work as a "Democratic campaign document" [11] did not prevent its being used as a source by Fleming and by many others.

In brief but practically complete outline, the pro-southern story appeared in E. Benjamin Andrews' popular general history published in 1895 and 1896. Drawing heavily from Herbert's "campaign document," Andrews used the following section headings for his chapter, " 'Carpet-Bagger' and 'Scalawag' in Dixie": The "Scalawag"; The "Carpet-Bagger"; Good Carpet-Baggers; Their Failings; Resistance; Northern

7 Wallace, *Carpetbag Rule in Florida: The Inside Workings of the Reconstruction of Civil Government in Florida after the Close of the Civil War* (Jacksonville, 1888).

8 Dunning, *Essays on the Civil War and Reconstruction and Related Topics* (New York, 1897).

9 William Watson Davis, *The Civil War and Reconstruction in Florida* (New York, 1913), 620, 625, 746.

10 Herbert (ed.), *Why the Solid South?, or, Reconstruction and Its Results* (Baltimore, 1890).

11 Fleming, *The Sequel of Appomattox* (New Haven, 1921), 305–306.

Sympathy with This; The Freedmen; Their Vices; Their Ignorance; Foolish and Corrupt Legislation; Extravagant Expenditures; Overthrow of Many Carpet-Bag Governments; Violence Still, But Often Exaggerated.[12] Thus the Dunning School presented an interpretation that already was familiar and that suited the spirit of the time.

In view of that spirit and of their own cultural heritage, most of the historians of the Dunning School were remarkably temperate and factual. This was especially true of the first of the group, James W. Garner. His *Reconstruction in Mississippi*,[13] published in 1901, tried to present an objective and balanced account of political, social, and economic developments in his native state in one of the most troubled periods of its history. Little that has been learned in the succeeding sixty years would serve greatly to alter or even to add to Garner's story. However, Garner did assume that Radical Reconstruction was wrong in principle and practice and that the restoration of native-white rule was essential to the peace and progress of Mississippi. These assumptions resulted in some lack of consideration of the experiences, needs, and aspirations of the Negro majority, and in tendencies to discredit the character and the testimony of those who took part in the Radical movement and to magnify the virtues of those who fought against it.

These characteristics are more apparent in Walter L. Fleming's *Civil War and Reconstruction in Alabama*.[14] Published in 1905, it was a product of tremendous labor, wide research, and great historical skill. William A. Dunning's evaluation of his student's work is interesting: "W. L. Fleming, *Civil War and Reconstruction in Alabama* (1905), is the most comprehensive of the group, presenting a great mass of social and economic as well as political facts, with a marked Southern bias in their interpretation." [15]

Fleming's "marked Southern bias" showed itself in lack of sympathy for aspirations of the Negro as man and citizen; emphasis on Negro ignorance, irresponsibility, and criminality; detailed and exaggerated exposure of extravagance and fraud in the Radical government, without

12 Andrews, *The History of the Last Quarter-Century in the United States, 1870–1895* (2 vols.; New York, 1895–1896) I, 111. Andrews was president of Brown University.

13 Garner, *Reconstruction in Mississippi* (New York, 1901).

14 Fleming, *Civil War and Reconstruction in Alabama* (New York, 1905).

15 Dunning, *Reconstruction, Political and Economic, 1865–1877* (New York and London, 1907), 353. In the same section, Dunning referred to James W. Garner's "rigidly judicial spirit."

mention of the participation of native Democrats; designation of the Reconstruction government as "negro rule"; and a tendency to deny or to justify the use of terrorism and violence against Negroes, carpetbaggers and scalawags.

The same attitudes mark Fleming's brief, but enormously influential survey, *The Sequel of Appomattox*, published in 1921. Here he declared again, with good reason, that "the negro is the central figure in the reconstruction of the South," and now, gratuitously, extended his hostility toward the Negro to include the "new" European immigrants:

The former good manners of the negro were now replaced by impudence and distrust. . . . Pushing and crowding in public places, on street cars and on the sidewalks, and impudent speeches everywhere marked generally the limit of rudeness. And the negroes were, in this respect, perhaps no worse than those European immigrants who act upon the principle that bad manners are a proof of independence.[16]

Even more influential than this work has been Fleming's *Documentary History of Reconstruction*.[17] It consists of a great number of brief extracts taken, inevitably out of context, from volumes which Fleming had read in some fashion. There can be quarrel with Fleming's methods of selection and labeling; and there can be serious quarrel with his introductory comments. But the important fact is that his brief extracts, used as "sources," are not genuine sources at all. They represent slivers of information which one man chose to regard as significant. All too often, they have served to allow the student or the writer to avoid the essential experience of going painfully through masses of basic materials and of forming his own judgment of what is valid and significant.[18] Thus, for many students, the value judgments of Walter L. Fleming have determined what was to be known and what was not to be known about the sources of Reconstruction history.

Fleming's attitudes did not characterize all the members of the Dunning School. C. Mildred Thompson, who wrote on Georgia, was, if anything, even more cautious, judicious, and temperate than Garner.

16 Fleming, *The Sequel of Appomattox*, 42–43.

17 Fleming (ed.), *Documentary History of Reconstruction: Political, Military, Social, Religious, Educational & Industrial 1865 to the Present Time* (2 vols.; Cleveland, 1906–1907).

18 In the "Bibliographical Note" in his *The Sequel of Appomattox*, Fleming suggested that "the general reader is usually repelled by the collections known as *Public Documents*." He could have added that this is also true of the general historian.

Her treatment of the work of the Freedmen's Bureau was sympathetic, or even generous. Her story of Reconstruction was no simple tale of good versus evil. She recognized and attempted to analyze the complexities to be found in men and social change. "On the whole," she said, "as far as personnel is concerned, the reconstruction administration of Georgia was not entirely bad, was even quite good in some members." She found evidence of fraud, but she recognized that it was not peculiar to the Reconstruction governments, and that leaders of the white Democracy were deeply involved. Her chapter on the Ku Klux Klan and social disorder shows insight and balance. There is little effort to discredit the entire Negro people, or to minimize the use of violence against them. "By intimidation and a thousand and one kinds of indirect influence, the negro was made to feel . . . that polling places were not healthy resorts for black men." Finally, Miss Thompson concluded that "in its largest sense, Reconstruction in Georgia meant a wider democratization of society." [19]

On the other hand, Joseph G. deRoulhac Hamilton's lengthy and vigorous *Reconstruction in North Carolina* has the tone of a white Democratic broadside against Negroes, carpetbaggers, scalawags, the Freedmen's Bureau, northern teachers, northern Radicals, and every objective and procedure of congressional Reconstruction. For a large portion of his material and his interpretations, Hamilton went to the Raleigh *Sentinel,* the newspaper that led the white Democratic attack. Its editor, Josiah Turner, was, according to Hamilton, "cunning as a serpent," and "relentlessly pursued . . . the chief aim of his existence, the overthrow of the Republican party in the State." In more than six hundred pages, Hamilton never quite faced the facts that Radical domination in North Carolina lasted only two years, and that, throughout the period of Reconstruction, North Carolina whites had a heavy majority in population, registered voters, and both houses of the legislature. Instead, he held that the Negro and Reconstruction were responsible for decades of political immorality.[20]

William Watson Davis, another of Dunning's students, was seldom positive in his judgments. His lengthy work, *Civil War and Reconstruction in Florida,* gives evidence of extended and diligent research, and of an effort to be judicious. Often, however, information and attitudes are drawn almost entirely from Wallace's *Carpetbag Rule* and from a Democratic newspaper, the *Floridian,* edited by Charles E. Dyke,

19 Thompson, *Reconstruction in Georgia, Economic, Social, Political, 1865–1872* (New York, 1915).
20 Hamilton, *Reconstruction in North Carolina* (New York, 1914).

whom Davis described as a "crafty, canny politician . . . a political leader and a maker of public opinion." Davis's relatively uncritical use of these materials gave to portions of his work a different tone from that which is found when he used such sources as official documents.

It is apparent that Davis, unlike many of his contemporaries, was troubled by the violence that accompanied the failure and overthrow of southern Reconstruction. One example is his concern about experiences of the Negroes:

The Southerner was certainly face to face with negro domination foisted upon him by Federal law . . . and in this contest for a very necessary supremacy many a foul crime was committed by white against black. Innocent people suffered. There is no mercy and scant justice in social adjustment. The negro was first freed, then enfranchised, then launched into practical politics, and then mercilessly beaten into reasonable subjection.[21]

Ella Lonn's *Reconstruction in Louisiana after 1868* [22] is of the Dunning type, although it was written as a doctoral dissertation at the University of Pennsylvania. After gathering material in Louisiana, Miss Lonn felt that some of the problems in that area were especially difficult because "the Gulf States had an element of extremely vicious negroes," who, in Louisiana, "were on the average less intelligent than those in most of the former slave States."

Although her sympathies are easily recognizable and clearly expressed, it is apparent that Miss Lonn understood the unusual difficulties of her task. In her preface, she said:

The attempt to disentangle the complicated story of Reconstruction in Louisiana needs no justification. Rather it is a matter of surprise that it has been left for a Northerner to do . . . .

The great extent and well-nigh inextricable confusion of the period explains why writers have veered away from a subject, otherwise dramatic and absorbing. Probably the truth can never be unveiled with regard to some of the details, particularly those in connection with the election of 1876, so that conclusions must always remain more or less a matter of opinion.

The Louisiana situation was so complicated by fraud, violence, perjury,[23] and multiple, shifting factions within the Republican and Demo-

---

21 Davis, *Civil War and Reconstruction in Florida* (New York, 1913), 586.
22 Lonn, *Reconstruction in Louisiana after 1868* (New York and London, 1918).
23 John Rose Ficklen, whose notes were used for the posthumous publication of his *History of Reconstruction in Louisiana (through 1868)* (Baltimore, 1910),

cratic alignments that it is difficult to follow Miss Lonn to 1876. Her bemused story of the election of 1872 and of a Louisiana canvass, which followed the election, seems almost unbelievable; but even a glance at sources indicates that the writer had time and space only to touch the surface of the chicaneries.

This is no suggestion that Miss Lonn lacked competence. It appears probable that a historian could spend a lifetime trying to unravel the evidence, including thousands of affidavits, and still be unable to determine who was betraying whom, or what the results of a full and fair vote in the Louisiana elections of 1872 and 1876 would have been. At least one thing is certain: the Republicans had a commanding lead in the mortality statistics.[24]

Without further analysis of Dunning-School or Dunning-type monographs,[25] it can be said that they adopted a framework of interpretation that had already gained general acceptance, and that in temperament, emphasis, and quality they differed widely among themselves.

It must also be said that most of them were remarkably temperate as

---

226, had already encountered this difficulty: "With the sworn testimony of the participants on both sides before us, it is extremely difficult if not impossible, to obtain an accurate account."

24 William Malvin Caskey, *Secession and Restoration of Louisiana* (Baton Rouge, 1938), 223, suggested that the Negroes were poor marksmen. Garnie William McGinty, *Louisiana Redeemed: The Overthrow of Carpet-bag Rule, 1876–1880* (New Orleans, 1941), 248, added to Ella Lonn's story a plaintive conclusion: "The Bourbon class of native whites, once more in office, made some effort to solve the economic problems, but the educational and social maladjustments were left undisturbed until recent years . . . . In short, the most significant factor in the transition was the absence of any outstanding change."

25 The "type," loosely interpreted, would embrace a large number of works, both old and new. The list might include, as examples: James Walter Fertig, *The Secession and Reconstruction of Tennessee* (Chicago, 1898); Hamilton Jones Eckenrode, *The Political History of Virginia during the Reconstruction* (Baltimore, 1904); John Schreiner Reynolds, *Reconstruction in South Carolina, 1865–1877* (Columbia, S. C., 1905); John Rose Ficklen, *History of Reconstruction in Louisiana (through 1868)* (Baltimore, 1910); Charles William Ramsdell, *Reconstruction in Texas* (New York, 1910); Thomas Starling Staples, *Reconstruction in Arkansas, 1862–1874* (New York, 1923); David Yancey Thomas, *Arkansas in War and Reconstruction, 1861–1874* (Little Rock, 1926); Paul Herman Buck, *The Road to Reunion, 1865–1890* (Boston, 1937); Robert Selph Henry, *The Story of Reconstruction* (Indianapolis, New York, 1938); William Best Hesseltine and David Leslie Smiley, *The South in American History* (New York, 1943); Ellis Merton Coulter, *The South During Reconstruction, 1865–1877* (Baton Rouge, 1947); Hampton McNeely Jarrell, *Wade Hampton and the Negro: The Road Not Taken* (Columbia, 1949); Nash Kerr Burger and John Knox Bettersworth, *South of Appomattox* (New York, 1959); William Curtis Nunn, *Texas Under the Carpetbaggers* (Austin, 1962).

compared with such northern giants as John W. Burgess and James Ford Rhodes, or even with Dunning himself.

In the same volume [26] in which Dunning ascribed "marked Southern bias" to Fleming and a "rigidly judicial spirit" to Garner, he departed from Garner's temperate judgments of Reconstruction in Mississippi, while accepting and, if anything, exaggerating Fleming's "biased" interpretations for Alabama. In each case, Dunning defended the black codes, exaggerated Negro political influence and corruption, and discounted the use of violence and intimidation by white Democrats.

Furthermore, the relatively mild discussions of "racial inequality" in the revised edition (1904) of the *Essays on the Civil War* [27] gave way to severer judgments in *Reconstruction* in 1907:

The Negro had no pride of race and no aspirations or ideals save to be like the whites. With civil rights and political power, not won, but almost forced upon him, he came gradually to understand and crave those more elusive privileges that constitute social equality. A more intimate association with the other race . . . was the end toward which the ambition of the blacks tended consciously or unconsciously to direct itself. It played a part in the demand for mixed schools, in the legislative prohibition of discrimination between the races in hotels and theatres, and even in the hideous crime against white womanhood which now assumed new meaning in the annals of outrage.[28]

It seems probable that one of the more important influences on Dunning and his students was the work of John W. Burgess, Columbia University political scientist who taught both Dunning and some of the Dunning students. In 1902, Burgess published his *Reconstruction and the Constitution, 1866–1876*.[29] In this brief work, he was able to combine declarations of the errors and evils of slavery and secession, a low evaluation of Andrew Johnson, a positive assertion that congressional control of Reconstruction was constitutionally correct, and a violent attack on the actual processes of congressional Reconstruction and on the Negro.

In earlier works, Burgess had developed elaborate assertions of semi-mystical, inherent qualities of the "Teutonic," "Celtic," "Latin," "Greek,"

26 Dunning, *Reconstruction, Political and Economic.*

27 Dunning, *Essays on the Civil War and Reconstruction and Related Topics* (Rev. ed.; New York, 1904), 384–85.

28 Dunning, *Reconstruction, Political and Economic*, 213–14.

29 Burgess, *Reconstruction and the Constitution* (New York, 1902). Burgess's influence was both positive and negative; Dunning and his students rejected a number of Burgess's assumptions.

"Slavic," and "negro" races, claiming always great superiority for the "Teutons," and denying any political rights to "barbaric populations." [30] Burgess returned to this theme again and again in *Reconstruction and the Constitution*. In any situation in which the race question was involved, his usually objective and often dull analyses of political and constitutional theories and issues gave way to emotional attack, with Reconstruction described as a "blunder-crime," or "the most soul-sickening spectacle that Americans had ever been called on to behold." In Burgess' opinion, "Life, property, happiness, honor, civilization, everything which makes existence endurable demanded that the decent white men of the South should stand shoulder to shoulder in defending their families, their homes and their communities from any return of the vile plague under which they had suffered so long and so cruelly."

There is no doubt that Dunning and his later students were influenced by the prestigious work of James Ford Rhodes.[31] On Reconstruction, as on almost all matters, Rhodes wrote with assurance and buttressed his assurance with documentation. Like Burgess and Dunning, he was inclined to defend and admire congressional seizure of the process of Reconstruction. This admiration was accompanied by merciless attacks on Andrew Johnson. But Rhodes's sympathy for congressional Reconstruction changed to hostility once Congress moved toward adoption of Negro suffrage. In every circumstance, he was obsessed with "the great fact of race," a phrase which he used over and over again. After defending the black codes as necessary for the control of "one of the most inferior races of mankind," Rhodes went on to declare that the Reconstruction Acts forced "negro rule" on the South at the point of the bayonet. He subscribed to the theory that it was a Negro characteristic to suffer diminution or cessation of mental development at thirteen or fourteen, or perhaps even earlier. He agreed with Louis Agassiz that Negroes were inherently "indolent," and "subservient," and that throughout history they had "groped in barbarism" and, of themselves "had never originated a regular organization."

There can be no wonder that, after tracing the ignominious story of

30 Burgess, *Political Science and Comparative Constitutional Law* (2 vols.; Boston, 1890), reprinted in part in his *The Foundations of Political Science* (New York, 1933).

31 Rhodes, *History of the United States from the Compromise of 1850 to the Final Restoration of Home Rule at the South in 1877* (7 vols.; New York, 1896–1906). In the preface to his *Reconstruction,* Dunning said, "The appearance of Dr. James Ford Rhodes's last two volumes, covering the years 1866–1877, in time to be used in the final revisions of my manuscript, is a mercy the greatness of which in a preface cannot be adequately expressed."

Reconstruction in the nation and in each of the southern states, Rhodes hailed the collapse of Reconstruction as "the final triumph of Southern intelligence and character over the ignorance and corruption that so long had thriven under Northern misconceptions." The general outcome had demonstrated that "the American people remained sound at the core."

With acceptance of the belief that Radical Reconstruction had been a tragic error, it became more and more difficult to maintain the generally low evaluation that had been given to President Andrew Johnson. Johnson had led the fight against congressional Reconstruction, stubbornly and desperately, at the cost of his reputation and political career. Why, then, should the leader of the good fight be written off as an incompetent villain?

In 1913, the aged James Schouler added a seventh volume to his *History of the United States under the Constitution,* covering the period 1865–1877.[32] The volume added little to the interpretation of Reconstruction already developed by Rhodes, but it differed sharply from Rhodes on the evaluation of Andrew Johnson, who began to emerge as hero and martyr. The rehabilitation was completed in the 1920's and 1930's in the violent prose of Claude Bowers [33] and the scholarly works of Robert W. Winston,[34] Howard Kennedy Beale [35] and George Fort Milton.[36]

By the 1930's, then, the orthodox story of southern Reconstruction was fully rounded out and accepted almost without question. Its villains, on the national scene, were identified as the congressional Radicals and the incompetent and deluded President Grant. The hero at the national level was Andrew Johnson. Within the South, the villains were carpetbaggers, scalawags (usually unidentified),[37] and a great, faceless mass

32 Schouler, *History of the United States under the Constitution* (7 vols.; New York, 1880–1913).

33 Bowers, *The Tragic Era.*

34 Winston, *Andrew Johnson, Plebeian and Patriot* (New York, 1928).

35 Beale, *The Critical Year: A Study of Andrew Johnson and Reconstruction* (New York, 1930).

36 Milton, *The Age of Hate: Andrew Johnson and the Radicals* (New York, 1930).

37 David Herbert Donald, "The Scalawag in Mississippi Reconstruction," *Journal of Southern History,* X (November, 1944), 447–60, an interesting and provocative article, names only one of the scalawags—the wealthy and conservative former Whig who was the Republican governor from 1870 until 1874. Allen W. Trelease, "Who Were the Scalawags?," *Journal of Southern History,* XXIX (November, 1963), 445–68, does not offer even one name or example in answer to his question. It seems probable, however, that a refined version of his statistical approach would be of value.

of ignorant, barbarous, and often ridiculous Negroes. The southern heroes were the whites who had suffered indignities with bravery and patience and who finally, with northern support, had overcome the rabble and restored the rule of virtue, intelligence, and property.

There is now a growing opinion that this interpretation of a violent and complicated phase of American history avoided discussion of basic issues by appeals to popular prejudice, and that much of it depended on popular and implausible anecdotes, political propaganda, and questionable testimony. General acceptance of such interpretations is not unusual in the history of history. The remarkable persistence of this one may be attributed to the fact that it was compatible with the practices, principles, beliefs, and prejudices that justified domination of the world by people whose origins were in northern and western Europe.[38]

When Coulter published in 1947 his definitive summary of the established story of southern Reconstruction, the beliefs and systems that had maintained the dominance and superiority of north European whites were already meeting terminal challenges. Both the United States and the world were facing the consequences of the breakdown. Yet, even then, leading American historians were almost unanimous in their endorsement of Coulter's work.[39]

Early protests against the hardening orthodoxy of Reconstruction history were highly defensive and received little attention. In 1909, in a paper read to the American Historical Association in New York, W. E. B. DuBois declared that "between the intense feeling of the South and the conciliatory spirit of the North" there was danger that grave injustice would be done to the Negro American in Reconstruction history. DuBois insisted that the Black Codes accurately reflected the general attitude of the white South at the close of the war, and that "no open-minded student can read them without being convinced that they meant nothing more or less than slavery in daily toil." He admitted the existence of incompetence and dishonesty in the Reconstruction governments. But he also asserted that reports had been greatly exaggerated, and that, furthermore, "dishonesty in public life has no monopoly of time or place in America." In support of the assertion, he reviewed the prewar record of Mississippi. Finally, DuBois claimed that most of

38 Paul Herman Buck, *The Road to Reunion, 1865–1890* (Boston, 1937), offers a generally sympathetic analysis of the surrender of northern sentiment to these principles and consequent acceptance of southern domination of the Negro.

39 John Hope Franklin, "Whither Reconstruction Historiography?" *Journal of Negro Education*, XVII (Fall, 1948), 446–61, outlines and attacks the favorable reviews of Coulter's book.

the Reconstruction governments had improved as they gained experience; and he credited them with substantial achievements in the building of schools, charitable institutions, jails, courthouses, and means of transportation, and in the writing of good constitutions and good laws, most of which were retained for years after the overthrow of Reconstruction.[40]

The next effort of any significance was made by John R. Lynch, a Negro who had been a Mississippi legislator and a congressman, and who continued to be active and influential in the Republican party until his death in 1939. Lynch's book, *The Facts of Reconstruction,* is a generalized defense of Republican policies, and it contained little to disturb the southern Democratic politicians with whom Lynch was still involved in mutually helpful relations.[41] Four years later, in 1917, Lynch published, in the *Journal of Negro History,* a provocative article entitled "Some Historical Errors of James Ford Rhodes." The article was republished in book form in 1922.

Lynch labeled Rhodes's story of Reconstruction "a compilation of untrue, unreliable and grossly exaggerated statements taken from political campaign literature." The Negroes, Lynch declared, did not draw the color line in politics; it was drawn against them by white Democrats who would limit or deny their political and civil rights. Lynch denied that Reconstruction in the South represented Negro domination or Negro rule, citing substantial facts to prove his point. Finally, Lynch insisted that congressional Reconstruction had not been a failure: "But for the adoption of their plan and the subsequent legislation of Congress along the same line, the abolition of slavery through the ratification of the 13th Amendment would have been in the name only—a legal and constitutional myth." [42]

In the 1920's, Alrutheus A. Taylor presented separate studies of the Negro in the Reconstruction of South Carolina and Virginia.[43] Taylor endeavored to show that most Negroes had continued to work during Reconstruction and that politically they had been instruments in the hands of militant factions of whites, enjoying few of the spoils. He

40 DuBois, "Reconstruction and its Benefits," *American Historical Review,* XV (July, 1910), 781–89.

41 Lynch, *The Facts of Reconstruction* (New York, 1913).

42 Lynch, *Some Historical Errors of James Ford Rhodes* (Boston and New York, 1922).

43 Taylor, *The Negro in South Carolina during the Reconstruction* (Washington, 1924), and *The Negro in the Reconstruction of Virginia* (Washington, 1926). Taylor's *The Negro in Tennessee, 1865–1880* (Washington, 1941), did little more than demonstrate that, politically, the Negro was able to play no positive role in the "reconstruction" of Tennessee.

asserted that most historical writings on Reconstruction were biased against the Negro and charged that any criticism of the established story was regarded as heresy.

In 1935 the brilliant and bitter W. E. B. DuBois made a frontal attack in *Black Reconstruction*.[44] The prevailing interpretation, he said, had been developed almost entirely by writers who were "passionate believers in the inferiority of the Negro," and who were guilty of maudlin sympathy for white Southerners and of deliberate distortion and suppression of evidence.

On some specific points, such as his attack on the black codes through simple and detailed quotation and his demonstration of the relatively slight participation of Negroes in the Reconstruction governments, DuBois was effective. In general, however, his polemic showed serious weaknesses. DuBois, no deep student of Reconstruction, had necessarily drawn most of his materials from books that were the objects of his attack. Furthermore, Marxist influence was apparent, and neither the rural Negro freedmen nor the southern poor whites, among whom DuBois included both Andrew Johnson and Abraham Lincoln, fitted the mold of Marxist theory. Similar weaknesses are found in the work of James Stewart Allen.[45]

But a substantial breach in the wall of Reconstruction orthodoxy had already been accomplished before DuBois made his sally. In 1932, Francis B. Simkins and Robert H. Woody published a new, detailed and expert study of Reconstruction in South Carolina. The South Carolina story in their study lost a great deal of its drama but became much more convincing. Throughout, there was objective analysis of men and measures of all parties. There was no effort to make the Black Code appear to be less harsh than it actually was. It was treated, as Garner had treated that of Mississippi, as a natural outcome of general belief in the inferiority of the Negro and in his unwillingness to work unless rigidly controlled. But there was the conclusion that "the interests of both races would have been better served had there never been a 'black code,'" and that "what was done would have been unwise had there been no Northern sentiment to take into account." There was full coverage of graft and corruption, but there was also consideration of the problems faced by the Reconstruction government and of serious efforts to meet the problems. Candid treatment was given to the use of

44 DuBois, *Black Reconstruction: An Essay toward a History of the Part which Black Folk Played in the Attempt to Reconstruct Democracy 1860–1888* (New York, 1935).
45 Allen, *Reconstruction: The Battle for Democracy* (New York, 1937).

intimidation and violence in the overthrow of the Republican government. Finally, there was a thoughtful and impressive analysis of the heritage of Reconstruction in South Carolina, with a provocative suggestion that the interpretation of Reconstruction developed by politicians and historians had been more harmful to the state than Reconstruction itself.[46]

To a large audience at the annual meeting of the Southern Historical Association in New Orleans in the fall of 1938, Francis B. Simkins read a paper entitled "New Viewpoints of Southern Reconstruction," beginning with the proposition that the main issue of Reconstruction was "the great American race question." In taking this position, he departed not at all from Fleming, or from Rhodes, or a hundred others. But Simkins went on to declare that "historians, sensing that the discrediting of the period in which the Negro most freely participated in politics justifies his subsequent exclusion from those activities, have condemned the Reconstruction measures as sweepingly as have the Southern politicians." He then asserted that Negro behavior in Reconstruction had to be explained on grounds other than race and that the time had come for more objective study of all phases of the period.[47]

In the same year, Horace Mann Bond had published a paper[48] that analyzed Reconstruction in Alabama and revealed a story of financial and political intrigue so complicated as to make Fleming's account of white Democratic virtue and black Republican sin seem naive.

Bond's paper was mostly a compilation of extracts from his book, *Negro Education in Alabama,* which was published in the following year. Three chapters of this carefully documented book are devoted to analysis of social, economic, and political forces in Alabama Reconstruction and of political leaders and their connections. Bond in a number of instances contradicted Fleming, who was, he said, "himself the son of a planter partially ruined by the war, and whose thesis, in some degree, was the expression of a class-attitude deeply affected by the events of the Civil War and Reconstruction." [49]

Shortly after the publication of Bond's book, Howard K. Beale,

46 Simkins and Woody, *South Carolina During Reconstruction* (Chapel Hill, 1932).

47 Simkins, "New Viewpoints of Southern Reconstruction," *Journal of Southern History,* V (February, 1939), 49–61.

48 Bond, "Social and Economic Forces in Alabama Reconstruction," *Journal of Negro History,* XXIII (July, 1938), 290–348.

49 Bond, *Negro Education in Alabama: A Study in Cotton and Steel* (Washington, 1939).

whose academic career had been built upon a defense of Andrew Johnson, read to the Southern Historical Association in Lexington, Kentucky, his controversial and influential paper, "On Rewriting Reconstruction History." [50] Drawing from the published works of Francis B.
Simkins and Robert H. Woody,[51] C. Vann Woodward,[52] Horace Mann
Bond,[53] Paul Lewinson,[54] Roger W. Shugg,[55] James S. Allen,[56] and
W. E. Burghardt DuBois,[57] and from the completed but then unpublished dissertation of Vernon L. Wharton,[58] Beale insisted that a much
too simple story of southern Reconstruction had been too generally
accepted and that there was need "to restudy Reconstruction in each
state, freed from preconceptions of the right and wrong of Reconstruction and determined to discover just what lasting influences Reconstruction exerted." [59]

Simkins' and Beale's challenges for new basic research have, as yet,
evoked little response. Such research would necessarily begin at town
and county level. It would require thorough review of materials that
generally have been undisturbed since the time of the Dunning students,
and of much greater masses of material which those students either did
not have available or did not use. There seems to be reluctance to spend
such labor on the rewriting of "state and local" history.

In the meantime, for the Reconstruction period, there has been no
general study of southern Negroes, carpetbaggers (including Negro
carpetbaggers), scalawags, or southern "redeemers." George R. Bent-

50 Beale, "On Rewriting Reconstruction History," *American Historical Review,*
XLV (July, 1940), 807–27.

51 Simkins and Woody, *South Carolina During Reconstruction.*

52 Comer Vann Woodward, *Tom Watson, Agrarian Rebel* (New York, 1938).

53 Bond, *Negro Education in Alabama.*

54 Lewinson, *Race, Class & Party: A History of Negro Suffrage and White
Politics in the South* (London, New York, Toronto, 1932).

55 Shugg, *Origins of Class Struggle in Louisiana: A Social History of White
Farmers and Laborers during Slavery and after* (Baton Rouge, 1939).

56 Allen, *Reconstruction.*

57 DuBois, *Black Reconstruction.*

58 Wharton, *The Negro in Mississippi, 1865–1890* (Chapel Hill, 1947).

59 A report of the meeting indicates that Francis Simkins, leading the discussion
of Beale's paper, expressed general agreement, but warned that class struggle
should not be emphasized at the expense of race consciousness in interpreting the
Reconstruction period. He believed that a balanced appraisal should take into
consideration other factors than political issues and their economic motivations,
and that there should be a fuller understanding of the emotional and psychological
causes of southern aversion to the experiment of the Negro in politics. James
Welch Patton, "The Fifth Annual Meeting of the Southern Historical Association,"
Journal of Southern History, VI (February, 1940), 83.

ley's recent *History of the Freedmen's Bureau*[60] uses new materials, but adds little important information to that presented by Paul S. Peirce in 1904.[61] Furthermore, there has been no synthesis of the revisionist point of view. For this purpose, Donald's cautious revision of Randall will not suffice; nor will John Hope Franklin's thoroughly revisionist, but brief and undocumented, *Reconstruction*.[62]

On the other hand, review of almost any new publication or new edition of American history textbooks and of recent essays on historiography indicates that most of the revisionist suggestions are being adopted, with or without any further detailed research. As Don E. Fehrenbacher has said, "Yet if the promise of the Simkins and Beale essays has been fulfilled only in piecemeal fashion, the day is fast disappearing when historians will treat the restoration of white supremacy as the happy ending of Reconstruction. For they know now that it was neither happy nor the ending." [63]

Other recent historiographers have taken a more extreme position. In 1959, Carl N. Degler, whose work[64] has been called by David M. Potter "just about the best one-volume interpretation of American history now extant," [65] attacked and rejected in detail the generally-accepted "myth" of Reconstruction history, with the blunt conclusion that "the tragedy of Reconstruction is that it failed." [66] For Donald Sheehan, writing in 1960, the failure of Reconstruction was a failure of the American people. He believed that there would be an increasing repudiation of "Dunning-ism," in part because "the doctrine of Anglo-Saxon superiority, so respectable in the 1890's, has been relegated to the dustbin." But Sheehan found little virtue in the approach of moderate historians, who were inclined to attempt to label the truth as the mid-point of two extremes, and to treat the poor qualities of Reconstruction legislators and the good qualities of their laws as matters of equal importance. Sheehan also rejected the increasingly popular economic

60 Bentley, *A History of the Freedmen's Bureau* (Philadelphia, 1955). Bentley goes beyond Peirce in emphasizing economic and political motivations of the Bureau, and in charging that it pushed the Negro into politics, sought too much for the Negro too soon, and "fed the flame of race hatred."

61 Peirce, *The Freedmen's Bureau* (Iowa City, 1904).

62 Franklin, *Reconstruction: After the Civil War* (Chicago, 1961).

63 Fehrenbacher, "Disunion and Reunion," in John Higham (ed.), *The Reconstruction of American History* (New York and Evanston, 1962), 116.

64 Degler, *Out of Our Past*, 217–28.

65 Potter, Review of Degler's *Out of Our Past*, in *Saturday Review*, XLII (February 7, 1959), 18.

66 Degler, *Out of Our Past*, 228.

interpretation of Reconstruction, with its proposal that the overthrow
was the result of bargains struck by politicians and businessmen. Instead, he declared, "For better or worse, the American people made the
decision to have the white South substantially control its own destinies."
And how, he asked, "do we evaluate a situation in which good American
principles [such as distaste for military control, regard for local self-
government, and acceptance of the recorded will of the majority]
consigned millions of people to second-class citizenship?" [67]

It will be noticed that the attitudes of Degler and Sheehan depart
significantly from the cautious suggestions of the "revisionists." There
is increasing evidence that moderate revisionism does not satisfy many
students of a new generation. Influenced by recent sociological, anthropological, psychological and political estimates of the nature of man,
possessed of new knowledge of what actually happened in the southern
states after their "redemption," [68] and profoundly disturbed by con-
tradictions between American doctrine and American behavior, some
of these students seek to find, once more, a simple, two-sided interpretation of the Reconstruction experience.

In these circumstances, the view taken by Henry Wilson in 1877 has
great appeal:

On the one side were those who would do justice to the black man, minister
to the pressing necessities, and carry out by appropriate legislation, and to
their [sic] legitimate results, the policy of emancipation; on the other were
those who brought to the discussion the still dominating influence of caste,
belittling the negro and his wants, and, with cruel insensibility, resisting
his claims upon either their sympathy, their humanity, or their sense of
justice.[69]

For those who adopt this interpretation there is again the temptation
to nominate sinners and saints, villains and heroes. Andrew Johnson,
as poor-white, racist southern demagogue, is a good candidate for
prime villain,[70] not for his failure to stop the Radicals, but for his

67 Sheehan, "Radical Reconstruction," in Sheehan and Harold C. Syrett (eds.),
Essays in American Historiography: Papers Presented in Honor of Allan Nevins
(New York, 1960), 37–49.
68 Woodward, *Origins of the New South 1877–1913,* describes in detail the evils
and disappointments that followed "redemption."
69 Wilson, *History of the Rise and Fall of the Slave Power in America* (3 vols.;
Boston and New York, 1872–1877), III, 491.
70 Eric Louis McKitrick, *Andrew Johnson and Reconstruction* (Chicago, 1960),
will not suffice for this purpose; McKitrick does little more than rejoin Burgess
and Rhodes in attributing the generally undesirable achievements of the congressional Radicals to the incompetence and intransigence of Johnson.

success in delaying and undermining their program until it had little chance of success. Furthermore, the reputation of Abraham Lincoln is vulnerable.

Acceptance of Henry Wilson's premise would suggest heroic status for the suffering and misinterpreted Thaddeus Stevens,[71] and for those Radical colleagues who risked or lost their political fortunes in the effort to establish democratic justice and the equality of man in America. The premise would also call for reappraisal and rehabilitation of carpetbaggers, scalawags, and southern Negro political leaders; and for many of them the rehabilitative material is readily available.

On the other hand, there must be warning that the great masses of background material do not reveal cleanly cut villains or heroes in any number. There can be little doubt that there were some people of heroic quality among the carpetbaggers, scalawags, and Negroes who fought the "battle for democracy" in the South; but most of them were little-known men who died on the line of battle. The records of survivors generally show either a successful leap into the white Democracy or a shoddy and pathetic struggle for very small messes of Republican political pottage.

In final warning, the attention of the future historian of southern Reconstruction, as he works with his "sources," is called to the following quotation from a report of General Lew Wallace, sent from Louisiana during the crisis of 1876: "Conscience offers no restraint. Nothing is so common as the resort to perjury. . . . Money and intimidation can obtain the oath of white men as well as black to any required statement. A ton of affidavits could be carried into the state house tomorrow and not a word of truth in them. . . . Now what can come of such a state of things?" [72]

---

71 Ralph Korngold, *Thaddeus Stevens: A Being Darkly Wise and Rudely Great* (New York, 1955), has already made this move for Stevens. For contrast, see Richard Nelson Current, *Old Thad Stevens, A Story of Ambition* (Madison, Wisconsin, 1942).

72 Randall and Donald, *The Civil War and Reconstruction*, 689, quoting from Harry Bernard, *Rutherford B. Hayes and His America* (Indianapolis, 1954), 327.

XIII

The "New South"

Paul M. Gaston

IN 1893, in a pioneer attempt to probe the meaning of the "New South," Amory Dwight Mayo, a northern exponent of new developments below the Potomac, found that there was "a good deal of unnecessary friction in the heated discussion of the question whether there really is a new South." Doubting his own ability to produce a definitive picture, Mayo offered little encouragement to the historians of the future. "Probably the time will never come," he predicted, "when the journalist, or even the average statesman, will be able to take an all-around view of a theme so large that it may be compassed only by many observations of many minds." [1] Since Mayo's time a good many historians, though not so many as one might wish, have set out to "compass" the "New South," but we today are likely to agree that they

1 Mayo, "Is There a New South?" *Social Economist*, V (October, 1893), 200.

have yet to produce the "all-around view" with which our guild can be permanently satisfied.

Part of the difficulty—and it is a problem that grows with the passage of time—lies in the extraordinary ambiguity of the term itself. C. Vann Woodward, for example, feels that it has caused so much "mischief" that, if possible, it ought to be abandoned entirely.[2] Most of the confusion stems from the fact that "New South" has customarily implied at least two quite different things. On the one hand, it denotes a particular ideology—thus the "New South School," referring to the Henry Gradys who were prophets of a "New South." On the other hand, it is used with equal, if not greater, frequency to mark off various, and vaguely defined, periods of southern history. It may signify the South since 1865; since 1877; from 1877 to 1913; since 1900, or simply the South of the present. Moreover, many writers who use the term to denote a particular period are not careful to state that "New South" has no connotative meaning. Or, conversely, the term may be implicitly invested with a vague meaning, stemming from the Grady ideology, and the progress of the region measured against achievement of those ideals. In this case one finds, in almost any post-Civil War period one investigates, that the "New South" is emerging, or must be resisted, or has triumphed, or, as Harry S. Ashmore put it a few years ago, is now "coming to reluctant maturity." [3] Finally, diverse groups have taken the term to describe themselves and their particular periodicals. Among these we find nineteenth-century journals devoted to industrialization and reconciliation, the familiar theme; a twentieth-century communist periodical; and the monthly publication of the Southern Regional Council, advocating a South free of racial discrimination.[4]

Clearly, then, before one can discuss the historiography of the "New South," some definitions and limitations must be established. As for the term itself, the position taken here is that it should be used almost exclusively as an adjective and seldom as a noun; and in its adjectival form it will be restricted largely to modification of the men of the post-Reconstruction years who first worked out in detail an ideology which was enthusiastically preached throughout the region. In addition, it will be used to describe the point of view of historians of a later period whose interpretations reflected the ideas of the original New South

2 Woodward, *Origins of the New South, 1877–1913* (Baton Rouge, 1951), ix–x.
3 Ashmore, *An Epitaph for Dixie* (New York, 1958), 14.
4 Winifred Gregory (ed.), *Union List of Serials in Libraries of the United States and Canada* (New York, 1943), 1979.

crusaders. As for periodization, the discussion will be restricted largely
to the period from the end of Reconstruction to the Populist Revolt, the
era in which the New South movement had its largest following and
made its greatest impact.

There is only one genuinely historiographical essay on this period, a
recent paper published by Professor Jacob E. Cooke.[5] Actually, his
"New South" extends from 1877 to 1914, and he finds that this period
"does not readily lend itself to historiographical discussion" because, he
explains, "few historians have presented a monistic interpretation which
gives unity and meaning to the varied facts of Southern experience."
Historians, he declares, have tended to emphasize different aspects of
the region's history—economic development, political practices, race
relations—and "few have argued that any single interpretive key would
unlock the door of this vast storehouse of historical material." [6] Perhaps, as a comment on recent studies, this judgment has merit. But
there was a time when, under the spell of the New South magic, historians found a central theme for most of the period and developed it
with great enthusiasm, conviction, and oftentimes elaborate documentation. If, by a "school" of historians we mean a group of scholars all
writing more or less toward the same end, there was in the years between 1900 and the Great Depression a group, composed mostly of
Southerners, deserving to be called the New South school of historians.

Albert Bushnell Hart, the Harvard historian, confronted one of the
principal characteristics of this group when he wrote, in 1910, that the
southern tendency toward exaggeration had to be understood before
one could properly evaluate southern writings. In the hands of southern
writers, he declared, "the clever but no-wise distinguished professor of
Latin is 'Probably the greatest classical scholar in the United States,'
the siege of Vicksburg was 'the most terrific contest in the annals of
warfare'; the material progress of the South is 'the most marvelous
thing in human history.' " [7] Later in the same volume, Hart exposed a
critical truth when he explained that the exaggerated statements of
southern material growth were widely believed in the region. "In every
discussion of Southern affairs," he declared, "an important thing to
reckon with is a fixed belief that the South is the most prosperous part
of the country, which fits in with the conviction that it has long surpassed

5 Cooke, "The New South," in Donald Sheehan and Harold C. Syrett (eds.),
Essays in American Historiography, Papers Presented in Honor of Allan Nevins
(New York and London, 1960), 50–80.
6 *Ibid.*, 51–52.
7 Hart, *The Southern South* (New York, 1910), 73–74.

all other parts of the world in civilization, in military ardor, and in the power to rise out of the sufferings of a conquered people." [8]

The themes of prosperity and power which Hart noted were rapidly becoming the stock-in-trade of writers on the South's recent history. Guy Carleton Lee, in the preface to Philip Alexander Bruce's *The Rise of the New South,* found the "subject of the South since the Civil War" to be an "inspiring one." Actually, he continued, the years since the war offered "such examples of heroic effort, such persistent struggle, such triumphant results, that the historian finds himself tending to an exaltation of the mind." Bruce's volume, praised by Lee as an authentic and comprehensive study of recent southern history, was "a vital narration of the progress of a mighty people, who, from adversity such as no other section of North America has ever experienced," had brilliantly "won the race with adverse fate and become the pride of the Union." [9]

Bruce's history stands as the capstone of the New South crusade itself; in fact, the New South school of historians, of which Bruce was the first major representative, had its origins in the promotional literature of the New South editors and publicists of the 1880's and 1890's. During these years the New South propagandists flooded the nation with an insistent literature in which historians of our generation find an astonishing mixture of fact and fancy, wish and reality. Few observers from the North were unimpressed by what they read. To cite a typical example, Charles Dudley Warner, writing in 1886, was persuaded that the South was in the throes of a mighty "economical and political revolution" whose story "will be one of the most marvellous the historian has to deal with." [10]

The marvel lies not so much in the history with which one must deal as in the descriptions that appeared in the eighties and nineties from the pens of the New South promoters. A New South creed, born in the seventies, nurtured in the early eighties, and brought to maturity with Grady's address before the New England Society of New York in 1886, was compounded of two distinct parts, the blending of which by the New South spokesmen accounts for numerous historiographical difficulties.[11] On the one hand was the doctrine that the South was poor,

8 *Ibid.,* 218.

9 Lee in Bruce, *The Rise of the New South* (Philadelphia, 1905), v–vi.

10 Warner, "Society in the New South," *New Princeton Review,* I (January, 1886), 1.

11 The ideas in this and the following two paragraphs are treated extensively in Paul Morton Gaston, "The New-South Creed, 1865–1900" (Ph.D. dissertation, University of North Carolina, 1961).

frustrated, and despised because it had, by decree of history, become entangled in wrong policies; the road to the future lay in abandoning one-crop agriculture, militant sectionalism, and outright repression of the Negro, and adopting instead a diversified industrial economy, a spirit of reconciliation, and a program of education providing separate independence for the Negro. The dream which they created was essentially a promise of American life for the South. It proffered all the glitter and glory and freedom from guilt that inhered in the American ideal. Sloughing off those characteristics which had marked him as poor, quarrelsome, unprogressive, guilt-ridden, and unsuccessful, the Southerner would—if he heeded the New South prophets—become a true heir of his heritage: prosperous, successful, confident of the future.

Before long, however, the promotional literature of the New South spokesmen included wondrous descriptions of a people who had already achieved, or were on the verge of achieving, all that had been promised as fruits of long toil. Testimony to the achievements of the new order was produced in copious quantity. From his headquarters in Baltimore, Richard Hathaway Edmonds, editor of the *Manufacturers' Record*, ground out statistics to substantiate his claim that the region was "throbbing" with industrial activity and that capitalists of the North and Europe were "looking to the South as the field for investment." [12] Henry Watterson thanked God that, at last, one could say of the South, "it is simply a geographic expression." [13] And, finally, a Vanderbilt professor declared that the "New South, which had first showed itself in 1880," had by 1886 "proved its name by evidences so powerful and convincing that only the blindest can fail to see them." [14]

Proclaiming the reality of an affluent and triumphant South, these spokesmen were equally fervent in depicting a South innocent of racial injustice. "Each has his own place," Grady declared of white and black, "and fills it, and is satisfied." [15] The program of paternalism, education, regulated franchise, and increasing segregation was advanced as the final solution to the conundrum presented by the demands of Negro freedom and the American tradition of equality. The New South image thus underwent in a short period a metamorphosis. Emerging from a

12 Edmonds, *Facts About the South* (Baltimore, 1907), 60–61, and *The South's Redemption: From Poverty to Prosperity* (Baltimore, 1890), 5.

13 Watterson, *The Compromises of Life* (New York, 1903), 289.

14 Wilbur Fisk Tillett, "The White Man of the New South," *Century Magazine,* XXXIII (March, 1887), 769–70.

15 Joel Chandler Harris (ed.), *Life of Henry W. Grady, Including His Writings and Speeches* (New York, 1890), 303.

program of action to save a despondent region from ruin, it evolved
into a declaration of triumph. Uncritically it could be assumed that,
because "facts" proved it, affluence and power were at hand and that
the Negro lived in the best of all possible worlds, righteously separated
from, but nurtured by, his white brethren. This was the intellectual tradition which historians of the twentieth century inherited; and with
certain exceptions, it was this tradition which dominated southern historical writing until the 1930's when the revisionist erosion set it.

Before that era of devastating reappraisal, however, a pattern of history was established which was comprehensive in scope and appealing
in tone. The New South school of historians developed, as the central
theme of their works, the concept of triumph over adversity, of steel
will and impeccable character overcoming staggering problems, often
against what seemed impossible odds. The South that was depicted
in most of these early histories rose from the extraordinary devastation
of the Reconstruction to a glorious plateau of achievement. Viewed
from the plateau, the story was one of hope and inspiration. Holland
Thompson, the first academic historian to write a general history of the
period, opened his work with the declaration that "somehow, some-
where, sometime, a new hopefulness was born and this spirit—evidence
of new life—became embodied in 'the New South.'" [16] To optimism
and cheerfulness was added the element of daring and romance. Broadus
Mitchell, in *The Rise of the Cotton Mills in the South,* enticed his
readers with the assurance that his story, properly understood, was "not
only an industrial chronicle, but a romance, a drama as well." [17] Here,
then, were powerful romantic elements to compete with the more popular
and more numerous histories of the gallant South that had fallen at Appomattox. And the histories of the new regime had the one virtue denied
chronicles of the Old South: they were success stories.

An essential ingredient was the element of strong moral fiber. While
the New South historians agreed that the new order differed from the
old in innumerable ways, few were willing to concede that the peculiar
moral superiority of the Southerner had perished with the Lost Cause.
As Bruce put it, the war and Reconstruction had shattered the South's
economic structure and visited economic ruin on the region; but they
had not destroyed the extraordinary "moral qualities of the people."
These, in fact, were strengthened in adversity and were the principal

16 Thompson, *The New South* (New Haven, 1919), 7.
17 Mitchell, *The Rise of the Cotton Mills in the South* (Baltimore, 1921), vii.

weapons available to Southerners to meet new challenges.[18] Ironically coupled with this sense of moral superiority was the common belief that the war and Reconstruction had emancipated the white South from the shackles of an old order that had barred material progress and prosperity. "The Civil War," Mitchell wrote, "brought into glaring view the absence of Southern economic self-sufficiency," and its outcome freed "not just the slaves, but the South as a whole." The "emancipated" whites, no longer fettered by the economic chains of the past but still endowed with the ancient traits of their forebears, were required to rebuild on new foundations. Driven by "moral incitement" and "civic piety," Southerners undertook the task of creating a prosperous industrial society. In response to a "moral stimulus," their leaders built cotton mills that provided work for impoverished poor whites and, one is almost led to believe, gave little thought to self-enrichment.[19]

It is important to remember that, almost without exception, New South historians wrote as confirmed nationalists and interpreted southern development within the context of national trends. Reconcilation and conversion to national ways and values were central to their histories. To Paul Herman Buck, the historian of reconcilation and, in many ways, a characteristic representative of the New South school, "the central theme of American life after the war . . . is not to be found in . . . sectional divergence. It was national integration which marked every important development in the years that followed." [20] This theme of national reconciliation is likely to be deceptive, and one should observe that it was never meant to imply a surrender of southern will to northern superiority. It signified, rather, a recognition in the South that the road to affluence and power led to the adoption of those national patterns which had accounted for American greatness. This is what Edwin Mims meant when he wrote, in his biography of Sidney Lanier that southern progress had been made possible by the "adoption of the national point of view"; [21] it is what Burton J. Hendrick, the biographer of Walter H. Page, had in mind when he declared that the new nationalism was the essential force underlying the South's resurgence, that "above all," the period of Page's crusading "was an era that witnessed the transformation of the backward Civil War South into a progressive

18 Bruce, The Rise of the New South, 4.
19 Mitchell, The Rise of the Cotton Mills, 53–54, 81, 153.
20 Buck, The Road to Reunion, 1865–1900 (Boston, 1937), vii.
21 Mims, Sidney Lanier (Boston, 1905), 275.

part of a united country." [22] A generation of New South historians was vindicated in 1937 when Buck concluded that, by 1900, "a union of sentiment based upon integrated interests had become a fact." [23]

New South historians, in stressing the theme of nationalism, were particularly careful to emphasize two complementary aspects. In the first place, they argued that the primary force binding the sections was the adoption by the South of what E. L. Godkin once called "the industrial stage of social progress." [24] To Buck, the South's new departure had brought about an "interlocking of economic dependence" which promoted similarity and destroyed particularism.[25] Broadus and George Mitchell, in *The Industrial Revolution in the South,* argued that the industrialization of the South destroyed "separatism" and invited "national consciousness." [26] In 1908, their historian father, Samuel C. Mitchell, attempted to place the movement toward American nationalism in a universal context, concluding of the South, "We have simply found out God's plan in our generation, and have fallen in line. . . . Whatever tends to equalize economic conditions in different sections of our country," he explained, "promotes similarity of view and identity of purpose." [27] Bruce also concluded that the industrial revolution in the South was the major factor in producing a republic "united in all its parts," free of debilitating antagonisms.[28]

In the second place, these historians were convinced that the resurgent southern economy had brought into existence a South of affluence, power, and independence which fully vindicated the New South spokesmen who had called the movement into being. As early as 1885, according to Mims, "factories were prospering, farm products were becoming more diversified, more farmers owned their own places, . . . the national spirit was growing, and . . . [a] day of hope, of freedom, of progress, had dawned." By the end of the century, Mims believed, the South was assured of a

22 Hendrick, *The Training of an American: The Earlier Life and Letters of Walter H. Page, 1855–1913* (Boston, 1928), v.

23 Buck, *The Road to Reunion,* viii.

24 Godkin, "The White Side of the Southern Question," *Nation,* XXXI (August 19, 1880), 126.

25 Buck, *The Road to Reunion,* 298.

26 Broadus and George Mitchell, *The Industrial Revolution in the South* (Baltimore, 1930), ix.

27 Samuel C. Mitchell, "The Nationalization of Southern Sentiment," *South Atlantic Quarterly,* VII (April, 1908), 110.

28 Bruce, "Social and Economic Revolution in the Southern States," *Contemporary Review,* LXXVIII (July, 1900), 72–73.

"brilliant future." [29] To other historians brilliance did not have to await future developments. Bruce was struck by a "recuperative power in the Southern people" which was "perhaps unsurpassed in history." [30] The Mitchells believed that there "arrived nearly overnight an Industrial Revolution as swift and as vigorous as that in England." [31] Buck pronounced the "economic revolution" to have been both "remarkable" and "sensationally rapid." [32] Reenforcing this sense of material greatness was the common belief that the South had been master of its own destiny, achieving its eminence virtually unaided. Moreover, nothing is so striking to the historian of today as the common absence of suggestions that the region was in any sense a colony of the North. Bruce, for example, noted the prominence of northern financiers in southern railroad development, but his analysis did not lead him to attach any special significance to the fact.[33] Buck, summing up the matter, could declare: "Thirty years after Appomattox there remained no fundamental conflict between the aspirations of North and South. The people of the United States constituted at last a nation integrated and united in sentiment." [34]

It would have been paradoxical in the extreme had these historians coupled their accounts of a pioneering, progressive, and energetic industrial leadership with an interpretation of political development which conceded the truth of the occasional northern charge that "Bourbon" politicians in the South stubbornly held to the past, refusing to adapt to the changing conditions of a new order. The truth is, such concessions were seldom made. The New South historians agreed with the editor of the Memphis *Appeal* who declared as early as 1875, "We do not know what a Bourbon Democrat means . . . unless it implies there is a class of politicians, who, . . . forgetting nothing and learning nothing, do not recognize any issues as settled by the war and are ready to inaugurate another rebellion. We know of no such Democrats." [35] On the contrary the early historians believed that the role played by the political leaders of the South was essentially the same as that played by the industrial leaders. Just as the latter had redeemed the South from economic error, so the former had redeemed the region from political error and, in addi-

29 Mims, *Sidney Lanier*, 279.
30 Bruce, *The Rise of the New South*, 279, 342.
31 Mitchell and Mitchell, *The Industrial Revolution*, 294.
32 Buck, *The Road to Reunion*, 178.
33 Bruce, *The Rise of the New South*, Chap. 19.
34 Buck, *The Road to Reunion*, 298.
35 Quoted in Willie D. Halsell, "The Bourbon Period in Mississippi Politics, 1875–1890," *Journal of Southern History*, XI (November, 1945), 519.

tion, had assured conditions which facilitated sectional reconciliation and material progress.

To understand this favorable interpretation of the "Redeemers," one must recapture something of the perspective from which the New South historians wrote. To them the experience of Reconstruction was a horror unique in American history and for this reason doubly noxious and degrading. Against this background, the Redeemers appeared virtually as knights in shining armor. Their primary task—indeed, their knightly duty—was to cut away the "poisonous growth," as Bruce put it, planted by a band of alien bandits and desecrators.[36]

Thus the image of the Redeemers is a relatively uncomplicated one. They began their careers in glory, especially those who participated in the noble act of securing definitive home rule as a result of the "Wormley House Bargain." They were, in contrast to the "aliens" who had ruled the South before redemption, the "natural" leaders of the region, men who had distinguished themselves during the Civil War. This is not to say that they were the old plantation aristocracy. Several New South historians recognized that many of the leaders came from the new commercial-industrial urban class rather than from the older planter class. In either case, however, they were *natural* leaders, men born to the region.

Their achievement, in the view of the New South historians, amply justified the trust that the masses confided in them. Responsible men, they reversed the corrupt and fraudulent practices of Reconstruction. Holland Thompson pronounced their administrations free from scandal of any kind. "No governments in American history," he wrote, "have been conducted with more economy and more fidelity." [37] Impeccable honesty was coupled with a high sense of fiscal responsibility. The ruinous taxes and extravagant appropriations of the carpetbag regimes were abolished as the Redeemers faced up realistically to the demands of recovery. Expenses were diminished by scaling down dishonest debts, eliminating unnecessary governmental positions, and lowering salaries. A new tax structure released capital for investment. In brief, an atmosphere was created in which business could thrive and men could exercise their initiative without fear of retaliation by a capricious government.

Moreover, none of these achievements would have been secured had the Redeemers not guaranteed freedom from political instability and

36 Bruce, *The Rise of the New South*, 3.
37 Thompson, *The New South*, 25.

resumption of Negro-Republican rule. It is in this sense that the New South historians generally applauded the Redeemer creation of a one-party, solid South. Taking the explanations of the political leaders more or less at face value, the historians gave credence to the simple formula that the South's suffering had come as a consequence of Republican domination resulting in "Negro rule." Bruce was convinced that, even after home rule, "an enormous number of black voters" continued to threaten "the stability of Southern institutions." [38] The threat could have become a reality, however, only if the Republican party had found support among native whites, and this could have occurred only if the whites had divided. Patriotism, loyalty to race and region, demanded, then, unswerving support of the Democratic party. The permanence of a "redeemed" South, in short, depended upon the maintenance of a "solid" South.

Thus it was that one-partyism, white supremacy, patriotism, morality in government, and the industrial revolution were all part of one pattern. Finding this connection, the historians of the early part of the century discovered much of which to be proud in the "New South": Reconstruction had been successfully undone, and a superior southern will had charted a prosperous, successful course for the once defeated and occupied land.

Reaction to this felicitous interpretation of the Redeemer era was bound to occur, and signs of dissent began to appear in the 1920's.[39] But it was not until the Depression that full scale revision began to take shape. The glowing picture of a prosperous and triumphant South made little sense to a region soon to be accurately, if somewhat undiplomatically, labeled the nation's "economic problem no. 1." The excruciating plight of the South provided new perspectives that helped to provide new interpretations of the Redeemer era.

The most eloquent and heated, if not the most thoroughly researched, interpretation emanated primarily from Nashville and is associated with the Vanderbilt Agrarian movement. The Nashville Crusaders, in their manifesto, *I'll Take My Stand,* wrote charmingly of an ordered, conservative, soil-oriented style of life, presumably characteristic of the Old South, which had been betrayed by the New South promoters.[40]

38 Bruce, *The Rise of the New South,* 446–47.

39 For a bitter indictment of the Redeemer regimes see William H. Skaggs, *The Southern Oligarchy: An Appeal in Behalf of the Silent Masses of Our Country Against the Despotic Rule of the Few* (New York, 1924).

40 Twelve Southerners, *I'll Take My Stand: The South and the Agrarian Tradition* (New York, 1930).

Lamenting the seduction of younger Southerners by the industrial gospel, the Agrarians called for a critical examination of the "advantages of becoming a 'new South' which," they insisted, would "be only an undistinguished replica of the usual industrial community." [41] Concerned with the present, wishing to launch the counterrevolution which they believed still had chances of success, they charged the New South historians with perpetuating original errors by failing to write genuinely critical history. What should be written, declared Donald Davidson in *The Attack on Leviathan,* was that America's need in 1900 was "to set off the tendencies that were leading the country straight into over-industrialization and social degeneracy." This could have been accomplished most effectively, he concluded, by "strengthening the conservative culture of the South, to the virtues of which [Walter Hines] Page and his followers were blind." [42]

Despite their appeal to traditional values rooted deeply in southern history, the Agrarians produced no historical studies of the Redeemer era, apart from occasional essays such as those by John Donald Wade on Henry Grady and Joel Chandler Harris.[43] Frank Lawrence Owsley, the most distinguished historian in the group, rediscovered the plain people of the Old South, but he did not investigate the social and economic history of this class after the Civil War. The significance of the Agrarians, then, lies primarily in the fact that they heightened awareness of an anti-New South tradition in the region and suggested to historians the profitability of exploring the patterns of conflict and antagonism in modern southern history.

The theme of conflict soon appeared in several works. Benjamin B. Kendrick and Alex M. Arnett, in *The South Looks at Its Past* (1935), found that "the quarter-century that followed the restoration of native white rule in the South was marked by a conflict between those who looked to the past and those who looked to the future." The Redeemer era could be described as a conflict between an Old-South party of agrarianism and a New South party of industrialism, with the former fighting a rear-guard action.[44] A similar interpretation was included in

41 *Ibid.,* x–xi.

42 Davidson, *The Attack on Leviathan: Regionalism and Nationalism in the United States* (Chapel Hill, 1938), 278.   ,

43 See, for example, Wade, "Henry W. Grady," *Southern Review,* III (Winter, 1938), 479–509, and "Profits and Losses in the Life of Joel Chandler Harris," *American Review,* I (April, 1937), 17–35.

44 Kendrick and Arnett, *The South Looks at Its Past* (Chapel Hill, 1935), 105–108.

William B. Hesseltine's general history of the South, first published in 1936.[45] To him, the South was beset by a conflict between the values of the Old South, embodied in Jefferson Davis, and the New South, embodied in Robert E. Lee, which left a lasting mark on the South. Hesseltine's conflict thesis was developed in more detail in his *Confederate Leaders in the New South*.[46]

However, the new views of conflict between an agrarian and an industrial tradition—a conflict that presumably reached its point of greatest intensity during the Redeemer era—resulted in relatively few serious monographic studies of that period. Commenting on the paucity of such studies, Judson C. Ward suggests that "the slower evolutionary processes of economic and social reconstruction carried on under one-party domination have not possessed for historians the dramatic appeal of the more spectacular period of the Civil War and Reconstruction which preceded this period or the Populist revolt which followed it." [47] Here Ward raises a point that is crucial in understanding the nature of the revisionism of the 1930's and 1940's. To many scholars of the Depression era, the Populist period held very special attraction. As C. Vann Woodward has pointed out, the two periods had much in common. There was, first of all, the common setting of depression and economic dislocation, coupled with a common antagonism toward the dominant business interests of the country. In addition, a sense of urgency and desperation infected large elements of the population. And, for Southerners, agricultural problems were among the most pressing and agrarian reform was at the center of much political and economic discussion.[48]

Southern scholars began asking themselves why the New South historians had almost uniformly passed over the Populist revolt, as though it were some form of temporary aberration, best neglected and forgotten. Could it be that, in minimizing the significance of southern populism, previous historians had missed a key element in post-Reconstruction history? More important, could it be true that the harmonious structure

45 Hesseltine, *A History of the South, 1607–1936* (New York, 1936). The most recent edition of this textbook is Hesseltine and David L. Smiley, *The South in American History* (Englewood Cliffs, N. J., 1960).

46 "Between the old South, which was, in its way the old Federal Union, and the New South, which subscribed to the concepts and practices of the new nation . . . there was a continuing conflict. . . . Eventually a working compromise was found . . . but the struggle left a long legacy of conflict in the life of the South." Hesseltine, *Confederate Leaders in the New South* (Baton Rouge, 1950), 41.

47 Ward, "The New Departure Democrats of Georgia: An Interpretation," *Georgia Historical Quarterly*, XLI (September, 1957), 227.

48 Woodward, *The Burden of Southern History* (Baton Rouge, 1960), 141–42.

of New South historiography, based on a general concept of unity, absence of conflict, and progress and reconciliation, might be dismantled by studies that exposed the proportions of the revolt against the New South regimes? Was the seething discontent of the nineties a reflection of agrarians struggling to maintain an old order, or did it represent a much more fundamental and comprehensive indictment of the power structure of the South? These and other questions were raised with increasing frequency in a decade in which thoughtful men found much to condemn in their own generation.

The point here is that the most searching revisionist studies of the Redeemer era—the ones upon which our present view of the period has been built—were primarily studies of Populism and not of the Redeemer era itself. It is true, of course, that some important studies of Populism were written before the Depression. Alex M. Arnett's *The Populist Movement in Georgia* (New York, 1922) is a good example. And John D. Hicks's standard work, *The Populist Revolt,* was published in 1931 at the very beginning of the Depression. But the most important works, which fundamentally challenged the New South view of the Redeemers, appeared after the onset of the Depression. A selective listing of these studies would include Roscoe C. Martin, *The People's Party in Texas* (Austin, 1933); Daniel M. Robison, *Bob Taylor and the Agrarian Revolt in Tennessee* (Chapel Hill, 1935); William D. Sheldon, *Populism in the Old Dominion* (Princeton, 1935); articles by James A. Sharp on Populism in Tennessee, published in 1937 and 1938; and articles by Kathryn T. Abbey on Florida, published in 1938;[49] Woodward, *Tom Watson* (1938); Francis B. Simkins, *Pitchfork Ben Tillman* (Baton Rouge, 1944); and Stuart Noblin, *Leonidas LaFayette Polk* (Chapel Hill, 1949).

The full impact of the revisionist departure was not apparent until 1951 when Professor Woodward, building on the new monographs and his own extensive research, published his *Origins of the New South.* It was the first general history of the post-Reconstruction South since Holland Thompson's brief volume of 1919 and the first detailed study since Bruce's work of 1905.[50] Resemblances between the new and older

49 Sharp, "The Entrance of the Farmers' Alliance into Tennessee Politics," *East Tennessee Historical Society Publications,* No. 9 (1937), 77–92, and "The Farmers' Alliance and the People's Party in Tennessee," *East Tennessee Historical Society Publications,* No. 10 (1938), 91–113; Abbey, "Florida Versus the Principles of Populism, 1896–1911," *Journal of Southern History,* IV (November, 1938), 462–75.

50 For an earlier formulation worked out for one state, consult C. Vann Woodward, "Bourbonism in Georgia," *North Carolina Historical Review,* XVI (January, 1939), 22–35.

works were difficult to find. Not only, of course, had Woodward written from a different perspective, but his skeptical, ironic approach to the materials was in direct contrast to the relatively uncomplicated and uncritical studies of the New South school. The results were generally devastating to the old tradition.

A significant clue to Woodward's approach was offered in a shorter book published earlier in the same year, *Reunion and Reaction,* a study of the Compromise of 1877 and the inauguration of the Redeemer regime. Its Beardian interpretation attacked the "Wormley House Bargain" legend and suggested that reunion was built, in large part, on a community of economic interests, with the Redeemers pledging support of nationalistic economic policies in return for economic aid to the South. Implicit in the settlement was an alliance of capitalists of the South and Northeast to preserve the status quo. Ironically agreeing with the New South historians that reunion was premised on the marriage of southern and northern capitalists, Woodward's revisionism lay in his assertion of the opportunistic and shortsighted motives that underlay the union.

Incorporating this interpretation in *Origins of the New South,* Woodward analyzed in detail the character of the Redeemer leadership, concluding that a high percentage of the new leaders were prewar Whigs, forced into the Democratic party because of the exigencies of white supremacy politics. Few, he found, came from the old planter class; nearly all, including most of those with agrarian connections, were oriented toward the commercial and industrial interests of the region. Redemption, then, was not a restoration of the old order but, rather, "a new phase of the revolutionary process begun in 1865. Only in a limited sense can it be properly called a 'counter-revolution.' " [51]

In describing the policies of the Redeemers, Woodward differed in almost every respect from the New South historians. Retrenchment, hailed by the earlier scholars as an indication of realism, was regarded by Woodward as an abdication of social responsibility. But perhaps a more permanent injury, he wrote, "was the set of values imposed upon the Southern mind by the rationalization of this neglect." [52] Equally devastating to the Redeemer reputation was the lengthy documentation of thievery in official places that marked the careers of many state administrations. Although finding that the stealing was less extensive than during the Reconstruction era, Woodward's history nonetheless

51 Woodward, *Origins of the New South,* 22.
52 *Ibid.,* 61.

tarnished another of the major claims made for the service of the Redeemers to their region.[53]

In dissecting the anatomy of the "Solid South," Woodward cut away
the shibboleths of white supremacy to reveal a politics of class and interest that cleverly exploited race and tradition to perpetuate its hold
over the region. Detailing the mounting grievances of various anti-
Redeemer elements within the South, he attributes the success of the
one-party machines to Machiavellian techniques that had been perfected
in the fight against the carpetbaggers. The result, at least until the
Populist revolt, was political apathy and despair, "a period of political
torpor more stultifying, perhaps, than any in . . . [the South's] long
history." [54]

But the New South promoters and the historians who followed in their
tradition had not built their image of a triumphant South on a basis of
political achievement alone. Political leaders, honest and loyal though
they might have been, were regarded as benefactors of the region chiefly
because they created the order and the atmosphere in which an industrial
revolution could take place. Here Woodward does not equivocate in
challenging completely the New South point of view. While conceding
that the South, in many respects, did hold its own in rates of relative
growth, he finds that, in absolute terms, the economic disparity between
North and South increased, rather than decreased, during the period
1880–1900. Moreover—and here was the unkindest cut of all—the
economy of the South became increasingly controlled by northern and
other outside capitalists. The South, Woodward concluded, "was limited
largely to the role of a producer of raw materials, a tributary of industrial powers, and an economy dominated by absentee owners." The
unhappy result was "low wages, lack of opportunity, and poverty." [55]

By 1951, then, the revisionist movement had found its spokesman in
a brilliant work, at once original and yet reflective of two decades of new
thought. In conclusion, one ought to ask where we stand today. Have
we reached a new consensus? Are counterrevisions of a major nature in
progress? Or, is the whole subject being neglected?

There is still much that we do not know. Woodward was struck by
the absence of adequate monographs when he wrote *Origins of the
New South,* and anyone who reads his "Critical Essay on Authorities"
may find that complaint documented in suggestions for numerous stud-

53 *Ibid.,* 66–74.
54 *Ibid.,* 106.
55 *Ibid.,* 311.

ies.[56] Other periods of southern history, it appears, are more inviting to the profession. Some years ago David Potter made a study of articles appearing in the *Journal of Southern History* from 1935 through 1949. Of those articles which he could classify by period, he found that 48.8 percent had been written on the period 1830–1865 while only 16.3 percent were devoted to the entire period since 1877.[57] During the period 1950–1963, the proportion on the period since 1877 has gone up slightly, to 21.9 percent of the total classifiable by period, but studies of the Redeemer era itself are disappointingly scarce.

We still lack, for example, good studies of the Redeemer era in most southern states despite an obvious need and the example of a few pioneer volumes of merit. Albert D. Kirwan's splendid analysis of Mississippi (which is not restricted to the Redeemer years) is a model to be emulated by students of other states. Works more limited in time span, such as Allen Going's monograph on Alabama, reveal what can be done to enrich our understanding of the period.[58] The Kirwan and Going volumes, both published in the same year that *Origins of the New South* appeared, largely support Woodward's revisionist generalizations. Should we have good studies of all the other states, however, the picture might become more complex, if not basically different. An analysis of South Carolina, for example, might well qualify the thesis that the conservative political regimes were dominated by commercial and industrial interests. In addition to the paucity of good state studies, another deficiency is in biography. Since 1951 good biographies of a few significant figures, such as James S. Hogg and George W. Cable, have been published, but equally important men still await biographers or invite reinterpretation by modern students.[59]

---

56 The present essay does not pretend to be a bibliography of the Redeemer period. To fill that need, the student is referred to Woodward, *Origins of the New South*, 482–515.

57 Potter, "An Appraisal of Fifteen Years of the *Journal of Southern History*, 1935–1949," *Journal of Southern History*, XVI (February, 1950), 25–32.

58 Kirwan, *Revolt of the Rednecks: Mississippi Politics, 1876–1925* (Lexington, 1951); Going, *Bourbon Democracy in Alabama, 1874–1890* (University, Alabama, 1951). Two particularly interesting articles which examine the nature of the conservative regimes in their respective states are Willie D. Halsell, "The Bourbon Period in Mississippi Politics, 1875–1890," *Journal of Southern History*, XI (November, 1945), 519–37; and Judson C. Ward, "The New Departure Democrats of Georgia: An Interpretation," *Georgia Historical Quarterly*, XLI (September, 1957), 227–36. Ward's article is based on his more detailed study, "Georgia under the Bourbon Democrats, 1872–1890" (Ph.D. dissertation, University of North Carolina, 1947).

59 Robert C. Cotner, *James Stephen Hogg: A Biography* (Austin, Texas, 1959); Arlin Turner, *George W. Cable: A Biography* (Durham, 1956). A selective list

For the most part, the work done in recent years has tended to support, rather than to challenge, the principal revisionist findings. There are exceptions. Nash K. Burger and John K. Bettersworth's *South of Appomattox* (New York, 1959) seems blithely unaware of revisionist findings and describes the Redeemers as highly motivated patriots, rescuers of an oppressed people. Thomas B. Alexander's study of Whiggery in the postwar South offers a more serious challenge to Woodward's view of the Redeemers. Examining the Hayes papers, where Woodward located much of the evidence for his economic interpretation of the Compromise of 1877, Alexander found "surprisingly few" items referring to economic matters. He does not press the point but suggests that "a more detailed study of the individual oldline Whigs in Congress might well establish the conclusion that the southern bloc would have acted as it did in 1877 had there been no railroad lobby involved." [60] On the other hand, Alexander's statistical study of former southern Whigs amply confirms the revisionist position that Whiggery was the dominant element in the Democratic party during the Redeemer era.

Alexander's careful study of political backgrounds has been matched by few other studies. We do not have a major general study of Redeemer politics, such as V. O. Key's pioneer masterpiece on twentieth-century politics, nor do we have sufficient monographs on the structure and process of politics to ease the burden of one undertaking such a task. Two recent interpretive books by T. Harry Williams and Dewey W. Grantham, both quite brief on the period, make stimulating reading but do not depart from the revisionist construction.[61] Indeed, Grantham's excellent account of the forging of the Solid South underscores the extent to which the revisionist position has triumphed.[62] Williams expresses reservations about some parts of the revisionist interpretation,

---

of candidates for good biographical studies would include Francis W. Dawson, Richard H. Edmonds, Joel Chandler Harris, Wade Hampton, and Daniel A. Tompkins, among others. Many of the standard biographies, most of which were written between the two world wars, could be profitably replaced by new studies.

60 Alexander, "Persistent Whiggery in the Confederate South, 1860–1877," *Journal of Southern History*, XXVII (August, 1961), 324–25. Other articles by Professor Alexander on the same subject are "Whiggery and Reconstruction in Tennessee," *Journal of Southern History*, XVI (August, 1950), 291–305, "Persistent Whiggery in Alabama and the Lower South, 1860–1867," *Alabama Review*, XII (January, 1959), 35–52, and "Persistent Whiggery in Mississippi: The Hinds County Gazette," *Journal of Mississippi History*, XXIII (April, 1961), 71–93.

61 Williams, *Romance and Realism in Southern Politics* (Athens, Georgia, 1961); Grantham, *The Democratic South* (Athens, Georgia, 1963).

62 With a reservation: Grantham, like several other historians, prefers to continue use of the term "Bourbon" rather than adopt "Redeemer."

arguing that Woodward erred in describing Redeemer politics as a politics of race and tradition, largely devoid of realistic concerns. Actually, the real difference between the two is slight.[63] The most notable recent advance of political history has resulted from two excellent studies of the Republican party and the South by Vincent P. DeSantis and Stanley P. Hirshson.[64] These works emphasize the continuing influence and importance of the GOP throughout the period, thus correcting occasional careless generalizations about the disappearance of the party in the South after Reconstruction. At the same time, they contribute to a fuller understanding of Redeemer opposition and the perfection of one-party politics.

Studies of race relations, the subject of another chapter in this volume, were pioneered by Vernon L. Wharton and George B. Tindall.[65] Woodward's *Strange Career of Jim Crow* (New York, 1955) added a new dimension to the subject by advancing the thesis that segregation laws came fairly late and by reemphasizing the degree to which the Redeemers were willing to forestall movements for proscription of Negro rights. Charles E. Wynes and Frenise A. Logan have tested the "Woodward thesis" for Virginia and North Carolina (with positive findings, in the main) and students of other states could follow suit with profit.[66] These recent studies accelerated the dismantling of the image of harmonious racial adjustment, predicated on subordination, given us by the New South school and, at the same time, revealed greater complexity in the political and economic aspects of race relations.

In the area of economic development one finds occasional echoes of the earlier writings. For example, John S. Ezell, though generally in

63 Williams declares that Woodward was "led to conclude that the politics of Redemption was of the romantic type, emphasizing tradition and demanding the subjection of all other issues to one while ignoring the future and denying issues of economics and self-interest." According to Williams, this interpretation is partly wrong, for the Redeemers "placed economics and power above questions of race." As proof of this point, Williams notes that the ruling whites did not disfranchise the Negro but manipulated his vote in order to preserve their own political power and enhance their own economic positions. Williams, *Romance and Realism*, 47–49. In fact, Woodward has developed this point in detail, but he would disagree with the implication that Redeemer opportunism belied a nonrational politics rooted in an appeal to race and tradition. Rather, the two are part of the same pattern.

64 DeSantis, *Republicans Face the Southern Question: The New Departure Years, 1877–1897* (Baltimore, 1959); Hirshson, *Farewell to the Bloody Shirt: Northern Republicans and the Southern Negro, 1877–1893* (Bloomington, Indiana, 1962).

65 Wharton, *The Negro in Mississippi, 1865–1890* (Chapel Hill, 1947); Tindall, *South Carolina Negroes, 1877–1900* (Columbia, South Carolina, 1952).

66 Wynes, *Race Relations in Virginia, 1870–1902* (Charlottesville, 1961); Logan, *The Negro in North Carolina, 1876–1894* (Chapel Hill, 1964).

agreement with Woodward, asserts one older view. He declares that the "crowning glory of the Bourbon era was its sensational success in attracting manufacturing to the South," adding that "the progress of Southern industrialization was little short of a miracle." [67] More commonly, however, scholars have tended to the revisionist position on this as well as on other subjects. Typical is the statement by Thomas D. Clark that the years between 1865 and 1914 were "lean and barren";[68] and revealing is William H. Nicholls' acceptance of the fact of industrial lethargy in the late nineteenth century and his attempt to explain continued economic backwardness in noneconomic terms.[69] Relatively little has been done with the problem of economic colonialism, raised poignantly by Woodward, but studies such as John F. Stover's *The Railroads of the South, 1865–1900* (Chapel Hill, 1955) show how it can be approached through a single industry. Stover's conclusion, in keeping with the revisionist finding, is that northern men and money extended their influence over virtually the entire railroad complex of the South.[70]

The whole field of southern economic growth badly needs attention, for many current generalizations rest on shaky foundations. Robert S. Smith's study of Danville cotton mills, though concerned primarily with the twentieth century, is an example of the kind of meticulous company history required in quantity.[71] Anthony Tang's study of economic development in the southern Piedmont, though, like Smith's work, largely devoted to the twentieth century, reveals what can be done by careful analysis.[72] Another welcomed approach would be a study within the framework of economic theory along the lines of Conrad and Meyer's essay on the profitability of slavery.[73] For the time being, as we await both the theoretical and empirical studies, an extraordinarily useful compendium of economic data to be exploited is Everett S. Lee and others, *Population Redistribution and Economic Growth: The United States, 1870–1950* (Philadelphia, 1957).

Tracing the shifting interpretations of the Redeemer era, as attempted

67 Ezell, *The South Since 1865* (New York, 1963), 136, 152.

68 Clark, *The Emerging South* (New York, 1961), 35.

69 Nicholls, *Southern Tradition and Regional Progress* (Chapel Hill, 1960).

70 See also Stover, "Northern Financial Interests in Southern Railroads, 1865–1900," *Georgia Historical Quarterly*, XXXIX (September, 1955), 205–20.

71 Smith, *Mill on the Dan: A History of Dan River Mills, 1882–1950* (Durham, 1960).

72 Tang, *Economic Development in the Southern Piedmont, 1860–1950, Its Impact on Agriculture* (Chapel Hill, 1958).

73 Alfred H. Conrad and John R. Meyer, "The Economics of Slavery in the Ante Bellum South," *Journal of Political Economy*, LXVI (April, 1958), 95–130.

in this essay, raises a number of intriguing questions. Studying the original New South idea leads one to wonder why it had such appeal and persistence, what gave its spokesmen their persuasiveness and ability to deceive others as well as themselves, and why it aroused such enduring partisanship and antagonisms in contemporaries as well as in their descendants.

In trying to understand the New South historians, one feels almost as though they were looking through a powerful telescope. The background against which their histories were written heightened the contrasts and exaggerated the images they saw. They saw southern economic achievements against a scene of grinding poverty, increasing political power and self-determination against an experience of galling powerlessness, attempts at reconciliation against the legacy of hatred and mistrust, and concessions to the Negro against a backdrop of slavery and black codes. It is not surprising that in describing their region's attempt to don the mantle of the American heritage they were lured into admiring the emperor's new clothes. Today, the South's more cosmopolitan historians see the region's history silhouetted against American and world experience; and bitter southern memories are no longer so potent. The most thoroughgoing of the revisionists reveal New South claims in all their factitiousness and find the era that gave birth to them barren and stultifying. Like the child in Andersen's fairy tale, they look at the emperor and exclaim, "But he has got nothing on!"

It is thus clear that New South historians and revisionists alike have shared a fundamental moral concern, a sense of the responsibility to judge, not simply describe, the past. In large measure, the "facts" upon which the changing interpretations have rested have not changed, but values have undergone a revolution. Thus, within the framework of their own value judgments, the earlier historians created an image of inspiration; later historians replaced it with a picture of near degradation. The trend of the future is uncertain. Increasing demand for detailed and impartial testing of current generalizations suggests that the next stage may involve less attention to ultimate meaning. On the other hand, the potent paradoxes and contrasts of the period itself will continue to confront historians with the perennial task of explaining the mentality of the era and the inheritance that it bequeathed.

XIV

Southern Negroes Since Reconstruction: Dissolving the Static Image

George B. Tindall

O NE of the most useful insights of historiography is summed up in the term "frame of reference." [1] With the best of intentions the historian cannot completely transcend the human limitations imposed by the temper of his times, his regional identification, his race, or causes that arouse his sympathies. His view of historical reality, the very selection of the facts with which he is concerned, inevitably will be shaped and distorted by the perspective in which he views them.

The student who ventures into American Negro historiography will repeatedly find his vision of the terrain blurred by these conditions. Equipped with the perspective of the 1960's, he may soon discover that a fundamental difficulty arises from the historical context in which the

1 The author wishes to express appreciation for a critical reading of this essay by Professors Lawrence Dunbar Reddick and the late Vernon Lane Wharton.

writing of Negro history had its origins. Except in the faintest begin-nings, it started in the twentieth-century age of segregation and has yet to escape the peculiarly static image of the Negro's status associated with that age. The new dispensation of white supremacy at the turn of the century very quickly acquired the sanctions of a supposedly hoary antiquity and the appearance of immutability—almost immediately after the upheavals of emancipation, Reconstruction, and Populism. The place of the Negro had been defined, at least in its major outlines. It was no longer an open question. "All such relationships will work themselves out gradually, naturally, quietly, in the long course of years," Ray Stannard Baker, a Northern journalist, wrote in 1908, "and the less they are talked about the better." [2]

The static image has seriously inhibited the development of Negro historiography, for history is fundamentally an evolutionary study and historians are strongly drawn to the investigation of evolutionary de-velopments and dynamic movements. These exist in abundance in Negro history, of course; the rise of slavery, antislavery, the Civil War and emancipation, Reconstruction. Yet, even in most studies of slavery the institution appears as a relatively stable social order and in most Recon-struction studies, as Vernon Wharton has pointed out, "the Negro ap-pears as intruder." [3] In the general American or southern historical studies, Negroes seldom appear as actors with vital roles or collectively as a positive social force. They appear as an undifferentiated background, as subjects to be acted upon, but not as people whose affairs have innate significance. Especially in post-Reconstruction historiography they have suffered less from racial prejudice than from a "bias by omission." [4]

For most of the nineteenth century the "Negro question," in terms of emancipation or Reconstruction, occupied a position so near the center of the stage that it could hardly be overlooked. After Reconstruction the Negro question ceased to be a consuming national issue. The subsequent diffusion of Negro life and development, though it marked the emerg-ence of a more complex culture, lacked the dynamic appeal of a central

2 Baker, *Following the Color Line: An Account of Negro Citizenship in the American Democracy* (New York, 1908), 305.

3 Wharton, "Historical Literature of the Negro as Freedman," paper delivered to the Southern Historical Association, Williamsburg, Virginia, November 10, 1949, p. 1.

4 Maurice M. Vance, "The Negro in the Literature of American History," in *The Negro in American Society* ("Florida State University Series," No. 28 [Talla-hassee, 1958]), 81. See also Marie Elizabeth Carpenter, *The Treatment of the Negro in American History School Textbooks* (Menasha, Wisconsin, 1941), which is broader in coverage than its title indicates.

public issue and so moved into the limbo of historiography. The Negro question was a social problem and therefore preeminently the subject matter of sociologists, amateur and professional, who were absorbed in contemporary conditions and slighted the temporal perspective of history.[5] Their focus gave a somewhat flat and static dimension to most of the literature on the Negro, and occasionally permitted serious misconceptions to develop regarding, for example, such issues as the evolution of segregation.[6] The result was that the latter decades of the nineteenth century, as they receded below the horizon of living memory, became the great *terra incognita* of Negro history, and the twentieth century became a kind of *terra sociologica.* It was only with the development of an increasing fluidity and militancy in Negro life that the temper of the times began to adjust historical perspectives into new focus.

The first efforts of white southern writers to treat systematically the Negro after Reconstruction were deeply affected by the static view. Early treatises by Philip Alexander Bruce and Alfred Holt Stone were based in large part upon observations of plantation labor in Virginia and Mississippi and heavily weighted with predilections for white supremacy and Negro inferiority.[7] Howard Washington Odum's first book was on the whole a grim and discouraging picture of Negro shortcomings, drawn in large measure from personal observations on folklore expeditions in Georgia and Mississippi.[8] None of these writers saw much hope for Negro advancement, and Bruce, in fact, saw a process of retrogression toward barbarism. In 1914 Odum's former teacher at the University of Mississippi, Thomas Pierce Bailey, plumbed the depths of pessimism by frankly expressing no hope for any real change or "solution" except by colonization. Roughly similar in outlook were the observations of the northern writers Ray Stannard Baker, Albert Bushnell Hart, George Spring Merriam, and Joseph Alexander Tillinghast shortly after the

5 No effort will be made here to survey the immense sociological literature although it contains much valuable material for historians. For basic bibliographies see Gunnar Myrdal, *An American Dilemma: The Negro Problem and Modern Democracy* (New York and London, 1944), 1114–80; and George Eaton Simpson and John Milton Yinger, *Racial and Cultural Minorities: An Analysis of Prejudice and Discrimination* (New York, 1958), 817–51.

6 Consult C. Vann Woodward, *The Strange Career of Jim Crow* (New York, 1955).

7 Bruce, *The Plantation Negro as a Freeman* (New York, 1889); Stone, *Studies in the American Race Problem* (New York, 1908).

8 Odum, *Social and Mental Traits of the Negro* (New York, 1910). Odum's outlook changed drastically in later years.

turn of the century.[9] None of these was or could be very well informed with a historical perspective on the New South.

One unusual book stands in striking contrast to these pessimistic accounts. Pasted together by a white Texas minister, the Reverend James Jefferson Pipkin, it drew from Negro sources a sympathetic account of individual Negro achievements, even in politics and military service; it included a variety of contributed essays and reprinted speeches. Pipkin undertook to show, in the spirit of Christianity and patriotism, "the Negro's capabilities, his honorable ambition to improve his enterprise, and his remarkable progress."[10] But his progressive image was more characteristic of Negro writers.

Other beginnings were sponsored by the Phelps-Stokes Fund. As one of its first projects, the fund in 1912 established endowments at the state universities of Virginia and Georgia "to stimulate . . . investigation and to encourage and guide a wider interest among students concerning the character, condition and possibilities of the Negro in the Southern States."[11] Most of the studies published by Phelps-Stokes Fellows at both institutions reflected the "problem" approach to current social and economic conditions, but the Virginia series as early as 1919 issued a monograph, *The Negro in Virginia Politics, 1865–1902,* that is still a useful guide to the facts but is informed by the author's conclusion that the "increasing harmony existing between the two races could only have come through the removal of the negro from sectionalism and politics."[12] But in all the twenty volumes of Virginia studies only three more were devoted to historical subjects.[13] At Georgia the score was only three

9 Baker, *Following the Color Line;* Hart, *The Southern South* (New York and London, 1910); Merriam, *The Negro and the Nation: A History of American Slavery and Enfranchisement* (New York, 1906); Tillinghast, *The Negro in Africa and America* ("Publications of the American Economic Association," 3rd Series, Vol. III, No. 2 [New York, 1902]). A convenient survey of the literature in the period by white authors may be found in Guion Griffis Johnson, "The Ideology of White Supremacy, 1876–1910," in Fletcher M. Green (ed.), *Essays in Southern History* (Chapel Hill, 1949), 124–56.

10 Pipkin, *The Story of a Rising Race: The Negro in Revelation in History and in Citizenship* (Saint Louis and New York, 1902), Preface.

11 *Lectures and Adresses on the Negro in the South* ("Phelps-Stokes Fellowship Papers," No. 1 [Charlottesville, 1915]), 3; James Hardy Dillard et al., *Twenty Year Report of the Phelps-Stokes Fund, 1911–1931* (New York, 1932), 57.

12 Richard Lee Morton, *The Negro in Virginia Politics, 1865–1902.* ("Phelps-Stokes Fellowship Papers," No. 4 [Charlottesville, 1919]), 6. For an extremely critical review, see *The Journal of Negro History,* V (January, 1920), 126–28.

13 William Henry Brown, *The Education and Economic Development of the Negro in Virginia* ("Phelps-Stokes Fellowship Papers," No. 6 [Charlottesville, 1923]); Raymond B. Pinchbeck, *The Virginia Negro Artisan and Tradesman*

historical studies out of fifteen, the earliest not written until 1930.[14]

If the Phelps-Stokes Fellows produced no historical studies of transcendent significance, they did add to the sociological literature that could serve future historians as sources. And they represented the slow evolution of concern with Negro life as a subject for empirical research. They were part of a trend toward more thoughtful and sympathetic attitudes among southern whites that began to flower into the interracial movement during the years from 1910 to 1919. This "New Reconstruction," as one of its leaders extravagantly labeled it, sought "better education . . . , higher moral ideals and a socialized religion, . . . increasing cooperation . . . , and greater publicity for those whose views are based on reason rather than prejudice and tradition," but it carefully avoided any challenge to disfranchisement and segregation.[15]

Willis Duke Weatherford of the Young Men's Christian Association was a central figure in the nascent interracial movement. Active during the first decade of the twentieth century in developing student study groups on the race problem, Weatherford produced the first textbook in the field in 1910.[16] In 1924 he published *The Negro from Africa to America,* which remains the best survey of Negro history by a white writer. The tone was that of history with a purpose. Like his earlier works, this book expresses with sympathetic understanding an interest in the Negro's betterment. It was "an attempt to help white men know the background, the traditional material on which the Negro race acts . . . an attempt to connect present conditions with the near and far past." [17] Nearly half the book was devoted to the Negro after slavery, with no

---

("Phelps-Stokes Fellowship Papers," No. 7 [Richmond, 1926]) ; Nancy Armstrong, *The Study of an Attempt Made in 1943 to Abolish Segregation of the Races on Common Carriers in the State of Virginia* ("Phelps-Stokes Fellowship Papers," No. 17 [Charlottesvile, 1950]).

14 John William Fanning, *Negro Migration* ("Phelps-Stokes Fellowship Studies," No. 9 [Athens, 1930]) ; Ralph Wilkinson Wardlaw, *Negro Suffrage in Georgia, 1867–1930* ("Phelps-Stokes Fellowship Studies," No. 11 [Athens, 1932]) ; Willard Range, *The Rise and Progress of Negro Colleges in Georgia, 1865–1949* ("Phelps-Stokes Fellowship Studies," No. 15 [Athens, 1951]).

15 William Oscar Scroggs, "The New Reconstruction," in *Lectures and Addresses on the Negro in the South,* 59–64.

16 Weatherford, *Negro Life in the South* (New York, 1910). See also his *Present Forces in Negro Progress* (New York, 1918). These were later supplanted by Thomas Jackson Woofter, Jr., *The Basis of Racial Adjustment* (Boston, 1925), Weatherford and Charles Spurgeon Johnson, *Race Relations* (Boston, 1934), and by standard sociological treatises for established credit courses on the Negro. See also William Winton Alexander, "Southern White Schools Study Race Questions," *Journal of Negro Education,* II (April, 1933), 139–46.

17 Weatherford, *The Negro from Africa to America* (New York, 1924), 20.

treatment of the Civil War or Reconstruction. From the readily-available sources and his own experience, Weatherford drew great catalogs of information on current economic and social conditions, the law, education, Negro self-expression and leadership, and the "constructive movements" for uplift, which did not include the National Association for the Advancement of Colored People, the National Urban League, or Negro nationalist movements. It was a useful compendium but scarcely either narrative or analytical history, and the *terra incognita* of the nineteenth century remained untouched.

The static image not only reflected the apparent realities of the situation, it also served an important function in the rationale of white supremacy. In the nature of things, it never so thoroughly inhibited the Negro writers as it did the white. Early Negro surveyors of conditions in the post-Reconstruction South, T. Thomas Fortune and Daniel Augustus Straker, drew broader pictures that included evidences of advancement and delineated more sharply the restraints imposed by white supremacy.[18] The first Negro historians also felt the inevitable compulsion to be "race men," to resurrect a usable Negro past that would serve the purposes of racial pride and undermine assumptions of Negro inferiority. In 1883 George Washington Williams, a Pennsylvania Baptist minister and veteran of the Civil War, published his monumental two-volume *History of the Negro Race in America from 1619 to 1880*, the first work on the subject to receive serious scholarly praise. But it scarcely touched the period after Reconstruction.[19] It was followed over the next three decades by a number of one-volume histories of the Negro which mostly conformed to the description given to one of them: "This volume is a controversial treatise supplemented here and there by facts of Negro life and history." [20] History as inspirational literature appeared in Booker Taliaferro Washington's two-volume *The Story of the Negro*.[21] The book is especially interesting for its wealth of

18 Fortune, *Black and White: Land, Labor and Politics in the South* (New York, 1884); Straker, *The New South Investigated* (Detroit, 1888).

19 Williams, *History of the Negro Race in America from 1619 to 1880* (2 vols.; New York, 1883).

20 J. O. Burke, review of Charles Victor Roman, *American Civilization and the Negro* (Philadelphia, 1916), in *The Journal of Negro History*, I (April, 1916), 218. See also William T. Alexander, *History of the Colored Race in America* (Kansas City, Missouri, 1887); Edward Augustus Johnson, *A School History of the Negro Race in America, from 1619 to 1890* (Raleigh, 1890); Harold McBride Tower, *The Negro in the History of the United States from the Beginning of English Settlement in America, 1607, to the Present Time* (Austin, Texas, 1905).

21 Washington, *The Story of the Negro: The Rise of the Race from Slavery* (New York, 1909).

anecdotes and illustrations drawn from the author's own career and contacts. It is notable, also, as the first to give much factual treatment to the post-Reconstruction period. Benjamin Griffith Brawley's *A Short History of the American Negro* moved argument to the background and marshalled facts into an organized pattern.[22] In the first edition, approximately a fourth of the space was given to the post-Reconstruction period; a pattern of Negro development emerged in subsequent editions, though it was never more than an outline and the book devoted much space to sketches of accomplished Negroes in various fields. Similar short histories followed over the years, mostly episodic chronicles for which there seemed to be a persistent market.[23]

Most of them were products of haphazard research, and at least through Brawley's earlier editions they challenged the static image of Negro life only by tracing the threads of individual achievements. In such histories, Lawrence Dunbar Reddick later complained, the "purpose-philosophy" of Negro historians took shape within a framework of naive Emersonian self-reliance, simple optimism, and patient regard for destiny. In the traditional story, "talented Negroes through hard work and high faith have leaped over all hurdles to success. Conditions are becoming better and better. If we will but work a little harder, save a little more, establish a few more businesses and *get educated,* we will some day receive our rightful place at the table of democracy, praise God from whom all blessings flow!" [24] But a new ferment in Negro historiography was at work soon after Brawley's first edition appeared.

The beginning of scholarly Negro studies came with the emergence of William Edward Burghardt DuBois and Carter Godwin Woodson. DuBois, the first Negro to earn a Harvard Ph.D., began in the 1890's a series of conferences on Negro problems at Atlanta University. Published annually from 1896 to 1914, the papers presented at these meetings have been described as "the first real sociological research in the South" constituting a "current encyclopedia on the American Negro

22 Brawley, *A Short History of the American Negro* (New York, 1913).

23 Edwin Rogers Embree, *Brown America: The Story of a New Race* (New York, 1931); Merl R. Eppse, *The Negro, Too, in American History* (Nashville, 1938); John George Van Deusen, *The Black Man in White America* (Washington, 1938); Roi Ottley, *Black Odyssey: The Story of the Negro in America* (New York, 1948); Anna Bontemps, *Story of the Negro* (New York, 1948); Jay Saunders Redding, *They Came in Chains: Americans from Africa* (Philadelphia, 1950).

24 Reddick, "A New Interpretation for Negro History," *The Journal of Negro History,* XXII (January, 1937), 23–24. See also Evarts Boutell Greene, "Perspectives in History," *The Journal of Negro History,* XVII (January, 1932), 8–18.

problems." [25] But DuBois, who wrote a distinguished study of the suppression of the African slave trade and later a controversial interpretation of Reconstruction, was soon drawn into an active life as a publicist and leader of Negro causes. He became himself a historical figure whose writings constitute an important source for historians of the Negro, but his own career as historian was somewhat limited.

A major milestone in Negro historiography was the founding in 1915 of the association for the Study of Negro Life and History. Carter G. Woodson, the founder and guiding figure until his death in 1950, was a native of Virginia, was graduated from Berea College in 1903, a year before the Kentucky legislature required it to segregate, studied at the Sorbonne and the University of Chicago, took a Harvard M.A. and Ph.D. and taught high school in Washington, D.C.[26] By the force of his own vigorous personality he stamped on the association the peculiar amalgam of race patriotism and historical professionalism that it has retained to this day. And by his persistent hammering year in and year out, he forged a revolution in Negro historiography.

Woodson boldly plunged his new association into debt in January, 1916, to bring out the first issue of *The Journal of Negro History,* which soon became one of the standard professional quarterlies. At the same time Woodson himself made some pioneering forays into special aspects of Negro history: books on antebellum education (1915), migration (1918), the church (1921), and various articles in the *Journal. The Negro in Our History* followed in 1922 and remained the most satisfactory survey for twenty-five years.[27] Fuller than Brawley's short history, it was also more militant in tone. Devoting about a fourth of its space to post-Reconstruction history, it recounted in those latter pages a summary of the Negro's wrongs together with some evidences of progress, gave a lengthy treatment of the Negro soldier in the First World War, and closed with a remarkable chapter outlining the militancy of the New Negro that was as much a summons to action as it was history.

25 Guy Benton Johnson, quoted in John Hope Franklin, *From Slavery to Freedom* (New York, 1947), 401.

26 *Who Was Who in America,* III, 1951–1960 (Chicago, 1960), 938; Charles Harris Wesley, "Carter G. Woodson—as a Scholar," *The Journal of Negro History,* XXXVI (January, 1951), 12–24.

27 Woodson, *The Education of the Negro Prior to 1861* (New York and London, 1915); *A Century of Negro Migration* (Washington, 1918); *The History of the Negro Church* (Washington, 1921); *The Negro in Our History* (Washington, 1922).

By 1921 the association was sufficiently well established to merit the confidence of the Carnegie and Laura Spelman Rockefeller foundations, each of which gave grants of $25,000 for the promotion of Negro studies. With additional grants from these and other sources, the association became in the 1920's and 1930's a fountainhead of monographs on Negro life and history.[28] Its investigators included Woodson, Alrutheus Ambush Taylor, Lorenzo Johnston Greene, Rayford Whittingham Logan, Charles Harris Wesley, Myra Colson-Callis, and James Hugo Johnston. Their subjects included the Negro in Africa and Spanish America, the free Negro in the United States, Reconstruction, and Negro wage earners, rural workers, the church, business, and professional men.[29] Woodson gathered a collection of more than five thousand manuscripts on Negro history and presented it to the Library of Congress. Meanwhile, the association also worked toward popularization of Negro history through observations of Negro History Week after 1926 and the publication of a monthly, *The Negro History Bulletin* after 1937.[30]

The beginnings inspired by Carter G. Woodson coincided with new dynamics in Negro life, the rise of the New Negro as reflected in militant race movements and the Negro Renaissance in literature.[31] These reinforced Woodson's efforts to loosen thought from its old framework. There was a new spirit of emancipation by the twenties, but it was not only a release from the "Emersonian" gospel of individual success. It was, paradoxically, at the same time an emancipation from race movements and static interracialism and all the anthropological polemics and theorizing that accompanied them. Monographic literature began to present empirical studies in the evolutionary development of Negro life. Negro history was falling into the hands of trained university men who viewed it in a larger social and economic framework. L. D. Reddick, under the contemporary spell of economic interpretation, put it this way: ". . . when we see the story of the Negro since Emancipation as the record of the clashes and rationalizations of individual and group impulses against an American social order

28 Woodson, "An Accounting for Twenty-five Years," *The Journal of Negro History*, XXV (October, 1940), 424–25.

29 See *ibid.*, 426–27, for a list of these studies. Those pertinent to this essay will be considered later.

30 *Ibid.*, 428–29.

31 Alain Le Roy Locke, *The New Negro: An Interpretation* (New York, 1925) is an anthology of the literary renaissance.

of an unfolding capitalism, within which operates [*sic*] semi-articulate arrangements and etiquettes of class and caste, we begin to understand the rise of, say, Booker T. Washington, the furore of lynching in the 1890's, and the attitude toward the black worker of the American Federation of Labor." [32] But it was broader than that. Historical monographs finally began in some detail to reclaim the *terra incognita* and *terra sociologica* and to reshape the old static image. In the process the contrast between white and Negro writers began to diminish.

The new dynamics in both Negro life and historiography paralleled the most significant development of twentieth-century Negro history, the "great migration" from the South. Beginning in the era of the First World War, it brought the net loss of some 323,000 Negroes from the Southeast, followed by another 615,000 in the twenties. By 1960 about 46 percent of all Negro Americans were living outside the South.[33] Dramatically altering the static image of Negro life, the migration also constituted in itself a conspicuously appropriate subject for study, and it became one of the most thoroughly documented developments of Negro history. Before it was well under way the Department of Labor sponsored a series of expert field investigations that were published in 1919.[34] The first overall secondary account, in 1920, was by Emmett J. Scott, former secretary to Booker T. Washington and wartime advisor to the Secretary of War.[35] A more analytical treatment, based on broad study of the voluminous sources, came in Henderson Hamilton Donald's account which filled an entire issue of *The Journal of Negro History* and later appeared as a book.[36] Woodson meanwhile set it in the broader perspective of a century's migrations.[37] Toward the end of the twenties Columbia University sponsored a study project that resulted in the most satisfactory account, summarizing what already had appeared,

32 Reddick, "A New Interpretation for Negro History," *The Journal of Negro History*, XXII (January, 1937), 26.

33 Rupert Baird Vance, *All These People: The Nation's Human Resources in the South* (Chapel Hill, 1945), 119. See also *Statistical Abstract of the United States, 1962* (Washington, 1962), 30.

34 U.S. Department of Labor, Division of Negro Economics, *Negro Migration in 1916–17* (Washington, 1919).

35 Scott, *Negro Migration During the War* (New York, 1920).

36 Donald, *The Negro Migration of 1916–1918* (Washington, 1921), reprinted from *The Journal of Negro History*, VI (October, 1921).

37 Woodson, *A Century of Negro Migration.* See also Anna Bontemps and Jack Conroy, *They Seek a City* (Garden City, New York, 1945) for a good popular account.

adding new materials, analyzing causes and effects and readjustments in the new communities.[38]

The great migration produced other effects on Negro historiography. In altering the static image it also diffused the Southern focus. Largely a migration of labor, it turned attention more strongly toward the Negro masses. Both of these influences were reflected in the pioneering history of Negro labor by Charles Harris Wesley, a Woodson protégé. Wesley demonstrated with some force that Negro labor, displaced in many of the old skills in the South, had found compensating outlets in new occupations. He strongly challenged with evidence the entrenched myth that Negroes were incompetent to operate machinery and traced in some detail their unsuccessful struggle for acceptance in organized labor.[39] Sterling Denhard Spero and Abram Lincoln Harris were less argumentative and wrote "neither a good will tract on race relations nor an attempt to offer a program for the solution of a vexing problem." [40] They concentrated on developments after the Civil War, giving special attention to the South in extensive treatments of longshoremen, coal miners, and railroad workers. A fuller overall picture was presented by Lorenzo Johnston Greene and Woodson in a book heavily weighted with statistics.[41] The paths opened by these historians, however, have not been followed since, though Horace R. Cayton and George Sinclair Mitchell study intensively the status of Negroes in organized labor during the thirties, centering on steel in the North, railroad car shops, and the Birmingham area.[42] A more extensive study by Herbert Roof Northrup traced the whole issue from its origins.[43]

The entrepreneurial side of Negro economic life was first considered in a careful analysis of Negro banking by Abram Lincoln Harris, which gave extensive attention only to Virginia in the South.[44] William

38 Louise Venable Kennedy, *The Negro Peasant Turns Cityward* (New York, 1930). The project also resulted in the publication of Frank Alexander Ross and Kennedy, *A Bibliography of Negro Migration* (New York, 1935) and three more specialized monographs including Clyde Vernon Kiser, *Sea Island to City* (New York, 1932), a study of migrants from Saint Helena Island, South Carolina, to New York City. The project was supported by the Social Science Research Council and the Columbia University Council for Research in the Social Sciences.

39 Wesley, *Negro Labor in the United States* (New York, 1927).

40 Spero and Harris, *The Black Worker: The Negro and the Labor Movement* (New York, 1931), vii.

41 Greene and Woodson, *The Negro Wage Earner* (Washington, 1930).

42 Cayton and Mitchell, *Black Workers and the New Unions* (Chapel Hill, 1939).

43 Northrup, *Organized Labor and the Negro* (New York and London, 1944).

44 Harris, *The Negro as Capitalist: A Study of Banking and Business Among American Negroes* (Philadelphia, 1936).

Johnson Trent's M.A. thesis, an account of Negro insurance companies, suffers from its brief scope. It was supplemented in 1940 with an extensive but uncritical compendium by the historian of the National Negro Insurance Association, Merah Steven Stuart.[45] The controversy over separation and integration in Negro business was given only a superficial coverage by Robert H. Kinzer and Edward Sagarin.[46] The Negro professional man received extended coverage in Woodson's *The Negro Professional Man,* based upon extensive field surveys and contracts, but its historical content is limited.[47]

In politics the consequences of the great migration were dramatically demonstrated by the election of the first northern Negro congressman in 1928, by a show of Negro power in preventing confirmation of John J. Parker for the Supreme Court in 1930, and by an abrupt shift of Negro voters to the Democratic party during the New Deal. In 1930 Paul Lewinson undertook to investigate Negro political activity and disfranchisement in the South, throwing some new light into the twilight period after Reconstruction and demonstrating that even after disfranchisement Negro political activity had continued, influencing local elections over many years in Memphis and San Antonio and at times in other cities.[48] William Felbert Nowlin's account of the Negro in national politics in the following year provided a useful collection of facts on southern Republicans but gave them little organization or analysis.[49] William Alexander Mabry in 1938 published at Duke University the results of extensive researches on Negro disfranchisement in four states and a later survey of the Negro in North Carolina politics.[50] Robert E. Martin narrated the disfranchisement movement in Virginia.[51]

New perspectives on Negroes in politics were presented by Luther Porter Jackson, who dredged up from obscurity Negro officeholders in

45 Trent, *Development of Negro Life Insurance Enterprises* (Philadelphia, 1932); Stuart, *An Economic Detour: A History of Insurance in the Lives of American Negroes* (New York, 1940).

46 Kinzer and Sagarin, *The Negro in American Business: The Conflict Between Separation and Integration* (New York, 1950).

47 Woodson, *The Negro Professional Man and the Community, With Special Emphasis on the Physician and Lawyer* (Washington, 1934).

48 Lewinson, *Race, Class, and Party. A History of Negro Suffrage and White Politics in the South* (London and New York, 1932).

49 Nowlin, *The Negro in American National Politics* (Boston, 1931).

50 Mabry, *Studies in the Disfranchisement of the Negro in the South* (Durham, 1938), and *The Negro in North Carolina Politics Since Reconstruction* (Durham, 1940).

51 Martin, *Negro Disfranchisement in Virginia* ("Howard University Studies in the Social Sciences," I [Washington, 1938]), 49–188.

Virginia and presented brief sketches designed to demonstrate that they were not universally ignorant and propertyless.[52] A more satisfactory and detailed monograph on Negro politics was Helen Gray Edmonds' study of North Carolina in the 1890's. Dealing with the period when Democratic division and Populist fusion with the Republicans brought Negroes into more significant political participation, Miss Edmonds demonstrated that the extent of their participation had been highly exaggerated in Democratic propaganda, that Negroes held a proportion of offices far below their proportion of population, and that this was a transitory phenomenon of the Populist era.[53] More recently, two excellent studies of southern Republican politics from Reconstruction to the nineties, while emphasizing national policy, have given complementary pictures of the Negro question in southern politics. Vincent P. DeSantis has focused upon the Republican search for a formula to rewin the South. Stanley P. Hirshson, by emphasizing the role of northern business (among other factors) in the eventual Republican abandonment of southern Negroes, has given support to Reddick's suggestion that developments of the period must be considered against a background of unfolding capitalism.[54] An altogether different theme was pursued by Elbert Lee Tatum, who surveyed a quarter century of lily-white ascendancy in the Republican party and Negro drift toward the Democrats, 1915–1940.[55] The failure of American Communists to lure Negroes into their camp was the subject of a more fully researched and satisfactory study by Wilson Record.[56]

Scholarly pursuit of institutional and cultural history encounters difficult obstacles in the diffuse nature of its subject and the fugitive quality of its sources. These problems are reflected in the uneven and diffuse quality of the first attempt at an intellectual history of American Negroes by Earlie Endris Thorpe. His book is not an integrated history of Negro thought but is, instead, a miscellany of essays held together

52 Jackson, *Negro Officeholders in Virginia, 1865–1895* (Norfolk, 1945).

53 Edmonds, *The Negro and Fusion Politics in North Carolina, 1894–1901* (Chapel Hill, 1951).

54 DeSantis, *Republicans Face the Southern Question: The New Departure Years, 1877–1897* (Baltimore, 1959); Hirshson, *Farewell to the Bloody Shirt: Northern Republicans and the Southern Negro, 1877–1893* (Bloomington, Indiana, 1962).

55 Tatum, *The Changed Political Thought of the Negro, 1915–1940* (New York, 1951).

56 Record, *The Negro and the Communist Party* (Chapel Hill, 1951). See also his *Race and Radicalism: The NAACP and the Communist Party in Conflict* (Ithaca, New York, 1964), and William A. Nolan, *Communism versus the Negro* (Chicago, 1951).

loosely by the author's thesis that "the central theme of Negro thought has been the quest for freedom and equality." [57] At the same time, he finds that the Negro masses, "southerners always, have been directly influenced by many of the same geographical and cultural factors which W. J. Cash so excellently outlined in his *The Mind of the South*." [58] Both the masses, through their folklore and occasional spokesmen, and race leaders appear in the broad panorama that Thorpe has developed from a diversity of original sources and secondary works.

A narrower area was treated more systematically and cogently by Rayford W. Logan in *The Negro in American Life and Thought: The Nadir, 1877–1901*. A study of the dismal period in Negro history after Reconstruction, it pictures the road to reunion as also the road to reaction. "The Terminal at the end . . . was massive and . . . ugly. On the pediments of the separate wing reserved for Negroes were carved Exploitation, Disfranchisement, Segregation, Discrimination, Lynching, Contempt." [59] The book elucidated some previously neglected aspects of the story and was particularly valuable for its treatment of national politics and racial attitudes in the North.

August Meier's *Negro Thought in America, 1880–1915*, carried the story on to that great watershed of Negro history marked by the death of Booker T. Washington, the great migration, and the emergence of the New Negro.[60] In the process he significantly illuminated the complex themes of racial ideologies within the Negro community, the paradoxes arising from the dual identity of a people both Negro and American, in the process of developing a racial pride and separate institutions without abandoning the ultimate goals of civil rights and integration. Meier explored the expressed thoughts of articulate Negroes, but he also pursued general trends through their institutional expressions: the convention movement, churches, schools, fraternal societies, and self-help groups. He undertook, on the whole successfully, to relate trends in racial ideologies to broader trends in the social thought and forces of the day. An important contribution for the period it covered, the book has also cleared the path and pointed the way for next steps toward examination of the New Negro and civil rights movements.

57 Thorpe, *The Mind of the Negro: An Intellectual History of Afro-Americans* (Baton Rouge, Ortlieb Press, 1961), xi.

58 *Ibid.*, xx.

59 Logan, *The Negro in American Life and Thought: The Nadir, 1877–1901* (New York, 1954), 314.

60 Meier, *Negro Thought in America, 1880–1915: Racial Ideologies in the Age of Booker T. Washington* (Ann Arbor, Michigan, 1963).

The obstacles to institutional and cultural history are less stubborn in the field of education than some others. Documentary materials, surveys, college histories, and biographical sketches of educational leaders abound. Among the earliest efforts to draw these materials into organized histories, the studies of higher education by Ullin Whitney Leavell and Dwight Oliver Wendell Holmes stand out as the most successful.[61] Identifying and tracing the major trends in the founding of Negro colleges and their emergence from secondary school status in the twenties, they present sound narratives of the major developments in philanthropy and higher education. The promise of broader perspectives on Negro education was offered by Horace Mann Bond, with a general history of Negro education followed by a more satisfying study of Alabama.[62] The latter, set in the broader perspectives of state politics and strongly emphasizing the economic context of the demand for cheap labor as a rationalization for inferior Negro education, is among the best histories of southern Negroes since Reconstruction. The excellence of Bond's state study unfortunately has been emulated in only one subsequent work, Willard Range's careful survey of the development of Negro colleges in Georgia out of the post-Civil War missionary schools, climaxed by the emergence of a modern university in Atlanta in the 1930's and 1940's. Charles H. Wilson's account of Mississippi schools is episodic, unscholarly, and excruciatingly roseate, while Lewis Kennedy McMillan's critique of higher education in South Carolina is the well-documented complaint of an angry scholar at the inadequacies of Negro education.[63] Louis R. Harlan developed another approach in his thorough and critical study of white supremacy influences in the early twentieth-century crusades for public education.[64] This book did not, however, reach into the period of increasing support for Negro schools after 1920.

Other aspects of institutional and cultural life have been less exten-

61 Leavell, *Philanthropy in Negro Education* (Nashville, 1930); Holmes, *Evolution of the Negro College* (New York, 1934).

62 Bond, *The Education of the Negro in the American Social Order* (New York, 1934), and *Negro Education in Alabama. A Study in Cotton and Steel* (Washington, 1939).

63 Range, *The Rise and Progress of Negro Colleges in Georgia, 1865-1949;* Wilson, *Education for Negroes in Mississippi Since 1910* (Boston, 1947); McMillan, *Negro Higher Education in the State of South Carolina* (Orangeburg, South Carolina, 1953). See also Luther Porter Jackson, *A History of the Virginia State Teachers Association* (Norfolk, 1937), and Lance George Edward Jones, *The Jeanes Teacher in the United States, 1908-1933* (Chapel Hill, 1937).

64 Harlan, *Separate and Unequal: Public School Campaigns and Racism in the Southern Seaboard States, 1901-1915* (Chapel Hill, 1958).

sively studied. Woodson's pioneering *History of the Negro Church,* largely devoted to beginnings and giving little attention to the New South, may be supplemented only by sociological studies, official and uncritical church histories, and inspirational biographies that constitute source materials rather than histories. The pioneering student of Negro authors was Benjamin Brawley, but critical attention to this field came with Vernon Loggins' survey of Negro writers to 1900, followed by the studies of Sterling Allen Brown, Hugh Morris Gloster, Blyden Jackson, Robert A. Bone, and Carl Milton Hughes.[65] The Negro press has been surveyed in an early encyclopedic volume by Irvine Garland Penn and a briefer critical survey by Frederick German Detweiler.[66] Both are now seriously out of date.

Negro contributions in music and the arts were surveyed by Alain Le Roy Locke and Mrs. Maud Cuney-Hare.[67] Perhaps the major contribution of southern Negroes to the arts, jazz, has become the subject of a tremendous popular literature and some critical history.[68] And Margaret Just Butcher has undertaken to survey the whole broad field of Negro contributions and influences in American culture.[69]

Jazz constitutes only the most spectacular aspect of a Negro folk culture that has proved a rich vein for sociologists and folklorists but has remained unworked by historians. The outstanding example of what may be done with a historical perspective in the field has been offered by Edward Franklin Frazier's sociological history of the Negro family, tracing its evolution from the matriarchal family of slavery and the rural South into the patriarchal family and development of middle class mores together with the unfettered life of roving men and women and the

65 Brawley, *The Negro in Literature and Art in the United States* (New York, 1918); Brown, *The Negro in American Fiction* (Washington, 1937), and *Negro Poetry and Drama* (Washington, 1937); Gloster, *Negro Voices in American Fiction* (Chapel Hill, 1948); Hughes, *The Negro Novelist: A Discussion of the Writings of American Negro Novelists, 1940–1950* (New York, 1953); Bone, *The Negro Novel in America* (New Haven, 1958).

66 Penn, *The Afro-American Press and Its Editors* (Springfield, Massachusetts, 1891); Detweiler, *The Negro Press in the United States* (Chicago, 1922).

67 Locke, *Negro Art, Past and Present* (Washington, 1936), and *The Negro and His Music* (Washington, 1936); Cuney-Hare, *Negro Musicians and Their Music* (Washington, 1936).

68 Marshall Winslow Stearns, *The Story of Jazz* (New York, 1956) includes a bibliography by Robert George Reisner that is expanded in the Mentor edition (New York, 1958), 242–54.

69 Butcher, *The Negro in American Culture,* based on materials left by Alain Le Roy Locke (New York, 1956). See also Brawley, *The Negro Genius: A New Appraisal of the Achievement of the American Negro in Literature and the Fine Arts* (New York, 1937).

disorganizing effects of the city. Frazier provided for the first time a "natural history" of the family in the United States and a study "of paramount significance for our understanding of the family" in general.[70]

The esoteric subject matter and fugitive sources easily explain the reluctance of historians to sink into the morass of folk history. Such obstacles cannot explain the absence of adequate studies of Negro improvement and protest organizations, which have left an abundance of documentation. There is no satisfactory critical history, for example, of Negro nationalist movements, the National Urban League, or the National Association for the Advancement of Colored People. Three books on the latter, by Robert L. Jack, Warren D. Saint James, and Langston Hughes provide only the barest sketch.[71] Their history can be followed far better in biographies and autobiographies of their leaders. Nor is there yet a published history of the Commission on Interracial Cooperation and other organizations of the southern interracial movement. Here, again, the story can best be followed in biography.[72]

In 1948 many of the results of the growing literature on Negro history to that date were incorporated into John Hope Franklin's *From Slavery to Freedom,* which supplanted Woodson's as the best overall survey of American Negro history.[73] It was an excellent, coherent, and lucid treatment, including sketches of early African history and the Negro experience in Canada and Latin America. Through the Reconstruction period its emphasis was largely on slavery and the freedmen in the South, but the later chapters reflected the newer conditions of Negro life and historiography in an increasingly national and even northern focus. Only three of the eleven post-Reconstruction chapters (excluding those on Canada and Latin America) dealt chiefly with the South. These covered the triumph of white supremacy, the rise of Negro educational, social, and religious organizations, the influence of Booker

70 Frazier, *The Negro Family in the United States* (Chicago, 1939). Quotations from Ernest Watson Burgess in Preface to the revised and abridged edition (New York, 1948), n.p.

71 Jack, *History of the National Association for the Advancement of Colored People* (Boston, 1943); Saint James, *The National Association for the Advancement of Colored People, a Case Study in Pressure Groups* (New York, 1958); Hughes, *Fight for Freedom: The Story of the NAACP* (New York, 1962).

72 Wilma Dykeman and James Stokely, *Seeds of Southern Change: The Life of Will Alexander* (Chicago, 1962). The best available history is Edward F. Burrows, "The Commission on Interracial Movement in the South" (Ph.D. dissertation, University of Wisconsin, 1955).

73 Franklin, *From Slavery to Freedom: A History of American Negroes* (New York, 1948). A revised edition appeared in 1956.

T. Washington, and the Negro's economic status. Another useful synthesis appeared the following year in E. Franklin Frazier's *The Negro in the United States*. Written by a sociologist, it undertook to deal "with the processes by which the Negro has acquired American culture and has emerged as a racial minority or ethnic group, and the extent to which he is being integrated into American society." [74] Although the emphasis was sociological, it was not static; and Frazier made use of historical studies in tracing the social evolution of American Negroes, with considerable attention to the South and with most of his space given to the post-Reconstruction era.

One of the most fruitful of the new approaches to southern Negro history has been the gradual reclamation of the late nineteenth century through state studies. Some beginnings may be found in the studies of South Carolina, Tennessee, and Virginia by Alrutheus A. Taylor, who not only began the revisionist study of Negroes during Reconstruction (see the Wharton essay elsewhere in this volume) but in some particulars carried over into the later period.[75] Treatments of South Carolina and Georgia by Asa H. Gordon were largely disconnected and based on limited research, but they broke new ground for the future historian.[76] Rousseve's history of Louisiana Negroes, in 1937, all too brief, gave only one chapter to the period after Reconstruction.[77] An all-Negro unit of the Virginia Writers' Project of the Work Progress Administration produced in 1940 an account of Virginia Negroes, about a third of which was given over to the post-Reconstruction period. It was disjointed and anecdotal, suffering from many of the faults of the WPA State Guide Series, which it resembled, but provided a helpful depository of information not elsewhere available.[78]

The promise of the state approach was first fulfilled in Vernon Lane Wharton's exhaustive study of Mississippi.[79] A study based on prodigious research and informed by mature judgment, it covered not only

---

74 Frazier, *The Negro in the United States* (New York, 1949). A revised edition appeared in 1957.

75 Taylor, *The Negro in South Carolina During the Reconstruction* (Washington, 1924); *The Negro in the Reconstruction of Virginia* (Washington, 1926); *The Negro in Tennessee, 1865–1880* (Washington, 1941).

76 Gordon, *Sketches of Negro Life and History in South Carolina* (Hammond, Indiana, 1929), and *The Georgia Negro, a History* (Ann Arbor, Michigan, 1937).

77 Charles Barthelmy Rousseve, *The Negro in Louisiana: Aspects of His History and Literature* (New Orleans, 1937).

78 *The Negro in Virginia,* compiled by Workers of the Writers' Program of the Works Projects Administration in the state of Virginia (New York, 1940).

79 Wharton, *The Negro in Mississippi, 1865–1890* (Chapel Hill, 1947).

political history but emancipation, adjustments in agriculture, other Negro occupations, the Negroes' legal status, disfranchisement, race relations, crime, education, religion, the Negro defective, and various aspects of social life. Its central theme was the evolution of white supremacy's new *modus vivendi* in the years after the destruction of slavery. The present writer followed the trail blazed by Wharton with a study of South Carolina Negroes after Reconstruction.[80]

In the state studies revelations that race relations had undergone a lengthy period of flux after Reconstruction contributed to the new insights of Woodward's pioneering history of racial segregation.[81] With a deft originality, Woodward attacked the entrenched myths that segregation marked a reversion to antebellum conditions and that it resulted altogether from a protracted accretion of folkways. He related its rise to the broader political and economic currents of southern history and traced the gathering of forces against segregation in the twentieth century. A subsequent state study of Virginia has validated for that state the Woodward thesis that segregation developed gradually out of circumstances in the late nineteenth century, although the color line stiffened more quickly in Virginia than in Mississippi and South Carolina because of different conditions. An excellent study, the work by Charles E. Wynes, is chiefly confined unfortunately to race relations and politics and does not seek to explore other aspects of Negro life.[82] A more recent work on North Carolina by Frenise A. Logan, on the other hand, covers a broader canvas and shows the Negroes of that state to have been in a relatively favorable position in comparison to Negroes in other states.[83]

The two major studies before Woodward's of racial segregation and discrimination, by Gilbert Thomas Stephenson and Charles Staples Mangum, Jr., were both narrowly legalistic in conception and essentially static in their view of race laws. A more evolutionary approach was reflected in Bernard Hamilton Nelson's excellent book on reinterpretations of the Fourteenth Amendment after 1920.[84] The darker aspects of Negro subordination have yet to be surveyed in historical monograph.

80 Tindall, *South Carolina Negroes, 1877–1900* (Columbia, 1952). It should be noted here that both the Wharton and Tindall studies were prepared under the direction of Professor Fletcher M. Green.

81 Woodward, *The Strange Career of Jim Crow.*

82 Wynes, *Race Relations in Virginia, 1870–1902* (Charlottesville, 1961).

83 Logan, *The Negro in North Carolina, 1876–1894* (Chapel Hill, 1964).

84 Stephenson, *Race Distinctions in American Law* (New York and London, 1910); Mangum, *The Legal Status of the Negro* (Chapel Hill, 1940); Nelson, *The Fourteenth Amendment and the Negro Since 1920* (Washington, 1946).

Several accounts of lynching have been written, and one of peonage, but there is no fully satisfactory analytical history.[85]

The accelerated changes in the status of Negroes since the 1930's have not yet been the subject of many histories. There is an unpublished study of the Negro and the New Deal, basically a narrowly administrative history based on materials in the National Archives, and three good studies of the Fair Employment Practices Committee, the March-on-Washington Movement that precipitated its establishment in 1940, and efforts to make it permanent by legislation.[86] A spate of polemical discourses, journalistic reports, travel accounts, and sociological investigations, together with the establishment of the *Race Relations Law Reporter* and the *Southern School News,* have made the Negro revolt of the mid-twentieth century the most thoroughly documented development of Negro history and a happy hunting ground for future historians. So far the only published studies that qualify as serious historical monographs are Hugh Douglas Price's survey of re-emergent Negro politics in Florida and Howard H. Quint's study of South Carolina reactions to the issue of school desegregation, both of which set high standards of research and analysis.[87]

The field of Negro biography has only begun to enter its period of emancipation. The pioneering treatments, like the earlier general histories by Negroes, were designed primarily to serve the function of developing racial pride. They were typically inspirational accounts of Negro builders and heroes. A considerable body of collections of short biographies in this vein have appeared in the twentieth century.[88] The same attitude

85 James Elbert Cutler, *Lynch-Law: An Investigation into the History of Lynching in the United States* (New York, 1905) ; Arthur Franklin Raper, *The Tragedy of Lynching* (Chapel Hill, 1933) ; Walter Francis White, *Rope & Faggot: A Biography of Judge Lynch* (New York, 1929) ; Walter Wilson, *Forced Labor in the United States* (New York, 1933).

86 Allen Francis Kifer, "The Negro Under the New Deal, 1933–1941" (Ph.D. dissertation, University of Wisconsin, 1961) ; Louis Ruchames, *Race, Jobs & Politics, the Story of the FEPC* (New York, 1953) ; Herbert Garfinkel, *When Negroes March, the March on Washington Movement in the Organizational Politics for FEPC* (Glencoe, Illinois, 1950) ; Louis Coleridge Kesselman, *The Social Politics of FEPC: A Study in Reform Pressure Movements* (Chapel Hill, 1948).

87 Price, *The Negro and Southern Politics: A Chapter of Florida History* (New York, 1957) ; Quint, *Profile in Black and White: A Frank Portrait of South Carolina* (Washington, 1958).

88 Some examples are Brawley, *Negro Builders and Heroes* (Chapel Hill, 1937) ; Edwin Rogers Embree, *13 Against the Odds* (New York, 1944) ; Elisabeth Ross Haynes, *Unsung Heroes* (New York, 1921) ; Mary White Ovington, *Portraits in Color* (New York, 1927) ; Ben Albert Richardson, *Great American Negroes* (New York, 1945).

generally characterizes a number of longer biographies of individual leaders.[89] A new approach toward a more integrated analysis of the evolution of Negro leadership has been presented by Richard Bardolph in *The Negro Vanguard*.[90]

In biographies of individual leaders the scholarly approach has commenced, appropriately, with the two great protagonists of accommodation and militancy, Booker T. Washington and W. E. B. DuBois. Washington has been studied by Basil Joseph Mathews and Samuel R. Spencer, Jr.; DuBois by Francis L. Broderick and Elliott M. Rudwick.[91] Mathews' biography of Washington is based upon considerable research but is frankly laudatory and somewhat discursive. Spencer, on the other hand, thoroughly examined the readily available sources and essayed a more critical appraisal of Washington's role. The personality that emerges from his pages is that of a man who was in many ways a characteristic figure of his era. His rise was the product of the luck and pluck which is typical of contemporary success literature, and his philosophy compounded the virtues of industry, morality, and the gospel of wealth. While recognizing the limitations of Washington's program for training craftsmen and small entrepreneurs in an increasingly industrialized society, Spencer felt that by overemphasizing vocational training Washington made a salutary break with the political preoccupation of Negro "radicals" and "highlighted the fact that economic progress offered a means to full integration no less important than political means. . . . His predecessors had taken their lead from Thomas Jefferson. Washington took his from Benjamin Franklin, and by doing so, introduced a strain into the Negro's Americanism which strengthened his claim to full citizenship." [92] Spencer also gave some attention to the argument that Washington's counsels of moderation emboldened the opponents of human rights for Negroes, but concluded that "to criticize his methods is to make the facile assumption that he had some choice in the matter.

89 Some examples are Emma Gelders Sterne, *Mary McLeod Bethune* (New York, 1947); Shirley Graham and George D. Lipscomb, *Dr. George Washington Carver, Scientist* (New York, 1944); Frederic Ridgely Torence, *The Story of John Hope* (New York, 1948); Dorothy Sterling, *Captain of the Planter: The Story of Robert Smalls* (Garden City, New York, 1948).

90 Bardolph, *The Negro Vanguard* (New York, 1959). The extensive bibliographical essay gives many additional examples of Negro biographies.

91 Mathews, *Booker T. Washington, Educator and Interracial Interpreter* (Cambridge, 1948); Spencer, *Booker T. Washington and the Negro's Place in American Life* (Boston, 1955); Broderick, *W. E. B. DuBois: Negro Leader in a Time of Crisis* (Stanford, 1959); Rudwick, *W. E. B. DuBois: A Study in Minority Group Leadership* (Philadelphia, 1960).

92 Spencer, *Booker T. Washington*, 197.

He did what was possible, given the time and place in which he lived, and did it to the utmost." [93]

The two studies of DuBois, despite Rudwick's subtitle, *A Study in Minority Leadership,* are basically biographies, and both were built chiefly from printed sources. The DuBois papers were closed to Broderick after he had examined them only to 1910. The books very largely overlap in their treatments and conclusions. Both find DuBois to have been chiefly a propagandist of protest, temperamentally unsuited to organizational leadership, and give illuminating analyses of the interweaving and sometimes contradictory themes of twentieth-century Negro leadership: accommodation, Negro nationalism, and the quest for integration into American life. Only Broderick, however, undertook to pursue DuBois into the long years of declining influence after the NAACP rejected his policy of Negro "self sufficiency" in 1934 to push for integration, the years during which DuBois drifted gradually toward Marxism and the Communists. His importance for Negro history, Broderick concluded, lay in two achievements of his earlier career: his role as "the loudest voice in demanding equal rights for the Negro and in turning Negro opinion away from the acceptance of anything less," and "his service to the Negro's morale" in holding up the ideals of liberal education and full citizenship.[94]

The fundamental issues involved in the leadership of Washington and DuBois will provide grist to the historical mills for many years to come. Excellent as are the existing studies, each man deserves a thorough and definitive biography. The basic raw materials for this work now repose in the extensive Washington papers at the Library of Congress and the DuBois papers recently deposited in the Fisk University Library.

In so hasty an expedition across the surface of Negro historiography it has been necessary to limit the coverage. Concentration on secondary works of some length necessitates neglect of the highly significant periodical, polemical, documentary, autobiographical, and sociological materials which so far present the only available glimpses into many aspects of Negro history. To survey the subject fully one would have to encompass the whole field of general history and monographs of the South, for there is no area of southern development that does not impinge upon Negro history. At the same time, in limiting the subject to *Negro* history *per se,* it has been impossible to limit attention entire-

93 *Ibid.,* 200.
94 Broderick, *W. E. B. DuBois,* 230–31.

ly to the South because so many significant developments have lapped over regional boundaries.

The record, while it reveals progress in many lines, is basically a record of historiographical deficiency. In practically every phase of Negro history that has been touched it is a record of pioneering surveys with only a few monographic forays into unknown territory. But the record, therefore, is also a prospectus of opportunity, for none of these fields has been exhausted. In Negro politics, for example, there is a need for extending the study of southern Republicans into the lily-white era of the twentieth century, for studies of southern Negroes and Populism, and fuller exploration of the Negro drift into the Democratic party. Business and labor history offer infinite possibilities, and Negro institutions of all kinds—social, economic, educational, and religious— provide ground that is not yet even plowed. Folk history may be too exotic for the common academic drudge, but is there no writer who can do for southern Negroes what Howard Odum did for southern white folk in his *American Epoch* or Wilbur Joseph Cash in his *The Mind of the South?* Is there none who can do for the Negro migrant what Oscar Handlin did for the European in *The Uprooted?* The interregional contacts of Negroes, as well as their adjustment to new environments, may provide stimulating insights. What, for example, has been the Negro's image of the South and of himself as Southerner and American? We know far more about the white Southerner's image of the Negro. The state study may seem to have exhausted its possibilities, for no strikingly new themes were added by the three that followed Wharton's book on Mississippi, but there undoubtedly would be interesting varia- tions in Louisiana with its Latin heritage, in Alabama with its relatively more significant Negro industrial labor, in Florida with its influx of Yankees, or in the border states with their tradition of moderation. And the twentieth century has not yet been subjected to state studies, al- though Charles E. Wynes now has in progress an extension of his Virginia study into the twentieth century. Historians have hardly scratched the surface of Negro protest movements, on the one hand, or of Negro accommodation leadership on the other. And among the darker aspects of Negro life, the southern practices of lynching and peonage have scarcely been brought under historical scrutiny at all.

Basic to all these opportunities is the need for bringing the focus of Negro history more upon Negroes themselves. Even in the best of the existing histories they are seen largely through white men's eyes. This has been forced by the imperatives of the sources, mostly of white origin, but Negro sources have become increasingly available in the last two generations. Useful compendia of significant events in the twentieth century are available in the *Negro Year Book* and *The Negro Handbook*.[95] In addition to the Carter Godwin Woodson collection of Negro manuscripts at the Library of Congress, great bodies of Negro material, printed and manuscript, have been collected at Howard, Fisk, Yale, and Atlanta Universities, at Hampton and Tuskegee Institutes, and in the Schomburg Collection of the New York Public Library, and even greater quantities in general archival and manuscript collections.[96] Files of Negro newspapers in some number have been located and microfilmed by the American Council of Learned Societies.[97] Among the bibliographical guides Monroe Nathan Work's standard bibliography is badly out of date, but it may be supplemented by Edgar Tristram Thompson's critical list of works in three major North Carolina libraries, by the Ross and Kennedy bibliography of Negro migration, and by a variety of bibliographies on special aspects of Negro life.[98]

One final conclusion seems to be justified. The historiography of American Negroes has been for some time not only in the process of emancipation from the static image that so long inhibited the historical approach, but also from the narrow treatment that ignored broad social forces and from commitment either to Negro advancement or white supremacy. Influenced perhaps by the rapid changes they have witnessed in recent years, historians have begun to reexamine the "static" decades of Negro history and to discover that while there were retreats on some

95 Monroe Nathan Work (ed.), *Negro Year Book and Annual Encyclopedia of the Negro*, 1912, 1913, 1914–15, 1916–17, 1918–19, 1921–22, 1925–26, 1931–32, 1937–38, 1941–46, 1947–52 (Tuskegee, Alabama, 1912); Jessie Parkhurst Guzman (ed.), *ibid.* [title varies], 1941–46 and 1947–52. Florence Murray (comp. and ed.), *The Negro Handbook*, 1942, 1944, 1946–47, 1949 (New York, 1942——).

96 Dorothy B. Porter, "Library Sources for the Study of Negro Life and History," *Journal of Negro Education*, V (April, 1936), 232–44; Lawrence Dunbar Reddick, "Library Resources for Negro Studies in the United States and Abroad," in William Edward Burghardt DuBois and Guy Benton Johnson, *Encyclopedia of the Negro: Preparatory Volume* (New York, 1945), 163–82; Paul Lewinson (compiler), *A Guide to Documents in the National Archives: for Negro Studies* (Washington, 1947).

97 The Library of Congress. Photoduplication Service, *Negro Newspapers on Microfilm: A Selected List* (Washington, 1953); Armistead Scott Pride, "Negro Newspaper Files and Their Microfilming," *Journalism Quarterly*, XXIV (June, 1947), 131–34.

98 Work, *A Bibliography of the Negro in Africa and America* (New York, 1928); Thompson, *Race and Region, A Descriptive Bibliography Compiled with Special Reference to the Relations Between Whites and Negroes in the United States* (Chapel Hill, 1949); Ross and Kennedy, *A Bibliography of Negro Migration*.

fronts and advances on others, there was also a gathering of forces beneath the surface for the new dynamics in Negro life.

Twenty years ago Gunnar Myrdal, in his monumental sociological survey of American Negroes, had the bold foresight to predict that the "period of stagnation was only a temporary balancing of forces which was just on the verge of being broken." [99] It does not require so bold a foresight to suggest that Negro historiography is only at the beginning of a similar release of forces. The next two decades will probably see an extensive historical invasion of areas that have been long forfeited to the sociologists.

99 Myrdal, "The Negro Problem: A Prognosis," *The New Republic,* CXLVII (July 9, 1962), 11. For the original prognosis in detail see Myrdal, *An American Dilemma: The Negro Problem and Modern Democracy* (New York and London, 1944), 997–1024.

XV

The Agrarian Revolt

Allen J. Going

THE high tide of the farmers' revolt occurred almost simultaneously with the beginning of interest in sectional history. Frederick Jackson Turner's seminal ideas were steering American historians away from cultural-institutional concepts and toward a more environmental approach to the nation's past. This interest soon prompted an outburst of writings on the South, but few authors in the early 1900's attached any significance to the southern agrarian revolt. Many, of course, reflected the contemporary suspicion, disdain, or contempt so frequently directed toward all agrarian reformers. The earliest scholarly analysis of Populism interpreted it as exclusively western and socialistic in everything but name.[1] Those who wrote more sympathetically in subsequent years confined their discussions largely to the West and accepted Turner's own explanation of Populism as "a manifestation of the old pioneer ideals of

1 Frank L. McVey, *The Populist Movement* (New York, 1896).

the native American, with the added element of increasing readiness to utilize the national government to effect its ends." [2]

The Populist movement failed to win the support of intellectuals in the 1890's, and Southerners writing soon after the event generally ignored it. Philip Alexander Bruce, in the first survey of the post-Reconstruction South by a competent scholar, made no mention of the farmers' revolt. He emphasized economic and social progress rather than political dissension. In *The South in the Building of the Nation,* the numerous essays dealing with late nineteenth-century politics likewise gave short shrift to the turbulent nineties. Most of the writers apparently agreed with Charles W. Ramsdell when he said that although the political history of Texas since Reconstruction was not devoid of interest, the student would find "far more attractive matter in tracing the social and material development of the mighty young republic." [3] The more perceptive William Garrott Brown anticipated some later interpretations by describing Populism as a combination of agrarian revolt and political insurgency of the "outs" against the "ins." He sensed a changed atmosphere in southern politics as a result of the upheaval; and, after the removal of the Negro from the political scene, he looked forward to more significant political divisions among the whites. [4]

The farm organizations themselves sponsored numerous official histories, leading one scholar to comment that "the farmers were threatened with an overproduction of history as well as field crops." [5] Although these works were usually highly partisan and hastily compiled, they did preserve much factual information that might otherwise have been lost. [6] In a somewhat similar category are accounts written by disillusioned

2 Frederick J. Turner, *The Frontier in American History* (New York, 1920), 155. For a discussion of the influence of Turner and others on the historiography of Populism, see Everett Walters, "Populism: Its Significance in American History," in Donald Sheehan and Harold C. Syrett (eds.), *Essays in American Historiography: Papers Presented in Honor of Allan Nevins* (New York, 1960), 217–30.

3 Bruce, *The Rise of the New South* (Philadelphia, 1905); Julian A. C. Chandler *et al.* (eds.), *The South in the Building of the Nation* (13 vols.; Richmond, 1909–13), IV, 425.

4 Brown, "Shifting the White Man's Burden," in *The Lower South in American History* (New York, 1902), 247–71.

5 James C. Malin, "Notes on the Literature of Populism," *Kansas Historical Quarterly,* I (Feb., 1932), 60.

6 Oliver H. Kelley, *Origin and Progress of the Order of the Patrons of Husbandry* (Philadelphia, 1875); Thomas C. Atkeson, *Semi-centennial History of the Patrons of Husbandry* (New York, 1916); Charles M. Gardner, *The Grange—Friend of the American Farmer: A Concise Reference History* (Washington, 1949); W. Scott Morgan ("official historian" of the Southern Alliance), *History of the Wheel and Alliance* (Hardy, Arkansas, 1891); William L. Garvin and S. O.

and embittered Populists. William H. Skaggs, who adhered to the monolithic interpretation of southern history, showed that the aristocratic oligarchy had survived every crisis. Joseph C. Manning, in two books that incorporated illuminating reminiscences of his experiences as a Populist in Alabama, bemoaned the failure of a Populist-Republican coalition and the continuation of Black-Belt, minority domination.[7]

The stream of scholarly history became deeper and broader during the second and third decades of the twentieth century. Emphasis on the "New History," reforms of the progressive period, and current agricultural problems—all stimulated interest in the agrarian and political upheavals of the late nineteenth century. Several surveys provided rather superficial treatments,[8] and two early works concentrated almost exclusively on the West.[9] Solon J. Buck, the first significant scholar of the agrarian revolt, produced two works of lasting value. *The Granger Movement,* based largely on materials collected by the Wisconsin Historical Society, gave some attention to the South but lacked any real grasp of southern history. His volume in the Yale *Chronicles* series, *The Agrarian Crusade,* is a readable synthesis based on the limited studies then available; it recognized the contribution of the Populist heritage to the progressive reforms of the early 1900's.[10] Holland Thompson's volume in the *Chronicles* series supplemented Buck's work by including the political activities of southern agrarians. With the characteristic confidence and optimism of a progressive "New Souther," he explained how the fresh political forces of the 1890's had ended the stultifying control of the Brigadiers and ushered in a new dawn of political and economic prospects for the white common man.[11]

While Buck could make use of only one serious work on Populism in

Daws, *History of the National Farmers' Alliance and Co-operative Union of America* (Jacksboro, Texas, 1887); Nelson A. Dunning (ed.), *Farmers' Alliance History and Agricultural Digest* (Washington, 1891).

7 Skaggs, *The Southern Oligarchy* (New York, 1924); Manning, *The Fadeout of Populism* (New York, 1928); Manning, *From Five to Twenty-five: His Earlier Life* (New York, 1929); W. Scott Morgan, *The Red Light* (Moravian Falls, N. C., 1904); Henry E. Tremain, *Sectionalism Unmasked* (New York, 1907).

8 John D. Black, *Agricultural Reform in the United States* (New York, 1929); William B. Bizzell, *The Green Rising: A Historical Survey of Agrarianism* (New York, 1926); Edward Wiest, *Agricultural Organization in the United States* (Lexington, Ky., 1923).

9 Frederick E. Haynes, *Third Party Movements Since the Civil War: With Special Reference to Iowa* (Iowa City, 1916); Ellis B. Usher, *The Greenback Movement of 1875–1884, and Wisconsin's Part in It* (Milwaukee, 1911).

10 Buck, *The Granger Movement* (Cambridge, Mass., 1913), and *The Agrarian Crusade* (New Haven, 1920).

11 Thompson, *The New South* (New Haven, 1919).

the South,[12] John D. Hicks, writing ten years later, could rely on a number of such studies. Most of these originated as dissertations in northern graduate schools and attempted to treat the subject with detachment, as free as possible from the prejudices and passions that still lingered in the wake of the upheaval. Two early state studies established excellent standards of quality. Alex M. Arnett hoped that his book on Georgia would be illustrative of the movement in the South and the nation, and he identified the attempts of the Populists to correct abuses in the democratic system with the aims of twentieth-century liberals and progressives. Francis B. Simkins' study of the Tillman movement documented the overthrow of the old aristocracy by the new democracy in South Carolina.[13] Two works on North Carolina went far toward revising the concepts that had equated Fusionism in that state with Radical Reconstruction. Both writers agreed that the impact of Populism had a profound effect on state politics. "The disappearance of the Negro in politics as the dominant issue," said Florence E. Smith, "left the Democratic party . . . free to take up much more important questions of education, prohibition, good roads, and public health." [14] John B. Clark, in his study of the farmers' revolt in Alabama, devoted considerable attention to twenty years of the state's history preceding Populism itself. The movement, he concluded, did not succeed because the opposition appealed to white supremacy, but its demands were ultimately satisfied by the Democratic party.[15]

These early state studies not only recognized the Populist contribution to twentieth-century reform but also counterbalanced the previous emphasis on the western origins and manifestations of the movement. They outlined some of the distinctive features of southern agrarianism, especially the presence of the Negro and a single-party political structure. H. C. Nixon brought into even sharper focus the differences between midwestern and southern Alliancemen. Anticipating the conclusions of later scholars, he contrasted the revolutionary character of the Southern Alliance with the moderate reforming spirit of midwestern

12 Melvin J. White, "Populism in Louisiana During the Nineties," *Mississippi Valley Historical Review,* V (June, 1918), 3–19.

13 Arnett, *The Populist Movement in Georgia* (New York, 1922) ; Simkins, *The Tillman Movement in South Carolina* (Durham, 1926).

14 Smith, "The Populist Movement and Its Influence in North Carolina" (Ph.D. dissertation, University of Chicago, 1929), 188. See also, Simeon A. Delap, "The Populist Party in North Carolina," Trinity College Historical Society *Historical Papers,* Ser. XIV (1922), 40–74.

15 Clark, *Populism in Alabama* (Auburn, Ala., 1927).

agrarians, and attributed at least some of the differences to the controversy over anti-oleomargarine laws.[16]

Interpretations of Populism during the past seventy years have
swung full cycle from distrust and suspicion to approbation and back
again to adverse criticism. The 1930's saw the appearance of an increasing number of favorable treatments beginning with Hicks' *The
Populist Revolt,* sometimes referred to as the definitive history of Populism. It is definitive only in the sense that it skillfully combines a synthesis of the material then available on the subject with the results of considerable original research. Although sparing in interpretation, Hicks
emphasized the large number of Populist demands that were ultimately
enacted. His major contribution, however, was a presentation of the
whole picture of Populism which established a pattern of development
followed by many others for years to come. His discussion of the
movement in the South recognized the unique features of its agrarian
background but was weak on the political implications. He viewed the
movement as contributing to the breakdown of aristocratic domination
that had carried over from a monolithic antebellum South. "Populism,"
he wrote, "may have had something to do with the withdrawal of political
power from the southern negro, but it also paved the way for the political emancipation of the lower class of southern whites." [17]

The Populist Revolt stimulated further research into the causes,
manifestations, and broad implications of the agrarian movement.
Scholars in the rapidly growing graduate schools of southern universities
concentrated intensively on the history of their own region, and some
turned their attention to the last quarter of the nineteenth century. The
New Deal atmosphere proved to be sympathetic to a study of the
South's problems and to the heritage of Populism. The intellectual controversy between the Nashville "Agrarians" and the Chapel Hill de-
fenders of southern urban and industrial growth likewise stimulated interest in similar arguments of the 1880's and 1890's. But perhaps the
strongest stimulus was the predominant Beard-Parrington conflict
theory of American history that seemed to point to the 1890's as the
final phase in the great struggle between agrarian and industrial-
urban forces.[18]

16 Nixon, "The Cleavage Within the Farmers' Alliance," *Mississippi Valley Historical Review,* XV (June, 1928), 22–33.

17 John D. Hicks, *The Populist Revolt* (Minneapolis, 1931), 412.

18 Beard made little distinction between the agrarian revolt in the South and
that in the nation as a whole and conceived of the movement as a revival of the
attempt by Jacksonian farmer-labor forces to curb industrial-financial powers.

Although still mindful of the connection between agrarian reform efforts and twentieth-century progressivism, more and more scholars investigated the background and causes of the upheaval in the South. Just as the concept of an Old South dominated by an aristocratic planter oligarchy was giving way to the concept of a dynamic economic democracy, the postwar period was emerging as the scene of a struggle between two politico-economic forces. Virginius Dabney, in his survey of liberalism in the South, showed some understanding of these conflicting forces and how their antagonisms led to the Populist upheaval. An even sharper picture of the cleavage was drawn by the Beardian progressive, Benjamin B. Kendrick, and his student, Alex M. Arnett. They depicted the post-Reconstruction period as one in which Old South agrarianism came into direct conflict with New South Bourbonism and its drive for industrialization and northeastern political ties. The Alliance-Populist movement stood for old southern ways, and its defeat meant the permanent imposition of the northern pattern on the South.[19] C. Vann Woodward, in his biography of Tom Watson, described the struggle of a Georgia agrarian rebel against "New Departure" Democrats who had betrayed the interests of the South to the forces of industrial capitalism. Daniel M. Robison explained that the Populists and so-called demagogues of the post-Populist period were in reality "spokesmen of the agrarian interests [who] more nearly represented a continuation of the political and economic ideas of the antebellum South than did the 'developers of resources' who were engaged in forming a New South."[20]

These works were beginning to reveal the broad implications of the southern agrarian revolt and to show that, far from being imported from the West, it had origins and dynamics of its own. They indicated a need for further study of the internal frictions beneath the surface solidarity of the post-Reconstruction South in order to grasp the significance and appreciate the impact of the turbulent nineties. Paul Lewin-

---

Charles M. and Mary R. Beard, *The Rise of American Civilization* (2 vols.; New York, 1927), 320–25. Vernon L. Parrington did not complete the projected sections on the "Hesitant South," but the headings, "The Aristocratic Clinging to the Romance of the Past" and "The Plebian Agrarian Joining with the Middle Border," suggest themes more fully developed later by C. Vann Woodward. *The Beginnings of Critical Realism in America*, Volume III of V. L. Parrington, *Main Currents in American Thought* (3 vols.; New York, 1927–30), xxxv.

19 V. Dabney, *Liberalism in the South* (Chapel Hill, 1932), 201–16; Kendrick and Arnett, *The South Looks at Its Past* (Chapel Hill, 1935), 105–41.

20 Woodward, *Tom Watson, Agrarian Rebel* (New York, 1938); Robison, "From Tillman to Long: Some Striking Leaders of the Rural South," *Journal of Southern History,* III (Aug., 1937), 289–310.

son delineated the important role played by Negro voting in this intra-party struggle. Other works on the Negro during this period made clear how the Democrats, as long as they were united, found ways of circumventing or controlling Negro votes, but how Negroes and white Republicans occupied a strategic position when Democratic schisms threatened.[21]

A number of state studies of political opposition to the Bourbon Democrats have recounted a story of fairly widespread independency and insurgency, especially in the late 1870's and early 1880's. The most fa-mous of these movements, that of the Readjusters in Virginia, was the subject of one of the earliest scholarly monographs on this period. Its author, Charles C. Pearson, credited William Mahone and his fol-lowers with ending the reactionary rule of the Brigadiers and injecting into Virginia politics a democratic spirit more amenable to popular wants. A later student of this same subject did not entirely agree that the Barbour-Martin machine, which overthrew the Readjusters, was quite so democratic, because it was still closely identified with urban business and railroad groups. The standard biography of Mahone made him the hero of virtually every incident and situation.[22] In addition to the Watson biography, a number of studies clarified anti-Bourbon move-ments in Georgia.[23] William P. Roberts' dissertation described the vigorous efforts of William H. Felton to break the grasp of the powerful Georgia Bourbon triumvirate. Felton emerged as a true idealist in all things save race relations; his "highly egotistical" nature led him, as well as a number of the other independents, to confuse "his desire to better government and society with his own political ambitions." [24]

---

[21] Lewinson, *Race, Class, and Party: A History of Negro Suffrage and White Politics in the South* (New York, 1932). For other studies of southern Negroes during the post-Reconstruction period, see George Tindall's essay above, pp. 337–61.

[22] Pearson, *The Readjuster Movement in Virginia* (New Haven, 1917); Allen W. Moger, "The Origin of the Democratic Machine in Virginia," *Journal of South-ern History,* VIII (May, 1942), 183–209; Nelson M. Blake, *William Mahone of Virginia* (Richmond, 1935).

[23] Judson C. Ward, "The Republican Party in Bourbon Georgia, 1872–1890," *Journal of Southern History,* IX (May, 1943), 196–209; Fletcher M. Green, "Ben E. Green and Greenbackism in Georgia," *Georgia Historical Quarterly,* XXX (March, 1946), 1–13.

[24] Roberts, "The Public Career of Dr. William H. Felton" (Ph.D. dissertation, University of North Carolina, 1952). Several other works have discussed Rebecca Felton who continued her husband's efforts well into the twentieth century. Josephine B. Floyd, "Rebecca Latimer Felton, Political Independent," *Georgia Historical Quarterly,* XXX (March, 1946), 14–34; Floyd, "Rebecca Latimer Felton, Champion of Women's Rights," *ibid.,* 81–104; John E. Talmadge, *Rebecca Latimer Felton* (Athens, Ga., 1960).

Two scholars have effectively described and analyzed the anti-Bourbon movements in Mississippi. Willie D. Halsell contrasted Mahone and James Chalmers, the leader of one independent movement, and finds the latter devoid of liberalism, unconcerned about the farmers, and interested only in his own immediate political advancement. Albert D. Kirwan, tracing the complete story of the overthrow of the Mississippi Bourbons, recognized the struggle as one between economic classes, interspersed with personal struggles of ambitious men. The opposition in Mississippi, he argued, unlike Mahoneism in Virginia, had little liberalizing effect on the Bourbons.[25] Independent movements did not develop in Tennessee, but heated political contests involved Republicans and three clearly defined factions of the Democratic party.[26]

Usually included in the general and state studies of Populism are discussions of the agricultural background, but postbellum agriculture itself is a neglected field. That volume of *The South in the Building of the Nation* which is on economic history devoted about one fourth of the entire work to agriculture; the information is factual and statistical with virtually no interpretation. The same is true of an older work on the economic history of the South.[27] Two definitive studies of particular commodities contribute to an understanding of certain special farm grievances. J. Carlyle Sitterson dealt with the battle between sugar planters and the sugar trust over tariff policy, while Nannie M. Tilley attributed the tobacco farmers' problems more to the warehousemen and leaf dealers than to the cigarette trust.[28]

Certain studies have revealed that the southern farmer faced special

25 Halsell, "James R. Chalmers and 'Mahoneism' in Mississippi," *Journal of Southern History,* X (Feb., 1944), 37–58; Halsell, "Democratic Dissensions in Mississippi, 1878–1882," *Journal of Mississippi History,* II (April, 1940), 123–35; Kirwan, *Revolt of the Rednecks: Mississippi Politics, 1876–1925* (Lexington, Ky., 1951).

26 Verton M. Queener, "The East Tennessee Republicans as a Minority Party, 1870–1896," East Tennessee Historical Society *Publications,* No. 15 (1943), 49–73; Daniel M. Robison, "The Political Background of Tennessee's War of the Roses," East Tennessee Historical Society *Publications,* No. 5 (1933), 125–41. Separate treatments of independent movements in other southern states are few. See Edward C. Williamson, "Independentism: A Challenge to the Florida Democracy of 1884," *Florida Historical Quarterly,* XXVII (Oct., 1948), 131–56; Frances Roberts, "William Manning Lowe and the Greenback Party in Alabama," *Alabama Review,* V (April, 1952), 100–21; Roscoe C. Martin, "The Greenback Party in Texas," *Southwestern Historical Quarterly,* XXX (Jan., 1927), 161–78.

27 Chandler *et al.* (eds.), *The South in the Building of the Nation,* VI, 17–174; Emory Q. Hawk, *Economic History of the South* (New York, 1934), 449–74.

28 Sitterson, *Sugar Country: The Sugar Cane Industry in the South, 1753–1950* (Lexington, Ky., 1953), 324–42; Tilley, *The Bright Tobacco Industry, 1860–1929* (Chapel Hill, 1948), 396–448.

problems peculiar to his own section in addition to those arising from
the generally depressed agrarian economy of the late nineteenth century.
An older concept, which had found its way into the Beards' *Rise of
American Civilization* and a number of textbooks, held that the Civil
War had brought about the breakup of the plantations into numerous
freeholds, and that the subsequent problems of southern farmers were
thus similar to those in other sections of the country. Even before the
1930's, however, a number of studies had pointed out some distinctive
regional features. In the 1890's Matthew B. Hammond blamed the
lien system, sharecropping, and overproduction for retarding the cotton
economy. Using a pseudo-muckraking approach reminiscent of Henry
D. Lloyd and Henry George, Charles H. Otken cited the crop-lien
system and the furnishing merchants as primarily responsible for the
southern farmer's troubles.[29] Two early works on Georgia agriculture
described the shift in that state from a plantation to a farmer-tenant
system of organization.[30] During the 1930's a number of articles, some
dealing with particular states, showed more clearly how the unique
features of southern agriculture contributed to growing farm grievances.
They pointed out that long after the abolition of slavery the plantation
structure continued to operate on a tenantry system and to emphasize the
single cotton economy.[31] Other articles elaborated on the various types
of tenantry and cropping and indicated that such systems were the
only feasible arrangements under the circumstances.[32]

The rural merchant has often been cited as a factor contributing to
the agrarian ills. Thomas D. Clark presented illuminating glimpses of the
southern country store during its heyday, 1865–1915, along with a discussion of the furnishing and supply system. In his opinion the merchant
has been "properly criticized" for his sins against southern agriculture,

---

29 Hammond, *The Cotton Industry: An Essay in American Economic History*
(New York, 1897) ; Otken, *The Ills of the South* (New York, 1894).

30 Enoch M. Banks, *The Economics of Land Tenure in Georgia* (New York,
1905) ; Robert P. Brooks, *The Agrarian Revolution in Georgia* (Madison, 1914).

31 Francis B. Simkins, "The Problems of South Carolina Agriculture After the
Civil War," *North Carolina Historical Review*, VII (Jan., 1930), 46–77; Simkins,
"The Solution of Post-Bellum Agricultural Problems in South Carolina," *North
Carolina Historical Review*, VII (April, 1930), 192–219; Roger W. Shugg, "Sur-
vival of the Plantation System in Louisiana," *Journal of Southern History*, III
(Aug., 1937), 311–25.

32 C. W. Tebeau, "Some Aspects of Planter-Freedman Relations, 1865–1880,"
Journal of Negro History, XXI (April, 1936), 130–50; Oscar Zeichner, "The
Transition from Slave to Free Agricultural Labor in the Southern States,"
Agricultural History, XIII (Jan., 1939), 22–32; Rosser H. Taylor, "Post Bellum
Southern Rental Contracts," *Agricultural History*, XVII (Feb., 1946), 121–28.

but he was actually "only a cog in an economic machine" which had fastened the one-crop commodity structure and all its attendant evils on the region.[33] Some scholars related agrarian conditions directly to the farmers' revolt. Hallie Farmer concluded that the southern Populist movement had to be interpreted as the protest of the small farmer against an intolerable economic situation. H. C. Nixon saw in the continuing emphasis on a cotton economy "a contest between hillbilly and planter over the distribution of the agrarian South's relatively small share of the income of American capitalistic society." [34] In many respects the most penetrating analysis of the agrarian background of the southern farmers' revolt is Roger W. Shugg's study of the class structure and antagonisms in Louisiana during the thirty-five year period, 1840–1875. He concluded that Populism was the political uprising of the poor and white who were finally driven to class-conscious action by their long and weary failures.[35] Although there is no comprehensive history of postbellum southern agriculture, Fred A. Shannon's survey incorporated most of the ideas that had been developed by 1945.[36]

A number of studies treating Populism and the agrarian revolt in the South appeared during the 1930's and the 1940's. The agrarian organizations themselves, even the Grange and the Alliance, lack adequate monographic treatment. Several articles dealt with such varied aspects of state Grange activities as interest in immigration and home manufacturing, cooperative ventures, political influence, and demands for railroad regulation, tax reduction, and economy in government.[37] An overall

33 Clark, *Pills, Petticoats, and Plows: The Southern Country Store* (Indianapolis, 1944), "The Furnishing and Supply System in Southern Agriculture Since 1865," *Journal of Southern History,* XII (Feb., 1946), 24–31.

34 Farmer, "The Economic Background of Southern Populism," *South Atlantic Quarterly,* XXIX (Jan., 1930), 77–91; Nixon, "The New South and the Old Crop," in Avery Craven (ed.), *Essays in Honor of William E. Dodd* (Chicago, 1935), 320–34.

35 Shugg, *Origins of Class Struggle in Louisiana* (Baton Rouge, 1939).

36 Shannon, *The Farmer's Last Frontier, Agriculture, 1860–1897* (New York, 1945), 76–124. Two recent syntheses of state agricultural history are Willard Range, *A Century of Georgia Agriculture, 1850–1950* (Athens, 1954); Samuel L. Evans, "Texas Agriculture, 1880–1930" (Ph.D. dissertation, University of Texas, 1960).

37 Ralph A. Smith, "The Grange Movement in Texas," *Southwestern Historical Quarterly,* XLII (April, 1939), 297–315, and Smith, "Cooperative Movements in Texas, 1870–1900," *Southwestern Historical Quarterly,* XLIV (July, 1940), 33–55; James H. Easterby, "The Granger Movement in South Carolina," South Carolina Historical Association *Proceedings* (1931), 21–32; James S. Ferguson, "The Grange and Farmer Education in Mississippi," *Journal of Southern History,* VIII (Nov., 1942), 497–512.

survey of the southern Grange concluded that it was less aggressive than its midwestern counterpart, especially on railroad regulation, and that it placed more emphasis on education and cooperative activities.[38] One of the few articles dealing with the Alliance as a whole decribed the emotional, if not always accurate, manner in which the organization changed the political thinking of the farmer, roused him to action, and impressed him with the necessity for governmental intervention.[39]

Various state studies have brought out differences and similarities in the general pattern of agrarian revolt. Daniel M. Robison's work on Bob Taylor provides an analysis of Tennessee politics from 1886 to 1899. The author notes the moderate character of the farmers' revolt and credits Taylor with winning his "wool hat" followers back into the Democratic party, thereby avoiding the fate of Fusionist North Carolina.[40] William D. Sheldon's study of Populism in Virginia also stresses the moderate course of the movement, attributing it in part to the more liberalized policies of the post-Readjuster Democratic party. He also pointed out that Virginia's balanced economy was more typical of a border state and that leading Democrats, like the popular John W. Daniel, were early advocates of free coinage of silver. Allen W. Moger likewise called attention to the border-state economy of Virginia that gave business and industrial forces unusual powers in the 1890's.[41]

A monograph on Texas Populism by Roscoe C. Martin, a political scientist, contains the most thorough analysis of the composition, organization, and methods of the People's party in any southern state.

38 Theodore Saloutos, "The Grange in the South, 1870–1877," *Journal of Southern History*, XIX (Nov., 1953), 473–87.

39 Homer Clevenger, "The Teaching Techniques of the Farmers' Alliance," *Journal of Southern History*, XI (Nov., 1945), 504–18. Alliance activities in certain states are treated in James A. Sharp, "The Entrance of the Farmers' Alliance Into Tennessee Politics," East Tennessee Historical Society *Publications*, No. 9 (1937), 77–92; Sharp, "The Farmers' Alliance and the People's Party in Tennessee," East Tennessee Historical Society *Publications*, No. 10 (1938), 91–113; Ralph Smith, "The Farmers' Alliance in Texas, 1875–1900," *Southwestern Historical Quarterly*, XLVIII (Jan., 1945), 346–69; James O. Knauss, "The Farmers' Alliance in Florida," *South Atlantic Quarterly*, XXV (July, 1926), 300–15; James C. Bonner, "The Alliance Legislature of 1890" in Bonner and Lucien E. Roberts (eds.), *Studies in Georgia History and Government* (Athens, 1940), 155–71; William W. Rogers, "The Farmers' Alliance in Alabama," *Alabama Review*, XV (Jan., 1962), 5–18.

40 Robison, *Bob Taylor and the Agrarian Revolt in Tennessee* (Chapel Hill, 1935).

41 Sheldon, *Populism in the Old Dominion: Virginia Farm Politics, 1885–1900* (Princeton, 1935); Moger, *The Rebuilding of the Old Dominion: A Study in Economic, Social, and Political Transition from 1880 to 1902* (Ann Arbor, 1940).

Martin accepted Turner's concept of the frontier origins of Populism but also attributed the upsurge to the refusal of the Democratic leaders to deal realistically with significant issues. He detects a strong religious element in the party, leanings toward prohibition, and little success in working with Negroes or "foreign" populations.[42] Francis B. Simkins' revision and enlargement of his study of Tillman emphasized that his subject was far from radical even though he did bring about a transformation in the South Carolina political scene. Kathryn T. Abbey focused on the liberal heritage of Populism in Florida, especially in bringing about more effective railroad regulation.[43] Two excellent studies of the agrarian revolt in Mississippi provide the most comprehensive coverage for any southern state. James Ferguson traced the movement from its origins in the dissatisfactions of the small farmers with the Bourbon regimes through the mild revolt of the Grange and the Relief to the aggressive tactics of the Alliance and the climax in the 1890's. He contended that the farmers did not question the basic values of the "New South" trends, but that they did object to the changes occurring at their expense and yearned for a greater share of the benefits of the new age. Although Populism itself was doomed to failure, the Bourbons were forced to modify their policies. Albert D. Kirwan, in tracing the rise of the common man to control of Mississippi politics, covered this same period of "almost incessant agrarian revolt" but concentrated more on the political ramifications. His primary purpose was to explain the origins of the twentieth-century demagogues, James K. Vardaman and Theodore G. Bilbo, who directed their appeal and based their strength on the same dirt farmers who had supported the Alliance-Populist, Frank Burkitt. Kirwan stressed the progressive influence of the demagogues despite their racist appeals which, he noted, the Bourbons themselves had utilized in a more genteel fashion.[44]

A few accounts have discussed particular aspects of the agrarian movements and efforts in the South during the first two decades of the

42 Martin, *The People's Party in Texas* (Austin, 1933). Additional information on Texas can be found in two more recent studies. Wayne Alvord, "T. L. Nugent, Texas Populist," *Southwestern Historical Quarterly*, LVII (July, 1953), 65–81; John S. Spratt, *The Road to Spindletop: Economic Changes in Texas, 1875–1901* (Dallas, 1955), 110–227.

43 Simkins, *Pitchfork Ben Tillman, South Carolinian* (Baton Rouge, 1944); Abbey, "Florida Versus the Principles of Populism," *Journal of Southern History*, IV (Nov., 1938), 462–75.

44 Ferguson, "Agrarianism in Mississippi, 1871–1900, A Study in Nonconformity" (Ph.D. dissertation, University of North Carolina, 1952); Kirwan, *Revolt of the Rednecks*.

twentieth century. Two early histories of the Farmers' Union brought out its similarity to the Alliance and its determination to avoid "betrayal by politicians" into a third-party movement.[45] A survey of agrarianism in the Southwest contains the best factual coverage of the union in Texas, especially after its split with the national organization in 1906. Two articles contain similar coverage of the movement in North Carolina, which claimed the largest membership of any state in 1912.[46] The only other significant work in this area deals with the limited influence of other farm organizations in the South and the early proposals by southern farmers and cotton interests of such later New Deal devices as acreage reductions and marketing quotas.[47] A neglected area is the crusade of the early 1900's to help the farmer help himself; virtually the only account to date is a biography of Seaman A. Knapp, the famous apostle of these ideas.[48]

Only two notable biographies of southern agrarian leaders have appeared in addition to those on Watson and Tillman. Stuart Noblin rescued L. L. Polk from the unjust connotations of Fusionism that had aroused such strong emotions in North Carolina and the South. The biography avoids far-reaching interpretations but helps to explain why a leading Southern Allianceman, who was anything but a wild-eyed, impractical dreamer, decided to support the third-party movement. Robert C. Cotner's recent lengthy biography of James S. Hogg, the Texas moderate agrarian reformer, contains much information on the politics of that state in the 1890's. Cotner depicts his subject as an honest, liberal-minded believer in effective government rather than a reformer or progressive.[49] Biographies of such influential figures as

45 Charles S. Barrett, *The Mission, History and Times of the Farmers' Union* (Nashville, 1909); Commodore B. Fisher, *The Farmers' Union* (Lexington, Ky., 1920).

46 Robert L. Hunt, *A History of Farmer Movements in the Southwest, 1873–1925* (College Station, Texas, 1935), 41–143; Charles P. Loomis, "The Rise and Decline of the North Carolina Farmers' Union," *North Carolina Historical Review,* VII (July, 1930), 305–25; Loomis, "Activities of the North Carolina Farmers' Union," *North Carolina Historical Review,* VII (Oct., 1930), 443–62.

47 Theodore Saloutos, "The American Society of Equity in Kentucky," *Journal of Southern History,* V (Aug., 1939), 347–63; Saloutos, "The Southern Cotton Association, 1905–1908," *Journal of Southern History,* XIII (Nov., 1957), 492–510; Gilbert C. Fite, "The Nonpartisan League in Oklahoma," *Chronicles of Oklahoma,* XXIV (Summer, 1946), 146–57; Fite, "Voluntary Attempts to Reduce Cotton Acreage in the South, 1914–1933," *Journal of Southern History,* XIV (Nov., 1948), 481–99.

48 Joseph C. Bailey, *Seaman A. Knapp, Schoolmaster of American Agriculture* (New York, 1945).

49 Noblin, *Leonidas LaFayette Polk, Agrarian Crusader* (Chapel Hill, 1949); Cotner, *James Stephen Hogg, A Biography* (Austin, 1959).

Hoke Smith, Walter Clark, John Sharp Williams, and others furnish helpful insights into the 1890's as a prelude to the period of their principal significance.

By 1950 a generation of historical scholarship had greatly expanded the knowledge and enhanced the significance of the agrarian revolt in the South. General summaries of southern history reflected these findings with some variations in emphasis and interpretation. William B. Hesseltine, in the limited space allocated the post-Reconstruction period, developed his account around the chronic controversy between the farmers and Bourbon governments that "had no consideration for the small farmer and the tenant." [50] Francis B. Simkins stated that the movement accomplished nothing for agrarian reform and was "merely an awkward interlude in the forward march of business." He concluded, however, that the overthrow of the Bourbon oligarchies and more effective participation by the common whites significantly affected political trends, and he cited the exploitation of emotionalism by demagogues and the disfranchisement of Negroes as reactionary results.[51]

Walter P. Webb, tracing the development of a colonial economic status for the South and the West, refers to the agrarian movements as "awkward, pathetic efforts" to stem the tide of northern industrialism and finance capitalism. W. J. Cash's famous work on the continuity of the southern mind rejects the concept of a dichotomy within the New South and its sharp break with the old. Cash did not attach much significance to the agrarian revolt, which he described as merely part of the national farmer movement against the East rather than a class movement within the South.[52]

C. Vann Woodward's widely acclaimed volume on the post-Reconstruction South provides the clearest understanding and most significant interpretation of the agrarian revolt. Based on exhaustive research as well as a discriminating use of secondary works, it embodied a freshness of view and shattered many popular but false notions. The Populist revolt served as the climax of the book and was preceded by a keen analysis of the institutional and social relationships of the post-Reconstruction years. There emerged a clear pattern of deeply rooted conflict between

50 Hesseltine, *The South in American History* (New York, 1943), 573.

51 Simkins, *The South Old and New: A History, 1820–1947* (New York, 1947), 254–69. A short summary of Populism, generally recognized as the Communist interpretation, noted the unique features of the southern movement but contained some questionable generalizations. Anna Rochester, *The Populist Movement in the United States* (New York, 1943).

52 Webb, *Divided We Stand* (New York, 1937), 181–82; Wilbur J. Cash, *The Mind of the South* (New York, 1941), 166–76.

the poverty-stricken masses, white and black, and the Redeemer leaders with their many deficiencies in state affairs and their conservative eastern alliance in national affairs. Woodward emphasizes the larger size and greater aggressiveness of the southern over the western movement and makes a convincing case for his contention that the southern revolt would have occurred even if there had been no western agitation. Although obviously sympathetic with many of the agrarian objectives, he concludes that the third-party attempt was doomed from the beginning because the controlling forces of an industrialized America were too strong. Woodward places less emphasis than others on the political effects of the revolt. The movement toward disfranchisement was simply accelerated, and the new Democratic leaders, most of whom had made concessions only on the silver question, often imitated Redeemer methods of government by vested interests. With the turn of the century the South found itself allied again with the North in the support of a "colonial economy," and most of the political aspirations and deeper needs of the masses remained unfulfilled.[53]

The few recent syntheses of the farmer movements recognize the importance of the southern phase.[54] In 1960 Theodore Saloutos, who has written extensively on agrarian history, published the first general synthesis of the southern agrarian movement. A little less than half the book covers the familiar ground of postwar agrarian conditions, the Grange, Alliance, and Populists, providing the most detailed summary yet available. The remainder of the book deals with the period after 1900 and is a major contribution, bringing into much clearer focus the shifting emphasis from politics to concerted economic action; it recognizes the importance of southern influence in national agrarian legislation. Saloutos develops the dominant theme that Southerners have contributed more to the agricultural thought of the nation than is generally realized. "The Southern Alliance," he writes, "perhaps the most underestimated agricultural organization . . . , was a reservoir of ideas that was to be tapped by Populists, Progressives, and urban and rural reformers for years to come." [55]

53 Woodward, *Origins of the New South, 1877–1913* (Baton Rouge, 1951). A number of writers, in attempting to explain current southern problems, have accepted Woodward's theory that the conservative triumph over a brief but radical agrarian revolt established basic patterns for the twentieth-century South. Harry S. Ashmore, *An Epitaph for Dixie* (New York, 1958) ; James M. Dabbs, *The Southern Heritage* (New York, 1958) ; William H. Nicholls, *Southern Tradition and Regional Progress* (Chapel Hill, 1960).
54 Fred A. Shannon, *American Farmers' Movements* (Princeton, 1957) ; Carl C. Taylor, *The Farmer's Movement, 1620–1920* (New York, 1953).
55 Saloutos, *Farmer Movements in the South, 1865–1933* (Berkeley, 1960).

As a result of these scholarly studies, particularly Woodward's stimulating analysis, the agrarian revolt in the South is generally recognized today as indigenous to the region, more radical than its western counterpart, and something of a watershed in post-Reconstruction history. It had its roots in the fundamental conflict between agrarians and the Redeemer governments, was aggravated by the sad state of farming in the South and in the nation, and bequeathed definite heritages to the twentieth-century South. Some very recent studies generally follow this basic interpretation and provide enlightening details for the states treated. William W. Rogers' work on Alabama is much more thorough and perceptive than Clark's older one. Rogers brings out the strength and breadth of the movement and the success of Populist-Republican fusion in local and congressional elections. Contrary to the conclusions of Saloutos and others, he argues that the leaders of the Grange were men of wealth and property and that many large landowners became prominent Populists.[56] William I. Hair's recent dissertation on Louisiana fills a gap of long standing. He stresses the valiant efforts made by white farmers and Negroes in their Populist-Republican coalition but finds that the cause was utterly hopeless because of the ruthless tactics of the conservative opposition. One result was a persisting biracial class consciousness unequaled in southern history.[57]

Although it is as yet too early to distinguish any clearly defined new "school of thought" on the agrarian revolt in the South, certain questions, implications, and suggestions have been raised. If these are pursued and elaborated, a new appraisal may develop. One of the tendencies is to broaden the period of reform activities to include both the agrarian revolt and the progressive period. Older works had, of course, recognized that the Populist demands were ultimately effected; but, beginning with Arthur S. Link's article in 1946, more recognition has been given to the role of southern agrarians in bringing about progressive reforms.[58] Eric F. Goldman's study of liberal reform since 1865 sees in progres-

56 Rogers, "Agrarianism in Alabama, 1865–1896" (Ph.D. dissertation, University of North Carolina, 1960).

57 Hair, "The Agrarian Protest in Louisiana, 1877–1900" (Ph.D. dissertation, Louisiana State University, 1962). Prior to this study by Hair, the only general work on Louisiana Populism was a published master's thesis. Lucia E. Daniel, "The Louisiana People's Party," *Louisiana Historical Quarterly,* XXVI (Oct., 1943), 1055–1149.

58 Link, "The Progressive Movement in the South, 1870–1914," *North Carolina Historical Review,* XXIII (April, 1946), 172–95. See also Link, "The South and the 'New Freedom,'" *American Scholar,* XX (Summer, 1951), 314–24; Anne F. Scott, "A Progressive Wind from the South, 1906–1913," *Journal of Southern History,* XXIX (Feb., 1963), 53–70.

sivism a continuation of the Populist emphasis upon economic opportunity and rights rather than liberty. He points to the fact that in the
South impoverished ex-Populists turned to demagogues who combined
reform efforts and racist attitudes. V. O. Key's thorough study of southern politics in the twentieth century essentially revolves around the
cleavage, fused in the fires of Populism, between the upcountry whites,
small farmer, labor faction with their tradition of radicalism and the
conservative Black Belters allied with merchants, bankers, and indus-
trialists.[59]

Joseph F. Steelman's recent study of the progressive movement in
North Carolina begins in the 1880's and shows that the Bourbons were
under increasing attack between 1884 and 1894 not only from farmers
but from protesting editors, lawyers, teachers, and "humanitarians of
every stripe and hue." He demonstrates that the pressure for progressive
reforms continued through the 1890's and on into the twentieth century,
sometimes resulting in changes, as under Fusionism, and sometimes
being thwarted by conservative reaction, as in 1898.[60] Chester M.
Destler has suggested sources of midwestern radicalism other than mere
agrarianism. Only a few articles, however, have attempted to treat non-
agrarian protest and reform efforts in the South prior to 1900.[61]

With the burgeoning civil rights movement, the 1950's witnessed increasing attention to the role of the Negro in the Populist revolt. Some
older studies written from the Negro point of view stressed how extensively the race issue and the Negro were used to defeat the third party
and to stabilize the solid Democratic South.[62] Woodward, however, emphasized the efforts made by some southern agrarians and Populists to
promote racial justice and political rights for Negroes. At the same time
he recognized, as have others, that the racism and anti-Negro diatribes
employed to defeat Populism contributed materially to the growth of

59 Goldman, *Rendezvous With Destiny* (New York, 1952); V. O. Key, Jr., *Southern Politics* (New York, 1949).
60 Steelman, "The Progressive Era in North Carolina, 1844–1917" (Ph.D. dissertation, University of North Carolina, 1955).
61 Herbert J. Doherty, Jr., "Voices of Protest from the New South, 1875–1910,"
Mississippi Valley Historical Review, XLII (June, 1955), 45–66; Jane Zimmerman, "The Penal Reform Movement in the South During the Progressive Era,
1890–1917," *Journal of Southern History*, XVII (Nov., 1951), 462–92; Arlin
Turner, "George W. Cable's Beginnings as a Reformer," *Journal of Southern
History*, XVII (May, 1951), 135–61.
62 J. L. Reddick, "The Negro and the Populist Movement in Georgia" (Master's
thesis, Atlanta University, 1937); Helen M. Blackburn, "The Populist Party in
the South, 1890–1898" (Master's thesis, Howard University, 1941).

segregation and disfranchisement.[63] Jack Abramowitz has also cited examples of Negro participation in Populism, but he acknowledges that Negro-white cooperation was accompanied by serious misgivings and that many agrarian leaders were not free from anti-Negro practices and statements.[64] A monograph that examines the role of the Negro in North Carolina during the Populist upheaval based its thesis on a somewhat different idea. Helen Edmonds, in support of her argument that the Conservative charge of Negro domination during Fusion was completely false, asserted that most Populists were dissatisfied Democrats whose racial attitudes were "avowedly anti-Negro." [65]

Some scholars who have studied the agrarian revolt in the same state have reached different conclusions about Negro-Populist relationships. The conflicting interpretations have resulted from at least two causes: first, the violent anti-Negro activities of some ex-Populists, such as Tom Watson, overshadowed their earlier efforts in behalf of racial cooperation; second, some Populists vacillated between a desire to promote a class struggle irrespective of race and their realization that such a policy made them vulnerable to conservative counterattack. Some still insist, however, that the most important aspect of Populism and race relations was the impetus that the reaction to the movement gave to disfranchisement and increased racism.[66]

In the last decade and a half new streams in American historical writing have been eroding the once-predominant concepts of conflict and polarity. Richard Hofstadter, a leading consensus historian, depicts Populism not fundamentally as a clash between liberal agrarian and conservative urban-industrial forces but rather as a movement stemming from farmers who had the same acquisitive goals and speculative temper as the business-commercial community. He plays down the "agrarian

63 C. Vann Woodward, *The Strange Career of Jim Crow* (New York, 1955); Woodward, "Tom Watson and the Negro," *Journal of Southern History*, IV (Feb., 1938), 14–33; George B. Tindall, "The Campaign for the Disfranchisement of Negroes in South Carolina," *Journal of Southern History*, XV (May, 1949), 212–34; Joseph H. Taylor, "Populism and Disfranchisement in Alabama," *Journal of Negro History*, XXXIV (Oct., 1949), 410–27.

64 Abramowitz, "The Negro in the Agrarian Revolt," *Agricultural History*, XXIV (April, 1950), 89–95; "The Negro in the Populist Movement," *Journal of Negro History*, XXX (July, 1953), 257–89; "John B. Raynor—Grass Roots Leader," *Journal of Negro History*, XXVIII (April, 1951), 160–93.

65 Edmonds, *The Negro and Fusion Politics in North Carolina* (Chapel Hill, 1951).

66 Rayford W. Logan, *The Negro in American Life and Thought: The Nadir, 1877–1901* (New York, 1954), 86; John H. Franklin, *From Slavery to Freedom, A History of American Negroes* (2nd ed.; New York, 1956), 332–33.

myth" which had implied that rural life and the goals of farmers were identical with democratic ideals. Hofstadter recognizes the impact of the movement in the areas of most acute agrarian distress, the Middle Border and the South, but he concludes that as a "political movement based upon the old phrases of agrarian ideology" it failed.[67]

Others have developed the idea that agrarian democracy, centered around ideals of equality and freedom, met its final defeat in the 1890's and that subsequent farmer organizations have developed around a power structure that actually repudiates the traditional nineteenth-century agrarian distrust of power.[68] Although such ideas have not yet been fully explored for southern Populism, David Potter has criticized southern historians for placing so much emphasis on the conflict between crass industrialism and a virtuous agrarian society. He contends that the southern economy and society have not been based predominantly on principles of small-farmer agrarianism, but rather on principles of commercial agriculture and the one-crop system.[69]

Some other recent studies have suggested a reevaluation of the Redeemer-agrarian conflict. Two students of the Mississippi Bourbons point out that the so-called triumvirate in that state was but "a pale replica" of the Georgia triumvirate which has often been accepted as the prototype for the entire South. James Z. George, one of the Mississippi trio, is described as more concerned with agrarian legislation than with special-interest measures for business and industrial growth.[70] These and other writings have implied that the Bourbon governments did not altogether neglect the farmer and his problems and that the "New South" creed gave considerable attention to agricultural improvements. Nash K. Burger and John K. Bettersworth, reminiscent of William W. Ball,[71] frankly admired the Bourbons and their accomplish-

67 Hofstadter, *The Age of Reform, From Bryan to F. D. R.* (New York, 1955), 23–93. For criticism of Hofstadter's methods and conclusions, see Norman Pollack, "Hofstadter on Populism: A Critique of *The Age of Reform,*" *Journal of Southern History,* XXVI (Nov., 1960), 478–500.

68 A. Whitney Griswold, *Farming and Democracy* (New York, 1948); Grant McConnell, *The Decline of Agrarian Democracy* (Berkeley, 1953); Charles M. Hardin, "Farm Politics and American Democracy," *Journal of Politics,* XVII (Nov., 1955), 651–63.

69 Potter, "The Enigma of the South," *Yale Review,* LI (Autumn, 1961), 142–51.

70 Willie D. Halsell, "The Bourbon Period in Mississippi Politics, 1875–1890," *Journal of Southern History,* XI (Nov., 1945), 519–37; May S. Ringold, "Senator James Zachariah George of Mississippi: Bourbon or Liberal?" *Journal of Mississippi History,* XVI (July, 1954), 164–82.

71 Ball, *The State That Forgot, South Carolina's Surrender to Democracy* (Indianapolis, 1932).

ments and censured the demagogue, the "spiritual descendants" of the embattled farmers. A similar effort to see the "other side of the coin" has cited evidence that the Alabama agrarians did not oppose the railroads.[72] It seems clear that there were decided differences between states in the post-Reconstruction political pattern, and some of the evidence tends to blur the lines of cleavage so sharply drawn by Woodward and others. One examination of these recent trends concludes that historians have probably been too quick to categorize southern leaders as *either* Bourbons *or* agrarians but cautions against unduly minimizing the agrarian protest in an effort to find consensus in the southern past.[73]

On the national level the current trend among many social scientists and a few historians is to cast the ideology of Populism in an unfavorable light. Hofstadter stresses the movement's alleged nativism and nationalism, with overtones of anti-Semitism and jingoism. Other urban-oriented writers, somewhat distrustful of mass, direct democracy, have gone further in identifying agrarians with antiliberal trends and even with ideas of the "radical right." Victor Ferkiss contends that American fascism owed much of its doctrine to the Populist tradition, and he cites the anti-Negro, demagogic ravings of Tillman and Watson as preparing the soil for fascist ideas of racism.[74] Another article points to the "latent nativism" in southern agrarian organizations as manifested in their opposition to unrestricted immigration.[75] Some strong rebuttals to these accusations have appeared. Woodward has warned of the danger "of swapping an old stereotype for a new one." He writes, "The old one sometimes approached the formulation that Populism is the root of all good in democracy, while the new one sometimes suggests that Populism is the root of all evil." [76] Two recent studies, both con-

72 Burger and Bettersworth, *South of Appomatox* (New York, 1959) ; James F. Doster, "Were Populists Against Railroad Corporations? The Case of Alabama." *Journal of Southern History,* XX (Aug., 1954), 395–99.

73 Dewey W. Grantham, "The Southern Bourbons Revisited," *South Atlantic Quarterly,* LX (Summer, 1961), 286–95.

74 Ferkiss, "Populist Influences on American Fascism," *Western Political Quarterly,* X (June, 1957), 350–73; "Populism: Myth, Reality, Current Danger," *Western Political Quarterly,* XIV (Sept., 1961), 737–40. For a criticism of Ferkiss' ideas, see Paul S. Holbo, "Wheat or What? Populism and American Fascism," *Western Political Quarterly,* XIV (Sept., 1961), 727–36.

75 Rowland T. Berthoff, "Southern Attitudes Toward Immigration," *Journal of Southern History,* XVII (Aug., 1951), 328–60.

76 C. Vann Woodward, "The Populist Heritage and the Intellectual," *American Scholar,* XXIX (Winter, 1959), 59.

fined to midwestern Populism, defend the movement as tolerant, forward looking, and committed to freedom and humanistic values.[77]

Much remains to be done on the agrarian revolt in the South, both in pursuing new lines of research and in synthesizing extant valid studies. Additional work on the independent and other anti-Bourbon movements would contribute to a clearer understanding of the political background of the revolt. Especially helpful would be more examinations of urban and labor developments and their impact on political history. Although much attention has been directed toward southern farm problems, the agrarian background of Populism is still incomplete. More studies of scientific agriculture, farm leaders, agricultural education,[78] and a general synthesis of postwar agrarian history are needed.

Adequate studies of the agrarian revolt are available for all southern states except Kentucky, Florida, and Arkansas. Still to be done, however, are comprehensive treatments of the regional agrarian organizations and biographies of such leaders as C. W. Macune, Reuben F. Kolb, and Lon Livingston. A synthesis of the third-party efforts in the South during the 1890's would clarify the similarities and the differences between the states. It might also focus attention on political maneuvering in an effort to understand how the thirty-party movement was undermined and what were the effects on the Democratic party.[79] The post-Populist period stands in need of many studies dealing with such subjects as agrarian movements and the subsequent role of ex-Populists in the progressive period.[80] In a rapidly urbanizing South, interest in agrarian history and agrarian causes has declined. Perhaps the study of such subjects from a more urbanized point of view will provide new insights and judgments for their overall significance in southern history.

---

77 Norman Pollack, *The Populist Response to Industrial America, Midwestern Populist Thought* (Cambridge, Mass., 1962) ; Walter T. K. Nugent, *The Tolerant Populists: Kansas Populists and Nativism* (Chicago, 1963).

78 See, for example, Chester M. Destler, "David Dickson's 'System of Farming' and the Agricultural Revolution in the Deep South," *Agricultural History,* XXXI (July, 1957), 30–39; Roy V. Scott, "Farmers' Institutes in Louisiana, 1897–1906," *Journal of Southern History,* XXV (Feb., 1959), 73–90.

79 For limited treatments of these ideas, see Allen J. Going, "Critical Months in Alabama Politics, 1895–1896," *Alabama Review,* V (Oct., 1952), 269–81; John E. Wiltz, "The 1895 Election: A Watershed in Kentucky Politics," *Filson Club Historical Quarterly,* XXXVII (April, 1963), 117–36.

80 One such study noted the divergent routes followed by Populist leaders and many Populist followers. Grady McWhiney, "Louisiana Socialists in the Early Twentieth Century: A Study in Rustic Radicalism," *Journal of Southern History,* XX (Aug., 1954), 315–36.

XVI

The Southern Mind
Since the Civil War

Horace H. Cunningham

FEW American historians have written with deeper understanding of the southern mind and spirit after the Civil War than C. Vann Woodward in his brilliant and authoritative *Origins of the New South, 1877–1913*. His chapter, "The Divided Mind of the New South," points up with rare discernment the battle between the old ideals centering around the "Lost Cause" and those which were being stridently proclaimed by the propagandists of industrialism and progress.[1] "As the economic and political conflict continued between advocates of the Old and New South," note two other perceptive observers, William B. Hesseltine and David L. Smiley, "it was also waged in the realm of culture: religion, education, journalism, and literature. . . . And as in economics and in politics, the New triumphed over the Old. In the last quarter of the century the South was a cultural colony drawing its intellectual and

1 Woodward, *Origins of the New South, 1877–1913* (Baton Rouge, 1951), 142–74.

literary values from the victorious East." Thus, conclude Hesseltine and Smiley, it became clear by 1900 that, while the Old South's defeat was not effected by the surrender at Appomattox, "the cultural surrender which followed it did make southern independence a Lost Cause." [2] And, Philip A. Bruce, writing almost half a century earlier than the foregoing, predicted that the Confederacy's defeat would eventually result in "the complete social unification of the United States" as the inevitable outcome "of the economic unification that followed almost immediately the destruction of the institution of slavery." [3]

The land of the South has been viewed with penetrating vision by other writers of distinction, and one of these, Francis Butler Simkins, has argued with considerable cogency that "despite changes which the catastrophe of 1865 made inevitable the distinctive culture of the section was never destroyed." Moreover, Simkins found himself speculating as to which section—North or South—would ultimately be the victor.[4] The continuity of the southern mentality is the thesis of Wilbur J. Cash's magisterial *The Mind of the South*. Entering the southern mind as no one else has done, impressing the reader throughout with his provocative ideas, and constantly displaying flashes of imaginative genius, Cash sees no significant conflict between the old ideals and progress in the postwar era. Indeed, he asserted at one point, "how essentially superficial and unrevolutionary remain the obvious changes [in the southern mind]; how certainly do these obvious changes take place within the ancient framework, and even sometimes contribute to the positive strengthening of the ancient pattern!" [5] It was in his skillful probing of the recent southern mind that Cash proved most stimulating. That one must use the singular "mind" with caution, however, was made evident by Earl E. Thorpe in a study of the Negro mind. Although he found similarities in the thought of the two races, Thorpe believed that in some respects "the mind of the South outlined by Cash is the Negro mind only in broadest outlines." [6] A more scholarly study by August Meier on a smaller segment of Negro thought provides significant background for the New Negro movement of the 1920's.[7]

2 Hesseltine and Smiley, *The South in American History* (2nd ed.; Englewood Cliffs, N. J., 1960), 435, 437.

3 Bruce, *The Rise of the New South* (Philadelphia, 1905), 435.

4 Simkins, *A History of the South* (3rd ed.; New York, 1963), 9, 11.

5 Cash, *The Mind of the South* (New York, 1941), 219.

6 Earl E. Thorpe, *The Mind of the Negro: An Intellectual History of Afro-Americans* (Baton Rouge, Ortlieb Press, 1961), xx.

7 Meier, *Negro Thought in America: Racial Ideologies in the Age of Booker T. Washington* (Ann Arbor, 1963).

While it is not the writer's purpose to join the continuing search for southern identity, one can hardly overlook in recent writings the recurrence of one particular theme: the experience of defeat and submission. C. Vann Woodward, in his presidential address before the Southern Historical Association in 1952, emphasized that the failure and humiliation suffered by the South represented "an experience that it could share with no other part of America." [8] And Louis D. Rubin, Jr., in a book resting upon the thesis that southernism ought to be preserved, concluded that the Civil War's impact upon the southern mind was "devastating and lasting," attributing to the memory of that conflict that which "more than anything else distinguishes the South from other areas of the country." An agrarian way of life and a Solid South possessed of a single mind were, according to Rubin, legacies of defeat and occupation.[9] "In defeat," echoed Robert Penn Warren while meditating upon the Civil War Centennial, "the Solid South was born. . . ." At "the moment of death the Confederacy entered upon its immortality." Thus, while the war's outcome retained the Confederacy for the Union, those states which had comprised it became more southern than ever.[10] In a book which some have called a sequel in miniature to Cash's masterpiece, Harry S. Ashmore explained that in any analysis of the southern mind one must remember that pride is involved, along with "the surprisingly durable memories of a lost war." [11] Such memories, others suggest, may have accounted for the region's early willingness to take up arms in behalf of Great Britain after the outbreak of the Second World War, as Southerners had been acquainted with defeat and did not want their cousins struggling against tyranny to have to undergo a similar experience.[12] There are, of course, additional explanations for "The Fighting South," but Virginius Dabney, writing in 1942, contended that the South had understood the real meaning of the Second World War sooner than any other part of the nation and alluded to the contrast between the almost unanimous support given by southern congressmen

8 Woodward, "The Irony of Southern History," *Journal of Southern History,* XIX (February, 1953), 5.

9 Rubin and Kilpatrick (eds.), *The Lasting South: Fourteen Southerners Look at Their Home* (Chicago, 1957), 7, 8.

10 Warren, *The Legacy of the Civil War: Meditations on the Centennial* (New York, 1961), 14–15.

11 Ashmore, *Epitaph for Dixie* (New York, 1958), 45.

12 See John Temple Graves, *The Fighting South* (New York, 1943), 8.

to extending the draft in 1941 and the overwhelming vote of congress-men from the Midwest in opposition to such extension.[13]

The imponderables in the southern mind and spirit, merely suggested by the foregoing, are indeed numerous and eclipse the concrete and the exact by a large margin. Nonetheless, Benjamin B. Kendrick and Alex M. Arnett based their *The South Looks at Its Past* upon the seem-ingly sound proposition "that indigenous to each region are certain his-toric and traditional culture patterns, certain physical and social capaci-ties and limitations, all of which must be taken into account in any rational scheme for a better order of life." [14] Accordingly, most of the emphasis in the remaining portion of this essay will be upon those studies which this writer believes will facilitate understanding of the social capacities and persistent cultural patterns of the South.

Not surprisingly, religion has occupied the attention of numerous writers. Simkins has asserted that conservatism in religion would rank close to "White Supremacy" in the list of significant causes for the regional distinctiveness of the land below the Potomac,[15] and other historians have said a loud "amen." Woodward's treatment of religion in the New South supported his judgment that no other facet of culture "could compare with religion in power and influence over the mind and spirit of the South." [16] In similar vein, John S. Ezell's chapter, "Re-ligion in the South," in his history of the postwar era has as its theme the mighty religious inclination of Southerners.[17]

The missionary campaign of northern Methodists during Reconstruc-tion is told in a readable and well-documented study by Ralph E. Mor-row.[18] An account by one who was an active participant in the crusade is Wesley J. Gaines's *African Methodism in the South*. Gaines saw the South as destined to become the great field of African Methodism and believed that the African Methodist Episcopal Church had done more for the Negro from 1865 to 1890 than any other denomination.[19] It would be difficult to find a more satisfactory monograph in the social history of the South from 1865 to 1900 than Hunter D. Farish's *The*

---

13 V. Dabney, *Below the Potomac: A Book about the New South* (New York, 1942), 285–87.

14 Kendrick and Arnett, *The South Looks at Its Past* (Chapel Hill, 1935), 3.

15 Simkins, *A History of the South*, 425.

16 Woodward, *Origins of the New South*, 448.

17 Ezell, *The South Since 1865* (New York, 1963), 355.

18 Morrow, *Northern Methodism and Reconstruction* (Lansing, 1956).

19 Gaines, *African Methodism in the South; or Twenty-Five Years of Freedom* (Atlanta, 1890), 268, 300.

Circuit Rider Dismounts, and more such studies for other denominations would be most welcome. Farish surveys the relationship of southern Methodism to social reform with considerable skill, and he concludes that the tolerant views of some church leaders "contributed much to the advancement of liberal thinking in the South." [20] However, according to Clement Eaton, it was Professor James Woodrow, Woodrow Wilson's uncle, who was responsible for initiating the spread of more enlightened thinking among southern theologians when in 1884 at the Presbyterian Theological Seminary, Columbia, South Carolina, he boldly defended Darwinian theories.[21] "Thereafter for nearly eighty years," Simkins noted, "the advocates of unyielding orthodoxy were in retreat." [22] Such challengers to orthodoxy were nonetheless forced to contend against a mind which Hesseltine and Smiley believe to have been closed by ignorance, poverty, and a deep fear of outsiders. Thus, it is contended, southern religionists were responsible for encircling the region with a new intellectual blockade, and the prevailing trends of American Christianity were rejected.[23]

The late nineteenth-century crusade to save traditional Christianity needs more study. Virginius Dabney's chapter, "Evolution and the Evangels," in his *Liberalism in the South,* underscored the intensity of that conflict as Methodists, Baptists, and Presbyterians "seized the banner of orthodoxy . . . and issued a resounding appeal to the faithful 'to rise in arms against Physical Science as the mortal enemy of all the Christian holds dear, and to take no rest until the infidel and atheistic foe has been utterly destroyed.' " [24] The extreme sensitivity of many Southerners to religious heresy was again illustrated by the Fundamentalist movement of the 1920's, which was interpreted by Kendrick and Arnett as "the Southern counterpart of the Northern red-hunt." [25] Maynard Shipley's *The War on Modern Science* showed, however, that anti-evolution agitation was by no means confined to the South and contended that embattled reactionaries, led by William Jennings Bryan, aimed ultimately at the virtual unification of church and state "under

20 Farish, *The Circuit Rider Dismounts: A Social History of Southern Methodism, 1865–1900* (Richmond, 1938), 367.

21 Eaton, "Professor James Woodrow and the Freedom of Teaching in the South," *Journal of Southern History,* XXVIII (February, 1962), 9–10.

22 Simkins, "The Rising Tide of Faith," in Louis D. Rubin, Jr., and James J. Kilpatrick (eds.), *The Lasting South: Fourteen Southerners Look at Their Home* (Chicago, 1957), 89.

23 Hesseltine and Smiley, *The South in American History,* 440.

24 V. Dabney, *Liberalism in the South* (Chapel Hill, 1932), 194.

25 Kendrick and Arnett, *The South Looks at Its Past,* 172.

sectarian-Fundamentalist-domination." [26] A more objective study of the Fundamentalist movement was that by Norman F. Furniss. He saw it as exemplifying the narrowness and provincialism of rural America in the 1920's and dealt with its impact upon the Baptists, Presbyterians, Methodists, Episcopalians, and Disciples of Christ.[27] Ray Ginger focused attention on the Scopes trial and interpreted it as involving recurrent problems of the democratic way of life,[28] whereas Edwin Mims, in his impressionistic *The Advancing South,* maintained that Bryan's uncompromising antievolution stand made conflict between science and religion irrepressible.[29]

The role played by religion in the election of 1928 has received shrewd and fair-minded attention from Edmund A. Moore in *A Catholic Runs for President.* Moore made it clear, however, that the religious issue was deeply entwined during the anti-Smith crusade with other issues such as prohibition, anti-urbanism, the liberal racial views of the Catholic church, and "Anglo-Saxon civilization." [30] Howard W. Odum, in his *An American Epoch,* furnished some interesting, and indignant, comment about the participation of "ecclesiastical politicians" in the 1928 campaign. "Again and again," he wrote, "the churches and their leaders slandered the Democratic candidate and his wife and family; again and again they presented downright falsehoods" and even suggested that the emblem of the Democracy be changed from the donkey to "a billy goat on a beer keg." Furthermore, he continued, while there was excoriation of evolution, materialism, atheism, recreation on Sunday, divorce, Catholics, Jews, Negroes, Yankees, cards, fiddling, theaters, crime, and youth, there was no protest against ignorance, hypocrisy, narrowness, intolerance, industrial wrongs, or discriminations of a racial character.[31]

Edwin McNeill Poteat, Jr., in an illuminating essay, agreed with Odum that the social vision of the southern churches had been extremely limited. Moreover, he underscored the illiberal character of theological

26 Shipley, *The War on Modern Science: A Short History of the Fundamentalist Attacks on Evolution and Modernism* (New York, 1927), 22.

27 Furniss, *The Fundamentalist Controversy* (New Haven, 1954).

28 Ginger, *Six Days or Forever? Tennessee v. John Thomas Scopes* (Boston, 1958).

29 Mims, *The Advancing South: Stories of Progress and Reaction* (Garden City, N.Y., 1926), 279–311.

30 Moore, *A Catholic Runs for President: The Campaign of 1928* (New York, 1956).

31 Odum, *An American Epoch: Southern Portraiture in the National Picture* (New York, 1930), 158–79.

training south of the Potomac by pointing to the fact that not a single southern theological school took a stand against the antievolutionist crusade.[32] Liston Pope's later dispassionate study of the role of the churches in the great Gastonia, North Carolina, textile strike of 1929 shed new and more intensive light on the church as an important agency in the local power structure.[33]

More recent studies of religion south of the Potomac have revealed some significant trends. Viewing the religious scene at mid-century, Simkins saw Southerners, white and Negro alike, catching up with Reinhold Niebuhr and other advocates of neo-orthodoxy. Having become increasingly pessimistic about the chances of fashioning an earthly kingdom of God, they were instead awaiting the Second Coming in a period of religious revival among all classes. Simkins also pointed to the strong influence of laymen in the church in keeping denominations from challenging the *status quo*.[34] In contrast, Thomas D. Clark, in *The Emerging South,* reported that Methodists and Presbyterians, in dealing with problems at their doorsteps, had learned the lessons of economics, political science, and sociology;[35] but Kenneth K. Bailey's *Southern White Protestantism in the Twentieth Century* concluded that religious faith, while remaining strong, was certainly not so pervasive in the 1960's as at the beginning of the century. Bailey thought, for example, that the influence of the southern clergy in meeting the great racial crises of the 1950's and 1960's was "clearly secondary."[36] Another authority affirmed that the subordination of the ministry and organized religion generally to established social patterns was the South's major religious problem, and he observed rather sorrowfully that churches were failing to give leadership to those seeking a way out of the racial impasse.[37] George B. Tindall, in a penetrating essay, agreed that southern churches were theologically conservative and socially remiss, but he argued that they had been important restraints "upon the most extreme expressions of racism, and have thereby contributed importantly to the erosion of the Southern Credo."[38] James Sellers, in

32 Poteat, "Religion in the South," in W. T. Couch (ed.), *Culture in the South* (Chapel Hill, 1934), 248–69.
33 Pope, *Millhands and Preachers: A Study of Gastonia* (New Haven, 1942).
34 Simkins, "The Rising Tide of Faith," *The Lasting South,* 84–103.
35 T. D. Clark, *The Emerging South* (New York, 1961). 248–70.
36 Bailey, *Southern White Protestantism in the Twentieth Century* (New York, 1964), 148.
37 Clyde L. Manschreck, "Religion in the South: Problem and Promise," in Francis Butler Simkins (ed.), *The South in Perspective* (Farmville, Va., 1959), 77–91.
38 Tindall, "The Central Theme Revisited," in Charles Grier Sellers (ed.), *The Southerner as American* (Chapel Hill, 1960), 120.

The South and Christian Ethics, envisions a victory for integration, but
he wonders about the moral problems subsequent thereto and whether
Christianity will be able to find a balm sufficiently potent to heal the
wounds torn open during years of racial conflict.[39]

There is a distinct need for more substantial work on particular religious groups, denominations, the rural church, and religious leaders.
Approximately one half of Carter G. Woodson's *History of the Negro
Church* [40] treated its post-Civil War development, but this work is undocumented and outdated, and there is a crying need for further research
and writing in this obviously important field.

The record of work on particular denominations and sects is more
impressive. Robert G. Torbet's *History of the Baptists* is a well-
documented and nearly inclusive study which does not neglect the relationship of this denomination's history to national and international developments.[41] Paul N. Garber's *The Methodists Are One People,*
although lacking documentation and a bibliography, is a valuable monograph about Methodist division and reunion.[42] Another denominational
study, that by George A. Singleton on the African Methodist Episcopal
Church, is far from definitive.[43] The Disciples of Christ has been the
object of a rather lengthy recent study by Earl Irvin West and an earlier
volume by Winfred E. Garrison and Alfred T. DeGroot.[44] A Different
kind of monograph is Elmer T. Clark's thoroughly researched examination of some one hundred smaller sects, many of which have southern
followings.[45] Little has been written about the southern country church
since the appearance of Jesse M. Ormond's *The Country Church in
North Carolina* in 1931. Conditions have changed so dramatically since
Ormond's research was done that new studies of the nature and future
of the country church within the region's social fabric are urgently
needed.[46]

A large body of biographical literature reveals the great influence of

39 Sellers, *The South and Christian Ethics* (New York, 1962).

40 Woodson, *The History of the Negro Church* (2nd ed.; Washington, 1945).

41 Torbet, *A History of the Baptists* (Philadelphia, 1950).

42 Garber, *The Methodists Are One People* (Nashville, 1939).

43 Singleton, *The Romance of African Methodism: A Study of the African Methodist Episcopal Church* (New York, 1952).

44 West, *The Search for the Ancient Order* (2 vols.; Nashville, 1957); Garrison
and DeGroot, *The Disciples of Christ* (St. Louis, 1948).

45 E. T. Clark, *The Small Sects in America* (Rev. ed.; Nashville, 1949).

46 Ormond, *The Country Church in North Carolina: A Study of the Country
Churches of North Carolina in Relation to the Material Progress of the State*
(Durham, 1931).

southern religious leaders since 1865, even though these works too often are uncritical and burdened with excessive detail. John Carlisle Kilgo, president of Trinity College from 1894 to 1910 and a vigorous leader of southern Methodism, is the subject of a well-researched study by Paul N. Garber.[47] Alfred M. Pierce has told the story of another giant among southern Methodist ministers and educators, Bishop Warren A. Candler of Atlanta. Pierce traces the life of this orthodox, combative, and determined leader through a stormy career which included an eight-year term as Emory University's first Chancellor and many more years of unyielding opposition to Methodist reunification; Candler "took his stand" on unification, Josephus Daniels is quoted as saying, "and was the lion in our path." [48] *Bishop Cannon's Own Story,* ably edited and with an excellent introduction by Richard L. Watson, Jr., is the memoir of still another contentious and powerful leader of southern Methodism, James Cannon, Jr.[49] It balances and somewhat answers the scathing indictment of Cannon in Virginius Dabney's *Dry Messiah.*[50] A scholarly biography of this controversial figure is an obvious need. John A. Rice's *I Came Out of the Eighteenth Century* provides some appealing glimpses of family life in Methodist parsonages and South Carolina's Female College, along with a number of memorable characterizations.[51] Extremely laudatory in tone are the "life and letters" volumes by Thomas C. Johnson on two staunchly conservative Presbyterian leaders whose lives spanned much of the nineteenth century: Robert L. Dabney and Benjamin M. Palmer. Dabney, unforgiving in his attitude toward the North and an opponent of public schools and evolution, was presented as one of the few really great theologians and philosophers produced in America.[52] Palmer "was one of the few greatest preachers of this century, and of the first nineteen centuries of the Christian era." [53] Briefer studies of the lives of Dabney and Palmer may be found in Henry A. White's

---

47 Garber, *John Carlisle Kilgo: President of Trinity College, 1894–1910* (Durham, 1937).

48 Pierce, *Giant against the Sky: The Life of Bishop Warren Akin Candler* (Nashville, 1948), 209.

49 Cannon, *Bishop Cannon's Own Story: Life as I Have Seen It,* ed. Richard L. Watson, Jr. (Durham, 1955).

50 V. Dabney, *Dry Messiah: The Life of Bishop Cannon* (New York, 1949).

51 Rice, *I Came Out of the Eighteenth Century* (New York, 1942).

52 T. C. Johnson, *The Life and Letters of Robert Lewis Dabney* (Richmond, 1903), 555–58.

53 T. C. Johnson, *The Life and Letters of Benjamin Morgan Palmer* (Richmond, 1906), 660.

Southern Presbyterian Leaders; all whose lives are included in the volume receive tender and loving attention.[54]

Educational development since 1865 is another aspect of southern cultural history which has commanded a not inconsiderable amount of attention. The influence of schools upon the mind of the South is almost beyond calculation. The guns were barely silenced before General Daniel H. Hill of North Carolina began a call for educational diversification, a call which was soon to be taken up as a part of the New South movement by Benjamin H. Hill, Henry W. Grady, Walter H. Page, and numerous others. Few would have taken issue with Philip A. Bruce when he wrote in 1905: "In public instruction . . . is to be discovered the firmest ground of hope for the moral and intellectual improvement of the Southern people as well as for the wisest use by them of the varied natural advantages which Providence has bestowed upon their region of country almost without stint." [55] Thirty years later, Arnett and Kendrick appraised the tax-supported schools, despite their many faults, "as the greatest contribution of the New South movement to the social and cultural life of the Southern people as a whole." [56] The southern educational story, Howard W. Odum declared in 1947, "is inseparable from the whole biography of the region in its American background." [57]

Most general histories of the South give a reasonable amount of space to education. Holland Thompson's *The New South* surveys educational progress through the second decade of the present century.[58] E. Merton Coulter furnishes a balanced treatment of Reconstruction's impact upon education in *The South During Reconstruction,*[59] and C. Vann Woodward carries the story through the New South to 1913—underscoring North Carolina's role in the origins of the great educational awakening.[60] Simkins, in his *History of the South,* while not failing to note the relative weakness of southern schools, emphasizes the widespread devotion to public education.[61] Thomas D. Clark, in *The Emerging South,* in-

---

54 White, *Southern Presbyterian Leaders* (New York, 1911).

55 Bruce, *The Rise of the New South,* 467.

56 Kendrick and Arnett, *The South Looks at Its Past,* 180.

57 Odum, *The Way of the South: Toward the Regional Balance of America* (New York, 1947), 219.

58 Thompson, *The New South: A Chronicle of Social and Industrial Revolution* (New Haven, 1919), 157–90.

59 Coulter, *The South During Reconstruction, 1865–1877* (Baton Rouge, 1947), 315–30.

60 Woodward, *Origins of the New South,* 61 and *passim.*

61 Simkins, *A History of the South,* 362–76.

cludes three chapters on the educational crusade, the Supreme Court's school decision in 1954, and subsequent regional developments in public education.[62] John S. Ezell's two chapters on education in *The South Since 1865* are well-written and informative.[63] Hesseltine and Smiley include stimulating sections on education in their volume and attribute certain southern peculiarities, such as demagoguery in politics, to education rendered deficient primarily by extreme poverty.[64]

General studies on public education have not been numerous, and this would appear to be a fruitful area for today's historians of the South. An illuminating analysis, published in 1922, was Edgar W. Knight's *Public Education in the South,* most of which dealt with the years before 1865.[65] In an essay written in 1934, Knight singled out the "social insanities" of "provincial prejudice and complacency" as major handicaps to overcoming the South's educational backwardness, and he called upon fellow Southerners to overcome their extreme sensitivity to criticism, examine themselves objectively, and forsake their tendency "to mistake the shadow for the substance of education." [66] Charles W. Dabney, in a well-researched, two-volume study of southern education, published fourteen years after Knight's book-length survey, also played upon the theme that education should be the chief function of a democratic nation. His second volume attempted to recount the story of the postwar southern educational movement largely through a series of biographical sketches and to show how the activities of educational foundations evoked other significant philanthropic activities aimed at the improvement of health, sanitation, and economic and social conditions generally.[67]

One of the first historical studies of Negro education was embodied in *Studies in Southern History and Politics,* edited by James W. Garner and inscribed to William A. Dunning. An essay therein, written by William K. Boyd, held that northern teachers of the freedmen "knew little of the delicate relations that exist between a lordly and a servile race." [68] A later scholarly and detailed account of these teachers by

62 T. D. Clark, *The Emerging South,* 149–205.

63 Ezell, *The South Since 1865,* 241–76.

64 Hesseltine and Smiley, *The South in American History,* 447–49, 593–96.

65 E. W. Knight, *Public Education in the South* (Boston, 1922).

66 E. W. Knight, "Recent Progress and Problems of Education," *Culture in the South,* 224, 225, 227.

67 C. W. Dabney, *Universal Education in the South* (2 vols.; Chapel Hill, 1936).

68 Boyd, "Some Phases of Educational History in the South since 1865," in James W. Garner (ed.), *Studies in Southern History and Politics* (New York, 1914), 282.

Henry Lee Swint revealed the strong southern reaction against them, though he concluded that the animosity which arose was not a reflection of opposition by southern whites to Negro education itself.[69] Of interest also in the realm of the Negro's postwar education is *Teach the Freeman,* edited by Louis D. Rubin, Jr., and devoted largely to the exchange of letters between President Hayes and the agents of the Slater Fund.[70] As Allen J. Going asserted in a well-ordered article, the heavy burden of educating the freedmen explained in part why many Southerners, mainly the New South champions, supported the ill-fated Blair education bill in the 1880's. In this division between educational modernists and fundamentalists, the latter won out, leaving, in Going's words, "the problem of public education in the South still unsolved." [71] Another important recent study, *Separate and Unequal,* by Louis R. Harlan, focuses on public educational crusades and racism in the Southeast from 1901 to 1915. Based upon careful scholarship, it discloses that as annual expenditures for education increased, flagrant discrimination in appropriations for Negro schools also increased. Harlan concludes, for example, that the Aycock era in North Carolina "was one of rapid deterioration in the concept of universal education, and of retrogression in the actual facilities provided for Negro schoolchildren." [72] Writing in 1939 about Negro education in Alabama, Horace Mann Bond also pointed up the wide difference in allotments for white and Negro schools. While wary about making predictions for the future, he thought that provisions for education might be affected by economic change or federal policy. The value of Bond's volume was enhanced by his superb evaluations of Booker T. Washington and Jabez L. M. Curry.[73]

Not all of the leaders of the educational crusade which developed during the New South period have received satisfactory biographical attention. George Peabody was the subject of a brief sketch prepared by Jabez L. M. Curry, himself one of the most distinguished figures in the educational movement. An important part of the book was Curry's ap-

69 Swint, *The Northern Teacher in the South, 1862–1870* (Nashville, 1941).

70 Rubin (ed.), *Teach the Freeman: The Correspondence of Rutherford B. Hayes and the Slater Fund for Negro Education, 1881–1887* (2 vols.; Baton Rouge, 1959).

71 Going, "The South and the Blair Education Bill," *Mississippi Valley Historical Review,* XLIV (September, 1957), 267–90.

72 Harlan, *Separate and Unequal: Public School Campaigns and Racism in the Southern Seaboard States, 1901–1915* (Chapel Hill, 1958), 110.

73 Bond, *Negro Education in Alabama: A Study in Cotton and Steel* (Washington, 1939).

praisal of the influence of the Peabody Educational Fund.[74] Jessie Pearl Rice's biography of Curry, while valuable, is relatively brief, and the writer did not succeed in showing Curry's relationship to the major developments of his era.[75] Louise Ware's biography of George Foster Peabody, treasurer of the General Education Board from 1902 until 1909, is based mainly upon interviews with friends of Peabody.[76] However, solid, full-length biographical studies, each a valuable addition to southern cultural history, have appeared for three leaders in the momentous educational awakening after 1900, Charles B. Aycock, Charles D. McIver, and Eugene C. Brooks.[77] An older study of one whose ideas and work helped prepare the way for the educational advancement is Burton J. Hendrick's skillful, sympathetic interpretation of Walter H. Page's earlier years. Page's doctrines, according to Hendrick, "injected an electric current into the life of North Carolina that . . . revitalized the State." [78] Complementing the Hendrick volume in several of its sections is Josephus Daniels' gossipy *Tar Heel Editor*.[79]

Much of the historical writing about higher learning in the South has centered on institutions. A pioneer, if undistinguished, study was John H. Reynolds' and David Y. Thomas' history of the University of Arkansas.[80] Philip A. Bruce's more detailed and authoritative history of the University of Virginia was published in the early 1920's.[81] Thomas P. Abernethy's brief sketch of the same university also merits recognition.[82]

Serious and really significant work in the history of southern higher education began in the 1930's. Walter L. Fleming's scholarly history of Louisiana State University from 1860 to 1896 appeared in 1936.[83] Soon

74 Curry, *A Brief Sketch of George Peabody and a History of the Peabody Education Fund through Thirty Years* (Cambridge, 1898), 25, 41.

75 Rice, *J. L. M. Curry: Southerner, Statesman, and Educator* (New York, 1949).

76 Ware, *George Foster Peabody: Banker, Philanthropist, Publicist* (Athens, Ga., 1951).

77 Oliver H. Orr, Jr., *Charles Brantley Aycock* (Chapel Hill, 1961); Rose Howell Holder, *McIver of North Carolina* (Chapel Hill, 1957); Willard B. Gatewood, Jr., *Eugene Clyde Brooks: Educator and Public Servant* (Durham, 1960).

78 Hendrick, *The Training of an American: The Earlier Life and Letters of Walter H. Page* (Boston and New York, 1928), 172.

79 Daniels, *Tar Heel Editor* (Chapel Hill, 1939).

80 Reynolds and Thomas, *History of the University of Arkansas* (Fayetteville, 1910).

81 Bruce, *History of the University of Virginia, 1819–1919* (5 vols.; New York, 1920–1922).

82 Abernethy, *Historical Sketch of the University of Virginia* (Richmond, 1948).

83 Fleming, *Louisiana State University, 1860–1896* (Baton Rouge, 1936).

afterward came David A. Lockmiller's histories of North Carolina State College and of the consolidation of the University of North Carolina.[84] Louis R. Wilson told the absorbing story of how the University of North Carolina became, from 1900 to 1930, "in a very true sense the principal instrument of North Carolina's educational, economic, and social well-being." [85] The history of Vanderbilt University was written with unusual clarity and literary skill by Edwin Mims.[86] A history notable for the objectivity of the author and the thoroughness of his research is that of the University of Kentucky, written by James F. Hopkins.[87] Two of the best histories of state universities are those by Daniel W. Hollis and John K. Bettersworth on the University of South Carolina and Mississippi State College, respectively. Hollis' history, largely administrative, relates the dramatic and well-documented account of a crisis-ridden institution first seeking a mission which would be acceptable both to itself and the citizenry of the state and then attempting to coordinate its efforts in moving toward implementation of the task ahead.[88] Bettersworth's well-conceived history of Mississippi State closely relates that institution's history to the development of the state, as does Hollis'.[89] A History of the University of Mississippi, by James A. Cabaniss, suffers somewhat by comparison with the Mississippi State volume, and it is hoped that a more thorough study of the former may be forthcoming soon.[90] Histories of Georgia Tech, the University of Georgia, Virginia Military Institute, and Eastern Kentucky State Teachers College, written or edited by Marion L. Brittain, Robert P. Brooks, William Couper, and Jonathan T. Dorris, respectively, are additional studies of state institutions.[91]

84 Lockmiller, History of the North Carolina State College of Agriculture and Engineering of the University of North Carolina, 1889–1939 (Raleigh, 1939); The Consolidation of the University of North Carolina (Chapel Hill, 1942).

85 L. R. Wilson, The University of North Carolina, 1900–1930: The Making of a Modern University (Chapel Hill, 1957), xviii.

86 Mims, History of Vanderbilt University (Nashville, 1946).

87 Hopkins, The University of Kentucky: Origins and Early Years (Lexington, 1951).

88 Hollis, University of South Carolina (2 vols.; Columbia, 1951, 1956).

89 Bettersworth, People's College: A History of Mississippi State (University, Ala., 1953).

90 Cabaniss, A History of the University of Mississippi (University, Miss., 1949).

91 Brittain, The Story of Georgia Tech (Chapel Hill, 1948); Brooks, The University of Georgia under Sixteen Administrations, 1785–1955 (Athens, Ga., 1956); Couper, One Hundred Years at V. M. I. (4 vols.; Richmond, 1939–1940); Dorris (ed.), Three Decades of Progress: Eastern Kentucky State Teachers College, 1906–1936 (Richmond, Ky., 1936).

Church-related and other type institutions of higher learning have also had their historians. Rhoda C. Ellison's history of Huntingdon College is a model of scholarly and graceful writing.[92] Randolph-Macon Woman's College has been given sound historical treatment by Roberta D. Cornelius, and Mary Baldwin College is the subject of a detailed history by Mary Watters.[93] David D. Wallace's history of Wofford College is a solid contribution to the history of the South over the entire first century of the college's existence.[94] A more exhaustive institutional history is that of Wake Forest College by George W. Paschal, a three-volume narrative of the college's triumphs and trials.[95] Valuable in many respects is Henry M. Bullock's history of Emory University; but the style is not consistently acceptable, and one fails to see Emory in its relationship to the social, political, and economic development of the southern region.[96] Trinity College's history receives scholarly treatment by Nora C. Chaffin, and it is possible to learn much about Coker College in George L. Simpson's *The Cokers of Carolina*.[97] The history of the University of Chattanooga is faithfully recorded by Gilbert E. Govan and James W. Livingood, but J. H. Easterby has written with less objectivity about the College of Charleston.[98] Elizabeth S. Peck's history of Berea College is competent.[99] A different approach is embodied in Charles D. Johnson's factual record of Southern Baptist work in the field of higher education.[100] Burton J. Hendrick's chapter on "Southern College Life in the Seventies" in the previously mentioned volume about Page is a brief, albeit informative, look at college life from the vantage point of the student.[101] This and other such accounts in the college and

---

92 Ellison, *History of Huntingdon College, 1854–1954* (University, Ala., 1954).

93 Cornelius, *The History of Randolph-Macon Woman's College: From the Founding in 1891 Through the Year of 1949–1950* (Chapel Hill, 1951); Watters, *The History of Mary Baldwin College, 1842–1942* (Staunton, Va., 1942).

94 Wallace, *History of Wofford College, 1834–1949* (Nashville, 1951).

95 Paschal, *History of Wake Forest College* (3 vols.; Wake Forest, 1935–1943).

96 Bullock, *A History of Emory University* (Nashville, 1936).

97 Chaffin, *Trinity College, 1839–1892: The Beginnings of Duke University* (Durham, 1950); Simpson, *The Cokers of Carolina: A Social Biography of a Family* (Chapel Hill, 1956).

98 Govan and Livingood, *The University of Chattanooga: Sixty Years* (Chattanooga, 1947); Easterby, *A History of the College of Charleston* (Charleston, 1935).

99 Peck, *Berea's First Century, 1855–1955* (Lexington, 1955).

100 C. D. Johnson, *Higher Education of Southern Baptists: An Institutional History, 1826–1954* (Waco, 1955).

101 Hendrick, *The Training of an American.*

university histories perhaps suggest the need for a good synthetic monograph.

Several writers have concerned themselves specifically with the Negro college. Dwight Oliver Wendell Holmes, in *The Evolution of the Negro College,* pointed out the defects and difficulties of the institutions open to Negro youth in 1934 and appealed for a sustained planning effort which would enable Negro colleges to measure up to the "American standard." [102] While the organization and style of Walter Dyson's detailed history of Howard University leaves much to be desired, it is an important study of a leading Negro educational institution.[103] Willard Range has described the metamorphosis of the Negro college in Georgia since 1865.[104]

Philip A. Bruce's intelligent volume about the New South contains the following perceptive observation: "Perhaps the most farseeing patriots in that part of the Union [the South] at the present time are to be found in the presidential chairs of its leading institutions of learning." [105] One also suspects that the statement is as applicable in the 1960's as it was in 1905. At any rate, it is a source of gratification to know that at least a few of those who served in such positions have received excellent biographical treatment.

It is fitting that two of the best biographies of southern leaders in higher education are those whose subjects labored so effectively at Vanderbilt University: Bishop Holland Nimmons McTyeire and Chancellor James H. Kirkland, whose administrations spanned more than sixty years of that institution's history. John J. Tigert, IV's well-documented and objective volume explains McTyeire's part in the founding and early history of Vanderbilt.[106] Edwin Mims's biography of Kirkland is a sympathetic interpretation by one who was an associate of his subject for more than fifty years. Kirkland's service as chancellor covered the period from 1893 to 1937, and his educational statesmanship is revealed throughout the Mims book in a profusion of quotations from both published and unpublished materials. One has no inclination to challenge Mims's assertion that Kirkland deserves a place among the

102 Holmes, *The Evolution of the Negro College* (New York, 1934), 202.

103 Dyson, *Howard University, The Capstone of Negro Education. A History: 1867–1940* (Washington, 1941).

104 Range, *The Rise and Progress of Negro Colleges in Georgia, 1865–1949* (Athens, Ga., 1951).

105 Bruce, *The Rise of the New South,* 467.

106 Tigert, *Bishop Holland Nimmons McTyeire: Ecclesiastical and Educational Architect* (Nashville, 1955).

leaders of the New South. His organization of the Southern Association of Colleges and Schools, his fight for high standards, and his unusual educational vision need only be mentioned to indicate his immeasurable contribution to southern education.[107]

Another valuable study is Dumas Malone's biography of Edwin A. Alderman. Alderman, more than any other individual after Jabez L. M. Curry, "became the symbol and spokesman of southern education." He served as president of the University of North Carolina and then of Tulane University before accepting a call to become the first president of the University of Virginia. "In his time," concluded Malone, "he was one of the prophets and builders of his section, and, more than any other single man, he embodied its educational history." [108] Thomas D. Boyd's life, including his thirty-one years as president of Louisiana State University, is given fairly satisfactory treatment by Marcus M. Wilkerson. There is much about Boyd's struggles to build an institution capable of meeting regional needs, but no attempt is made to evaluate fully his overall contribution.[109] *McIver of North Carolina*, by Rose H. Holder, is the first full-length biography of another educator who left to his people a legacy of college education for girls as well as boys.[110]

Trinity College, later Duke University, has had able leaders. One of these, John C. Kilgo, is the subject of the competent biography by Paul N. Garber cited earlier. Kilgo's crusade in support of Christian education, his part in the conflict between the state and denominational colleges, his fight against professionalism in college athletics, and his stand in the Bassett controversy, are all related in an absorbing fashion. Garber's contention that Kilgo held advanced social, economic, and political views seems, however, to be somewhat in conflict with the facts.[111] The papers and addresses of William P. Few, Duke University's first president, have been competently edited by Robert H. Woody. In a biographical appraisal, Woody states that Few's greatness lay "in an inspired vision of the future and the quiet and patient determination to bring that vision into reality." [112]

Important studies have been made of several Negro leaders who oc-

107 Mims, *Chancellor Kirkland of Vanderbilt* (Nashville, 1940).

108 Malone, *Edwin A. Alderman: A Biography* (New York, 1940), 26, viii.

109 Wilkerson, *Thomas Duckett Boyd: The Story of a Southern Educator* (Baton Rouge, 1935).

110 Holder, *McIver of North Carolina.*

111 Garber, *John Carlisle Kilgo.*

112 *The Papers and Addresses of William Preston Few, Late President of Duke University,* ed. Woody (Durham, 1951), 141.

cupy high rank among southern educational administrators. Outstanding among these is Booker T. Washington, who did more than any other individual to persuade the white South to accept higher education for his race. His own autobiography, of course, is a classic—over two hundred pages relate to his years at Tuskegee—and there is another volume which includes his significant public addresses.[113] There is no completely satisfying biography of Washington, even though several volumes of a biographical character, beginning with the undocumented and uncritical work by Emmett J. Scott, Washington's secretary for a number of years, and Lyman B. Stowe, have been published.[114] Basil Mathews' study of Washington is a good portrayal of his twin role as educator and interracial interpreter, but there is no bibliography, and the interpretation is quite favorable to Washington throughout.[115] More scholarly and authoritative is Samuel R. Spencer's brief biography, which attempts to relate Washington and his work to the general southern milieu.[116] A volume in tribute to Washington's successor at Tuskegee, Robert R. Moton, has been edited by William H. Hughes and Frederick D. Patterson.[117] Moton, an outstanding educator, deserves a full-length biography.

That facet of cultural development in the South which has commanded most attention nationally has been the consistently vigorous and sometimes brilliant quality of its literature. Paul H. Buck's *Road to Reunion, 1865–1900,* left no doubt about the impact of southern fictional writers upon the northern mind in helping to bridge the chasm between the sections in the postwar years. Literature, contended Buck, dispelled the completely hostile northern picture of the South and proved to be more important than any other factor in restoring sectional harmony.[118] A similar note was struck by Edwin Mims in the still-useful series, *The South in the Building of the Nation,* when he concluded that writers like Thomas Nelson Page and Joel Chandler Harris had been "among the

---

113 B. T. Washington, *Up from Slavery: An Autobiography* (Garden City, N.Y., 1901) ; *Selected Speeches of Booker T. Washington,* ed. E. D. Washington (Garden City, N.Y., 1932).

114 Scott and Stowe, *Booker T. Washington: Builder of a Civilization* (Garden City, N.Y., 1916).

115 Mathews, *Booker T. Washington: Educator and Interracial Interpreter* (Cambridge, 1948).

116 Spencer, *Booker T. Washington and the Negro's Place in American Life* (Boston, 1955).

117 Hughes and Patterson (eds.), *Robert Russa Moton of Hampton and Tuskegee* (Chapel Hill, 1957).

118 Buck, *The Road to Reunion, 1865–1900* (Boston, 1937).

prime forces in revealing the South to the nation and the nation to the South, thus furthering one of the most important tasks of the present generation—the promotion of a real national spirit." [119]

Southern literary activity is not neglected in the two-volume *Literary History of the United States,* edited by Robert E. Spiller and others; and the volumes in the "American Guide Series" of the Federal Writers' Project on southern states and cities include articles about their literature.[120] The general studies of southern history do not usually slight literature. Both Coulter and Woodward, in volumes cited previously, contain numerous shrewd comments about southern fictional writing and other literature from 1865 to 1913. Coulter terms the literature of Reconstruction one of defense "against anything Northern," which no doubt explains why Cash spoke of it as "a propaganda." [121] Woodward is not unappreciative of those writers who were responsible for the southern revival in the 1880's, but he complains about the lack of realistic portrayal in their work.[122] On the other hand, it may be that Edmund Wilson was right in saying that no one in this period cared particularly to have the realities portrayed.[123] Arthur M. Schlesinger considers "The Renaissance in Letters and Art" in *The Rise of the City, 1878–1898,* and Simkins, by way of concluding a fine chapter on literature in *A History of the South,* suggests that "a wide reading of Southern literature yields a complete and profound understanding of the region." [124] Ezell's chapter on "The Southern Literary Renaissance" in *The South Since 1865* is a solid piece of writing.[125] Hesseltine and Smiley give a different emphasis, noting a continuation into the twentieth century of "conflict between literary modernists and fundamentalists." [126] Significant also are the

119 Mims, "Southern Fiction after the War of Secession," in Julian A. C. Chandler *et al.* (eds.), *The South in the Building of the Nation* (13 vols.; Richmond, 1909–1913), VIII, p. lxiv.

120 Spiller *et al.* (eds.), *Literary History of the United States* (Rev. 3rd ed.; 2 vols.; New York, 1963); see *Catalog American Guide Series Federal Writers' Project* (Washington, 1938).

121 Coulter, *The South During Reconstruction,* 283; Cash, *The Mind of the South,* 142.

122 Woodward, *Origins of the New South,* 168.

123 E. Wilson, *Patriotic Gore: Studies in the Literature of the American Civil War* (New York, 1962), 613.

124 Schlesinger, *The Rise of the City, 1878–1898* (New York, 1933); Simkins, *A History of the South,* 453.

125 Ezell, *The South Since 1865,* 277–95.

126 Hesseltine and Smiley, *The South in American History,* 525.

two chapters on literature and journalism in Virginius Dabney's *Liberalism in the South.*[127]

Nothing like a comprehensive and historical survey of southern literature since the Civil War has been made; perhaps one should not even be attempted, as Louis D. Rubin, Jr., suggests, while "modern Southern literature and the Southern Literary Renascence . . . [are] still very much alive and changing." Rubin believes, however, that one phase of the renascence, which began with the Nashville Fugitives, came to an end with the death of William Faulkner.[128]

Several studies which grew out of the literary renascence deserve at least passing mention. One of these, by C. Alphonso Smith, appraised in 1927 a number of contemporary southern fiction writers who, Smith believed, were writing southern history because they were "interpreting Southern life." [129] Donald Davidson presented an essay on the trend of literature in 1934, but refused to believe that a literary revival was under way in the region.[130] Five years later, Shields McIlwaine, in an excellent monograph, ventured a compelling literary interpretation of the "poor whites." [131] And, in 1954, Jay B. Hubbell's massive *The South in American Literature, 1607–1900,* received acclaim as one of the signal achievements of historical scholarship; Hubbell, however, accorded thorough treatment to only seven post-Civil War writers.[132]

Objective historical study is needed on the luminous band of Nashville Fugitives and the Agrarian protest of the twenties and thirties. In his misleadingly titled *Southern Writers in the Modern World,* Donald Davidson has penned only a brief literary memoir of the Fugitives and Agrarianism.[133] Louise Cowan's recent history of the Fugitive group draws upon unpublished letters of its members to provide insights concerning their literary accomplishments, and she includes extracts from *The Fugitive* in a valuable appendix.[134] *Fugitive's Reunion,* edited by Rob Roy Purdy, contains the record of what the Fugitives themselves

127 V. Dabney, *Liberalism in the South.*

128 Rubin, *The Faraway Country: Writers of the Modern South* (Seattle, 1963), xiii, 235.

129 C. A. Smith, *Southern Literary Studies* (Chapel Hill, 1927), 70.

130 Davidson, "The Trend of Literature: A Partisan View," in Couch (ed.), *Culture of the South,* 186.

131 McIlwaine, *The Southern Poor-White: From Lubberland to Tobacco Road* (Norman, Okla., 1939).

132 Hubbell, *The South in American Literature, 1607–1900* (Durham, 1954).

133 Davidson, *Southern Writers in the Modern World* (Athens, Ga., 1958).

134 Cowan, *The Fugitive Group: A Literary History* (Baton Rouge, 1959).

said about the movement during a three-day reunion at Vanderbilt in 1956. A discussion there between the Agrarians brought to light some historically important information about the Agrarian Manifesto, *I'll Take My Stand*. The Scopes trial was pointed to as strongly influencing the decision to write the book, and there was general agreement that the choice of the term "Agrarian" was not a good one. Frank L. Owsley considered their revolt to be against materialism and stereotyped living, whereas Robert Penn Warren remembered the protest as one against loss of the individual's role in society, and thought that they were attempting to discover "a rational basis for a democracy." [135] *I'll Take My Stand,* however, presented the forces of industrialism and agrarianism as representing exclusive ways of life, with agrarianism offering the only hope for maintaining the charm and humanity characteristic of the Old South.[136] Similar ideas were expressed with lyric beauty in William A. Percy's *Lanterns on the Levee.*[137]

The South's literary figures have not fared particularly well in the field of biography. Alluding to this fact in 1947, Gregory Paine declared that "nearly every author of essays and fiction needs a new biography, a bibliography of his writings, and some competent critical evaluation based upon full information." [138] William P. Trent's life of William Gilmore Simms, published in 1892, dealt quite sketchily with the famous South Carolinian's postwar years.[139] Sidney Lanier, another whose work extended from the Old South into the New, has received admirable biographical and critical treatment at the hands of Aubrey H. Starke.[140] The best known members of the "local color" contingent of the 1880's have not been overlooked. George W. Cable, who strongly attacked various aspects of southern life after achieving fame as a writer of Creole stories, has been the object of sound treatment by Lucy Leffingwell Cable Biklé, Arlin Turner, and Philip Butcher. Mrs. Biklé, a daughter of Cable, was able to harmonize the apparently diverse elements of the writer's personality through her skillful use of his letters, works, and diaries.[141] Few, if any, biographies of southern

135 Purdy (ed.), *Fugitive's Reunion: Conversations at Vanderbilt, May 3–5, 1956* (Nashville, 1959), 206–13.

136 Twelve Southerners, *I'll Take My Stand: The South and the Agrarian Tradition* (New York, 1930).

137 Percy, *Lanterns on the Levee, Recollections of a Planter's Son* (New York, 1941).

138 Paine, *Southern Prose Writers* (New York, 1947), vi.

139 Trent, *William Gilmore Simms* (New York, 1892).

140 Starke, *Sidney Lanier: A Biographical and Critical Study* (Chapel Hill, 1933).

141 Biklé, *George W. Cable: His Life and Letters* (New York, 1928).

writers are more discriminating, authoritative, and scholarly than Turner's volume, one which shows plainly his subject's true significance for the historian.[142] Butcher's emphasis is upon Cable as social reformer.[143] The best existing biographies of James Lane Allen and Charles Egbert Craddock (Mary Noailles Murfree) are those by Grant C. Knight and Edd W. Parks, respectively.[144] There are as yet no satisfactory biographical studies of Joel Chandler Harris and Thomas Nelson Page. A rather interesting record of Harris' life, by his daughter, and the only book-length portrayal of Page, by his brother, will no doubt be useful to future biographers of these two romanticists who continued to write lovingly and longingly of a society which perhaps had never really existed.[145] Other studies worthy of note are Daniel S. Rankin's rather detailed examination of the life and work of Kate Chopin and Edward L. Tinker's candid picture of Lafcadio Hearn's twenty years in America, ten of which were spent in New Orleans.[146] Critical and authoritative biographies of Ellen Glasgow and southern literati of the present century, while needed, have not as yet made their appearance.

Magazines, a rich source for the social historian, for many years have furnished the region's writers a medium for their literary output. Frank L. Mott's detailed and well-ordered *History of American Magazines* has overlooked neither the South's magazines nor the continuing indifference of the southern people toward this literary form.[147] Briefer though not unimportant studies have been James P. Wood's *Magazines in the United States* and Theodore Peterson's *Magazines in the Twentieth Century,* the latter concerning itself only with the popular magazine.[148] An intelligent study devoted solely to southern magazines was Jay B. Hubbell's essay in *Culture in the South.* While asserting that magazines represented perhaps the best expression of the region's mind,

142 Turner, *George W. Cable: A Biography* (Durham, 1956).

143 Butcher, *George W. Cable* (New York, 1962).

144 G. C. Knight, *James Lane Allen and the Genteel Tradition* (Chapel Hill, 1935); Parks, *Charles Egbert Craddock (Mary Noailles Murfree)* (Chapel Hill, 1941).

145 Julia Florida (Collier) Harris, *The Life and Letters of Joel Chandler Harris* (New York, 1918); Rosewell Page, *Thomas Nelson Page, A Memoir of a Virginia Gentleman* (New York, 1923).

146 Rankin, *Kate Chopin and Her Creole Stories* (Philadelphia, 1932); Tinker, *Lafcadio Hearn's American Days* (New York, 1924).

147 Mott, *A History of American Magazines* (4 vols.; Cambridge, 1930–1957).

148 Wood, *Magazines in the United States* (2nd ed.; New York, 1956); Peterson, *Magazines in the Twentieth Century* (2nd ed.; Urbana, 1964).

Hubbell, like Mott, alluded to their inhospitable reception and expressed the view that the southern magazine's future would be no less interesting than its past.[149]

Wendell H. Stephenson, in *The South Lives in History,* paid high tribute to the *Sewanee Review* and William P. Trent, its founder and first editor.[150] *Fifty Years of the South Atlantic Quarterly,* edited by William B. Hamilton, indicated that this excellent journal and its founder, John Spencer Bassett, became as important as their predecessors in promoting the South's social and cultural development.[151] Additional publications of this kind would be helpful in enabling one to comprehend more clearly the full impact of the literary journal upon the southern mind. Virginius Dabney, in his short analysis of such periodicals, expressed the opinion that they were in part responsible for the southern literary renascence.[152]

Frank L. Mott's *American Journalism,* a truly herculean effort to present a history of the nation's newspapers from 1690 to 1950, did not overlook the southern press.[153] Most general histories of the South also give some attention to its journalism, but book-length studies of newspapers and editors are scarce. Coulter, in his brief but incisive treatment of the Radical and Democratic press during Reconstruction, saw Democratic editors wielding influence beyond even the control of the military authorities.[154] The chapters which dealt with journalists in Virginius Dabney's *Liberalism in the South* were broad in scope, and yet they contained absorbing interpretations of the postwar journalistic giants. Allusion was made to "Marse Henry" Watterson's considerable influence, as editor of the Louisville *Courier-Journal,* in bringing about sectional reconciliation; to Francis W. Dawson's "sane, intelligent, and liberal" effect upon the southern mind during his editorship of the Charleston *News and Courier;* and to the "lasting contribution" which Walter Hines Page made to the development of liberal thought while editor of the Raleigh *State Chronicle.* Writing from the vantage point of 1932, Dabney believed that the southern press had moved from

149 Hubbell, "Southern Magazines," in Couch (ed.), *Culture in the South,* 159–82.

150 *Ibid.;* Stephenson, *The South Lives in History: Southern Historians and Their Legacy* (Baton Rouge, 1955), 3.

151 Hamilton (ed.), *Fifty Years of the South Atlantic Quarterly* (Durham, 1952).

152 V. Dabney, *Liberalism in the South,* 396.

153 Mott, *American Journalism: A History of Newspapers in the United States through 260 Years: 1690 to 1950* (New York, 1950).

154 Coulter, *The South During Reconstruction,* 289.

provincialism and partisanship at the end of the nineteenth century to a tone which equalled "if indeed it does not surpass, that of any other section of the United States in forthrightness and in liberalism." [155]

W. J. Robertson, in his chapter on the press, in *The Changing South,* reached conclusions similar to those of Dabney and thought that the southern newspaper was an important factor in teaching the region "that many of its political, social and religious notions, which it has held for so many years, do not belong in an up-to-date civilization." [156] There were dissenting voices, however, and one of these was that of John D. Allen, who wrote the chapter titled "Journalism in the South" for the Couch volume. Writing at about the same time as Dabney, Allen injected the jarring note that the distinctive qualities which southern journalism and culture generally had once possessed had been lost in the materialistic and mechanistic culture of the New South. "The great majority of southern newspapers," he stated, "are smug class organs, standardized, superficial, often unfair in the presenting of news, and worse than useless as interpreters of the present scene or as guides to the future." [157] Studies are now needed to bring this particular dialogue up to date so that the quest for truth concerning journalism's history in the South may continue along a brighter path.

Illumination could perhaps be provided by more histories of leading southern newspapers. Sam Acheson's history of the Dallas *Morning News,* the oldest business institution in Texas, is interesting, but it frequently gets lost in the history of Texas. One may also need to go beyond the files of a newspaper to show its full impact upon the area in which it circulates.[158] An enthusiastically written and factual chronicle which needed better organization is Thomas E. Dabney's centennial history of the New Orleans *Times-Picayune,* almost half of which is devoted to the period before 1865.[159] Another study of a single paper is that by E. L. Bell of the Augusta *Chronicle.*[160] An excellent description of the influence of rural or small town editors and their weekly papers in various aspects of life is given by Thomas D. Clark in

155 V. Dabney, *Liberalism in the South,* 228–37, 398.

156 Robertson, *The Changing South* (New York, 1927), 164.

157 Allen, "Journalism in the South," in Couch (ed.), *Culture in the South,* 158.

158 Acheson, *35,000 Days in Texas: A History of the Dallas News and Its Forbears* (New York, 1938).

159 T. E. Dabney, *One Hundred Great Years: The Story of the Times-Picayune From its Founding to 1940* (Baton Rouge, 1944).

160 Bell, *The Augusta Chronicle: Indomitable Voice of Dixie, 1785–1960* (Athens, Ga., 1960).

The Southern Country Editor.[161] Negro journalism in the South still awaits its historian.

Southern achievement in the realm of the nonliterary arts has been disappointing when contrasted with the remarkable literary output, as is revealed by the comparative paucity of writing pertaining to the former. One of the best general sources for this subject is the "American Guide Series" of the Federal Writers' Project, and Oliver W. Larkin's *Art and Life in America* is not completely devoid of references to southern artistic achievement.[162] Nowhere is there a more satisfactory introduction to the fine arts below the Potomac than Simkins' treatment of the region's meager accomplishments in this field in *A History of the South.*[163] Of worth also is Ula Milner Gregory's essay in *Culture in the South;* she hopefully noted in 1934 a growing regional consciousness of certain art forms. With reference to architecture, however, she observed that the South, living on memories, had failed to make a single original contribution since 1865 despite the extensive building that had taken place therein.[164]

S. Fiske Kimball's *American Architecture* stresses the theme that art must change if it is to live, but allusions to southern architecture since the Civil War are limited to Biltmore in western North Carolina, where an effort was made to create a French chateau, and to Florida, where a return to local Spanish traditions was inaugurated.[165] *The South in Architecture,* by Lewis Mumford, is also rather fragmentary insofar as it concerns the recent South, but Mumford's explanation of true regional architecture is an enlightening one, as is his statement that in those instances when "social interests have been paramount in our architectural planning, the results have been decisively good." [166] A penetrating examination of contemporary architecture's genesis in the Southeast is supplied by Edward and Elizabeth Waugh in their richly illustrated *The South Builds.* Viewing the sameness of southern cities as a commentary on the region's aesthetic debasement, the Waughs conclude that architectural grace can be recaptured only by total environmental planning. Such planning envisions the architect and other professionals working together in designing the future development of the

161 T. D. Clark, *The Southern Country Editor* (Indianapolis, 1948).
162 Larkin, *Art and Life in America* (New York, 1949).
163 Simkins, *A History of the South,* 455–69.
164 Gregory, "The Fine Arts," in Couch (ed.), *Culture in the South,* 270–98.
165 Kimball, *American Architecture* (Indianapolis, 1928), 127, 129.
166 Mumford, *The South in Architecture* (New York, 1941), 143.

South's towns and countryside.[167] The Waughs would no doubt sym-
pathize with Donald Davidson's complaint in *I'll Take My Stand* that
the architect had too often in the past surrendered his artistic function
under the impact of industrialization.[168] They would surely find themselves supporting an eloquent plea for a return to gracious living, as
voiced by Medora F. Perkerson in *White Columns in Georgia*.[169] The
architecture of New Orleans is the subject of a study by Nathaniel C.
Curtis, who also decries the post-Civil War decline in architectural taste
and thinks that modern work suffers in comparison with the "solidity,
elegance and restraint about the old architecture." [170]

Historical writing about southern music, aside from some worthwhile
volumes on jazz and spirituals, is surprisingly desultory in view of the
region's generally satisfactory performance in this particular art form.
William C. Handy's *Father of the Blues* is a highly engrossing and informative memoir.[171] In addition to explaining in colorful prose how the
blues began and how the great jazz classics came to be written, this
autobiography of the famous folk-music composer, born "eight years
after surrender," recounts much also about Negro life in the South. A
foreword by Handy is an important feature of George W. Lee's *Beale
Street: Where the Blues Began,* a journalistic account which touches
upon various aspects of life on the "Main Street of Negro America,"
including the jazz bands and their leaders, the theater, churches, politics,
business, and the Negro press. The narrative becomes less satisfactory
as it treats more recent developments.[172] Louis Armstrong, perhaps the
greatest trumpeter of jazz, traces in *Swing That Music* the route which
jazz followed after moving up the Mississippi from New Orleans.[173]
An authentic study of one band is the well-written volume by H. O.
Brunn, a former Dixieland band leader himself, who regards jazz as
the only original American art form.[174] *Jazzmen,* headlining the jazz
musicians themselves, is a compilation by Frederic Ramsey and Charles
E. Smith accompanied by a good text and numerous rare illustrations.[175]

167 Edward and Elizabeth Waugh, *The South Builds: New Architecture in the
Old South* (Chapel Hill, 1960), 142–43.
168 Davidson, "A Mirror for Artists," in *I'll Take My Stand,* 50.
169 Perkerson, *White Columns in Georgia* (New York, 1952).
170 Curtis, *New Orleans: Its Old Houses, Shops and Public Buildings* (Philadelphia, 1933), 208.
171 Handy, *Father of the Blues, An Autobiography* (New York, 1941).
172 Lee, *Beale Street: Where the Blues Began* (New York, 1934).
173 Armstrong, *Swing That Music* (New York, 1936).
174 Brunn, *The Story of the Original Dixieland Jazz Band* (Baton Rouge, 1960).
175 Ramsey and C. E. Smith (eds.), *Jazzmen* (New York, 1939).

An extremely impressive and valuable history of Negro music's development and progress is Maud Cuney-Hare's *Negro Musicians and Their Music*.[176] The Negro spiritual as true American folk song is the major focus in a study titled *The Carolina Low-Country;* the volume includes nearly fifty low-country spirituals and their histories.[177] George P. Jackson's *White Spirituals in the Southern Uplands* brings to light an interesting musical version of the grim regional struggle between fundamentalism and modernism. The determined endeavor of shape-note rural singing groups, employing an antiquated solmization associated with a surviving primitive, vocal-musical theory and practice, all inherited from England, to maintain their existence against indifference, urbanization, and other more natural enemies makes an absorbing and not unimportant story.[178] Arthur P. Hudson, in his well edited *Folk Songs of Mississippi and Their Background,* presents folk songs recovered from white Mississippians throughout the state. The ballads in the volume, Hudson avers, "have sustained an intimate relation to the lives, character, and interests of the folk who sang them." [179] Folklore with a broader regional flavor makes up the attractive fare which is set before the reader in B. A. Botkin's *A Treasury of Southern Folklore*.[180]

While no effort will be made to draw sweeping conclusions from the foregoing presentation, it appears evident that the South since 1865 could be brought into sharper focus by a greater quantity of scholarly writing about religion, education, literature, magazines, journalism, and the fine arts. Yet relatively few of the South's historians who are making really significant contributions to the business of research and publication seem to be working in these fields. A cursory examination of the publications of the history alumni of a distinguished southern graduate school from 1952 to 1964, for example, discloses that less than 25 of a total of nearly 650 items are concerned directly with the South's cultural history. Such disclosure, one suspects, simply mirrors the situation prevailing generally among those who are writing southern history. It is surely enough to suggest the strong need for a more productive interest in the cultural realm if historians are to contribute more materially to a deeper understanding of the South, its institutions, and its thought.

176 Cuney-Hare, *Negro Musicians and Their Music* (Washington, 1936).
177 Smythe, Sass, *et al., The Carolina Low-Country* (New York, 1931).
178 Jackson, *White Spirituals in the Southern Uplands* (Chapel Hill, 1933).
179 Hudson, *Folk Songs of Mississippi and Their Background* (Chapel Hill, 1936), vii.
180 Botkin (ed.), *A Treasury of Southern Folklore: Stories, Ballads, Traditions, and Folkways of the People of the South* (New York, 1949).

XVII

The Twentieth-Century South

Dewey W. Grantham, Jr.

IN our own day the South easily qualifies as the most thoroughly reported and intensively analyzed part of America. No period offers more abundant materials for the writing of the region's history than the recent past, yet historians have scarcely begun to confront the southern experience in the twentieth century. This can partially be attributed to the chronological hiatus that usually separates the historian and the period he is investigating. But a more fundamental factor may be a swift disappearance in recent years of the old regional distinctions. The very process of change and fragmentation which stimulated the writings of social scientists and journalists has made it more and more difficult for the historian to portray the region in clear-cut and comprehensible terms. Yet the recent South offers the historian an unsurpassed opportunity. The South's rapid transformation in the twentieth century and its steady drift toward national conformity may complicate his work, but these changes also challenge him to broaden his focus and to write about state or region in a more meaningful context.

The pioneer historians who began in the late nineteenth and early twentieth centuries to write scholarly histories on southern themes naturally wrote of an earlier South.[1] The historian, after all, was concerned with the past, and emphasis on sectionalism in the writing of American history led him unerringly to the role of the section in the nineteenth century. There was conflict and drama in that period and, equally important for the regional historian, a focus provided by the events themselves which would never exist for the historian of the more recent South. These early historians did occasionally bring their accounts into the twentieth century. Thus the authors of *The South in the Building of the Nation* commented on various aspects of southern life during the first decade of the century, and their survey of contemporary economic institutions and conditions is still a valuable source for that period.[2]

The first interpreters of the twentieth-century South were not the historians, however, but the travelers, journalists, and critics who found fascinating materials in the region. Hundreds of travelers were visiting the South every year by 1900, and a great many of them described their impressions in books and articles. The social problems of the "backward South" provided the focus for some of these accounts and for innumerable articles in such national magazines as the *Independent* and *Outlook*. In the 1920's this social criticism took on a more astringent tone, and the stereotype of a "savage South" became a commonplace in American thinking.[3] Meanwhile, the treatment of southern problems in such works as Edgar Gardner Murphy's *Problems of the Present South* (New

1 For an excellent characterization of the first scholarly generation of southern historians, see Wendell Holmes Stephenson, *The South Lives in History: Southern Historians and Their Legacy* (Baton Rouge, 1955).

2 Julian A. C. Chandler and others (eds.), *The South in the Building of the Nation* ... (13 vols.; Richmond, 1909–1913). Philip Alexander Bruce's *The Rise of the New South* (Philadelphia, 1905), which treats the period from Reconstruction to 1905, is similarly useful as a survey of southern economic and social conditions early in the twentieth century. Holland Thompson, in his influential volume in the Chronicles of America Series, *The New South: A Chronicle of Social and Industrial Evolution* (New Haven, 1919), attempted some years later to describe the social and economic aspects of the region's progress during the era from Reconstruction to the First World War.

3 Frank Tannenbaum, *Darker Phases of the South* (New York, 1924), a biting sociological survey of such phenomena as the Ku Klux Klan, textile mill villages, southern prisons, and one-crop agriculture, provides a good example of this criticism.

York, 1904) demonstrated that the South was producing some critics of its own. Contemporary topics were being discussed in books like Alfred Holt Stone's *Studies in the American Race Problem* (New York, 1908) and Horace Kephart's *Our Southern Highlanders* (New York, 1913). There was also an outpouring of articles and books by Southerners on the theme of southern progress through industrialization, agricultural diversification, and education.[4]

Most of these writings were characterized by a decided contemporaneity and, in the case of the southern progressives, a prophetic quality. The first serious attempt to relate the changing currents of twentieth-century life to the broad stream of southern history came, surprisingly enough, from a talented group of literary critics and writers of fiction. In the early twenties young writers in Nashville and New Orleans and other places were revolting against the literary expression of their region, against what C. Hugh Holman has called "the dark night of Southern writing" between 1865 and 1920.[5] They were the first to sense the deepening fault that began to shatter the surface of southern life about the time of the First World War. Their work revealed a kind of dialecticism in which the disruptive forces of economic and social change provided the fore-history to a past in which the region's culture appeared to be integrated and whole. There was a "peculiarly historical consciousness" in their approach, as Allen Tate has pointed out, for they sought to find in history a key to the bewildering present. Their art, as Louis Rubin has remarked, "mirrored the transition from one kind of life to another." [6]

If the Southern Renascence was a literary expression of regionalism, regional self-consciousness was also an important factor in the early development of sociology and other social sciences in the South. The growth of these disciplines in the 1920's and 1930's reflected the widespread conviction during the early years of the century that the region's problems could be solved through science and education. This attitude became a major part of the rationale underlying Howard W. Odum's approach to the region as a cultural area and as a valuable concept of

4 With variations, the version of a progressive South became a constant refrain in the columns of such journals as Richard H. Edmonds' *Manufacturers' Record* and Walter Hines Page's *World's Work*, as well as in books like Edwin Mims, *The Advancing South: Stories of Progress and Reaction* (New York, 1926) and William J. Robertson, *The Changing South* (New York, 1927).

5 Holman, "Literature and Culture: The Fugitive-Agrarians," *Social Forces*, XXXVII (October, 1958), 16.

6 Rubin, "The South and the Faraway Country," *Virginia Quarterly Review*, XXXVIII (Summer, 1962), 445.

social analysis. Odum's pioneering work in public welfare, his establishment of the journal, *Social Forces* (1922), and his organization of the Institute for Research in Social Science (1924) made the University of North Carolina the center for the first systematic scientific study of southern society.[7] By the time the Great Depression began to tighten its grip on the American economy, the new regionalism had inspired the publication of numerous articles and monographs on southern economics, race relations, mill villages, tenancy, and prisons.

Three developments greatly broadened the scope and significance of regionalism during the 1930's. In the first place, the growing professionalization of the social sciences, and of such related fields as educational administration and public welfare, added recruits to social and institutional analysis, and the South's peculiar problems and continued distinctiveness frequently provided a regional framework for such studies. Indeed, the South as a sort of academic laboratory received increasing attention from scholars and investigators in other sections. In the second place, the Great Depression worsened a regional economic situation already under great strain as a result of the collapse of the cotton economy and widespread agrarian distress. The poverty-ridden South—framed in numerous monographs dealing with farm tenants and mill hands and in Franklin D. Roosevelt's well-remembered phrase, "the nation's number one economic problem"—heightened the strain of meliorism that social analysts brought to their subjects. Finally, the New Deal stimulated the southern regionalists by promoting a broad spirit of critical inquiry and promising action and social planning. It struck fire in what William B. Hesseltine has referred to as regionalism's "political instrumentalism." [8]

Never had an American region been subjected to more intensive scrutiny. Discussion of the "southern problem" became a kind of na-

7 Odum's sociology of regionalism was also influenced by his studies of Negro folklore and his interest in folk portraiture, as well as his role in the preparation of the President's Research Committee on Social Trends, *Recent Social Trends in the United States* (2 vols.; New York, 1933), which encouraged him to think of the South in a national setting, and by his strong dislike for what he considered to be the destructive sectionalism of the agrarian manifesto, Twelve Southerners, *I'll Take My Stand: The South and the Agrarian Tradition* (New York, 1930). For a valuable article on Odum's work and influence, see George B. Tindall, "The Significance of Howard W. Odum to Southern History: A Preliminary Estimate," *Journal of Southern History*, XXIV (August, 1958), 285–307. See also Rupert B. Vance and Katharine Jocher, "Howard W. Odum," *Social Forces*, XXXIII (March, 1955), 203–17.

8 Hesseltine, "The Status and Future of Regionalism—A Symposium," *Journal of Southern History*, XXVI (February, 1960), 32.

tional parlor game, and Southerners themselves were acutely aware of the investigations and the ferment taking place in their midst. "All around the South social experiments are going on, some planned and some just happening," reported a southern sociologist in the mid-forties. "The people are talking and asking questions, more concerned about the future than southern folk usually are thought of as being." [9] The nationalizing influence of the Second World War and the cold war that came in its wake, the growing prosperity of the region, and the increasing pace of economic change within its borders all contributed to the eventual decline of regionalism. "Regionalism has come to appear in perspective," writes George B. Tindall, "as a sort of way station on the road from Southern sectionalism toward integration into the national culture—and not as a permanent phenomenon." [10] Yet regionalism brought into being a significant body of literature analyzing southern society during the second quarter of the twentieth century, and the very changes that undermined its appeal have provided a theme for the work of contemporary sociologists and other interpreters.

These currents of professional growth and social change influenced the thinking and writing of historians as well as social scientists and popular writers. The professionalization of history had in fact preceded and contributed to the development of clear-cut disciplines in the social sciences. But the study of southern history on a systematic and scientific basis did not really come of age until the 1920's and 1930's. This was demonstrated in the collection of historical materials in state archives and university libraries, organization of strong historical commissions and societies, appearance of good historical journals, courses on the South in colleges and universities, and publication of an increasing number of books and articles on southern history. The revival of political liberalism during the New Deal years and the international ideological conflicts of the forties and fifties have undoubtedly contributed to the historian's mounting interest in the role of the common man and the course of democracy in an earlier South. At the same time, this historiography reflected a certain amount of cross-fertilization from the new regionalism [11] and a gradually developing interest in the twentieth-century South as a field of historical research.

9 Edgar T. Thompson, "Sociology and Sociological Research in the South," *Social Forces*, XXIII (March, 1945), 364.

10 Tindall, "The Significance of Howard W. Odum to Southern History," 306.

11 The interpretive volume by Benjamin Burks Kendrick and Alex Mathews Arnett, *The South Looks at Its Past* (Chapel Hill, 1935), was designed as a kind of historical preface for the regional studies emanating from Chapel Hill.

Nevertheless, historians were slow in bringing their narratives into the twentieth-century South. When David M. Potter surveyed the first fifteen volumes of the *Journal of Southern History* in 1949, he could not find a single article devoted to southern industrialization in the twentieth century and few articles on any aspect of the region's history since 1900.[12] Almost a decade later Charlton W. Tebeau could still assert that twentieth-century Florida history was "almost untouched in articles or books" of a scholarly character.[13] Yet a remarkable change has been taking place since 1945. Whereas the American Historical Association's list of dissertations in progress in 1940 included no more than eight or ten on topics having to do with the twentieth-century South, that of 1961 listed some fifty-five such studies in process or recently completed.[14] A large number of articles and books on various aspects of the southern experience during the years 1900–1920 have appeared during the last decade and a half. And C. Vann Woodward's impressive *Origins of the New South, 1877–1913* (Baton Rouge, 1951), the ninth volume in "A History of the South," provided the first comprehensive treatment of the early years of the twentieth century.

The most substantial contribution that historians have made to a greater understanding of the twentieth-century South has been their work on the first two decades of the century. Much of this historical writing has dealt with one aspect or another of southern progressivism, an amorphous movement broadly related to the pervasive forces that gradually coalesced into a nationwide drive for social and political reform. The southern phase of this movement owed a good deal to the agrarian revolt of the late nineteenth century, and some historians who were drawn first to that revolt have illuminated the southern historical landscape during the early twentieth century by exploring the later careers of its leaders and the influence of its heritage. Thus Alex M. Arnett, in his history of Populism in Georgia, noted as early as 1922 that the leaven of agrarian radicalism "was working in all parties" during the 1900's, and that "the popular faction [in the various southern states] has advocated reforms along the general lines of those urged

12 Potter, "An Appraisal of Fifteen Years of the Journal of Southern History, 1935–1949," *Journal of Southern History*, XVI (February, 1950), 25–32.

13 Tebeau, "Historical Writing on Twentieth Century Florida," *Florida Historical Quarterly*, XXXVII (October, 1958), 174.

14 *List of Doctoral Dissertations in History Now in Progress at Universities in the United States and the Dominion of Canada* (Richmond, 1940) ; William Lloyd Fox (comp. and ed.), *List of Doctoral Dissertations in History in Progress or Completed at Colleges and Universities in the United States since 1958* (Washington, D.C., 1961).

by the Populists in the nineties." [15] C. Vann Woodward and Francis B. Simkins in their biographies of Tom Watson and Ben Tillman, two of the leading agrarian reformers, have not only shown how the movements these men led encouraged the liberalization of southern politics after the turn of the century but also the way in which the insurgency of the 1890's was often transmuted into disillusion, reaction, and prejudice in later years.[16] These biographies throw revealing light on the problem of political leadership in the New South and suggest the importance of such elements as class feeling, agrarian conflict, and white supremacy.

Another study that explores the relationship between the agrarian upheaval of the late nineteenth century and the progressivism of the early twentieth is Albert D. Kirwan's *Revolt of the Rednecks*. Kirwan's realistic and admirably conceived monograph analyzes the complicated conflict for political power in a social context of class, race, and party. The central theme in Mississippi politics for fifty years following Reconstruction, writes Kirwan, was "a struggle between economic classes, interspersed with the personal struggles of ambitious men." [17] While Kirwan's book merely adumbrates the nature of legislative action and reform content, his objective study of the fifty-year struggle for control of the Democratic party in Mississippi between the "wool hat boys" and their social betters who represented the Delta planters and the new corporate interests demonstrates both the demagogic uses of such power and, ironically, the constructive and socially responsible achievements of leaders like James K. Vardaman and Theodore G. Bilbo. In many ways the work is a model that might well be used in the analysis of political developments in other southern states.

The continuing revolt of southern farmers after the turn of the century and the political and economic significance of farm organizations like the Farmers' Union have not yet been adequately investigated by

15 Arnett, *The Populist Movement in Georgia: A View of the "Agrarian Crusade" in the Light of Solid-South Politics* (New York, 1922), 212-13. In a chapter on the "Aftermath," Arnett traces the impact of Populist leaders and ideas on the convolutions of Georgia politics during the first decade of the twentieth century.

16 Woodward, *Tom Watson: Agrarian Rebel* (New York, 1938) ; Simkins, *Pitchfork Ben Tillman: South Carolinian* (Baton Rouge, 1944). A third outstanding southern reformer of the 1890's, James S. Hogg of Texas, is the subject of Robert C. Cotner's comprehensive biography, *James Stephen Hogg: A Biography* (Austin, 1959).

17 Kirwan, *Revolt of the Rednecks, Mississippi Politics: 1876-1925* (Lexington, Kentucky, 1951), 307. There are almost no studies of socio-economic groupings in the South over long periods of time. One such work of political ecology that attempts to correlate election returns with behavioral patterns is Perry H. Howard, *Political Tendencies in Louisiana, 1812-1952* (Baton Rouge, 1957).

historians.[18] Some indication of what was happening among southern farmers is revealed in Joseph Cannon Bailey's enthusiastic biography of Seaman A. Knapp, about half of which is devoted to Knapp's pioneering work in farm demonstration methods during the years 1902–1911.[19] More important is Theodore Saloutos' careful study of farm movements in the region from the Civil War to the early 1930's.[20] Saloutos has performed a useful service by placing these movements in historical perspective, but his most valuable contribution is his evaluation of twentieth-century organizations—the Farmers' Union, the cotton and tobacco associations—and the reaction of southern farmers to the farm programs of the 1920's. He shows the influential role played by agrarian spokesmen of the South in the enactment of the Wilsonian agricultural legislation, and he argues convincingly that "southerners have contributed more to the agricultural thought of the nation than is generally realized." [21]

The first historian to demonstrate the existence of a widespread progressive movement in the South during the first decade and a half of the twentieth century was Arthur S. Link, who published an influential article in 1946 on reform activities in the region during the period 1870–1914.[22] Link attributed this reformism in part to the impact

18 On occasion these agrarian revolts in the twentieth century led to outright war, as in the tobacco regions of Kentucky and Tennessee, or to the outbreak of rural Socialism in states like Oklahoma and Louisiana. (See, for example, John G. Miller, *The Black Patch War* [Chapel Hill, 1936]; James O. Nall, *The Tobacco Night Riders of Kentucky and Tennessee, 1905–1909* [Louisville, 1939]; and Grady McWhiney, "Louisiana Socialists in the Early Twentieth Century: A Study of Rustic Radicalism," *Journal of Southern History*, XX [August, 1954], 315–36.) In general, however, southern farmers abandoned independent political action and concentrated upon means of increasing farm efficiency and productivity. Nevertheless, they served as a strong liberalizing force in the politics of this period.

19 Bailey, *Seaman A. Knapp: Schoolmaster of American Agriculture* (New York, 1945).

20 Saloutos, *Farmer Movements in the South, 1865–1933* (Berkeley, 1960).

21 *Ibid.*, v. For examples of significant articles on various aspects of farm organization in the twentieth-century South, see Charles P. Loomis, "The Rise and Decline of the North Carolina Farmers' Union," *North Carolina Historical Review*, VII (July, 1930), 305–25; Loomis, "Activities of the North Carolina Farmers' Union," *North Carolina Historical Review*, VII (October, 1930), 443–62; Gilbert C. Fite, "Voluntary Attempts to Reduce Cotton Acreage in the South, 1914–1933," *Journal of Southern History*, XIV (November, 1948), 481–99; and Roy V. Scott, "Farmers' Institutes in Louisiana, 1897–1906," *Journal of Southern History*, XXV (February, 1959), 73–90.

22 Link, "The Progressive Movement in the South, 1870–1914," *North Carolina Historical Review*, XXIII (April, 1946), 172–95.

of the agrarian crusade of the 1880's and 1890's, but he made the significant point that twentieth-century progressivism in the South, like
American progressivism in general, was basically urban and middle-class
in its orientation and leadership. In an illuminating series of articles
published at about the same time, Link established the correlation between the political factions that supported Woodrow Wilson for the
Democratic presidential nomination in 1912 in almost every southern
state and the progressive elements in a bifactionalism that often traced
back a decade or more.[23]

Numerous articles and monographs have appeared since the publication of Link's pioneering essay, but there is as yet no comprehensive
study of the progressive movement in the South. Woodward's *Origins
of the New South* provides the best general treatment of the various
phases of the movement, including a chapter appropriately entitled
"Progressivism—For Whites Only." [24] Herbert J. Doherty, Jr., has
written a suggestive article on southern dissident spirits and social critics
during the late nineteenth and early twentieth centuries.[25] Anne Firor
Scott has shown that southern congressmen were more reform-minded
during the years 1906–1913 than earlier students had assumed.[26] And
in several books and articles Professor Link has emphasized the impor-

23 These articles, which appeared in many southern historical journals, were based
on Link's Ph.D. dissertation, "The South and the Democratic Campaign of 1912"
(University of North Carolina, 1945). They are summarized in the first volume of
Link's biography of *Wilson: The Road to the White House* (Princeton, 1947).

24 Woodward interprets the progressive movement in the South as "a pretty strictly
indigenous growth, touched lightly here and there by cross-fertilization from the
West." Woodward, *Origins of the New South,* 371. An older work that throws
some light on twentieth-century southern liberalism is Virginius Dabney, *Liberalism
in the South* (Chapel Hill, 1932).

25 Doherty, "Voices of Protest from the New South, 1875–1910," *Mississippi
Valley Historical Review,* XLII (June, 1955), 45–66. See also Doherty, "Alexander
J. McKelway: Preacher to Progressive," *Journal of Southern History,* XXIV
(May, 1958), 177–90; Allen J. Going, "The Reverend Edgar Gardner Murphy:
His Ideas and Influence," *Historical Magazine of the Protestant Episcopal Church,*
XXV (December, 1956), 391–402; E. Charles Chatfield, "The Southern Sociologi-
cal Congress: Organization of Uplift," *Tennessee Historical Quarterly,* XIX
(December, 1960), 328–47, and Chatfield, "The Southern Sociological Congress:
Rationale of Uplift," *Tennessee Historical Quarterly,* XX (March, 1961), 51–64.

26 Scott, "A Progressive Wind from the South, 1906–1913," *Journal of Southern
History,* XXIX (February, 1963), 53–70. See also the comprehensive study this
article summarizes, Scott, "The Southern Progressives in National Politics, 1906–
1916" (Ph.D. dissertation, Radcliffe College, 1957). Another valuable unpublished
dissertation is by John W. Davidson, "The Response of the South to Woodrow
Wilson's New Freedom, 1912–1914" (Yale University, 1953).

tance of the southern contribution to Wilsonian liberalism during the years 1913–1917.[27]

Scholarly biographies of such reform governors as Charles B. Aycock of North Carolina and Napoleon B. Broward of Florida have helped to clarify the nature of the reform movements in the various southern states and to outline the pattern of political conflict in the region.[28] One of the most significant biographical contributions is Joseph L. Morrison's perceptive examination of Josephus Daniels' role in North Carolina journalism and politics during the two decades before he entered Wilson's Cabinet in 1913.[29] No historian has succeeded better than Morrison in explaining the interplay of race, party, and political reformer in the fashioning of southern progressivism. "If Daniels remained something of a nonconformist by reason of his progressivism," observes Morrison, "it was only within the framework of a larger [southern] conformity." [30] While some of the more important southern progressives have received biographical treatment, many others still await scholarly studies, including Walter Clark, Walter Hines Page, Alexander McKelway, Edgar Gardner Murphy, and a host of lesser figures.[31] Nor have

27 See, especially, Link's article, "The South and the 'New Freedom': An Interpretation," *American Scholar*, XX (Summer, 1951), 314–24, and his two books: *Woodrow Wilson and the Progressive Era, 1910–1917* (New York, 1954) and *Wilson: The New Freedom* (Princeton, 1956). Link's interpretation has been challenged by Richard M. Abrams, "Woodrow Wilson and the Southern Congressmen, 1913–1916," *Journal of Southern History*, XXII (November, 1956), 417–37. Southern conservatism in Congress is also revealed in Howard W. Allen, "Geography and Politics: Voting on Reform Issues in the United States Senate, 1911–1916," *Journal of Southern History*, XXVII, (May, 1961), 216–28.

28 Oliver H. Orr, Jr., *Charles Brantley Aycock* (Chapel Hill, 1961); Samuel Proctor, *Napoleon Bonaparte Broward: Florida's Fighting Democrat* (Gainesville, 1950). See also Dewey W. Grantham, Jr., *Hoke Smith and the Politics of the New South* (Baton Rouge, 1958). For a good study of a leading border state progressive, see Louis G. Geiger, *Joseph W. Folk of Missouri* (Columbia, Missouri, 1953). Two other studies of southern reform governors worthy of mention are William E. Larsen, *Montague of Virginia: The Making of a Southern Progressive* (Baton Rouge, 1965), and an unpublished study, Robert M. Burts, "The Public Career of Richard I. Manning" (Ph.D. dissertation, Vanderbilt University, 1957).

29 Morrison, *Josephus Daniels Says . . . : An Editor's Political Odyssey from Bryan to Wilson and F.D.R., 1894–1913* (Chapel Hill, 1962). Unfortunately, Morrison gives little attention to Daniels' role in national politics.

30 *Ibid.*, 173.

31 Aubrey Lee Brooks, *Walter Clark: Fighting Judge* (Chapel Hill, 1944), is a friendly and undocumented biography of the outstanding progressive among southern jurists. See also the valuable edition of Clark's papers edited by Aubrey Lee Brooks and Hugh Talmage Lefler, *The Papers of Walter Clark, 1857–1924* (2 vols.; Chapel Hill, 1948–1950). Examples of other biographies of southern political

the so-called demagogues of this period been the subject of scholarly scrutiny, as is shown in the cases of Vardaman, Bilbo, and Coleman L. Blease. Southern conservatives have been even more neglected; only Joseph W. Bailey of Texas and John Sharp Williams of Mississippi have received adequate biographies.[32]

Aside from the better biographies and Kirwan's study of Mississippi politics, there is still no comprehensive treatment of southern progressivism on the state level, nothing to compare with such a book as George E. Mowry's *The California Progressives,* published in Berkeley and Los Angeles in 1951. There are, however, two first-rate unpublished studies on Texas and North Carolina, and others are in progress.[33] As for municipal progressivism in the South, the only significant monograph is William D. Miller's study of Memphis during the progressive period.[34] By examining the campaigns for clean elections, efficient administration, equitable taxation, improved public service, and various social reforms, Miller makes it clear that Memphis experienced a significant reform movement during the first two decades of this century.

---

leaders of this period, mostly uncritical, include James E. Palmer, *Carter Glass: Unreconstructed Rebel* (Roanoke, Virginia, 1938); Anna Mary Moon and Joe Phillips, *John A. Moon: Father of the Parcel Post* (Chattanooga, 1941); and Harold B. Hinton, *Cordell Hull, A Biography* (Garden City, 1942). A more scholarly work is Alex Mathews Arnett's *Claude Kitchin and the Wilson War Policies* (Boston, 1937), a study of an independent North Carolina congressman written in the spirit of World War I revisionism.

32 Sam Hanna Acheson, *Joe Bailey: The Last Democrat* (New York, 1932); George Coleman Osborn, *John Sharp Williams: Planter-Statesman of the Deep South* (Baton Rouge, 1943). For the views of two other southern conservatives, see J. Fred Rippy (comp. and ed.), *F. M. Simmons, Statesman of the New South: Memoirs and Addresses* (Durham, 1936), and Anthony Harrigan (ed.), *The Editor and the Republic: Papers and Addresses of William Watts Ball* (Chapel Hill, 1954).

33 James Aubrey Tinsley, "The Progressive Movement in Texas" (Ph.D. dissertation, University of Wisconsin, 1953); Joseph Flake Steelman, "The Progressive Era in North Carolina, 1884–1917" (Ph.D. dissertation, University of North Carolina, 1955). Two older studies that are still useful for Virginia during the progressive era are F. A. Magruder, *Recent Administration in Virginia* (Baltimore, 1912), and Ralph Chipman McDanel, *The Virginia Constitutional Convention of 1901–1902* (Baltimore, 1928). A recent study by Robert F. Durden, *Reconstruction Bonds & Twentieth-Century Politics: South Dakota v. North Carolina (1904)* (Durham, 1962), is not only the story of a celebrated interstate lawsuit but also a revealing example of the way in which Reconstruction and Populist animosities continued to influence southern politics after 1900.

34 Miller, *Memphis During the Progressive Era, 1900–1917* (Memphis, 1957). For some account of southern involvement in the movement for new forms of municipal government, see James Weinstein, "Organized Business and the City Commission and Manager Movements," *Journal of Southern History,* XXVIII (May, 1962), 166–82.

An example of the machines the municipal reformers frequently sought to overthrow is provided in an earlier work on New Orleans by George M. Reynolds. Reynolds analyzed the operation of the Choctaw Club of that city and the leadership of its boss, Martin Behrman.[35]

Several specialized studies have been published on important aspects of southern progressivism and many others are currently under way. James F. Doster has written a valuable monograph on railroads in Alabama politics in which he reveals the significant role of the movement for railroad regulation in bringing Alabama progressivism into focus.[36] Elizabeth H. Davidson's painstaking study of child labor legislation in the southern textile states is notably successful in showing the gradual erosion of laissez-faire assumptions on the part of a region engaged in an almost desperate search for economic progress through industrialization.[37] Although historians have neglected the origins of social welfare programs in the South,[38] valuable studies of the prohibition movement on the state level and of the woman suffrage campaign in the southern states have contributed to a better understanding of the region's progressive movement.[39]

35 Reynolds, *Machine Politics in New Orleans, 1897–1926* (New York, 1936).

36 Doster, *Railroads in Alabama Politics, 1875–1914* (University, Alabama, 1957). An older regional study is Maxwell Ferguson, *State Regulation of Railroads in the South* (New York, 1916). For two good unpublished Ph.D. dissertations, see Albert Neely Sanders, "State Regulation of Public Utilities by South Carolina, 1879–1935" (University of North Carolina, 1956), and Robert L. Peterson, "State Regulation of Railroads in Texas" (University of Texas, 1960).

37 Davidson, *Child Labor Legislation in the Southern Textile States* (Chapel Hill, 1939).

38 But see Jane Zimmerman, "The Penal Reform Movement in the South during the Progressive Era, 1890–1917," *Journal of Southern History*, XVII (November, 1951), 462–92, and Zimmerman, "Penal Systems and Penal Reforms in the South Since the Civil War" (Ph.D. dissertation, University of North Carolina, 1947); Fletcher Melvin Green, "Some Aspects of the Convict Lease System in the Southern States," in Green (ed.), *Essays in Southern History Presented to Joseph Gregoire de Roulhac Hamilton . . .* (Chapel Hill, 1949), 112–23; Lyda Gordon Shivers, "Twentieth Century South-wide Civic & Lay Organizations for Human Welfare," in Vera Largent (ed.), *The Walter Clinton Jackson Essays in the Social Sciences* (Chapel Hill, 1942), 187–207; Arthur W. James, *Virginia's Social Awakening: The Contribution of Dr. Mastin and the Board of Charities and Corrections* (Richmond, 1939); Anne Gary Pannell and Dorothea E. Wyatt, *Julia S. Tutwiler and Social Progress in Alabama* (University, Alabama, 1961); and Elizabeth Wisner, *Public Welfare Administration in Louisiana* (Chicago, 1930).

39 For the prohibition movement, see James Benson Sellers, *The Prohibition Movement in Alabama, 1702 to 1943* (Chapel Hill, 1943); Daniel Jay Whitener, *Prohibition in North Carolina, 1715–1945* (Chapel Hill, 1945); and John Evans Eubanks, *Ben Tillman's Baby: The Dispensary System of South Carolina, 1892–1915* ([Augusta, Georgia, 1950]).

Books and articles on the development of education are also helpful in understanding southern progressivism and southern patterns of thought early in the twentieth century. Indeed, the educational renaissance during the first part of the century mirrored as did few other movements the region's growing faith in progress; the manner in which education became the *raison d'être* of political liberals, social welfare advocates, economic expansionists, and northern philanthropists for the remaking of southern commonwealths; and the sectional and racial overtones that characterized the crusade for educational advancement.

Woodward's *Origins of the New South* contains a brilliant interpretation of the educational crusade in this context, and Charles William Dabney, himself one of the leading educational reformers in the South, has written a comprehensive but uncritical account, *The Southern Education Movement.*[40] Most of the southern states have been the subject of monographs dealing with the public education movement.[41] Although many of these studies are informative in their delineation of educational problems and progress in the late nineteenth and early twentieth centuries, they tend to dwell on the organizational and administrative phases of the movement to the neglect of important social and political considerations. Unfortunately, the professional historian has been reluctant to enter directly into this field, which is surely one of the most significant aspects of social history in the modern South. Historians have

---

A. Elizabeth Taylor has written a book and a series of scholarly articles on the woman-suffrage movement in various southern states, of which the following are examples: *The Woman Suffrage Movement in Tennessee* (New York, 1957); "The Woman Suffrage Movement in Arkansas," *Arkansas Historical Quarterly,* XV (Spring, 1956), 17–52; "The Woman Suffrage Movement in Texas," *Journal of Southern History,* XVII (May, 1951), 194–215; and "The Woman Suffrage Movement in North Carolina," *North Carolina Historical Review,* XXXVIII (January and April, 1961), 45–62, 173–89. See also Lee N. Allen, "The Woman Suffrage Movement in Alabama, 1910–1920," *Alabama Review,* XI (April, 1958), 83–99; John E. Talmadge, *Rebecca Latimer Felton: Nine Stormy Decades* (Athens, 1960). For a suggestive essay on the significance of women in southern reform movements, see Anne Firor Scott, "The 'New Woman' in the New South," *South Atlantic Quarterly,* LXI (Autumn, 1962), 473–83.

40 C. W. Dabney, *The Southern Education Movement,* Volume II of his *Universal Education in the South* (Chapel Hill, 1936). *The General Education Board: An Account of its Activities, 1902–1914* (New York, 1915) is a valuable official report of the GEB's various activities in the South.

41 For examples, see Frederick Eby, *The Development of Education in Texas* (New York, 1925); Andrew D. Holt, *The Struggle for a State System of Public Schools in Tennessee, 1903–1936* (New York, 1938); Frank L. McVey, *The Gates Open Slowly: A History of Education in Kentucky* (Lexington, 1949); and Dorothy Orr, *A History of Education in Georgia* (Chapel Hill, 1950).

studied some of the principal leaders in the educational crusade, and useful biographies of such men as John C. Kilgo, James H. Kirkland, Edwin A. Alderman, and Charles D. McIver have been published.[42] Willard B. Gatewood's careful study of Eugene C. Brooks is especially valuable for educational advances in North Carolina and as a model for the integration of educational and political history.[43]

In the realm of higher education in the South, the last two decades have witnessed the publication of dozens of college and university histories, some of which devote considerable space to recent developments. But all too often these histories are narrowly institutional, uncritical, and poorly written. There are exceptions, however, as is proved by Daniel W. Hollis' history of the University of South Carolina and Louis R. Wilson's study of the University of North Carolina during the years 1900–1930.[44] The second volume of Hollis' well-written and judicious history is notable for its success in placing the university in the perspective of the state's evolution. Wilson is less successful in discussing the relationship between the university and the state; his achievement is a richly detailed account of the way in which the University of North Carolina emerged as a great institution of higher learning.[45] Two volumes that deserve comment for the light they throw on special aspects of southern education are Horace Mann Bond's *Negro Education in Alabama,* a penetrating analysis of the social and economic forces affecting education in that state, and Louis R. Harlan's *Separate and*

42 Paul Neff Garber, *John Carlisle Kilgo: President of Trinity College, 1894–1910* (Durham, 1937); Edwin Mims, *Chancellor Kirkland of Vanderbilt* (Nashville, 1940); Dumas Malone, *Edwin A. Alderman: A Biography* (New York, 1940); and Rose Howell Holder, *McIver of North Carolina* (Chapel Hill, 1957). See also Marcus M. Wilkerson, *Thomas Duckett Boyd: The Story of a Southern Educator* (Baton Rouge, 1935); Charles L. Lewis, *Philander Priestley Claxton: Crusader for Public Education* (Knoxville, 1948); Louise Ware, *George Foster Peabody: Banker, Philanthropist, Publicist* (Athens, Georgia, 1951); George Lee Simpson, *The Cokers of Carolina: A Social Biography of a Family* (Chapel Hill, 1956); and Robert Watson Winston, *Horace Williams: Gadfly of Chapel Hill* (Chapel Hill, 1942).

43 Gatewood, *Eugene Clyde Brooks: Educator and Public Servant* (Durham, 1960).

44 Hollis, *College to University* (Columbia, 1956), Volume II of Hollis, *University of South Carolina* (2 vols.; Columbia, 1951–1956); Wilson, *The University of North Carolina, 1900–1930: The Making of a Modern University* (Chapel Hill, 1957).

45 Another useful university history is Edwin Mims, *History of Vanderbilt University* (Nashville, 1946). For examples of superior college histories, see John K. Bettersworth, *People's College: A History of Mississippi State* (University, Alabama, 1953); Elisabeth S. Peck, *Berea's First Century, 1855–1955* (Lexington, 1955).

Unequal, a well-documented study of the repressive influence of racism in the southern crusade for education during the progressive era.[46]

As a whole, this body of historical writing represents a significant contribution to southern historiography and to the study of the progressive movement in the United States. The work on North Carolina is particularly impressive. Nevertheless, the treatment of the progressive movement and of other aspects of human endeavor in the South during the first two decades of the twentieth century is still fragmentary. The period remains a frontier for the historian. Many important leaders in public affairs, agriculture and business, journalism, education, religion, and social welfare need to be studied. Few southern states and municipalities have been the subject of works like Steelman's unpublished dissertation on North Carolina or Miller's study of Memphis. Little attention has been given to the South's involvement in national politics, and almost none to its reaction to foreign affairs. The role of women, the public health movement, social welfare activities, and regulatory agencies remain largely unexplored. And much more can be done on the educational aspects of southern progressivism.

If historians are just beginning to produce scholarly books and articles on the early twentieth century, they have scarcely ventured at all into the period after 1920. Except for a few studies like Reinhard H. Luthin's sketches of several modern southern demagogues, most of the writing on recent southern politics has been the work of political scientists and popularizers.[47] There is no study of a southern state in the 1920's done in the manner of Joseph Huthmacher's *Massachusetts People and Politics, 1919–1933* (1959),[48] though Preston J. Hubbard

46 Bond, *Negro Education in Alabama: A Study in Cotton and Steel* (Washington, D.C., 1939) ; Harlan, *Separate and Unequal: Public School Campaigns and Racism in the Southern Seaboard States, 1901–1915* (Chapel Hill, 1958). See also Luther L. Gobbel, *Church-State Relationships in Education in North Carolina since 1776* (Durham, 1938), which is important for the early twentieth century.

47 Luthin, *American Demagogues: Twentieth Century* (Boston, 1954), which contains essays on Bilbo, the Fergusons, Eugene Talmadge, William H. Murray, and Huey P. Long, is a work of considerable merit. For the southern demagogues, see also Daniel M. Robison, "From Tillman to Long: Some Striking Leaders of the Rural South," *Journal of Southern History,* III (August, 1937), 289–310; T. Harry Williams, "The Gentleman from Louisiana: Demagogue or Democrat," *Journal of Southern History,* XXVI (February, 1960), 3–21. An uncritical volume of some value is William T. Cash, *History of the Democratic Party in Florida, Including Biographical Sketches of Prominent Florida Democrats* (Tallahassee, 1936). Dewey W. Grantham, Jr., *The Democratic South* (Athens, Georgia, 1963), tries to place recent southern politics in historical perspective.

48 George B. Tindall has suggested some of the opportunities historians will find in the 1920's in his article, "Business Progressivism: Southern Politics in the Twenties," *South Atlantic Quarterly,* LXII (Winter, 1963), 92–106.

has written an excellent monograph on the origins of the Tennessee Valley Authority, and some of the decade's more spectacular aspects have received attention.[49] As for the South and the New Deal, Elmer L. Puryear's study of Democratic factionalism in North Carolina and Seth Shepard McKay's volume on W. Lee O'Daniel and Texas politics are almost the only works published by historians.[50]

The changing southern economy and the economic revolution so apparent in the region during the past two decades will no doubt exert an increasing attraction for the southern historian. But, as yet, he has contributed little to the illumination of this chapter of southern history. Several histories of particular industries and businesses have appeared, but no comprehensive historical treatment exists.[51] A brief work by Jack Blicksilver traces the evolution of the South's leading industry to mid-century, and Robert S. Smith's somewhat pedestrian business history of Dan River Mills provides a meticulous record of a major textile enterprise.[52] There are no comparable histories of mining and heavy

49 Hubbard, *Origins of the TVA: The Muscle Shoals Controversy, 1920–1932* (Nashville, 1961), is an example of the effective integration of regional and national political history. For other historical writings on the twenties, see Charles C. Alexander, *Crusade for Conformity: The Ku Klux Klan in Texas, 1920–1930* ([Houston], 1962); Arnold S. Rice, *The Ku Klux Klan in American Politics* (Washington, D.C., 1962); Norman F. Furniss, *The Fundamentalist Controversy, 1918–1931* (New Haven, 1954); Ray Ginger, *Six Days or Forever? Tennessee v. John Thomas Scopes* (Boston, 1958); Virginius Dabney, *Dry Messiah: The Life of Bishop Cannon* (New York, 1949); Richard L. Watson, Jr. (ed.), *Bishop Cannon's Own Story: Life As I Have Seen It* (Durham, 1955); and Wilma Dykeman and James Stokely, *Seeds of Southern Change: The Life of Will Alexander* (Chicago, 1962).

50 Puryear, *Democratic Party Dissension in North Carolina, 1928–1936* (Chapel Hill, 1962), is a revealing analysis of one-party politics during a significant period, but it does not adequately demonstrate the impact of the New Deal on North Carolina politics. McKay, *W. Lee O'Daniel and Texas Politics, 1938–1942* (Lubbock, 1944), is an informative work based on printed sources. For another useful book by McKay on twentieth-century Texas politics, see *Texas Politics, 1906–1944, With Special Reference to the German Counties* (Lubbock, 1952).

51 Emory Q. Hawk, *Economic History of the South* (New York, 1934), was too sketchy on the development of the New South to be very helpful even at the time it was published. For a more comprehensive treatment of one state in the recent period, see Ralph Wright Steen, *Twentieth Century Texas: An Economic and Social History* (Austin, 1942).

52 Blicksilver, *Cotton Manufacturing in the Southeast: An Historical Analysis* (Atlanta, 1959); Smith, *Mill on the Dan: A History of Dan River Mills, 1882–1950* (Durham, 1960). See also Broadus Mitchell, *The Rise of Cotton Mills in the South* (Baltimore, 1921); Broadus Mitchell and George Sinclair Mitchell, *The Industrial Revolution in the South* (Baltimore, 1930); Benjamin F. Lemert, *The Cotton Textile Industry of the Southern Appalachian Piedmont* (Chapel Hill,

industry in the modern South, although Ethel M. Armes, *The Story of Coal and Iron in Alabama* (Birmingham, 1910), is still useful for developments early in the century; and H. H. Chapman and others, *The Iron and Steel Industries of the South* (University, Alabama, 1953), is a comprehensive economic survey.[53] The modern tobacco industry in the South has been dealt with more adequately, particularly in Nannie May Tilley's large-scale work on the cultivation, marketing, and manufacture of bright-leaf tobacco.[54] J. Carlyle Sitterson's excellent history of the region's sugar cane industry, though most thorough on the nineteenth century, brings the story of that industry into the modern period.[55] Nollie Hickman, in a sound study of the longleaf pine industry in southern Mississippi, traces this phase of southern lumbering into its golden age during the early part of the twentieth century.[56] The oil industry in the Southwest has been the subject of several histories, preeminent among which are Carl Coke Rister's valuable full-length account and an admirable study of the Humble Company by Henrietta M. Larson and Kenneth Wiggins Porter.[57] The rise and collapse of the leading

---

1933); and Gerald W. Johnson, *The Making of a Southern Industrialist: A Biographical Study of Simpson Bobo Tanner* (Chapel Hill, 1952).

There is no adequate history of the agricultural side of the modern cotton industry, although some information is contained in a popular account by David L. Cohn, *The Life and Times of King Cotton* (New York, 1956). The role of cotton farming and of agriculture generally in one southern state is treated in Enoch M. Banks, *The Economics of Land Tenure in Georgia* (New York, 1905); Robert P. Brooks, *The Agrarian Revolution in Georgia, 1865–1912* (Madison, Wisconsin, 1914); and Willard Range, *A Century of Georgia Agriculture, 1850–1950* (Athens, 1954).

53 For the sulphur industry, see Robert H. Montgomery, *The Brimstone Game: Monopoly in Action* (New York, 1940); Williams Haynes, *Brimstone, the Stone that Burns: The Story of the Frasch Sulphur Industry* (Princeton, 1959).

54 Tilley, *The Bright-Tobacco Industry, 1860–1929* (Chapel Hill, 1948). One of the author's most arresting conclusions is that the speculators and the loose-leaf auction system, rather than the American Tobacco Company and other large corporations, were responsible for the generally low prices received by tobacco farmers. For two biographies of a leading southern entrepreneur in tobacco, see John W. Jenkins, *James B. Duke: Master Builder* (New York, 1927); John K. Winkler, *Tobacco Tycoon: The Story of James Buchanan Duke* (New York, 1943).

55 Sitterson, *Sugar Country: The Cane Sugar Industry in the South, 1753–1950* (Lexington, 1953). For another rather restricted southern industry, see James T. Hopkins, *Fifty Years of Citrus, The Florida Citrus Exchange: 1909–1959* (Gainesville, 1960).

56 Hickman, *Mississippi Harvest: Lumbering in the Longleaf Pine Belt, 1840–1915* (University, Mississippi, 1962). Several other historical studies of southern lumbering are now in process.

57 Rister, *Oil! Titan of the Southwest* (Norman, 1949); Larson and Porter, *History of Humble Oil and Refining Company: A Study in Industrial Growth* (New York,

southern security house in the 1920's is described in John Berry Mc-
Ferrin's *Caldwell and Company*.[58] Thomas D. Clark's entertaining study
of the southern country store follows the fortunes of that institution
down to the First World War; and a few accounts of individual merchants and firms have been published, but, for the most part, historians
have given little attention to the development of merchandising in the
twentieth-century South.[59] Nor have they concerned themselves with the
history of labor in the recent South. Ruth A. Allen's objective study of
lumber workers in East Texas stands almost alone in that category.[60]

Social and cultural trends in the twentieth-century South have received even less attention from historians than have political and economic developments. Education, at least in an institutional sense, has
not been neglected, but the same cannot be said for religion.[61] The his-

1959). Rister describes the origin and development of the oil business in Texas,
Oklahoma, Louisiana, and Arkansas, as well as in Kansas and New Mexico. For
other petroleum studies, see Gerald Forbes, *Flush Production: The Epic of Oil in
the Gulf-Southwest* (Norman, 1942); James A. Clark and Michel T. Halbouty,
Spindletop (New York, 1952); John Joseph Mathews, *Life and Death of an Oil-
man: The Career of E. W. Marland* (Norman, 1951); George Sweet Gibb and
Evelyn H. Knowlton, *History of Standard Oil Company (New Jersey): The Resurgent Years, 1911–1927* (New York, 1956); John L. Loos, *Oil on Stream! A
History of Interstate Oil Pipe Line Company, 1909–1959* (Baton Rouge, 1959);
and John O. King, *The Early History of the Houston Oil Company of Texas,
1901–1908* ([Houston], 1959).

58 McFerrin, *Caldwell and Company: A Southern Financial Empire* (Chapel
Hill, 1939). There are several state studies of banking and fiscal policy, including
Marce C. Rhodes, *History of Taxation in Mississippi (1798–1929)* (Nashville,
1930); Stephen A. Caldwell, *A Banking History of Louisiana* (Baton Rouge,
1935); James E. Thorogood, *A Financial History of Tennessee Since 1870* (Nashville, 1949); and J. E. Dovell, *A History of Banking in Florida, 1828–1954* (Or-
lando, 1955).

59 See Clark, *Pills, Petticoats and Plows: The Southern Country Store* (In-
dianapolis, 1944), and the following examples: Le Gette Blythe, *William Henry
Belk: Merchant of the South* (Chapel Hill, 1950); Charles Howard Candler,
Asa Griggs Candler (Emory University, 1950); Henry Givens Baker, *Rich's of
Atlanta: The Story of a Store Since 1867* (Atlanta, 1953); and George Lee
Simpson, *The Cokers of Carolina: A Social Biography of a Family* (Chapel Hill,
1956).

60 Allen, *East Texas Lumber Workers: An Economic and Social Picture, 1870–
1950* (Austin, 1961). A slender volume of some value as history is George Sinclair
Mitchell, *Textile Unionism and the South* (Chapel Hill, 1931). For a significant
personal account, see Lucy Randolph Mason, *To Win These Rights: A Personal
Story of the CIO in the South* (New York, 1952). Freddie Ray Marshall, "History of Labor Organization in the South" (Ph.D. dissertation, University of
California at Berkeley, 1955), is one of several useful unpublished studies.

61 Although some denominational histories give space to the twentieth century,
few of them possess much historical merit. A work that catches the spirit of
popular religion in the South is Archibald T. Robertson, *That Old-Time Religion*

tories of several newspapers of the modern South have been published as well as Thomas D. Clark's study of the southern country editor.[62] A sizeable body of writing exists on the literature of the recent South, but this is largely the work of literary critics and literary historians.[63] Although it can hardly be classified as history, a symposium on contemporary civilization in the South, published in 1934, provides a comprehensive portrayal of southern culture.[64]

Recent historical writing of a more general nature has begun to give more consideration to the twentieth century. Yet much of this work is ephemeral and filled with local pride, and the number of genuinely good volumes of this kind by historians is surprisingly small. In the field of local and urban history, for example, few studies are as good as *The Chattanooga Country* by Gilbert E. Govan and James W. Livingood, and even that history concentrates on the period before 1900.[65] Rare indeed

---

(Boston, 1950). A provocative essay by James Sellers, *The South and Christian Ethics* (New York, 1962), comes to grips with the southern heritage while analyzing the present situation.

62 Clark, *The Southern Country Editor* (Indianapolis, 1948). Clark's volume is a mine of information on the southern weekly newspaper during the period 1865–1948, but, unfortunately, it does not provide much chronological analysis. For examples of newspaper histories, see Sam Hanna Acheson, *35,000 Days in Texas: A History of the Dallas News and Its Forbears* (New York, 1938); Thomas Ewing Dabney, *One Hundred Great Years: The Story of the Times-Picayune from Its Founding to 1940* (Baton Rouge, 1944); Herbert Ravenel Sass, *Outspoken: 150 Years of the News and Courier* (Columbia, 1953); and Earl L. Bell and Kenneth C. Crabbe, *The Augusta Chronicle: Indomitable Voice of Dixie, 1785–1960* (Athens, 1960). For the history of a leading southern magazine, see William B. Hamilton (comp.), *Fifty Years of the South Atlantic Quarterly* (Durham, 1952).

63 A collaborative volume summing up the Southern Renascence at mid-century and placing the movement in its historical and cultural setting is Louis D. Rubin, Jr., and Robert D. Jacobs (eds.), *Southern Renascence: The Literature of the Modern South* (Baltimore, 1953). Other works that illuminate writing in the modern South are Shields McIlwaine, *The Southern Poor-White: From Lubberland to Tobacco Road* (Norman, 1939); Louise Cowan, *The Fugitive Group: A Literary History* (Baton Rouge, 1959); Louis D. Rubin, Jr., and Robert D. Jacobs (eds.), *South: Modern Southern Literature in Its Cultural Setting* (Garden City, 1961); and John M. Bradbury, *Renaissance in the South: A Critical History of the Literature, 1920–1960* (Chapel Hill, 1963).

64 W. T. Couch (ed.), *Culture in the South* (Chapel Hill, 1934). Such cultural phenomena as the fine arts have been little studied. But for one aspect of southern culture, see Harry O. Brunn, *The Story of the Original Dixieland Jazz Band* (Baton Rouge, 1960).

65 Govan and Livingood, *The Chattanooga Country, 1540–1951: From Tomahawks to TVA* (New York, 1952). In a revision of this work (Chapel Hill, 1963), the authors have added a chapter on the recent period. Among other above-average local histories important for the recent period are William Kenneth Boyd, *The*

is the social history of a small community written with the engaging style and eye for regional values of Herman Clarence Nixon's *Possum Trot: Rural Community, South* (Norman, 1941).[66] One noteworthy example of recent local history is the Virginia Second World War History Commission's series of studies dealing with the communities and people of that state during the war.[67]

Some of the numerous multivolume state histories published during the twenties and early thirties gave attention to the early twentieth century, but in general these works were unbalanced and uncritical in evaluating recent events. Two state histories published by professional historians in 1934—those of David Duncan Wallace on South Carolina and Albert Burton Moore on Alabama—were remarkable for their handling of the recent period.[68] Wallace, for instance, was as concerned with the times of Tillman and Blease as he was with those of Calhoun and Hampton. In the 1940's and 1950's several one-volume state histories were able to transcend the usual impressionistic treatment of the twentieth century. Outstanding among these studies were Hugh Talmage Lefler and Albert Ray Newsome's scholarly and balanced history of North Carolina and Ernest M. Lander's revealing survey of South

---

Story of Durham: City of the New South (Durham, 1925); Thomas J. Wertenbaker, *Norfolk: Historic Southern Port* (2nd ed.; Durham, 1962); Angie Debo, *Tulsa: From Creek Town to Oil Capital* (Norman, 1943); and Adelaide L. Fries *et al., Forsyth: A County on the March* (Chapel Hill, 1949).

66 See also Nixon, *Lower Piedmont Country* (New York, 1946), a volume in the American Folkways Series devoted to the Chattanooga-Atlanta-Birmingham triangle. For an interesting study of an unusual southern community, see Paul E. and Blanche R. Alyea, *Fairhope, 1894–1954: The Story of a Single Tax Colony* (University, Alabama, 1956).

67 For examples, see Marvin Wilson Schlegel, *Conscripted City: Norfolk in World War II* (Norfolk, 1951); Charles F. Marsh (ed.), *The Hampton Roads Communities in World War II* (Chapel Hill, 1951); Gertrude Dana Parlier and others, *Pursuits of War: The People of Charlottesville and Albemarle County, Virginia, in the Second World War* (Charlottesville, 1948). For another specialized war study, see Spencer Bidwell King, *Selective Service in North Carolina in World War II* (Chapel Hill, 1949).

68 Wallace, *The History of South Carolina* (4 vols.; New York, 1934); Moore, *History of Alabama* (University, Alabama, 1934). For two recent multivolume histories that give space to the twentieth century, see J. E. Dovell, *Florida: Historic, Dramatic, Contemporary* (4 vols.; New York, 1952); Stanley J. Folmsbee, Robert E. Corlew, and Enoch L. Mitchell, *History of Tennessee* (4 vols.; New York, 1960). Some older histories that are useful for the modern period are Dunbar Rowland, *History of Mississippi: The Heart of the South* (2 vols.; Chicago and Jackson, 1925); R. D. W. Connor, *North Carolina: Rebuilding an Ancient Commonwealth, 1584–1925* (4 vols.; Chicago and New York, 1929); and Philip M. Hamer (ed.), *Tennessee: A History, 1673–1932* (4 vols.; New York, 1933).

Carolina during the period 1865–1960.[69] A few of the many informal interpretations are worthy of note for their insight into the patterns of cultural change in the modern South. For example, Marshall W. Fishwick's awareness of the role of tradition and mythology in twentieth-century Virginia is suggested by some of the chapter titles in his *Virginia: A New Look at the Old Dominion* (New York, 1959) : "F.F.V.'s," "Marse Chan vs. the N.A.A.C.P.," "Restoration Blues," and "The Virginia Lady." [70]

Meanwhile, several general histories of the region attempted to deal seriously with developments during the first half of the twentieth century. Francis B. Simkins' *A History of the South* is especially valuable for its detailed treatment of social and cultural as well as economic trends in the modern period.[71] Equally broad in approach, if somewhat less detailed, is John Samuel Ezell's fresh and informed *The South Since 1865* (New York, 1963). A third general history important for the recent period is *The South in American History,* a concise evaluation of main trends by William B. Hesseltine and David L. Smiley.[72] The most informative work on social and economic changes in the region since 1920 is Thomas D. Clark's sprightly volume, *The Emerging South* (New York, 1961).

No student of the South's recent past should overlook the work of the social scientists. The sociologist, economist, and political scientist have usually been concerned with contemporary social analysis, and

69 Lefler and Newsome, *North Carolina: The History of a Southern State* (Chapel Hill, 1954) ; Lander, *A History of South Carolina, 1865–1960* (Chapel Hill, 1960). Other southern state histories that are distinguished for their handling of recent themes are Rupert Norval Richardson, *Texas: The Lone Star State* (New York, 1943) ; and Edwin C. McReynolds, *Oklahoma: A History of the Sooner State* (Norman, 1954).

70 See also John Gould Fletcher, *Arkansas* (Chapel Hill, 1947) ; Alfred Jackson Hanna and Kathryn Abbey Hanna, *Florida's Golden Sands* (Indianapolis, 1950) ; Frank Goodwyn, *Lone-Star Land: Twentieth Century Texas in Perspective* (New York, 1955) ; George Melvin Fuermann, *Reluctant Empire* (Garden City, 1957) ; and William Francis Guess, *South Carolina: Annals of Pride and Protest* (New York, 1960).

71 Simkins, *A History of the South* (3rd ed.; New York, 1963). Simkins' emphasis is on the New South and the influence of tradition and conservatism in conditioning attitudes and institutions in the region. His organization of material is sometimes disjointed, but his book is nevertheless a pioneering work of synthesis and interpretation on the twentieth-century South.

72 Hesseltine and Smiley, *The South in American History* (2nd ed.; Englewood Cliffs, New Jersey, 1960). For a volume on the Southwest that covers some of the states in the larger South, see W. Eugene Hollon, *The Southwest: Old and New* (New York, 1961).

they did not begin to employ the regional concept until long after historians had incorporated the section as a theme in their interpretations. Even so, the value of the work of the social scientists for an understanding of the modern South can scarcely be overemphasized. Research in southern universities during the 1930's, whether on cultural trends, community problems, race relations, or ecological studies, was usually cast in a regional mold.[73] The same was true to a considerable extent of the anthropological field studies of northern investigators.

The most important influence in the regional analysis of southern problems was the work of Howard W. Odum and his colleagues in sociology at the University of North Carolina. Odum's regionalism was a synthesis of all the social sciences and, to some extent, of the humanities as well. He emphasized what he called the concept of "folk-regional society," an approach to the region in a broad sense as a cultural area, a gestalt "in which all factors are sought out and interpreted in their proper perspective." [74] Odum's most signal contribution to the literature on regionalism was his monumental *Southern Regions of the United States* (Chapel Hill, 1936), a tour de force in the use of cultural-statistical data in regional analysis.[75] In this impressive volume Odum not only made clear the conceptual framework for his approach to the study of American regions but also fashioned from a wealth of statistics an appraisal of the Southeast on the basis of which a program of reconstruction could be initiated. It became a sort of Bible for the regionalists and a work of incalculable importance in the study of the southern region.

The contributions of some of the other sociologists at the University of North Carolina were almost as great as Odum's. Rupert B. Vance's *Human Geography of the South,* published during the early thirties, was a masterly treatment of the region in terms of its cultural heritage,

73 It is significant that the Southern Economic Association, the Southern Sociological Society, and the Southern Political Science Association, two of which published their own journals, were organized in the 1930's. It should also be noted that this remarkable experimentation in social research within the framework of a major region was supported by many other organizations—the Commission on Interracial Cooperation, the Southern States Industrial Council, the Southern Policy Committee, the Southern Conference for Human Welfare, the TVA, and various New Deal agencies.

74 Odum, "From Community Studies to Regionalism," *Social Forces,* XXIII (March, 1945), 253.

75 Gerald W. Johnson, *The Wasted Land* (Chapel Hill, 1937), provides a summary of Odum's book and a trenchant interpretation of his own.

geographic setting, and people.[76] His *All These People,* which appeared
in the mid-forties, was a worthy supplement to Odum's *Southern
Regions of the United States.* It brought the earlier volume up to date,
extended its analysis, and in many respects improved on it as a vigorous
and original synthesis in its own right.[77] In *Southern Industry and
Regional Development* (Chapel Hill, 1940), Harriet L. Herring applied regionalism's principle of "optimum production" to manufacturing
in the Southeast in an effort to suggest a desirable economic balance for
the region. By 1945, when the Institute for Research in Social Science
of the University of North Carolina published a list of its research, the
institute could boast that eighty-seven books and monographs had been
published and scores of unpublished studies completed, covering a wide
range of regional topics.[78]

Some of the work by sociologists did not fall into the pattern of
Odum's regionalism, but, even so, it frequently illuminated significant
aspects of southern culture. One very important body of writings by
sociologists dealt with rural life: the ravages of the depression, the
status of landlord and tenant, the impact of New Deal policies, and the
chances of rehabilitating the southern farmer.[79] The picture these
studies presented was not a pretty one, but some of them were extraordinarily revealing in their descriptions of living conditions in the
agricultural regions.[80] For example, Arthur F. Raper's *Preface to*

76 Vance, *Human Geography of the South: A Study in Regional Resources and
Human Adequacy* (Chapel Hill, 1932). For a work that attempts to describe the
civilization of the South in terms of its economic and geographic aspects, see A. E.
Parkins, *The South: Its Economic-Geographic Development* (New York, 1938).

77 Rupert B. Vance in collaboration with Nadia Danilevsky, *All These People:
The Nation's Human Resources in the South* (Chapel Hill, 1945). For an able
treatment of more recent population changes in the South, see John M. Maclachlan
and Joe S. Floyd, Jr., *This Changing South* (Gainesville, 1956).

78 "Institute for Research in Social Science: Publications and Manuscripts (Ar-
ranged Chronologically)," *Social Forces,* XXIII (March, 1945), 309–28. See also
Howard W. Odum and Katherine Jocher, *In Search of the Regional Balance of
America* (Chapel Hill, 1945); and Edith Webb Williams, *Research in Southern
Regional Development* (Richmond, 1948).

79 On the theme of regional research and land tenure, see Harold C. Hoffsommer,
*Regional Research Cooperation: A Statement of Regional Research Procedures as
Developed by the Regional Land Tenure Project* (Chapel Hill, 1949), and Hoff-
sommer (ed.), *The Social and Economic Significance of Land Tenure in the South-
western States: A Report* (Chapel Hill, 1950). See also Charles S. Mangum, *The
Legal Status of the Tenant Farmer in the Southeast* (Chapel Hill, 1952).

80 Charles S. Johnson, Edwin R. Embree, and W. W. Alexander, *The Collapse
of Cotton Tenancy: A Summary of Field Studies & Statistical Surveys, 1933–35*
(Chapel Hill, 1935), 14, characterizes the cultural landscape of the agrarian South
as a "miserable panorama of unpainted shacks, rain-gullied fields, straggling fences,
rattle-trap Fords, dirt, poverty, disease, drudgery, and monotony."

Peasantry: A Tale of Two Black Counties (Chapel Hill, 1936) was a detailed inquiry into every aspect of life in two Georgia counties. His *Tenants of the Almighty* (New York, 1943) was probably the most intensive case study ever done in the field of rural southern life, as well as a reasonably good social history of Greene County, Georgia.[81] Two of the more interesting works published since 1950 on rural life in the South are Morton Rubin's *Plantation County* (Chapel Hill, 1951), one of the Field Studies in the Modern Culture of the South directed by John Gillin, and James H. Street's study of the mechanization of cotton production, *The New Revolution in the Cotton Economy: Mechanization and Its Consequences* (Chapel Hill, 1957).

Another valuable group of sociological studies has been concerned with the conditions of industrial workers, particularly in the cotton textile industry. The work of Harriet L. Herring on the mill village and Herbert J. Lahne's study of *The Cotton Mill Worker* (New York, 1944) are notable examples.[82] Liston Pope's *Millhands & Preachers: A Study of Gastonia* (New Haven, 1942) is not merely an account of the role of the church in the social and industrial control of Gastonia; it is also a comprehensive analysis of the city's cultural and social structure. John Kenneth Morland's *Millways of Kent* (Chapel Hill, 1958), to cite one other example, is a perceptive anthropologist's report in a series of studies devoted to the Piedmont mill town of "Kent."

The sociologists have produced a variety of other works on the

81 For other examples, see Rupert B. Vance, *Human Factors in Cotton Culture: A Study in the Social Geography of the American South* (Chapel Hill, 1929); Wilson Gee and William Henry Stauffer, *Rural and Urban Living Standards in Virginia* (University, Virginia, 1929); Charles S. Johnson, *Shadow of the Plantation* (Chicago, 1934); T. J. Woofter, Jr., *Landlord and Tenant on the Cotton Plantation* (Washington, D. C., 1936); Herman Clarence Nixon, *Forty Acres and Steel Mules* (Chapel Hill, 1938); Margaret Jarman Hagood, *Mothers of the South: Portraiture of the White Tenant Farm Woman* (Chapel Hill, 1939); William C. Holley and others, *The Plantation South, 1934–1937* (Washington, D. C., 1940); Arthur F. Raper and Ira De A. Reid, *Sharecroppers All* (Chapel Hill, 1941); Paul W. Wager, *One Foot on the Soil: A Study of Subsistence Homesteads in Alabama* (University, Alabama, 1945); Rupert B. Vance and Gordon W. Blackwell, *New Farm Homes for Old: A Study of Rural Public Housing in the South* (University, Alabama, 1946).

82 Herring, *Welfare Work in Mill Villages: The Story of Extra-Mill Activities in North Carolina* (Chapel Hill, 1929), and *Passing of the Mill Village: Revolution in a Southern Institution* (Chapel Hill, 1949). For other examples, see Jennings J. Rhyne, *Some Southern Cotton Mill Workers and Their Villages* (Chapel Hill, 1930); Marjorie A. Potwin, *Cotton Mill People of the Piedmont: A Study in Social Change* (New York, 1927); Horace R. Cayton and George S. Mitchell, *Black Workers and the New Unions* (Chapel Hill, 1939); Glenn Gilman, *Human Relations in the Industrial Southeast: A Study of the Textile Industry* (Chapel Hill, 1956).

South, ranging from the studies of Negro folklore and folk culture by Odum, Guy B. Johnson, and others to interpretations of individual states like those of S. Huntington Hobbs and G. Croft Williams.[83] Other important categories include population studies of state and city, evaluations of public welfare activities, surveys of church and community, and community studies by the anthropologists.[84] The quickening pace of urbanization in the South caused some sociologists to investigate its impact on the rural community and led to the publication in 1954 of *The Urban South,* a collaborative work that traced the rise of urbanism in the region and attempted to interpret its broader implications.[85]

A regional survey undertaken in the late 1950's by the Southern Appalachian Studies resulted in the publication of the most comprehensive analysis ever made of an area that had been bypassed by many of the modern currents of economic and social change.[86] Yet, significantly,

---

83 Examples are T. J. Woofter, Jr., *Black Yeomanry: Life on St. Helena Island* (New York, 1930); Guy B. Johnson, *Folk Culture on St. Helena Island, South Carolina* (Chapel Hill, 1930); Howard W. Odum, *American Epoch: Southern Portraiture in the National Picture* (New York, 1930); S. Huntington Hobbs, *North Carolina: Economic and Social* (Chapel Hill, 1930), and Hobbs, *North Carolina: An Economic and Social Profile* (Chapel Hill, 1958); G. Croft Williams, *A Social Interpretation of South Carolina* (Columbia, 1946).

84 For illustrative volumes, see John Ballenger Knox, *The People of Tennessee: A Study of Population Trends* (Knoxville, 1949); Chalmers Alexander McMahan, *The People of Atlanta: A Demographic Study of Georgia's Capital City* (Athens, 1950); Roy M. Brown, *Public Relief in North Carolina* (Chapel Hill, 1928); Frank W. Hoffer, *Counties in Transition: A Study of County Public and Private Welfare Administration in Virginia* (University, Virginia, 1929); Wiley B. Sanders, *Juvenile Courts in North Carolina* (Chapel Hill, 1948); Jesse Marvin Ormond, *The Country Church in North Carolina: A Study of the Country Churches of North Carolina in Relation to the Material Progress of the State* (Durham, 1931); Gordon W. Blackwell, Lee M. Brooks, and S. H. Hobbs, Jr., *Church and Community in the South: Report for the Committee on Re-study of Religious Education of the Presbyterian Church in the United States* (Richmond, 1949); Joseph Henry Fichter, *Southern Parish: Dynamics of a City Church* (Chicago, 1951); John Dollard, *Caste and Class in a Southern Town* (New Haven, 1937); Hortense Powdermaker, *After Freedom: A Cultural Study in the Deep South* (New York, 1939); Hylan Lewis, *Blackways of Kent* (Chapel Hill, 1955).

85 Rupert B. Vance and Nicholas J. Demerath (eds.), *The Urban South* (Chapel Hill, 1954). See also Reuben Hill, J. Joel Moss, and Claudine G. Wirths, *Eddyville's Families: A Study of Personal and Family Adjustments Subsequent to the Rapid Urbanization of a Southern Town* (Chapel Hill, 1953); and F. Stuart Chapin, Jr., and others, *In the Shadow of a Defense Plant: A Study of Urbanization in Rural South Carolina* ... (Chapel Hill, 1954).

86 Thomas R. Ford (ed.), *The Southern Appalachian Region: A Survey* (Lexington, 1962). For an older report on this region, see U. S. Department of Agriculture, *Economic and Social Problems and Conditions of the Southern Appalachians* (Miscellaneous Publication No. 205 [Washington, D.C., 1935]). A recent popular

most of the recent studies of southern society have turned away from regionalism, concentrating instead upon race relations and problems of desegregation, social mobility, and decision making.[87] The trend toward the convergence of regional and national status, observes Rupert B. Vance, "has dulled the edge of regional claims and reduced the drive of regionalism as a social movement." [88]

One of the most important contributors to the popularization of the regional concept and its identification with the South has been the Tennessee Valley Authority, which not only exerted itself to promote the scholarly study of regional problems,[89] but became the subject of numerous analyses by social scientists within the regional framework its creation ordained. Joseph Sirera Ransmeier's economic analysis of TVA's multipurpose stream planning, C. Herman Pritchett's administrative study of the Authority, and David E. Lilienthal's vibrant "inside story" of the experiment were only the forerunners of scholarly investigations of many other aspects of this venture in regional rehabilitation.[90]

Some economists subscribed to the tenets of Howard W. Odum's regionalism, but in general the economists were less likely to be regional-

---

account of a depressed subregion is Harry M. Caudill, *Night Comes to the Cumberlands: A Biography of a Depressed Area* (Boston, 1963).

87 See, for example, Robin M. Williams, Jr., and Margaret W. Ryan (eds.), *Schools in Transition: Community Experiences in Desegregation* (Chapel Hill, 1954); Melvin M. Tumin, *Desegregation: Resistance and Readiness* (Princeton, 1958); Floyd Hunter, *Community Power Structure: A Study of Decision Makers* (Chapel Hill, 1953); M. Elaine Burgess, *Negro Leadership in a Southern City* (Chapel Hill, 1962).

88 Vance, "The Status and Future of Regionalism—A Symposium," *Journal of Southern History,* XXVI (February, 1960), 47.

89 For the TVA's early interest in regional analysis, see William E. Cole, "Personality and Cultural Research in the Tennessee Valley," *Social Forces,* XIII (May, 1935), 521–27.

90 Ransmeier, *The Tennessee Valley Authority: A Case Study in the Economics of Multiple Purpose Stream Planning* (Nashville, 1942); Pritchett, *The Tennessee Valley Authority: A Study in Public Administration* (Chapel Hill, 1943); Lilienthal, *TVA: Democracy on the March* (New York, 1944). See also Herman Finer, *The T.V.A.: Lessons for International Application* (Montreal, 1944); Philip Selznick, *TVA and the Grass Roots: A Study in the Sociology of Formal Organization* (Berkeley, 1949); Norman I. Wengert, *Valley of Tomorrow: The TVA and Agriculture* (Knoxville, 1952); Robert S. Avery, *Experiment in Management: Personnel Decentralization in the Tennessee Valley Authority* (Knoxville, 1954); Gordon R. Clapp, *The TVA: An Approach to the Development of a Region* (Chicago, 1955); James Dahir, *Region Building: Community Development Lessons from the Tennessee Valley* (New York, 1955); John R. P. Friedmann, *The Spatial Structure of Economic Development in the Tennessee Valley: A Study in Regional Planning* (Chicago, 1955); and Roscoe C. Martin (ed.), *TVA, The First Twenty Years: A Staff Report* (University, Alabama, 1956).

ists than were the sociologists. Nevertheless, many economists were involved in the study of regional problems, and almost by necessity their
investigations revolved around the colonial character of the southern
economy and such things as freight-rate discrimination, wage differen-
tials, and monopolistic exploitation.[91] An excellent case study of the
restrictive effects of northeastern policies on the South is presented in
George W. Stocking's volume on the basing point system in the iron
and steel industry.[92] Some economists, moreover, were involved in the
regional planning activities of such groups as the National Planning Association Committee of the South.[93]

Significant aspects of the regional economy were analyzed in many
articles appearing in the *Southern Economic Journal* and in monographs
dealing with industry, labor, and agriculture.[94] Such subjects as the
public regulation of transportation, the effect of taxation on manufacturing, and state and local trends in fiscal policy have also received attention from southern economists.[95] The historian of the modern South

---

91 See, for example, Clarence Heer, *Income and Wages in the South* (Chapel
Hill, 1930); William H. Joubert, *Southern Freight Rates in Transition* (Gainesville, 1949); and Robert A. Lively, *The South in Action: A Sectional Crusade
against Freight Rate Discrimination* (Chapel Hill, 1949). In Walter Prescott
Webb, *Divided We Stand: The Crisis of a Frontierless Democracy* (New York,
1937), a mass of data is used in attempting to explain the contrast in economic
ramifications between the position of the South and the West, on the one hand, and
that of the North, on the other.

92 Stocking, *Basing Point Pricing and Regional Development: A Case Study of
the Iron and Steel Industry* (Chapel Hill, 1954).

93 See, for instance, John V. Van Sickle, *Planning for the South: An Inquiry into
the Economics of Regionalism* (Nashville, 1943); and Albert Lepawsky, *State
Planning and Economic Development in the South* (Washington, D.C., 1949).

94 For examples, see James A. Morris, *Woolen and Worsted Manufacturing in
the Southern Piedmont* (Columbia, South Carolina, 1952); H. H. Chapman and
others, *The Iron and Steel Industries of the South* (University, Alabama, 1953);
Olin S. Pugh and others, *The Food and Kindred Products Industries of South
Carolina: Their Position, Problems and Prospects* (n.p., 1962); Abraham Berg-
lund, George T. Starnes, and Frank T. De Vyver, *Labor in the Industrial South:
A Survey of Wages and Living Conditions in Three Major Industries of the New
Industrial South* (University, Virginia, 1930); George Talmage Starnes and John
E. Hamm, *Some Phases of Labor Relations in Virginia* (New York, 1934); John
Leonard Fulmer, *Agricultural Progress in the Cotton Belt Since 1920* (Chapel Hill,
1950); Donald Crichton Alexander, *The Arkansas Plantation, 1920–1942* (New
Haven, 1943).

95 See Clyde C. Carter, *State Regulation of Commercial Motor Carriers in North
Carolina* (Chapel Hill, 1958); James W. Martin and Glenn D. Morrow, *Taxation
of Manufacturing in the South* (University, Alabama, 1948); Joe Summers Floyd,
Effects of Taxation on Industrial Location (Chapel Hill, 1952); Joseph M. Ray,
Alabama's State Dollar (University, Alabama, 1942); James W. Martin, *Southern
State and Local Finance Trends and the War* (Nashville and Lexington, 1945);

will find much to use and to ponder in three recent contributions by economists. One is the comprehensive and balanced report on southern economic resources and policies by Calvin B. Hoover and Benjamin U. Ratchford.[96] It presents a valuable picture of an older agrarian region slowly coming into economic maturity. A second contribution is a significant monograph by Anthony M. Tang entitled *Economic Development in the Southern Piedmont, 1860–1950: Its Impact on Agriculture* (Chapel Hill, 1958). Tang is interested in determining how agriculture and farm income fared in developed as compared with underdeveloped areas. His study clearly demonstrates that urbanization and industrialization have been beneficial to southern agriculture.[97] William H. Nicholls, under whom Tang studied at Vanderbilt University, is the author of a thoughtful book on *Southern Tradition and Regional Progress* (Chapel Hill, 1960). He argues that the region's lag in per capita incomes results from its relatively slow pace of industrial-urban development, and that its lag in industrialization is largely attributable to the long-time adherence to a set of cultural values inconsistent with rapid industrial development.[98]

The political equivalent of Odum's *Southern Regions of the United States* is V. O. Key, Jr.'s *Southern Politics in State and Nation* (New York, 1949). Already a classic in political writing, this comprehensive work contains a penetrating analysis of power structures and the operation of the political process.[99] While it emphasizes the historic role of the black belts in perpetuating southern sectionalism, Key's book also dispels the old notion that all southern states fall within the same pat-

and John Littlepage Lancaster, *County Income Estimates for Seven Southeastern States* (Charlottesville, 1952).

96 Hoover and Ratchford, *Economic Resources and Policies of the South* (New York, 1951). The book organizes a vast amount of material, criticizes certain generally accepted policies, but is optimistic in its broad outlook.

97 For similar studies of other areas, see Frank T. Bachmura, "Migration and Factor Adjustment in Lower Mississippi Valley Agriculture: 1940–50," *Journal of Farm Economics*, XXXVIII (November, 1956), 1024–42; and William H. Nicholls, "The Effects of Industrial Development on Tennessee Valley Agriculture, 1900–1950," *Journal of Farm Economics*, XXXVIII (December, 1956), 1636–49. For the delineation of another subregion, see Herman Frederick Otte, *Industrial Opportunity in the Tennessee Valley of Northwestern Alabama* (New York, 1940).

98 Nicholls is perhaps unduly harsh in his criticism of southern traditions, but his discussion is suggestive and his positive recommendations are valuable.

99 In addition to a state-by-state interpretation of politics in the ex-Confederate states, Key's book examines the mechanisms and procedures of the one-party system, analyzes the composition of the southern electorate, discusses the restrictions on the franchise, and treats the role of the South in national politics.

tern. A valuable complement to Key's volume is Alexander Heard's *A Two-Party South?* (Chapel Hill, 1952). Heard, who had assisted Key in the preparation of *Southern Politics in State and Nation,* did not neglect the role of tradition and nonrational motivation in the one-party South; but he detected many signs of fissure in the old party loyalties, and he was optimistic about the chances for a two-party system below the Potomac. He presented a careful and thorough treatment of southern Republicans, an analysis of recent tendencies in political opinion in the South, including the "Dixiecrat" movement, and a study of the Negro's role in the political affairs of the region.[100]

Another general work of importance on southern politics grew out of a broad survey of the political scene in the South published in the *Journal of Politics.*[101] Jasper B. Shannon attempted a general interpretation in a series of lectures published under the title *Toward a New Politics in the South* (Knoxville, 1949). His characterization of "The Governing Class of a Southern County Seat" is particularly discerning. One of the volumes in the five-volume study of presidential nominating politics in 1952 provides a wealth of information on recent party activities in all of the southern states.[102] Allan P. Sindler's *Huey Long's Louisiana,* an analysis emphasizing bifactionalism in Louisiana politics during the period 1920–1952, and John H. Fenton's perceptive study of politics in the border states are examples of the best work on the state level.[103] Cortez A. M. Ewing and other scholars have studied primary

---

100 For recent southern Republicanism, see Donald S. Strong, *Urban Republicanism in the South* (University, Alabama, 1960).

101 These articles appeared in book form in Taylor Cole and John H. Hallowell (eds.), *The Southern Political Scene, 1938–1948* (Gainesville, 1948).

102 Paul T. David, Malcolm Moos, and Ralph M. Goldman (eds.), *The South,* Volume III of *Presidential Nominating Politics in 1952* (5 vols.; Baltimore, 1954). See also L. Vaughan Howard and David R. Deener, *Presidential Politics in Louisiana, 1952* (New Orleans, 1954); and Jasper B. Shannon and Ruth McQuown, *Presidential Politics in Kentucky, 1824–1948: A Compilation of Election Statistics and an Analysis of Political Behavior* (Lexington, 1950).

103 Sindler, *Huey Long's Louisiana: State Politics, 1920–1952* (Baltimore, 1956); Fenton, *Politics in the Border States: A Study of the Patterns of Political Organization, and Political Change, Common to the Border States—Maryland, West Virginia, Kentucky and Missouri* (New Orleans, 1957). For two other valuable state studies, see Joseph L. Bernd, *Grass Roots Politics in Georgia: The County Unit System and the Importance of the Individual Voting Community in Bifactional Elections, 1942–1954* (Atlanta, 1960); and William C. Havard and Loren P. Beth, *The Politics of Mis-Representation: Rural-Urban Conflict in the Florida Legislature* (Baton Rouge, 1962).

elections and other features of the electoral process in the South.[104] In addition to a number of works on the role of the Negro in American politics generally, several books have recently been published which deal with the race question in southern politics.[105] Hugh D. Price's compact study of Negro registration and voting participation in Florida makes impressive use of data available in that state.[106]

Political scientists have made detailed studies of all of the state governments in the South. The volumes in the American Commonwealth Series, while essentially studies of administrative procedures at the state level, throw much light on state politics. The student of recent southern history will also find valuable material in some of the numerous books on local and municipal governments in the South. The regional point of view and cooperative regional analysis are reflected in several significant studies of resource management at the state level in the South.[107] Finally,

104 See Ewing, *Primary Elections in the South: A Study in Uniparty Politics* (Norman, 1953) ; L. M. Holland, *The Direct Primary in Georgia* (Urbana, 1949) ; Alexander Heard and Donald S. Strong (eds.), *Southern Primaries and Elections, 1920–1949* (University, Alabama, 1950) ; Frederic D. Ogden, *The Poll Tax in the South* (University, Alabama, 1958).

105 For the Negro voter in the nation at large, see Henry Lee Moon, *Balance of Power: The Negro Vote* (Garden City, 1948) ; Wilson Record, *The Negro and the Communist Party* (Chapel Hill, 1951) ; Elbert Lee Tatum, *The Changed Political Thought of the Negro, 1915–1940* (New York, 1951) ; James Q. Wilson, *Negro Politics: The Search for Leadership* (Glencoe, Illinois, 1960). For the race question in southern politics, see Paul Lewinson, *Race, Class & Party: A History of Negro Suffrage and White Politics in the South* (New York, 1932) ; C. Vann Woodward, *The Strange Career of Jim Crow* (New York, 1955) ; and a valuable symposium, "The Negro Voter in the South," *Journal of Negro Education*, XXVI (Summer, 1957), 213–431. Aspects of the legal controversy surrounding race relations are discussed in Robert J. Harris, *The Quest for Equality: The Constitution, Congress and the Supreme Court* (Baton Rouge, 1960) ; and Jack Walter Peltason, *Fifty-Eight Lonely Men: Southern Federal Judges and School Desegregation* (New York, 1961).

106 Price, *The Negro and Southern Politics: A Chapter of Florida History* (New York, 1957).

107 This literature is voluminous, but for illustrative volumes, see James Karl Coleman, *State Administration in South Carolina* (New York, 1935) ; William H. Combs and William E. Cole, *Tennessee: A Political Study* (Knoxville, 1940) ; Robert B. Highsaw and Charles N. Fortenberry, *The Government and Administration of Mississippi* (New York, 1954) ; Robert S. Rankin, *The Government and Administration of North Carolina* (New York, 1955) ; Joseph M. Ray and Lillian Worley, *Alabama's Heritage: A Study of the Public Administration of Natural Resources* (University, Alabama, 1947) ; Lee S. Greene and others, *Rescued Earth: A Study of the Public Administration of Natural Resources in Tennessee* (Knoxville, 1948) ; R. L. Carleton, *Local Government and Administration in Louisiana* (Baton Rouge, 1935) ; Karl A. E sworth, *Black Belt County: Rural Government in the Cotton Country of Alabama* (University, Alabama, 1941) ; Tennessee Valley Authority, *County Government and Administration in the Tennessee Valley*

the writings of the politicians themselves should not be overlooked, for they include such distinctive volumes as the memoirs of Josephus Daniels and Cordell Hull as well as an occasional perspicacious interpretation like Ellis G. Arnall's *The Shore Dimly Seen* (Philadelphia, 1946).[108]

While the social scientists have done the most to make the modern South the best documented region of the country, a numerous band of less scholarly writers has made its contribution through the publication of regional and state interpretations, travel accounts, and reminiscences of a regional character. Many of these works are valuable for the information they present on the changing South. Thus Katharine Du Pre Lumpkin's *The South in Progress* (New York, 1940) and Virginius Dabney's *Below the Potomac: A Book about the New South* (New York, 1942) are useful surveys of the region's development during the 1930's. Jonathan Daniels, Hal Steed, Angie Debo, and others have written informal but revealing interpretations of individual southern states.[109] Some of the southern contributions to the American Folkways Series and the Rivers of America Series, such as Harnett T. Kane's saga of the Deep Delta and Wilma Dykeman's charming story of the French Broad, are effective blending of fact and folklore.[110]

States (Washington, D.C., 1940); Melvin Clyde Hughes, *County Government in Georgia* (Athens, 1944); Weldon Cooper, *Metropolitan County: A Survey of Government in the Birmingham Area* (University, Alabama, 1949).

108 Four of the volumes in Daniels' remarkable autobiography (5 vols.; Chapel Hill, 1939–1947) deal with the twentieth century. Other memoirs and personal accounts of southern political leaders include: *The Memoirs of Cordell Hull* (2 vols.; New York, 1948); Charles Seymour (ed.), *The Intimate Papers of Colonel House* (4 vols.; Boston, 1926–1928); William H. ("Alfalfa Bill") Murray, *Memoirs of Governor Murray and True History of Oklahoma* . . . (3 vols.; Boston, 1945); Maury Maverick, *A Maverick American* (New York, 1937); Fuller Warren, *How to Win in Politics* (Tallahassee, 1949); Aubrey Lee Brooks, *A Southern Lawyer: Fifty Years at the Bar* (Chapel Hill, 1950); Tom Connally, *My Name Is Tom Connally* (New York, 1954); James F. Byrnes, *All in a Lifetime* (New York, 1958); Luther H. Hodges, *Businessman in the Statehouse: Six Years as Governor of North Carolina* (Chapel Hill, 1962). Special note should be taken of the valuable series of messages, addresses, and public papers of North Carolina governors published by the North Carolina Council of State.

109 Daniels, *Tar Heels: A Portrait of North Carolina* (New York, 1941); Steed, *Georgia: Unfinished State* (New York, 1942); Debo, *Oklahoma: Foot-Loose and Fancy-Free* (Norman, 1949); Agnes Rothery, *Virginia: The New Dominion* (New York, 1940).

110 See, for example, Kane, *Deep Delta Country* (New York, 1944), and *The Bayous of Louisiana* (New York, 1943); Dykeman, *The French Broad* (New York, 1955); and Henry Savage, Jr., *River of the Carolinas: The Santee* (New York, 1956).

And many recent publications are concerned with the theme of race relations.[111]

The student of the recent South should not ignore the state and city guides prepared by the Federal Writers' Project of the Works Progress Administration. Nor should he neglect the travel accounts. A recent bibliography of southern travel accounts listed 627 books for the years 1900–1955.[112] Many of these are of little value but some of them are important social documents, full of insight as regional and subregional interpretations. Consider, for example, Jonathan Daniels' *A Southerner Discovers the South* (New York, 1938), an urbane and brilliantly written report of a trip through the region; J. Saunders Redding's *No Day of Triumph* (New York, 1942), an angry, honest, and compassionate picture of Negro life in the South as it appeared to an educated northern Negro; and Carl T. Rowan's *South of Freedom* (New York, 1952), a powerful and moving account of a profound personal experience and of a perceptive journalist's observations. Another chronicle of a journey through the South is Wilma Dykeman and James Stokely, *Neither Black Nor White* (New York, 1957), a probing and compelling search for a comprehensive regional portrait. Other examples range from such foreign accounts as those of Ursula Branston and Clare Leighton to the classic documentaries of southern sharecroppers by James Agee, Erskine Caldwell, and Margaret Bourke-White.[113]

Popular attempts at regional portrayal are as diversified as Howard W. Odum's amorphous but lyrical interpretation of the South's cultural pattern in *American Epoch: Southern Portraiture in the National Picture* (New York, 1930); the articulate reaffirmation of agrarian prin-

111 Among these are Robert Penn Warren, *Segregation: The Inner Conflict in the South* (New York, 1956); Howard H. Quint, *Profile in Black and White: A Frank Portrait of South Carolina* (Washington, D.C., 1958), Martin Luther King, Jr., *Stride toward Freedom: The Montgomery Story* (New York, 1958); William Peters, *The Southern Temper* (Garden City, 1959); Brooks Hays, *A Southern Moderate Speaks* (Chapel Hill, 1959); Hodding Carter, *The South Strikes Back* (Garden City, 1959); P. D. East, *The Magnolia Jungle: The Life, Times and Education of a Southern Editor* (New York, 1960); Benjamin Muse, *Virginia's Massive Resistance* (Bloomington, 1961); Bernard Taper, *Gomillion versus Lightfoot: The Tuskegee Gerrymander Case* (New York, 1962); Louis E. Lomax, *The Negro Revolt* (New York, 1962).

112 Thomas D. Clark (ed.) *The Twentieth-Century South, 1900–1955: An Era of Change, Depression, and Emergence,* Volume II of *Travels in the New South: A Bibliography* (2 vols.; Norman, 1962).

113 Branston, *Let the Band Play "Dixie"! . . . Improvisations on a Southern Signature Tune* (London, 1940); Leighton, *Southern Harvest* (New York, 1942); James Agee and Walker Evans, *Let Us Now Praise Famous Men* (Boston, 1941); Caldwell and Bourke-White, *You Have Seen Their Faces* (New York, 1937).

ciples in Twelve Southerners, *I'll Take My Stand: The South and the Agrarian Tradition* (New York, 1930); and Wilbur J. Cash's brilliant essay on the southern character in *The Mind of the South* (New York, 1941).[114] Another category of popular writings important for an understanding of the present South is more personal in nature, including such volumes as Carl Carmer's *Stars Fell on Alabama* (New York, 1934); Ben Robertson's, *Red Hills and Cotton: An Upcountry Memory* (New York, 1942); and Hodding Carter's *Where Main Street Meets the River* (New York, 1953).[115] At their best, these books illuminate the conflict that often attended the impact of social change upon traditional values. Thus William Alexander Percy, in *Lanterns on the Levee: Recollections of a Planter's Son* (New York, 1941), has written a poignant interpretation of the Delta aristocracy and the passing of a way of life. Katharine Du Pre Lumpkin's *The Making of a Southerner* (New York, 1947), and Ralph McGill's *The South and the Southerner* (Boston, 1963), to cite two other examples, are warm and knowing accounts of their coming of age in the early twentieth-century South, and of how the South changed and changed them.

The greatest value of this popular literature lies in the comprehensive reportorial coverage it provides for the recent South. But it also has other values, including many courageous expressions of regional self-criticism. Some of these books are also distinguished by an undeniable literary charm, reflecting a combination of regional self-consciousness and genuine creative ability on the part of their authors. Their approach to the region is revealing, for they have shown a peculiar awareness of the relationship between the past and the present, of the community, of the concreteness of human relationships, of what Harry S. Ashmore describes as a "sense of identity with time, place, and the past." [116] However deficient their scholarship, these journalists and professional

114 The variety of the regional portraits may be suggested in these examples: Clarence Cason, *90° in the Shade* (Chapel Hill, 1935); Lillian Smith, *Killers of the Dream* (New York, 1949); John Temple Graves, *The Fighting South* (New York, 1943); Stetson Kennedy, *Southern Exposure* (Garden City, 1946); Hodding Carter, *Southern Legacy* (Baton Rouge, 1950); William T. Polk, *Southern Accent: From Uncle Remus to Oak Ridge* (New York, 1953); Harry S. Ashmore, *An Epitaph for Dixie* (New York, 1958); James McBride Dabbs, *The Southern Heritage* (New York, 1958); and Henry Savage, Jr., *Seeds of Time: The Background of Southern Thinking* (New York, 1959).

115 See also Clayton Rand, *Ink on My Hands* (New York, 1940); Rebecca Yancey Williams, *The Vanishing Virginian* (New York, 1940); Marjorie Kinnan Rawlings, *Cross Creek* (New York, 1942); David L. Cohn, *Where I Was Born and Raised* (Boston, 1948); Louis Cochran, *Hallelujah, Mississippi* (New York, 1955).

116 Ashmore, *An Epitaph for Dixie*, 176.

writers often surpassed the scholars in their ability to encompass within their regional portrayals both the progressive fragmentation of the South and the continuing relevance of the southern heritage.

It should be clear from this survey of writings on the twentieth-century South that this chapter of southern historiography is largely an unfinished one. Social scientists and popular interpreters have produced a magnificent body of literature in the form of regional description and analysis, but thus far the historian's contribution has been modest. Although historical scholarship has begun to reconstruct the materials of human endeavor in the South during the first quarter of this century, it is significant that this treatment of the region's past is highly compartmentalized. It is no disparagement of the scholarly monographs and biographies devoted to this period to say that the modern South has resisted synthesis at the hands of the historian.

It is precisely at this point that the historian of the recent South will find his greatest opportunity. The opportunity is not without its perils, for as he moves forward in time the concept of the distinctive South becomes progressively less useful. Yet who if not the historian is to describe the interaction of man and his institutions—in the South or anywhere—in the temporal perspective that gives history its special function? Surely the wealth of published materials, especially on the period since the 1920's, and the rapidly accumulating sources in archives and libraries are grist for the mill of the southern historian. Furthermore, the historian will discover more than source materials in the accounts of the social scientists and the popular writers. He will find, even as the distinctive South disappears, illuminating approaches to the region—in the use of the culture concept and the correlation of folkways and regional attitudes, in the analysis of regional problems in a national context, in the study of sectional erosion and national integration. Regionalism may have served its purposes for the sociologist, but for the historian it suggests a fruitful avenue to an area that retains an unusual heritage as it moves toward national conformity. The work of the popular writers is also suggestive, for they have frequently demonstrated an eye for the broad pattern and a synthesizing skill that the historian might well emulate. Finally, the historian of the recent South would do well to follow the southern writers of fiction into the domain of myth and legend, not as a source of factual information but as a special kind of reality with enormous potency in the shaping of regional and national attitudes.

"In a time when nationalism sweeps everything else before it, as it does at present," C. Vann Woodward declared in an address to fellow historians of the South in the fall of 1952, "the regional historian is likely to be oppressed by a sense of his unimportance." As a standpoint from which to write American history, Woodward continued, the South "is regarded as eccentric and as a background for a historian something of a handicap to overcome." [117] There is doubtless much truth in this observation, but it is less true today than it was a decade ago, in part because of Woodward's own impressive demonstration of how American history can be illuminated by the imaginative reconstruction of a region's past. The important point in considering the twentieth-century South, as Fletcher M. Green pointed out more than twenty years ago, is that the region "is now *a part of* as well as in the Union, and its development is such an integral part of the United States that it has no real separate history." [118] The historian of the South should think of himself as an American historian, for however small his subject he can, if he will, contribute to the ongoing historical quest for an understanding of the interaction of time and place in the evolution of American society. History is not always concerned with conflict and change, but surely the historian of the twentieth-century South will find his most challenging theme in the momentous transformation of the region since 1900.

117 Woodward, "The Irony of Southern History," *Journal of Southern History,* XIX (February, 1953), 3.
118 Green, "Writing and Research in Southern History," *Proceedings of the South Carolina Historical Association, 1942* (Columbia, 1942), 16.

Fletcher Melvin Green:

A Bibliography

THIS BIBLIOGRAPHY covers the published works of Fletcher
Melvin Green through December, 1964. No attempt has been made to
include titles of papers read before numerous institutional and professional groups unless these appeared later in published form. In 1949,
for example, Green delivered the Walter Lynwood Fleming Lectures at
Louisiana State University; in 1962 he was one of the lecturers for the
Institute of Southern Culture at Longwood College; and in 1964 he
gave the J. P. Young Lectures at Memphis State University. He has
also lectured at the U.S. Military Academy, Connecticut College, Agnes
Scott College, and many other institutions. One can only regret that
such manuscripts have not been printed.

In compiling the list of Green's writings one finds no place for the
"Presidential Campaign and Election of 1832" which was his master's

thesis, completed in 1922. Even though this remains a typed manuscript I mention it here not only because it was written by Green, but also because it was directed by Joseph Grégoire de Rouhlac Hamilton.

Fletcher Green has established a reputation as a teacher, and particularly as a sympathetic and skillful—not to say exacting—guide of graduate students. Few people, however, realize how much writing he has done, nor have they been aware of the range of his interests as here revealed.

J. ISAAC COPELAND

Books and Pamphlets

Constitutional Development in the South Atlantic States, 1776–1860. Chapel Hill: University of North Carolina Press, 1930. (Originally a Ph.D. dissertation.)

Heroes of the American Revolution. (University of North Carolina *Extension Bulletin,* XI, No. 5.) Chapel Hill: University of North Carolina, 1931.

Romance of the Western Frontier. (University of North Carolina *Extension Bulletin,* XI, No. 8.) Chapel Hill: University of North Carolina, 1932.

Studies in Confederate Leadership. (University of North Carolina *Extension Bulletin,* X, No. 8.) Chapel Hill: University of North Carolina, 1931.

A Style Book for Theses and Dissertations. Chapel Hill: Department of History, University of North Carolina, 1954.

————. Revised edition. Chapel Hill: Department of History, University of North Carolina, 1959.

Edited Works

Blackford, John. *Ferry Hill Plantation Journal, January 4, 1838–January 15, 1839.* Edited, "with an introduction and notes," by Fletcher Melvin Green. (James Sprunt Studies in History and Political Science, XLIII.) Chapel Hill: University of North Carolina Press, 1961.

Douglas, Henry Kyd. *I Rode with Stonewall.* Edited, with an introduction, "The Author and His Book," and "Notes," by Fletcher Melvin Green. Chapel Hill: University of North Carolina Press, 1940.

Green, Fletcher Melvin (ed.). *The Chapel Hill Methodist Church: A Centennial History, 1853–1953.* Chapel Hill, 1954.

[————.] *Essays in Southern History Presented to Joseph Grégoire de Roulhac Hamilton . . .* (James Sprunt Studies in History and Political Science, XXXI.) Chapel Hill: University of North Carolina Press, 1949.

————. *The Lides Go South . . . and West: The Record of a Planter Migration in 1835.* (South Caroliniana Sesquicentennial Series, No. 2.) Columbia: University of South Carolina, 1952.

University of North Carolina, Department of History, *News Letter.* Fletcher Melvin Green, editor, 1952——— (Nos. 1–2 with Loren C. MacKinney.)

Works Edited in Collaboration with Others

Fletcher Melvin Green, Departmental Editor, Southeastern United States, 1957–1962. *Encyclopaedia Britannica.*

The Graduate School Dissertations and Theses. Edited, with a foreword by James L. Godfrey, Fletcher M. Green, and W. W. Pierson. (University of North Carolina Sesquicentennial Publications.) Chapel Hill: University of North Carolina Press, 1947.

"James Sprunt Studies in History and Political Science." Fletcher Melvin Green, member of Board of Editors, 1939———, and Chairman, 1953———.

Articles

"American Lawlessness and Civic Responsibility," *Wesleyan Christian Advocate*, XCIX-A (April 5, and April 12, 1935), 10–12, 10–11.

"Annual Report of the Secretary Treasurer," *Journal of Southern History*, III (February, 1937), 91–98.

"Annual Report of the Secretary Treasurer," *Journal of Southern History*, IV (February, 1938), 68–71.

"Annual Report of the Secretary Treasurer," *Journal of Southern History*, V (February, 1939), 76–80.

"Annual Report of the Secretary Treasurer," *Journal of Southern History*, VI (February, 1940), 89–94.

"Ben E. Green and Greenbackism in Georgia," *Georgia Historical Quarterly*, XXX (March, 1946), 1–13.

"Cycles of American Democracy," *Mississippi Valley Historical Review*, XLVIII (June, 1961), 3–23.

"Democracy in the Old South," *Journal of Southern History*, XII (February, 1946), 3–23.

"Duff Green: Industrial Promoter," *Journal of Southern History*, II (February, 1936), 29–42.

"Duff Green, Militant Journalist of the Old School," *American Historical Review*, LII (January, 1947), 247–64.

"Electioneering 1802 Style by William Lenoir," [edited] *North Carolina Historical Review*, XX (July, 1943), 238–46.

"Fools," *Emory Phoenix*, XXXV (December, 1919), 70–72.

"General Jackson's Campaigns in Florida and Alabama," Brewton (Alabama) *Trade Record*, V (June, 1934), 4–6.

"George Davis, North Carolina Whig and Confederate Statesman, 1820–1896," *North Carolina Historical Review*, XXIII (October, 1946), 449–70.

"Georgia's Board of Public Works, 1817–1826," *Georgia Historical Quarterly*, XXII (June, 1938), 117–37.

"Georgia's Forgotten Industry: Gold Mining," *Georgia Historical Quarterly*, XIX (June and September, 1935), 93–111, 210–28.

"Georgia's Oldest Monuments. Who Built the Gray Tabby Ruins Along the Georgia Coast?" Atlanta *Journal*, January 5, 1936, magazine section.

"Gold Mining: A Forgotten Industry of Ante-Bellum North Carolina," *North Carolina Historical Review*, XIV (January and April, 1937), 1–19, 135–55.

"Gold Mining in Ante-Bellum Virginia," *Virginia Magazine of History and Biography*, XLV (July and October, 1937), 227–35, 357–66.

"Green Family Has Played Stalwart Role in History of Dalton and Nation," Dalton (Georgia) *Citizen*, August 25, 1932, section 3, p. 7.

"Introduction: William Watson Davis," in William Watson Davis, *The Civil War and Reconstruction in Florida*. Gainesville: University of Florida Press, 1964. Pp. xiii-xliii.

"James S. Calhoun: Pioneer Georgia Leader and First Governor of

New Mexico," *Georgia Historical Quarterly,* XXXIX (December, 1955), 309–47.

"Lincoln: 'the taste of the Presidency is in my mouth a little,' " *South Atlantic Quarterly,* LIX (Autumn, 1960), 510–20.

"Listen to the Eagle Scream: One Hundred Years of the Fourth of July in North Carolina, 1776–1876," *North Carolina Historical Review,* XXXI (July and October, 1954), 295–320, 529–49.

"Northern Missionary Activities in the South, 1846–1861," *Journal of Southern History,* XXI (May, 1955), 147–72.

"On Tour with President Andrew Jackson," *New England Quarterly,* XXXVI (June, 1963), 209–28.

"Origins of the Credit Mobilier of America," *Mississippi Valley Historical Review,* XLVI (September, 1959), 238–51.

"A People at War: Hagerstown, Maryland, June 15–August 31, 1863," *Maryland Historical Magazine,* XL (December, 1945), 251–60.

"Presidents on Parade," *Social Science Reporter,* VIII (May 15, 1960), 1–2.

"Resurgent Southern Sectionalism, 1933–1955," *North Carolina Historical Review,* XXXIII (April, 1956), 222–40.

"Some Addenda to 'Walter Lynwood Fleming: Historian of Reconstruction,' " *Journal of Southern History,* XI (August, 1945), 424–25.

"Some Northern Wartime Attitudes Toward the Post-Civil War South," *The United States, 1865–1900: A Survey of Current Literature,* III (January 1, 1944–December 31, 1944), 169–70. (Abstract of George Winston Smith's article of this title.)

"The South and Its History," *Current History,* XXXV (November, 1958), 287–91.

"The South Looks Abroad," *The South and World Affairs,* V (September, 1943), 6–7, 17.

"The Spirit of '76," *Emory University Quarterly,* XI (June, 1955), 65–82.

"Transplanted Georgians: Their Roles in the Development of the Gulf States," *Emory University Quarterly,* IV (June, 1948), 76–86.

"Walter Lynwood Fleming: Historian of Reconstruction," *Journal of Southern History,* II (November, 1936), 497–521.

"Women of the Confederacy in War Times," *Southern Magazine,* II (September, 1935), 16–20, 47–48.

"Writing and Research in Southern History," in South Carolina Historical Association, *Proceedings, 1942,* 3–17.

Essays in Cooperative Works

"Address of the Southern Delegates," in James Truslow Adams (ed.), *Dictionary of American History.* 5 vols. and index. New York: Charles Scribner's Sons, 1940. I, 10.

"Albion Winegar Tourgée," in Joint Committee of the North Carolina English Teachers Association and the North Carolina Library Association, *North Carolina Authors: A Selective Handbook.* Chapel Hill: University of North Carolina Library, 1952. Pp. 121–22.

"Benjamin Edwards Green," in Allen Johnson and Dumas Malone (eds.), *Dictionary of American Biography.* 21 vols. New York: Charles Scribner's Sons, 1928–1936. VII, 538–39.

"Calhoun's Exposition," in James Truslow Adams (ed.), *Dictionary of American History.* 5 vols. and index. New York: Charles Scribner's Sons, 1940. I, 269.

"Calhoun's Exposition (1828)," in James Truslow Adams (ed.), *Concise Dictionary of American History,* edited by Wayne Andrews. New York: Charles Scribner's Sons, 1962. P. 129.

"Charles Pinckney," in *Encyclopaedia Britannica.* 24 vols. Chicago: Encyclopaedia Britannica, Inc., 1963. XVII, 932–33.

"Charles Cotesworth Pinckney," in *Encyclopaedia Britannica.* 24 vols. Chicago: Encyclopaedia Britannica, Inc., 1963. XVII, 933.

"Confederacy, Public Opinion in the South During the Civil War," in James Truslow Adams (ed.), *Dictionary of American History.* 5 vols. and index. New York: Charles Scribner's Sons, 1940. II, 4.

"Confederate States, Public Opinion in the South," in James Truslow Adams (ed.), *Concise Dictionary of American History,* edited by Wayne Andrews. New York: Charles Scribner's Sons, 1962. P. 227.

"Dixie," in *Encyclopaedia Britannica.* 24 vols. Chicago: Encyclopaedia Britannica, Inc., 1963. VII, 522–23.

"Duff Green," in Allen Johnson and Dumas Malone (eds.), *Dictionary of American Biography.* 21 vols. New York: Charles Scribner's Sons, 1928–1936. VII, 540–42.

"Duff Green," in *Encyclopaedia Britannica.* 24 vols. Chicago: Encyclopaedia Britannica, Inc., 1963. X, 851.

"George Michael Troup," in Allen Johnson and Dumas Malone (eds.), *Dictionary of American Biography.* 21 vols. New York: Charles Scribner's Sons, 1928–1936. XVII, 650–51.

"George Walton," in Allen Johnson and Dumas Malone (eds.), *Dictionary of American Biography.* 21 vols. New York: Charles Scribner's Sons, 1928–1936. XIX, 403–405.

"George Washington Bonaparte Towns," in Allen Johnson and Dumas Malone (eds.), *Dictionary of American Biography.* 21 vols. New York: Charles Scribner's Sons, 1928–1936. XVII, 615.

"Hinton Rowan Helper," in Joint Committee of the North Carolina English Teachers Association and the North Carolina Library Association, *North Carolina Authors: A Selective Handbook.* Chapel Hill: University of North Carolina Library, 1952. Pp. 56–57.

"The Historical Background of the Constitution," in *The Federal Constitution; Addresses Delivered at the Ninth Annual Institute, March 30–April 2, 1936.* (Emory University Bulletin, XXII, No. 7, May, 1936.) Atlanta: The University, 1936. Pp. 5–14.

"John Reed," in Allen Johnson and Dumas Malone (eds.), *Dictionary of American Biography.* 21 vols. New York: Charles Scribner's Sons, 1928–1936. XV, 450.

"John Tyler," in *Encyclopaedia Britannica.* 24 vols. Chicago: Encyclopaedia Britannica, Inc., 1962. XXII, 639–41.

"Linton Stephens," in Allen Johnson and Dumas Malone (eds.), *Dictionary of American Biography.* 21 vols. New York: Charles Scribner's Sons, 1928–1936. XVII, 580–81.

"Lynching and Lynch Law," in *Encyclopaedia Britannica.* 24 vols. Chicago: Encyclopaedia Britannica, Inc., 1961. XIV, 526–27.

"Middle Passage," in James Truslow Adams (ed.), *Dictionary of American History.* 5 vols. and index. New York: Charles Scribner's Sons, 1940. III, 395.

"Middle Passage," in James Truslow Adams (ed.), *Concise Dictionary of American History,* edited by Wayne Andrews. New York: Charles Scribner's Sons, 1962. P. 612.

"Nashville Convention," in James Truslow Adams (ed.), *Dictionary of American History.* 5 vols. and index. New York: Charles Scribner's Sons, 1940. IV, 55.

"Nashville Convention," in James Truslow Adams (ed.), *Concise Dictionary of American History.* 5 vols. and index. New York: Charles Scribner's Sons, 1940. V, 91–93.

"Nullification," in *Collier's Encyclopedia.* 24 vols. New York: Crowell-Collier Publishing Co., 1962. XVII, 758–61.

"Nullification," in James Truslow Adams (ed.), *Dictionary of American History.* 5 vols. and index. New York: Charles Scribner's Sons, 1940. IV, 153–54.

"Nullification," in James Truslow Adams (ed.), *Concise Dictionary of*

American History, edited by Wayne Andrews. New York: Charles Scribner's Sons, 1962. P. 691.

"Peculiar Institution," in James Truslow Adams (ed.), *Dictionary of American History.* 5 vols. and index. New York: Charles Scribner's Sons, 1940. IV, 238.

"Pierce Manning Butler Young," in Allen Johnson and Dumas Malone (eds.), *Dictionary of American Biography.* 21 vols. New York: Charles Scribner's Sons, 1928-1936. XX, 633-34.

"Proslavery Literature," in James Truslow Adams (ed.), *Dictionary of American History.* 5 vols. and index. New York: Charles Scribner's Sons, 1940. IV, 364.

"Proslavery Literature," in James Truslow Adams (ed.), *Concise Dictionary of American History,* edited by Wayne Andrews. New York: Charles Scribner's Sons, 1962. P. 773.

"Secession, The Right of," in James Truslow Adams (ed.), *Dictionary of American History.* 5 vols. and index. New York: Charles Scribner's Sons, 1940. V, 50-51.

"Secession, Right of," in James Truslow Adams (ed.), *Concise Dictionary of American History,* edited by Wayne Andrews. New York: Charles Scribner's Sons, 1962. Pp. 860-61.

"Slave Trade, The American," in James Truslow Adams (ed.), *Dictionary of American History.* 5 vols. and index. New York: Charles Scribner's Sons, 1940. V, 91-93.

"Slave Trade, American," in James Truslow Adams (ed.), *Concise Dictionary of American History,* edited by Wayne Andrews. New York: Charles Scribner's Sons, 1962. Pp. 876-78.

"Slavery in Orange County," in Hugh Talmage Lefler and Paul Woodford Wager (eds.), *Orange County, 1752-1952.* Chapel Hill, 1953. Pp. 95-106.

"Solid South, The Democratic Party in the," in James Truslow Adams (ed.), *Dictionary of American History.* 5 vols. and index. New York: Charles Scribner's Sons, 1940. V, 118.

"Some Aspects of the Convict Lease System in the Southern States," in Fletcher Melvin Green (ed.), *Essays in Southern History Presented to Joseph Grégoire de Roulhac Hamilton.* . . . Chapel Hill: University of North Carolina Press, 1949. Pp. 112-23.

"The South in Reconstruction, 1865-1880," in Thomas Dionysius Clark (ed.), *Travels in the New South.* 2 vols. Norman: University of Oklahoma Press, 1962. I, 3-126.

"Star of the West, The," in James Truslow Adams (ed.), *Dictionary of American History*. 5 vols. and index. New York: Charles Scribner's Sons, 1940. V, 160.

"Tariff of Abominations (1828)," in James Truslow Adams (ed.), *Dictionary of American History*. 5 vols. and index. New York: Charles Scribner's Sons, 1940. V, 223–24.

"Tarpley Letter, The (July 9, 1849)," in James Truslow Adams (ed.), *Dictionary of American History*. 5 vols. and index. New York: Charles Scribner's Sons, 1940. V, 224.

"Thomas Pinckney," in *Encyclopaedia Britannica*. 24 vols. Chicago: Encyclopaedia Britannica, Inc., 1963. XVII, 933.

"Thomas Spalding," in Allen Johnson and Dumas Malone (eds.), *Dictionary of American Biography*. 21 vols. New York: Charles Scribner's Sons, 1928–1936. XVII, 426–27.

"Uncle Tom's Cabin; or, Life among the Lowly," in James Truslow Adams (ed.), *Dictionary of American History*. 5 vols. and index. New York: Charles Scribner's Sons, 1940. V, 337.

"Uncle Tom's Cabin; or, Life among the Lowly," in James Truslow Adams (ed.), *Concise Dictionary of American History*, edited by Wayne Andrews. New York: Charles Scribner's Sons, 1962. P. 971.

"Walter Lynwood Fleming," in Allen Johnson and Dumas Malone (eds.), *Dictionary of American Biography*. 21 vols. New York: Charles Scribner's Sons, 1944. XXI, 302–303.

"Wanderer, The," in James Truslow Adams (ed.), *Dictionary of American History*. 5 vols. and index. New York: Charles Scribner's Sons, 1940. V, 395.

"Webster-Hayne Debate," in James Truslow Adams (ed.), *Dictionary of American History*. 5 vols. and index. New York: Charles Scribner's Sons, 1940. V, 431–32.

"Webster-Hayne Debate (January, 1830)," in James Truslow Adams (ed.), *Concise Dictionary of American History*, edited by Wayne Andrews. New York: Charles Scribner's Sons, 1962. Pp. 1005–1006.

"Wiley Thompson," in Allen Johnson and Dumas Malone (eds.), *Dictionary of American Biography*. 21 vols. New York: Charles Scribner's Sons, 1928–1936. XVIII, 474–75.

"William Tatum Wofford," in Allen Johnson and Dumas Malone (eds.), *Dictionary of American Biography*. 21 vols. New York: Charles Scribner's Sons, 1928–1936. XX, 440–41.

Book Reviews

Adams, James Truslow (ed.), *Album of American History*, Vol. II, 1783–1853, in *Mississippi Valley Historical Review*, XXXII (March, 1946), 600–601.

Atherton, Lewis Eldon, *The Southern Country Store, 1800–1860*, in *Social Forces*, XXIX (December, 1950), 218–19.

Barnhart, John Donald, *Valley of Democracy: The Frontier Versus the Plantation in the Ohio Valley, 1775–1818*, in *Mississippi Valley Historical Review*, XLI (December, 1954), 506–507.

Beale, Howard Kennedy (ed.), *Charles A. Beard: An Appraisal*, in *North Carolina Historical Review*, XXXII (January, 1955), 126–28.

Bemis, Samuel Flagg, *John Quincy Adams and the Union*, in *Journal of Southern History*, XXII (November, 1956), 521–23.

Berger, Max, *The British Traveler in America, 1836–1860*, in *Journal of Southern History*, X (February, 1944), 106–107.

Bond, Beverly Waugh, *The Civilization of the Old Northwest: A Study of Political, Social, and Economic Development, 1788–1812*, in *Georgia Historical Quarterly*, XVIII (December, 1934), 381.

———, in *Political Science Quarterly*, L (September, 1935), 454–56.

Brown, William Adam, Jr., *The Future Economic Policy of the United States*, in *The South and World Affairs*, V (November, 1943), 18–19. (Published unsigned.)

Calder, Isabel MacBeath (ed.), *Colonial Captivities, Marches and Journeys*, edited under the auspices of the National Society of the Colonial Dames of America, in Atlanta *Constitution*, December 29, 1935, section M, p. 10.

Capers, Gerald Mortimer, *John C. Calhoun, Opportunist: A Reapraisal*, in *Mississippi Valley Historical Review*, XLVIII (March, 1962), 703–704.

Carroll, John Alexander, and Mary Wells Ashworth, *George Washington, A Biography*, Vol. VII, completing the biography by Douglas Southall Freeman, in *Mississippi Valley Historical Review*, XLV (June, 1958), 130–32.

Clark, Blanche Henry, *The Tennessee Yeomen, 1840–1860*, in *Social Forces*, XXI (December, 1942), 259–60.

Clark, Thomas Dionysius, *The Emerging South*, in *Louisiana History*, III (Fall, 1962), 375–76.

———, *The Southern Country Editor*, in *Georgia Historical Quarterly*, XXXIII (June, 1949), 183–85.

———, *The Southern Country Editor* and *The Rural Press and the*

New South, in *American Historical Review,* LIV (April, 1949), 621–23.

Trans-Mississippi West: Papers Read at a Conference Held at the University of Colorado . . . , edited by James F. Willard and Colin B. Goodykoontz, in *North Carolina Historical Review,* VIII (October, 1931), 482–85.

Coulter, Ellis Merton, *Auraria: The Story of a Georgia Gold-Mining Town,* in *North Carolina Historical Review,* XXXIV (April, 1957), 291–92.

——, *A Short History of Georgia,* reviewed with Lawton Bryan Evans, *All About Georgia,* and Ralph Betts Flanders, *Plantation Slavery in Georgia,* in *Social Forces,* XIII (March, 1935), 466–67.

——, *Thomas Spalding of Sapelo,* in *Georgia Historical Quarterly,* XXV (March, 1941), 83–84.

——, *Wormsloe: Two Centuries of a Georgia Family,* in *North Carolina Historical Review,* XXXII (October, 1955), 592–93.

Craven, Avery Odelle, *The Coming of the Civil War,* in *Journal of Southern History,* VIII (November, 1942), 564–65.

——, *The Growth of Southern Nationalism, 1848–1861,* Volume VI of Wendell Holmes Stephenson and Ellis Merton Coulter (eds.) "A History of the South," in *Mississippi Valley Historical Review,* XL (December, 1953), 534–36.

Curti, Merle Eugene, *The Roots of American Loyalty,* in *Mississippi Valley Historical Review,* XXXIII (September, 1946), 313–14.

Dabney, Virginius, *Below the Potomac,* in *South Today,* VII (Spring, 1942), 66.

Dangerfield, George, *The Era of Good Feelings,* in *Social Forces,* XXXI (December, 1952), 175–76.

Demaree, Albert Lowther, *The American Agricultural Press, 1819–1860,* in *Journal of Southern History,* VIII (February, 1942), 119–20.

Dodd, William Edward, *The Old South,* Vol. I, in *Social Forces,* XVII (December, 1938), 290–92.

Doster, James Foster, *Railroads in Alabama Politics, 1875–1914,* in *Alabama Review,* XII (July, 1959), 235–36.

Driver, Mrs. Leota Stultz, *Fanny Kemble,* in *Journal of Southern History,* I (May, 1935), 219–20.

Dumond, Dwight Lowell, *Antislavery: The Crusade for Freedom in America,* reviewed with his *A Bibliography of Antislavery in America,* in *North Carolina Historical Review,* XXXIX (Summer, 1962), 387–89.

Eaton, Clement, *A History of the Southern Confederacy,* in *Pennsylvania Magazine of History and Biography,* LXXVIII (October, 1954), 525–26.

Evans, Lawton Bryan, *All About Georgia,* reviewed with Ralph Betts Flanders, *Plantation Slavery in Georgia,* and Ellis Merton Coulter, *A Short History of Georgia,* in *Social Forces,* XIII (March, 1935), 466–67.

Farish, Hunter Dickinson, *The Circuit Rider Dismounts: A Social History of Southern Methodism, 1865–1900,* in *Social Forces,* XIX (October, 1940), 131–33.

Flanders, Ralph Betts, *Plantation Slavery in Georgia,* in *Georgia Historical Quarterly,* XX (March, 1936), 94–95. Also reviewed in *Social Forces,* XIII (March, 1935), 466–67.

Floan, Howard Russell, *The South in Northern Eyes, 1831 to 1861,* in *North Carolina Historical Review,* XXXVI (January, 1959), 112–13.

Foreman, Grant, *Indian Removal: The Emigration of the Five Civilized Tribes of Indians,* in *North Carolina Historical Review,* XI (April, 1934), 155–58.

Franklin, John Hope, *The Militant South, 1800–1861,* in *Mississippi Valley Historical Review,* XLIV (June, 1957), 140–41.

———, *Reconstruction: After the Civil War,* in *North Carolina Historical Review,* XXXIX (Spring, 1962), 238–40.

Fraser, Hugh Russell, *Democracy in the Making: The Jackson-Tyler Era,* in *Journal of Southern History,* V (August, 1939), 397–98.

Freeman, Douglas Southall, *George Washington, A Biography,* Vols. I and II, in *Mississippi Valley Historical Review,* XXXVII (September, 1950), 311–12.

———, Vols. III and IV, in *Mississippi Valley Historical Review,* XXXIX (June, 1952), 107–109.

———, Vol. V, in *Mississippi Valley Historical Review,* XXXIX (March, 1953), 755–57.

———, Vol. VI, in *Mississippi Valley Historical Review,* XLI (March, 1955), 699–701.

Gabriel, Ralph Henry, *Main Currents in American History,* in *Journal of Southern History,* IX (May, 1943), 257–59.

Gara, Larry, *The Liberty Line: The Legend of the Underground Rail-*

road, in *American Historical Review,* LXVII (October, 1961), 229–30.

Gardiner, Mrs. Mabel Henshaw, and Ann Henshaw Gardiner, *Chronicles of Old Berkeley: A Narrative History of a Virginia County from its Beginnings to 1926,* in *Social Forces,* XVIII (October, 1939), 145.

Geiger, Vincent Eply, and Wakeman Bryarly, *Trail to California: The Overland Journal of Vincent Geiger and Wakeman Bryarly,* edited by David Morris Potter, in *Emory University Quarterly,* II (March, 1946), 62–63.

Ghent, William James, *The Road to Oregon, A Chronicle of the Great Emigrant Trail,* in *North Carolina Historical Review,* VII (January, 1930), 162–63.

Govan, Gilbert Eaton, and James Weston Livingood, *The University of Chattanooga: Sixty Years,* in *Mississippi Valley Historical Review,* XXXIV (March, 1948), 699–700.

Graves, John Temple, *The Fighting South,* in *The South and World Affairs,* V (September, 1943), 18. (Published unsigned.)

Haines, Charles Grove, *The Role of the Supreme Court in American Government and Politics, 1789–1835,* in *Mississippi Valley Historical Review,* XXXI (March, 1945), 598–99.

Hatcher, William Bass, *Edward Livingston, Jeffersonian Republican and Jacksonian Democrat,* in *North Carolina Historical Review,* XIX (January, 1942), 107–109.

Hays, Louise (Frederick), *Hero of Hornet's Nest: A Biography of Elijah Clark, 1733 to 1799,* in *Georgia Historical Quarterly,* XXX (December, 1946), 358–59.

Heard, Alexander, *A Two-Party South?,* in *Carolina Quarterly,* IV (May, 1952), 61–62.

Heartsill, William Williston, *Fourteen Hundred and 91 Days in the Confederate Army. A Journal Kept by W. W. Heartsill for Four Years, One Month and One Day. Or, Camp Life, Day by Day, of the W. P. Lane Rangers from April 19, 1861 to May 20, 1865,* edited by Bell Irvin Wiley, reviewed with William Howard Russell, *My Diary, North and South,* in *American Historical Review,* LX (January, 1955), 388–89.

Hesseltine, William Best, *The South in American History,* in *The United States, 1865–1900: A Survey of Current Literature,* II (September, 1942–December, 1943), 248–50.

Hockett, Homer Carey, *The Constitutional History of the United States,* Volume II of *A More Perfect Union,* in *Journal of Southern History,* VI (August, 1940), 408–409.

Hoopes, Alban W., *Indian Affairs and Their Administration, with Special Reference to the Far West, 1849–1860,* in *Social Forces,* XIII (December, 1934), 318–19.

Hughes, Rupert, *George Washington,* Vol. III, in *Carolina Magazine,* I (May 18, 1930), 5.

Hutchins, Robert Maynard, *Education for Freedom,* in *The South and World Affairs,* V (October, 1943), 18–19. (Published unsigned.)

Hutchinson, William Thomas, *Cyrus Hall McCormick,* Vol. I, in *North Carolina Historical Review,* IX (April, 1932), 206–207.

James, Marquis, *Andrew Jackson, the Border Captain,* in *North Carolina Historical Review,* X (October, 1933), 333–35.

Jefferson, Thomas, *The Papers of Thomas Jefferson,* Vol. VIII, 25 February to 31 October 1785, edited by Julian P. Boyd and others, in *North Carolina Historical Review,* XXXI (July, 1954), 435–36.

Johnson, Amanda, *Georgia as Colony and State,* in *Georgia Historical Quarterly,* XXIII (June, 1939), 208–10.

Johnson, Thomas Cary, Jr., *Scientific Interests in the Old South,* in *North Carolina Historical Review,* XV (January, 1938), 88–89.

Jones, John Beauchamp, *A Rebel War Clerk's Diary at the Confederate States Capitol . . . ,* with an introduction and historical notes by Howard Swiggett, 2 vols., in Atlanta *Constitution,* August 25, 1935, section K, p. 2.

Kirk, Russell, *Randolph of Roanoke: A Study in Conservative Thought,* in *American Historical Review,* LVII (April, 1952), 693–94.

Krout, John Allen, and Dixon Ryan Fox, *The Completion of Independence, 1790–1830,* Volume V of Arthur Meier Schlesinger and Dixon Ryan Fox (eds.), *A History of American Life,* in *William and Mary Quarterly,* II (October, 1945), 413–15.

Lanning, John Tate, *The Diplomatic History of Georgia: A Study of the Epoch of Jenkins' Ear,* in *Hispanic American Historical Review,* XVIII (November, 1938), 539–41.

Milton, George Fort, *The Eve of Conflict: Stephen A. Douglas and the Needless War,* in Atlanta *Constitution,* April 7, 1935, section B, p. 8.

Montgomery, Horace (ed.), *Georgians in Profile: Historical Essays in Honor of Ellis Merton Coulter,* in *Journal of Southern History,* XXIV (November, 1958), 494–95.

Moore, Arthur Keister, *The Frontier Mind: A Cultural Analysis of the Kentucky Frontiersman,* in *American Historical Review,* LXIII (July, 1958), 1071.

Myers, Gustavus, *The History of American Idealism,* in Nashville *Ban-*

ner, March 29, 1925, "Society, Editorial and Other News," p. 10. (Published unsigned. "First Book Review ever published by F M G." This memorandum found in Professor Green's manuscript notes.)

Nevins, Allan, *Ordeal of the Union,* 2 vols., in *Mississippi Valley Historical Review,* XXXV (June, 1948), 128–29.

Nixon, Raymond Blalock, *Henry W. Grady, Spokesman of the New South,* in *Georgia Historical Quarterly,* XXVIII (March, 1944), 53–54.

——, in *The South and World Affairs,* VI (January, 1944), 14, 17.

Nugent, Mrs. Nell Marion, *Cavaliers and Pioneers: Abstracts of Virginia Land Patents and Grants, 1623–1800,* Vol. I, 1623–1666, in Atlanta *Constitution,* August, 18, 1935, section K, p. 3.

Overdyke, William Darrell, *The Know-Nothing Party in the South,* in *North Carolina Historical Review,* XXVIII (October, 1951), 531–32.

Parks, Joseph Howard, *Felix Grundy, Champion of Democracy,* in *North Carolina Historical Review,* XVIII (July, 1941), 307–308.

Pearce, Haywood Jefferson, *Benjamin H. Hill, Secession and Reconstruction,* in *The Emory Alumnus,* V (January, 1929), 8–9.

Posey, Walter Brownlow, *The Development of Methodism in the Old Southwest, 1783–1824,* in *Georgia Historical Quarterly,* XVIII (March, 1934), 92–93.

Pratt, Fletcher, *Ordeal by Fire: An Informal History of the Civil War,* in Atlanta *Constitution,* September 8, 1935, section B, p. 7.

Ramsdell, Charles W., *Behind the Lines in the Southern Confederacy,* in *The South and World Affairs,* VI (May, 1944), 13. (Published unsigned.)

Rippy, James Fred, *Joel R. Poinsett, Versatile American,* in Atlanta *Constitution,* January 12, 1936, section A, p. 12.

Robinson, William Morrison, Jr., *Justice in Grey: A History of the Judicial System of the Confederate States of America,* in *American Historical Review,* XLVII (April, 1942), 641–43.

Russell, William Howard, *My Diary, North and South,* reviewed with William Williston Heartsill, *Fourteen Hundred and 91 Days in the Confederate Army,* in *American Historical Review.*

Saye, Albert Berry, *A Constitutional History of Georgia, 1732–1945,* in *William and Mary Quarterly,* VI (July, 1949), 552–53.

——, *New Viewpoints in Georgia History,* in *Georgia Historical Quarterly,* XXVIII (December, 1944), 285.

Schachner, Nathan, *Thomas Jefferson, A Biography,* 2 vols., in *Journal of Southern History,* XVIII (November, 1952), 538–41.

Sears, Louis Martin, *Jefferson and the Embargo,* in *North Carolina Historical Review,* V (April, 1928), 245–47.

Simkins, Francis Butler, *The Everlasting South,* in *North Carolina Historical Review,* XLI (Summer, 1964), 394–96.

———, *The South Old and New: A History, 1820–1947,* in *South Atlantic Quarterly,* XLVII (July, 1948), 398–400.

Skinner, Constance Lindsay, *Beaver, Kings and Cabins,* in *North Carolina Historical Review,* XI (April, 1934), 153–55.

Skipper, Otis Clark, *J. D. B. DeBow, Magazinist of the Old South,* in *American Historical Review,* LXIV (July, 1959), 1017.

Smith, William Ernest, *The Francis Preston Blair Family in Politics,* 2 vols., in *Social Forces,* XIV (October, 1935), 156–57.

Staudenraus, Philip J., *The African Colonization Movement, 1816–1845,* in *Florida Historical Quarterly,* XLII (October, 1963), 184–86.

Stephenson, Wendell Holmes, *Isaac Franklin, Slave Trader and Planter of the Old South,* in *North Carolina Historical Review,* XVI (October, 1939), 463–65.

———, *The South Lives in History: Southern Historians and Their Legacy,* in *American Historical Review,* LXI (July, 1956), 983–84.

Strickland, Reba Carolyn, *Religion and the State in Georgia in the Eighteenth Century,* in *Georgia Historical Quarterly,* XXIV (September, 1940), 281–82.

Strobel, Philip A., *The Salzburgers and Their Descendants,* in *Georgia Historical Review,* XXXVIII (June, 1954), 204–205.

Sullivan, Mark, *Our Times: The United States, 1900–1925,* Vol. III, in *Carolina Magazine,* LX (December 16, 1930), 5.

Tansill, Charles Callan, *The Congressional Career of Thomas Francis Bayard, 1865–1885,* in *North Carolina Historical Review,* XXIV (October, 1947), 546–47.

Taylor, Richard, *Destruction and Reconstruction: Personal Experiences of the Late War,* edited by Richard B. Harwell, in *Georgia Historical Quarterly,* XXXIX (September, 1955), 297–98.

Temple, Mrs. Sarah Blackwell (Gober), *The First Hundred Years: A Short History of Cobb County in Georgia,* in *Journal of Southern History,* I (November, 1935), 514–16.

Thomas, Alfred Barnaby (ed. and tr.), *After Coronado: Spanish Exploration Northeast of New Mexico, 1696–1727,* in Atlanta *Constitution,* July 7, 1935, section A, p. 14.

Thomas, Mrs. Ruby Felder (Ray), *Historic Spots and Places of In-*

terest in Georgia, in Atlanta *Constitution,* May 12, 1935, section A, p. 12.

Trenholme, Mrs. Louise (Irby), *The Ratification of the Federal Constitution in North Carolina,* in *Social Forces,* XI (May, 1933), 609–11.

Truett, Randle Bond, *Trade and Travel Around the Southern Appalachians Before 1830,* in *North Carolina Historical Review,* XII (October, 1935), 384–86.

Warren, Charles, *Jacobin and Junto: Or, Early American Politics as Viewed in the Diary of Dr. Nathaniel Ames, 1785–1822,* in *Social Forces,* XII (October, 1933), 151–52.

Warren, Harris Gaylord, *The Sword Was Their Passport, A History of Filibustering in the Mexican Revolution,* in *The South and World Affairs,* V (October, 1943), 18. (Published unsigned.)

Washington, George, *The Autobiography of George Washington, 1753–1799,* edited by Edward C. Boykin, in Atlanta *Constitution,* September 1, 1935, section A, p. 13.

Wender, Herbert, *Southern Commercial Conventions, 1837–1859,* in *Social Forces,* X (March, 1932), 459–60.

White, Leonard Dupee, *The Jacksonians: A Study in Administrative History, 1829–1861,* in *Journal of Southern History,* XXI (August, 1955), 414–16.

Whitehill, Walter Muir, *Independent Historical Societies: An Enquiry into Their Research and Publication Functions and Their Financial Future,* in *Journal of Southern History,* XXIX (November, 1963), 513–15.

Wiley, Bell Irvin, *The Plain People of the Confederacy,* in *The South and World Affairs,* VI (May, 1944), 13. (Published unsigned.)

Williams, Alfred Brockenbrough, *Hampton and His Red Shirts,* in Atlanta *Constitution,* April 21, 1935, section K, p. 6.

Williams, Thomas Harry, *Romance and Realism in Southern Politics,* in *Journal of Southern History,* XXVII (August, 1961), 424–25.

Articles about Green

Almonte Charles Howell, "Fletcher Melvin Green," in his *The Kenan Professorships.* Chapel Hill: University of North Carolina Press, 1956. Pp. 236–39.

"Professor, Writer, Golfer and Fisherman," University of North Carolina *Alumni Review,* XXX (May, 1942), 238.

"These Three Men Head Departments Teaching Many Students," University of North Carolina *Alumni Review,* XLV (May, 1957), 222.

INDEX

463